Dimitri Mitropoulos

Dimitri Mitropoulos, 1896–1960. Photo by Eventon, 1944.
Courtesy Richard Frahm.

Priest of Music

THE LIFE OF
DIMITRI MITROPOULOS

by

William R. Trotter

AMADEUS PRESS
Reinhard G. Pauly, General Editor
Portland, Oregon

Copyright © 1995 by William R. Trotter
All rights reserved.

Published in 1995 by Amadeus Press
(an imprint of Timber Press, Inc.)

ISBN 0-931340-81-0

Printed in Singapore

AMADEUS PRESS
The Haseltine Building
133 S.W. Second Avenue, Suite 450
Portland, Oregon 97204 U.S.A.

Library of Congress Cataloging-in-Publication Data

Trotter, William R.
    Priest of music: the life of Dimitri Mitropoulos / by William R. Trotter.
        p.   cm.
    Includes bibliographic references (p.465) and index.
    ISBN 0-931340-81-0
    1. Mitropoulos, Dimitri, 1896–1960. 2. Conductors (Music)—Biography. I. Title.
ML422.M59T76   1995
780'.92—dc20
    [B]   94-23928
                                                                            CIP
                                                                            MN

Table of Contents

The Forgotten Giant

At the time of conductor Dimitri Mitropoulos's death on November 2, 1960, more than one hundred Mitropoulos-led performances were listed in the American record catalogues; a decade later, there were a dozen.

When he died, Mitropoulos was generally regarded as one of the most important and influential musicians ever to work in the United States. Yet only seven years later, when critic Harold C. Schonberg (who had attended many of Mitropoulos's concerts) published a book entitled *The Great Conductors*, Mitropoulos rated a mere two paragraphs.

To measure this fall from grace—a process that has caused not only the man's reputation but the very record of his achievements to become only the dimmest wisp of cultural memory—one need only consider the briefest outline of his American career.

He became music director of the Minneapolis Symphony Orchestra in 1937 and remained in that post until 1949. He transformed a decent provincial orchestra into an organization worthy to be ranked just below the first tier of American symphonic ensembles; and in the process—often to the bewilderment of his good-willed but basically conservative midwestern audiences—he made Minneapolis an internationally known center for contemporary music. He supported, not just morally but in many cases financially, dozens of musicians who later became famous, among them composer David Diamond and conductor Leonard Bernstein, thus profoundly changing and immeasurably enriching American musical culture.

For a decade, beginning in 1949, he was either music director or principal conductor of the New York Philharmonic Orchestra, and was for several seasons the most important conductor to appear at the Metropolitan Opera. He gave either the world or the United States premieres of more than one hundred works, many of them now regarded as truly significant (Gustav Mahler's Sixth Symphony, Samuel Barber's *Vanessa*, Shostakovich's Tenth Symphony). Against monolithic inertia and occasional outright hostility, he modernized the repertoire of the New York Philharmonic and made it, for the first time in decades, an institution of immediate and powerful relevance. And when he guest-conducted in Boston and Philadelphia, he not only electrified audiences but also won the passionate devotion of the hard-to-impress musicians in both orchestras. He was a man of deep spirituality and profound intellect, an intensely private man who could also be a spell-binding conversationalist. In the words of Isaac Stern, "There was a *scope* to him" which was acknowledged even by his enemies.[1]

And yet, as the centennial of his birth in 1896 draws near, Dimitri Mitropoulos is virtually forgotten in the very land where he achieved his greatest triumphs. Such is certainly not the case in Europe, where Mitropoulos is remembered with the same awe that is attached to the memories of Wilhelm Furtwängler and Arturo Toscanini, and where many extraordinary live performances have been issued on compact discs.

This book attempts, for the first time, to set straight the record of Mitropoulos's career, his failures as well as his successes, and perhaps in the process to shed light on the peculiar, sad, and ironic circumstances that deposed him, in a condition of near-disgrace, from the New York Philharmonic, that laid waste to his once-powerful body, that broke his vast and generous heart, and that ultimately killed him at a comparatively early age.

His story is more than the chronicle of a great conductor's career; it is the moving human account of a noble but tragically vulnerable man, and it is also, in part, a chronicle of two dynamic, colorful, and adventurous decades in the cultural history of the United States.

Research for this book was begun in 1983 by Oliver Daniel, who was uniquely qualified to tell this story. If fate had been kinder, he, not I, would have written this book. For the better part of twenty years, Oliver produced the radio broadcasts of both the Boston Symphony and the New York Philharmonic, and in the latter capacity he attended most of the Philharmonic's rehearsals and concerts during the tenure of Mitropoulos. He also worked for the Columbia Broadcasting System as producer of two influential and stimulating radio programs, "Invitation to Music" and "Twentieth-Century Concert Hall." He served for several years as vice president of Broadcast Music, Inc., (BMI) and was a regular contributor to the pages of *Saturday Review*. He was among the founders of CRI Recordings, a label that has done more to document twentieth-century American music than any other. With Leopold Stokowski, he cofounded the Contemporary Music Society, and in 1982 he published a monumental thousand-page biography of that conductor entitled *Stokowski: A Counterpoint of View* (Dodd, Mead & Company, now sadly out of print.) That definitive account met with great critical acclaim, and soon after its appearance, Oliver began work on a proposed biography of Mitropoulos, with the same dogged, painstaking research that had rendered the earlier book so authoritative. But prolonged and finally chronic illness made his progress slow and sporadic; he lived long enough to write the first draft of a single chapter, but his death in December 1990 seemed to doom the project.

The honor and responsibility of completing this task fell to me, ironically, because of my interest in Leopold Stokowski, whose lush, seductively dramatic style lured me into a love affair with classical music at age fourteen. That conversion led to a life-long interest in the performing styles of the so-called Golden Age of Conducting, which eventually led to a record collection of five thousand items, a twelve-year stint as a music and record critic, three years as program annotator for the Eastern Music Festival, and a delightful four years as author and co-host of "The Collectors' Corner," a weekly program broadcast by the National Public Radio affiliate of Wake Forest University.

It also led to research for a proposed biography of Stokowski, starting in 1961, my freshman year in college, and lasting until Oliver's book appeared in 1982. The moment I picked up Oliver's book and flipped through its pages, I knew that there was no point in continuing my research; Oliver had done *the* book on Stokowski—anything else would be superfluous and no other author could hope to match Oliver's credentials or equal his amazing degree of access to musicians, famous or otherwise.

Nevertheless, my interest in Stokowski continued unabated, only now in the form of a hobby. During the 1980s, I wrote several interpretive articles that were published in *Toccata*, the journal of the British Leopold Stokowski Society, as was a 120-page chunk of my own biographical material, and when the American Stokowski Society was founded by Robert M. Stumpf in 1983, I contributed occasional reviews to its lively quarterly journal, *Maestrino*.

One evening in the summer of 1991, I received a phone call from Bob Stumpf asking if I had any interest in Mitropoulos. Yes, of course, I replied. Bob then told me about Oliver Daniel's unfinished biography and urged me to contact Don Ott, Oliver's longtime friend and the executor of his estate. After several exploratory phone calls, Ott sent me a sample of the letters and interviews in Oliver's files, while I simultaneously sent him samples of my own musical writings.

I read Oliver's material with increasing excitement. I realized that although I had been quite aware of who Mitropoulos was, I really did not know this man. Through those documents I made the acquaintance of a rare and radiant spirit, and from reading the selection of yellowing reviews, I began to suspect that I, and many other music lovers, had taken Mitropoulos too much for granted, that we had missed something special the first time around, and that this story simply had to be told. The power of Dimitri's personality, as reflected in his letters, compelled me to set aside all other projects. Don Ott and I soon came to an agreement, a contract was drawn up, and I began systematically indexing Oliver's material while Don finished transcribing the last of more than three hundred hours of taped interviews.

Thus came about this collaborative book. Most of the research is Oliver's; the writing is mine. The project was made all the more challenging by the paucity of information about Mitropoulos's youth and by the loss of several major collections of material: the files of Trudy Goth, Mitropoulos's European secretary; the notes of Louis Stanley, a freelance writer who in the mid-1950s began but never finished a biography; all but a few fragments of the files of Arthur Judson, the conductor's agent; and the hundreds of letters Mitropoulos wrote to Maria Negroponte.

On the other hand, Oliver's approximately 150 interviews—many of whose subjects, alas, are no longer living—and the more than four thousand reviews and clippings he collected furnished a strong documentary foundation for this book, as did the information Oliver gathered during two trips to Greece, in 1984 and 1985. Although a surprising amount of information, most notably the dissertation of Apostolos Kostios, has become available since his death, the heart and soul of the book remains Oliver Daniel's superlative research. For the interpretation of events and the style in which the information is presented, I alone am responsible, for better or worse.

This narrative contains ideas and anecdotes that have not appeared in print before, including some that are surprising and controversial. After three years' acquaintance with the material, I am satisfied as to the accuracy of what appears on these pages.

I approached this project with absolutely no preconceptions, no agenda, no prejudices. Ultimately, my treatment was dictated by the material. Not far into the book, most readers will understand that Mitropoulos's is a story about which the participants and even the observers *did not feel neutral*. What Rudolf Serkin said about Mitropoulos, "Mitropoulos could never be indifferent," could be said of those who knew him, whether they agreed with him or not. The interviewees spoke in utter candor, and occasionally, when speaking about sensitive matters, on condition of anonymity.

Many good people have rendered help and support during the writing of this book. Special thanks, however, are due:

To Eve Goodman, for her devoted and inspired editing;

To Don Ott, for entrusting me with this project and sustaining me with his faith and his dedication;

To Robert M. Stumpf, president of the American Leopold Stokowski Society, for midwifing the project;

To composer Nicolas Roussakis, for stimulating Oliver's initial interest in a Mitropoulos biography;

To John and Linda Plevrites, who translated important parts of the Maria Christopoulou biography;

To William Walker, who obtained the Kostios dissertation from the University of Vienna and who translated every word of it onto cassettes;

To Dr. Michael Heymel, who generously granted permission to use his notes of interviews with Leonard Bernstein, Gottfried von Einem, and several other important but otherwise inaccessible persons;

To Nick Nickson, who probably knows more about Mitropoulos's recordings than anyone else in the United States and who happily shared his expertise as well as a complete set of the CDs he has privately produced to document the Greek maestro's art;

To David Diamond for his hospitality, his forbearance, and his willingness to share his memories and letters;

To Andreas Nomikos, for permission to reproduce his exquisite drawing of the conductor (page 297), done from life in Mitropoulos's study at the Great Northern Hotel in New York;

To Sam Norkin, author of *Drawings, Stories: Theater, Opera, Ballet, Movies* (Heinemann, 1994), for permission to reproduce his drawings of the conductor in rehearsal (pages 97, 464);

To the memory of Dennis Quick, a fine photographer whose expertise rescued a number of problematical old photographs for this book, and who died of AIDS only weeks after the manuscript was completed;

To Louis B. Hurvitz, of Minnesota Public Radio, for his valuable work in locating and copying five years' worth of Minneapolis reviews and clippings;

To David S. Cooper, son of Mitropoulos's close friend William Cooper, for his unflagging support and enthusiasm;

To Paul Gunther, librarian of the Minnesota Orchestra, whose cooperation went far beyond the call of duty during the research phase and who reviewed the manuscript with an eagle eye;

To Barbara Haws, director of the New York Philharmonic Archives, and Robert Tuggle, director of the Metropolitan Opera Association Archives, for reviewing portions of the manuscript;

To my aunt, Mary Eva Johnson, for letting me use her St. Paul apartment as temporary headquarters;

To Joan Peyser, for sharing her insights into the convoluted relationship between Mitropoulos and his most famous protégé, Leonard Bernstein;

And to my beloved wife, Elizabeth Lustig, who understood why I had to put every other project aside for three years in order to write this book (and who knew, before I did, that I was going to).

William R. Trotter
Greensboro, North Carolina

PART ONE

"I Am a Greek— Good for Everything."

CHAPTER ONE

Origins

From 1950 until the end of his life, Dimitri Mitropoulos spent most of each summer guest-conducting in Europe. While the headline engagements were those at the Salzburg and Florence Festivals, he also conducted many successful concerts with various European radio ensembles, enjoying particularly fine results with the first-class ensemble of Cologne Radio.

At some point during the summer of 1958 or 1959—the exact date has proven elusive—the conductor found time to write a short but illuminating autobiographical sketch which was later included in a volume of similar essays, published in Germany circa 1960.

One question Mitropoulos often faced from European interviewers concerned his decision to remain in the United States, even though several eminent European orchestras had offered themselves to him unconditionally. In the final paragraphs of his essay, the conductor addressed this matter with his usual directness and candor:

> I feel right at home in Europe, like a fish swimming in its accustomed waters, although it is true that I regard myself as a cosmopolitan—at home everywhere. I don't know homesickness. As for my special affinity for America, well, there are special reasons for that.
>
> The Europeans don't need me as much. They are self-assured in matters of art; theirs is a long history and the riches of their culture are even greater than they realize. It is always gratifying for an artist to meet people who are willing to learn. That is why I believe I can be of much greater influence in America than in Europe.
>
> It is therefore a question of morality, not art, which causes me to stay in America. Here I still conduct the [New York] Philharmonic from time to time. And here it was that fate willed finally that I should begin conducting operas in the 55th year of my life, a task for which I was sufficiently prepared by my years as Assistant at the Berlin Staatsoper. The Metropolitan Opera invited me, because there were always too many "specialists" in the orchestra pit: French conductors for French music, Germans for German music, Italians for Italian music.
>
> But I am a Greek—good for everything.[1]

There is an old Greek folk tale that recounts how God, when He was making the world, put all the earth through a sieve and took one handful of good soil to make this country, another to make that country, and so on, until the world was formed. But when He was finished, He still had left all the grit and rocks which would not fit through the sieve. He shook all of these out into His hand and threw them over His shoulder. That was the origin of Greece.

An aerial view of the Peleponnesus might serve to confirm the wry truth behind that folk tale. Shaped like a vast leaf, its stem formed by the Isthmus of Corinth, the Peloponnesus comprises 8287 square miles of extremely rugged land, a peninsula that forms the southern part of the Greek mainland. Named for Pelops, son of Tantalus, the region is densely packed with four thousand years of history. Doric columns dot the hills, and so do the domes of Byzantium. This was the land of Agamemnon.

Greek civilizations throve here during the half-legendary age of the Mycenaens. Sparta evolved from a dusty village into a city-state whose armies were powerful enough to halt forever, in the fifth century, the expansionist ambitions of the Persian Empire. It was in the Peloponnesus that the first Olympic games were held, and it was there, in the city of Patros in 1821, that Greek nationalists first raised their flags of revolt against the Ottoman Empire.

The eastern-central district of the Peloponnesus is called Arcadia, from which name derives an English-language adjective, *arcadian*, that denotes pastoral beauty. In the real Arcadia, one of the best-watered regions in Greece, there are indeed many areas—sloping valleys lushly shaded by cherry orchards and olive groves—to which that adjective can certainly be applied.

On the whole, however, it is the sterner elements of the Arcadian landscape which predominate and which leave the strongest impression on a traveler's memory. Rising from those olive groves and valleys are myriad sharp-edged ridges, painted violet and pink and salmon under the white glare of the Mediterranean sun; and above these, in many places, are taller pine-clad mountains. Ruins lie scattered in these mountains, for this is a land that has been much fought over down through the centuries, and the dominating terrain is often crowned with the remains of castles and fortifications—sometimes layered, like palimpsests of stone, by the succession of empires under whose sway a particular peak happened to fall. In a single site, the traveler may contemplate the crumbling ramparts of a Frankish castle of the fourteenth century, constructed in part from the remnants of a temple looted by the Spartans in the sixth century, B.C., then sacked again by Alaric's Goths in the fifth century A.D., and yet again during the War of Independence by Ibrahim Pasha's Egyptian Janissaries.

The late nineteenth- and early twentieth-century revival of Hellenic culture was characterized by the same sort of unruliness and fitful progress that characterized the rebirth of the Greek nation itself.

For four hundred years, following the fall of Constantinople in 1453, Greece and the Balkan countries were reduced to a condition of vassalage under the Ottoman Turks. Culturally and economically, Greece—once the envy of the pre-Christian world and fount of the Renaissance—became a backwater state, isolated from mainland Europe, its culture, politics, and economy placed in a state of suspended animation.

Greek Independence Day is observed on March 25, for it was on that day in 1821 that the archbishop of Patros unfurled the national flag and proclaimed a state of revolution in the Peloponnesus. Inspired by the French Revolution and quietly supported by the Russian tsar, the Greek uprising was among the great romantic actions of the nineteenth century. It lured adventurous souls from all over Europe, the most notable of whom was Lord Byron, who died on Greek soil in 1824.

Warfare dragged on for almost a decade and was characterized by extreme cruelty on both sides. Motivated by genuine sympathy as well as cold-blooded ambition to achieve political gains at small cost to themselves, three powerful European states (Russia, France, and Great Britain) formed the Triple Alliance and weighed in on the side of Greece in 1827. The combined Allied fleets destroyed the Turkish Navy later that year in the Battle of Navarino. The Turks never recovered—without sea power, they could not sustain the war. Greek independence was formally recognized in 1829, through the instrument of the Treaty of Adrianople.

Now calling themselves the Protecting Powers, the Allies began looking for a monarch to rule this new/ancient country. Prince Otto of Bavaria, whose father, Ludwig I, was a passionate student of classical Greek culture, was approached about the job, and he accepted the proffered crown in 1832 at the age of seventeen. The day-to-day running of the country was managed by a council of Bavarian regents.

As is so often the case, winning a revolution proved to be much simpler than governing the country begotten by that revolution. Greece was backward and impoverished, and the hills swarmed with heavily armed ex-rebels who were forced, for economic reasons, to become brigands. What would today be called the national infrastructure was virtually nonexistent.

In view of these circumstances, King Otto's decision to import experienced Bavarian bureaucrats seems merely sensible. To the Greeks, however, the system was a constant source of irritation and resentment. Consequently, even though Otto himself seems genuinely to have cared about Greece, he was never very successful at running things. He dawdled endlessly over the writing of a new constitution, and in 1862, as tired of the Greeks as they were of him, Otto abdicated.

A plebiscite held afterward revealed an overwhelming desire by the Greeks that their next ruler be British. The British government nominated Prince George of Denmark, who was related by marriage to Prince Edward, heir to Queen Victoria's throne, and the Greeks accepted him as their king.

In 1863, George I was duly crowned King of the Hellenes, even though large parts of "Hellas," including Crete, still remained under Turkish domination. Upon his ascension, George quickly endorsed the newly revised constitution, and he stuck by that document faithfully for the next half-century, becoming in fact a very model of a modern constitutional monarch.

To some degree, the vitality and coherence of musical culture in modern Greece has always been influenced by the stability and coherence of the nation's politics. Political upheavals in Athens, social and economic instability, and numerous wars, both in the Balkans and in Asia Minor, all conspired to retard the growth of a robust indigenous Greek musical culture.

Four centuries of Turkish domination had left Greece culturally withered, the artistic dreams of its people nourished on the echoes of ancient glories. The nourishing streams of European musical traditions had bypassed Greece altogether. Aside from folk songs, the only music to be heard in the new Greek state of 1830 was the ancient monophonic vocal chants of the Byzantine church.

Things began to change when Otto moved south to assume the Greek throne. Not surprisingly, given the background of events, the first European music heard in Greece was played by a fine Bavarian band imported by Otto to the new capital of Athens in 1834. So popular did the band's concerts prove to be, that a touring company was formed from its ranks in 1841 and sent forth to give concerts in Argos, Messolongi, and other important towns. Along with the usual marches, galops, and waltzes, the full band is known to have performed excerpts from the basic orchestral repertoire, including movements from popular symphonies. Beethoven, Mozart, and Rossini were surely played, for some of their music would have been in the active repertoire of any self-respecting royal band in Europe. These concerts, whether held in Athens or in more remote locations, gave the people of Greece their first exposure to the polyphonically structured music of mainstream European culture.

The impact of this exposure, at least among the more cultivated and curious minds of the new Greek state, was profound. A veritable band-craze swept Greece. By the end of the century, most major cities in Greece, along with some not-so-major ones, boasted their own municipal band; these ensembles were called *Philarmonikes*, and because lots of people wanted to play in them, there arose a need for music schools. By far the most important of these was the Athens Conservatory, founded in 1871. After twenty years of more or less provincial activity, the school came into its own in 1891 with the appointment of an inspired administrator named Georgios Nasos. Among Nasos's most effective actions were the reorganization of the conservatory orchestra on a semiprofessional basis and the importation of a distinguished Belgian composer and pedagogue, Armand Marsick, in 1908, to be its director.

A competing establishment, the Hellenic Conservatory, was founded in 1919 by the intensely nationalistic composer Manolis Kalomiris—a man who, in later years, would prove himself to be no friend of Mitropoulos.

Throughout the remaining years of the nineteenth century, both curriculum and performances would emphasize operatic rather than symphonic fare, especially Italian opera, which had been brought into the country by touring troupes of Italian singers, even before Athens was designated the capital. So far as is known, the first complete opera given in Athens (in 1837) was Rossini's *Barber of Seville*, which was followed three years later by Donizetti's *Lucia di Lammermoor* and then by a host of other productions.

As time went by, many of those touring Italian musicians, sensing good employment opportunities in a congenial environment, chose to settle in Greece, as was exactly the case with Dimitri's first piano teacher. Eventually many of these musicians organized themselves into performing ensembles, such as the Euterpe Philharmonic Society of Athens (1871), the Terpsichore Society of Navplion (1872), the Philharmonic Society of Piraeus (1873), and the Athens Philharmonic Society, forerunner of the orchestra Mitropoulos would direct during his Athenian period, which was founded in 1888.

Dimitri Mitropoulos's family came from the tiny village of Vresthena, located near the center of Arcadia, in the foothills of the Parnon mountain range, about five miles east of the main road between Sparta and Tripoli. The place cannot be found on maps of recent vintage, and according to Greek sources, the village is no longer inhabited.[2]

Unlike Stokowski, Mitropoulos did not seek actively to hide his origins behind mythic veils; to his closest friends, he sometimes spoke about his family's Peloponnesian beginnings. Only a few fragments of recollected conversation have survived, but little as it is, the information contained in them suggests that life in nineteenth-century Vresthena must have been harsh. So verminous were most of the village dwellings that the local priest mixed insecticide with the holy water he used for blessing houses. Hard conditions bred rugged people, however, and Mitropoulos's own grandmother once gave birth outdoors while gathering firewood, then carried both the baby and the bundle of wood nearly a mile uphill before she could reach home and lie down.[3]

Yannis Mitropoulos, the conductor's father, was born in Vresthena in 1867, the first-born son of the village's Greek Orthodox priest. Indeed, the family's strong religious faith had a profound influence on its members' destinies. In 1892 Yannis's uncle, Ierotheos (b. 1840), was ordained bishop of Patros—an important city on the northwestern coast of the Peloponnesus—and remained so until his death in 1903. Yannis had two brothers, Constantine (b. 1868) and Georgios (b. 1870), both of whom entered the church and both of whom spent part of their lives in the great monastic enclave on Mount Athos. Constantine eventually left Mount Athos and entered a monastery on the island of Poros, apparently living out the remainder of his days there. Georgios, however, chose to remain on Mount Athos, where in 1912 he was elected secretary of the Holy Community itself, an honorific that speaks highly of both his intelligence and his piety.

Vresthena was a tiny village in a poor and backward region; the only work generally available was subsistence-level farming and prospects for economic betterment were virtually nil. Yannis therefore moved to Athens in 1893, just one of many thousands of Greek peasants who were being lured from the impoverished countryside into the new capital city. In Athens, opportunities could be found in trade and manufacturing which were starting to generate a sizable middle class where none had existed before. Once settled in Athens, Yannis opened a leather goods shop at No. 15 St. Mark's Street.

Two years later, in April 1895, Yannis married Angeliki Anagnosto-poulu, an attractive twenty-nine-year-old woman who was the fourth of six children. Angeliki's father was a coachman in the service of King George I, and therefore a man of considerable respectability. The connection to roy-alty may have been more than a simple matter of employment, if one cares to give credence to an exceptionally stubborn rumor that Dimitri Mitro-poulos was the illegitimate son of King George. A comparison of portraits does in fact reveal striking similarities; more so, it could plausibly be ar-gued, than a comparison between Dimitri and Yannis. After the passage of a century, it is extremely doubtful that such an allegation could either be proven or not. The matter is largely irrelevant, except for the fact that clan-destine royal assistance would go a long way toward explaining why the Mitropoulos family enjoyed a markedly higher standard of living than could logically have been expected from the earnings of a shopkeeper who worked hard but whose business acumen appears to have been nothing special.

Whatever the precise biological antecedents and despite the fact that his mother had more than a dozen miscarriages, Dimitri was born on Feb-ruary 18, 1896—that was the date given in many early interviews and pro-grams, at any rate. American sources, however, list the birth date as March 1, 1896, and that is the date Mitropoulos himself always cited in interviews. The discrepancy can be partly explained by the Greek adoption of the Gre-gorian calendar only in 1924. But herein lies an additional inconsistency, since the difference between the old and new calendars was thirteen days, which would yield a "new" birth date of March 2, or working backward, an "old" birth date of February 19. In an effort to sort things out, the Greek musicologist Apostolos Kostios delved into the Athenian archives, but he was unable to turn up either the original birth records or any copies. Even-tually, he gave the matter the scholarly equivalent of a shrug and moved on to more important topics.

The conductor himself had a typically candid explanation, which he offered during an interview before his sixtieth birthday:

"Actually," he said, "next Saturday isn't my birthday at all. I'm not quite sure *when* I was born. I was born in Greece, you know, and they weren't very good at keeping records of that sort of thing."

What happened, Mr. Mitropoulos said, was that when he left Greece 20 years ago, he needed a birth date for his papers, and just made that one up.

"My mother decided I was about forty years old . . . and that's what we put down. I certainly am not less than 60, but I may be even four years older. Who knows?"[4]

Nine years later, a sister named Heleni was born. Until that event, the family had been living in an apartment near the leather shop on St. Mark's Street. These quarters were now too small, so in 1910 Yannis purchased an attractive house located at No. 13 Triton Street, in the seaside suburb of Palarion (Old) Faleron.

Old Faleron and New (*Neon*) Faleron faced each other across a sickle-shaped bay that formed the southern flank of the bustling port of Piraeus. At the time the Mitropoulos family moved to Triton Street, Old Faleron was part suburb and part economy-class resort, populated by some five thousand people. Its waterfront was dotted with small seaside cafes and nightclubs, and the water was not yet too polluted to swim in.

Historical associations were plentiful, and in later years Mitropoulos would often express pleasure in having grown up close to the birthplace of Thucydides. Clay from the Faleron district was highly prized by the potters and sculptors of ancient Athens, and local legend had it that the beach was once covered with the washed-up wreckage of Persian ships that had been destroyed in the Battle of Salamis.

The Greece Mitropoulos was born into was a nation of approximately two million people. There were but three real urban centers: Athens, of course, along with its almost-contiguous port of Piraeus, and Patros, the Peloponnesian city where Dimitri's uncle served as bishop of the Orthodox Church.

At the time Yannis Mitropoulos moved there, the population of Athens was about 160,000. By the early twentieth century, Piraeus was the fourth-busiest port in Europe. By the time Dimitri entered primary school, the University of Athens had become a flourishing institution, the center of all Greek intellectual life; and the first stirrings of artistic endeavor, mostly nationalistic in flavor, were generating excitement, especially among the sons of the growing middle class.

By the time he was five or six, Dimitri had carved a wooden flute and taught himself how to play it. He was precocious, lively, and naturally musical. He had blond hair and blue eyes of exceptional clarity and depth. Angeliki shamelessly doted on him and sought to protect him in ways that were both practical and superstitious. When they walked together, she was quite likely to turn the child around and rush him into an alleyway because she had spotted some stranger trying to cast an evil eye on the lad. She hovered over conversations about Dimitri, admonishing friends and family alike not to voice over-lavish praise on the boy, lest God be offended.

Sometimes, she reverted to ancient tradition by using the term *gods* rather than the more up-to-date singular. If the family chanced to go out together at night, Angeliki always insisted on entering the house first, leaving the others outside while she searched for any evil spirits that might be lurking within.

Spiritual matters of a different sort had become a profound concern for her son even before his tenth birthday. Whatever peccadillos Angeliki may have committed in her youth, she had by now become an intensely devout woman, as well as a superstitious one. What with his mother's hovering influence, his two prelate uncles, and a father who inclined more toward religion as he grew older, Mitropoulos's family was already a kind of religious community unto itself. Young Dimitri absorbed much from this environment, but even before adolescence, he had gone beyond the boundaries of the family in his quest for spiritual sustenance.

He visited nearby monasteries and daydreamed about becoming a monk. He carried his devotions a step further and fantasized various scenarios in which he became venerated as a great anchorite, a cave-dweller, a pole-sitter, a bearded hermit with some kind of direct line to the cosmos. Sometimes the fantasies spilled out, and Dimitri would form his own little religious order with neighborhood children as his monks, acting out elaborate homemade rituals of devotion and self-abnegation. Other times, he could be found actually delivering impromptu sermons to whatever audience of ragamuffins he could assemble. When his parents looked in on the boy, they were apt to find him either composing music or saying prayers for the souls of his friends, for his family, for himself.

Of course Dimitri's curiosity was not, at this stage of his life, strictly of an aesthetic or intellectual bent. Like most boys, he wanted to know how things worked. As he recalled in an interview:

> When I was a boy, I loved to tinker with watches. I remember the first time I took a watch apart and then tried to reassemble it. I should say that a quarter of the parts were still left on the table when I finally put the lid back on the watch. I nevertheless tried again and again, and each time thereafter the number of parts left over diminished until I could assemble the complete watch and knew every detail of its workings. [In a similar way], I make no distinction between learning a score and memorizing it. By the time I have learned a composition, I have also memorized it.[5]

His mother called him Dimitrakis, a diminutive of Dimitri, and was seldom able to stay angry at him for long—not that he gave her many reasons, for he was generally well behaved. In two areas, however, he seemed incorrigible. One involved his instinctive gifts as a mimic—he would often imitate other people, sometimes to the acute embarrassment of his parents.

The other area was a compulsion to perform acts of charity. Starting at the age of eight, he unhesitatingly gave away articles of clothing to poor children in the neighborhood, sometimes taking a brand new shirt from his back and simply handing it over to a less fortunate child. Toys, even new ones, often vanished for the same reason. When he reached adolescence and was allowed to make what he called excursions—walking tours of the city or hikes into the countryside, perhaps to visit a monastery—he often came back at night without the same inventory of clothing he had worn in the morning, having given away various garments to paupers he passed during the day. On several occasions, he took the very shoes from his feet and handed them to some impoverished child he met along the way, happy to return home barefooted, even if it meant a scolding from Angeliki.

Dimitri's first formal music instruction consisted of piano lessons, starting at age nine, administered by an Italian named del Buono who played salon music for a living in a seaside coffee house and supplemented this meager income by giving lessons during the daytime. The fact that the Mitropoulos family could afford to own a piano does suggest that there must have been some source of income other than the proceeds from the leather goods shop.

After finishing primary school, Mitropoulos entered secondary school —equivalent to junior high school—at the Varvakian Gymnasium. His graduation certificate survives, showing that he matriculated in the summer of 1912 with a 5.5 grade average, approximately a B. By that time, however, his formal musical education was already well under way.

One day when Dimitri was ten years old, he was playing some of his own compositions when a dapper gentleman named Armand Marsick strolled by the open window. Marsick also happened to be on the faculty of the Athens conservatory, and he was so impressed by what he heard that he knocked on the door, introduced himself, and declared to Angeliki that he would personally see to it that her son was accepted into the conservatory at the earliest possible date.

lunchtime assignations with male partners, while in their "real lives" distinctly proper behavior was expected.

There is no doubt that Mitropoulos also went through, at about this time, a period of intense religious and philosophical turmoil. His weekend pilgrimages to monasteries had become more important as his freedom of movement increased with age. If he learned about an out-of-the-way chapel or hermitage anywhere within reach, he would go there and see what he could learn. He slept on straw pallets and stone floors, ate coarse black bread and soup with the monks or hermits, and talked about spiritual matters.

On several occasions, over holiday weekends and during vacations, Mitropoulos went to visit his uncles in the Holy Community of Mount Athos. These visits to the sacred peninsula were milestones in the conductor's life, but frustratingly little is known about them. There were approximately two dozen active monastic communities on Athos in the years before World War One, but we do not know with any certainty which ones Mitropoulos stayed with. In the mid-1950s he did send out Christmas cards depicting the monasteries of Meteora and Varlaan, so it is reasonable to suppose that he may have made one or both of these places his headquarters during his visits; so great was his interest in the Holy Community, however, that he must have visited every facility and hermitage he could.

Even modern-day visitors who do not consider themselves especially religious fall readily under the spell of Mount Athos. It is truly a place where time has stood still, with its crown of monasteries threaded atop stark mountainous cliffs, its groves and gardens so exquisitely tended and so riotous in color and fragrance, its whole setting bathed in glorious light and surrounded by the island-dotted sea—this is what much of Greece must have looked like in the time of Homer, before centuries of over-grazing denuded so much of the land. To young Mitropoulos, this contrast between the ascetics of architecture and the sensual radiance of nature would have been intoxicating on every level of his being.

On a personally physical level, however, these sojourns on Athos could be quite uncomfortable. On one visit, Mitropoulos was kept awake at night by bedbugs falling from the ceiling (the insects' only means of gaining access since the four legs of the bed were resting in cans of kerosene).[2] On another occasion, he was required to sleep at night on a bare stone floor. As it happened, that night was dank and chilly in the mountains, yet despite the discomfort, he once recalled to conductor Paul Strauss, "when I got up that morning, I was greatly invigorated with the sacrifice I had made!"[3]

Part of what made a monk's life so appealing to him was, in fact, these denials of creature comforts. Mitropoulos was intensely, mystically, drawn toward an early Christian ideal of self-sacrifice that tended to embrace even the extremes of self-denial and discomfort, a medieval proposition that one's spiritual strength grows greater in direct proportion to one's denial of the flesh. There is no question but that this same impulse, when it manifested itself in later decades, sometimes approached outright masochism, but for the adolescent pilgrim seeking a purer existence and feeling himself inexorably drawn toward a very personal vision of the Godhead, the ideal of a monastic life was quite romantic in its appeal—especially in the setting of Athos, so isolated from the outside world that it might as well have been in an alternate universe.

Mitropoulos was at a crossroads. In one direction lay music, which fulfilled him as no other human activity could; in the other direction lay either the priesthood or the life of a monastic. He had to find out, before wholly committing himself once more to the conservatory, if there were not some way to combine these two callings.

At the climax of this internal crisis, Mitropoulos had what must have been a Dostoyevskian dialogue with a member of the Greek Orthodox hierarchy. The person was not one of his uncles, or at least was never identified by Mitropoulos as such, but he may well have been a trusted spiritual advisor to whom the uncles directed this young pilgrim. Mitropoulos gave identical accounts of this event in dozens of interviews.

He opened the dialogue by describing his love for music and his belief in its spiritual power, yet he also confessed that he was drawn, with equal force, toward the ideals of monastic life. He sought some assurance that this might not be an either/or choice, that the church might steer him into a religious career that would accommodate both of his passions.

No, said his advisor. Although the Greek Orthodox Church has a heritage of vocal music that is both vast and glorious, it permits no instrumental music in its services.

Surely the church would not mind if he pursued music on his own, in his free time, Mitropoulos countered.

That, too, would not be possible, replied the priest. The church allows no musical instruments on sacred ground.

Mitropoulos responded that he would be content if he could just have a little harmonium in his cell.

Not even a harmonium, said the priest.

"I knew then," the conductor later recalled in numerous interviews, "that I just could not do it."

But he did find a way to combine these seemingly contradictory choices. He brought to the podium a sense of religious dedication, a fierce, uncompromising zeal on behalf of music he deemed unjustly neglected or that others deemed too difficult for the average listener; and over the years as he strove to fulfill this mission, he pared down his own lifestyle to the severe and essential, avoiding most of the comforts and perquisites his status and salary entitled him to.

And if commentators or colleagues chose to refer to him as "monkish," he did not mind in the least.

Armand Marsick (1877–1959), although almost forgotten today, was a well-known and highly regarded musician at the time Mitropoulos came under his tutelage. A pupil of Guy Ropartz, Marsick began his career as a violinist and soon became concertmaster of a major Parisian orchestra. Lured by a good salary and the chance to have an orchestra of his own at the Athens Conservatory, he joined the faculty of that institution, teaching composition as well as conducting. His compositional output was not large—some forty works, most of them written before 1914—but it was of high quality, skillfully blending the combined influences of Wagner and Franck and expertly orchestrated. There was much that young Mitropoulos could learn from such an experienced musician.

Marsick found in Mitropoulos the kind of pupil who illuminates an entire teaching career, a young man of musical genius whose broader intellectual potential seemed unbounded, quick and keen to learn; even at age sixteen, even while struggling privately with moral crises whose dimensions were greater than those of mere adolescence, young Mitropoulos seemed to have a center, a clear and focused concept of who he was and what he wanted to accomplish.

For such a pupil, the classroom is only a beginning, a portico, and Marsick was determined to broaden Mitropoulos's horizons at this sensitive point in the young man's life, in a most dramatic way.

In the summer of 1912, therefore, Marsick invited Dimitri and a fellow student named Georgios Sklavos to be his guests, until October and the start of the new school year, in the city of Rome. Marsick's wife was Italian, the couple owned a spacious, attractive residence in the city, and they took pains to assure that their young guests became deeply immersed in the historical and cultural ambience of the city.

This was Mitropoulos's first exposure to a great European city, and the experience was an intoxicating one. He made passionate pilgrimages to Rome's great monuments and art works, and was deeply moved to behold with his own eyes the statues, paintings, and edifices about which he had read for so many years. Musical life in Rome, of course, was a dazzling banquet for his senses, and he attended dozens of concerts, recitals, and operatic productions of a quality simply not encountered in Athens. His sense of what was artistically possible expanded to vast new horizons. Most enjoyable of all, he performed in chamber music soirees held in the Marsick apartment, taking the piano part while Marsick himself played the violin, and some of Europe's finest musicians took turns filling out the various ensembles. His own creativity, not surprisingly, was stimulated by such an environment, and he composed a piano work, his Scherzo in E-flat Major, while living with the Marsicks.

If Rome nourished the intellectual and the artist, the Holy City provided an equal stimulus for the philosopher and the mystic. While the dogmas of the Catholic Church—or any other set of dogmas, for that matter—did not appeal to Mitropoulos, the richness of its history, tangible as marble on every side, exerted a powerful allure. He had always been profoundly attracted to the spiritual quest that lies at the heart of all religions, and now he found himself in a city whose inhabitants had delved into those mysteries for two thousand years. The past reached out to embrace him and it resonated with his inner quest.

Nothing that happened to Mitropoulos in Rome had a more powerful effect than his discovery of the life and writings of Francis of Assisi. Dimitri Mitropoulos had found his personal patron saint, and from that summer until the last day of his life, he strove to live according to the principles of St. Francis, a man who was born into worldly circumstances near the end of the tumultuous twelfth century, but who in his relatively short life, in the words of one modern biographer, "almost managed to turn the Christian ideal into a triumphant fact."[4]

The more Mitropoulos studied the biographies of St. Francis, the closer became his identification. Although there would be mean-spirited men who mocked Mitropoulos, sometimes to his face, for his open, unashamed allegiance to a medieval ideal, Mitropoulos succeeded in living up to the ideal of St. Francis nearly as well as Francis lived up to the ideal of Christ. And while Mitropoulos received good professional training by the standards of his country at that time, he was spiritually and philosophically, like Francis, a theodidact—a God-taught man.

Given Mitropoulos's youth during this Roman summer, it is likely that he identified most strongly with the *young* Francis, at least on an emotional level. Both young men loved the sheer physical beauty of the world; and both loved music. Francis, in his reckless and relatively debauched teenage years, was a noted troubadour whom early accounts describe as having a sweet and powerful voice. Many of the ballads Francis sang, and no doubt some that he composed, were highly erotic in content. Francis was a rake, a party-goer, and his family's wealth, combined with his own swaggering persona, afforded plenty of opportunities to enjoy lavish dinners and balls. Even after Francis underwent his spiritual transformation, this love of music continued—his early followers were sometimes called "minstrels of God" and are often described in terms of their joyous singing.

Both men had a strong streak of carnality, which both suppressed. In the young Francis, Mitropoulos recognized the same tension between flesh and spirit as he felt within himself. That tension became the dynamo that fueled his accomplishments; for most of his adult life, he managed to channel everything into music, even as Francis subordinated every extraneous thing to faith. Already, by mid-adolescence, Mitropoulos had acquired the same bedrock belief in the value of sacrifice and the comparative worthlessness of worldly goods, the same ideal of a dedicated and therefore necessarily austere style of life. Mitropoulos gave himself to Music, allowed himself to become possessed by it, to become *inhabited* by it, in much the same way as Francis gave himself over to Christ. And there would be plenty of times, when he burned with zeal to communicate the essence of some new and difficult composition, that the conductor must have envied St. Francis preaching to the birds.

In the relationship between St. Francis and St. Clare, Mitropoulos found a model for his idealization of the interaction between conductor and orchestra: the love of equals in a common search for an Ultimate Love that is beyond their separate identities but that may be attainable, or at least glimpsed, through their mutual commitment.

Mitropoulos's manner of rehearsing an orchestra was also derived from his study of St. Francis, particularly the eighth precept set down in his "Letter to the Faithful," a set of eleven guidelines probably written in 1215 and widely circulated not only among Franciscans, but throughout the church. Precept number eight, entitled "How Those Who Command Should be Humble" reads, in part: "Anyone who has the right to give orders should remember that 'the greater should be as the lesser'; he should be a servant to his brothers and deal with them mercifully, as he would wish to be treated if he were in their place. Nor should he rage against a brother who sins, but patiently and kindly counsel him and help him."

In many interviews, Mitropoulos referred to St. Francis as a guide and mentor, but in 1956, in an article he wrote for an obscure musical publication, he discussed his youthful discovery of Francis from the viewpoint of his own career, summarizing the Franciscan influence with clarity and eloquence:

> Art must reach out to people. The artist who stands on temperament— who demands that the public understand *him*—is traducing a basic principle. . . . I am not inclined to argue this point because my mind is thoroughly made up. To wit, the artist has replaced the politician and the businessman as the teacher and leader in our confused time. And he must accomplish his task, it seems to me, by setting an example, by doing. This has been my position for a very long time. At an early age, while studying in Italy, it was revealed to me by a great spiritual figure who has been a source of faith and inspiration to me ever since. I refer to Francis of Assisi.
>
> In a day when church corruption had made a mockery of religion, this man of wealth chose to give away everything and to appear on the streets in the humblest clothing, convinced that he could most effectively spread the ideal of Christ by emulating it himself.
>
> Over the years I have always found peace of mind and soul—to whatever extent we can achieve this state—by likewise striving at all times as I would have others strive, by acting as I would have others act. Francis taught me that to cajole or to threaten is never as effective as to set an example yourself.[5]

Neither Mitropoulos nor St. Francis was an especially practical man, but Francis at least lived in an age when such impracticality could be valued on its own terms. Mitropoulos lived in an age when true humility and open spiritual commitment made people uneasy and drew from them scorn and ridicule, especially from the hard-bitten, frequently ill-used men of the New York Philharmonic, who tended to take gross advantage of any conductor who did *not* tyrannically cajole and threaten them. It was easier to be God's Fool in twelfth-century Umbria than in twentieth-century Manhattan.

But Mitropoulos believed with all his heart that if God asked a man to do hard things, then God would provide that man with the strength to do them. For many years, this belief sustained him. But when his body began to betray his will, when the cumulative physical effects of the tensions under which he lived and worked began to manifest themselves, the shock bruised his soul. Yet he persevered to the end, and it could be said of him what a modern biographer of St. Francis said of the man from Assisi: "As the one whom he loved so much had done, he kept silent in the face of the human hounds baying at him. Lost in prayer, he marched forward."[6]

CHAPTER THREE

The Young Composer

Although Mitropoulos was sorry to leave Rome, he was happy to reenter the Athens Conservatory for the academic year 1912–1913. His studies in theory were now closely guided by Marsick, and his piano technique was already exceptional. He composed his second work during this school year, *Un Morceau de concert*, for violin with piano accompaniment. Marsick was so impressed with his progress, both as a composer and as a performer, that he scheduled his star pupil on the conservatory's concert series. Mitropoulos therefore made his first public appearance, as both composer and pianist, on March 22, 1913, and repeated the program on April 4. The work was his own new concert piece, and Marsick played the violin part.

During his third year at the conservatory, 1913–1914, Mitropoulos progressed to the intermediate level in his piano studies. He also took advanced harmony under Marsick and broadened his coursework to include choral music.

Honors and recognition began to come during his fourth year of formal study, when he received a prize for attaining the highest grades in counterpoint of any student in the academy's history. He continued piano study, now at the advanced level, and he composed energetically, completing three works during the academic year 1914–1915, including his first work for orchestra, a tone poem entitled *Tafi* (or *Gospel*, based on Matthew 27:59; the score is apparently lost, for the work is not included in any published list of Mitropoulos's compositions). The other two works were *Okorniostos* for male chorus and *Danse des faunes*, subtitled Scherzo fantastique, for string quartet.

The year's most significant event, however, took place at a concert of the conservatory orchestra on April 19, 1915, when Mitropoulos made his public debut as a conductor, leading the orchestra through his own tone poem, *Tafi*.

In his fifth year at the Athens Conservatory, 1915–1916, in addition to his continuing study of piano technique and counterpoint, Mitropoulos took classes in orchestration and chamber music. He composed at least one work during this academically busy year, his Scherzo in F Minor, which would later be featured on his examination program in the spring of 1916.

At this point in the conductor's life, politics and world events elbowed their way into the pleasantly self-contained world of musical academia. Greece had doubled in size by the start of World War One, thanks to the success of King George's newly modernized army in the First and Second Balkan Wars—most of the ethnic regions that had remained under Ottoman control after the founding of modern Greece had been redeemed during those confused and bloody mountain campaigns; only the large Greek population in Thrace, and an even larger enclave in Asia Minor, centered around the port of Smyrna, remained under the heel of the Turks.

Good King George was assassinated by a lunatic in 1912, and was succeeded by his son, Constantine. Although a militarist by nature (his hero was Kaiser Wilhelm), Constantine was blocked from joining the Germans in 1914 by a strong prime minister and a liberal government. When the Greeks' former enemies, the Bulgarians, came in on the German side in September 1915, the Greeks were compelled to mobilize—on the Allied side.

Mitropoulos's political views in 1916, when he was twenty, are not known. Clearly, however, he was prime material for conscription. He did not wish either to interrupt his studies or to be labeled as a shirker; neither did he wish to get himself killed on some barren mountainside in Salonika. He volunteered before he could be drafted. Draftees served for a period of two years; enlistees served for five years, but those with special skills had some degree of choice about where they would be stationed. Certainly, by this time, Mitropoulos had enough connections in high places to make sure he would not end up as cannon fodder.

On July 25, 1916, he was posted to the band of the Athenian garrison with the (rather amusing) rank of Musician Fourth Class. The only vacancy in the band was for the timpani, an instrument Mitropoulos had never before studied but one which he quickly mastered. His official responsibilities turned out to be surprisingly light, so that he was able to continue his formal studies during off-duty hours, and he was discharged honorably in the spring of 1920.

In fact, his musical studies do not seem to have been more than inconvenienced by his military service. School records show him listed as a percussionist in the Conservatory Orchestra for the year 1916–1917. Indeed he took to the percussion so readily that he played in that section—and dominated it—until his graduation. An eyewitness described Mitropoulos working the battery:

Diagonally, up high across from the sweeping violin bows and behind the woodwinds and trumpets, appeared an unmistakable blond head. There stood Mitropoulos in the midst of his battery—tambourines, cymbals, large bells and small, triangles, drums, and gongs—everything within the reach of those long, long arms. He was so constantly in motion, so nervously, with such physical strength, that he seemed to be the virtual center of the music, marking its heartbeat and its very breath, giving it not only color but soul. The whole orchestra seemed to create the performance from his example.[1]

More than that: when a conductor less competent than Marsick was on the podium, as was frequently the case, the orchestra simply took the beat from Mitropoulos, who was so charged with energy during a performance that his body continued to conduct the music even when he had no percussion parts to play. This early experience with the timpani, together with his virtuosity on the piano, may well account for the preference Mitropoulos later showed, as a conductor, for explosive, percussive accents. Mitropoulos's career as a timpanist is still honored by the Minnesota Orchestra—the timpanist's position in that orchestra is permanently endowed as the Dimitri Mitropoulos Principal Timpani Chair.

Mitropoulos's second solo public performance took place on February 18, 1917, in a war-charity event sponsored by King Constantine. This was an all-Mitropoulos affair, featuring the twenty-two-year-old musician as both composer and performer, an indication that he was already regarded as a rising star on a national scale. On the program were a piano sonata in E-flat major entitled *My Soul*, the Scherzo in F Minor, and a brand new composition for piano entitled *Pictures from Barracks Life*. Mitropoulos was at the keyboard for that work, as well as for the concluding two songs ("Last Song" and "A Mother's Heart,") which were performed by soprano Maria Stratou. Centerpiece for the concert was Mitropoulos's Sonata in C Minor for violin and piano, performed by faculty artists.

For a composer whose style would soon take a great leap to an advanced contemporary idiom, Mitropoulos was still writing music in a surprisingly romantic style at age twenty-two. The three movements of his E-flat major piano sonata, for instance, were entitled "Love," "Pain," and "Belief." This concert marked Mitropoulos's first appearance before an audience not composed almost wholly of conservatory people, and listeners were captivated by both his piano technique and his striking appearance. "Gasps could be heard while he was playing the sonata," according to Maria Christopoulou, who interviewed several elderly audience members during the early 1980s.[2]

Mitropoulos shared the podium with a faculty conductor on May 11, 1917, conducting two works that would later become concert specialties during his American years: Mozart's Overture to *Don Giovanni* and Alexander Glazunov's *Overture on Greek Themes*, Op. 3. This concert was held beyond the confines of the conservatory, at the National Theater in Athens, and the event was well covered by the press.

He was supposed to graduate at the end of the spring trimester of 1918 but was unable to do so because of surgery (the nature of the operation is not recorded). His creative energy remained high even as his body recuperated, for he began working long hours on his most ambitious project to date, an opera entitled *Soeur Béatrice*. A concert version of Act One was performed on April 12, 1918, under Mitropoulos's direction. The leading roles were sung by professionals—Béatrice by soprano Maria Mesolora and Bellidor by tenor Kimon Triantafilou—and the remaining parts by vocal students from the conservatory.

Mitropoulos also appeared for the first time that spring as an orchestral soloist, playing the piano part in Vincent d'Indy's *Symphony on a French Mountain Air* at a Conservatory Orchestra concert on January 21 under Marsick's baton, and again, on April 15, in César Franck's *Symphonic Variations* for piano and orchestra. Marsick by this time may have begun to suspect that his star pupil's gifts as a conductor were potentially equal to his other musical abilities, for on March 18, he entrusted to Mitropoulos a performance of his own tone poem *La Source*, a ripe specimen of late romanticism reminiscent of Franck.

Altogether, during his years at the Athens Conservatory, Mitropoulos performed publicly at the piano on fourteen occasions: four times accompanying a violinist, nine times as a vocal accompanist, and once in a chamber music program. He played perhaps three times as many concerts in off-campus events, often at the behest of other, smaller music academies, and during his last two years at the conservatory, he was in constant demand by his colleagues as a rehearsal accompanist.

Mitropoulos graduated from the Athens Conservatory in the spring of 1919 at the age of twenty-three. His final exam was a traditional graduation recital, for which he chose:

Beethoven	Sonata in A-flat Major, Op. 110
Franck	Prelude, Aria, and Finale
Chopin	Preludes Op. 10, No. 12; Op. 25, No. 9 and 12
Chopin	Impromptu in F-sharp Minor
Liszt	Sonata in B Minor
Mitropoulos	*For Crete: Festivals and Joy*

This was an arduous program even for an experienced virtuoso, but both Mitropoulos's technique and stamina were equal to its demands. He graduated with the highest honors on June 25, 1919, and at that time he was awarded, by unanimous vote of the faculty, a special gold medal. Even after winning his diploma, Mitropoulos continued to study theory with Marsick, as a private pupil, for another year.

During that exciting summer following graduation, the young musician's attention was focused on two important things: composition and love. By midsummer, he had written a special song, entitled "Kassiani," which he dedicated to Madame K. Paxinou.

Katina Paxinou was a nineteen-year-old student of voice and piano, who had recently enrolled in the Athens Conservatory following studies in drama at the Geneva Conservatory. A native of Piraeus, she gained early fame as a specialist in classical Greek drama. She was on tour with the

Greek National Theater when World War Two broke out and she ended up in America, where she distinguished herself in several Broadway productions before Paramount offered her a movie contract. Her first role—as Pilar, the tough, canny, but tender-hearted guerrilla in *For Whom the Bell Tolls*—earned her an Academy Award in 1943. Her screen career thereafter was one of solid accomplishment on both sides of the Atlantic, until she returned to Athens in 1956 and devoted the remaining seventeen years of her life to the Royal Theater of Athens. Although she and Mitropoulos never rekindled their physical intimacy after 1920, they remained devoted friends for the rest of his life.

Katina was the sort of woman usually described as striking rather than conventionally beautiful. She was big-boned and somewhat angular of face; she moved with great physical energy—her reach across a table was enormous—but always with the grace imparted by her theatrical training. She had an earthy mane of raven's-wing hair, a sensual mouth, and eyes like black suns.

She and Dimitri had met when he was assigned to be her accompanist, possibly as early as the autumn of 1918. They had much in common, these two young artists: energy, idealism, and the explosive creativity of youth. What began as a passionate friendship evolved, by the summer of 1920, into a passionate love affair. Although Mitropoulos was then, and would always remain, primarily homosexual, he was not exclusively so during his late adolescence and early manhood. In later life, he would sometimes say: "Don't think I have not known the love of women," or variants to that effect. Certainly Katina was the woman whose sexual love he knew best and for the longest time; there may have been at least one other.

Working together, Katina and Dimitri hatched an ambitious plan to mount a fully staged production of Mitropoulos's opera *Soeur Béatrice*, with Katina in the title role. Given the operatic resources available in Athens at this time, the undertaking was bold. Fortunately, Katina came from a wealthy family, and most of the money raised for the project came from her resources. Dimitri not only planned to conduct, but he managed and directed the production as well.

Of course, neither of them had the slightest practical experience in mounting theatrical productions, so the project was plagued by delays and compromises and stress for all concerned. At some point along the way, Mitropoulos realized he was spreading himself too thin and accepted Marsick's offer to take over in the orchestra pit.

Though its production values were still rough, the opera nevertheless opened on schedule on May 11, 1920. *Soeur Béatrice* did not showcase a compositional style of path-breaking originality; indeed, for the newspaper *Estia*, Marsick himself wrote: "Mr. Mitropoulos is like all young people who have not yet put the stamp of individualism on their music. He therefore, and quite naturally, reflects the many influences he has been exposed to during his studies."[3] The reviewers all agreed that some pages of the opera sounded like Debussy; a few were unkind enough to say the opera sounded like "school music." But the audience responded warmly to the production, and the consensus was that even if Mitropoulos tended to reflect numerous influences, at least he did so with remarkable craftsmanship, self-assurance, and musicality.

Response to the first performance was encouraging enough, at any rate, to justify a second performance, on May 13. Fate was sitting in the audience that night, in the person of the elder statesman of French music, Camille Saint-Saëns, who had been in Athens on unrelated business, had heard interesting things about this young multitalented musician, and had decided on the spur of the moment to attend. He, at least, was not grudging in his praise, for when he returned to Paris, he wrote an article about his Greek sojourn which contained a number of extremely flattering remarks about Mitropoulos and his youthful opera.

This may very well have marked the first occasion when a Greek musician, educated and trained on home soil, had received a good review in Paris, and when Saint-Saëns's remarks were reprinted in the Athenian papers, the entire city reverberated with praises for its young native son.

The results, in terms of Mitropoulos's career, were immediate and profound. At a special meeting of the conservatory's administrative committee on June 14, the decision was made to award Dimitri Mitropoulos a stipend for further study, to be undertaken in Marsick's home town, Brussels. Clearly the young man had absorbed all the musical education Athens could offer, and the time had come for him to seek broader horizons. This grant amounted to seven hundred drachmae a month, barely enough for Mitropoulos to live decently. There was, however, one very large string attached: in return for this generosity, Mitropoulos was supposed to concentrate on the study of organ music, so that he might return home and inaugurate a course of study in that instrument at the Athens Conservatory.

Mitropoulos had no particular interest in the organ, but if studying that instrument would enable him to live in Brussels, he was certainly willing to do so. He signed the necessary papers, bade goodbye to his friends and to Katina, and made ready to depart in the waning days of August 1920.

Financial aid, on a rather considerable scale, was also forthcoming from a wealthy Athenian banker named Miltiades Negroponte, who took a very active interest in furthering the young man's career, probably at the insistence of his wife, Maria, who had quite fallen under Mitropoulos's spell. While Mr. Negroponte remains a shadowy figure, Mrs. Negroponte became a devoted friend and remained so until her death. An educated and well-read woman, she was fascinated by Mitropoulos's talent and mesmerized by his appearance on the podium, by the physical force of his gestures, by the strength and beauty of his outsized hands. However she may have regarded him in the sanctuary of her heart, she proved to be an ideal combination of friend, mother, and benefactor.

Even Katy Katsoyanis, who fancied herself as the only woman in Mitropoulos's life and who could be fiercely resentful of anyone whom she
saw as competition for the conductor's affections, paid tribute to the Negroponte relationship:

> Maria Miltiadou Negroponte, that exceptional woman, was the most
> important person in Mitropoulos's life. From his youthful years she
> and her husband were for him a support, guide, benefactor, helper. She
> brought him up. Widely educated and a gracious soul, she knew how
> to combine dignity with enthusiasm, her sense of duty toward herself
> with an understanding of others.[4]

Without question, Mitropoulos loved her, for he found the time to write
her virtually every day for twenty years (except, of course, during the war).
At the time of her death, in the late 1960s, she had hundreds of letters from
him, some of them brief notes, others quite detailed and confessional. Mitropoulos poured out his heart to this generous and sympathetic woman—
more so, even, than he did in his celebrated published correspondence with
Katy Katsoyanis—and taken as a whole, that correspondence comprised
an intimate autobiographical chronicle.

Intimate it would remain; when she realized that she had but a short
time to live, Maria Negroponte burned the entire collection, justifying
the act to Katy Katsoyanis by saying that "private letters are not for public
consumption."

CHAPTER FOUR

Berlin and Studies with Busoni

Music lovers familiar with the mature Dimitri Mitropoulos—the legendary black-clad "monk" with the gangling frame, bald cranium, and somber, downcast features—would scarcely have recognized the twenty-four-year-old student who moved to Brussels in August 1920. His overall appearance was more bohemian than monkish. He wore his fine-stranded medium-blond hair long, either parting it in the middle or, more often, brushing it straight back in the classic, partless pompadour often adopted by European intellectuals of the day. His complexion was medium in tone, and his skin was clear. One met him first, even before the handshake, by means of his extraordinary eyes: Aegean blue, they projected a gaze of utter clarity and openness and anyone who walked into the room could feel their impact.

Blessed with good health all his youth, Mitropoulos had kept himself extremely fit even during the conservatory years, through regular hiking excursions and mountain-climbing treks. While he was not conventionally muscular, he possessed enormous wiry strength. When Katy Katsoyanis met and fell in love with him in 1925, the attraction was definitely physical as well as intellectual: "He had so much physical strength that he could drive a nail into the wall with his finger, and his hand was so steady he could draw an absolutely straight line on paper."[1] For all his radiant good health and vigor, Mitropoulos did not give bone-crusher handshakes, nor limp ones—the initial touch of his hand, whether the recipient was man or woman, imparted a sense of delicacy and, above all other qualities, gentleness; "like the touch of cotton," was how one friend described the sensation.[2]

According to the records of the Conservatoire Royal de Musique Bruxelles, Mitropoulos stayed in the city for two years. One of his most painstaking Greek biographers, Kostios, cites other sources that indicate that, while Mitropoulos might have been carried on the rolls at the conservatory, he did not in fact stay in Brussels much longer than fifteen or sixteen months. Although according to the terms of his stipend agreement Mitropoulos was supposed to be enrolled as a student of organ, his conservatory records indicate no emphasis on that instrument. He did study organ privately with Alphonse Desmet, but the effort was surely half-hearted. For a young musician as dynamic as Mitropoulos, the idea of becoming a professor of organ music must have seemed a fairly dismal future, especially now: Brussels was close enough to the heart of European musical life for Mitropoulos to gain far more exposure to contemporary developments than he ever got in Greece. Musical earthquakes were erupting regularly in Paris and Berlin as nineteenth-century ideals crumbled and new, revolutionary concepts struggled for their place in the musical sun. Mitropoulos read and heard about these exciting events, and about the controversial Stravinskys and Weills and Schoenbergs who were the standard-bearers of contending modern trends; probably no musical endeavor could have seemed less relevant to him than playing the organ.

Much more important to Mitropoulos's development were the composition classes he took under Paul Gilson. Gilson (1865–1942) was at this time in disgrace for allegedly collaborating with the German occupation authorities and had been forced to resign from the conservatory, although many believed he was more guilty of naiveté than treason. He was, in any case, a formidable musician and a master of orchestration. After winning the Prix de Rome in 1889, he had held important academic posts in Brussels and Antwerp, and before the war he was the most influential music critic in Belgium. Mitropoulos admired Gilson and pitied his current predicament. "He was penniless, but a very nice person," recollected the conductor many years later. "After I had been studying with him for one year, he suddenly said: 'My dear man, what are you still doing here in Brussels? Go to Germany!'"[3]

Probably the only thing holding Mitropoulos to Brussels, after Gilson's encouraging remark, was the need to finish a large-scale composition before interrupting his life with another major move. The composition, *A Greek Sonata*, was Mitropoulos's greatest piano work, a monumental fifty-minute blockbuster in the great virtuoso tradition of the B Minor Sonata of Franz Liszt or Rachmaninoff's Sonata No. 2, Op. 36. Mitropoulos completed the work on October 15, 1920. Before packing his bags for Berlin, he booked a recital hall in Brussels and gave the world premiere of this sonata. The work then languished for seventy years, until May 1990, when the adventurous young British pianist Geoffrey Douglas Madge programmed the work and brought down the house with it.

So extravagant are the colors and sonorities of this work that it could only have been conceived orchestrally. In scope and emotional range, the first movement alone—about seventeen minutes long—is virtually a piano symphony. In the second movement, a lyrical vein, edged with harmonic vinegar, hints of familiarity with Bartók; the slow third movement reaches a spectacular climax.[4] In the last movement, Maestoso, Allegro (non troppo), Mitropoulos throws in references to everything that was on his creative mind in 1920, from Greek dance rhythms to parodistic quotations from Stravinsky's *Petrushka*.

Mitropoulos was an active composer for some fifteen years, with one large hiatus when he was adjusting to new responsibilities as conductor of the Athens Conservatory Orchestra as well as trying to digest the staggering amount of new musical input he had been exposed to in Brussels and

Berlin. The *Greek Sonata* is the centerpiece of his career as a composer, a work of explosive creativity that expresses both his Greek heritage and his innate cosmopolitanism. While his colleagues in Athens were composing nationalistic works (such as Kalomiris's *Levendia Symphony*—a sort of Greek "Ilya Murometz"—or Petros Petridis's *Greek Symphony*), Mitropoulos was evolving an intense, harmonically bristling personal style that gleamed like Bauhaus chrome and veered giddily toward the *terra incognita* of atonality. As a composer, Mitropoulos was already plunging toward serialism in 1920, when even the hardiest disciples of modernism were still hedging their bets with neoclassicism. In the five years between Mitropoulos's graduation and his return to Athens in 1924, he struck out on his own and achieved a compositional style as advanced and as personal as those of Berg or Stravinsky, while during that same time, his former Greek colleagues were laboring righteously and self-consciously, but no doubt with a sense of mission equal to Mitropoulos's own, to establish the Greek National Music movement. Small wonder that many of those colleagues, happily writing warm, folk-flavored romantic music, regarded Mitropoulos as an avant-garde subversive, an incoherent Futurist, or a dangerous disciple of the musical anti-Christ, Arnold Schoenberg. And Mitropoulos, for his part, probably felt as though he has set foot on a strange planet, not all of whose inhabitants were friendly.

In the autumn of 1920, however, he was content to have finished his sonata and to have performed it at least once. He was under no illusions as to the potential popularity of the sonata, but he knew that it was a landmark work in his own creative evolution and he was eager to learn how it would be regarded, not by the public but by his colleagues in Berlin.

If Paris was the Mecca of postwar literature, Berlin was the center of musical gravity. By 1920 there was a small Greek colony already established in the city, students and artists mostly, including one friend from conservatory days, Antonis Skokos, and another young Greek composer—perhaps the best his nation produced in the first half of the century—named Nikos Skalkottas; it would be Skalkottas, most notably in his symphony *The Return of Ulysses*, who would come closest to blending Greek nationalism with contemporary musical techniques.

Once Mitropoulos was settled in Berlin, Skokos introduced the new arrival to his own piano instructor, Egon Petri, marking the start of a long artistic and personal relationship. Petri was on the threshold of a major virtuoso career; with a virtuoso's eye he studied the score of the *Greek Sonata*, and with a virtuoso's ear he listened to Mitropoulos blaze through its knuckle-breaking octaves.

Impressed by what he heard, Petri recommended that Mitropoulos become a pupil of Petri's own former teacher, the great Ferruccio Busoni, who was then presiding over a master class at the Prussian Academy of the Arts. Mitropoulos made an appointment with Busoni, arrived at the proper time, and played through the entire work. Busoni listened patiently for the better part of an hour, saying nothing until the last thunderous chords had died away, at which point he glared belligerently at Mitropoulos and pronounced: "Too much passion! Go back to Mozart in order to learn purity of form!"

Mitropoulos recalled:

> I was deeply shocked, for he seemed to be saying that music and passion are two things better kept separate. I tried to find hidden irony in his words, but there was none. He meant it, and I had not misunderstood him. But what could I do, when my entire nature is full of passion and fire? Busoni's remark gave me some difficult days and weeks!
>
> My entire being had been devoted to composing [that sonata]. It had been passionate and sensual music-making. But now, mulling over Busoni's lecture, I felt like a sinner. I could no longer compose, yet I had to find my peace of mind again. I had to find the equilibrium between my heart, my nature, and my reason. Really, this was a decisive moment. If conducting had not come to the fore in the meantime, who knows? Perhaps my involvement with music might have come to an end.[5]

Earlier biographical sketches have stated that Mitropoulos was a member of Busoni's master class, and Mitropoulos himself often spoke, offhandedly, of being "a pupil of Busoni's," but the arrangement must have been private and informal, not in an academic setting, for the records of Busoni's class exist and they contain no mention of Mitropoulos. What is certain is that Mitropoulos rapidly became a member of Busoni's inner circle of pupils and admirers and that he attended many gatherings in Busoni's home, where he mingled with some of the brightest musicians, artists, and writers in Berlin. Among his closer acquaintances in this setting were Kurt Weill, Vladimir Vogel, Phillip Jarnach, and Gisella Selden-Goth—who would briefly become Busoni's mistress and whose daughter, Trudy Goth, would become Mitropoulos's European secretary during the last decade of his life.

Selden-Goth was also present when Mitropoulos met Béla Bartók in Berlin:

> It was in February 1923 that I met Dimitri Mitropoulos for the first time. The unforgettable Béla Bartók, who had just started to attract the attention of the progressive musical world, had come there to present his compositions in a series of chamber music concerts. He was then at the full height of his youthful powers, producing new, unusual, and fascinating music. Among other scores, he had brought with him his ballet *The Miraculous Mandarin*. Regarding the piano version as unworkable for a single player, he had arranged the work for four hands, but had not been able to find a partner sufficiently familiar with the new tech-

niques to try it out with him. He asked me to find someone in Berlin who could muster the necessary qualifications. It seemed . . . a nearly hopeless task. One day, however, I succeeded in presenting to him a very thin, shy, close-mouthed young man who was studying with Busoni and who had been mentioned by this master as having a knack for performing anything, however impracticable or crazy. Bartók sat down at the keyboard with him rather skeptically. After a dozen bars, he stopped and said quietly: "This man is all right."[6]

Busoni's stunning admonition to Mitropoulos—"Too much passion! Go study Mozart!"—was typical of his flamboyant style as a pedagogue. He often used such pithy, jabbing aphorisms to make important points, sometimes tossing out intentionally contradictory or ambiguous statements, much like Zen *koans*, intended to get the pupil's mind up to speed or simply to break the pattern of old habits. "The old and the new are the same!" was one classic Busoni-ism that made the rounds of his inner circle.

Mitropoulos the pianist was stimulated, sometimes awed, by Busoni's technical prowess and by the panache with which he illuminated familiar masterpieces:

> I was completely fascinated whenever he demonstrated at the piano during composition lessons. He had an incredibly artistic way of playing certain passages, sometimes using entirely novel finger placement. It gave him pleasure to demonstrate his virtuosity. . . . I remember also being shocked by the way he performed the Beethoven Fourth Concerto. In the first movement, he played the chromatic accompaniment of the left hand in octaves. This suited him; it was brilliant, stunning, but it was also quite unnecessary.[7]

Busoni's style of piano playing also influenced Mitropoulos's conducting philosophy. American composer Otto Luening, who was a Busoni pupil from 1917 to 1920, described his teacher as the consummate virtuoso who

> avoided strict metrical playing in all performances; he was interested in projecting the form of each piece so that it could be remembered. This concept resulted in *rubato* playing based on the phrase relationships within each piece. Because these varied in each work, his style of interpretation also varied from work to work and in different performances of the same pieces. His sense of phrase affected his tempi, so he never played a piece fast just to dazzle listeners.[8]

Busoni encouraged his pupils to be independent of trends, to accept traditions while striving to transform those traditions into the music of today and tomorrow. He described himself as an artist who sought to create a multifaceted personal style that incorporated the best cultural traits of both the Italians and the Germans.

Mitropoulos was seeking a similar synthesis, for his own creative development was certainly marked by an attempt to reconcile the passion of his Mediterranean blood with a decidedly European concern for form and architecture. He was deeply stimulated by his contact with Busoni the teacher, and perhaps even more so by Busoni the composer; the purity of intent and the transparency of means displayed in Busoni's best works were qualities that the young Greek also sought, whether as a pianist, composer, or conductor. Again, Otto Luening:

> Busoni was more than a mentor—he was an *animator*. . . . He would size you up and then give you support as an artist whether you were a pianist or a composer. He was interested in your personality, and if there was a seed in your personality that could be developed, that's what he went for. He did that with everybody who came into contact with him and he did, I'm sure, have a terrific influence on Mitropoulos.[9]

Indeed, from the moment Busoni said "Too much passion!" Mitropoulos's inner priorities began to shift. Until his contact with Busoni, he had wanted more than anything else to be a composer, a creator. Now, gradually, he began to think of his musical career more in terms of re-creation. He did not give up composing all at once—several of his most original compositions were yet to be written—but he no longer focused as much energy on writing music as he did on performing it.

In later years, when audiences and critics alike were charmed by Mitropoulos's image as "musical monk," this important connection to Busoni and Berlin in the 1920s was seldom mentioned. Indeed, Busoni himself was little known and less understood in America, where only Mitropoulos championed his music. Only one major critic was astute enough, or knowledgeable enough, to mention the connection. Writing about Mitropoulos in 1953, music historian Roland Gelatt suggested that it was the tension between Mitropoulos's inherently romantic and passionate style of composing and his simultaneous intellectual attraction to Busoni's neoclassical principles of lucidity and moderation that attracted Mitropoulos to the conducting profession in the first place. Taking this theory one step further, Gelatt described Mitropoulos as "a kind of Bauhaus conductor," an embodiment of the principle of form following function. His insatiable appetite for the new and modern in music, his physical mirroring of the scores he led, his streamlined and uncluttered style of living, all struck Gelatt as qualities that "reflect the very form and figure of our age."[10]

Berlin was a more expensive city to live in than Brussels, and at times Mitropoulos had to rely on his growing network of connections, rather than on pocket money, to gain admission to concerts and operas that interested him. Busoni had complimentary tickets to everything, it seemed, and he generously distributed them among his favorite students. One such concert left a lasting impression on Mitropoulos: the Berlin premiere of Stravinsky's

L'Histoire du soldat, under the formidable baton of Hermann Scherchen. "It was some evening!" Mitropoulos stated in his autobiographical essay, recalling that the audience was outraged by Stravinsky's bristling, densely packed idiom—they began booing, stamping their feet, and whistling, even before the piece was finished. The one highly visible exception was the box where Busoni and his entourage were sitting. "Busoni alone understood the greatness of this 'cold' music," Mitropoulos recalled.[11] While the rest of the audience seethed, Busoni stood and applauded with the greatest enthusiasm, seconded by Mitropoulos, who would one day champion this very score before similarly skeptical, though not quite so openly hostile, American audiences.

Through the help of a Greek friend, the set designer Panos Aravantinos, Mitropoulos was able to hear a sold-out performance of Wagner's *Parsifal* at the Berlin Staatsoper. Aravantinos simply let his friend in through the stage entrance and arranged for an extra chair to be placed discreetly behind the percussion section. The only person in a position to see the interloper in this unobtrusive spot would be the conductor, Fritz Stiedry, and he of course would be too preoccupied to pay much attention.

Everything went smoothly until the house lights began to dim. Mitropoulos was sitting in shadow behind the kettle drums, and once the timpanist took his place, the eavesdropping student would be effectively hidden even from the conductor. Applause rippled through the hall as Stiedry strode into the pit, took a perfunctory bow, and raised his baton. The seraphic sounds of the orchestral prelude began, and Mitropoulos basked in them luxuriantly.

Suddenly a look of alarm crossed Stiedry's face. Mitropoulos quickly came out of his Wagnerian reverie, realizing that the conductor was looking straight at him—or rather, at the empty spot where the timpanist was supposed to be standing. It was too late, now, to delay the concert, and there was no sign of the percussionist. Although Mitropoulos had not played the timpani since his last concert in the Athens Conservatory orchestra, he calmly rose from his seat, picked up the drum sticks, found his place in the score, and came in perfectly. He played through the entire first act without a single mistake and thereby earned the gratitude of Stiedry and the admiration of his colleagues in the orchestra pit—the real timpanist showed up during the first intermission, but Mitropoulos was allowed to stay for the remainder of the opera.

With glowing recommendations from both Stiedry and Busoni, Mitropoulos landed his first job as a conductor: assistant conductor at the State Opera, Unter den Linden. The contract was for one year, and his duties were clearly enumerated: he was to conduct choral rehearsals as needed; to provide piano accompaniment for rehearsals, and to play the piano, harpsichord, or any other keyboard instrument, including the organ, when and if called for by the score; likewise, he would conduct any bands or ensembles, onstage or off, when called for by the score. Mitropoulos happily signed the contract, and Max von Schillings signed for the management of the opera house.

Mitropoulos was joyful about getting the job, and he performed his various duties with exceptional diligence. His contract was renewed for the 1923–1924 season, and orchestral rehearsals—much to the young conductor's delight—were added to his responsibilities.

Busoni was glad that his pupil's career had been launched, but occasionally he grew testy when Mitropoulos's duties came into conflict with Busoni's teaching schedule. On one occasion, Mitropoulos arrived at Busoni's somewhat late and without the compositional exercises Busoni had given him at their last session.

"What's the matter with you?" Busoni snapped.

"I'm sorry, Maestro, but I had rehearsals for 'The Ring'."

To Mitropoulos's surprise, Busoni exclaimed: "When will people finally stop listening to all that Wagnerian rubbish!"[12]

Mitropoulos worked in the theater as well as the opera house, and sometimes found himself playing and conducting incidental music to productions of Shakespeare and Ibsen. He logged more and more hours of orchestral rehearsal and even led the orchestra in a concert of ballet music from various operas. He also played the solo piano parts, under other conductors, in works such as *Petrushka* and Scriabin's *Prometheus*.

Just as important to his artistic development was the opportunity to observe closely the technique of eminent conductors: Erich Kleiber, Bruno Walter, Leo Blech, Richard Strauss, Otto Klemperer, Wilhelm Furtwängler —all were active at this time in or near Berlin. Fritz Stiedry—a truly underrated conductor—ended up at the Metropolitan Opera, in charge of the German repertoire. He claimed that the two best assistants he had in Berlin were George Szell and Mitropoulos, whom he contrasted as the coolly intellectual Apollonian and the passionate Dyonisian: "They were as different as day and night, because one"—here he put the side of his hand against his adam's apple—"because one was from the neck up and the other from the neck down."[13]

While the years 1921 and 1922 were exciting and artistically fulfilling, they also brought a double measure of personal sorrow.

Early in 1921, Mitropoulos's younger sister, Heleni, was stricken by tuberculosis. He loved her very much and she had played an important role in the musical life of the Mitropoulos household, for she too was gifted. Dimitri had nurtured her fledgling talents and had done whatever he could to further her musical interests; thanks to him, several manuscripts of Heleni's music are still preserved in the archives of the Athens Conservatory. There is enough substance in them to permit speculation about what the future might have brought if she had lived.

After her diagnosis, Heleni was sent to a clinic in Switzerland, where she received the best care available. She seemed to rally after her initial treatments, but after a period of several months, her condition began to deteriorate. When the clinic could do no more for her, Dimitri went to Switzerland and brought her back to Berlin. There he nursed her and comforted her as best he could until her death on May 7, 1922.

Another blow struck not long after that date, although Mitropoulos would not feel it until some weeks after the fact, because of the political and social chaos in Greece at this time. Acting entirely without Allied support, King Constantine launched a ramshackle military expedition to liberate the Greek population of Asia Minor—the largest and most prosperous Greek enclave still under Turkish rule. Under the canny leadership of Mustafa Kemal, the Turks lured the Greek forces deep into the countryside, away from their supply base at Smyrna, then sprung a gigantic ambush and sent the invaders reeling back in panic.

Driving the routed Greek remnants before them, the Turks swept into Smyrna on September 9, 1922, and commenced a barbarous revenge on its Greek inhabitants. Scenes from the Dark Ages were reenacted, replete with rape, torture, and wholesale slaughter that spared neither women nor children. With the city in flames behind them, thousands of Greek refugees fled Smyrna on anything that could float. Elsewhere in Asia Minor, the situation was the same; by land and by sea, tens of thousands of Greeks fled the wrath of the Turks. Athens alone was swollen with 1.3 million refugees, and Constantine's government collapsed. Conditions in Athens were chaotic, but in some of the coastal cities, they verged on the medieval.

Yannis Mitropoulos was too old to serve in the Greek army, of course, and in the time since Dimitri had left Athens, he had become more and more obsessed with religion, expressing the wish that he had followed his brothers into the church. The house in Old Faleron became a meeting place for devout laymen and clerics alike, and Yannis became fixated on the idea of taking religious orders. Whether his state of mind was delusionary or not, he began to behave as though he were a priest and he became an outspoken critic of the Greek government's policy in Asia Minor.

After the sack of Smyrna, Yannis left home and went to some of the largest refugee camps, where conditions were squalid, brutal, and desperate. He presented himself as a priest, and those who sought comfort from him believed that he was. There was little that one man, of modest financial means, could do in such a sea of human misery, but Yannis gave everything he had to give. He comforted the sick, bought whatever medicine and food he could afford, often at greatly inflated prices from the black marketeers who had sprung up around the refugee camps, and said prayers for the dying. And he joined loudly in condemning the government officials whose policies had created a disaster of biblical proportions but who were now too corrupt or too incompetent to provide for the innocent victims of their mistakes.

So outspoken did Yannis Mitropoulos become that one day in the summer of 1922, he was arrested, possibly on charges of sedition, and thrown into an overcrowded detention facility where conditions were even more dreadful than they were in the refugee camps. Yannis continued his work as a lay priest, unable to offer more than spiritual comfort now, but ministering to people who were grateful even for that. He seemed, in the last weeks of his priestly career, a man on fire with the presence of God, burning from within and gauntly radiant. While ministering to dying internees in the charnel house that passed for the prison's infirmary, Yannis contracted typhus and died.

Shattered by the deaths of her daughter and husband, Angeliki Mitropoulos moved to Berlin and lived with her eldest son.

In the spring of 1924, an emissary arrived from the Athens Conservatory, bearing an invitation for Mitropoulos to return and assume the post of music director of the orchestra. "We need you. You must come," said the man.[14]

Mitropoulos later admitted that his first impulse was to say no. The prospect of leaving Berlin, the musical capital of Europe, and returning to Athens, where the already provincial musical climate was poisoned by a rancid atmosphere of political influence peddling, did not appeal to him, however proud he was of his Greek blood. Angeliki threw her considerable influence behind the Athenian proposal. Now that she had recovered from her grief, she had turned her full motherly attention toward berating her son for wanting to live in such a sinful place as Berlin instead of back home in Greece.

"Think of Greece!" she admonished, when she learned of the invitation from the conservatory, "Think of Greece and comply!"

The next day, after a routine rehearsal at the opera house, Mitropoulos went to see its current music director, Erich Kleiber, an artist for whom the young man had profound respect. He explained the situation to Kleiber and finished by saying: "You don't know Greek mothers! They are queens who demand obedience!"

Kleiber clapped him on the back and replied, "Well then, you'd better do as she wants. Go for a year, get it over with, and then I'm sure you'll come back to us."[15]

With Kleiber's support, Mitropoulos had no trouble obtaining a year's leave of absence. Angeliki was delighted. Mitropoulos spent the waning days of spring arranging his affairs, saying goodbye to his many friends, and mentally preparing himself for his new responsibilities. In the early summer of 1924, he and his mother returned to Athens. He was still convinced that this would be a one-year sideshow, intended to mollify his mother and perhaps also to make up for the fact that he was not returning as an organ professor, as he had promised to do when he accepted the stipend that allowed him to leave Athens in the first place.

But Athens was destined to be his home base, and its orchestras to be his ensembles, for the next fifteen years.

CHAPTER FIVE

Athenian Challenges

The Greece Mitropoulos returned to was a troubled and politically turbulent state. After the debacle at Smyrna, King Constantine was overthrown and replaced by his weak-willed and vacillating son, George II. George reigned, if that is the word for it, only two years and was forced to abdicate in 1924, the year Mitropoulos returned to Athens. Greece's constitutional monarchy was replaced by a republic, but the new form of government seemed only to make things more disorderly and inefficient. Unceasing party strife among Liberals, Royalists, Republicans, and the small but vociferous Communist Party resulted in a dreary parade of impotent, squabbling, eminently forgettable governments.

It was against this background of constant political instability that Mitropoulos and other prominent figures in the postwar Hellenic cultural revival struggled to create professional orchestras, theaters, literary journals, and the other institutions of European culture. Well-paying, prestigious positions within the academic and artistic communities were few; political interference, influence-peddling, and petty treachery were constant, ugly facts of life. An artist or an institution favored by highly placed bureaucrats and willing to dance to whatever tune the government was playing from month to month could at least struggle along. Those who were not willing to play such power games, or who attempted, as Mitropoulos did, to keep themselves above the intrigue and back-stabbing, would find themselves obstructed, vexed, and sometimes powerless to affect their own destinies. There were times when Mitropoulos despaired for his beloved Greece and, increasingly, for his own chances of sustaining an honorable and effective career in his native land.

A friend recalled a letter the conductor had written during the early to mid-1930s, apparently to an influential person, revealing just how intolerable conditions had become in Athens: "Please help me to find a place—anywhere—the remotest place on earth that has an orchestra, and I will go there and work, and work so well that they will thank you for having sent me there. But please help me to get away from Greece!"[1]

In the summer of 1924, however, he was idealistic, bursting with energy and ideas. He was returning to one of the world's most historically cultured cities, a city with a population of almost a half-million (not counting the

51

refugees from Asia Minor). There seemed no logical reason why he could not, in such a city with such a heritage, build his conservatory forces into a first-class symphony orchestra.

But politics—of the academic variety—intervened from the start. Although Mitropoulos had not yet decided irrevocably on a career as a conductor, both his actions and his conversations with friends make it clear that he was strongly inclined in that direction. Since an emissary from the Athens Conservatory had already approached him in Berlin to offer him the job as conductor of the school's orchestra, Mitropoulos naturally supposed that the position was being held for him, and that all he needed to do was to go through the motions of formally applying for the job.

He quickly learned that some individuals in both the administration and the faculty resented his not returning to Greece as a certified organist, as he had more or less promised to do; the vague outlines of an anti-Mitropoulos clique could be discerned, comprising people who took umbrage at the way the former boy-genius had blithely pursued his own agenda, and some people who were simply jealous of his ability.

His staunchest faculty ally, Armand Marsick, was no longer in Athens —he had moved on to a more appealing job as director of the Bilbao Conservatory in Spain. Orchestral concerts at the Athens Conservatory were now firmly under the control of three professors: Philoctates Economidis, José de Bustinduy, and Jean Boutnikoff. While none of these gentlemen was, or would ever become, a podium celebrity, each had sound credentials, each had worked hard to get where he was, and none had any intention of stepping aside in favor of a young man whom many considered to have been unduly pampered by circumstances and connections.

When Manolis Kalomiris, director of the rival Hellenic Conservatory, heard that Mitropoulos was back in town and unexpectedly jobless, he immediately contacted the young conductor and offered him the job of leading the Hellenic Conservatory's orchestra. Mitropoulos accepted, even though he must have known that the Hellenic ensemble would not be as good as the orchestra he had been promised. His first appearance as conductor of the Hellenic Conservatory Orchestra was on October 21, 1924; during the 1924–1925 season, he led seventeen concerts. Thereafter the orchestra disbanded.

The reasons appear to have been both financial and political. By this time, many refugees who had originally gone into camps near the coastal cities had elected to press on to Athens, in the mostly illusory hope of better job opportunities; the city was now bursting at the seams with two million impoverished newcomers, straining the government's resources and aggravating the already chaotic political climate. Politically, the balance of power was held by the small but well-organized Communist Party, in alliance with a much larger bloc of socialists, giving Athenian government a decidedly left-wing flavor.

With so many destitute people crowded into shanty towns around the city, there was considerable resentment toward any funding for the fine arts. Ideologues and pamphleteers railed against symphony concerts, describing them as an elitist and superfluous pastime, unworthy of "the People's" financial support. Many Athenians conceded that they had a valid point, insofar as the two rival conservatories were concerned. The logical approach would have been to combine the best players from both schools into a single ensemble; but for reasons of pride and prestige, both schools insisted on having their own ensembles and on mounting weekly concerts with them. Given the pressure-cooker atmosphere in Athens at this time, the Hellenic orchestra, which was considerably less well-funded than the Athens Conservatory ensemble, did remarkably well by surviving a full season.

A committee of music-loving businessmen, chaired by Mitropoulos's wealthy patron Miltiades Negroponte, tried to put Athenian concert life on a rational basis by organizing and financing a plan to combine the two academic ensembles into a single ensemble named the Orchestra of the Concerts Society—thus tactfully avoiding mention of *any* music school. Two series of concerts were planned, and the responsibility for leading them was carefully balanced between Greek and foreign conductors. The regular series of subscription concerts would be led by Mitropoulos and Jean Boutnikoff, and a series of lighter-weight "pops" concerts, ecumenically named the People's Concerts, would be conducted by José de Bustinduy and Philoctates Economides.

Any animosity these other conductors may have felt toward Mitropoulos when he first returned to Greece was soon dispelled when they saw how hard he worked and heard the playing he obtained from the orchestra. And while Mitropoulos would later become extremely bitter about many of his Greek colleagues, he singled out his three co-conductors for praise. "Of course my colleagues were much older than I. But all of them were not only nice to me, they were helpful in any way they could."[2]

Mitropoulos inaugurated the new orchestra's activities on October 17, 1925, and conducted fourteen more concerts with them during that first season. A second, shorter, season began in October 1926, during which Mitropoulos led twelve concerts. There was no third season; in the spring of 1927, the Orchestra of the Concerts Society simply fell apart. Antagonism between musicians from the two music schools proved as stubborn as it was irrational. Wrangling for advantage between partisans of the two conservatories was bitter and divisive, not at all in the spirit of harmony and collaboration envisioned by Mitropoulos and heavily underwritten by Negroponte, pulling the ensemble's artistic standards into the gutter and seriously undermining its morale. Under the circumstances, just getting a coherent performance out of the musicians was all Mitropoulos or any other conductor could do. By the end of the second season, everyone agreed that this orchestra had no chance of ever achieving an autonomous creative identity. As the quality of the concerts declined, the box office receipts plummeted, creating a budget deficit too large even for Negroponte's deep pockets. By May 1927, therefore, Athens had gone from having too many orchestras to having none at all.

Since the older and more stable Athens Conservatory was weathering these hard times better than its rival, an attempt was made, in the autumn of 1927, to revive its orchestra. Mitropoulos had by now amply demonstrated that he was by far the best conductor in the city, so he was invited to head the new conservatory group and was asked to lead as many concerts as the other three conductors put together. This time the orchestra survived, and Mitropoulos would be its conductor for the next ten years—which is not to say that the conservatory orchestra enjoyed smooth sailing. Each season, the papers published dire predictions about its imminent collapse for one reason or another. Many of its problems came from its lack of cohesiveness—when there was a drachma to be made playing at a coffee house or in the pit of a silent movie house, that's where the musicians could be found, rather than at the low-paying symphonic rehearsals. At the end of each season, there was always a deficit and private funds never quite covered the gap. There was also, still, intense rivalry between the two music schools. Kalomiris gradually turned against Mitropoulos, for he was struggling to revive his own school's orchestra as a matter of prestige, and he was a strong proponent of overtly nationalistic music, recognizably "Greek" in its use of folk tunes and dance rhythms, whereas Mitropoulos and the Athens Conservatory were aesthetically more progressive, espousing a more international and cosmopolitan outlook.

When Kalomiris finally launched his new orchestra, he immediately tried to hire away the better players from Mitropoulos's band. Kalomiris's sources of funding, however, proved to be sporadic, and as a consequence the Hellenic Orchestra's concerts were also sporadic; some musicians who left the Athens Conservatory ensemble in order to join the rival orchestra found themselves unemployed for long periods and unable—because of the resentment their desertion had caused—to return to the fold.

For players and conductors alike, this was a period of artistic and financial insecurity. The situation went from strained to ludicrous when yet a third music academy opened, calling itself the National Conservatory. In all of Greece, never mind just Athens, there were not enough professional orchestral musicians to staff three symphony orchestras. Rivalry for the services of the best players became so bitter that if a musician signed on with one conservatory, he would be blacklisted by the other two.

Things reached such a state that Mitropoulos, in October 1928, wrote a letter to Prime Minister Eleutherios Venizelos, evidently in the hope that the government might compel the three competing schools to cease their internecine warfare or suffer financially:

In Athens at this moment, for better or worse—and according to my way of thinking, for worse—there are three conservatories, serving between three and four thousand students. This situation is seriously fragmenting the pool of native Greek talent, for each of these three schools is trying to devour the other in order to get more money for their individual symphony orchestras. They see these orchestras as manifestations of the glamour and prestige of their schools, but as it stands now, they're spending all their time and energy competing for the glamorous acquisition of the best orchestra, instead of applying themselves to their primary responsibility, which is to *teach music*.[3]

Mitropoulos found the general situation intolerable, but he labored heroically to instill in his orchestra, at least, a sense of communality and identity, even going so far as to pay the difference, out of his own pocket, when the better musicians were tempted to take more lucrative work elsewhere. His personal example, his dynamism and dedication, certainly attracted many players, but the centrifugal forces were too strong for one man to oppose consistently and the orchestra's morale was usually rather shaky. Audiences were likely to witness individual players simply get up in the middle of a symphony and walk offstage with their instruments, so they could catch that night's gig at a night club or a cinema.

When the deficit caught up with the orchestra, at some point during the spring concert season, there was only one way to save money: by cutting the number of rehearsals, sometimes to one per concert, and by cutting back on the number of string players, with easily imagined effects on the quality of the concerts. Mitropoulos had the power to fire as well as hire, an act that caused him great personal distress, and sometimes he was pushed to that extreme for the good of the ensemble. But no matter how slack or unprofessional a fired player might be, his dismissal left yet another hole in this patchwork orchestra's ranks.

To make matters worse, most of the personnel had to perform on cheap, student-quality instruments that sounded inferior at their best and were frequently in need of repair. The orchestra's budget, however, allowed for neither repairs nor replacements. Here again, Mitropoulos did what he could, sometimes actually buying new instruments, out of his own paycheck, for his best players.

Moreover, the musicians were not anonymous servants to the will of the man on the podium. Mitropoulos shunned the very idea that a conductor should be a dictator and that the men playing for him should be depersonalized servants. Despite his own youth, he thought of the musicians as his children and encouraged them to come to him, at any time, when their personal problems interfered with their music making. When the players realized that the conductor really cared about their welfare, they began to respond in kind. Quietly, without any publicity attached to his actions, Mitropoulos helped with financial, medical, and emotional problems.

Such a relationship between players and conductor was rare in any city, at any time, and as the months went by, Mitropoulos gradually won the loyalty of a steady core of musicians; as the personnel roster stabilized and morale rose, the concerts improved, the audiences got larger and more enthusiastic.

After his first few seasons, Mitropoulos instituted changes that solidified the orchestra's position in the greater community. He opened its rehearsals to all music students, free of charge; he built the orchestra's concerto repertoire not only around famous celebrities but also around deserving young soloists who were graduates of the local conservatories; he arranged for pops concerts to be held, free of charge, at various public squares in and around Athens.

He also worked tirelessly to modernize the orchestra's repertoire and to broaden the taste of his audience. He took the plunge into outright modernism on January 28, 1928, by giving the Athens premiere of Stravinsky's L'Histoire du soldat—an undertaking that required more than three months of rehearsal. Decades later, in an exceedingly mellow and optimistic mood, Mitropoulos recalled: "The reaction in Athens to all this new music was not bad; on the contrary, the public at the subscription concerts had progressive tastes."[4] Some of the people interviewed for this book remembered things differently and insisted that the public response, especially to the uncompromising Stravinsky work, was vociferously negative.

Nowadays, when Mitropoulos is quite properly regarded as a Greek national hero, his countrymen tend to look back through the gauzy lens of nostalgia and refer to the late 1920s as the Golden Age of Mitropoulos. However, it was not until Mitropoulos gained fame beyond the borders of Greece, that is from 1930 until he emigrated to America, that he enjoyed circumstances that enabled to him give performances in Athens that were of international caliber—when his fame and prestige were big enough to silence his more vocal critics and to allow him to do his work in relative peace.

No recordings are known to exist of the Athens orchestra during the late 1920s, so no realistic judgment can be formed about its playing. No doubt, there were nights when everything fell into place, when there was a full complement of players and Mitropoulos succeeded in galvanizing them and compelling them to play beyond themselves. But given the myriad difficulties the orchestra struggled with at this time, the average concert would probably sound, to modern ears, painfully scrappy and raw-toned.

The Athenian critics were no help. Most of them were puffed-up provincials who owed their jobs to patrons who expected their personal agendas to be advanced, their own favorite composers and performers to be lauded. Even though there was only one orchestra now, there were still three competing music academies, and critics shamelessly tried to advance one native composer, or one music school, over another. The orchestra owed its very existence to well-heeled "music lovers" who used their patronage, or the threat of its withdrawal, to influence programs and the choice of soloists. Behind the scenes, the bickering and character assassinations continued.

Mitropoulos was able to curb the worst excesses simply because everyone now knew that he was utterly incorruptible and fair-minded. But every time he wanted to program a work by a Greek composer, he had to brave a firestorm of interference from partisans of rival composers. These struggles so exasperated him that, later in the United States, he used his influence only rarely and very selectively on behalf of Greek composers. He remained faithful to many old Greek friends all of his life, but he carried forward no abiding fondness for the Athenian music scene as a whole. Although he loyally refrained from taking long-range pot-shots at old enemies, usually preferring to keep silent about that whole pre-1930 period, he did speak frankly on rare occasions, to very close friends, and when he did, he usually referred to Athens as "an awful nest of intrigue" and allowed that he was well out of it.

Some sense of the cultural climate in pre-1930 Athens can be gained from the tenor of surviving reviews. Whenever Mitropoulos programmed works by Debussy, Milhaud, or Stravinsky—never mind Schoenberg, whose works began to show up occasionally in the late 1920s—the critics would denounce the music as "Communistic," "subversive," and "decadent." During the first few years, Mitropoulos met resistance even when he performed composers that the rest of Europe had long since taken for granted. The Athenian critics found Wagner "hard to digest"; Brahms, "boring"; Schumann, "impoverished in his ideas"; Beethoven's "Pastorale" Symphony was dismissed as "over-long and exhausting to listen to" while the "Eroica" was described as being "full of wrinkles," whatever that might mean.[5]

By the time Mitropoulos moved back to Athens in 1924, his bohemian mane of hair was a memory; the onset of baldness was as rapid as it was total. That smooth glowing cranium would be a lifelong trademark, and the surviving hair around the base of the head formed a tonsure-like frame. This arrangement gave, so to speak, a crowning touch to the conductor's public image as "the musical monk."

Baldness also accentuated the fascinating purity of his blue eyes, the proud promontory of his nose, and the coarse sensuality of his full lips. His ears were proportionally as large as his nose, and he never grew sideburns or lengthened his fringe of hair to detract attention from them; features which would have earned another man the description "jug-eared" became on Mitropoulos a set of monumental antennae, as though the outsized ears had been God-given for the purpose of gathering in music. Although his face was still unlined, lacking the cragginess of his maturity, its separate and rather homely elements formed a whole that was compelling to look upon and that underscored dramatically the surge of emotions within. His frowns had the weight of thunderheads, and his smile possessed such presence, such physicality, that it could lift the mood of everyone within its ambit. Persons who were drawn to him, of either sex, tended to be powerfully attracted and to feel vitalized in his company, as if life itself had suddenly become more precious and their spirits somehow freer.

Instantaneous and compulsive attraction marked the start of the longest, most enduring, and best-documented friendship of Mitropoulos's life, when he met, at an after-concert reception in the winter of 1925, a beautiful and cultured young woman named Katy Katsoyanis. "We immediately established a close relationship," wrote Katy, in her introduction to the published collection of their letters, adding "I may say that there was not even a period of simple acquaintanceship, for we became friends right away and this lasted to the end of his life."[6]

During the next twelve years of his Greek period, Mitropoulos saw Katy nearly every day. They dined together, took long walks together, and had epic conversations. She attended most of his rehearsals and concerts, went with him to Berlin when he debuted there with the Berlin Philharmonic, and again accompanied him to Paris in 1932 when he made his first appearances in that city. In 1938 and 1939, when he returned to Greece from his post in Minneapolis, he spent whatever free time he had each summer at Katy's house in Kifissia, a suburb northeast of Athens. The villa was spacious and airy, with terraces that offered postcard views of the countryside, and lush, manicured gardens bordered by stately cypress trees. Katy's home, like Katy's company, was an oasis for Mitropoulos, a place on the land and in the heart where he could let down his guard, be totally himself, speak his mind, and be refreshed in body and spirit.

Katy Katsoyanis was a petite woman with chestnut hair, a fair complexion, a queenly Nefertiti neck, a pretty and expressive mouth, and immense dark liquid eyes; in several early photographs she looks not unlike the young Anaïs Nin. She moved with the alert grace of a dancer and was quite capable of keeping up with Mitropoulos's loping, league-devouring stride. She was musically literate, broad-minded, and immensely well-read. Fluent in at least four languages, she could converse knowledgeably about poetry, art, and philosophy, and in her marathon conversations with the conductor, any and all of these topics were likely to be covered.

In their epic thirty-year correspondence, they continued these conversations on paper, and Katy's letters reveal a wide-ranging, sharply focused intelligence, capable of holding its own on the highest level of intellectual discourse, able to discuss everything from dodecaphony to the writings of Gide with equal ease. No feminine deference is found in her writing, either: when she thought Mitropoulos was wrong about something or someone, she was capable of fierce debate, to the extent, now and then, of scolding.

In a lovingly written introduction to the published edition of the Mitropoulos-Katsoyanis correspondence, musicologist and critic Louis Biancolli captured perfectly the nature and essence of the relationship:

One would have to search far in the realm of letter-writing for any parallel correspondence to this. It would be only partly accurate to cite the Tchaikovsky–Madame von Meck exchange, since they scarcely met and were not passionate in their avowals of affection. The letters of Dimitri and Katy, for much of the period covered, however "platonic" or spiritual the relationship remained, are those of very intimate friends, or of brother and sister, almost, if not quite, of husband and wife. They met from time to time, in New York, in Greece, but their physical confrontation was not essential to the rapport and reciprocal concern maintained in their correspondence. The two were really of a higher order of man and woman, absorbed in the deepest values in life and music, both thinkers forever exploring their own mind and each other's. Sex, family, children were not of the essence. Each had his or her own world in such matters. The world they inhabited together was pure and free, shared over long distances, even over long periods of imposed silence. True human contact surmounts geography.[7]

The question naturally arises: were they lovers? It is possible, in the early years, that they were. Although Mitropoulos was basically, and after about 1930 exclusively, homosexual in orientation, his lengthy affair with Katina Paxinou proves that he was not exclusively so in his early manhood. At this stage of his life, he could have answered certain questions the way his beloved St. Francis did, when in the early years of his ministry he candidly blurted out: "Do not be in such a hurry to make a saint out of me—I am still perfectly capable of fathering a child!"

Given his visibility and the unceasing intrigues which swirled about him during his first decade in Athens, his sexual proclivities made him frighteningly vulnerable to gossip, blackmail, and the constant possibility of unendurable public shame. He had already established a pattern of sublimating his physical desires into his work, of going for long periods of time in a state of truly monkish self-denial. A conventional affair, while not something to be publicly flaunted, did not carry the same risks, and indeed the suspicion that he was Katy's lover would have gone a long way toward deflecting other, more perilous speculations. On those occasions when his true sexuality refused to obey his will any longer and the accumulated weeks of self-denial exerted unbearable pressure, he sought release by leaving Athens and roaming, as incognito as someone of his appearance and fame could become, the waterfront districts of Piraeus.

Biancolli addresses this matter candidly in his introduction to the Katsoyanis letters:

Was there room for a wife in this man's life? Do we detect half-confided longings for the more usual commitments of the heart, or do they confirm what we discern in the letters and conversation notebooks of Beethoven—that, however strong the pull towards marriage and its paternal joys, he was wedded, for better or worse, to Music. That was the

bride that sustained and nourished him and gave him so much in return. Did this argue a monastic or ascetic turn of mind? Many believed
so, and lightly dismissed his casual attachments.

The truth is that his enslavement to the bride-mistress Music left no
room for serious enduring attachment, call it physical, call it sexual,
call it romantic. Yet he did not practice mortification of the flesh. He
yielded, though sparingly, to its urgencies. One had only to hear him
conduct a Schumann symphony or a Wagner excerpt to know the man
was far from carnally deprived. He savored that side of life by his own
code, just as for escape and relief from the demands of his devouring intellect he indulged in a taste for attending midnight movies, and not
always of any real quality.[8]

Katy Katsoyanis, for her part, encouraged people to think that there
had been an erotic element in their relationship, even though she clearly
knew about Mitropoulos's essentially homosexual nature; indeed, she
seems to have been not-so-privately proud of the notion that she had been
woman enough to redirect those basic drives, at least for a time. As she grew
older, alas, she grew more and more obsessed with the conviction that she
was not just his soulmate but his actual spouse. In her old age, she turned
her house into a kind of Mitropoulos museum, and would lead visitors
around like a curator, pointing out various spots on the terrace and in the
garden and saying: "He used to sit and read here during the afternoon," or
"This is where we used to have tea and discuss music."

When preparing their letters for publication, she took it upon herself to
delete any passages in which Mitropoulos spoke critically of people or circumstances in Athens. When others, including Maria Christopoulou,
sought to publish biographical studies of the conductor, she not only refused to cooperate with their research, but actively tried to thwart them. In
her final years, she would not tolerate any opinion, however factual, that
conflicted with her own idealized version of things. When someone finally
worked up the nerve to ask her point-blank about the conductor's homosexuality, she became quite indignant and replied: "That could not possibly
be true. I was his wife."[9]

If these two people were indeed lovers, that phase of the relationship
probably did not last more than a few years. Mitropoulos seemed to acknowledge as much in a letter he wrote in 1938, at the start of his second season as conductor of the Minneapolis Symphony: "As for the 'abyss' that
separates us in some things, I know it, alas, only too well! Besides, I've always felt this abyss isolating me from the whole world, so that I am and
will remain *always* alone, even when I am near those who love me."[10]

Whatever the particulars of their early involvement with one another,
their relationship matured into an extraordinary friendship, intellectually
rich and spiritually vibrant. The correspondence documenting that friendship is unique in the annals of twentieth century music. Katy's feelings of

exclusivity made the decision to publish those letters very difficult, but eventually she, too, was overpowered by their uniqueness and by the knowledge that Maria Negroponte had burned all of *her* letters, so that the letters to Katy formed the only candid, day-by-day chronicle of Mitropoulos's personal life, the only tangible embodiment of his questing and omnivorous intellect. She was encouraged to publish, she said in her introduction, by a passage in a letter from the conductor dated April 23, 1940: "All your letters arrived numbered, ready to go to the printers for the great book that will appear at the end of the year and which will be titled *The Metaphysics of Friendship.*"[11]

Yet she also cautioned the reader not to "imprison him in his own words":

> One needed a lot of time to get to know him well. Only then could one
> ... find out that under the surface contradictions the character line was
> uniform, the man remained the same from the starting point to the pinnacle of his career: the same austere principles, the same love of art, the same feeling of responsibility, the same honesty, the same magnanimity, the same humanity, the same self-consuming anguish, the same incredible unselfishness.[12]

During his Athenian career, Mitropoulos conducted 127 concerts, most of them exciting and the later ones executed at a higher level of cohesion and technical polish than many listeners to the early events would have thought possible.

Mitropoulos also continued to act as an accompanist for visiting vocal soloists. The quality of these recitals could be very high when a pianist of his caliber performed with soloists such as Ninon Vallin, Joseph Rogatschewsky, Elisabeth Schumann, Lotte Lehmann, and George Thill. As might be supposed, Mitropoulos also played with many Greek singers and instrumentalists during this period—an extensive list indeed, but one whose names are unlikely to be familiar even to the most ardent American or European connoisseurs of Lieder.

Mitropoulos performed as soloist in d'Indy's *Symphony on a French Mountain Air* in 1925, with Boutnikoff on the podium. In January 1926, Boutnikoff again accompanied Mitropoulos for a performance of Scriabin's *Prometheus*. In December 1927, Mitropoulos was at the keyboard again for Franck's *Symphonic Variations*, Bustinduy conducting.

That concert was the last in which Mitropoulos played while someone else conducted. The next time he essayed the Franck piece, only a few days later, Mitropoulos directed the orchestra from the keyboard—a feat no one in Athens had ever seen before, and which proved sensationally popular.

He was, perhaps, showing off just a little bit and having a wonderful time doing it. His keyboard technique was sufficiently masterful, and the orchestra, by this time in their relationship, was disciplined enough and alert enough to follow cues given by eyes, nose, and chin, as well as hand. This stunt also served a practical purpose, in that it afforded audiences a chance to hear interesting works that few celebrity pianists were willing to perform.

Other works he played and conducted simultaneously, with performance dates: Respighi's Toccata for Piano and Orchestra (1934 and 1935), Milhaud's Etudes for Piano and Orchestra (1933), Ravel's Concerto in G Major (1933 and 1934), Roussel's Piano Concerto in G Major, Op. 36 (1936), Malipiero's Concerto No. 1 (1936 and 1937), and Louis Albert's Fantasy for Piano and Orchestra in D Minor, Op. 8 (1937). On two occasions, in 1932 and again in 1933, he even tried to accommodate the titanic Second Piano Concerto of Brahms, but the scale of that work made it unsuitable for conducting from the keyboard. The other works, only one of which (the Ravel) has ever achieved repertoire status, became Mitropoulos specialties, and he enjoyed great success whenever he programmed them, whether in Europe or in the United States.

In 1924, when he finally came to terms with Busoni's admonition, Mitropoulos began once more to compose music as well as conduct it. First from his pen was the Passacaglia, Preludio, e Fuga for Piano, written in the late summer of 1924; and shortly thereafter, *Four Kytheran Dances*, also for piano.

In June 1927, the conservatory sponsored a concert of all-Greek music. Two Mitropoulos compositions were on the program, his Ostinata in Three Parts for Violin and Piano and the work that is generally regarded—by the handful of persons who are familiar with Mitropoulos's compositions—as his masterpiece, *Ten Inventions on Poems of Cavafy* for soprano with piano accompaniment. In both these works, Mitropoulos was exploring expressive and technical possibilities more advanced than those of even the most devoted Schoenbergians, and was doing so, moreover, entirely on his own, without contact or encouragement from any school of like-minded composers. The Ostinata, in three movements, is pure twelve-tone music—nothing tentative about it—making it, if nothing else, a pioneering work. It leapfrogs over Schoenberg in places and lands somewhere in the general vicinity of Stockhausen. The *Ten Inventions*, while not strictly serial compositions, are free of conventional tonality. Taken in one dose, these must have been strenuous listening indeed for an audience that was just starting to feel comfortable with Brahms and Wagner. The overall sound recalls Alban Berg—the ear distinguishes tonal centers of gravity and thematic curvatures. There is remarkable delicacy, restraint, and concentrated beauty in these songs, and contemporary vocalists, in Europe at least, began to perform them with some frequency in the 1990s.

To the Athenian audience of 1927, however, these works sounded severely modernist; a sizable percentage of the audience reportedly got up and walked out. Critical response ranged from mild indignation to revulsion. "He really ought not to be surprised if we don't understand this music," wrote one critic, while others accused Mitropoulos of "aesthetic degeneracy," of having been "seduced by aesthetic psychopathy," and of having "no sense of cultural roots in his music," the last, clearly of the self-inflating Greek National School, adding, "Where is he taking us?"[13]

Mitropoulos wrote surprisingly little for the full orchestra. Aside from the very early tone poem *Tafi*, there is another presumably programmatic work dating from 1925 entitled *The Burial*; and from 1928, a substantial orchestra piece entitled Concerto Grosso, dedicated to Negroponte. In this piece the guiding spirit is Stravinsky rather than Schoenberg; the idiom is compact, tightly argued neoclassicism, and the form—as one might expect from the title—is basically baroque. It is tough-fibered music, tonal but laden with dissonance, with a particularly ferocious timpani part in the final pages and some brooding string passages that presage the symphonic writing of Honegger.

There are four movements, in which slow tempos alternate with fast ones, in keeping with the baroque concerto grosso form. A Largo opens the work, scored only for strings and two horns in F; an Allegro movement follows, fashioned as a sort of *fugato* and scored for cornet, strings, and a pair of trumpets; static antiphonal string writing provides the foundation for the third movement, Largo (Chorale), with clarinets and bassoons playing in canonical fashion; a fugal Allegro concludes the work in a bright, aggressive manner—kettledrums and piano jump in to punctuate the strings, trumpets, and horns.[14]

As a composer, Mitropoulos found his personal voice with the Concerto Grosso, the Ostinata, and the Cavafy song cycle. Tapes of these works, and Geoffrey Douglas Madge's staggering traversal of the *Greek Sonata*, suggest a brilliant and utterly individual musical voice; had Mitropoulos continued to write music, his reputation today as a composer would likely match those of the composers who influenced him in the 1920s. Yet even as he was writing these tremendously impressive pieces, his ambition to compose began to cool. His isolation from sympathetic peers may have contributed; no doubt the incomprehension and hostility of the Athenian audiences had something to do with this change as well. Most likely, his interest in composing began to wane as he came to see his destiny in re-creating the music of others, in serving as a missionary for other composers whose music was neglected or misunderstood. He was, after all, just a single human being; no matter how hard he drove himself, he could not hope to be equally successful as composer, pianist, and conductor. There was a rite of self-sacrifice involved, too, as if by immolating Mitropoulos the composer, he might increase the persuasive powers and efficacy of Mitropoulos the crusading conductor. He expressed this complex process in very plain words in a letter to Katy dated March 4, 1929: "I feel so full of other people's music, that I cannot create my own."[15]

His composing did not suddenly cease, of course, but after the Concerto

Grosso, its level of energy and commitment gradually diminished. He made the transition by means of some orchestrations of earlier composers' music. His arrangements of Bach's Fantasia and Fugue in G Minor and of the Prelude and Fugue in B Minor are leaner than the orchestrations of Stokowski, Respighi, or Elgar, but they are as full-blooded and stirring as anyone else's symphonic Bach. For strings alone, he also arranged *Prelude and Death of Dido* from Purcell's *Dido and Aeneas* (the title is Mitropoulos's; the music is based on that of the well-known "Dido's Lament.") In 1931, he produced an ambitious string-orchestra arrangement of Beethoven's String Quartet No. 14, Op. 131, which Leonard Bernstein recorded, gorgeously, with the strings of the Vienna Philharmonic in the late 1970s.

For the five years following 1931, he composed nothing. In 1936 and 1937, his interest revived briefly. With as much nationalistic pride as any of the more conventional Greek composers, he composed incidental music for new productions of *Electra* by Sophocles and *Hippolytus* by Euripides.

Interestingly, Mitropoulos the conductor did very little to keep alive the reputation of Mitropoulos the composer. He programmed his orchestral works a few times during guest engagements in Europe during the 1930s, but did not conduct them at all in Minneapolis or New York. In America, his compositional efforts were represented solely by his Bach and Purcell orchestrations, which audiences liked and critics tended to dismiss, just as they tended to dismiss Stokowski's. So self-effacing was he about his own compositions—he never mentioned them in any American interviews—that many of the musicians Oliver Daniel interviewed for this book were unaware that Mitropoulos had ever composed anything and were startled to learn that a total of forty-five works existed.

1   Mitropoulos as a child, ca. 1905.
Courtesy Maria Christopoulou.

2   At about age ten. Oliver Daniel
collection.

3   Working on his score to *Soeur Béatrice*, 1919. Courtesy Jim Dixon.

4   Mitropoulos in Paris, ca. 1916. Courtesy Jim Dixon.

5　The onset of baldness was as quick as it was total: a portrait taken in Brussels, April 8, 1920; compare to appearance in Figure 4.

6 Mitropoulos's father, Yannis Mitropoulos, ca. 1920. Courtesy Maria Christopoulou.

7 Mitropoulos with his mother, Angeliki, ca. 1922. Courtesy Maria Christopoulou.

8   House of the Mitro-
poulos family in the
Old Faleron district of
Athens. Courtesy Maria
Christopoulou.

9   Mitropoulos's talented but tragically short-lived sister, Heleni, ca. 1921; taken
in Swiss tuberculosis sanitarium. Courtesy Maria Christopoulou.

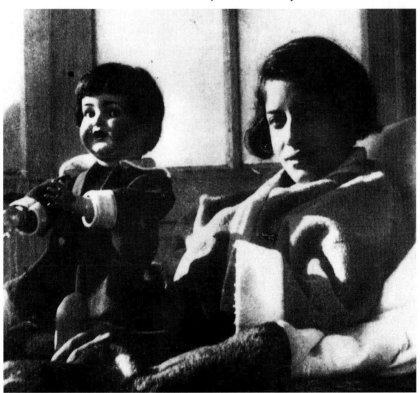

10   Mitropoulos and companions relaxing on the shore, May 1932. Courtèsy Mrs. Theodore Vavayannis.

11   With faculty colleagues, ca. 1932. Mitropoulos on right, in sailor cap, arm around Katina Skokos. Kneeling in front is John Vavayannis; on Mitropoulos's right is his protégé Theodore Vavayannis. Courtesy Mrs. Theodore Vavayannis.

12 Studio portrait, 1934. Courtesy Maria Christopoulou.

13 Katy Katsoyanis as she appeared when she met and fell in love with Mitropoulos. Oliver Daniel collection.

14　Mitropoulos with students from the Athens Conservatory Orchestra, ca. 1935. Courtesy Mrs. Theodore Vavayannis.

15　Mitropoulos, center, with colleagues before embarking for Italy, ca. 1935. Courtesy Mrs. Theodore Vavayannis.

CHAPTER SIX

Mountains to Climb

Although Mitropoulos did not conduct outside of Greece from 1924 until 1930, his reputation spread far beyond his homeland. By 1929, the Athens orchestra had gone from being a raw provincial band to being at least a good, sometimes better-than-good, second-rank ensemble. The stability Mitropoulos had worked for so diligently began to pay off, and guest artists of the highest caliber began scheduling Athenian concerts as they would engagements in any other European capital. When these world-class soloists went to Athens, they found an inspiring conductor who did everything he could to accommodate the interpretive wishes of the visiting artist. When they left Greece, artists such as Bronislaw Hubermann, Wilhelm Backhaus, Artur Rubinstein, Artur Schnabel, and Alfred Cortot brought with them praise for the Greek conductor. Mitropoulos was someone to watch, a diamond in the rough, a man capable of leading any orchestra, anywhere.

Those who managed the Athens orchestra's finances discussed in 1928 and again in 1929 the possibility of arranging a European tour by the group, but Greece's chronic economic and political instability made this unfeasible. At this juncture, Miltiades Negroponte decided that if the orchestra could not tour, at least its conductor could. Using his own money entirely, Negroponte began making inquiries, and by the end of 1929, he had engaged the entire Berlin Philharmonic Orchestra for a concert under Mitropoulos on February 27, 1930.

Six years after he had resigned his position with the Unter den Linden Opera, Mitropoulos returned to Berlin, determined to make the most of this opportunity. He chose the program carefully: his own Concerto Grosso, the Third Piano Concerto of Prokofiev, and the Symphony in C Major of Paul Dukas, a charming and colorful work which would be new to Berlin audiences, as would the other two works on the program.

For the soloist in the Prokofiev work, Mitropoulos engaged the celebrated virtuoso Egon Petri whom Mitropoulos had known and liked during his apprentice days in Berlin. Not long before rehearsals were scheduled to begin, Petri notified Mitropoulos that, because of illness and fatigue, he simply did not have the time or energy to master the difficult Prokofiev work. A bit of investigation on the part of Mitropoulos's Berlin agent, Louise Wolff, revealed that Petri was being disingenuous—he had taken one look at the bristling, hammer-and-tongs piano part in the Prokofiev Third Concerto and decided that he hated it. Mitropoulos, when he learned the truth, was furious; he felt that Petri had let him down.

A flurry of telephone calls from Wolff to various other pianists produced no results—not a single virtuoso would, or could, tackle so formidable a work in the time remaining. Five days before the scheduled performance, Mitropoulos listened glumly while his agent read out the list of famous and near-famous pianists who had declined. Then he gave a tentative smile and said, "Mrs. Louise, what would you say if *I* played it?"

"Can you play it?"

"Yes, I know this work very well."

"But then, who will conduct?"

"I will."[1]

It was this small twist of circumstance—Egon Petri's dislike of the Prokofiev concerto and the reluctance of any other pianist to fill in for him—that turned the February 27 concert into the most memorable event of the Berlin season. When the members of the Philharmonic arrived for rehearsal three days before the concert, they found Mitropoulos sitting serenely at the keyboard of a grand piano from which the lid had been removed. When he announced to them the change of soloists, many of the players exchanged skeptical glances. But that skepticism vanished within minutes, once Mitropoulos gave the downbeat and plunged into the keyboard pyrotechnics of the first movement.

In terms of sheer showmanship, Mitropoulos pulled off the musical coup of his early career. He not only delivered a virtuoso account of this fiercely demanding concerto, he provided a spectacle. During the orchestral passages he conducted with his usual vigor, stabbing out cues and flaying the air for tuttis; then, at the split-second before the piano part resumed, his clawlike hands would plummet unerringly to the right keys. While playing, he continued to conduct with his eyes, his mouth, and the hypnotic bob and weave of that regally shining head, creating a picture of phenomenal energy, concentration, and timing. It was a tightrope act without a net, and he not only negotiated the trick, but he also did it with superb flair. The jaded Berlin audience went wild at the conclusion.

The critics took due notice, of course. This event was not just another concert—this was *news*. Alfred Einstein, a leading German critic, wrote: "The manner in which he played the Prokofiev Third Concerto and conducted from the keyboard, was one of the strongest displays of sheer talent I have ever witnessed." Less laudatory were the comments on Mitropoulos the composer, when his composing was noted at all. Many found the Concerto Grosso lacking in the very qualities that made its composer so appealing as a performer/conductor. The composition was described as "brutal and coarse," with "confused and deliquescent tonal language, barren dissonances and a poverty of emotion."[2] Yet critics and audience certainly took from the concert an indelible memory of the electrifying concerto and the blazing performance of the Dukas symphony that concluded the program.

This Berlin experience marked the moment when Mitropoulos began to define himself almost exclusively as a conductor, occasionally a pianist—but no longer an active composer. Referring to the Berlin concert, Mitropoulos later wrote: "Without my really thinking about it, fate willed it that I should be successful as a conductor from the very start. I remained with this profession and completely gave up composing."[3]

After the stunning success in Berlin, one other thing was clear: as Miltiades Negroponte and the conductor's other supporters had intended, Mitropoulos had taken the first and most important step beyond the confining cultural boundaries of his native land. Rather strangely, in view of the sensation he had made in Berlin, two more years would pass before he received an invitation to conduct outside of Greece, this time with the Paris Symphony Orchestra, on February 14, 1932. According to Kostios, the Paris engagement was arranged by Alfred Cortot, at the behest of Cortot's friend, the Greek composer Petros Petridis; in return for this favor, Mitropoulos agreed to conduct a Petridis orchestral work on the program. Something misfired, however—or the Parisian management may have balked—and Mitropoulos was unable to conduct anything by Petridis. Although there was nothing to indicate double-dealing on Mitropoulos's part, Petridis considered himself betrayed and from then on, even after the conductor's death, treated Mitropoulos as an enemy despite Mitropoulos's effort to make amends by conducting a Petridis composition in Monte Carlo several years later. The Paris concert went on as scheduled, despite this last-minute skirmish.[4]

This time out, Mitropoulos played his strongest hand quite calculatingly, making the Prokofiev Third Concerto the centerpiece of a program that also included his own orchestrations of Bach's Fantasia and Fugue in G Minor and of Franck's Prelude, Chorale, and Fugue, concluding with the vividly theatrical music to Florent Schmitt's ballet *La Tragédie de Salomé*. The concert was a well-rounded success, for the conductor's orchestrations were received with much more enthusiasm than the Concerto Grosso had been in Berlin. Once again, his showmanship and pianistic prowess in the Prokofiev provided his enthralled Parisian audience with a memorable spectacle.

Mitropoulos had brought Florent Schmitt's opulent ballet score to pulsating, voluptuous life; in a lengthy critique, Schmitt described Mitropoulos as " a vibrant orchestral conductor combined with an extraordinary pianist . . . a musician rarely gifted by the gods." Critic Léon Moreau described the concert as "a revelation! Here is a conductor both fiery and exact." He was also called, quite simply, "a force of Nature!"[5]

Fresh from this triumph in Paris, Mitropoulos crossed the Channel and made his English debut conducting the Halle orchestra in Liverpool. He found the city charming but working conditions intolerable. "Ah! That rehearsal!" he wrote to Katy Katsoyanis on the night before the concert—

"Never before have I had such a disorderly rehearsal." While rehearsing, he had the distinct impression that half the orchestra were mentally packing baggage rather than focusing on their parts. That impression was correct, as the men were scheduled to play a concert that night in Manchester, and as time drew near for the last train that could deliver them on time in the other city, the musicians began glancing nervously at their watches and, finally, slipping off stage well before the end of rehearsal. "We bundled through the Dukas symphony as badly as possible, and I've only got tomorrow's rehearsal for us to look at, or rather run through, all the rest! I'm very upset by this, but there's nothing to be done!"[6]

Perhaps it was coincidence, but Mitropoulos did not conduct again in Great Britain until 1951, as music director of the New York Philharmonic.

During the 1932–1933 season, Mitropoulos performed more widely, first in the Augusteo in Rome with the Santa Cecilia Orchestra, then in two more concerts in Paris, and finally in Venice. In contrast to his Liverpool experience, Mitropoulos enjoyed himself in Rome. The orchestra, he wrote to Katy, was "a wonder! The musicians, full of feeling, gave of themselves like a woman gives herself to her lover."[7]

The four concerts of this season served to consolidate Mitropoulos's European reputation, proving him to be a musician of breadth and stature, not just a one-trick showman. Only his attempt in Paris to play and conduct the Brahms Second Piano Concerto backfired, described by one critic as "an accomplishment more athletic than musical," and he never tried that particular stunt again. Yet his Paris concerts—the Brahms experiment notwithstanding—sparked so much excitement that Pierre Monteux remained jealous even after both conductors had transferred their careers to America.

Mitropoulos's involvement with opera was severely limited during these years; no foreign opera house made him an offer and both financial constraints and internecine squabbling made opera productions a rarity in Athens. Nevertheless, at the conservatory he did conduct Offenbach's *Les Contes d'Hoffmann* in 1931. Three operas representing the Greek National School also came under his baton, beginning in 1927 with *Kyra Frosini* by Georgios Sklavos. The other two were by Kalomiris (*The Master Mason* in 1930 and *The Mother's Ring* in 1931).

Musical horizons broadened for Mitropoulos yet again during the 1933–1934 season as he conducted in Belgrade, Florence, Turin, Rome, Venice, Monte Carlo, Brussels, Paris, Bologna, Warsaw, and finally in Moscow and Leningrad before concluding in Milan. The Turin concert, incidentally, marked the first known occasion that Mitropoulos directed a piece of "American" music—the world premiere of Daniele Amfitheatrof's *American Panorama*. Amfitheatrof had never been to America, but that didn't stop him from writing a substantial tone poem about the place; a melange of musical cliches that would have embarrassed the most talentless Hollywood hack.

In Venice he both played and conducted the first Italian performances

Mitropoulos's passport from 1935, a time when the young conductor's foreign engagements were increasing. Courtesy Jim Dixon.

of Respighi's Toccata for Piano and Orchestra and Milhaud's Etudes for Piano and Orchestra. After the Brussels concert, Mitropoulos enjoyed an emotional reunion with his three former teachers: Gilson, Marsick, and Desmet, then continued on to Paris and eastward. By May he was back in Paris and wrote Katy his impressions of Russia:

> If I had stayed any longer in the Soviet Union, I would have ended up forgetting there are people who dress well, eat well, and are clean. The impression of misery and filth that one gets down there is something indescribable. But you get used to this quickly and then you are left with the charm of this people who have nobility of heart, grace of soul, and limitless enthusiasm—and are artists through and through. I think nowhere else can such perfect music be made as in that country.[8]

Guest engagements in the touring season of 1934–1935 included stops in Florence, Turin, and Paris, where he conducted the famed Lamoureux Orchestra for the first time. He added Ravel's G Major Concerto to his dual conducting/playing repertoire. For the second year in a row, he was asked to return to Monte Carlo for a long visit and fifteen concerts. At the end of April, he returned to Italy before going back to Greece, and conducted the orchestras of Naples, Bologna, and Milan.

What sort of conductor was this fiery young Greek who had captured the attention and affection of two of Europe's greatest musical capitals? An intensely physical one, to begin with. As Roland Gelatt later described him: "he conducts with his body. When the music soars, he is a bird in flight; when it droops, he huddles as though broken in spirit."[9] This mirroring of the musical score and its changes by means of constantly shifting physical analogies was spontaneous and natural, an irrepressible function of the tremendous internal dynamism that possessed Mitropoulos when he conducted. On a strictly analytical level, Mitropoulos candidly admitted that while "I wouldn't recommend that a conductor deliberately make his gestures with an audience in mind," nevertheless "It is easier for the audience to understand the meaning of music if the conductor is a bit of an actor."[10]

While he was working with the opera house in Berlin, Mitropoulos used a baton, but he seems to have abandoned the baton in favor of a two-fisted, bare-handed style shortly after his return to Greece. The earliest known reference to a batonless Mitropoulos concert occurs in a review dated November 11, 1925. For the next seven or eight years, he seems to have waffled, using a stick for one concert, conducting bare-handed the next. By 1933, however, he seems to have made up his mind, and he conducted for the next twenty years exclusively without one. "The baton," he was wont to say when interviewers questioned him about the matter, "can achieve ensemble, but it cannot be expressive." He did return to the baton in the final stages of his career, in 1954, for two reasons. First, his cardiologist informed him, during his recovery from his first heart attack, that con-

ducting with the stick would put less strain on his heart than did his previous, recklessly physical style. The second reason, and perhaps the more
compelling, was Mitropoulos's late-blooming dedication to the opera pit.
He found out quickly that batonless conductors simply could not achieve
the desired unanimity of ensemble when leading from the submerged orchestra pit and attempting to cue not only the players around them but the
soloists and chorus moving on the stage above. Having made the switch
back to the baton, he remained faithful to it until his death.

During the Greek and European stages of his career, Mitropoulos's
hands usually moved independently of one another, except during climactic crescendos, when—like Stokowski—he would often extend both arms in
the manner of an urgent embrace to shape a smooth, intensifying wave of
sonority. Ordinarily, his right hand gave the beat, with independent fingers adding stresses to the rhythm. The right hand usually launched instrumental attacks as well, expanding or contracting to indicate changes in
the dynamics. To the left hand went the task of shaping the phrases. And
like Furtwängler, Stokowski, and Koussevitzky, he often preferred to beat
phrases or paragraphs rather than measures.

This description could apply to many other famous conductors, but
what made Mitropoulos look so different—the quality that led reviewer
after reviewer to describe his podium style as "odd," "unorthodox," "individual," or "strange"—was the involvement of his entire body. Whereas
the conductor most like Mitropoulos in style, Leopold Stokowski, would
never move from the waist down, Mitropoulos, at least during this stage of
his career, involved every part of his body. Head, eyes, shoulders, arms,
legs, waist—all contributed something to the visual analogy he was attempting to draw. For musicians and listeners unused to such an athletic
style, their first sight of Mitropoulos in action was an occasion for amazement. Verbal descriptions tend toward the comic ("like a Greek bartender
vigorously shaking cocktails," wrote Winthrop Sargent in *The New Yorker*)
or lapse into caricature, as though a Mitropoulos performance were some
sort of grand mal seizure; nevertheless, when one was sitting in the orchestra—or even today, when watching Mitropoulos on archival video
footage—one could *see* the music passing through his body as if by a process of superconductivity. Orchestra players understood what he wanted as
they saw him move, saw his conception of the music—real-time, dynamic,
organic, flowing powerfully from his intellect and forming an intensely personal physical response to the information contained in the score.

Wrote Boston critic Rudolph Elie: "He will live every part, personally
direct the entrance of every voice, shape and focus every phrase, build up
every climax, underscore every rhythm and blend all elements of music together in unanimity and concord . . . using every part of his body from his
head to his feet, and everybody who sees him knows precisely what he
means."[11] The conductor's left hand seemed to become, in the words of another reviewer, "almost gigantic" as it delineated the curve and twist of a

phrase: "in the finely-nerved play of its fingers, Mitropoulos had an apparatus for conjuring nuance of the highest sensitivity."[12]

During his American career, Mitropoulos was famous for being the one top-ranked conductor who rarely used a score (the exceptions can literally be counted on the fingers of one hand); not merely in concert—that was common enough when the basic repertoire was being played—but also in rehearsal. At some point in his early career—possibly after seeing Toscanini during the 1920s—Mitropoulos decided to commit every score, no matter how complex, to memory before performing it.

Because he gravitated into conducting, only gradually detaching himself from composing and from a potentially grand career as a concert pianist, Mitropoulos viewed his profession humbly, without the slightest delusion as to its publicly perceived glamour; he did not encourage younger colleagues to set their sights on a conducting career but rather encouraged them to study conducting as a means to broaden and season their total knowledge of music. In a letter to a young colleague identified only as Dino, written near the end of his tenure with his Athenian orchestra, Mitropoulos had this to say:

> The idea of studying conducting is, in my opinion, neither good nor bad, because above all conducting is useful to every musician. It is harmful to those who look at it as an end in itself, and not as something useful to the general and more perfect education of a musician. Don't misunderstand these words of mine. I shouldn't like even you, whom I appreciate so much, to let conducting make you sick and unhappy in all your life, continuously complaining if for one reason or another you aren't given the opportunity to have an orchestra at your disposal.
>
> So then: go on and study conducting too; learn all the secrets of the art of conducting, but let your purpose be to enrich your knowledge and to let no secret of the art of Music go unrevealed to you! Then, if chance decides to make things easy for you, you shall be fully equipped for the purpose; but if that doesn't happen, you will still know the pride of having gained that much more knowledge and clarity about the complex workings of the art of Music.[13]

In addition to his duties as music director of the Conservatory Symphony Orchestra, Mitropoulos also taught a well-attended course in musical form, using his own Greek translation of what was at that time the standard textbook on the subject, Richard Stohr's *Musikalische Formenlehre*.

Students found Mitropoulos a stimulating classroom instructor and a trusted, approachable counselor, whether they wanted to discuss music or ask his advice about personal matters. His comments were compassionate and sensible; to genuine concerns, sincerely expressed, he brought genuine empathy.

Mitropoulos took part in the social life of the academy when his schedule permitted. The mother of Athenian music critic George Leotsakos could still remember, when asked for her recollections in 1985, going to numerous parties at the home of professor Antonis Skokos at which Mitropoulos was present. Skokos and his wife Katina were among Mitropoulos's closest friends at the conservatory, so he was more likely to abandon his monkish demeanor in their company than he would have been at most faculty functions. Mrs. Leotsakos remembered several parties at which Skokos and Mitropoulos alternated at the piano, trying to play tangos and fox trots so the students could dance. Both faculty members, it turned out, were hopelessly "square" when they tried to play in pop-music styles, displaying a sense of rhythm that was "stiff and clumsy" until the students politely but firmly banished them from the piano and took matters into their own hands.[14]

When George Leotsakos began reviewing music for a major Athenian newspaper in 1959, he discovered that, to the average Greek music lover, "Mitropoulos was already a legendary, unworldly creature, beyond history and beyond any criticism, as perfect and as faultless as a God!"[15]

That was certainly not the case in February 1933. On the twenty-third day of that month, Mitropoulos was elected to a chair in the Academy of Athens, an honorary and ceremonial organization patterned after the French Academy. This was a signal honor, one that brought enormous prestige to its recipient and a bitter reaction from the musical right-wing.

By this time, practitioners of the Greek National School had upgraded their own status by forming the Union of Composers—which could be joined by just about anyone musically literate enough to write down a C major scale. Time after time, the Union had sought to persuade or browbeat Mitropoulos into conducting scores that he considered unworthy of a public hearing. Some members of the Union of Composers vilified Mitropoulos in print and in backstage smear campaigns, labeling him as "unpatriotic." Darker, slimier accusations were put into circulation about the conductor's supposed "moral turpitude." Mitropoulos was a very public figure and hence quite vulnerable, but he risked shame rather than compromise his artistic standards.

Shortly after Mitropoulos's election to the Academy of Athens, six members of the Composers Union bought space in all the Athenian papers and publicly denounced the academy's action. Of the six composers who signed this proclamation, only one—Manolis Kalomiris—is remembered today, a fact that goes some distance toward confirming Mitropoulos's opinion that most of the music churned out by the nationalists was inferior stuff. Kalomiris, at least, knew better, for Mitropoulos had performed his works, including two fully staged operas; surely the appearance of Kalomiris's name on this document must have been a stab-wound to Mitropoulos. The document read, in part:

This is a proclamation of Greek Composers regarding the election of Mr. Mitropoulos to the Academy: We the undersigned ... were stunned to learn that Mr. Mitropoulos had been elected to a chair reserved for a "Greek composer." We do not wish to lessen Mr. Mitropoulos's stature as a conductor and pianist, which is praiseworthy, but as a composer, he has no presence of any value—neither as to the quality of his music nor the quantity of it that he has produced. Therefore, it is impossible to justify the election of him to the seat . . . in the Academy. It is impossible for us to understand how the Academy could have made such a decision when there are other Greek composers who have produced better and more numerous works than Mr. Mitropoulos. . . . we believe that neither the Concerto Grosso nor the Inventions for voice and piano to the erotic poems of Cavafy are of sufficient inspiration. If composers were judged as seriously for admission to the Academy as academicians and scientists, then better criteria would be used than the amount of press attention that composer has received.[16]

There was one Greek composer, though, whose works Mitropoulos logically should have championed: Nikos Skalkottas. Born in 1904, Skalkottas studied violin in Athens, then went to Berlin in 1924 to study with Weill, Schoenberg, and Phillip Jarnach. He and Mitropoulos just missed each other in Berlin, and Skalkottas confessed somewhat enigmatically to a mutual friend—pianist John Papaioannou—that "it was probably just as well" the meeting hadn't come off.[17] Evidently someone had told Skalkottas something about Mitropoulos that prejudiced Skalkottas against him. Homophobia is ruled out by the ambivalence of Skalkottas's own sexual preferences. Nor did Skalkottas cease admiring Mitropoulos as a composer, even going so far as to dedicate one of his own pieces to Mitropoulos and to orchestrate the conductor's *Four Kytheran Dances* for piano.

When Skalkottas returned to Athens, he carried with him the ideology and the techniques of Schoenberg and employed them in a number of colorful and ambitious orchestral works, most notably in the one-movement symphony *The Return of Ulysses*. If Mitropoulos was looking to program Greek music that could compete on an international level, all he had to do was glance to his left when he was conducting the Athens Conservatory Orchestra and he would have seen the impoverished Skalkottas dutifully sawing away in the back row of the violin section, eking out a living while he composed scores no one was interested in performing.

Mitropoulos did eventually take into his repertoire four of Skalkottas's marvelous (and decidedly, though quirkily, tonal) *Greek Dances*, which he conducted spectacularly and even recorded for Columbia Records. All efforts to interest him in one of Skalkottas's longer works, particularly the Schoenbergian *Ulysses* symphony, proved fruitless. When Mitropoulos was visiting Katy Katsoyanis in 1955, she and Papaioannou obtained several Skalkottas scores from the conservatory archives and left them prominently displayed on various surfaces of the living room furniture. Only once during his visit did the conductor even flip idly through the pages and when

Katy asked him pointblank why he did not take one of them back to New York and program it, Mitropoulos muttered: "Yes, well, you know I would have to get the approval of the Board of Trustees to do something this unfamiliar, so I'm just not interested in new things right now."[18]

For a conductor who had spent his entire career championing "new things," this was an astonishing statement. But by 1955, Mitropoulos was experiencing periods of gloomy self-doubt, when he felt that he had wasted too much of his life fighting battles on behalf of difficult or neglected composers, and had too few tangible results to show for it.

His attitude toward Skalkottas seems even stranger in view of the fact that he defended the Greek composer (who died, still poor and unrecognized, in 1949) vehemently in a radio interview broadcast by the Voice of America, lashing out with uncharacteristic bitterness at the Greek intellectual establishment for its treatment of Skalkottas. "They killed him, you know, Skalkottas. They killed him. And if I hadn't left, they would have killed me, too."[19]

Like St. Francis, like Gustav Mahler, Mitropoulos felt closer to heaven when he was most enraptured by the beauties of the Earth. To that end, he climbed mountains. The more arduous the climb, the more refreshing to his spirit would be the view from the top. In the wind that blew across a summit, he heard the reverberation of the All, and in the ritual of the ascent itself, he found a perfect metaphor for Life, at least for Life as he knew it. Botanist William Cooper of the University of Minnesota—at whose Colorado lodge Mitropoulos often stayed during part of the summer—climbed with him many times and had this to say: "His motive in climbing was uniquely his own. The mountain to him was a symbol: a goal to be gained through struggle, against difficulties to be overcome. Attainment of the summit was a spiritual rather than a physical goal; it matched with the complete mastery of a new and difficult score."[20]

Mitropoulos was a member of the Greek Mountaineering Society, and by the time he moved to the United States he had mastered most major Greek ascents: Parnon, Chelmos, Ziria, Parnassus, Parnitha, and of course Olympus itself.

Tassos Zappas was a member of the nine-man party that ascended Olympus in September 1932. He recorded the conductor's remarks and observed his behavior in a memoir written a half-century later. Mitropoulos, Zappas recalled, was so excited by the prospect of the climb that he had scarcely slept the night before. "I feel like a child again!" he exclaimed, eyes bright and sun-vulnerable head covered by a sporty beret. "This is glorious, like being reborn without any cares or sorrows!"[21]

Mitropoulos climbed with a "steadfast rhythm," Zappas recounted. The thirty-six-year-old conductor was "lean and strong. . . . He climbed with the prudence of a wise and experienced climber, not frantically as was the case with some other people."

On the climbers' left spread out the rich valley of Enippea. They encountered patches of early snow and bushes laden with wild strawberries, which they picked and ate. By twilight, they had reached the climbers' shelter at the 6900-foot contour line. From this site, the view was magnificently panoramic. Once firewood had been gathered, they ate a frugal meal and watched the deepening of darkness all around and below them.

At six in the morning, the party started out again, their objective being to conquer the summits of both Scolio and Mytica peaks. As they neared the summit of Scolio, Mitropoulos said: "You would think that this peak was placed here precisely to reward the bravest climbers with the greatest possible compensation." Of the precipice that separated Scolio from Mytica and the Throne of Zeus, Mitropoulos observed: "A place so wild and inaccessible could only be an abode of the gods, and yet when we stand here, we too feel like gods."

Later on, after the climbers had reached the peaks and started down again, Mitropoulos led some of them on a detour to inspect the cave called the Asylum of the Muses where a famous hermit-artist named Vasilis Ithakissios had lived. The way led through a dense forest of beech trees, their canopy so thick that the sky could not be glimpsed between their branches. All was silent inside this lush oasis, except for the soft song of a brook meandering through the mossy rocks at their feet.

"This is the perfect place for a writer to write or a musician to compose," observed Zappas.

"I disagree," said Mitropoulos, "for the most ardent desire to create, the sharpest inspiration, comes not from being in direct contact with such a place, but while being away from it. It's the feeling of absence that kindles the imagination. As with a woman—you feel the greatest longing for her, the most ardent desire, when she's not close at hand."

When Mitropoulos spoke like that, Zappas later wrote, his Arcadian soul revealed itself. In the next breath, however, the conductor revealed something else about his soul: "When I'm on a high peak, I feel the joy of life overflowing in me . . . but at the same time, I get a taste of the proximity of death. I hope that when the moment of my death comes, I may die by falling from the summit of some great peak."

CHAPTER SEVEN

Triumph in Boston and a Fateful Encounter with Leonard Bernstein

Whenever Mitropoulos performed and simultaneously conducted Proko-fiev's Third Piano Concerto, audiences went wild—these performances were great theater and musically they left nothing to be desired. The pound-ing motoric rhythms of the concerto and its stretches of tart lyricism were perfectly suited for Mitropoulos's gifts as a pianist. Wherever he had played the work once, he was asked to play it again in subsequent seasons; invita-tions for first-time performances came in steadily, from places as far away as Rio de Janeiro and Tokyo.

One person who did not appreciate the Greek conductor's *coup de théâtre* was Serge Prokofiev. As it happened, Prokofiev had been earning a fair part of his income by appearing as a soloist in that very concerto; he had never dared to conduct it at the same time, of course, and now that Mi-tropoulos had done so, to sensational effect, demand suddenly declined for the more conventional arrangement. When Mitropoulos played the Third Concerto for the first time in Paris, Prokofiev was in the audience, eager to witness firsthand the phenomenon he had been reading and hearing about. At the conclusion of the performance, Prokofiev turned to a companion and said, above thunderous applause: "Well, Mitropoulos has taken it over completely. I guess I'll just have to write another concerto for myself."[1]

Indirectly, Mitropoulos's identification with the Prokofiev concerto led to his American debut in 1936. As it happened, the rights to the score of the Third Concerto were owned by the publishing house that Serge Kousse-vitzky had established in Paris before he emigrated to Boston. As a matter of routine business, Koussevitzky received clippings about performances of works published by his firm, and the sudden spate of notices piqued his in-terest in this unknown Greek.

Since taking the podium of the Boston Symphony in 1924, Kousse-vitzky had made himself and the Boston Symphony Orchestra synony-mous. Though lacking in any formal training as a conductor, Koussevitzky was a stupendously gifted natural musician, with a seemingly supernat-ural ability to coax passionate, committed playing from his superb instru-mentalists. He did not rely on famous soloists to fill Symphony Hall—his

Mitropoulos for his feelings about the popular Finnish composer. Mitropoulos had only performed Sibelius one time, in fact (the Second Symphony, in Monte Carlo), and would seldom perform his music in either Minneapolis or New York. His response to this question was frank and to the point: "I would rather conduct his music than listen to it. I have not the patience to listen to Sibelius, though I admit that it's beautiful and grand. Personally, I prefer Mahler."

Reports of Mitropoulos's first BSO concert (in Providence, Rhode Island) confirmed that something special was in store farther north when Mitropoulos made his Symphony Hall debut before the most staid and complacent of Boston audiences, the Friday Afternoon Regulars—hundreds of ladies who held season tickets as a matter of social custom and who had become quite content with the status quo, smugly secure in the knowledge that they had the world's greatest orchestra and certainly one of the three greatest conductors in America.

But the Friday afternoon audience also had a large contingent of students and ordinary music lovers, known as the Fifty-centers after the price of their top-balcony seats and leftovers. What this audience lacked in social status, it made up for in genuine passion and receptiveness. Such was the curiosity about Mitropoulos that people began lining up on the front steps of Symphony Hall early in the morning and waited expectantly until the doors opened at half past two, at which time a real scramble began for the fifty-cent seats.

When the lights dimmed, all eyes turned toward the left side of the stage, where the conductor would make his entrance. Unlike Koussevitzky, who ambled to the podium with the measured, dignified tread of one who is about to lead a sacred ritual, Mitropoulos bounded on stage like a thoroughbred coming out of the starting gate. With no score, no music stand, and no baton to impede him, he clawed the air with his big, taut hands, giving the downbeat for Beethoven's *Leonore* Overture No. 2. The concentrated energy emanating from the podium riveted the attention of everyone present, from the blue-haired matrons to the students in the balcony.

The program Mitropoulos had chosen was somewhat offbeat, in keeping with the spirit of the whole enterprise. Following the Beethoven came the *Overture for a Don Quixote* by Jean Rivier, and to close the concert's first half, Debussy's *La Mer* (a bit of a dare, that one, since *La Mer* was a Koussevitzky specialty). On the second half of the concert, there was but a single work: Richard Strauss's *Symphonia domestica*.

Audience response was long, loud, and unusually demonstrative. Critical reaction was just a bit tentative, however—those gentlemen had been conditioned to the Koussevitzky way, and some of them carped at what they perceived to be exaggerated dynamics, a tendency on Mitropoulos's part to demand *pianissimo*s that verged on the inaudible and *forte*s that seemed strident.

During the days between his first and second Boston programs, Mitropoulos made a quick side trip to New York. As was his habit, he simply checked in at a hotel and went out on his own to see the sights and get a feel for the place. One location he definitely wanted to see was world-famous Carnegie Hall. When he reached Fifty-seventh Street, he learned from the posters on display that Stokowski and the Philadelphia Orchestra would be in town that very night. He went in and bought a ticket. That concert, he later averred, "was one of the most extraordinary musical experiences of my life. I did not know that sounds like that could come out of an orchestra!"[6]

As if to make up for their hesitancy in reviewing Mitropoulos's first Boston concerts, the critics unleashed a thesaurus full of adjectives describing his second pair of appearances. This time, his program began with Mahler's First Symphony, a work that had not been heard in Boston for thirteen years, and concluded with two unashamedly colorful works, Florent Schmitt's *La Tragédie de Salomé* and the conductor's own orchestration of Bach's Fantasia and Fugue in G Minor.

New Yorkers would read in the words of Olin Downes, visiting to see what all the fuss was about, that Mitropoulos "is more than a kindling virtuoso. He showed a microscopic knowledge of [the] strongly contrasted scores, and his temperament is that of an impetuous musician. [He] addressed himself with complete comprehension and with blazing dramatic emotion."[7]

National coverage came when Boston critic Alexander Williams wrote two reviews for the *Musical Courier*, offering, in the second of these, "high praise" for Mitropoulos's "fanatical devotion to the art of music, . . . governed by good taste and intelligence."[8]

Because of the astonishing success this unknown Greek visitor had enjoyed and because of where he achieved it, rumors had indeed begun to circulate even before he left America. Some suggested, as Richard Dyer had reported in the *Boston Herald* in February, that Mitropoulos was already being lined up to succeed Koussevitzky; many believed that Koussevitzky became so jealous of Mitropoulos that he refused to ask the Greek conductor back and had to be overruled by the BSO board of directors. Certainly, Koussevitzky may very well have been unnerved by the ease and totality of Mitropoulos's triumph, but the Russian conductor's most authoritative biographer, Moses Smith, states that Koussevitzky rushed backstage after the Saturday night concert, embraced Mitropoulos, and invited him, in front of numerous witnesses, to return the following year. When a reporter made reference to Mitropoulos's stunning effect on the Boston audience, Koussevitzky responded graciously but somewhat slyly: "That makes me happy. He is a great talent, and I am glad that they appreciate my sending him to them."[9]

Even before the dates for Mitropoulos to return had been scheduled, George Judd received an urgent telephone call from Mrs. Carlyle Scott, manager of the Minneapolis Symphony Orchestra. Were the reports true, Scott asked; was the Mitropoulos fellow really something special? Judd assured her that he was. Could Minneapolis have a look at him after he was through in Boston? Indeed Minneapolis could. Dates were finalized just before Mitropoulos embarked for the return voyage to Europe. He would appear in Boston again on January 14 and 15, 1937, then take a train out to Minnesota, where he would conduct the Minneapolis Symphony Orchestra for the first time on January 29.

Mitropoulos did not have time to savor his American triumph, for he was due back in Berlin in late February, to guest-conduct the Philharmonic. After Berlin, he headed south for his now-customary sojourn in Monte Carlo. This season, he directed ten concerts there and added to his dual-capacity repertoire the G Major Piano Concerto of Albert Roussel and Gian Francesco Malipiero's Piano Concerto No. 1.

He did not care for Monte Carlo. "As soon as I arrived here this morning," he wrote Katy on March 1:

> I was seized by a black depression at the thought of having to stay for a month and a half in this hole. The [management] doesn't want new things . . . and if I want to do something interesting, of course it doesn't exist in the orchestra's library and I'm obliged to pay myself for the rental of the orchestra's material! . . . If this didn't bring me some money and if the orchestra weren't good, I must confess that it would be absolutely unbearable.[10]

By the end of his stay in Monte Carlo, he was feeling somewhat better. He wrote Katy and apologized for the self-pitying tone of his earlier letter, saying that "when the environment bothers you, you become neurotic." It is difficult to tell from the letters just what, in particular, irritated Mitropoulos so. Probably the languid, hedonistic ambience of that sunny principality just clashed with his own fairly Calvinistic sense of propriety. It is hard to imagine Mitropoulos hanging about in the casinos or enjoying tennis and cocktails with the idle rich who came to spend their money.

He derived a lot of pleasure from the Monte Carlo orchestra, at least, and described it to Katy as "the best in France." Despite his complaints, he managed to program quite a few novelties and challenging works, such as the Bruckner Fourth Symphony, Busoni's *Indian Fantasy,* Max Reger's *Isle of the Dead* (from *Four Tone Poems after Böcklin*), Mahler's First Symphony (and the Adagio movement from the Ninth Symphony), and Schoenberg's *Transfigured Night.* Nor did he neglect the music of his countrymen. During the years he was a regular in Monte Carlo, he directed performances of symphonies by Kalomiris and Petrides, four of the exuberant *Greek Dances* of Skalkottas, and shorter works by Spiro Samara and Harilaos Perpessa.

At the turn of the new year 1937, Mitropoulos sailed for the United States and two events that would dramatically change the direction of his life: his debut concert with the Minneapolis Symphony Orchestra on January 29 and his initial meeting with Leonard Bernstein, then a handsome, dazzlingly talented, consumingly ambitious sophomore at Harvard University. As a result of that encounter, Bernstein would become Mitropoulos's protégé, many years later his colleague and rival, and eventually his betrayer.

The meeting with Bernstein came about as a consequence of Mitropoulos's return engagement with the Boston Symphony. In accordance with the details worked out a year earlier, the Grecian guest was slated to conduct two pairs of concerts in Boston (January 15 and 16, 22 and 23) after an opening night in Cambridge on January 14.

Bernstein was nineteen when he met Mitropoulos. Bernstein's friendship with Koussevitzky was still several years in the future, making Mitropoulos the first and for a long time only conductor of significant repute whom Bernstein knew well. For Mitropoulos, the initial meeting seems to have been a charming and slightly flirtatious interlude; one cannot be more specific than that—most of his recorded comments about Bernstein date from the years after their relationship had become clouded with, at the very least, ambiguity.

For the young Bernstein, however, the 1937 encounter was an emotional earthquake. One year after the event, he wrote a thinly fictionalized account of the incident for his course in English composition, entitling the story "The Occult." To his English professor and classmates, the story would have seemed pure fiction (albeit daringly direct in its homoerotic overtones), if only because the setting is California and not Boston. But in 1973, Bernstein resurrected the tale and allowed it to be published, without offering a word of comment, in his autobiographical grab bag of a book, *Findings*.[11] Given the frankly confessional nature of the story (*Findings* appeared five years before Joan Peyser's controversial biography provided the general public with the truth about Bernstein's sexual orientation) and the absence of any commentary about it by its author, one can only speculate on Bernstein's reason for including it. Exhibitionism, certainly—that element was always present in his public acts—but perhaps also an act of contrition for his cruelty to a man on whom he had once had a gigantic crush. Whatever Bernstein's motives for allowing "The Occult" to be published, many details found in it have been corroborated by Bernstein's longtime friends. The exchanges of dialogue between Bernstein and Mitropoulos, while doubtless polished in the writing, have the ring of plausibility and may be taken as a reasonable facsimile of what the two men actually said to each other; in the following discussion, all quotations dealing with their initial meetings are excerpted from Bernstein's story unless otherwise noted.

When Mitropoulos arrived in Cambridge, he was approached by representatives of Harvard's Helicon Society, accompanied by Raphael Demos, Alford Professor of Philosophy and Acting Master of Adams House. This delegation wanted very much to put on a reception in honor of the visiting maestro, attendance strictly limited to students and faculty who were involved in the Greek society. The approach was made diffidently—the word had already gone out that Mitropoulos disliked "social functions"—but the conductor agreed, provided the affair was not open to the public and the guest list was limited to people affiliated with the Helicon Society. The event was scheduled for the following Friday night, just before Mitropoulos was scheduled to return to Boston, and the location was the Phillips Brooks house. An abundant array of canapes and sweets was laid on by the ladies of the Greek community. Admission was by Helicon Society membership card only, and anyone who showed up at the door without that document would be tactfully but firmly turned away.

Leonard Bernstein had attended the January 15 Mitropoulos concert in Boston, and, in his own words, "had gone bananas" in response to the Greek conductor's intense music-making.[12] He was now determined to meet Mitropoulos. Bernstein was already well known on campus as a pianist, and he was invited by a Helicon Society member, Leonidas Demeter, to provide musical background for the reception. Bernstein had already been figuring his chances of crashing the party, so this opportunity came as a delightful surprise.

It was also a last-minute one, evidently, for Bernstein had to arrange a ride with his mother, Jennie, on very short notice, so short that Jennie Bernstein was in the middle of baking when her son burst in and, with characteristic exaggeration, announced that she simply had to drop what she was doing and drive him to Harvard because "Mitropoulos wants to meet me and it has been arranged!"[13] Always eager to indulge her son, Jennie washed the dough from her hands, threw a fur coat over her housedress, and headed for campus, Lenny chattering excitedly beside her in the family's Plymouth.

Guarding the door at the Phillips Brooks house was Professor Demos's wife, Jean, who had already turned away several erstwhile gate-crashers and who knew nothing about a student pianist coming to play. "I was approached to make an exception for a lady with her undergraduate son, who seemed somewhat embarrassed by his mother's insistence, but I was firm," recalled Mrs. Demos many years later. Having stood her ground and closed the door in the Bernsteins' faces, she went back into the party and circulated. The next time she looked up, there were the same two people, already in conversation with the guest of honor. "The officious faculty-wife was thwarted by the courageous mother," recalled Mrs. Demos.[14]

In "The Occult," the piano-playing protagonist is named Carl Fevrier and the star conductor is given the name Eros Mavro. Bernstein/Carl enters the crowded room and spies "the great Greek conductor for whom this reception was being given," and the descriptions of Mitropoulos/Eros begin with a line about "a great dome of a hairless head which reflected the brilliant California sun like a halo."[15]

Bernstein was introduced, or introduced himself. When Mitropoulos was speaking, Bernstein "saw the wide, full mouth . . . the strong nose . . . a disarming gentleness in the small blue eyes." Some perfunctory remarks were exchanged between conductor and sophomore, after which Bernstein sat down at the piano and played for approximately a half-hour. He began with the Nocturne in F-sharp Major by Chopin, presumably played another classical selection or two, then segued into some of his own keyboard compositions. Mitropoulos was clearly impressed by the young man's talent, and he was not unaware of Bernstein's still-somewhat-adolescent good looks. At the end of the party, as they were shaking hands, Mitropoulos invited Bernstein to attend his Boston Symphony rehearsals the following week. "If they will not allow you in, ask to see me," were his parting words.

Although semester exams were only a few days away, Bernstein went in to Boston. He had no trouble getting into the rehearsal—Mitropoulos had already seen to that. At first, Bernstein took a seat respectfully back in the darkened rows of Symphony Hall, beyond the penumbra of the stage lights, but when Mitropoulos entered, he motioned for Bernstein to sit down front, then handed him his own copies of the scores so that the younger musician could follow in detail. At that moment, Bernstein was staggered by the realization that Mitropoulos did not need the scores—"the music was all in Mavro's incredible head."

In a rare display of approval, the Boston Symphony applauded when their guest stepped onto the podium. There was a cane-bottomed chair on the podium, and at one point during the rehearsal, in order to signify a sudden, dramatic diminuendo, Mitropoulos dropped onto the chair so hard he broke the bottom out of it. According to Bernstein, the conductor literally didn't miss a beat, but rose from his undignified fall smiling and still conducting, "too full of the music to stop even for an instant."

Bernstein thought the rehearsal sounded "glorious," but he was too excited and too nervous to stay around afterward—in one morning, Mitropoulos had become Leonard Bernstein's idol. After the next rehearsal he worked up his nerve to approach the conductor, both to congratulate him and to ask if he might show Mitropoulos the score to one of his own recent compositions. He jumped up on stage just as Mitropoulos was exiting. Bernstein followed, and suddenly the two men collided.

"I was just coming back to look for you," Mitropoulos said. "Will you take lunch with me?"

This was the first time the two men had had a chance to be alone and simply talk to one another. Leonard Bernstein, as millions of Americans would learn from watching his *Omnibus* television programs, could be a spellbinding conversationalist, but on this occasion, he was willing and happy to subordinate himself to the older man. Their talk ranged over many subjects and the more Bernstein saw and heard, the more he was convinced that he was in the presence of "a truly great man, with the sort of greatness that embodies liberalism, complete tolerance, unbounded enthusiasm for and devotion to his art."

At length, after much stimulating and increasingly intimate conversation, Mitropoulos made the heavily loaded gesture of offering Bernstein an oyster from his own fork. The implied symbolism of the act, as well as its sheer class, impressed young Bernstein deeply, although perhaps not as drastically as his fictional alter-ego Carl, who "nearly fainted" when the quivering bit of seafood was proffered. Fictional Carl's response to the gesture is not recorded, but real-life Leonard did not hesitate to accept the oyster, along with whatever implications of a relationship went along with it.

Without, one suspects, any overt calculation toward seduction, Mitropoulos had made the whole luncheon encounter into a dizzying occasion for his new friend. The oyster-sharing ritual flattered the sensualist in Bernstein, and the words Mitropoulos spoke a few moments later kindled a fierce glow that bypassed Bernstein's rapacious sexuality and went directly to the ego centered within it.

"Do you know," Mitropoulos said slowly, "the moment I set eyes on you, I felt a something—a feeling of the presence of—greatness; of something—genius." There it was, openly spoken by his new idol: the G-word. At the sound of those words, intoned with the added majesty of Mitropoulos's beautiful continental accent, Bernstein was rendered "limp with realization. The man had spoken it. . . ."

All too soon after the utterance of those intoxicating words, Mitropoulos went back to work with the orchestra, and Bernstein, no doubt distractedly, went off to study for exams. The two men would not spend any more time alone until after the final Boston concert.

For his program of January 14–15, Mitropoulos offered fresh and varied fare indeed. On the concerts' first half, he conducted two of his own arrangements: *Prelude and Dido's Lament* from Purcell's *Dido and Aeneas* and the string-orchestra version of Beethoven's Op. 131 string quartet. Oliver Daniel was fortunate enough to be in the audience for the January 15 concert and thought both transcriptions "deeply moving," the BSO's playing radiant.[16] After intermission, the Greek visitor accomplished one of those spectacular two-for-one feats by playing and conducting Respighi's Toccata for Piano and Orchestra. The program ended with a lively and colorful suite drawn from Alfredo Casella's *La donna serpente*.

During the second week of concerts, Mitropoulos again did his balancing act, this time playing and conducting the Piano Concerto of Gian Francesco Malipiero. Critic Moses Smith found this tour de force "remarkable simply as a stunt" and hastened to emphasize that "Mitropoulos himself strikes one as the farthest thing in the world from a trickster."[17]

At the final pair of concerts Bernstein was hypnotized by the "poignancy and fire" of Ravel's *Rapsodie espagnole*, and "felt that he would burst with a terrifying mixture of pride and despondency" at the tenderness with which Mitropoulos unfolded the slow movement of Schumann's Second Symphony.

When the last concert ended, Symphony Hall rocked on its foundations as the audience vented its enthusiasm. The overflow crowd roared and shouted, joined by the lathered musicians in the orchestra; ladies threw their corsages at the podium. Mitropoulos was recalled thirteen times; he applauded the musicians, who had played like gods for him, and then he picked up all the flowers on stage, one by one, and kissed them. Retired Boston Symphony players, interviewed by Oliver Daniel a half-century later, still spoke of those last two Mitropoulos concerts in terms of glory.

Dazed and trembling with emotion, Bernstein joined the tide of well-wishers flowing backstage to congratulate the guest conductor. The dressing room, of course, was packed with people, all crowded around a glowing, sweat-glazed Mitropoulos who could scarcely find room to light a cigarette. Despite the press of people, he spotted Bernstein almost the instant he entered the room. Their eye contact arced across the room like a spark. Pushing his way through the crowd, Mitropoulos reached Bernstein's side; he took the younger man's shoulder and guided him—rather to the astonishment of the crowd—straight into the bathroom, the only place in reach where the two of them might exchange a few words in private.

Mitropoulos closed the door, then put his hands on Bernstein's shoulders.

"You must make me proud of you one day," Mitropoulos said. "It is plain to me you have every talent for a composer. You are sensitive in an ideal way—I know, don't say a word. You must work, work very hard. You must devote all your time to your art. You must keep yourself pure. Do not let friends spoil you with flattery. You have everything to make you great. It is up to you only to fulfill your mission."

He took an inscribed photo from inside his jacket and handed it to Bernstein, saying: "This is for you. Do not fail me." The inscription read "Very sympathetically. D. Mitropoulos."

Bernstein promised he would try to live up to his mentor's hopes. Mitropoulos promised to write after he returned to Europe; then he said goodbye and went back outside to sign autographs. Bernstein remained in the bathroom for a while, flushed and sweating with malarial profusion. He leaned helplessly against the cool tiles on the wall, holding the photo, and laughing in quiet hysteria.

"You know, it's very strange," Leonard Bernstein remarked to an early biographer, "that in my conducting I'm always compared to Koussevitzky or Reiner. But nobody ever realizes how much of it is Dimitri—deep, deep —because it was the first conducting I ever really watched carefully and listened to carefully."[18]

Jennie Bernstein attributed her son's podium career directly to that initial 1937 encounter with Mitropoulos. Until the moment he burst into the kitchen on that wintry Friday night, she had nurtured a very different vision of her son's future. "I wanted him to be a great pianist. That was my dream for him. When he met Mitropoulos all that changed."[19]

The Mitropoulos influence could be seen most clearly in Bernstein's podium style. The choreographic ecstasies, the sheer physicality, the trance-like and utterly subjective involvement with the music—the concept of a great performance being the end product of a metaphysical, sexual encounter between conductor and orchestra—all of these dominant characteristics in Bernstein's conducting style can be traced directly to Mitropoulos's influence.[20]

In a documentary film about himself (*Reflections*, a 1978 production directed by Peter Rosen for the United States Information Agency), Bernstein gave the most expansive of his numerous commentaries on his Mitropoulos connection:

> The influence of Mitropoulos on my life, on my conducting life, is enormous and usually greatly underrated or not known at all, because ordinarily the two great conductors with whom I studied are the ones who receive the credit for whatever conducting prowess I have; namely, Serge Koussevitzky and Fritz Reiner. . . . But long before I met either one of them, I had met Dimitri Mitropoulos . . . and watching him conduct those two weeks of rehearsals and concerts with the Boston Symphony laid some kind of conductorial passion and groundwork in my psyche which I wasn't even aware of until many years later. I remember every piece he did. All that I do is proof enough of that influence . . . those pieces that Mitropoulos played, nobody will ever forget who played them or attended them.[21]

One lesson Bernstein learned during those two weeks in Boston was that the profession of conducting, traditionally an ironclad bastion of maleness, was not necessarily closed to a homosexual. He had witnessed the Boston Symphony Orchestra, as macho a band as any in America, play as though possessed, under the leadership of a man who had made no effort to hide from Bernstein the fact of his being gay. That the rest of Boston did not share this knowledge was irrelevant; Bernstein, at age nineteen, had found his most singular and powerful role model. In later years, he even adopted Mitropoulos's habit of taking favored guests into the backstage bathroom for private *tête-à-têtes* after his concerts—only in this mannerism, Bernstein went Mitropoulos one better by sometimes greeting his dressing-room visitors stripped to the waist, a towel slung casually over one shoulder.

(Mozart), *Egmont* (Beethoven), *Anacreon* (Cherubini), *Ruy Blas* (Mendelssohn), *Rosamunde* (Schubert), *Euryanthe* (von Weber), and *Die Fledermaus* (Johann Strauss). The occasion was Mitropoulos's first pops concert, and he was serving notice to everyone that these concerts would not be musically inconsequential, however lighter and more playful they might be than the more symphonic programs.

Given the format for the pops concerts at this time, a certain amount of zaniness in the programming was probably in order. Each such concert was divided into three parts: during the first and third parts, the MSO performed its concert fare, and sandwiched in the middle was a half-hour radio broadcast with the Lake-Wobegon-ish title "The March of Minnesota" (that week's episode: "The Early History of St. Cloud").

As adventurous, even risky, as the seven-overtures program was, it proved extremely popular with both listeners and reviewers. There was sufficient contrast among the overtures, and their unusual juxtaposition offered a fresh perspective. The experience, wrote John Sherman, was "like hearing seven masterpieces by the seven greatest composers of all time." Why had this oddball program worked so well? The answer resided in a key element of Mitropoulos's style:

> Mitropoulos packs so much meaning into everything he plays, gives it such potency of phrase and illuminates it throughout with such a wealth of revealing touches that the choice of music, in itself, has far less to do with the listener's enjoyment than is usually the case. That's a strange situation, but there it is. You've nothing else to do than accept it joyfully.[10]

As the season progressed and sheer intoxication became diluted by routine, of course the range of critical and popular response widened. When, at the end of January, the new conductor presented his interpretation of Beethoven's "Eroica" Symphony, some critics finally took issue with his highly individual conception. Some found it bracing, praising its clarity and "lack of bluster"; others found it disappointingly dry, oddly detached, lacking in gravity, and—in the Funeral March especially—too brisk in its tempos. The same style, however, wrought a very different impression when Mitropoulos essayed Beethoven's Fifth Symphony two weeks later. By eschewing all bombast and presenting the work in a lean, muscular, propulsively energetic style, he made this overfamiliar symphony breathtakingly fresh again. "I have never heard the work given more sinew, more kinetic force and momentum, more incisiveness of stroke," wrote Sherman in his *Star* review.

January's programs reached an emotional peak with an all-Strauss program (first half by Richard, second half by Johann) which brought back critical unanimity and superlatives. Mitropoulos's Don Juan seemed no mere rake, but an existential hero grappling with destiny; as Sherman described it, "under Mitropoulos's flailing fists, the story was given a fire, a passion and sting that made the score smoke."[11] And his traversal of *Death and*

Transfiguration ranged the emotional extremes, taking the music absolutely at face value from its tenebrous opening pages—darkness made audible in this interpretation—to climaxes of terrifying intensity to a closing of seraphic relinquishment. That night, the Minneapolis audience learned a truism about Dimitri Mitropoulos: the man never gave a bad performance of Richard Strauss's music. As for Johann, well, one wouldn't want to dance to these performances (the way one might to Ormandy's Johann Strauss), but by virtue of the point and filigree Mitropoulos brought out in them, one could happily listen to them all night.

Mitropoulos ended his first full month as the MSO's music director by coupling a safe warhorse (Beethoven's Fourth Piano Concerto, with Artur Rubinstein as the much-appreciated soloist) and a massive work that had not yet been accepted anywhere in America: Gustav Mahler's Symphony No. 1. Where Mahler was concerned, Mitropoulos was already a zealot, preaching with all the skill he could command to a public predisposed to skepticism. Mahler's music had a reputation—even among listeners who had never heard any of it—for heaviness and length, bombast and bathos dished out in massive Teutonic helpings. Ormandy had gone to enormous trouble and expense to program the Second Symphony, and Oberhoffer had essayed the tuneful, unthreatening Fourth, but neither work had made a strongly favorable or lasting impression on the Minneapolis audience. No conductor before Mitropoulos had ever programmed the First Symphony.

On this occasion the audience was pleasantly surprised. When Mitropoulos cued all seven French horns to stand up and cut loose in the final measures of the work, the Minneapolitans finally discovered how gloriously, vulgarly exciting Mahler could be. Never mind all the metaphysical claptrap with which the program notes described his symphonies, here was the nineteenth-century symphony orchestra in its fullest glory, sweeping everything before it like an elemental tempest. The thunder on stage was echoed by a standing ovation in Northrop Auditorium.

The Minneapolis critics were generally not yet able to see Mahler's style as anything other than a discontinuous parade of orchestral episodes, some glorious, some banal, some mystifying. Sherman, chief Mahlerphobe among local reviewers, confessed, though, that Mitropoulos came closer than any other conductor ever had to convincing him that Mahler was a great composer. And James Davies wrote:

> The discussions about Mahler pro and con roll merrily along without reaching any definite conclusion. . . . As we heard him at this concert, he is a great composer, if we measure greatness by the effects produced. Would his music have risen before us to such gigantic proportions with any other conductor? . . . we are constrained to believe that under the directions of a master conductor like Mitropoulos his symphonies could win their way into favor and he would be universally regarded as a great composer.[12]

By the midpoint of this spring season, a clear consensus had formed among audience members, critics, and even ordinary citizens who did not usually pay much attention to these matters, that something extraordinary was happening in Minneapolis. The Twin Cities may have been in a culturally backward region, but most touring orchestras, ballet companies, chamber groups, instrumental virtuosos, and vocalists stopped off there as they crossed the country, affording the Twin Cities' critics ample opportunity to measure any local performances against the highest national standards. Nor should it be forgotten that, in some respects, even the average citizen of Minneapolis had better access to great live music-making in 1938 than he or she would have today—one had only to cut on the family radio set during any week of the season to hear Toscanini and the NBC Symphony live, Stokowski in Philadelphia, or Koussevitzky in Boston. Allowing for some degree of hometown boosterism, the reviews of Mitropoulos's first season still convey a remarkable sense of occasion, of something unprecedented happening, and happening on such a scale that even people who did not attend concerts were aware of it and touched by enthusiasm.

Most salient, perhaps, was the opinion that the Minneapolis orchestra was playing, week in and week out, with a precision, subtlety, and vibrancy never before heard; that Mitropoulos had taken a good orchestra and made it superlatively good, consistently, in the widest possible range of the orchestral repertoire. "Here let me say what is apparent to all who have heard the orchestra under Mitropoulos," wrote James Davies in the *Tribune*. "There has been a notable improvement throughout the organization; the men play with a concentration we never dreamed possible and yet through it all there is no evidence of strain, the tones flow easily and freely with added power, or at the other extreme, with beautiful refinement in point and quality."[13]

As for the conductor himself, there was an almost gleeful feeling that Minneapolis had been lucky to discover Mitropoulos and wise to hire him. "Pardon my one-track mind," John Sherman wrote in an informal, unbuttoned appreciation written for the *Star* in early January 1938: "but . . . *Have you heard Mitropoulos conduct?* I've shot that question to so many friends, acquaintances and total strangers that I might as well repeat it here. And to prove I haven't lost all semblance of critical balance and poise, not one person I've button-holed has accused me of over-enthusiasm."[14]

The intense communal excitement, Sherman extolled, had given Minneapolis's music lovers some idea of what "the brotherhood of men would be like, if and when it comes." Professional rivals and enemies, people who ordinarily took pains to avoid one another in public, could be seen rushing up to each other at intermission, shaking hands, back-slapping, and radiating shared enthusiasm for what they had just heard and seen. Socialites who used to attend concerts primarily to show off their new clothing, jewels, or hairdos, could now be seen huddled together, hands waving, passionately discussing the nuances of the evening's performances. Sherman likened this phenomenon to a kind of communitywide "spiritual awaken-ing." Nor were the orchestral musicians themselves immune—Sherman talked to dozens of veteran players, and they all said more or less the same thing: "I'm damned if I know how he does it, but even up there on the stage, in the middle of the orchestra, we can hear how good we are, and it's better than we thought we could possibly do!"

In essence, Mitropoulos's charisma and his painstaking, layered meth-ods of rehearsal, with their emphasis on secondary voices, illuminating the harmonic skeleton, and phrasing long lines with unexpected rhythmic hair-pins fully audible, were creating a whole new concept of interpretation, of re-creative art. His vivid perception of every detail and nuance in a score suggested to Johan Egilsrud of the *Minneapolis Journal* "that somehow, mi-raculously, the music was being born at the very moment one heard it."[15]

By the end of January, it was clear that this phenomenon was not a tem-porary thing, but was the essence of Mitropoulos's style. As it happened, the week Mitropoulos gave his all-overture concert was the same week Tos-canini performed the *Magic Flute* Overture on his weekly NBC concert, and several critics thought Mitropoulos's reading had even more scintillation and excitement. Comparison, though surely premature, was already being made by Sherman, who believed from the start that "Some day [Mitropou-los] will be spoken of the country over with the same awe and devotion which are now given to Toscanini."[16]

News of the death of Maurice Ravel occasioned a memorial concert on February 17, comprising two suites (*Le Tombeau de Couperin* and *Ma Mère l'Oye*), the Piano Concerto in G Major, with Mitropoulos in the dual role of soloist/conductor, and climaxing with both suites from *Daphnis and Chloe*. Ravel has long been entered into the pantheon of great composers, but in 1938 he was still very much a contemporary force: "Whether he will be en-rolled among the immortals . . . must be left to posterity. We can at least say of this man that he was never dull," wrote James Davies in the *Tribune*.[17]

Quite the sensation of the evening was Mitropoulos's blazing per-formance of Ravel's Piano Concerto in G. He gloried in the work's prismatic shifts from percussive giddiness to insinuating charm, its modulations from exquisite tenderness to glittering show-off pyrotechnics. Whatever the mood, Mitropoulos was clearly having a wonderful time and the orchestra responded with an edge-of-the-seats ebullience that sent sparks flying through Northrop Auditorium. As might be expected, the concluding *Daphnis and Chloe* was an orgiastic knock-out that brought the full-house audience to its feet, cheering.

An undisputed highlight of Mitropoulos's first season was his February 20 performance of Mendelssohn's "Scottish" Symphony, a work which most reviewers, then as now, tended to greet with a yawn. Mitropoulos, however, envisioned it as a painting, in tone, of a rugged, wind-swept nordic landscape. His bright, hard-edged accents, his athletic phrasing, full of swagger and stride, and his startling rhythmic tension, all combined to blow the cobwebs from what usually sounds like a polite Victorian genre-piece and turn it into a virile, coruscating delight.

An all-Wagner program on March 6 gave audience and critics a chance to hear Mitropoulos interpret Wagner. Mitropoulos ran hot and cold on Wagner all his life, sometimes professing to dislike his music intensely, at other times revealing himself to be its powerful advocate. On this occasion, Mitropoulos won praise for the "fervor and surge" of his interpretations.

Despite John Sherman's only half-mocking suggestion that the city charter be amended to make it illegal for more than one Mahler work to be performed in a season, Mitropoulos again ventured into progressive territory by programming the Fourth Symphony on Friday night, March 10. In the fourth movement, the soprano part was fetchingly sung by Irena Opava, wife of the MSO's first flutist. While admitting that much of the symphony was "sweet-spirited—benign, childishly joyful, droll, piquant" and all that, Sherman confessed that Mahler still made him "squirmy" and that the symphony's third movement was "long, lovely, and *long*." Yet by now Mahler was being received more warmly, even enthusiastically, by reviewers and audiences—much to the conductor's gratification. Egilsrud perhaps had the last word: "If Mahler could be interpreted so well as he was last night by Mitropoulos, there would be no need for a Mahler Society to create an interest in the composer."[18]

The conductor made his first foray into Brahms on March 18, with a performance of the Third Symphony—to mixed notices. His interpretation was certainly refreshingly different, but its odd stresses and curious points of emphasis seemed inexplicable to some listeners. For instance, Mitropoulos might suddenly throw a sonic spotlight on the cello part when the obvious thing happening at that moment was a repetition, in the violins, of the main theme; at other places in the score, he would bring into bold relief certain basic foundation chords in the brasses, changing the color of the music and adding a spikiness to textures that other conductors sought to make as smooth as possible. To many in the hall, these effects were "exciting and evocative," but exactly what was being evoked, other than a sense of differentness for its own sake, no one could say. Mitropoulos's restlessness when conducting Brahms would become noticeable and would be held against him in later years, especially in New York, where his Brahms symphonies tended to be erratic in both concept and quality of execution. For his loyal and forgiving Minneapolis audience, there was no problem—they did not expect him to do everything equally well, and he had already amply demonstrated the tremendous range of his musical sympathies.

During this first Minneapolis season, Mitropoulos performed a wide variety of music, but most of it was within the parameters of the accepted repertoire: a ballet suite by Nicolas Nabokov, his own string-orchestra transcription of Beethoven's String Quartet No. 14 in C-sharp Minor, a Norwegian Rhapsody by Johann Svendsen, Glazunov's spicy *Overture on Greek Themes*, and a short orchestral work (the Prelude to *Lara*) by his old friend and mentor, Armand Marsick. These were novel scores but they were accessible; he did not yet think the time was ripe for Schoenberg or other difficult moderns.

It was in the foyer of Northrop Auditorium that a particularly telling remark was offered after Mitropoulos had climaxed the season by leading Act One of *Die Walküre*, with Helen Traubel, Lauritz Melchior, and Emanuel List. The performance was sensational, as were the post-intermission performances of "Wotan's Farewell" and the "Magic Fire Music." As critic John Davies was exiting, a somewhat stuck-up New York acquaintance, a concert manager as it happened, sidled up to him with a rueful expression on his face and said, "You know, we don't have such conducting as that in New York."[19]

After the close of the Minneapolis season, Mitropoulos took a train east for his one guest engagement of the spring. He had turned down several earlier requests, feeling that it would be improper and psychologically bad for the Minneapolis orchestra if he left, even for a week, so soon after taking over. The one engagement he decided to take, between the end of the Minneapolis season and the date he was booked to sail back to Europe, was an important one: he had been invited to conduct Toscanini's orchestra, the NBC Symphony, on May 28. This would be his New York debut.

His program for the occasion began with his own transcription of Purcell's "When I am Laid in Earth" from *Dido and Aeneas*; Glazunov's *Overture on Greek Themes*; his calling-card symphony, Schumann's Second; and a pair of Chopin works, the *Revolutionary Etude* and the Polonaise in A-flat Major as transcribed for orchestra by an otherwise-unknown Russian composer named Dimitri Rogal-Lewitzki.

Before Mitropoulos could proceed with serious rehearsing, however, he had to pass a rite of initiation planned by some of the more skeptical NBC musicians, those who doubted that the conductor *really* memorized every score. The trap was sprung by Harry Berv, a member of the horn section. Berv waited until the conductor had stopped to give instructions to another section, then raised his hand to get Mitropoulos's attention. Once he had it, he asked in wide-eyed innocence if the third horn part at bar number so-and-so was to be played *con sordino* (with a mute inside the bell of the horn) or in the usual open manner.

Mitropoulos knew instantly what was going on. With an expression of blue-eyed innocence fully equal to Berv's, he replied: "I really don't understand why you stopped us to ask that question at this point. We passed that bar a long time ago. As a matter of fact, it should be marked *con sordino* in red crayon. I put it in your part myself."

The other musicians began to shuffle their feet rhythmically to signal approval at the silkiness with which Berv had been trumped. From that moment on, the NBC players gave Mitropoulos their full cooperation.[20]

Still, his style took some getting used to after Toscanini's. "At first it was difficult to follow him," recalled cellist Alan Shulman, "because he had a very erratic, fluid beat—a completely different technique from Toscanini's. But it was a sensitive beat, it was not choreographic in the show-biz sense, like Bernstein's was, but it was still very fluid. Eventually, we got together with him, though, and then we gave some very good performances."[21]

First impressions were important to New York audiences and critics, and Mitropoulos made a good one, earning "an unusually fervent ovation" from the audience in Studio 8-H. "The impression gathered from reports from Massachusetts and Minnesota that he is a director of unusual ability and interpretive personality was borne out last night by his first concert in New York, which left reason to hope that there will be opportunity to hear another concert or two under his direction in this series next season," wrote Francis D. Perkins in the *New York Herald Tribune*. According to one account, several well-known conductors were in the audience, checking out the new talent, but unfortunately they are not identified by name.

Details in the Schumann symphony occasioned some discussion, but on the whole the Manhattan reviewers agreed that Mitropoulos's interpretation was an imposing one, of great depth and emotional range, and wholly dedicated to the spirit of the composer. Writing in the *Post*, Samuel Chotzinoff, as passionate a Toscanini partisan as the city contained, fussed about some Mitropoulos tempo modifications, chiding him sternly for a whopping *ritardando* at the conclusion, "which caused the ending to be ludicrous rather than impressive."[22]

Every reviewer dumped scorn on the Chopin transcriptions. Even though the *New York Times* reviewer called the final moments of the concert "a timpanists' and trombonists' holiday, and a technical tour de force for the orchestra" he added that "the spirit of Chopin was light-years away from Radio City. At least one hopes so."

All the reviews described the new conductor's unorthodox podium style and appearance. Chotzinoff:

> Mr. Mitropoulos is tall, wiry and bald. Dispensing with stick and score, he takes full possession of his men with his arms and hands, which are as eloquent as those of a snake dancer. Yet if his left hand is extravagant, his right is always there with the downbeat. It takes a few minutes to get accustomed to the picturesque convolutions of the left, but there is never any question of the sincerity of the man. Passionate vitality is his chief characteristic, but one gets the feeling that it is controlled by an exhaustive knowledge for, and a creative sympathy with, musical art. . . . Mr. Mitropoulos is undoubtedly a conductor of great talent and force, and his presence on the American scene is bound to be salutary.[23]

CHAPTER NINE

Summer and Winter 1938:
Greek Machinations, Feats of Memory,
and a Christmas Visit from Lenny B.

During his summer weeks in Greece, Mitropoulos conducted only once, on August 1, 1938, a pension fund concert for the musicians of the Athens Conservatory Orchestra. He was still officially the conductor of this ensemble, but the conservatory directors voted him a year's sabbatical so that he might pursue his new American career without encumbrance—on the face of it, a generous gesture. Behind the scenes, schemes were already being hatched by rivals and enemies to use this as the opening wedge of a campaign to maneuver Mitropoulos out of power in Greece for good. They struck during the crisis years of the German occupation, redrawing the charter of the Conservatory Orchestra so that no one could be its music director unless that person had been active in the conservatory faculty for ten consecutive years—thus thwarting any later plans by Mitropoulos to return, in triumph, to reclaim his Athenian post. In practice, these machinations were moot, for the last thing Mitropoulos wanted by that time was to immure himself again in the Athenian snake-pit, but the motives behind them were petty and vindictive, and the implementation of the scheme created a schism in Greek musical life whose aftershocks were still rattling the china twenty years after Mitropoulos's death.

The first concert of the Minneapolis Symphony's 1938–1939 season was scheduled for the evening of November 8; Mitropoulos arrived in town about a week before that and immediately plunged into rehearsals. By this time, the orchestra players had gone through an intense half-season with their new director, followed by a summer's respite during which they could reflect on the experience and consolidate their opinions about Mitropoulos. Even so, even knowing what the new season's rehearsals were going to be like, they were once again startled and fascinated by their Greek leader's style.

In fact, however willing the musicians were, many found that the unique Mitropoulos approach still took some getting used to. Sigurd Bockman, clarinetist with the MSO (and later with the NBC Symphony and New

106

York Philharmonic), commented during a 1986 interview with Oliver Daniel:

> Mitropoulos came into town like a breath of fresh air—into this conservative midwestern town where so many people came from Scandinavian backgrounds. He was so novel, he just astounded the natives. The men in the orchestra—well, we had to get used to his conducting. . . .
>
> The most difficult thing was when he played the piano and conducted simultaneously. We had to read signals not only from his hands but also from his *shoulder muscles*. . . . I would say it took the average orchestra player about a year to really become comfortable with the way Mitropoulos conducted.[1]

As concertmaster of the Minneapolis Symphony from 1944 to 1949, violinist Louis Krasner observed Mitropoulos at close range, week after week. Mitropoulos, Krasner averred, would

> absorb the score and then project it. He did not conduct from the page—he absorbed the music and then recreated it with his body and his hands. . . . His manner of beating left some players perplexed—all they wanted was for someone to tell them "play piano here" and "play loud there," up-bow or down-bow, downbeat or upbeat—that's the way they'd been trained to do it, but Dimitri couldn't respond that way.[2]

During one especially tricky, rhythmically complex modern score, a player asked "Maestro, tell me, at this point do we come in on the fourth beat—is that an up-beat sign you're giving us or is it a sideways motion of your head?" Mitropoulos honestly could not answer the question. "Look," he finally responded, "never mind how my beat is. If you don't come in, it's my fault and you shouldn't worry about it. The conductor has to do it by telepathy, and if the telepathy doesn't work, then it's the fault of the sender, not the receiver."[3] Sometimes the sender resorted to extraordinary means to illustrate a point. Such was definitely the case at a 1940 rehearsal of Beethoven's Ninth, when, in order to make a point to the chorus, Mitropoulos got down on all fours and crawled back and forth across the stage, in time with the music, "leaping like a rabbit" on the notes he wanted heavily accented.[4]

More often than not, however, Mitropoulos's motions and expressions clarified by projecting a physical analogy of something—music—that is in fact utterly incorporeal. Christopher Constantakos, an early biographer of Mitropoulos, vividly described the conductor's style:

> his whole body was vibrating, from head to toe. . . . His heels would come up, and he would go up and down so that the entire spine and body seemed to be expressing the beat, and his hands were very, very loose and very limp—sort of relaxed—while his body was in this vibrating mode. It was a fantastic way of conducting, the likes of which I have never seen again, even to this day.[5]

Sometimes he would move beyond an especially troublesome passage in a score by saying to the players: "Never mind—we'll understand each other when this time comes during the performance," and more often than not, they did.

In matters of tempo, he tended to be brisk, sometimes disconcertingly so. When questioned about his seeming inability to conduct an adagio that did not turn into an andante, Mitropoulos simply stated that "every man has his own tempo," then followed up with some abstruse remarks about his own pulse rate.

For all the frenetic excitement of his best concerts, there were times when the new music director's style seemed overdone ("over-accented and over-guided . . . jerked and flagellated," in the words of critic Virgil Thomson), giving rise to a new adjective: Mitropoulized. Seldom was a piece of music, however modest its scope and no matter what its historical style, simply allowed to speak for itself. Everything was focused through the lens of the conductor's personality, resulting in occasional performances that were "so violently personal as to prevent the original intentions of the music from coming through on their own terms."[6]

While the intense physicality of Mitropoulos's conducting style was unquestionably instinctive, some of its more extreme manifestations—the hand-clapping, foot-stomping, and occasional airborne leaps—can probably be traced back to his apprentice years as a conductor, when he worked entirely with student orchestras or ill-disciplined ensembles that mixed students with indifferently motivated professionals.

To players and observers alike, Mitropoulos's animated, at times wild, rehearsal manner made even the theatrical Ormandy seem sedate. He danced, yelled, clapped, sang, hunkered down for *pianissimo* effects, then leaped into the air for the big climaxes. If there was excess here, there was also method, as the members of the Minneapolis Symphony Chorus discovered when they stumbled during a rehearsal, quite unable to produce an effect called for in the score: a sharp, cutting, *sforzando* (a forced note) on top of a full-throated *fortissimo*. Several times they tried and raggedly failed to achieve that treacherous effect. Finally, at that moment in the score, Mitropoulos jumped off the stand, still facing the musicians, and caused the startled choristers to produce a *sforzando* effect by pure reflex, which they were able to repeat once they realized that they could do it.

Brenda Ueland was a music-loving Twin Cities socialite, poet (and friend of Carl Sandburg), and essayist who contributed chatty, personable columns to the local papers from 1937 to 1961. She caught the mood of the early Mitropoulos seasons, as they were perceived by the Twin Cities public, in her description of a 1939 rehearsal:

> Mitropoulos wore a light blue sweater, his shoulders powerful and relaxed. ("He is a faun on Mt. Olympus . . . and like Savonarola," we whispered). He is before them without music score or baton. And he is

happy because he is working again (he is devoured by jackals and hyenas when he isn't) and he cannot keep from shining smiles of happiness like a child when Christmas is imminent. And he can't keep the love out of his voice, the inclusive feeling he has for them all, almost as though he were the father of adorable children. . . . ("I think they are so wrong" we whisper in the darkness, "to say he doesn't need to use his body so much. Why it just IS the music.") How utterly flabbergastingly extraordinary he is! . . . His face lighted with joyful excitement (I see spokes of rays in wheels about his head), he springs down among the violins, pulling out their theme, bounds to point with a fierce index finger to the horns. To whip the rhythm he leaps high, stamps his heels in pistol shots. It makes the heart leap to see the terrific and wild exaggeration of his rehearsals.[7]

Thus did Ms. Ueland and thousands of other listeners undergo musical experiences that were transcendental in nature, and that they talked about in metaphysical language, without the slightest embarrassment.

For all the vehemence of his gymnastics, Mitropoulos seldom expressed wrath unless things went seriously and stubbornly wrong; when a detonation did occur, it was usually followed by a quick apology. His response to a bad rehearsal was more often akin to open despair than to anger. During one particularly unproductive rehearsal, he held his head in his hands for a moment, then said in a plaintive voice: "Today I am having a very bad day. Today I don't just hear what I *think* I hear; today, I hear what you actually sound like!"[8]

In that remark, the conductor acknowledged a striking aspect of his personality, a phenomenon that was both a strength and a glaring weakness. His powerful ability to focus, his note-perfect memory of every score he set out to perform, gave him a mental conception so vivid, so concentrated, so fixed, that it could mask many imperfections of orchestral execution. As veteran MSO trombonist Burton Paulu put it: "I think he had an idealized conception of the scores in his mind, so strong a conception that much of what was actually going on in the orchestra was not conscious to him. A lot of little mistakes crept in and went unnoticed, and uncorrected, because he heard *what he wanted to hear* rather than what was actually being played."[9]

Every former MSO member interviewed for this book agreed that the rehearsals, for all of the conductor's civility toward the players, could be drainingly intense. Some players even complained that they felt "played-out" by the time the actual concert rolled around on Friday. Still, the men knew their leader was pushing himself harder than he pushed them—after all, his conducting from memory, his liberation from the printed page, imposed an extra layer of stress on him, not on them.

His preferred method, always, was to interact with the musicians in the manner that came naturally to him: reasoned argument, persuasion, the setting of an example. His players were treated as professionals, colleagues, and reasonable people, not as hod-carriers or automatons. In return, the men felt genuine warmth and affection toward him. There were, of course, two or three exceptions, most notably principal horn Waldemar Linder who would talk back to Mitropoulos, sometimes quite nastily. Flutist Anton Winkler recalled:

> It used to make me furious that he would dare talk back to that sainted man, Mitropoulos. But Mitropoulos had the sort of personality that really hard-boiled musicians could step all over—as they did in New York. At times, he needed to be the kind of steely disciplinarian that George Szell or Fritz Reiner was. But Mitropoulos never came down hard on Linder, the way he should have; he just didn't have the personality for it. He should have said something like: "Shut up and do your job, buddy, and I'll do mine," but that was not his way. He was always polite, even to this belligerent, know-it-all smart-aleck; and there's something about having a kind answer and having someone in authority be polite that just eggs on people like that.[10]

Composer John Verrall, a Minneapolis native who knew many of the MSO players, remembered that

> Mitropoulos was very friendly with the players, and some of the smarter people saw that this could be a serious problem. His friendly approach worked fine for the really top-notch players who had real quality of personality, but with the cynical players it worked very much against him. I saw rehearsals where the hard cases really talked back to him, and it bothered me very much. Mitropoulos was aware of it, of course, but he didn't know what to do—he simply did not want to be a martinet over his players.[11]

Sometimes the conductor's philosophy of kindness and compassion led him to try things that were truly impractical. One short-lived experiment in 1939 or 1940 involved shuffling the seating arrangement in the violin section so that the weaker, less-experienced players were paired with the more adroit veterans. Presumably the objective was to improve overall polish and security, with the strong helping the weak. In practice, however, the system was a disaster—the good players resented being paired with the second-rate ones, and the weak players just became more insecure and self-conscious. The plan was quietly abandoned midway through the season.

The players, even the ones who did not agree with everything he did, generally knew how fortunate they were to be working under a man of Mitropoulos's character. Their good will increased when it was learned that the new conductor had eschewed the posh living quarters to which his status and salary entitled him. Indeed, Mitropoulos quartered himself, for the first two or three seasons, in a suite of small, spartanly furnished rooms—little more than a student dormitory would have provided—in a University of Minnesota building (officially known as the Center for Continuation Studies) whose only distinction was its proximity to Northrop Auditorium. The building's only other inhabitant was the basketball coach who lived on the ground floor. Even the furnishings were spare: bookcases, a few chairs, a studio bed, an upright piano, two trunks, the bare essentials of kitchen ware—distinctly monklike. The monastic dwelling, the black turtleneck sweaters and tunics he often wore to rehearsal, the tonsured appearance of his formidable head, his familial connection to the Greek Orthodox hierarchy (of which the Minneapolis newspapers made much), his tendency to discuss music-making in metaphysical terms, the large crucifix he always wore next to his heart, the fact that he could sometimes be seen praying in his dressing room before concerts, all contributed to the popular notion that Dimitri Mitropoulos actually *was* a monk, or at least a practicing mystic.

One aspect of Mitropoulos's style truly struck many musicians as supernatural: his memory. John Verrall got an unforgettable glimpse of the conductor's powers of concentration when he took Mitropoulos the score of his First Symphony. Mitropoulos asked Verrall to come to his dressing room during the fifteen-minute break in a Friday-morning rehearsal. Just as Verrall handed Mitropoulos the score, a lady stuck her head through the door and engaged the maestro in two or three minutes' worth of routine conversation. Finally, when she had gone, Mitropoulos had a chance to sit down and look at Verrall's score, which was 108 manuscript pages in length: "He started turning page by page, rather rapidly—I would say he only spent perhaps ten seconds on each page. I thought, good heavens, he must not like it—he's going so *fast*! Finally he flipped the last page, closed the book and came to me with a big smile."

"We'll start rehearsals next Monday."

"That's wonderful, but at some point during the weekend, I'll need my manuscript so I can copy out some more instrumental parts."

"Oh, you can take it now," said Mitropoulos. "I don't need it any more."

On the following Monday, Mitropoulos conducted the rehearsal from memory:

> I don't mean he knew the score in some kind of general overall way. I mean *he knew the score*. He knew it so exactly, he could turn to me and say things like "on page twenty-seven, how loudly do you want the woodwinds to play those three measures?" He knew the work as well or better than I did. It was one of the most remarkable things I've ever witnessed.[12]

Mitropoulos always insisted, when asked about his phenomenal ability to commit complex scores to memory, that his was not literally a photographic memory but rather a memory that he had trained as an athlete would train his body. There was no easy, freak-of-nature solution—the man simply worked very hard until he had developed a power of concentration that could be focused like a laser beam. Through the years, he also developed various personal systems to aid in these feats of memorization. William Cooper witnessed the conductor's study methods during the weeks Mitropoulos stayed at the Coopers' summer lodge in Colorado:

> His favorite seat was by the big window with the view of Long's Peak, the score on a music stand in front of him. For memorizing, he devised an elaborate system based on numbered slips of paper. Other activities in the room, even conversation, disturbed him not at all. If something being said interested him, he could offer a comment. As a result of such concentrated study, he was able at rehearsals to lift from his memory the exact page, bar, and rehearsal number at which something had gone wrong.[13]

Leonard Rose, the great cellist, also had a peek at Mitropoulos's study techniques when the conductor was out of the room: "I saw a lot of little pieces of paper in Mitropoulos's living room, and there were things written on them like 'P, Q, 15 in the middle'—stuff like that. Parts of it looked like stock market quotations."

"What's all this?" asked Rose, when Mitropoulos entered the room, bearing tea.

"Oh, that's the way I memorize," replied the conductor.

"You mean you don't have . . ."

Chuckling, Mitropoulos finished the sentence for him:

> "A photographic memory?" No, I don't. And I don't believe there is such a thing. Mine is certainly not photographic. I know the bars. The scores that give me the most trouble are those that have bar numbers instead of rehearsal letters, because the ones with letters usually follow the form of a piece pretty closely, with new numbers corresponding to important entrances or changes.[14]

Having observed the conductor's memorization system, Rose began to see how often during a rehearsal Mitropoulos would close his eyes and tap his forehead with the fingers of his right hand, mentally turning score pages and counting bars until he reached the spot that needed work.

Interviewers would ask Mitropoulos why he had made memorization such a fundamental part of his art, even when the music was obscure, fearsomely difficult, or a once-in-a-career blockbuster—surely, no one could fault him for using a score in those situations.

"Yes," Mitropoulos would answer; "I'm sure they couldn't. But for me, it's very simple. I feel the need to liberate myself from the printed score just as an actor does from the script. You would not expect someone to play Hamlet in front of a paying audience with the script in his hands—it's the same thing with me and music."

Mitropoulos once told flutist Anton Winkler that he also kept a mental count *between* movements: "if something was in 3/4 time, he then began to count in the time of the movement that was coming afterwards. He mentally kept time between movements so that the breathing space between each bloc of music was very carefully factored in, within his mind, with the whole architectural structure of the piece."[15]

Considering the staggering amount of time and mental energy required to memorize a score such as *Wozzeck*, one encounters in Mitropoulos a deep underlying current of self-abnegation, perhaps of masochism. It was not fun to memorize those scores. For Mitropoulos, the act of performing music was not just a symbolic mountain-climb, an act of achievement—it could also be an act of expiation. It seemed to those who knew him well that the more difficult and demanding the score, the more sleepless hours of study demanded of him to master it, the greater the sacrifice required to do justice to the music, the more satisfaction Mitropoulos derived from the purging rite of actual performance. After observing Mitropoulos for many years, personally and professionally, John Sherman concluded that this entire memorization process constituted a kind of self-immolation, "a duty the gifted must assume, as payment for being gifted, and as an example for the world."[16]

To open the fall 1938 season, Mitropoulos programmed two warhorse symphonies: Tchaikovsky's Fifth and Brahms's Third. Ticket sales were brisk (4600 seats were filled out of a possible five thousand) and expectations high.

As some had suspected during the previous season, Brahms brought out the eccentric in Mitropoulos; throughout his entire career he tended to overconduct this composer, accenting unusual secondary, or even tertiary voices while allowing the grand overall line more or less to take care of itself. Each critic who reviewed this opening night concert reacted differently to the Brahms symphony—one man praising its "lucidity and calm strength," another arguing that the conductor's obsessive highlighting of details, his fascination with timbral chiaroscuro, diluted the symphony's vigor. The Tchaikovsky symphony finished a decided second-best for Egilsrud of the *Minneapolis Journal*, who found it "obvious, frantic, and over-emphatic." Still, Mitropoulos's interpretation was "animated by a surging passion, a dramatic vigor and an abandon which, in the climaxes, made chills run down the spine from sheer nervous reaction to the intensity of the sound."[17]

For some unknown reason, Mitropoulos loaded the autumn season with orchestral transcriptions of string quartets—Grieg's Quartet in G Minor, Franck's Quartet in D Major, and Beethoven's Op. 95 in F Minor—as well as Nicolas Nabokov's orchestration of Bach's *Goldberg Variations*. Popular response to these curios was warm, critical reaction decidedly mixed. The climax of the autumn 1938 season was an incandescent performance of Rachmaninoff's First Piano Concerto, played by the composer.

By the end of 1938, the Minneapolis audiences had grown used to their fiery and colorful new conductor. Some music lovers responded to Mitropoulos's presence on the scene in remarkably emotional ways. A socialite columnist named Sidney Baldwin devoted sixteen column-inches to an open love letter to the Greek conductor, beginning with a swooning poem:

DIMITRI MITROPOULOS

> They take their places—all those silent men
> Whose lives are spent in music.
> One single A sounds from a far-off string,
> Muted behind the scenes.
> The audience in fur and velvet, tuxedo and tails,
> Have found their seats. The whole assemblage waits for
> That master of them all.
> Master of those who make the music real,
> Master of those who listen avidly. . . .
> From slender fingers one can almost see
> The rays of tone from instrument to man
> That fuse and joining fill the room, the world—
> So delicate, so soft, so powerful.
> And by some strange and magic alchemy
> The music pours, not from his hands but from mine,
> Who move with him, one in his rhythmic beat
> And with my heart-strings follow where he wills.

Sidney Baldwin would not be the last woman to develop a crush on Dimitri Mitropoulos. That one of the Minneapolis papers could publish such stuff with a straight face reveals just how emotional was the relationship that had developed between the Twin Cities and their orchestra's new conductor.

On Christmas Eve, 1938, Mitropoulos penned a revealing and emotional letter to Katy Katsoyanis:

> Your letter, so optimistic, so full of nice plans, managed to give the *coup de grace* to my soul which is troubled by so many problems and dilemmas that have presented themselves lately. And this, right at the moment when I was making inquiries about the possibility of becoming an American resident or citizen. Can you imagine? One thing is certain, my dear child, that whether here or down in our country, I'll always be unhappy. But here, at least, I'll be less unhappy. Here, although I suffer morally, I am morally pure! It wouldn't be the same, alas, in Athens. I know it all too well. In Athens I am morally attacked on two sides; here, at least, I suffer from my own troubles, which will exist for me in every corner of the earth. But Athens would mean my total ruin if I were to return for a long while. Here, at least, I feel purified, helped in transforming my weaknesses, because the people are innocent and full of

religious feelings. In our country or in Europe people are suspicious and they can make you disgusted of even your purest intentions. They soil you! This way one loses one's courage.[18]

One of the "problems and dilemmas that have presented themselves lately" was Leonard Bernstein. Now a junior at Harvard, Bernstein had kept a torch burning for Eros Mavro during the months since their first dramatic meeting in Cambridge. On Bernstein's work desk stood the autographed photo Mitropoulos had given him backstage, after the triumphant Boston Symphony concerts. At that time, too—presumably while they were closeted in the men's room—Mitropoulos had promised to write. He had not done so, however; not so much as a card. A year had passed since their first meeting.

When Bernstein read in the musical press that Mitropoulos had returned to Minneapolis, he decided to reopen communications by means of a letter. Mitropoulos responded with typical emotion; Bernstein can be forgiven for interpreting affection as passion: "My dear, dear boy, believe me your letter touched me very deeply. I never forgot you. I was only busy this past year . . . dear friend, is that so, is it true, that you believe so much in me: Have I really failed you, have I really left you in a void after our last meeting? This thought drives me crazy, and so happy that I dare not believe it."[19]

Mitropoulos also responded by wiring Bernstein two hundred dollars, along with an invitation for the young man to spend Christmas with him in Minneapolis. Bernstein was given a room right next to Mitropoulos's.

Because of the erotic overtones of their initial encounter in Boston (the oyster offering, their tête-à-tête in the bathroom), and the tortured, Saul-and-David relationship the two men shared as their professional fortunes waxed and waned, there has long been speculation that a sexual relationship was started during this visit, and that its rapid deterioration contributed to the eventual estrangement of the two conductors. A close study of the evidence—most of it admittedly anecdotal—leads to a rejection of this durable rumor.

The fact that Mitropoulos had not written to Bernstein since their first meeting indicates that the conductor was either having second thoughts about his erstwhile protégé or, at the very least, had become ambivalent. How that ambivalence worked itself out in a dorm room in Minneapolis is a question of some import. Several possibilities suggest themselves.

As the Christmas Eve letter to Katy suggests, Mitropoulos was evidently settled into his celibate mode during this period—a circumspect thing for him to do, considering the conservative standards of the local community. While Mitropoulos did possess a strong element of carnality, he sublimated and fiercely restrained that element for long periods of time; immersed in his work, channeling his sexual energy into the act of performance rather than the act of love, he became in fact the monk that people considered him to be.

During the interval between the first meeting with Bernstein and the Christmas visit, Mitropoulos may well have experienced some cooling of enthusiasm. While he acknowledged the younger man's brilliance—and indeed, was the first authority figure to call him "a genius" to his face— Mitropoulos must have found some aspects of that genius unpalatable: Bernstein's consuming egotism, the shamelessness of his ambition, the compulsive exhibitionism—these traits would have been distasteful to Mitropoulos, recalling in his mind the sort of conniving and fighting-for-position that had made the Athenian cultural scene so repugnant.

Nor would it have taken more than a few minutes for Bernstein's politics to rub Mitropoulos the wrong way. Instinctively, Mitropoulos knew that if war came to Europe, Greece would be dragged in willy-nilly, and he feared for his homeland. Bernstein at this time had a tendency to spout cocktail-party socialism, to express the then-trendy notion that Europe was welcomed to drown itself in blood again as long as the U.S.A. stayed out of it. Given the very real threat to Mitropoulos's homeland—and to those great European capitals he knew and loved so well—such opinions would have been an irritant.

While there must have been considerable erotic tension between Bernstein and Mitropoulos, there was no sexual intimacy; no advances made or rebuffed. Composer David Diamond, who was uniquely qualified to know the details of this Christmas visit by virtue of his close friendship with both parties, has refuted the notion in no uncertain terms:

> There was no sexual relationship at all; absolutely not. That story gained momentum because the homosexual community wanted it to be so for one set of reasons and the heterosexual musicians wanted it to be so for totally different reasons. They did not sleep together, and I'll tell you why: Lenny was not Dimitri's *type*, and Dimitri was not Lenny's. Lenny was never attracted to older, homely, men. Now, from the neck up, Bernstein was very handsome, and in the photographs you don't see how bandy-legged he was. Dimitri told me, after meeting Lenny, "That is a genius-boy. He's too good looking, but he is proportioned badly. He will have great difficulties because he is so narcissistic."
>
> Dimitri had absolutely Greek ideals about the male body—it had to be Apollonian. At the same time, there was this element of Dionysian torment within him. He must have sensed that Lenny could not answer that need.[20]

What did the two musicians do, what did they discuss, during this week-long interlude? Much of their time was spent backstage at Northrop Auditorium. Mitropoulos gave Bernstein scores to sight-read, and there was much piano playing, solo and duet. Again, David Diamond had access to the accounts of both men:

There was a lot of discussion of music, of interpretations, going over scores, discussing Lenny's future and what he ought to do, but mainly it was Dimitri advising Lenny that he must watch his behavior. Dimitri felt that he was already out of control—the ego, the ambition, the narcissism—and on the first occasion Dimitri took him out to dinner, Lenny embarrassed the hell out of him. Ten minutes after he was introduced to their hosts, Lenny sat down at the piano and began banging out the Ravel concerto, singing all the orchestral entrances, showing off, jazzing it up, cigarette dangling from the corner of his mouth, making it impossible for anyone else in the room even to have a conversation. This kind of exhibitionism simply horrified Dimitri. He came to me a while later and said, "Dear, you must really talk to him. He does not need to show off that way."

So I did talk to Lenny, who looked at me innocently and said: "Am I really *that* bad?"[21]

Regardless of who did or did not make a pass at whom during that Christmas interlude, the outcome of it was a decided distancing of Mitropoulos from his tempestuous admirer. Whether Bernstein was motivated by pique at having been sexually rejected, or whether he just felt like being a jerk, the last few days of his visit brought an unwelcome sense of chaos to Mitropoulos's ordered, disciplined, hermitic existence.

After the acute discomfort of that first dinner party, Mitropoulos (who was quite uninterested in hob-nobbing to begin with) was loathe to take Lenny out into polite society again. They spent their afternoons making music or talking about it, they dined together, and afterward Mitropoulos would bid the younger man good night and retire to his own rooms. For Lenny, the night was still young. On the last two or three nights of his visit, Bernstein went out on his own, checked out some local taverns, and returned with a crowd of drunken revelers who proceeded to party into the wee hours, while poor Mitropoulos, separated from the noise only by one thin dormitory wall, tried to study his scores.

Whatever friction there was during the last days of his Minneapolis visit, Bernstein returned home full of enthusiasm. His father, Sam Bernstein, recalled: "He came back and said, 'Papa, I'm going to make music my life.' Mr. Mitropoulos had said he would give him a job with the Minneapolis Symphony as soon as he graduated from college."[22]

Mitropoulos, at this time, issued no specific job offer to Bernstein—he had no authority to do that on his own and no discernable reason to extend false hopes. For whatever causes, the temperature of the relationship, at least on Mitropoulos's part, went down a few degrees after this Christmas visit. It is at least plausible that propinquity, along with a certain amount of immature behavior, caused Mitropoulos to sense in Bernstein an ambition so enormous, a personality so driven by its passion for acclamation, as to make him cautious about joining forces with Bernstein in any professional capacity. Mitropoulos may also have felt an unwelcome taint of jealousy, an intimation that those same objectionable elements in Bernstein's personality—which would, after all, be among the reasons Bernstein would succeed in taming the New York Philharmonic not so long after Mitropoulos was broken by that same ensemble—were among the factors that would enable Bernstein to surpass Mitropoulos's achievements. No man, however compassionate his heart and noble his motives, could be immune to the dread such an intuition delivers.

CHAPTER TEN

War Clouds Gathering

Minneapolis took Mitropoulos to its heart. For decades, America's midwestern citizens had chafed under a cultural inferiority complex, embarrassingly aware that the average New York intellectual regarded any location west of the Mississippi River as a wasteland inhabited by Bible-thumping bigots and thick-skulled clodhoppers. Now there was cultural thunder out of Minneapolis, and America was taking notice, sometimes with unconcealed envy. Great was the pride in the Twin Cities, when magazines such as *Time* began, in the spring of 1939, to print articles praising the accomplishments of their "slippery-skulled Greek" and informing the world that "some of the most brilliant U.S. conducting since the peak days of Stokowski and Toscanini was being done in snow-crusted Minneapolis."[1]

Indeed it was, and if some stuffier citizens were occasionally offended by Mitropoulos's plebeian habits, by a lifestyle that some considered undignified, a far greater number of people cherished those very qualities. When a gaping budget deficit loomed at the end of the spring 1939 season, Mitropoulos addressed the issue bluntly, in remarks that got prominent exposure in the press: "Never mind my dignity. If necessary to continue the orchestra, I'll take my men to the corner of Seventh and Nicollet and we'll play there and just pass the hat."[2] And sure enough, in the Nicollet Hotel's ballroom, Mitropoulos and his band played a fundraising concert of Strauss waltzes and did pass the hat—into which some four hundred of the Twin Cities' more prominent citizens deposited twenty thousand dollars in checks and cash, along with enough pledges to cover the Minneapolis Symphony's annual budget for the next two years. After this demonstration, the incidence of griping about Mitropoulos's lack of "dignity" diminished considerably.

At the end of the spring season, Mitropoulos signed a new, three-year contract.

Until the start of 1939, Mitropoulos had not ventured radically or often from the standard repertoire, with the notable exception of his advocacy of the music of Gustav Mahler—and much of the unfamiliar music he had performed was quite accessible. Beginning with the first concert of 1939, he made a subtle shift of priorities toward contemporary works of greater substance and challenge, for both the orchestra and the audience.

119

On the January 6 program was the Concerto Grosso for String Orchestra by American composer-conductor Albert Stoessel. The piece went over fairly well with the audience, but critical opinion was sharply bifurcated. Egilsrud, writing in the *Tribune*, proclaimed it "concentrated, lean and vital music played with zest," whereas John Sherman thought the same work a sterile and scholarly fabrication "betrayed in the end by its own cleverness."[3]

There was sharp disagreement over the other big-scale work on the program, Beethoven's Symphony No. 2; indeed, the various reviewers' reactions were a paradigm of the way Mitropoulos's Beethoven interpretations were usually received: those who liked them tended to revel in their idiosyncrasies, and those who did not like them tended to find them grossly overconducted—"mannered, over-handled, and almost tedious in the myriad accents and inflections given it," in the words of John Sherman.[4]

On the next program, played the evening of January 20, Mitropoulos served up the coldest and most recondite of all the Sibelius symphonies, the grim-visaged Fourth. The audience, as usual, didn't quite know what to make of this stark, forbidding work, but the reviews were unanimous in their praise of the way Mitropoulos handled the score—brutal but sympathetic.

Five days later, Mitropoulos earned warm praise for his performance of another modern American work, the orchestral Rhapsody by young John Verrall. By far the most significant and controversial contemporary work was Aaron Copland's *Dance Symphony*, given a crackling performance on March 17. A majority of the critics praised the symphony's energy and color. A diametrically opposite response was voiced by James Davies, who reacted to the music as though stuck with a goad. In his fulminating review of March 18, he articulated the feelings of many less-adventurous members of the Minneapolis audience. Indeed, his review staked out a loyal opposition whose voice would grow louder over time and that would crescendo into yowls of rage and dismay when Mitropoulos finally steered his orchestra into the shoals of dissonance and past the rocks of atonality:

> I am heartily in sympathy with the movement to give American music a fair chance if it is worth the trouble. I very much question whether this Copland music *is* worth the trouble. It bears the title "A Dance Symphony", for some reason or other. It was neither dance nor symphony, in fact, while straining every nerve to be sympathetic to efforts like this, I have no desire to suffer a nervous breakdown. . . . it is vague. It never touches the hem of beauty's dress . . . a solemn, sobbing, deeply melancholy, slightly incoherent and depressing statement about nothing in particular.[5]

That Davies was not just a hidebound reactionary was proven on April 1, when he joined all of his colleagues in praising the first Minneapolis performance of Paul Hindemith's symphony *Mathias the Painter* (as *Mathis der Maler* was identified in the program notes). As Sherman wrote:

The old and the new continue to mingle on Dimitri Mitropoulos' programs, giving us the thrills both of recognition and discovery. Fortunately, even the most provocative of modern works never seems to im-
part a warmed-over flavor to the classics that share the evening with
them . . . the reason for that is simple: Mitropoulos never uses warming-
over methods. His music is always fresh, vital.[6]

Also in the audience for this concert was Boston music critic Moses
Smith, who had dropped in to write a Mitropoulos update for his Boston
readers. Smith found the Hindemith interpretation "startlingly brisk" compared to the plusher interpretation Koussevitzky had given the piece, but
added that the Greek conductor's tempos seemed entirely justified by the
results. As for the Minneapolis Symphony itself, Smith reported "no ragged
edges" in the ensemble, and praised both the fullness of string tone and the
"rugged sonority of the brass."

Like Toscanini, Mitropoulos will go to the greatest lengths to insure
clarity of line and fine balance among the choirs, so that every detail
may be heard as clearly as possible. . . . His obsessing passion seems to
make music in the best way he knows how. If he notices the audience,
it is by virtue of their participation in the proceeds, not because he is
putting on a show for them. The heartening thing is that such an audience, fairly remote from the center of musical culture in America,
should respond to such ministrations with the greatest enthusiasm.[7]

On April 14, Mitropoulos gave one of the most interesting concerts of
his entire Minneapolis tenure: a scorching performance of Berlioz's *Harold in
Italy* (the viola part played by David Dawson, the MSO's first-chair viola,
then in his final season with the orchestra) coupled with several works by
contemporary Greek composers. Included were excerpts from the *Hellenic
Suite* by Kalomiris, a tone poem entitled *The Eagle* by Georgios Sklavos, and
three of Skalkottas's *Greek Dances*. This earthy, strongly rhythmic music was
greeted with enthusiasm by the audience and sympathetically described by
the reviewers. Notice of this concert did appear in the Athens press, but Mitropoulos's efforts on behalf of his countrymen did nothing to lessen the animosity and jealousy heaped on him even in his absence. Mitropoulos
always sought to avoid even the suggestion of favoritism; perhaps overly
sensitive to the limitations of the Greek National School, Mitropoulos never
again devoted such a chunk of program time to Greek music, although he
kept the Skalkottas dances in his active repertoire and showcased individual
Greek works later in New York, not always with the happiest results.

A sold-out finale ended the spring season on April 21, when the orchestra was joined by the incomparable Kirsten Flagstad for an evening of
Wagner performances whose glories remained vivid in the minds of retired
MSO players half a century later. In the audience were Crown Prince Frederick and Princess Ingrid of the royal house of Denmark.

By the end of the spring 1939 season, the Minneapolis critics could say little that was new about Mitropoulos and his style; but if novelty had worn off, a constant sense of adventure and discovery remained associated with the MSO's concerts. In late February, a new battery of critics—the notoriously sharp-knifed reviewers of Chicago—got their first look at the Greek conductor and their first chance to hear how the Minneapolis orchestra sounded under his leadership.

Mitropoulos pulled out all the stops for this Chicago engagement, scheduling himself as soloist/conductor in Malipiero's Second Piano Concerto, after first handing out a kind of aural business card—his melodramatic orchestration of Bach's Fantasia and Fugue in G Minor. The program climaxed with Brahms's Fourth Symphony, and Richard Strauss's *Till Eulenspiegel* was thrown in for good measure. The Chicago critics had heard the Minneapolis band before, under Ormandy and Verbrugghen, and their reviews were uncolored by any of the self-congratulating hype that had attended the Minneapolis discovery of Mitropoulos. Herman Devries, writing in the *Chicago American*, was favorably impressed by the orchestra's "titanic leader" and the "many changes for the better" in the orchestra's basic sound.[8] But Edward Barry of the powerful *Chicago Daily Tribune* was less dazzled. "Mr. Mitropoulos does strange things to the music," he said; the performance of *Till Eulenspiegel* struck him as particularly episodic, "with each phrase seeming to be torn convulsively from the conductor's vitals." On the orchestra, however, Barry heaped cautious praise: "accurate, sonorous, and capable of the most amazingly beautiful tonal effects. Again and again a listener would become so entranced by the sheer sensuous glory of sound that it would be a full minute before he could pull himself together and declare argumentatively, 'This ain't Bach' or 'This ain't Brahms.'"[9]

It was the Brahms Fourth, however, that brought Mitropoulos's style into the clearest focus. Eugene Stinson, critic for the *Chicago Daily News*, had hitherto known Mitropoulos's work only through press accounts. Now he took the opportunity to write a perceptive essay. The Fourth, he averred, got a highly interesting reading, now lush, now severe and chaste, with many of its time-values "re-edited" by Mitropoulos, so that the net effect of the interpretation was "rather baroque."

> The performance was a big one . . . yet even so, it did not find the true bigness of the symphony; we could not see the mountain for the molehills. . . . The only constancy in Mr. Mitropoulos's line is inconstancy. He is indeed so charged with alertness and so keen in his perception of minutiae that he is by temperament a man whose workmanship must consist of departure from the norm. . . . His was the art, if not the aim, of the caricaturist.[10]

During the entire season of 1938–1939, Mitropoulos conducted thirty concerts in Minneapolis, six of which were repeated in St. Paul, along with the

one Chicago concert on February 21 and two highly successful over-the-border forays to Winnipeg, Canada, in late March. His only out-of-town appearance during this time was a December 15 concert in Cleveland, in which he and Joseph Szigeti presented the world premiere of the Bloch Violin Concerto.

On his way back to Athens in early June 1939, Mitropoulos stopped over in Naples for a spectacular performance of the Berlioz Requiem, using the combined orchestras of the Teatro San Carlo and the San Pietro Conservatory. Upon returning to Athens, he plunged into work again, helping with plans for the establishment of a new Athens Festival. In July, he conducted four well-attended outdoor concerts at the Theater of Herodus Atticus. These proved to be the last concerts he would conduct in Greece for sixteen years.

The coming of war almost overtook him. He did not leave Europe until August 31. He later described that trip as one of the most wretched experiences of his life. The ship was old, foul, and dangerously overcrowded; it was a freighter with limited accommodations for only one hundred passengers. More than five hundred were jammed aboard. Mitropoulos slept for the entire nineteen-day voyage on a pad unrolled beneath the grand piano in the ship's saloon. Much of the crossing was rough, the ship rolled constantly, and the food was disgusting. Nevertheless, Mitropoulos did what he could to make the trip bearable for his fellow refugees, spending several hours each day playing music for them on the same piano he slept under.

Among the passengers on this last ship from prewar Greece were some friends of an oboist named Leonard Burkat, who had been a friend of Leonard Bernstein's since high school. Burkat's friends had in turn befriended Dimitri Mitropoulos during the long, dismal voyage; there were handshakes and introductions all around as the passengers waited for their baggage to be unloaded.

"Leonard Burkat," mused Mitropoulos, "Why I met a bright young fellow at Harvard not too long ago who had very similar name. Leonard Bernstein."[11]

Burkat brightened instantly; he and Lenny Bernstein, he declared, had been friends since they were teenagers. Mitropoulos asked how Lenny was doing and what he was doing. Burkat did not know quite what to say, since one of the things Lenny Bernstein had been doing was sitting around waiting to hear from Mitropoulos about a conducting job in Minneapolis.

Mitropoulos read nothing into Burkat's discomfited silence, however. In parting, he asked Burkat to tell Bernstein that he would be staying in New York for a week or so, before going out to Minnesota to begin rehearsals.

As soon as Bernstein got the news, he swung into action. Being broke at the time, he hitched a ride with a friend and was soon standing in the lobby of the Commodore Hotel, calling Mitropoulos on the house phone. As Bernstein himself recounted the story of this fateful meeting, Mitropoulos greeted him at the door of his suite with the somewhat disingenuous remark: "Well, what has happened to you?"

"Well, what's happened to me is that I've finished Harvard. I've had a marvelous education. I've had great teachers. I've studied the piano all along with Helen Coates and Heinrich Gebhard and I'm playing pretty well. I write music. But I can't find a job. What shall I do?"

Mitropoulos did not hesitate. "I know what you should do. You must be a conductor."

"Fine. Well, how does one become a conductor?"

"You study."

"Where do you study conducting?"

"There's the Juilliard School, and there is a marvelous man named Albert Stoessel who teaches conducting there. Perhaps you can get into his class."

As it happened, he couldn't; enrollment for Stoessel's class was already full. In dismay, Bernstein called Mitropoulos again, just before the older man was about to depart for Minneapolis.

"Now what should I do?"

This time, the advice Mitropoulos gave him turned out to be provident indeed. Mitropoulos had just heard about a new conducting class that Fritz Reiner was forming at the Curtis Institute in Philadelphia, and according to the musicians' grapevine, there were still some openings.

After borrowing enough money to buy some study scores, Bernstein took a train to Philadelphia and after a typically brusque and businesslike audition for Fritz Reiner, he was accepted into the new conducting class.

Although Bernstein always gave Mitropoulos full and even generous credit for steering him into a conducting career, Bernstein was probably already going in that direction on the advice of Aaron Copland.[12] This meeting with Mitropoulos, if not quite as fateful as Bernstein made it out to be, did serve to reinforce confidence—Mitropoulos had placed a seal of approbation upon his young colleague's choice of careers.

Leonard Bernstein, at least partly propelled by the advice of Mitropoulos, was now embarked on one of his profession's most astonishing careers. The ascending curve of the younger man's fortunes, gathering force like a rocket as it moved through the musical universe, would intersect once more with the peculiar and eccentric orbit of Mitropoulos's own destiny. The impact of that collision would change musical history.

During the first wartime season, 1939–1940, Mitropoulos conducted twenty-seven concerts with the Minneapolis Symphony; he also participated in the orchestra's first Winter Tour, a trek that lasted nineteen days, starting on February 5, and encompassed twenty-two concerts in sixteen cities. Mitropoulos conducted eighteen of these programs; the other four were children's concerts directed by William Mueble, who was ordinarily the assistant first horn.

From the prevailing tone of the reviews, the 1939–1940 season was greeted by more settled emotions than its two predecessors had been. There is less a sense of discovery than of renewed, trusted pleasures. People expected the concerts to be good, and they were. The critics paid much attention to the excellence of Mitropoulos's programs—their balance, contrast, tone, and weight. Indeed, he seems in this season to have found an ideal groove: the old and the familiar were made fresh by means of imaginative juxtapositions with the new and unfamiliar.

Opening night was October 27. With bracing tempos and unusually powerful climaxes, Mitropoulos blew the cobwebs off Franck's Symphony in D Minor. Egilsrud in his review remarked that Franck would "probably have been terrified by the intensities."[13]

John Sherman was reflective: "Dimitri Mitropoulos continues to be the vibrant, commanding man on the platform, whose energy is volcanic and inexhaustible. Last night he led his men through music of varied styles, drawing forth an eloquence and beauty of tone which lifted the listener to the heights."[14]

The November 17 concert featured Yehudi Menuhin's performance of the newly discovered Violin Concerto of Robert Schumann, a dullish and overlong work that has never really caught on but which the Minneapolis audience welcomed with respect if not affection.

There was unanimous critical agreement that Beethoven's "Pastoral" Symphony, played on the night of December 8, was extraordinarily fine. Jack Conklin, a new reviewer writing for the *Minneapolis Morning Tribune*, described what was different about Mitropoulos's Beethoven:

> Most striking of all was Mitropoulos' handling of the storm. This is usually taken in something of a rush with much pounding of the timpani and clatter of brass and, to cite one descriptive detail, the flash of lightning in the piccolo is too often drowned in the general downpour. Last night, all this was taken at a comparatively slow tempo, from the first mutterings of the basses, to the full climax. . . . Each detail was worked out for its full pictorial possibilities, and the result was a surprisingly vivid and impressive whole.[15]

For Mitropoulos himself, the highlight of the fall–winter season came during the concert of December 22, when he conducted Alban Berg's difficult *Lyric Suite* and convinced the public that this was music of stature and importance. "It doesn't take long for great quantities of musical water to flow under bridges," commented Frances Boardmann on this new acceptance of the Berg work:

> Alban Berg, not so many years ago, was looked upon as a wild-eyed Leftist of an incomprehensible and probably seditious sort; that, at least,

was the view of the conservatives, who viewed his dallying with the twelve-tone scale as darkly suspect.

Friday's performance of his music seemed beautiful, imaginative, and altogether adapted to the evocation of mystic ideas and dimensions. And for this state of things unreserved credit must go to Mr. Mitropoulos' absolute control of the situation, and to the surpassingly beautiful performance of the string orchestra.[16]

Sherman and Egilsrud, too, had nothing but praise for the performance and gratitude to Mitropoulos. These reviews appeared on December 23, and on the same day, the conductor dashed off an ebullient letter to Katy Katsoyanis:

> Last night, my dear friend, I felt the greatest relief I've ever felt in my life: I managed to make the audience and the musicians understand, love, and warmly applaud the Alban Berg Suite that is so full of problems. It's a victory and a sure measure of my persuasive forcefulness of expression. You must understand that all the tragic and passionate element was projected with magnifying lenses, and so they couldn't resist me. I managed to hypnotize them, like a real Yogi.[17]

The winter–spring 1940 season began on a note of sadness with the death of James Davies, music critic of the *Minneapolis Times-Tribune* for over a quarter-century. Mitropoulos respected Davies and performed one of the late critic's favorite works, Grieg's melancholy *The Last Spring* as a memorial tribute. Professor Davies's place was taken by his wife, Grace.

A significant new American work figured on the program of January 26, the Symphony No. 1 in E Major by John Verrall. At this point Verrall was teaching piano and composition at Hamline University in St. Paul. His musical background was first rate, including a degree from the Royal College of Music in London and private study in Budapest with Zoltán Kodály. Neoclassical in style, his first symphony proved to be a cogently constructed and handsomely orchestrated piece, welcomed enthusiastically by both audience and critics. Johan Egilsrud saw the performance in a larger context: "it marked an epoch in the musical life of Minneapolis—the first official recognition by the symphony orchestra of the importance of the local composer as a contributor to our musical culture. For this sign of cultural maturity we must thank Dimitri Mitropoulos."[18]

On February 5, the MSO began its midseason tour. So ingrained had the ritual of concert attendance become, that for many Minneapolis citizens the sudden absence of their orchestra left a social and cultural void. Dispatches from the tour cities, including quotes from local reviews, allowed the Minneapolis Symphony's fans to follow the triumphant progress of the band, and many did so with the enthusiasm usually bestowed on winning football teams. Rave review followed rave review. After the February 11 concert in Columbus, Ohio, a reviewer for the *Columbus Citizen* proclaimed "the discovery of a great conductor . . . by the time [Mitropoulos] had finished conducting a splendid program on Saturday night at Memorial Hall, he had the town's musical gentry running off cadenzas of acclaim in the lobby and turning critical cartwheels in the street. He was THAT good."[19]

After the final concert in Columbus, the conductor was presented with an enormous floral basket, courtesy of the local Greek-American community. On the following morning, in a typical gesture, Mitropoulos made sure that the flowers were taken to a local hospital and distributed to the patients.

Mitropoulos made himself available to local journalists throughout the tour, despite the draining schedule. He was frequently asked whether Arthur Judson was grooming him to take over the New York Philharmonic—speculations had blazed higher than ever when the news was released that Mitropoulos would guest conduct the New York orchestra for an entire month in his next season. The conductor squelched these rumors firmly whenever they arose, stating that he had no plans to leave Minneapolis and loyally speaking up for his adopted city, proclaiming it to be a metropolis-in-the-making and predicting that it would be recognized, if it was not already, as a major center of musical culture.

When a reporter in St. Louis asked him if he now considered himself to be a Greek or an American, Mitropoulos cagily responded: "Well, Greece is a fine country, but my true nationality is music. And my orchestra is my family."

When asked about the state of music in America, Mitropoulos was thoroughly enthusiastic. "America is the El Dorado of musicians as it once was the El Dorado of the conquistadors. You have more and better musicians being trained in this country than one can find anywhere else in the world."

And what did the illustrious Greek conductor think of "swing" music? "Oh, it has value, like every other form of art. It should not, however, be played on the same program with symphonic compositions."[20]

Another St. Louis reviewer stated flatly that the MSO performance was the most exciting musical event to hit town since Arturo Toscanini had brought the La Scala Orchestra on tour, twenty years earlier.

Particularly gratifying were the Chicago reviews, for all the critics remarked that Mitropoulos had matured greatly as an interpreter in the space of a single year, and that his orchestra had also improved. The strings sounded more uniform and more vibrant, the brass mellower, and woodwinds less pipey. The conductor's podium style, observed the *Daily Tribune*'s critic, "seemed less extreme than last year, and there is no doubt that he lets the music take a smoother course."[21]

Columnist Eugene Stinson, bowled over by the MSO performances of Dukas's *La Peri* Overture and the Rachmaninoff Third Symphony, also discussed the changes in Mitropoulos's style: "Mr. Mitropoulos had drastically curbed the quite hysterical style of conducting he revealed to us last spring. He furthermore conducted in a much bigger and imposing line than before and the splendid qualities of his musicianship have a far more fitting and effective setting."[22]

Back home in Minneapolis, both orchestra and conductor were given a rousing welcome at their first post-tour concert, on March 1. On this occasion, the hometown audience heard the orchestra in a new seating plan Mitropoulos had adopted for the tour: first and second violins separated into two columns, facing each other across the podium; cellos arrayed where the second violins had previously sat, on the conductor's left. The programming was even more unusual than the novel seating plan: Handel's *Water Music* suite, Max Reger's *Four Tone Poems After Pictures of Böcklin*, and Ravel's orchestration of Mussorgsky's *Pictures at an Exhibition*, a composition that has become a lathered warhorse indeed to modern ears but which at that time was still quite a novelty (the first American performance had been on November 7, 1924, in Boston). The Minneapolis audience's response was thunderous, and special bravos were given to concertmaster Harold Ayres, whose soaring violin solo in Reger's tone poem *The Fiddling Hermit* brought down the house. Mitropoulos was called back on stage several times to acknowledge the standing ovation given him not only by the listeners but by the orchestra as well.

Critical response was more cautious, indicating that there were two contradictory ways to judge this concert. On one hand, the playing of three episodic and pictorial works offered more variety than two or three more conventional programs. On the other hand, the same program—three works in a row, each of them subdivided into several serial parts—struck some listeners as being patchy and nervous. All told, there were eighteen parts, and many in the audience spent as much time poring anxiously over their programs, trying to identify tags and titles, as they did listening.

At the close of the April 7 concert, Mitropoulos surprised everybody by announcing from the stage that there would be an encore for this evening, a complete performance of Copland's *El Salón Mexico*. "I have placed it at this point in the program, " he explained from the podium, "so that any of you who object to this school of composition may quietly leave before we begin to play it." Under such public circumstances, to do that would have amounted to an admission of musical philistinism, so that relatively few listeners availed themselves of the opportunity; those who did rather shamefacedly scuttle for the exits missed a performance of drop-dead brilliance.

No dissent was voiced about the final program of the spring 1940 season, a rendition of Beethoven's Ninth Symphony. The message of Beethoven's titanic score took on new urgency in the context of a burgeoning world war, and Mitropoulos seemed especially inspired.

At about the same time that he was conducting the final rehearsals for the Beethoven Ninth, Mitropoulos was also composing a curious telegram to Leonard Bernstein. Bernstein was now enrolled at the Curtis Institute in

Philadelphia, studying conducting under Fritz Reiner and still assuming that, at the end of the academic year, he would have an assistant's job waiting for him in Minneapolis. He had good reason to expect good news from Minneapolis, because in December Mitropoulos had outlined, in a very definite manner, a job description: Bernstein would more or less apprentice himself to Mitropoulos, much as Mitropoulos, in his twenties, had served under Erich Kleiber at the Unter den Linden Opera. He would play piano parts in any scores that called for that instrument, he would attend all rehearsals, run errands, and be Mitropoulos's understudy if accident or illness prevented the older musician from conducting.

On April 13, 1940, however, he received a telegram from his mentor: "DON'T LEAVE YOUR CLASS FOR NEXT SEASON. SOME DIFFICULTIES HERE BECAUSE OF MY ENGAGEMENT IN NEW YORK AND ONE MONTH OF ORCHESTRA TOUR AND SOME GUEST CONDUCTORS. AM VERY AWFULLY SORRY."

Although the telegram but stated the truth about the situation in Minneapolis, Bernstein read into it every dire imagining he could think of, and in a letter to his friend David Diamond, he poured out his heart. Everything he had been doing, he swore, was based on the assumption that he would be going to Minneapolis: "April is the cruelest month. I received a wire from Dimitri that knocks my world completely to hell. . . . The prospect of next year . . . was for me the one, single motive of my activity . . . every move, every note studied, person loved, hope ignored, was a direct preparation for next year. From the scores I chose to study, to the sexual life which I have abandoned—all."[23]

In despair, Bernstein wrote directly to Minneapolis, asking for clarification and reassurance. Three days later, in his reply, Mitropoulos explained the situation in detail, blaming himself for being naive and for making premature promises. In utter good faith, he had offered Bernstein the assistant's job, only to learn later that union rules forbade the hiring of anyone not from Minnesota for any administrative job. Nor would the Minneapolis Symphony Orchestra's board of directors allow Mitropoulos to hire an untried student who had no experience in the day-to-day running of a large professional orchestra. The tone and substance of Mitropoulos's reply took some of the sting out of Bernstein's disappointment, and in a letter to David Diamond—who at this point in his career had a powerful streak of cynicism with regard to any type of authority figure—he reaffirmed his faith in Mitropoulos: "Dimitri is no false promiser. He has an integrity that is *sans pareil*. He's simply up against a strong machine."

Dimitri was in fact confused, embittered, and frustrated. Events in Europe were spinning into an abyss. A mighty civilization was being consumed in blood and fire, devouring itself, as though Germany—a nation Mitropoulos knew and loved—had made some terrible Faustian pact with the worst demons of Niflheim. Mitropoulos felt isolated, psychologically as well as emotionally, because he alone seemed to perceive the magnitude of evil that had been let loose upon western culture. His perceptions were so different, so infused with rage and impotence, compared to the people he worked with every day, with their infuriating business-as-usual attitude. All around him, Americans were clucking their tongues ruefully at Hitler's actions, yet also prattling witlessly about staying aloof from the holocaust. Gone for the moment was his ardent infatuation for all things American. Doubtless, the Greek conductor was uncomfortable with himself for feeling such altered emotions, but the scale of the horror unfolding in Europe had unbalanced him and thrown him into a depression whose depth and darkness was not suspected by his colleagues.

To Katy, he could unburden himself, and in a letter written in June—the same month that Bernstein spent writing desperate letters to Diamond and waiting for the phone to ring with a call from Minneapolis—he revealed the extent of his bitterness, as well, perhaps, as some of the reasons why his attitude had hardened toward his brilliant but pushy protégé:

> I am alone, completely alone, practically locked up in my room reading books and scores. If I manage to survive this time, then I'll never be in danger again of needing the company of any human being. It is the hardest test I've ever had in my life. I've explained to you that since I haven't been able, up to now, to relate spiritually with any American being, this means that it will never happen to me. I came to this country at too mature an age, and it is now quite impossible for me to link myself completely with the environment and with the people. Most of all, the absence of romanticism, of warmth, makes me feel far more alone than if I chose to be alone in a warm environment. Maybe you'll be amazed at what I write here, after all I told you in person about my impression of this country and its people. I've discovered that, up to now, most of the time I colored them with my imagination and saw them not as I wanted them to be, but as, unfortunately, they are not.[24]

A week later came the shattering news that France had surrendered, prompting Mitropoulos to write an even more despairing letter:

> I'm writing you today with a very heavy heart. France has fallen, Paris even, into the hands of the barbarians! I've stopped believing in anything, I doubt that there's any humanity left! My God, why, at such a time is there no one near me to give me courage, but only cold-blooded Americans who still think it is not their business to get involved in European events. I'm disgusted with all of them, and, to tell you the truth, I wish with all my heart that they'll taste the sweetness of Hitlerian influence in their country. There's selfishness everywhere; all is well as long as America is not affected. They're intoxicated with *comfort* and nothing else interests them. The ambition of every one of my musicians is to buy a car. The students are signing petitions to keep America *out of the war!* This is the daily motto. They discuss Hitler with a certain respect *for his grandeur*. It doesn't surprise me, because that's also how

they admire the heroism of their gangsters! The only ones who hate and condemn Hitler are the Jews!!

Then long live human morality!!! Let this humanity perish then, it isn't worthy of existence! All that is left for us is to find refuge outside of time and place, according to Thomas Mann! Everything he predicted has happened.

I don't have the courage to continue. I can only kiss you with all my shattered heart.[25]

Just before Mitropoulos embarked on the strenuous 1941 edition of the now-traditional midwinter tour, one routine matter needed attention. Between the day Mitropoulos returned from New York and January 28, when the tour departed, the Minneapolis Symphony's management held a press conference to announce that the conductor's contract had been extended for another two years. The timing of this announcement was not accidental—so rife had speculation grown about a possible move to the New York Philharmonic that the Minneapolis public desperately wanted someone to tell them it was not so. Not yet, at least.

The tour covered twenty-one cities in twenty-nine days, a schedule that left both orchestra and conductor exhausted. Among their stops were: Ann Arbor, Toledo, Chicago, Columbus, Birmingham, Nashville, Montgomery, New Orleans, Houston, Galveston, Dallas, Springfield, Davenport, Cedar Rapids, Omaha, and Ames, Iowa. As on previous occasions, the orchestra did not simply dust off a handful of pieces and reshuffle them slightly from town to town, but took instead a whole trunkful of scores, performing more than two dozen major pieces.

Certain elements of this tour were different, however. For one thing, every city with a sizeable Greek-American population had its own aid-for-Greece committee, and Mitropoulos felt duty-bound to lend his name and prestige to their activities. This in turn meant that he was not only keeping a grueling professional regimen, but spreading himself thin socially as well, something he was generally loath to do. He was always cornered by reporters at these affairs, and he always took the time to answer their questions courteously, no matter how exhausted he was.

"Although they can be unbelievably cruel," Mitropoulos said in response to a question about Germany, "the German people are romantic sentimentalists at heart and I have found them to be the best concert audiences in the world. They listen as though they were attending a religious service." He was asked repeatedly about job offers from New York, and he repeatedly squelched any speculation that he would be moving from Minneapolis. He was asked, sometimes rather tactlessly, why he was not married. "I am not married, and I don't intend to get married. I married my art," was the crisp reply, or words to that effect. Was Maestro Mitropoulos bothered about the way several high-powered Chicago critics had taken him apart during that leg of the trip? "Everyone is free to say what he likes, and I'm free to do what I like. I have to act according to my own nature, to be sincere. And I don't have to get angry because someone doesn't agree with me. I'm happy to see that someone has a different idea." Was it true that Maestro Mitropoulos had originally intended to be a monk, and how does that aspiration jibe with his present secular occupation? "I like to think there are two kinds of monks—those that stay at home and pray, and those who become missionaries. I consider myself one of the missionaries."[26]

With the notable exception of Chicago, the reviews the MSO received on this tour were overwhelmingly enthusiastic. The sheer dynamism, the gut-level excitement, of a Mitropoulos concert was something beyond these listeners' normal experience, and they tended to let themselves be bowled over uncritically. Wartime similes abound, with the concerts being described as "Greek conquests" and "musical blitzkriegs."

Only in Chicago, where the Mitropoulos phenomenon had been studied for several seasons, did the touring maestro come under serious intellectual scrutiny. Chicago critic Cecil Smith took the lead. While admitting Mitropoulos's power to electrify an audience, while making it clear that he did not for one instant doubt the Greek conductor's sincerity and dedication to music, Smith had begun to harbor serious reservations about some larger aspects of Mitropoulos's art.

"He has trained [the MSO]," wrote Smith, "to make percussive accents like pistol shots, and he has impressed upon them the belief that no phrase, however short, is ready for public consumption until a sharp crescendo or diminuendo has been imposed upon it . . . not a moment is ever calm. Even the points of relaxation are grotesquely over-relaxed." Both the Schumann Second Symphony and Debussy's *La Mer*, Smith continued, suffered badly from being torn into "tattered little short phrases," each one bombarded with intense colors and accents, but none ever coalescing again into a seamless long line or, for that matter, into any semblance of basic structural integrity. Finally, Smith launched at the Minneapolis conductor the most serious arrow yet:

> It was a program, therefore, in which we never heard Mozart's style, or Schumann's, or Debussy's. We were not allowed to become acquainted with their purposes, because Mr. Mitropoulos's purposes stood in the way. And, as I have indicated, it is my sincere and profound conviction that Mr. Mitropoulos's interpretive aims have less to do with the great realities of musical expression than with the aims of any other major conductor I have ever heard.[27]

A bombardment of angry letters rocked Smith's office after this review appeared, mostly from concertgoers who felt that Mitropoulos offered something more vital, more stimulating, more life-affirming than the austere and proper virtues Smith wanted him somehow to acquire. The pattern emerges once again: listeners who were emotionally tuned in to Mitropoulos's personal wavelength became addicted to the high-voltage excitement of his style and believed that all other considerations paled to insignificance; listeners who approached music more with their intellect than with their gut or heart or central nervous system were likely to have reservations.

So intense was the controversy stirred by Smith's review that the critic devoted twenty-two column inches, more than a week after the concert, to a more detailed and thoughtful analysis of what he saw as Mitropoulos's weaknesses. No other critic, in any city, had ever written such a piece before. From the manner in which he presents his argument, it is clear that he wrote not out of defensiveness or malice, but out of sincere conviction and at least some hope that a man of Mitropoulos's intelligence might give thought to the points raised and perhaps make some changes in his way of doing things. It seems clear from the evidence, both written and recorded, that Mitropoulos gradually did just that; he never showed pique at serious, thoughtful criticism, and he worked hard to mellow his own worst excesses, succeeding to such an extent that recordings documenting his late 1950s appearances in Europe reveal a steadiness, a command of overall architecture, a depth of feeling, on a totally different plane from his sometimes overanxious style in Minneapolis or his wildly erratic style in New York. Ironically, of course, the conductor made this conceptual and stylistic breakthrough, achieved the full maturity of his potential, only a few years before he died.

Cecil Smith prefaced his remarks by describing the four main duties of a conductor: first, to create a single, unified, balanced, flexible musical instrument out of the hundred or so musicians in the orchestra; second, to reproduce, with their proper interrelationships and balances, the combinations of sounds that a composer of any given work intended to be heard; third, to present any piece of music in such a way as to make sure its unique structural features may be clearly understood; and fourth, to present music eloquently, with the degrees and qualities of emotional stress implied by the score. A conductor who fails in any of these tasks is, *ipso facto*, not fully adequate at his job. The reason for the shortcomings may be a lack of technical competence or a deficiency of intuitive feeling. Overdoing the second, third, and fourth items, in Smith's opinion, was nearly as great a failing as not being able to do them at all.

Smith went on to analyze, point by point, the conducting of Mitropoulos. His conclusions:

• Dimitri Mitropoulos was a stupendously gifted artist who had, for whatever reasons, simply taken a wrong turn, and that because of his remarkable ability to get what he wanted from an orchestra, his present style threatened to divert public attention from "the conductor's proper sphere of usefulness."

• Mitropoulos was a conductor who had gone much too far in the fourth of Mr. Smith's categories, without sufficiently disciplining himself in the first three, upon which the fourth depends.

• Although his Minneapolis orchestra was capable of great things, especially in terms of its rhythmic alertness, its sections' tone tended to go muddy whenever the conductor turned his specific attention elsewhere; the brasses tended to over-blow everything written for them, and when Mitropoulos conducted the inner voices, they stood out in sculptured relief; when he did not, they went gummy and slack.

• In his recent Chicago visit, Mitropoulos "most conclusively" did not reproduce the proper combinations of instrumental sound and timbre indicated in the various scores he led. His Mozart did not have "the bright, effortless glitter and the disarming simplicity of tone color" required. His Debussy did not "gleam quietly with the half lights, the restrained effects of evocative tone color, the aristocratic spurning of everything bombastic or fat sounding" as it had in guest-conducted performances by Koussevitzky and Ansermet. Instead of stylistic appropriateness, Mitropoulos "imposed one intensely taut nervous sonority" on every composer he conducted.

• To present music—any music—in its proper intellectual context of form and structure, a conductor should treat momentary effects and incidents so that they remain just that, momentary and incidental. Mitropoulos, however, just bashed away, from one accent or inflection to the next, seldom achieving enough real continuity to fix the attention on large-scale rhythmic form or on long-breathed melodic phrases. Each piece, regardless of its style, emerged as a mosaic of tiny musical shards, some of them marvelous, but the total of which seemed never to coalesce into any larger musical statement.

This situation, Smith concluded, had come about because Mitropoulos failed to discipline both himself and the orchestra so that the fundamentals of orchestral execution would register adequately with his hometown orchestra. "I do not say that he cannot attain these ends, or that he does not wish to. But as yet he has not attained them."

Aware that this critique would not sit well with listeners who knew about the Greek conductor's recent triumphs in New York, Smith hypothesized that Mitropoulos would sound at his best when directing an orchestra that was already well-grounded in the first three of his four conductorial principles—training which Toscanini had thoroughly flogged into the New York band during his long reign in Carnegie Hall.

Thus a picture emerges of Mitropoulos as an enormously interesting musical personality, gifted in one area—physical coordination and the ability to compel an orchestra to play as he wished—to the point of genius. As yet however, his was a lopsided genius, sorely lacking in certain fundamental elements of musical communication. Smith ended his piece by wondering whether Mitropoulos on his next trip to Chicago would have focused on his weaknesses, or whether he would display an increased determination "to exploit his own nervous energy and his own special idiosyncrasies to a more sensational degree than ever."[28]

Mitropoulos knew this was no ordinary critical hatchet-job, and he may have pondered Smith's remarks deeply. Indeed, he had enough respect for Smith's article to send a copy to Katy Katsoyanis for her files, along with all the other laudatory and far more perfunctory notices the MSO garnered on this winter tour. John Sherman welcomed the orchestra back with a newspaper article that boasted some impressive statistics. Minneapolis now officially had the largest per capita concert audience in America. Counting both home and road concert dates, the MSO played forty-eight concerts in the 1940–1941 season, before a total of approximately 350,000 listeners. No other orchestra or conductor at that time had such numbers, and Minneapolis was entirely justified in patting itself on the back.[29]

While America's other major orchestras were trimming back their out-of-town engagements to meet wartime exigencies, the MSO logged more miles on the road than ever. Six tours were undertaken during the period 1941–1945, during the course of which the orchestra played 171 concerts in approximately fifty cities, from Rochester to New Orleans. By the end of its 1945 tour, the Minneapolis Symphony Orchestra had given a total of 2647 out-of-town concerts in 379 American and eighteen Canadian cities, and one concert in Havana, Cuba.

Conditions made these tours very rugged affairs, tough on the instruments as well as the personnel. The men traveled in tourist-class coaches or buses—for short hops—and slept in Pullman cars; only Mitropoulos and the orchestra management had hotel accommodations on a regular basis. Trains could be delayed, rerouted, or have their rolling stock requisitioned for military needs, leaving the orchestra to muddle-through from one town to the next as best it could.

"These tours made for a very grubby existence," recalled flutist Anton Winkler, "particularly after we'd been on the road a couple of weeks. Mitropoulos would turn his hotel room over to the men, whenever he was not actually working there, so they could use his bathtub."[30]

Mitropoulos rode and sometimes slept in the same buses and coaches as the men. For the first two or three years, he carried everything he needed (except his conducting tails and dress shirts) in a mountaineer's rucksack on his back. He was a familiar and beloved figure in those days, cigarette eternally dangling from his paw, full rucksack slung over his big, raw-boned frame, a dapper little beret perched atop his big, bald head, standing on the station platform, joking and chatting with the musicians, loping down corridors, or sprawled out in some dismal midwestern waiting room, reading Thomas Mann or Tolstoy from a dog-eared paperback. He looked, as one witness put it, more like a hitchhiking vagrant than a world-famous conductor. That's what Arthur Gaines—who replaced Mrs. Carlyle Scott as the orchestra's manager when Mrs. Scott retired in 1938—thought, too, and one of Gaines's first acts was to scold Mitropoulos for his plebeian appearance on tour. Gaines extracted from the conductor a promise to cut a more "dignified" figure when he was on the road. Mitropoulos compromised as far as substituting a regular suitcase for his knapsack, but he never gave up his shaggy overcoat or his little beret or his fraternization with the players.

So good was the conductor's disguise during his knapsack days that he was once stopped from boarding a coach car by an overzealous conductor who grabbed him by the arm as he was stepping aboard and said: "Here, you! You can't get on that train—it's reserved for the Minneapolis Symphony!"[31]

Mitropoulos ate what his men ate and suffered the delays and hardships and long hours with them, allowing himself only the luxury of a bottle of Minnesota spring water which the stage manager had to keep perpetually refilled from a container carried in the baggage car.

Several cities looked forward to their annual MSO visitation so keenly that the ensemble found itself adopted as honorary members of communities as far apart as Winnipeg and New Orleans. In towns where the audience behaved boorishly—Chattanooga was particularly noisy and ill-mannered on the orchestra's first visit—Mitropoulos simply waited for the noise to subside, however long this took. If it did not, he walked offstage and came back a few minutes later, repeating the process two or three times, if necessary, until the audience found its manners.

In the winter of 1943, the orchestra undertook its longest tour, a seven-thousand-mile odyssey that represented the longest North American tour given by any orchestra during the entire decade (and still one of the longest on record). Midway through this trek, the stress began to manifest itself. Lacking regular sleep or food, never sure whether they could make their next engagement on time and with all of their instruments, the musicians became daytime zombies, coming to life fully only when Mitropoulos gave the downbeat. Following one particularly brutal eighteen-hour stretch without sleep or decent food, during which some of the men were forced to ride standing in the aisles of their railroad car, two musicians got into a vicious fistfight and had to be expelled from the orchestra. Going from Birmingham to Tuscaloosa, the musicians once had to ride in a converted prison car with bars on the windows.

At another location, the first cellist, Nikolai Graudon, suffered a painful eye injury when he was struck by a lollipop hurled from the audience by a restless child. Mitropoulos himself broke a toe one night while stumbling around in a blacked-out sleeping car, and had to conduct the rest of the tour in considerable pain. A failed alarm clock caused him to be stranded in Savannah, and he was forced to take a taxi to Augusta in order to catch up in time for the next concert.

Of course, there were moments of serendipitous pleasure, too, when, for example, an ample supply of fresh oranges and grapefruit was brought to them by local citizens during the Florida leg of the trip; or the night when the entire orchestra was so delayed by a blizzard that it arrived in Johnstown, Pennsylvania, unable to eat before the start of the already-late concert. Upon learning of the musicians' plight, some local people solicited aid from nearby restaurants and when Mitropoulos and his frazzled men went backstage at intermission, they found two hundred fresh sandwiches and gallons of hot coffee waiting for them.

True to form, Mitropoulos did not take just a handful of well-rehearsed greeting-card pieces on tour. Instead, he reserved the right to shuffle things around as the mood took him, so that the orchestra's long-suffering librarian, Herman Boessenroth, had to keep up with the parts for as many as thirty-five works, including eleven symphonies.

Especially gratifying for musicians and conductor was the enthusiasm of the crowd both in Boston, a city which had never heard the Minneapolis Symphony before, and in the toughest room of all, New York City, where the Minnesotans had not ventured since 1927. While Virgil Thomson sniffed disdainfully at the Rachmaninoff Second Symphony (he leaned over to his companion's ear as the first lugubrious bars were being played by the low strings and whispered: "Strained stool!"), he and the other Manhattan critics agreed that the Minneapolis Symphony had become "altogether big league"—the sweetest words the Minnesotans could have read.[32]

CHAPTER ELEVEN

The War Years in Minneapolis

America's entry into World War Two naturally disturbed the stability of the Minneapolis Symphony Orchestra, as was the case for any organization staffed, in part, by draft-age men. The constant turnover in personnel made Mitropoulos feel that he was starting from scratch at the first rehearsal of each season. Every season began with a rough period as the newcomers settled in and the older players adjusted their sense of continuity. "Every year," Mitropoulos wrote to Katy Katsoyanis soon after their correspondence resumed, "the good results began to show only at the end of the season, exactly when I had to dismiss the orchestra for the summer."[1] But despite these chronic personnel problems, the war years proved to be golden ones for Mitropoulos and the Minneapolis Symphony. Together they scored many triumphs in both the conventional and the exceptional repertoires.

The autumn season of 1941 got underway with a meat-and-potatoes concert (Berlioz, Brahms, Ravel, and Schumann) on October 24. "New" music, relatively speaking, appeared on the November 7 concert in the form of Sibelius's Sixth Symphony, one of the most elusive works in that composer's oeuvre. Sibelius always found a welcome audience in the Twin Cities, however, and this Minneapolis premiere found Mitropoulos doing his utmost for music that was basically uncongenial to him.

It may seem odd to regard Borodin's Second Symphony as new music, too, but indeed it was new to both orchestra and audience when Mitropoulos directed it on November 14, 1941. This symphony had occupied a special place in Mitropoulos's heart ever since the first time he conducted it, in Russia in 1934. At the end of that concert, a rumpled, unshaven, badly dressed man had shambled backstage and embraced the conductor with tears in his eyes. "I haven't heard that symphony played with such understanding and such feeling since my friend, the composer, played it years ago," said the man, who then identified himself as Mikhail Ippolitov-Ivanov, who had heard Borodin lead the work in the mid-1880s. Now, many years later, Mitropoulos gave a stirring interpretation, one which was recorded—in cramped, miserly sonics—on the day Pearl Harbor was bombed.

On November 11, Marian Anderson sang arias from Monteverdi and Verdi, along with a clutch of gussied-up spirituals. Novelties on the concert included Aaron Copland's breezy *Outdoor Overture* and a Pastorale for Orchestra by an obscure Cypriot composer named Anis Fuleihan; reviewers' descriptions of the latter piece make one curious to hear the music. How *did* he come up with some of these things?

Nothing atonal appeared during the autumn 1941 season, but Schoenberg did make an appearance, in the form of *Verklärte Nacht*, which the Minneapolis program annotator translated as *Radiant Night*, instead of the more common *Transfigured Night*. Was there a suspicion that "transfigured" might be too foreboding an adjective? In any case, the score writhed and twitched and sobbed under Mitropoulos's hands, so that even patrons who didn't especially like the music had to admit that the performance was a knock-out.

On January 16, 1942, a few days after returning from guest engagements in New York, Mitropoulos opened the spring season, with Hindemith's *Mathis der Maler* Symphony. Critical response to the Hindemith was mixed, with Grace Davies articulating the most skeptical viewpoint. Davies credited the conductor with "laboring valiantly and with wonderful assurance" to make the Hindemith work convincing, then closed her remarks by saying that "Perhaps in the post-war days it may seem astonishing that Hindemith was hard to understand. I wonder!"[2]

On January 30, the MSO essayed Shostakovich's Fifth Symphony for the first time. From the perspective of the mid-1990s, it seems incredible that this now-overplayed work was roundly hissed when Koussevitzky premiered it in Boston in 1941. Koussevitzky responded by promising to "ram it down the ears" of its critics until they acknowledged it as a modern masterpiece. In Minneapolis, the symphony sparked an unusual demonstration of between-the-movements comments throughout the audience, but its overall impact was staggering. "It created a veritable sensation," wrote the conservative Grace Davies, "[and] if all of the twentieth-century music were as clearly stated as that heard last night, we would be willing to subscribe to the inevitable rebirth of musical thinking."[3]

In February, the orchestra went on tour. No sooner had the train pulled out of the station than rumblings began to be heard from a nascent "Dump Dimitri" faction that had coalesced among mostly older and deeply conservative listeners. Even though three-fourths of the programs in each Mitropoulos season had been devoted to the conventional repertoire (or to lesser-known works that were easy on the ears), the perception had emerged that Mitropoulos was dishing out too much modern stuff—a perception that surely derived much of its power from the conductor's zealous, outspoken advocacy of those difficult works he did choose to perform.

John Sherman opened up the pages of the *Star-Journal* to his readers, and printed a number of vigorous comments, pro and con. His own opinion was that Mitropoulos's eccentric programs were stimulating rather than alienating, but he did express a wish that Mitropoulos would occasionally relax, that too much severity would eventually backfire. Hundreds of letters poured in after Sherman's initial article, in which he invited readers to voice their own opinions. Statistically, the pros and cons were about even, and many readers articulated the same general comments:

- The world is depressing enough without having to listen to austere and unfamiliar music, they wrote;
- Mitropoulos had made Minneapolis famous, and his audience, like it or not, was considered one of the most sophisticated and responsible in the U.S.A. As for those who complained about "too much" modern music—how much was too much? What they really meant, wrote some, was that *any* amount of modern music was too much; and finally,
- For all his technical mastery, Mitropoulos's programs were unbalanced and featured too many weird juxtapositions. Over-stimulation could be as exhausting, after a while, as over-sedation from too many popular works.[4]

Sherman's open forum gave the average audience member a public voice. Nothing was resolved by this discussion, of course, but most music lovers, whether they loved Mitropoulos's programs or hated them, agreed that such a spirited debate was itself a sign of cultural maturity.

Regular subscription concerts resumed on March 8, only two days after the musicians returned from their winter tour. Mitropoulos lost no time in demonstrating that he was evolving as an interpreter. His one previous Minneapolis performance of Tchaikovsky's Fifth Symphony had been a frontal assault, dispatching the entire work in a feverish thirty-three minutes. This time, he took almost ten minutes longer with the piece, and its climaxes were considerably more powerful for this additional breadth.

Only a few days later, the conductor spoke out against some hardline pronouncements by composer Percy Grainger, who was then composer-in-residence at Gustavus Adolphus College in St. Peter, Minnesota. Grainger, who harbored racial prejudices scarcely less venomous than those found in the average SS officer, had urged a total ban on German music for the duration of the war.

Mitropoulos, the international artist, replied:

> If the enemy has something in his civilization which makes him strong, we should be able to borrow from him. Of course, if I have to choose between doing American composers and German composers, I will take the Americans . . . because the Americans need our help. . . . I hate political Germany, but I am sorry Percy Grainger feels as he does about German music.[5]

Joseph Szigeti, one of the conductor's favorite partners in the concerto repertoire, joined the MSO on March 27 for a performance of the rarely heard Busoni Violin Concerto. "The concerto did not put much strain on the conservative listener," wrote one reviewer. John Sherman neatly summarized most listeners' reactions to Busoni: "This consecrated approach to the Busoni work . . . did not dispel, however, the conviction that it is almost totally a cerebral product—something which issued from a well-stocked, cultivated, musician's brain that could do virtually anything but create a commanding musical idea."[6]

Oscar Levant, the wise-cracking radio personality and pianist, appeared on the season's closing pension-fund concert on April 15, performing two Gershwin works and his own piano concerto. Some weeks earlier, when Mitropoulos was dining with Levant and his wife, Mitropoulos had frozen all conversation by remarking that the concerto was "full of hate and masturbation."

Angrily, Levant snapped: "Then don't play it!"

Mitropoulos, ever the unflappable, merely smiled and said, "That is the first time in my career I've heard those words from a composer." The actual performance was described by Levant this way:

> The concerto's opening measures are for piano alone. I waited for the downbeat. . . . Mitropoulos turned to me and smiled. I returned the smile. Mitropoulos nodded and smiled again. Not to be outdone, I returned the second smile. We kept grinning at each other while the audience waited. Finally, it dawned on me that the smile was the signal to begin.[7]

Both conductor and soloist might have saved themselves the trouble. Not one reviewer liked the piece, although Sherman took the rhetorical prize by saying that "The Levant concerto ranks somewhere between an indiscretion and a monstrosity."[8]

During the 1941–1942 season, Mitropoulos headed a campaign to install a much-needed acoustical shell behind the stage of Northrop Auditorium. The device was patterned after one that Stokowski had designed and used with great success during his recent cross-country tour with the All American Youth Orchestra. So urgently was this improvement needed, in the maestro's opinion, that the usual process of committees and fundraising benefits was bypassed. Mitropoulos jump-started the campaign by contributing ten percent of the total cost out of his own paycheck. He also demonstrated that when the cause was sufficiently energizing, he could be surprisingly adept at soliciting funds from the MSO's wealthier patrons. Construction costs were fully pledged less than a month after the campaign began; Mitropoulos celebrated by taking a train out west and climbing Mt. Shasta and Mt. Whitney.

When the new acoustical framework debuted, it was an instant success. The previous canvas drapery had absorbed volume, blurred dynamics, and cast an occasional veil over the individual timbres of woodwinds and strings. Everyone agreed that the new shell made the orchestra's sound deeper, cleaner, more vivid, and allowed solo passages to emerge with much more character. The installation also placed an additional ten thousand pounds on a stage that was already strained by fourteen thousand pounds of personnel and more than a ton of instruments; two years after the shell went up, the stage itself had to be strengthened. At that point, the appearance of the hall itself was improved by replacing its dingy institutional yellow with a pleasing color scheme of dark blue-greys.

Wartime conditions really began to affect the Minneapolis Symphony at the start of its autumn 1942 season. A dozen players went into the armed forces; eight new and not necessarily better players replaced them. Gas rationing forced many symphony fans to carpool. And as early as October, the MSO began giving concerts intentionally designed as morale-boosters for servicemen, starting with an "Allied Nations" program at Fort Snelling on October 23, consisting of Beethoven's "Victory" Symphony, the Fifth, framed by smaller works of Norwegian, English, and Russian origins, climaxed with a performance of Tchaikovsky's *1812 Overture* for which the University of Minnesota Band and at least one cannon joined in to make a stirring racket.

Like every other major orchestra in America, the MSO had its turn performing the Shostakovich Seventh ("Leningrad") Symphony. Tremendous hype attended the November 11, 1942, Minneapolis premiere, and given the wartime context, it is not surprising that otherwise sober-minded critics jumped on the bandwagon—one of them pointed out to his readers that in the interval between the opening downbeat and the final chord, hundreds of people would die in the fighting for Leningrad.

Many listeners had already heard the symphony; Toscanini and the NBC orchestra had broadcast its American premiere on July 19. And in the opinion of many who heard both performances, Mitropoulos gave by far the better interpretation. "Put me down as a man who claims that Mitropoulos far excelled Arturo Toscanini," wrote John Sherman, "not only in understanding and projecting the work, but in holding it together and welding its many diverse elements into one stirring and dramatic utterance."[9]

Mitropoulos made his own contribution to the war effort, first by buying a truckload of powdered milk which the Red Cross managed to get distributed to needy Greek children in the Athens region, and then by volunteering for a Red Cross mobile blood unit at the end of the 1943 spring season. This latter job involved his giving up a summer's worth of guest appearances, along with the much-needed salary accruing therefrom, but the experience boosted his spirits immensely. "Believe me," he wrote to David Diamond,

> during these three months when I have been doing completely different work, I felt for the first time in my life that I was doing something really useful, and it gave me the opportunity to refuse a lot of attractive sum-

mer engagements, where I could have had the extreme delight of chewing the endless and unendless gum of classic-romantic concoctions. Every time I wash the tubes which have been used to transfer the blood of a human being from his veins to a little jar, I feel more hopeful and more real, and even sometimes I find myself dreaming of quitting my abstract, smug profession. Now don't be again mad at me for my exhibition of paradoxes—I am in the mood to be strange and seeking for freedom—freedom from routine, although I know that, like an old alcoholic, sooner or later I will come back to my onions.[10]

His official designation was "blood custodian." Every morning for three months, Mitropoulos and his driver would start out for a specified location within a seventy-five-mile radius of Minneapolis—that was as far as they could go, because each day's supply of donated blood had to be shipped to Chicago for neutralization within twenty-four hours. A doctor and several nurses would arrive at the donation site later in the morning and work would begin. Mitropoulos was responsible for setting up sixteen iron cots for the donors, for washing test-tubes and other equipment, for storing the cloth blood-bags in their refrigerated containers, for cleaning up after the donors had gone, and for doing whatever scutwork had to be done, from filling out forms to sweeping floors. These chores made for twelve-to-fourteen-hour days, but Mitropoulos swore he had never been happier in his life than he was during that summer. The blood unit job was truly a Franciscan sort of labor, and it brought him into daily contact with hundreds of ordinary Americans, many of whom had no idea that the gentle bald man with the pleasant foreign accent was a world-famous conductor. It was reported in the Minneapolis papers that Mitropoulos also played piano for the blood donors at several locations.

When interviewed by the *New York Post* at the end of the summer, Mitropoulos claimed that the bloodmobile job had left him more relaxed than he had ever felt. Beyond the moral satisfaction of the work itself, he attributed remarkable therapeutic benefits to a humble garment, the overall:

If I am more relaxed, working in overalls is the reason. What a joy to wear your oldest shoes and comfortable clothes when you work! The overall is the new symbol of humanity—and I really mean that! How I would love to conduct in overalls—that stiff shirt and white tie business really is passé—but I don't dare do it yet. Many times, we wouldn't get back to Minneapolis until nine o'clock, so I had no time to change; I went to the movies in my overalls. And I'm telling you, I found people were much more friendly than if I were dressed up in my best suit.

When I offered my services to the Red Cross, you know, I was surprised, they jumped on me. . . . One of the biggest thrills was going to the St. Cloud Reformatory for boys, where 116 young men voluntarily gave their blood. They seemed like a fine lot of kids . . . one would never imagine they had done anything wrong. One boy made me a present of an exact miniature model of the ambulance we used in the blood unit.

According to the interviewer, Mitropoulos paused at this point to light a cigarette. He stared intently at his own outsized hands. When he spoke again, there was a "deep seriousness" in his voice: "Now I have had the privilege of using these hands for a glorious purpose. Every day we came back with four iron containers filled with 160 pints of blood. Each pint meant a life saved. I carried those containers with love in my heart, just as I conduct a great work of Beethoven with love."[11]

Thanks to his lack of European engagements and his demanding but satisfying work for the Red Cross, Mitropoulos enjoyed a vacation from music during the summer of 1943. Batteries charged, he returned to open the 1943–1944 season with full vigor.

The most demanding work on the early fall schedule was Bartók's Violin Concerto (with Menuhin as the soloist on November 6), coupled with Shostakovich's First Symphony. The Bartók was judged "severe" but was accorded much respect, and the impish Shostakovich work had actually become popular with many listeners. Much of the new music heard that autumn consisted of first Minneapolis performances of such easily digested pieces as Griffes's *Pleasure Dome of Kubla Khan*, Hindemith's fizzy overture to his 1929 opera *News of the Day*, Tchaikovsky's colorful Symphony No. 2 in C, and Morton Gould's delectable *Spirituals for String Choir and Orchestra*. One piece that did not go down so smoothly with some listeners was Prokofiev's Suite from *The Love for Three Oranges*, which offended critic Grace Davies by virtue of its "gruesome subtleties," whatever those might be.

Looking over the autumn schedule as a whole, one senses that Mitropoulos was possibly hoarding credit with the audience before unleashing on them Ernst Krenek's fiercely uncompromising Symphony No. 2, on December 3.

By this stage of Mitropoulos's tenure, the concert seasons had acquired a definite tone and shape. What one got out of them depended on what kind of mood one took to them. Except for the truly calcified reactionaries, the audience had learned to accept the experience of hearing new and challenging music, even if the price for that stimulation was occasional bafflement or irritation. The audience generally had come to terms with the fact that their conductor was a missionary, not an entertainer, and most were agreeable to the situation because of the high drama of the conductor's presentations. But friction occurred on different nights for different people. Mitropoulos was always "on," but there were nights when even the most tolerant listeners simply did not feel like following him to the mountaintop; when even listeners with broad taste and high intelligence just wanted to sit there and be diverted, taken out of themselves for two hours; when going to a concert needed to be a relaxing ritual of pleasure rather than an act of faith.

For the new year, 1944, Mitropoulos programmed mostly hardy and accessible fare: an all-Wagner concert with Helen Traubel, Rudolf Firkušný playing the Dvořák Piano Concerto—and a few unintimidating novelties, such as Milhaud's *Suite Provençale*, and Reger's sunny *Variations and Fugue on a Theme of Beethoven*. The program for March 24 was loopy even by Mitropoulos's standards: Krenek's *Cantata for Wartime*, Debussy's *Nocturnes*, Handel's Concerto Grosso, Op. 6, No. 10, Stravinsky's *Circus Polka*, and the Seventh Symphony of Jean Sibelius. Even the conductor's staunchest admirers were hard-pressed to see any design in this higgledy-piggledy melange of musical styles. Bohuslav Martinů's Second Symphony appeared on the program of April 7, along with Copland's *A Lincoln Portrait* (narrated, in a barely audible manner, by Carl Sandburg). It is a measure of how attitudes have changed that the reviewers treated the Copland work in a cavalier manner that would be unthinkable today: "The Copland music for 'A Lincoln Portrait' was such as we have come to expect from this composer—angular, dissonant, and, as a setting for Lincoln's noble words, anachronistic."[12]

The season ended on April 14, with an all-Brahms program.

In September 1944, the Minneapolis Symphony got a new concertmaster: Louis Krasner. Renowned as a tireless champion of modern music, Krasner has also earned a permanent niche in music history as the man for whom Alban Berg composed one of the twentieth century's greatest violin concertos.

As Krasner told the story, he and Mitropoulos almost didn't connect:

> I went to a concert in New York, not long after my wife and I emigrated to America. Heifetz was playing and Mitropoulos conducting. I went backstage to say hello to Heifetz and Mitropoulos—whom I had not met before—was standing nearby. When he overheard my name, he broke off his own conversation and said: "Louis Krasner?" "Yes?" I answered. He actually bowed to me and said: "We should light a candle for you, for all that you have done for music. I admire you so much." Well, I was embarrassed because there was Heifetz standing there, suddenly no longer the center of attention. "Where are you playing now?" Mitropoulos asked. "Wherever it is," he went on, "we simply must get together and play something." Then he passed on.[13]

At that time, Krasner was assistant concertmaster in Pittsburgh, under Fritz Reiner. Hans Heinsheimer of Schirmer's was acting as Krasner's agent at that time, and he soon approached Krasner with an offer for the job of concertmaster in Indianapolis, under Fabien Sevitzky. Krasner had just signed the contract when he received an unexpected call from Mitropoulos.

"Are you free to come be my concertmaster next September?"

"I'd love to," Krasner responded, suddenly wishing he had not signed the Indianapolis contract.

"Come to Minneapolis and we'll perform all the great modern concertos together," Mitropoulos urged.

"Can you give me until tomorrow?" Krasner finally said, stalling for time.

Mitropoulos said he could, and that Mr. Gaines, the MSO's manager, would telephone Krasner the next day with details of the contract. Krasner immediately called Heinsheimer and said: "Here I have this wonderful offer from Mitropoulos, and yet I've agreed to go work for Sevitzky."

"Where's that contract?" Heinsheimer asked.

"In my pocket."

"Tear it up. Do you think, if Sevitzky suddenly got an offer from the Boston Symphony, that he would hesitate just because he had a contract with Indianapolis?"

Krasner tore up the document and started making plans to move to Minnesota.

Ticket sales were unusually brisk before the start of the autumn 1944 season. A fair number of new and novel pieces appeared on the programs, but none of them, to judge from the reviews, seems to have presented difficulties for even the more conservative members of the audience: Ralph Vaughan Williams's *A London Symphony*, Milhaud's *Le Boeuf sur le toit* (given a real down-and-dirty, sawdust-on-the-floor performance, to judge from the MSO's spectacular 1945 recording), a quasi-impressionist suite by Robert Casadesus, the first of Shostakovich's two piano concertos, David Diamond's zestful *Rounds for String Orchestra*, and Charles Mills's *Appalachian Mountains: An American Folk Rhapsody*. A significant number of these "novelties" eventually entered the working repertoire.

Perhaps it was the energizing presence of Louis Krasner, perhaps it was the looming Allied victory in Europe, but Mitropoulos's spring 1945 season was among the most far-reaching, provocative, and stimulating of his entire Minneapolis period.

Things began on a clangorous note on January 5, when the brilliant young William Kappell introduced the Khachaturian Piano Concerto. The performance, in John Sherman's words, was "perfectly incredible," and the concerto—now generally held in contempt for its populist gestures and supposed movie-music cliches—set the audience ablaze. Two days later, the Russian mood was rekindled when cellist Yves Chardon played the solo role in Alexander Tcherepnin's *Rhapsodie georgienne*—Borodin with an overlay of Ravel.

Before Krasner and Mitropoulos served up the Minneapolis premiere of Alban Berg's Violin Concerto on January 12, both men sought to prepare the audience through extensive newspaper and radio interviews; Krasner also offered several preconcert talks about his role in the creation and premiere of this twentieth-century masterpiece.

Minneapolis gave the concerto a mixed reception. John Sherman estimated that eighty percent of the audience didn't like it, but that there was wide respect for the work's manifest integrity and for Krasner's authoritative handling of the solo part. Less daunting, but also less interesting by a goodly measure, was William Walton's Violin Concerto, given its Minneapolis premiere on January 26 by Heifetz.

Mitropoulos made one of his most eloquent pleas for tolerance toward modern music at the conclusion of a March 17 concert. He had just presented another new and substantial work that both audience and critics found harrowing: Alexandre Tansman's Fifth Symphony. After the conductor's from-the-stage appeal for more blood donors, he asked:

> What sense does it make to embrace modern inventions and conveniences, modern films and radio shows, but to utterly reject modern sounds? Could you take a sporting interest in these contemporary works? That is to say, could you not accept the challenge of *listening* first and then deciding, on a piece by piece basis, what to embrace and what to discard? Listening to a new work of music is an *experiment*, and as any scientist can tell you, an experiment can be its own reward, at least in terms of intellectual satisfaction. We don't have to ask that all modern works we hear should be supremely great works of art. Most of them aren't, and we would be naive to expect them to be, but we are more naive if we close our ears to them.[14]

For the next concert, on March 23, Mitropoulos programmed another tolerance-tester: a string-orchestra arrangement of Schoenberg's Quartet No. 2 in F-sharp Minor, Op. 10. The arrangement includes a very demanding vocal part for soprano, sung in this case by a young artist of Norwegian birth, Nancy Ness. When she arrived for her first rehearsal, Mitropoulos handed over her music with the diffidence of someone loaning out an original copy of the Magna Carta. "Be careful of it," he admonished, "because this is the only copy of it in America. And you must learn this so well that you can sing it with a Stravinsky record playing full blast behind you."[15]

Ms. Ness sight-read the music with some trepidation, telling a rehearsal visitor that "this is harder than *Götterdämmerung!*" A visiting journalist recorded some colorful details of the rehearsal:

> When she comes to the climax of the Litany, a prolonged high C, there is a terrible, beautiful, prolonged shriek and then it suddenly drops to a low B. Mitropoulos, smiling in his kind of incandescent eagerness, tells her how he wants it: "Deep down at once. Dee-deeda—" and singing it in his hoarse voice and expressing just how she should do it with his spasmodic violent body. . . . And one time in a beautiful

mysterious blur of sound, he said to the violins, "Gentlemen, this A-sharp—hold it through the G until it resolves and comes out again. It is beautiful, this harmony."[16]

Artur Rubinstein came to town late in March, to rehearse and perform the Symphony Concertante by Karol Szymanowski. He and Mitropoulos took in some movies together, and the two musicians were once overheard in a spirited argument about the proper symbolism of a small dog which was featured in a Fred MacMurray–Claudette Colbert movie called *Practically Yours*.

Mitropoulos closed the spring season on a showmanly note, on April 6, 1945, playing and conducting Respighi's Toccata for Piano and Orchestra.

One casualty of the war years was the Minneapolis Symphony's revered patron, Elbert Carpenter, who died on January 29, 1945, after a long, gradual decline. For several years, his attendance at the concerts had been sporadic, and finally, when he could no longer attend in person, the orchestra placed a dedicated microphone at the front of the hall and piped the music directly into Mr. Carpenter's home. Although his share of hands-on management of the orchestra's daily affairs had become less and less, his absence was a blow, for he was, in several senses, the father of the orchestra. He had taken a shaky, provincial band, nursed it through repeated financial crises, and lived to see it internationally recognized, debt-free, and in very good shape for the future. Concert attendance, in fact, remained strong during the war years, despite the sometimes prickly nature of the repertoire and the wartime entertainment tax that jacked ticket prices up by about twenty percent.

Fundraising, of course, remained an ongoing problem, war or no war, as it was and continues to be for every American orchestra. Direct from-the-stage solicitations (always delivered midway through an especially crowd-pleasing program), fund drives, pension concerts, raffles, symphony balls, parties, and dances—all were employed. Activities on behalf of his orchestra were the one category of extracurricular event in which Mitropoulos was willing to participate. At one of these affairs, the conductor demonstrated how good a sport he could be, when the cause was dear to his heart, by leading an ensemble of MSO players through a theatrical skit. Mitropoulos was costumed as an eighteenth-century *Kapellmeister*, complete with frock coat, periwig, a three-foot baton, and spectacles balanced precariously on the end of his monumental nose, while the orchestra members indulged in all sorts of Marx Brothers japery. On this occasion and several similar to it, close observers noted how much Mitropoulos seemed to enjoy dressing up and stepping, for a few hours at least, outside of his own customary persona; more than one patron voiced the opinion that, had Maestro chosen another line of work, he might well have been a very fine character actor.

Like many ordinarily pacifistic citizens, Mitropoulos followed wartime military affairs with naive enthusiasm. Some acquaintances had the rather startling experience of being subjected to lectures on military strategy, coupled with lists of suggestions on how the Allies could manage their campaigns better, all based on the conductor's fervent rereading of Thucydides. He told one friend that he was going to send copies of the Greek historian's writings to Roosevelt and Winston Churchill; whether he actually did so is unknown.

CHAPTER TWELVE

The War Years: Guest Engagements

By far the most momentous musical event of the 1940–1941 season occurred not in Minneapolis but in New York, where Mitropoulos made his official debut with the New York Philharmonic on December 19, 1940. He was scheduled to conduct nineteen concerts (December 19–20, 22, 26, 27; January 2–5, 8, 10–12), a substantial chunk out of the midseason period. Of course, he had already debuted in that city with the NBC Symphony in 1938, but that was before an invited audience, and in the minds of New Yorkers, a debut only mattered if it was given before a paying crowd.

At this time, the New York Philharmonic was in the doldrums. When Toscanini left in 1936, Arthur Judson—who managed both the orchestra and the fearfully powerful Columbia Artists Management Agency—chose to replace him not with the great Wilhelm Furtwängler but with a then-unknown English conductor named John Barbirolli. Barbirolli was a musician of taste and ability, but he was too much of a gentleman to handle the Philharmonic. The band played like brigands for him, no one bought the records he made with them, and ticket sales, by 1940, had slipped badly. By mid-1940, it was clear that Barbirolli's days were numbered; there was much speculation about who might be named to replace him.

Minneapolis regarded the upcoming Mitropoulos debut with mixed emotions. On the one hand, there was great civic pride that the hometown guy was being given a chance to show what he could do with the premier orchestra in the land. The mood in the papers was not unlike that preceding the hometown ball club's elevation to the World Series—extensive summaries of the New York reviews would be greedily devoured by Minneapolis readers, every critical metaphor turned inside out so that its entrails could be read. On the other hand there was a certain trepidation: most Minneapolitans were resigned to the knowledge that sooner or later their beloved Dimitri would be lured away by a greater orchestra, although they devoutly hoped it would be later. John Sherman spoke for everyone when he wrote, just before Mitropoulos's departure: "Now we'll be watching for the New York reviews and hoping the Philharmonic won't get too possessive."

As for the conductor himself, he was undergoing great emotional turmoil, torn between the quotidian reality of his own life and the ghastly greater reality of what was happening to his beloved Europe. Mussolini was already massing troops to wrest the Albanian provinces from Greece and would in fact declare war on October 28—only to have the stalwart Greeks beat him to a standstill and then roll back his legions in a series of humiliating defeats. For most of his adult life, Mitropoulos had disliked newspapers and was proud to claim that he disdained to read them (although he did keep extensive files of his own reviews and clippings—not for reasons of egotism, but so that he could send everything to Katy, as she had asked him to do), but now he devoured every headline, every war story, every twitch of the campaign arrows in the maps, keeping himself obsessively informed, even though the act of doing so only deepened his depression. He knew that, even if the Greeks could hold off the Italians, it was only a matter of time until the Germans waded in, and the Greeks had no hope of beating them. He worried about his mother, about Katy, about Maria Negroponte, about the very civilization to which he was heir; most of all, he wondered if his life's work really mattered when compared to the cataclysm unfolding overseas.

Added to this torment was a very real anxiety about his New York debut. He was content in Minneapolis and loyal to its orchestra, but the idea of eventually commanding one of the two greatest ensembles in the United States (the Boston Symphony or the New York Philharmonic) had lodged itself in his heart as a metaphoric mountain peak. And he was by nature a conqueror-of-peaks, a strider-after-the-unattainable (what his German friends described as *ein Gipfelstürmer*). If the summit were within his grasp, he would throw himself toward it with all his might. But the aching doubt remained: would that be enough? In a series of intense letters written during the summer and autumn of 1940, he revealed his anguish to Katy Katsoyanis:

> If you only knew in what state of despair I find myself! Both over the events in Europe as over my personal problems. I implore you, concentrate all your critical mind and give me an answer to what I have to say below. I have now been abroad so many years and have done all I could to improve my art, and I think I have arrived at a fairly high degree of maturity, even of fame. Must I then, because of this, be condemned to shrivel up and die far away from my country? If my future is to become the head of the Boston or New York Philharmonic, when I reach that point, if I ever do, there won't be a drop of blood left in my veins! I understand that it is my duty to sacrifice my whole life for art, but even sacrifice has its limits. Alone as I am over here, it is no longer a sacrifice, but a wasting away, a complete destruction of myself. I'm not afraid of my isolation, but there are limits to isolation, and when one goes beyond them, one risks destroying what is human in each of us.[1]

About a month before he left for New York, he wrote in even more despairing terms: "comments on the European situation, I assure you . . . have a desperate effect on my nerves. I am seized with such a mania of hate that I'm disgusted with myself."[2]

He even found himself repelled by Bach and Beethoven, who at this stage in history represented to him "the systematized thought of the destructive German race." How can one not despise "the crocodile tears of Richard Strauss' sentimentality?" he asked Katy rhetorically. "I need great strength to resist the temptation to banish from my programs, if I could, this destructive spirit of the human race." He went even farther and admitted to Katy something he never admitted to the public or to his colleagues: "Contemporary art in general gives me the impression of a ridiculous and sterile masturbation, and it is only with great effort that I maintain my faith in it."[3] He wrote:

> I feel such spiritual fatigue sometimes from always drawing on my own resources, trying to make the hours of the day and night bearable, from trying not to be disgusted with the constant re-reading of the same scores, the routine of my art, from trying not to despair of life completely, from trying not to let my heart and my love dry out. I find my presence in the New York Orchestra ironic at a time when others, maybe better than me, go hungry or are mercilessly killed by the forces of Evil. Courage, you may say, but what else do we do in life but draw constantly on our courage and then arrive exhausted at the grave that waits for us.[4]

By the end of October however, his mood had lightened, despite the news of the Fascist attack on Greece. He was looking forward keenly now to the concerts in New York. "This time," he wrote Katy on October 16, "it will be the debut of a famous man, and you can imagine with what eyes and ears they will listen to me."[5] His mood was brightened by the chance to see Charlie Chaplin's *The Great Dictator*. He fell so in love with the film that he saw it four times in the same week, marveling at the great comedian's achievement. The film soothed and uplifted him with what he described as its "vibrant perfection," and viewing it changed his entire outlook. As long as one great artist could create such a work, there was perhaps hope for mankind. The ebullient letter he wrote to Katy about the movie, dated October 25, 1940, was the last full-length communication the two would share until after the war and Greece's liberation. Only occasional brief Red Cross–carried messages and telegrams got through for the next four-and-a-half years.

Mitropoulos had scheduled as few social events as possible during his four-week engagement in New York, but there was no way to escape the press. Aside from the predictable questions, to which Mitropoulos gave the now-predictable answers, there was one query of particular interest. Reporters had noted that Mitropoulos's program included two works by living Italian composers (Alfredo Casella and Mario Castelnuovo-Tedesco, the former still living in Italy, the latter by then residing in the United States). How could he, the reporters asked, conduct Italian music when Mussolini's armies were invading Greek soil? Considering how bitterly Mitropoulos had written about the matter to Katy, the conductor's answer was remarkably calm and civilized: "I planned to do it, and I do it because I admire the Italian compositions and I love Italy like my own country. I know that the invasion is the mistake of one person and not of a whole people. I know the Italians very well. They are born for art and music, and not to be conquerors."[6]

His first rehearsal with the Philharmonic was on the morning of December 17. The orchestra was on its best behavior, something that would not have been the case if Mitropoulos had come from a rival podium in Boston or Philadelphia, cities whose orchestras had regularly sold-out Carnegie Hall during the 1930s, often when the hometown band played to half-empty halls. As was now his custom, Mitropoulos had taken the trouble to memorize most of the players' names, and his courteous, cooperative approach to rehearsals was initially quite appealing to the Philharmonic members. His ability to remember every single bar of even the most complex scores also elicited exclamations of wonder even from the most cynical veterans of the orchestra.

After two days of intense but productive rehearsals, the opening concert on December 19 went very well indeed. According to the review that appeared in *The New Yorker*, "every conductor not professionally occupied that evening seemed to be in attendance. If Mr. Mitropoulos had become exhausted during the course of his labors and somebody had shouted, 'Is there a conductor in the house?' there would have been collisions in the aisles."[7] Half the program was familiar (Beethoven's seldom-played *Leonore* Overture No. 2 and the Fourth Symphony), and the concluding half featured a single orchestral blockbuster, the *Symphonia domestica* of Richard Strauss, a work that had not been played in the city since the composer directed it during a visit in 1922.

At the conclusion of the Strauss work, which ends with a glorious full-throated double fugue, the audience went berserk, leaping up and cheering, clapping with rolled up programs, stamping their feet, whistling. When Mitropoulos asked the members of the Philharmonic to rise and share the ovation, they spontaneously remained in their seats, adding their own cheers and applause to the general din. The conductor was recalled numerous times before the demonstration exhausted itself.

The august Olin Downes of the *New York Times* began his morning-after review in no uncertain terms, with what amounted to a demand that somehow, sooner or later, Dimitri Mitropoulos had to become the Philharmonic's music director:

Hopes, long famished, of a conductor of commanding qualities to direct the Philharmonic-Symphony Orchestra of New York were gratified last

night when Dimitri Mitropoulos appeared for the first time in a public
concert in this city as guest conductor of that body in Carnegie Hall.

Conducting without score or baton, with a strange eccentric technique all his own, Mr. Mitropoulos quickly proved his energy and fire
as a leader and his remarkable control of his players. He did as he
pleased with the orchestra. The orchestra . . . obeyed him implicitly,
and sounded like an entirely different body than the one we have been
listening to in late months. This is not said in malice, but in plain fact.[8]

The intellectuals' darling among critics, composer Virgil Thomson, was
never very fond of what he called "the Wow! technique" by conductors—at
the end of Mitropoulos's debut concert, Thomson's unnamed companion of
the evening turned to the critic and remarked: "My, he must be tired!"—but
Thomson acknowledged that the Greek visitor had "succeeded beyond any
imaginable success." He then tempered his praise with a seemingly gratu-
itous sourness, saying that the Greek simply made "a dull Strauss piece interesting . . . and a dullish Beethoven symphony vaguely exciting":

> he merely lifted them out of their semi-oblivion and used them as what
> the theatrical world calls "vehicles." It was interesting to hear what he
> could do *with* the Strauss, less interesting to hear what he did *to* Bee-
> thoven. . . . Nevertheless, a really good time was had. Mr. Mitropoulos
> conducts the wrong pieces magnificently, shows them a whale of a
> time. This listener had a whale of a time, too. Maybe that is the right
> way to conduct second-class works. It will be interesting to hear what
> he does *with* or *to* Mozart, Schubert, or Debussy.[9]

The next wholly new program was given first on December 26. Violinist Albert Spalding joined the orchestra for the Sibelius Violin Concerto;
also performed was Mitropoulos's string-orchestra arrangement of the Beethoven Op. 131 string quartet, which was received rapturously by the audience but which occasioned the usual sniffy responses from the critics.
"One marveled at what the conductor did," wrote Olin Downes in his *Times*
notice, "and then one asked oneself why on earth he did it."

Midway through the New York engagement, Mitropoulos submitted to
a formal interview by feature writer Ross Parmenter of the *Times*. News
had just arrived that the under-gunned Greek forces had trounced the Black
Shirt legions on the Albanian front, sending them reeling in a series of ferocious counterattacks. Mitropoulos was not gloating (at least not publicly;
it is difficult to imagine that he did not feel glad in his heart); indeed, he
cautioned that the Italians were as good fighters as any in Europe when de-
fending their own soil—they simply weren't eager to spill their blood in
the name of Mussolini's dreams of territorial expansion.

Parmenter solicited, and duly received, the now-traditional story about
how Mitropoulos turned from religious orders to the podium "because they
wouldn't let me have a little harmonium in my cell" (readers in New York

gobbled up the story with the same eagerness as those in Minneapolis had four years earlier), then went on to give a sharp sketch of the man he was interviewing:

> Yet Mr. Mitropoulos still suggests a monk, for he has the deep-set eyes and the lean cheeks of an ascetic, and although he is only 44, his hair has retreated so that only a tonsure remains. But perhaps it would be more exact to say that he suggests an early Renaissance humanist such as Holbein might have drawn, for like those humanists, though he still carries the stamp of an almost medieval religious background, he is also a free-thinker, an internationalist, a man of wit, and one who is at home in the world of affairs.[10]

In addition to an unfamiliar work by Richard Strauss, Mitropoulos included a wide range of novel works that were generally well received. Most significant of the lot was Alexander Zemlinsky's 1933 Sinfonietta. After fleeing Vienna in 1938, Zemlinsky had settled in New Rochelle, New York, and had largely disappeared from public awareness. He was known, if at all, primarily as Arnold Schoenberg's brother-in-law and as a teacher. Little of his music had been performed outside Europe, the Sinfonietta not at all. The work comes close to the ambiguous tonality of early Schoenberg but is still comfortably Viennese in idiom, and the New York audiences appreciated it for that quality. In this as in many other instances, Mitropoulos was far ahead of his time—not until the 1980s, when most of Zemlinsky's output became available on recordings, did the musical establishment reevaluate his standing and acknowledge that he was indeed a significant figure of the period between the world wars.

The spring 1941 season started with a January 2 world-premiere performance of Nicolas Nabokov's (cousin of the great writer Vladimir) *Sinfonia biblica*. The score, sounding rather like a blend of Stravinsky, Milhaud, and Ernest Bloch, a tailor-made vehicle for Mitropoulos, was enthusiastically received, with the composer on hand to acknowledge several curtain calls. Adding to the richness of the program mix was Castelnuovo-Tedesco's Overture to *The Merchant of Venice,* a brilliantly orchestrated score played to the hilt. Again, Mitropoulos showcased works that were both contemporary and wholly accessible—yet again, he failed to light more than a passing flicker of interest.

Joining the orchestra for the concluding half of this January 2 concert was Jascha Heifetz, playing the Beethoven Violin Concerto. This time, in contrast to their hot-and-cold reception of the Beethoven Fourth, the critics praised Mitropoulos's handling of the orchestral part. Olin Downes concluded his review by saying: "Mr. Mitropoulos treated certain details in the score . . . in his own way, but the orchestral part has seldom sounded with such transparency and such release from the routine, which is sometimes considered synonymous with classicism."[11]

The final concert of Mitropoulos's four-week engagement featured two finely contrasted symphonies, Albert Roussel's bracing Third and Gustav Mahler's First. As with the first concert, both audience and orchestra joined to give a rousing standing ovation to the man who had brought to town the most stimulating concerts New Yorkers had heard in many a season. Mitropoulos's debut made national news as well; *Time Magazine* gave the event a full column under the subhead "Gifted Greek" and described with relish how Mitropoulos's "glabrous dome would shake like a furiously boiling egg."[12]

During the war years, the range of Mitropoulos's guest appearances broadened to include new orchestras and quite a bit of new repertoire. In June 1941, he conducted the New York Philharmonic for the first time at its summer home, Lewisohn Stadium. He returned to Manhattan in October, for two dates with Toscanini's NBC Symphony Orchestra, and again from December 13 to January 12, 1942, for a series of programs with the Philharmonic that included one American and one world premiere: the Piano Concerto of Carlos Chavez (Eugene List, soloist) and Aaron Copland's *Statements for Orchestra*.

By far the most significant concerts of this New York engagement were the December 21, 1942, premiere of David Diamond's Symphony No. 1 and the all-Busoni program given two weeks later. Diamond had begun composing his first symphony after returning to the United States from two years of study in Paris, with Nadia Boulanger, and had completed it at the artists' colony of Yaddo, where he resided in company with Katherine Anne Porter, Delmore Schwartz, and Carson McCullers. Once the score was complete, he sent telegrams to three conductors, offering them the premiere rights. Mitropoulos answered first, and in the affirmative.

Diamond was eager to hear the first rehearsal—it is no small event when a young composer first hears the New York Philharmonic play his music—but the occasion was compromised by a curious incident. Only a few bars into the Diamond rehearsal, Diamond saw a tall, familiar man leap out of his seat and bolt for the nearest exit. The fleeing man was Sergei Rachmaninoff, and Diamond was left with the uncomfortable conclusion that it was his music that had driven the legendary Russian from the hall. After the rehearsal, Mitropoulos sought an explanation from Rachmaninoff, who had expected the rehearsal to begin with his own Third Symphony.

"Please tell Mr. Diamond," Rachmaninoff explained, "that it was nothing personal and no reflection on his symphony. I simply don't have time to spend listening to new music by American composers."

Diamond's First Symphony was performed at a Sunday matinee concert to laudatory if not overly perceptive reviews. Diamond contributed a lengthy and eloquent essay on Busoni and his legacy, printed in the *Herald Tribune* on December 27, as an introduction to Mitropoulos's all-Busoni concert given on the following Sunday. Included were the *Indian Fantasy for Piano and Orchestra* (with Egon Petri), the Violin Concerto (with Szigeti), the

Suite No. 2 for Orchestra, and excerpts from *Doktor Faust*. Mitropoulos was praised for his advocacy, but the critical consensus remained what it was before (and to a large extent still is)—that Busoni was an "interesting" composer of agreeable, well-groomed, but not terrifically memorable scores.

At the summertime Ravinia Festival of 1942, Mitropoulos led the Chicago Symphony Orchestra for the first time, performing several personal favorites (Mendelssohn's Third, Schumann's Second, the orchestral inflation of Grieg's String Quartet in G Minor, and one fairly new work that was already making its way into the popular repertoire, the Fifth Symphony of Shostakovich. The Chicago reviewers, doubtless mindful of Cecil Smith's sharp-eyed analysis of Mitropoulos's faults and virtues, paid close attention to the Greek visitor's style. At least one critic thought Mitropoulos had heeded Smith's criticisms:

> Intensity can be enhanced by avoiding minor explosions. Mr. Mitropoulos, with all his nervous gymnastics, conveys that impression in his conducting, in general. He gives the impression that he could be a lot more nervously agitated if he didn't hold himself in, and this feeling he managed to inject into his direction of the Shostakovich symphony.[13]

Edward Barry, critic for the *Chicago Daily Tribune*, had become somewhat fixated on the Mitropoulos style and on its place both in musical culture in general and in the pantheon of contemporary podium stars in particular. On the night of July 1, he was nonplussed by the conductor's orchestration of Bach's Fantasia and Fugue in G Minor, finding it even more outlandish than the infamous Stokowski transcriptions:

> the terrific violence of the accents and the theatrical quality of the sudden pianissimos helped strengthen one's suspicions that this was an original composition and not a transcription at all. The fugue, as it approached its climax, became a succession of over-poweringly brilliant chunks of tone, each one hurled at the audience with demonic energy. The flow of the music—what one might call its horizontal quality—disappeared completely.[14]

Five days later Mr. Barry was back, gnawing the same rhetorical bones and identifying the conductor's Achilles' heel:

> When Mr. Mitropoulos deals with a score which has, legitimately and in its own right, the kind of tense, supercharged drama he loves, his conducting of it is good and perhaps great. It is only when he has to manufacture this drama himself, and set it to compete with and eventually destroy the inherent character of the piece, that he puts himself into difficult artistic positions.[15]

When Mitropoulos reached New York again, on December 17, 1942, an Associated Press reporter was waiting to interview him. In answer to the inevitable question about whether he was in line for the Philharmonic's directorship, Mitropoulos expressed a not-altogether-convincing lack of interest. "The schedule was too grueling," he said, adding "A musician has to stop and clean himself. If he does not, the dirt collects on him until finally he is not fit for the job. It is too much to rehearse and conduct four concerts a week."[16]

The opening concert, featuring Sergei Rachmaninoff playing his own *Rhapsody on a Theme of Paganini*, went very well indeed. For the second concert, however, both Virgil Thomson and Olin Downes brought out the rhetorical knives. While giving credit to Mitropoulos for conducting the first New York Philharmonic performance of Gershwin's *Rhapsody in Blue*, both leading critics found much to carp about in his readings of Bach's Orchestral Suite No. 3 and Brahms's Third Symphony.

Thomson prefaced his remarks by reminding his readers that Mitropoulos had so far given his New York audiences only music that was "laborious or unfamiliar," and that the real test would come when he "eventually got around to playing some music that was made of song . . . that simply cannot be manhandled." On this occasion, he did: Bach and Brahms.

> The result was what one had foretold. There was the same centralization of everything in the conductorial gesture and the same authoritarian control of every sound. The discipline was perfect. There was about as much spontaneity as there is in the building of a battleship. There was no song, no ease, no letting of the music have its say, no confidence in the ability of any instrumentalist to utter a brief phrase without the conductor molding it for him. . . . This kind of performance is diverting when the music played is not very interesting in itself. It is insupportable when the music is more than skin deep. It is fatal with the music of Brahms, which only blossoms at all under gentle treatment.[17]

Downes dismissed the Bach performance with quick contempt ("a good example of ways in which Bach should not be played"); then he too assailed the Brahms interpretation:

> [there were too] many nuances of tempo and shading where they are not indicated; [too] much italicizing of detail, hauled to the forefront instead of relegated to its proportionate place in the tone-picture can hardly be called characteristic of the composer's thought, whatever the conductor's idea of it.[18]

Mitropoulos began 1943 by directing the New York premiere of Roy Harris's *Folksong Symphony*. Really more a suite than a symphony, this painfully self-conscious exercise in art-for-the-masses comes about as close as any American composer managed to Socialist Realism. It was judged as the weakest of Harris's four symphonies at the time it was written, and his subsequent production of three more did nothing to change that verdict. Mitropoulos was at least given credit for presenting the work sympathetically. Of far greater value was the first complete performance of Aaron Copland's *Statements for Orchestra*, a fine example of the tough-fibered side of Copland's oeuvre and a work that Copland himself brought to Mitropoulos's attention.

For his final concert in New York, Mitropoulos put together a strong program and delivered it in top form: Haydn's "Military" Symphony (No. 100 in G), Prokofiev's Third Piano Concerto, and the brand-new Fourth Symphony of Ralph Vaughan Williams. Since one of the main critical guns fired at Mitropoulos during his declining years in New York was his supposed ineptitude in the classical repertoire, it is interesting to note that on this occasion the critics were unanimous in their praise for his Haydn. "He directed [it] with energy and all precision," wrote Virgil Thomson.[19] "In the aggregate," said Olin Downes in the *Times*, "this was a delightful and finished performance, one that did rare justice to the lustiness, the wit, and the effervescent humor of the music." About the Prokofiev concerto, which was both played and conducted by Mitropoulos, Downes said:

> The performance . . . was in all respects phenomenal and of a nature which made it clear that in this conductor the public has lost a conquering virtuoso. And yet we doubt if there is another conductor or virtuoso either who could accomplish what Mr. Mitropoulos achieved on this occasion. . . . He ate the music alive. He played horse with it, with the complete and reckless mastery of the one brain that contained every note of the score, and with exultant power and fire and prodigality of sarcastic energy that galvanized the score.[20]

Vaughan Williams's Fourth relates to the rest of his pastoral-pictorial oeuvre the way Sibelius's Fourth does to his—a grim work of the tautest, most inward-reaching construction; no crowd-pleaser, but rather a harrowing musical journey across a lonely granite-veined landscape. The Vaughan Williams work ends with a single massive, jagged chord which Mitropoulos weighted and shaped like a great fist slamming into plate glass. If he was temperamentally about as unsuited to the bucolic works of Vaughan Williams as any conductor could be, he was the ideal maestro for this recondite and savage opus, and his commercial recording of the Fourth is among his finest studio achievements.

Mitropoulos accepted no conducting engagements during the summer of 1943 when he was working for the Red Cross mobile blood unit. But in the summer of 1944, he appeared for the first time with the Philadelphia Orchestra at the orchestra's summer home, Robin Hood Dell. He opened the summer season, the Dell's fifteenth, with an all-Russian concert on June 20. Bad weather plagued the first two concerts—rain on one night and a sudden plunge from 78 degrees Fahrenheit to 65, in only two hours, for the next—but two thousand people sat through the rain and three thousand shivering souls sat through the chill. More seasonal conditions prevailed after the first two concerts, and the crowds ranged from five thousand to seven thousand each night—rather extraordinary, considering the trolley strike in the city and the two- or three-mile walk required for many of the attendees to reach the Dell. Almost nine thousand showed up for a gala concert featuring the Don Cossack Choir and Borodin's Second Symphony.

Chemistry between Mitropoulos and the Philadelphia players was strong. At his final concert, the musicians added their applause to that of the audience. After the final concert, the orchestra awarded Mitropoulos a gold-plated baton—the first such honor bestowed on any conductor in the thirteen-year history of the Robin Hood Dell concerts.

From Philadelphia, he journeyed to California and led five concerts at the Hollywood Bowl with the Los Angeles Philharmonic. This particular guest engagement found Mitropoulos in the most ebullient of moods (in newspaper photographs he wears an ear-to-ear grin); the movie addict was at last in Hollywood! Katina Paxinou, fresh from winning an Oscar for her performance as Pilar in *For Whom the Bell Tolls*, threw a grand party for Mitropoulos and introduced him to Gary Cooper, Errol Flynn, Mary Pickford, and Tallulah Bankhead, to name but four of the many celebrities in attendance. Mitropoulos enjoyed himself hugely, especially when a representative of Metro-Goldwyn-Mayer offered him one hundred thousand dollars to appear in a movie based on the life of Brahms (he was evidently to be cast as conductor Hans Richter, a rotund, heavily bearded man whom Mitropoulos resembled about as much as he resembled Mickey Mouse). Mitropoulos turned down the offer, not without regrets.

At the end of summer 1944, a press release from the Philadelphia Orchestra announced that Dimitri Mitropoulos had been appointed "permanent conductor" of the Robin Hood Dell summer concerts. As protocol dictated, Mitropoulos sent Eugene Ormandy a letter, expressing pleasure at having the chance to work with "your marvelous orchestra." Ormandy, who was going to make sure it remained *his* orchestra, wrote back: "I want you to know that it will be a source of great satisfaction to me to know that the standards for which we work during the winter will be carried on in the summer concerts."

In December 1944, Mitropoulos returned for the last time to the Boston Symphony. Koussevitzky was stung by suggestions, however well founded they might have been, that he was jealous of Mitropoulos's early success with the Boston Symphony, and hoped, by means of this Christmastime engagement, to prove that he was not afraid to let Mitropoulos back in front of his orchestra. Perhaps he was hoping that, this time, the Greek guest would not be such a novelty and would not garner the same extravagant praise he had enjoyed during his first two visits. If so, Koussevitzky was in for a disappointment.

Rudolph Elie, Jr., critic for the *Boston Herald*, wrote an energetic account of a Mitropoulos rehearsal, dubbing the visitor's style the "Quivering Ganglion school of conducting." Mitropoulos came on stage wearing an old blue sweater and gray flannel trousers, made his way to the podium with his "strange, bouncing gait," leaped upon it, waved his hands for silence and said: "Good morning, jehnl-men. Let's begin at letter *M*." Giving the men several seconds to find their place,

> Mr. Mitropoulos gathers himself together like a cougar stalking a deer, and, passionately humming the measure of music leading up to "M," he unleashes the most amazing physical energy ever contained (it would seem) in the body of a human being. From then until he stops the orchestra, which may be after ten bars or not until the movement's end, he is the personification of music itself. . . . He certainly holds the standing high jump among conductors. I swear I saw him spring four feet into the air without bending his knees first and he is certainly the only man on earth who can give you the impression he has spun completely around without moving his feet. The movement of his shoulders and his arms is incomparably expressive, while his crouch prior to driving home a climax is not less than hair-raising. Watching Mr. Mitropoulos conduct is, in fine, one of the most astonishing demonstrations of physical vigor, endurance, and ingenuity it is possible to imagine.[21]

For his programs, Mitropoulos had chosen a number of specialties (Rachmaninoff's Second Symphony, de Falla's dances from *The Three-Cornered Hat*, Mendelssohn's "Scottish" Symphony), a couple of novelties (Krenek's *Variations on a North Carolina Folk Song* and Morton Gould's *Spirituals*), and one classical work, Schubert's Second Symphony, that, strange to say, had never been programmed in Boston before.

Since the Boston critics had last seen Mitropoulos in 1938, there was ample opportunity to observe any changes in his style. They not only found him as arresting this time as he had been six years earlier, but they also detected a certain maturing, a fleshing-out, of his interpretations, and went out of their way to say so. Nor was their basic enthusiasm tempered, as the New York reviews were, with nit-picking. "His music making with the Boston Symphony Orchestra," wrote Rudolph Elie, Jr., in his review of the opening concert, "was a continuous miracle, a revelation, you might say, of a musical world of strange tempestuous beauty, a world which is not better than the one we know, but which is different and startling and fascinating." Elie continued:

> Take the "Scottish Symphony," for example. We are accustomed to hearing it in the most well-bred and elegant fashion (which is doubtless the way Mendelssohn intended for us to hear it). But Mr. Mitropoulos, evidently recalling that knuckle-end of Britain and the "sweep of its broad claymore" goes at the symphony as though it really were Scottish through and through, and gad, if it doesn't sound so. In any case, it suddenly comes alive and you find yourself completely immersed in it, not floating politely on top of it.[22]

Elie also wrote a vivid essay entitled "Mitropoulos, A Mighty Man is He, Part 2," based on a long interview with the conductor just before he left Boston. Mitropoulos could not keep his hands still when he talked, Elie wrote, giving the impression that he was "conducting" the dialogue, and that he was every bit as absorbed by the conversation as he would be interacting with a Mahler symphony.

At a distance, Elie thought, the conductor's fierce aquiline nose, severe jaw, and startlingly bald head gave him the imperious look of an Egyptian king. But at close range the severity of his features softened, and Elie was disarmed by the blueness of his eyes and the warmth of his expression. "The moment he looks at you his personality begins to radiate like an electric sunbowl, and you suddenly realize how it feels to be putty." His accent, Elie thought, was not so much Greek as it was pan-European, and his voice was both soft and pleasant, modulated very expressively with the emphasis of someone who truly loves good conversation and regards it as "both a necessity and a grace." He was also a superb listener: "he listens to what you say as though you were giving instructions on how to make a million dollars in three minutes."

> He loves to tell stories and tells them charmingly, characterizing every episode and all the dialogue while adding frank and witty asides. He finds the greatest delight in the witticisms, the gaieties and the frivolities of music, yet his approach to serious music is sober, even humble. This quality of humility pervades his character in every way, and he talks to waiters with the same warmth, the same friendliness and the same interest as he talks to university presidents. (I can't think of any more of a tribute to a man, either, than that he is beloved of waiters.)
>
> A conductor, he said, . . . is a universal catalytic agent for music. He may have his personal tastes in music, obviously, and he may have his personal convictions and preferences. But he must bear his responsibility as the interpreter of all music, and he must range the widest possible extent of the repertoire to give all worthy music its chance and all composers their hour.[23]

So great was Mitropoulos's success during this return engagement to Boston that rumors immediately resurfaced about his being groomed as Koussevitzky's heir. For a while, the prospects looked so good that Mitropoulos himself even began to hope and believe. Sadly, if he had gone to Boston (or Philadelphia or San Francisco or Chicago) his fate would probably have been very different from the destiny that waited for him in New York.

Mitropoulos returned to Philadelphia in the summer of 1945 and conducted before audiences of up to eleven thousand people. He once more scored a tremendous success with the Prokofiev Third Concerto, a work which he subsequently recorded with the Philadelphia Orchestra.

The rapport between Mitropoulos and the Philadelphians had grown remarkably during two short summer seasons. Marcel Tabuteau, first oboe of the orchestra beginning in 1928 and among the greatest woodwind play-ers of all time, once said to his friend Ben de Loache: "As for Stokowski, never did a conductor rise and live in the realm of the angels as did Stokowski . . . but the greatest conductor *qua* conductor I ever played under in my life was Dimitri Mitropoulos."[24] Eugene Ormandy had not yet be-come the icon he would be by the 1950s. There was, in fact, a great deal of restlessness among the players, especially those who had experienced the Philadelphia's glory days under Stokowski. From the summer of 1945 until Mitropoulos's Robin Hood Dell contract expired in 1948, there was real ag-itation in the orchestra to have Mitropoulos appointed music director. Or-mandy, of course, learned of this and stewed about it—he knew that if he lost Philadelphia, anywhere else he might go would be a demotion. While Ormandy could not blame Mitropoulos—who had nothing to do with the rumors and straw polls being taken—he did publicly complain that every summer when he returned to the Philadelphia podium after the closing of the Dell concerts, he had to "retune" the orchestra to correct its degener-ated state after Mitropoulos's visits.

In 1945, Mitropoulos came east during December and scored two tri-umphs with the Rochester Philharmonic before going to Manhattan for four outstanding concerts with the NBC Symphony, including the first New York performance of Alban Berg's Violin Concerto (with Joseph Szigeti as soloist). Even Virgil Thomson had to admit that this NBC concert was one of "unaccustomed distinction" and praised conductor and soloist for their "inimitable comprehension and care of execution."[25]

These NBC concerts were not without incident. Toscanini happened to drop by during rehearsal for the Berg concerto. He reacted to the music by having a temper tantrum, storming backstage, gesturing toward Mitropou-los and Joseph Szigeti, and screeching: "What are those two bald heads doing there?? What are those two bald heads doing??" Exactly what they had been engaged to do, replied the orchestra's management. Toscanini was hustled out of the studio, still fuming and spewing Italian invective; when he had calmed down a few days later, he asked the NBC Symphony's librarian to send a copy of the Berg score to Riverdale, presumably so he could study it. How much interest Toscanini actually had in this atonal masterpiece is conjectural; he certainly did not attempt to conduct it, then or ever.

A new theme appears in Mitropoulos's letters by the end of World War Two. Monetary constraints and wartime personnel problems had forced him to attempt prewar standards of performance with constantly chang-ing musicians and curtailed rehearsal time. The cumulative strain had begun to show by the war's final year. Parallel to this contraction of scope in Minneapolis, Mitropoulos was now regularly conducting three of Amer-ica's finest orchestras (four, in the year he went back to Boston), and no mat-ter how great his loyalty to Minneapolis, the contrast between what he could achieve there and what he could achieve in Boston or Philadelphia was gradually having an effect. A decided restlessness surfaced in one of his first letters to Katy following the reestablishment of regular mail service to Greece:

> I lead the life of an unhappy dog, to whom a wonderful juicy bone is presented each time right at his nose. He smells it, he looks forward to the enjoyment, and at the last minute someone takes it away from him. That is just how it is with me, to have those wonderful instruments at my disposal, to see the possibility of a perfect performance, and to remain unsatisfied because of lack of time to fulfill what I dream.
>
> In spite of my evident success, there has not yet been an opportunity for me to go away from Minneapolis and have permanently one of the big four orchestras. Not that mine is not good, especially trained with my blood, but the others are much better and are in towns where the musical *niveau* is higher. I never stop hoping. I only wish that if such a thing ever occurs, it will happen before I am too old and unable to suck this wonderful bone.[26]

CHAPTER THIRTEEN

There Were Giants . . .

Never before, or since, has the American public heard so much truly great recreative music making as it did during the so-called Golden Age of Conducting, that period of cultural history—lasting approximately from 1910 to the mid-1950s—when titans bestrode the podiums of the land, and the popular image of the superstar conductor coalesced from equal parts of Stokowski, Toscanini, and Koussevitzky. These men looked, spoke, and acted as the public thought conductors should. With the advent of electrical recording technology in the mid-1920s, the consumer could actually hear the tonal qualities these conductors drew from their ensembles—subtleties of color, nuance, and dynamics which could only be dimly suggested by acoustic recordings. Moreover, in circumstances that today seem unbelievably utopian, the interested citizen had only to turn on his or her radio to hear the great ones "live."

In the nineteenth century, most conductors were regarded as time keepers and traffic cops. The late-romantic era did have its prima donnas, to be sure, such as Mahler, von Bülow, and the incomparable Artur Nikisch, but relatively few music lovers actually were able to experience their art in person; one read about these gentlemen, one heard stories, but unless one actually lived near the cities where they practiced their art, one did not experience the music they made.

By 1940, all that had changed. Stokowski was shaking hands with Mickey Mouse on movie screens across the nation, and his wonderfully hammy performance opposite Deanna Durbin in the 1937 film *One Hundred Men and a Girl* had actually saved Universal Pictures from bankruptcy. Toscanini, as his sycophants never stopped reminding people, was aloof from such nonsense; in the name of musical purity, he was able to rage at his terrified musicians like a thwarted six-year-old and be considered the greater artist for it. Koussevitzky seemed, in some ways, the most Olympian of the lot, if only because nobody could understand half the things he said; he ruled Boston as a benevolent dictator.

When *Coronet Magazine* ran a special feature on conductors in its August 1939 edition, the piece was unabashedly entitled "Gods of the Stick." To the public, these were not mere mortals—they were supernatural beings who lived in a rarified realm of glory, adulation, instant sexual

165

gratification (at least in the case of Stokowski and Toscanini), and material luxury. They could, and often did, behave like perfect swine, but because they were great artists, the rules of behavior that bound the average earthling did not apply to them. And all they really did was stand in front of an orchestra and *wave their hands*! Small wonder that so many ordinary people drew the shades, locked the doors, cranked up their Victrolas to full volume, and waved a pencil in time with the records, just to indulge, for a few glorious moments, in the fantasy of being Toscanini or Stokowski.

This aura of mysterious grandeur was sustained, in part, because no major practitioner of the podium art ever talked much about it. When asked a direct question about his job, Toscanini's customary response was a growl of Italian invective; Stokowski, when an interviewer asked blunt questions about what he did in front of an orchestra, tended to deliver whimsical *non sequiturs* instead of straight answers. He at least wrote a book (*Music For Us All*, 1943), but in between his breathless descriptions of Tibetan monks chanting prayers and J. S. Bach composing fugues, he too talked about the conducting profession as though the only proper response the layperson could make was humility before the ineffable.

Dimitri Mitropoulos, too, could be a showman selling the music to his audience, and his podium style was among the wildest-looking, the most literal physical representation of the music, of any conductor in the world.

But unlike the other demigods, he did write and speak about his profession, not only in terms the public could understand but also, on occasion, by means of analogies that angered and alienated his colleagues. The tenor of his many remarks, both as responses to interviewers' queries and in the form of articles that appeared in magazines, provides an accurate and detailed picture of how Mitropoulos viewed himself in relation to his profession, and how he viewed that profession itself.

To the public at large, he often said, the conductor appears to be a very fortunate man indeed. All the advantages are his. When a pianist hits the wrong keys, when the French horn sounds a clam, most of the audience is aware of that mistake instantly—a telepathic wave of embarrassment sweeps through the hall. But the conductor performs with his back to the audience; if he gives a wrong cue and an audible mistake results, it is the player who gets blamed, not the conductor. At the end of the performance, although he alone has contributed nothing audible to the proceedings, it is the conductor who receives and acknowledges the applause.

"Definitely," wrote Mitropoulos in his essay "The Making of a Conductor," "the role of conductor looks attractive. It appears not only easy but gratifying, in a cowardly way, and if you add to that his opportunity to satisfy the natural human desire to be 'the boss,' it is not surprising that many young people ask what they must do to become conductors."[1] Indeed, that sort of question popped up so often, and the public image of the superstar conductor eventually became so outlandish, that Mitropoulos coined a word for the whole phenomenon: "conductomania."

There was a hidden price for that position, Mitropoulos declared—the conductor should, in fact, work harder and study more than any of his players. No one even had the right to stand in front of an orchestra, he averred, without first having proven himself as a performer on at least one instrument. "In other words, he has to prove his ability to recreate a work from beginning to end and to communicate it to an audience before he can hope to communicate it to an orchestra." His own instrument, the piano, was especially useful because of its polyphonic possibilities, its ability to give experience in dealing with many simultaneous musical voices and complex rhythmic patterns, but any other instrument would do.

As for the mechanical aspects of his profession—the standard inventory of gestures used to start and stop the orchestra, to cue entrances, to indicate rhythm, and to control dynamics—"they are the simplest part of a conductor's equipment, and they can be learned in half an hour. But that is not conducting!"

To project a piece of music faithfully, the conductor should also have as much contextual knowledge as possible about the cultures in which various composers lived. What ideas influenced them? What books did they read? What political circumstances had impact upon their lives? Broad, deep, general cultural knowledge was a hidden ingredient to good interpretations. In this assertion, Mitropoulos was taking a stand at polar opposites from Toscanini, who insisted that everything one needed to know about a piece of music was in the score. "To some people, this is about Napoleon," he once snarled to an interviewer, referring to the score of Beethoven's "Eroica," "and to some it's about Hitler or Mussolini; but to me, it's just *allegro con brio!*"[2]

Such broad knowledge, Mitropoulos insisted, was also necessary for yet another aspect of the conductor's job: that of evaluating and selecting for presentation contemporary works that had not yet stood the test of time.

> The best conductors, I think, are those who have the coordinated ability to think musically and convey it simultaneously through motions, by the intensity of their thought and by their establishment of a rapport with their men. Those who have this gift will make conductors. Without it, one may become a fine scholar, a musicologist, a composer—but never a good conductor.[3]

For any glory-besotted young musician who dreamed of becoming the next Stokowski or the next Toscanini, Mitropoulos had harsh words: "I will advise him to forget about it entirely!"

In the first place, one cannot deliberately set out to become a conductor; that ambition produces the same sort of conductor as the ambition to be a professional politician produces senators. There is little room at the top and so few opportunities for advancement that to have such an ambition almost assures a life of frustration and bitterness, a life which might otherwise be productively and happily spent in some other form of musical activity.

Mitropoulos cautioned, "Not many conductors are needed, really. But good musicians, on the other hand, are always needed."

A person consumed by ambition to become a famous conductor, Mitropoulos concluded in his essay, is embarked on a quest for power rather than a quest for musical excellence, and " a hidden lust for power . . . is a devastating thing."

Setting aside for a moment the obvious fact that Dimitri Mitropoulos's patron saint was Francis of Assisi, the philosophical foundation from which the Greek conductor operated, his deepest principles as summarized in these remarks, precluded his treating *any* orchestra, even the New York Philharmonic at its most thuggish and intractable, in a tyrannical manner. From Mitropoulos, such an attitude would be patently hypocritical, unsustainable, and would be understood as such by the musicians; for better or worse, he was trapped within his own philosophical principles no less than by the innate gentleness of his character. That his beliefs and personality could leave him vulnerable was something he understood early in his career and accepted without reservation.

Indeed, from the earliest days of that career, Mitropoulos carried two quotations in his wallet. One of course was from St. Francis: "God grant that I may seek rather to comfort than to be comforted, to understand rather than to be understood, and to love rather than be loved." The other was from Socrates: "If I must choose between doing an injustice and being unjustly treated, I will choose the latter."

How this philosophy related specifically to conducting was addressed by Mitropoulos in an interview with a Greek magazine correspondent soon after he moved from Minneapolis to New York:

> The conductor does not stand alone on the podium; he finds himself between the orchestra and the audience. He can move his listeners by the performed work only if he has previously comprehended each musician as an individual human being, at the same time that he leads the orchestra as an entity. I believe he can do this only if he steps down from the podium and communicates to his musicians the feeling that he is not a dictator but an apostle. The interpretation represents a communal effort; it requires unity, and in no case does it move from the conductor's baton to a pack of subjugated slaves. Only when the conductor makes an obeisance full of love to every musician, only when he shows an open-hearted interest in each musician's psychological and personal situation, can he make the orchestra into a true medium for the composer's message. Only in this manner can he hope to carry the audience along with him and establish communication. In the history of music, there are only two main types of conductor: the tyrant and the colleague. For myself, I choose to be the second type.[4]

When Mitropoulos spoke of "An obeisance full of love to every musician," he was venturing into metaphor as well as metaphysics. In numerous interviews during his American career, Mitropoulos revealed the sensual side of his nature in his often surprisingly explicit references to the sublimated sexuality of a conductor's relationship with an orchestra—that the leader and the musicians engaged in a form of intercourse, which in effect produced a third party, a "child," in the form of the musical performance itself. Each gives to the other, he would say: the conductor attempts like a skillful lover to draw forth the innermost responses of the ensemble, and the players respond with music-making that surpasses their ordinary level of accomplishment. From the procreative heat of this exchange springs a great interpretation.

By working with his orchestras from these moral and philosophical bases, Mitropoulos believed he was not only being true to his own nature and to the nature of music as a communicative art, but also that he was furnishing an example of total commitment, total devotion. He took it as a given that intelligent musicians would understand this and respond in kind. In Minneapolis, for the most part, they did. In New York, even among the many players who understood full well what Mitropoulos was doing and why, the response was often grudging and tainted with tough-guy contempt.

No one, in either orchestra, ever accused Mitropoulos of wasting time or of being less than prepared. The power of conviction he strove for by conducting from memory would have backfired if the orchestra personnel had felt that they were being asked to do more than their fair share as a consequence of that idiosyncrasy. An orchestra resents nothing more than the shabby spectacle of a conductor burning up valuable rehearsal time to do his basic homework. Even the Philharmonic players who were glad to see Mitropoulos leave could never accuse him of that sin.

Some artists maintain one set of standards when speaking to the press but present a less idealistic image when talking shop with their colleagues. Mitropoulos did not. Examples of his consistency abound. When Katy Katsoyanis wrote in the waning days of 1939 to inform Mitropoulos that his place at the Athens Conservatory had been taken by Swiss conductor Hermann Scherchen, Mitropoulos replied in a manner that not only demonstrates his customary respect for colleagues but also shows how clear-eyed he was about his own weaknesses as a conductor, how determined he was to improve:

> At last Athens has a real conductor: Scherchen! I was sure that you'd like him and I've no doubt you'll realize how great he is, what immense knowledge he has, and how far removed I am myself from his fantastic technical knowledge. He has the most important technical resources for being a conductor, which unfortunately, in spite of all my efforts, I will never acquire. That's why I never believed that I could have any claim to being one of the really great artists. What makes me appear to approach them is the intensity of my expression, my logical rhythmic

construction, and the convincing forcefulness I have sometimes, when I'm at my best. But deep down I'm always fighting all kinds of natural deficiencies . . . with which God has endowed me.[5]

In a profession notable for the bloated—and in the cases of Herbert von Karajan and Leonard Bernstein, truly monstrous—egos of its practitioners, Mitropoulos was capable of writing to composer Leon Kirchner:

> I wish you good luck in your new conducting assignments and that you also get the delight of that unusual and cowardly occupation—to lead other people to play for you and perform compositions that are written by others. That is why most people prefer to be conductors rather than composers or instrumentalists. In spite of everything that you may have as an argument, there will always remain this one: that with a little personality and salesmanship, it is the easier way out to be a conductor. I always realized this fact. That is why I never denied my embarrassment at being promoted by the fates or destiny to follow this profession. One cannot be humble enough before such a privilege of getting glory and acclaim, not only from using someone else's emotions, but also from having someone else to express them for you.[6]

Violinist Louis Krasner, the Minneapolis Symphony Orchestra's concertmaster during the last five years of Mitropoulos's tenure, remembered an equally astounding conversation he had with the conductor following a sensational performance of Rachmaninoff's Second Symphony, an intensely melodramatic work which Mitropoulos loved unapologetically and passionately. On this occasion, Mitropoulos had been unable to wriggle out of a postconcert dinner party being given by an important patron of the orchestra. Krasner noticed, as he circulated through the crowd, that the conductor had disengaged himself from all well-wishers with unseemly haste and was now ensconced in a corner, brow thunderously furrowed, palpably uninterested in his surroundings.

Finally the hostess approached Krasner and said: "Will you please go talk to Dimitri and see what's wrong? Nobody else can."

Krasner went over to the corner and said, "The concert was a great success, but these good people are worried that you seem so concerned. Are you dissatisfied?"

"No, no," replied Mitropoulos, shaking his head as though clearing away cobwebs. "Tonight it went very well." He hesitated for a moment before continuing, a look of genuine anguish passing over his features. "The Rachmaninoff was wonderful. It's just that I feel that tonight I've given them too much of myself. I feel like a prostitute. I get swept up in the music, but then afterwards, I feel so embarrassed, so guilty."[7]

Yet he also saw noble purpose in his work. Not long after this incident, Krasner was present when an elderly woman came backstage after the concert and grasped Mitropoulos in a familiar way as he was on his way into his dressing room. After a moment's hesitation, the conductor returned her embrace with a smile of recognition. It transpired that this woman was from Greece and had been a friend of the Mitropoulos family.

"Dimitri," she said happily, "you recognized me!" Turning to the room at large, she gestured expansively and announced: "I haven't seen him all these years since the days of the priests! You know that as a young man he went to Mount Athos!" Turning back to the conductor, she wagged her finger remonstratively at him. "Look at you now! And you were supposed to become a priest! What happened?"

Mitropoulos smiled broadly and pointed to the podium: "Well, here I am and there is my pulpit."

Until the start of World War Two, the programs Mitropoulos had been offering his Minneapolis audiences were generally praised for their freshness, variety, and balance—however unconventional the latter quality may have been from time to time. Beginning with Frances Boardman's reaction to the March 1, 1940, program (the one subdivided into no fewer than eighteen titled sections), one detects a gradual increase in negative criticism directed at the programming. Did the conductor sporadically lose the internal compass that should have guided his selections of pieces and their juxtaposition? The criticism in Minneapolis would never be as severe or as carping as the New York notices eventually became, but its presence was constant enough to raise questions about the conductor's programming philosophy. Yet postmortem discussions of Mitropoulos's career that assume he had little basic instinct for programming are surely oversimplifications.

Part of the problem was that Mitropoulos seemed to regard each composition as a discrete entity to be performed and digested by the audience as a thing-unto-itself, not necessarily related to what came before or after it, either on the same evening or within the context of an entire season. He did *not* sit down and methodically plan a whole season's music around a single theme, not even around a single school or a single composer. His programs could be didactic, lopsided, even hectoring in their weight and distribution. If three obscure or difficult works happened to take his fancy on a given week, then the audience would hear all three, bang-bang-bang. If the majority of his listeners happened to be on the same wavelength as the conductor, so much the better. If not, too bad.

Mitropoulos was keenly aware of the criticisms leveled at his programming, and he had a ready explanation. He sometimes responded with an uncharacteristic trace of testiness, simply declaring: "A concert is not a place to relax. You (meaning the listener) have to give your collaboration. A good audience listens hard."[8]

Mostly, he was fighting against what he called the ghetto-ization of the new and the unfamiliar. He instinctively saw where this could lead—where in fact it *has* led in today's abysmal, boring, self-defeating emphasis on the tried and true—and he felt morally obligated to oppose the phenomenon:

The position which has been entrusted to me also entails an educational task. I feel strongly responsible for the public's taste. By introducing contemporary works, I want to familiarize all with the expression of our time in music. . . . To someone like myself, who wanders through the forest of music year in and year out, and is privileged to serve as guardian of the giant trees, it is a duty not only to care for those trees, but also to devote time, effort, and affection on those that are still fighting to find their place in the sun. It is an obligation to be undertaken gladly, sometimes even against public judgment.[9]

Sometimes the conductor intentionally threw in programs designed and touted as audience-pleasers, such as an all-Puccini evening featuring soprano Eleanor Steber. As John Sherman remarked, "there were a few occasions when he pleased his hearers so assiduously . . . that some suspected he was banking good will against the day of withdrawals."[10] It was one thing to create a buffer of good will to cushion the shock of his next evening of Krenek or Schoenberg, but some of his programs just seem capricious (those seven overtures back-to-back, or two Strauss tone poems together, as if they were movements of a mega-symphony).

The balance sheet, in Minneapolis at least, was summarized by John Sherman:

twelve years of stimulating, irritating, uplifting, exhausting concerts . . . programs of unprecedented severity and thorny content, of music and conducting that made the city for a time both a laboratory and an international capital of contemporary, experimental and unconventional music. . . . It is not always comfortable to live with a genius, but to take and to understand what he gives is a lucky opportunity for those who want to grow.[11]

Maybe so, but Mitropoulos's championship of the unfamiliar in time generated a curious backlash. Going on the theory that what the audiences didn't know wouldn't hurt them (or the ticket sales), the MSO's management finally stopped identifying "first performances" as such on the program notes, having seen plenty of evidence that the mere appearance of an asterisk or two after a work's title was enough to make many listeners raise their intellectual shields before hearing a single note.

Ironically, today's music lovers can only feel great envy for the listeners in Minneapolis in 1940 or for those in New York a decade later. What a contrast Mitropoulos provides to the bland, predictable routines of most contemporary orchestras, whose directors have succumbed to the formula that pits three comfortable works against, at most, one unfamiliar one; music directors who, whether through intellectual laziness or a craven capitulation to the know-nothingism of their local boards, seem to have infinitely less knowledge of accessible twentieth-century repertoire than does any moderately experienced record collector.

What's more, if Dimitri Mitropoulos gave his audiences heavy doses of Krenek and Schoenberg, he also gave them Vaughan Williams, Mahler, Gould, Malipiero, Respighi, Milhaud, and a host of other eminently listenable composers, artists who require no more of an audience than the sort of willingness to stretch one's taste buds that makes Chinese restaurants so popular. Can anyone today seriously maintain that Mitropoulos's eccentric programming philosophy, for all its fretful asymmetry, was not better for the institution of music as a whole than today's suffocating emphasis on the same One Hundred Masterpieces, with its gradual effect of debasing both the masterpieces it relies on and the very act of concertgoing itself?

Recording activity in the United States had become all but moribund by the mid-1930s as radio gained overwhelming acceptance in American households. RCA Victor's contract with the Minneapolis Symphony Orchestra lapsed at about the time Ormandy left town. By the year Mitropoulos arrived however, the domestic recording industry had started to show signs of renewed life.

Yet it was also radio exposure that breathed vitality into the classical music scene; tens of thousands of listeners, having grown fond of hearing the New York Philharmonic, the Boston Symphony, and the Philadelphia Orchestra during their weekly live broadcasts, began to seek their favorite compositions in a permanently replayable format. The availability of very inexpensive add-on turntables, crude but rugged devices that just plugged into the radio, spurred an ever-growing demand for records.

As the recording industry's two giants, RCA and Decca, forged ahead, the also-ran Columbia label entered the doldrums in 1937. Its classical catalogue was dependent on European sources which were rapidly drying up as European commerce girded itself for war. A dramatic turnaround came in 1938, however, when William S. Paley of the Columbia Broadcasting System spent seven hundred thousand dollars to acquire the entire Columbia Records operation. Paley immediately began signing up every major orchestra in the United States that was not already under contract with RCA: the San Francisco Symphony under Pierre Monteux, the Cleveland Orchestra under Rodzinski, the All American Youth Orchestra under Stokowski, the Chicago Symphony under Stock, and, beginning in 1940, the Minneapolis Symphony under Mitropoulos.

If by 1948—the year the long-playing record was introduced to the U.S. market by Columbia—the record-buying public had come to the conclusion that Mitropoulos and the Minneapolis orchestra were a less-than-first-rate attraction, the blame can be laid squarely at Columbia's door. RCA's engineers had at least been able to achieve reasonably decent sound in their Northrop Auditorium sessions with Ormandy, but it had taken a lot of tweaking and experimenting—the sheer size of the hall militated against its use as a recording venue, and before the installation of the new acoustical shell the walls and ceiling of the place soaked up both volume and tone color.

174 THIRTEEN

While RCA's engineers had eventually found the secrets to obtaining decent recordings in Northrop, that same secret would elude Columbia's engineers like the Loch Ness Monster—it was there, somewhere, but nobody was quite sure how to coax it forth. As heard in their 78-rpm incarnations, most recordings made in Northrop sound awful: flat, dry, nasal, boxy, one-dimensional, drained of tone color, and so restricted in dynamic range that in half of them the Minneapolis Symphony does not sound as though it had either a percussion section or double-basses. Columbia evidently hoped the public would not notice, but the public did. America's foremost record collector at that time was critic David Hall, whose magnificent encyclopedic work *The Record Book*—a fourteen-hundred-page tome describing and evaluating every classical recording available as of late 1947—was the bible of record collectors in the 78 era. Hall had this to say in his introductory remarks:

> Turning back to America once more, the Greek conductor of the Minneapolis Symphony Orchestra, Dimitri Mitropoulos, is one of those who have suffered scandalously at the hands of the recorders. Still in the prime of life, Mitropoulos's brilliance as conductor, pianist and all-around musician is such that he could become the Toscanini of his generation. Yet, of the very considerable catalog of recordings he has made for the Columbia label in Minneapolis, only one comes anywhere near doing justice to his work, namely the Mahler First Symphony. The others almost without exception are marred by faulty instrumental balance, lack of room resonance, or both. This is not to say that Mitropoulos himself has not been without fault; for there are times when his readings seem erratic and explosive, but we have heard too many superb concert hall performances by this artist to have any other conviction but that most of his Columbia discs are a gross misrepresentation. As this book is being written, Mr. Mitropoulos has switched his allegiance to Victor, and remembering the excellent discs which the company made with the Minneapolis Symphony under Eugene Ormandy, we are inclined to be quite optimistic.[12]

If only Mr. Hall's prediction had come true, Mitropoulos might today be accorded some of the respect and admiration he deserves. The truth is that, after he took over the New York Philharmonic, which was under contract to Columbia instead of RCA Victor, Columbia ranked him and treated him and his orchestra as second-stringers, while spotlighting the glitzier and more profitable Ormandy-Philadelphia team. Mitropoulos rarely got to record what he wanted to, and of the discs Columbia did make with him, a scandalous percentage have him and the Philharmonic relegated to the role of accompanist for more bankable solo performers.

As for the reasons that so many of the Minneapolis Columbias sound wretched, theories abound. One possibility is that the then-new Columbia Masterworks series suffered under the leadership of Moses Smith, whose background was musical (he was a former Boston newspaper critic) rather than technical—but such a man, surely, could not have listened to Columbia's products without realizing instantly how manifestly inferior they were to RCA's orchestral recordings, to say nothing of what had been done before the war by EMI and Telefunken.

At the time, when reviewers such as Hall took them to task, Columbia tried to blame the inferior sound of its records on a wartime shortage of high-grade record shellac, and certainly that was a contributing factor. A likelier culprit was Columbia's corporate goal at the start of the 1940s: to market its records at a retail cost of one dollar per disc, effectively undercutting RCA and Decca. To trim overhead costs, Columbia sent equipment to Northrop Auditorium that was utilitarian rather than state of the art; the engineers—though competent—were not the best or most experienced in the field and some had had little or no experience in making commercial recordings before they went to Minneapolis.

Indeed, most of the recording engineers Columbia sent to Minneapolis were "radio men" whose paradigm for orchestral sound was that obtainable on the inexpensive AM radios so many Americans had hooked up to their record players. This meant a dry, assertive, upper-mid-range sound, with no real thought of realistic bass timbres or subtleties of hall ambience, which the average AM radio simply could not reproduce. Played on a cheap add-on turntable, through the speaker of an inexpensive AM radio, the Minneapolis Symphony's recordings at least came through loud and clear, and that, apparently, was all Columbia's engineers cared about.

Almost as harmful was Columbia's decision to cut production costs still further by simply leaving out some of the costlier ingredients in its record-making compound, such as silver nitrate. This decision resulted in 78s that were noisy, pinched and coarse in tone, narrow in dynamic range, and prone to excessive wear—discs which, given the yo-heave-ho state of home playback equipment, would audibly deteriorate after only a few playings. In fact, when Columbia started reissuing their old Minneapolis recordings in the then-new LP format, from 1948 to about 1951, as a stopgap to fill their catalogue until new recordings could be made, the original matrixes were cleaned up, quiet high-grade vinyl was used for the pressings, and many of those same performances turned out to be surprisingly listenable, even though the endemic dryness and lack of ambience remained as annoying as ever.

Whatever the reasons, most Columbia recordings of the Minneapolis Symphony simply cannot be taken as accurate documentations of what the Minneapolis Symphony actually sounded like in the concert hall. Unfortunately and frustratingly, there do not seem to be any extant air-check recordings of live Minneapolis performances even though radio broadcasts were made during much of Mitropoulos's tenure.

Mitropoulos was no help, either. Recording was a new game to him—he was forty-four before he ever faced a recording microphone. He seems not to have been averse to it on principle (as Toscanini was, much to the detriment of his legacy), and he understood the value of recordings as good advertisements for the orchestra, but he found the stop-and-start nature of the process both alien and irritating. When Mitropoulos had built up a full head of steam on the podium, it was incredibly vexing for him to put the brakes on at four-minute intervals so that the engineers could cue up a new recording master.

As David Hall said in *The Record Book*, among the finest achievements in the Minneapolis discography was the Mahler First Symphony, waxed in 1940, before the wartime-shortages excuse became relevant. The finished product is intensely vital and very well played. This was the first recording of a work that has now become a repertoire staple, even with second-tier orchestras. The LP incarnation, circa 1950, is especially good; the taut, lithe playing gives no hint of the chaos that characterized the recording sessions. Even before the microphones were turned on, the MSO players were tense; they had not been in a recording session since the Ormandy days, and they were required to take off all metallic jewelry—watches, cufflinks, anything that might make an extraneous noise. Even the Minneapolis-to-Chicago train, the Chicago and Northwest *400 Streamliner*, scheduled to depart at noon, was delayed briefly so that the engineers could get a usable take of one more quiet passage. As for Mitropoulos, he was overwound to the point of detonation, and no matter how hard he tried, he kept conducting beyond the limit imposed by the engineers' stopwatches. A dozen acetate masters had to be scrapped for every side that was usable. By the end of the first two-hour session, the band was still bogged down midway through the first movement and Mitropoulos was verging on apoplexy.

Another factor made the Mahler sessions stressful. Mitropoulos had fought a long and frustrating battle with Arthur Gaines and the board of directors for their permission to make this particular recording. The MSO's management was skeptical to say the least—the project would cost the then-astronomical sum of twelve thousand dollars (about the cost of twenty minutes' studio time for a major orchestra today), and who would buy a Mahler recording anyway? As it turned out, lots of people: by 1945 the initial pressing was sold out and a second, larger, pressing had to be ordered. Between sales of the 78s and even brisker sales of the early LP version, the Minneapolis Symphony made a substantial profit.

Mitropoulos never saw a penny from this or any other Minneapolis recording. He donated his services, for the good of the orchestra and in the name of spreading the gospel of music. Not until 1946, when he conducted the accompaniment of duo-pianists Whittemore and Lowe's recording of the Poulenc Concerto for Two Pianos, did the conductor receive any remuneration for his services in the studio—the princely sum of five hundred dollars.

35   A gentle moment with Napoleon, Eleanor Peters's poodle, 1955. Although his lifestyle precluded personal pets, Mitropoulos had a Franciscan love for animals. Photo by Fred Plaut, courtesy Eleanor Peters.

33   Mitropoulos, John Corigliano (NYPO concertmaster), and Guido Cantelli, ca. 1950. Photo by Magnum Photos, Inc., courtesy Dorle Soria.

34   Studying a score, 1951. Photo by Susan Hoeller, courtesy Maxim Gershunoff.

31 Mitropoulos, Jenny Cullen, and Jim Dixon, 1951. Courtesy Jim Dixon.

32 Katy Katsoyanis, Mitropoulos, unidentified companion, and Jim Dixon, Italy, ca. 1950. In Maria Christopoulou's biography of the maestro, this photograph shows Katy's image obscured by a crude drawing of a huge, prickly cactus, undoubtedly revenge for Katy's attempt to block Christopoulou's research efforts. Courtesy Jim Dixon.

29 Making the ascent during a mountain-climbing expedition, mid-1940s. Courtesy Jim Dixon.

30 Mitropoulos and Jim Dixon, Twin Sisters Mountain, Colorado, summer 1949 or 1950. Courtesy Jim Dixon.

28   Mitropoulos studying a score on the front steps of Tapiola, the Colorado vacation home of William Cooper, ca. 1945. Courtesy Jim Dixon.

26   At the piano
rehearsing Krenek's
Third Piano Concerto.
Courtesy Jim Dixon.

27   Mitropoulos rehearsing
at the Goethe Festival, Aspen
1949.

24 Candid portrait, ca. 1945, inscribed to Monty Loucks. Courtesy Richard Frahm.

25 Mitropoulos with Nathan Milstein, Gregor Piatigorsky, and the MSO at the Goethe Festival, Aspen, 1949. Photo by Franz Berko, courtesy Aspen Music Festival.

22　Minneapolis Symphony rehearsal, early 1940s: Mitropoulos with Egon Petri and Joseph Szigeti. Courtesy Jim Dixon.

23　"Weekend with Music" program on CBS, ca. 1945. Left to right: Oliver Daniel, two unidentified guests, Mitropoulos, and Jim Fassett, announcer for NYPO radio concerts.

21　A studio portrait.

19   Mitropoulos studying a score—one of his favorite pictures of himself. Oliver Daniel collection.

20   In Minneapolis, 1940. Oliver Daniel collection.

17 Mitropoulos
and John (Buddy)
MacKay, ten-year-
old piano soloist
with the MSO, 1945.
Courtesy John
MacKay, Jr.

18 Mitropoulos and
John MacKay, Sr., prin-
cipal trombonist of the
MSO, ca. 1941. Courtesy
John MacKay, Jr.

16   Mitropoulos, in a portrait that shows his intense blue eyes.

CHAPTER FOURTEEN

American Friends, American Ways

As was the case for so many other immigrants before him, Mitropoulos felt energized and somewhat overwhelmed by America and its lifestyle. He plunged into this new culture without reserve, even managing to survive his first full Minneapolis winter with a smile that bespoke both stoicism and good sportsmanship. Some of his enthusiasm surfaced in a bubbly letter he wrote to Katy during the winter of 1938:

> Here is why America is better. There is everywhere an encouraging breath—for work, for morality. When they see you as a god, an apostle, a leader, you feel the need to be as pure as possible before people who are ready to adore you, to follow you, to respond to you. All these things seem childish in Europe. Here, even the gangsters have some glory, some idealism in them, and are a thousand times more interesting than the European *blasés*.[1]

By the time this letter was written, Mitropoulos had already begun to think about settling permanently in the United States. Wartime exigencies, along with some degree of uncertainty on Mitropoulos's part, made permanent citizenship difficult to obtain, so the conductor traveled to the U.S. Embassy in Winnipeg, where he obtained an emigrant visa that permitted him to live in the United States for an indefinite period. This arrangement worked well enough during the war years, and by the time the shooting had finished, it was manifestly clear to Mitropoulos that America would be his base of operations for the remainder of his career. He therefore applied for full citizenship, and on March 13, 1946, became a U.S. citizen. John MacKay, the MSO's first trombonist, stood up for him.

There was one thing in American culture that Mitropoulos loved more than anything else: the movies. He adored them, reveled in them, soothed his over-worked brain by slipping into a theater the way another man might slip into a warm bath. Sometimes he would call up a friend or two—including orchestra members, of course—and invite them along; often he would go alone at odd hours of the day or night and sit through double or even triple features. He was utterly, joyously, indiscriminate about what he watched—comedies, dramas, gangster sagas, monster movies—to him, all the Hollywood genres combined to form a bottomless stewpot of sensory impressions from which he gulped greedily. Given the rigors of his daily schedule—self-imposed or otherwise—and his intense dislike of parties and socialite small-talk, Mitropoulos's marathons of movie-watching became a condensed, streamlined way for him to absorb big dollops of American popular culture, for him to lose himself, as heedlessly and wide-eyed as a ten-year-old boy, in a whole smorgasbord of fantasies. The European intellectual who read Thomas Mann and Proust while waiting for a concert to begin, the somber hermit who pondered Kierkegaard in the wee hours in his spartan dorm room, could sit mesmerized through any new film that came his way, no happier with *Citizen Kane* than he was with the latest Hopalong Cassidy western. Movies, he often said, were to him a form of "canned life." Before the end of the 1938–1939 concert season, every ticket-seller and usher in Minneapolis was on friendly terms with the Maestro.

"When I go to the movies," he told one musician, "I can be anything I want to be. I can be a lover, a sailor, a hero, a cowboy. I can live all those lives I don't normally have."[2]

His favorite genre was the western. Horse operas were to him delightfully encapsulated morality plays, in which the entire Manichaean concept of good and evil was rendered down to its essence: the guys in black hats against the guys in white hats. Critic John Sherman occasionally went to the movies with Mitropoulos and always had a wonderful time. Sherman recalled how the conductor "chortled with naive delight" the first time he saw a cowboy hero leap from a second-story balcony onto the back of his horse.

Clarinetist Sigurd Bockman recalled:

The thing that remains vivid in my mind is how gung-ho he was to become American. I knew him when he had his first stick of chewing gum. He embraced avidly every experience that was part of American culture—I'm sure, if he had been alive in the Sixties, he would have gotten into rock and roll! He did everything he could to immerse himself in things that we took for granted—like double-feature movies. And he was intensely physically active while he was doing it, very hard to keep up with him—I never saw him climb a flight of stairs one at a time. He would always bound up two or three steps at a time.[3]

Eventually, Mitropoulos was coaxed from his gloomy dorm rooms on the University of Minnesota campus and ensconced in a more comfortable—but still far from luxurious—apartment located at 510 Groveland Street. Hostesses still found it all but impossible to lure him to any kind of dinner party, but the ordinary citizens of Minneapolis saw him often—walking to the local drugstore for cigarettes, waiting for a bus, standing in line for a movie, or going to church on Sunday. To the delight of Minneapolitans of all faiths, their illustrious and mystical conductor, the same man who had dwelt on legendary Athos and who always wore a silver Greek Orthodox cross on a chain next to his heart, became a regular member of the congregation of the Westminster Presbyterian Church. Calvinism, after all, was something he instinctively comprehended; more to the point, he very much liked the rhetorical style and personality of the Presbyterian church's pastor, Dr. Arnold Lowe, with whom he enjoyed many stimulating conversations.

When Mitropoulos arrived in Minneapolis, he made clear to the city's social establishment how he wanted to be treated: "Do you want me to be as much as possible a perfect musician or do you want me to be a society man? You can have an agreeable, entertaining conductor to decorate your dinner parties and you will also get bad music making. If you leave me alone to study my scores, you will have good music."[4] The word quickly got out to the city's prominent hostesses: if invited, he will probably not come; if he comes, you will probably wish he hadn't. By and large, to an extent that would seem blissful to a contemporary conductor, they left him alone.

Throughout his adult life, Mitropoulos tended to compartmentalize his friendships, perhaps consciously. There would be an enclave of friends in one part of town, another enclave six blocks away; the two would not mix socially, unless by accident, and might not even be aware of each other's existence. He did this not in order to play favorites, but because the arrangement gave him the most flexibility and control over his time and whom he spent it with. Those he did spend time with found him excellent company, as John Sherman recalled:

> With friends of his own choosing whom he liked, where the conversation took quick flight in speculation about music and the world, he was happy and talkative; his darting mind and deep sympathies, his keen logic and bold deductions, all making a breathtaking experience for those who talked to him—and tried to keep up with him. Against those who voiced fallacies and prejudices, he could quickly marshal an adroit and demolishing argument that would outpoint his adversary every step of the way.[5]

Mitropoulos was genuinely fond of Elbert Carpenter (founding chairman of the MSO's board of directors) and his wife, and would dine with them in their home at 314 Clinton Avenue on a weekly basis. These meals would always start with a favorite dish of the conductor's, a thick fish soup Mrs. Carpenter prepared carefully from scratch. The Carpenters' son, Leonard, carried into adulthood his own memories of those dinners: "His conversations were always interesting, because in addition to being a musician, he was really a philosopher—he had many theories about human points of view and human attitudes."[6] Sometimes in the summer, Mitropoulos would stay in a small guest house on the Carpenters' property. There was a baby grand piano in the cottage, and he would spend his mornings either studying scores or exercising on the lawn. In the evenings after supper, he would play a card game called Russian Bank with Mrs. Carpenter.

Lunch and dinner were the two meals Mitropoulos usually took on-the-run. He divided his attentions equally between high-class restaurants and neighborhood greasy spoons. He loved hamburgers (cooked rare), leg of lamb, and all manner of seafood and poultry dishes. His appetite was at times gargantuan, at other times, parsimonious. He sometimes displayed amusingly plebeian habits, such as dunking his dinner rolls in salad dressing.

His morning routine never varied, except, of course, when he was on tour. He rose every day at five in the morning; his breakfast consisted of two raw eggs (he punctured the shells and sucked them, as though they were oysters, straight down his gullet) and strong black coffee. He then stripped to his shorts and basked for thirty minutes under a sun lamp. This ritual complete, he lit the first of the day's two-and-a-half packs of cigarettes and addressed himself to score-study. Rehearsals at Northrop began at ten in the morning. Lunch would be taken somewhere on impulse—he might meet someone at a specific location downtown or he might ask his taxi driver to pull up beside a humble beanery that happened to take his fancy while he was driving by (the Minneapolis cabbies loved to have him as a passenger because he always tipped them ten dollars). The afternoon was again devoted to study. Sometimes he took a half-hour catnap around five in the afternoon, then got up either for dinner or for the concert, with dinner afterward, depending on his mood. On evenings when there was no concert, he either read for pleasure or went to the movies.

During the period when the conductor lived on the University of Minnesota campus, he became a familiar figure to the students and never failed to spend a few moments chatting with any who approached him. In April 1941, the student body paid a most unorthodox tribute to their favorite maestro by inviting him to a meeting of the campus Boogie Woogie Club to hear a piece that had been composed in his honor. When Mitropoulos was settled—sitting cross-legged on the floor surrounded by cute coeds in bobby sox—composers Ken Green and Sid Smith cued their dance band in the opening measures of "Beat Me, Dimitri (Eight to the Bar!)":

> A certain Maestro on his concert job
> Has to cater to a long-hair mob.
> He'd like to lead some boogie-woogie kicks
> But boogie-woogie and Bach don't mix.
> So when no one's about, the boys swing out
> And "beat me Dimitri!" are the words they shout.

Mitropoulos took it all in like a good sport, and when the applause died down, he took the microphone and thanked the students for their homage. "This is the most touching tribute I have received since I have been on campus," he began, and then—probably kicking himself mentally as he did so—he could not refrain from the same sort of honesty he displayed in rehearsals with his orchestra. "The song is very good, as far as it goes, but the same musical ideas could be carried out with more elaboration and improvement in the orchestration." At that point, he became apologetic and sat back down, leaving the creators of "Beat Me, Dimitri" somewhat confused as to how their number had gone over. Mitropoulos stayed sitting on the floor through two or three additional swing pieces, then slipped quietly out of the room. The Minneapolis papers had a field day with the incident.

Composer John Verrall's house was a favorite Mitropoulos haunt—few people knew that, which meant he could escape the demands on his time and spend some hours relaxing with other musicians. Since Verrall worked with numerous members of the MSO, several men from the orchestra were usually on hand. Verrall recalled:

> Some nights, he would turn up and just announce: "Come on, boys, we're going to the movies!" There might be six or eight of us, but we would all pack into the car and drive to the nearest theater, a kind of second-rate Minneapolis music hall, and Dimitri would leap out and run to the ticket window shouting "We can just make the second show!" He would buy a long string of tickets for everybody and we would go in and have a grand time watching whatever show was on, good or bad didn't really matter.[7]

The longest and deepest friendship Mitropoulos formed in Minneapolis was with William Cooper and his family. The two men met first during the spring of 1937 when Cooper was heading a fundraising drive for the orchestra on the university campus. "They hit it off," recalled son David Cooper. "There was an empathy between them which lasted for Mitropoulos's entire life."[8] The conductor invited the professor to sit in on rehearsals, which Cooper did whenever his academic schedule permitted.

In return, the Coopers—after much hesitation, due to the conductor's reputation as a hermit—invited Mitropoulos to the first of many dinners he was to enjoy at their home. The guest list was small and select and included Dr. Laurence McKinley Gould, a professor of geology at Carleton College who had been second-in-command on Admiral Richard Byrd's first polar expedition. David Cooper, only fifteen at the time, was not invited to the adults' dinner party, but he was allowed to ride in the backseat of the Coopers' car when his father went to pick up the guest of honor. As it happened, Mitropoulos's recent performance of Mahler's First Symphony had driven young David into a state of ecstasy, so the maestro and the teenager had a long and passionate discussion about that composer during the drive. Mitropoulos did not talk down to young people, and the memory of that shared enthusiasm stayed bright in David Cooper's mind for half a century.

Also in attendance at this dinner was violinist Jenny Cullen, the Minneapolis Symphony's only full-time female player. A native of Glasgow, Cullen was an accomplished artist who had been, in her youth, a protégé of Henri Verbrugghen. She had followed the dapper Belgian to Australia (where he founded a music school in New South Wales) and thence to Minneapolis, where she had stayed, at an address within walking distance of Mitropoulos's own on Groveland. She was in her late fifties at the time she and Mitropoulos met, and she had a mothering instinct that seemed to strike a sympathetic note in the solitary conductor. They often went to the movies together and usually turned up together at the Presbyterian church where Mitropoulos chose to worship. Cullen enjoyed picking playful fights with Mitropoulos; on the very night they first were introduced, they enjoyed a brisk but thoroughly friendly argument about the merits of arranging string quartets for full orchestra. After debating the aesthetics of the matter for a while, Mitropoulos finally admitted that he had an ulterior motive for programming these transcriptions: the string section of the MSO was its weakest choir, and these arrangements gave the string players an extensive workout which, the conductor hoped, would build their tone and refine their precision.

After their first meeting, Cullen often had him over for dinner, along with the Coopers, and usually served one of the maestro's favorites: brains. William Cooper could handle the dish, actually liked it in fact, but Mrs. Cooper was always provided with alternative fare. According to David Cooper, the inordinate amount of time the bachelor and the spinster spent together caused some tongues to wag at first, but eventually their friendship was recognized for what it was.

> Jenny's relationship with Mitropoulos began in our living room on the night of the celebrated dinner party. She and Mitropoulos had an animated discussion about orchestral arrangements of string quartets sparked by Mitropoulos's performance of Beethoven's Op. 131. Jenny had a "thing" about conductors, feeling that she understood them better than their wives. Mrs. Verbrugghen she categorized as "cold." In Jenny, Mitropoulos found a discerning professional, and one who was on his intellectual level; theirs was a really close friendship. Years later, I asked a close friend, a former president of the MSO board of directors, if people had ever been concerned about Mitropoulos's homosexuality. Not at all, he said, but they were worried about his relationship with Jenny! They had nothing to fear; if Jenny Cullen wasn't a virgin, I'm a monkey's uncle.[9]

His friendship with the Coopers gave Mitropoulos a summertime haven, at the Coopers' lodge (named Tapiola, in homage to Sibelius), located near Long's Peak, Colorado. From 1946 until 1951, Mitropoulos spent at least two weeks at Tapiola every summer. He alternated score-study with physical labor. "He helped replenish the fireplace wood," wrote William Cooper in a private memoir. "At one end of a two-man saw, he was reasonably proficient; when he wielded an axe we were apprehensive."[10] The rustic lodge, surrounded by tall pines and birches and offering spectacular alpine views in all directions, proved an ideal setting for the kind of intensive study Mitropoulos performed on difficult scores. He accomplished so much during these visits that he eventually began listing his intellectual conquests on the pages of the Coopers' guest book.

In 1947, for example, when Mitropoulos actually rented the lodge for a month and a half, he left the following inventory of major works studied and absorbed:

> Mahler: Sixth Symphony
> R. Strauss: Eine Alpensinfonie
> Ernst Krenek: Fourth Symphony
> Samuel Barber: Cello Concerto
> Roger Sessions: Violin Concerto
> Béla Bartók: Dance Suite
> Arnold Schoenberg: Quintet for Wind Instruments

Tapiola was the starting point for many mountaineering expeditions. As early as the summer of 1940, the conductor had tackled both Mt. Whitney and Mt. Shasta, and one of them at least was beyond his level of skill—he had to be rescued and helped down by professional guides. In Colorado, Mitropoulos generally matched himself against peaks he could handle, and always with experienced companions. William Cooper, after several summers of observation, finally concluded that the conductor was an "ardent" climber but not an especially skilled one. Cooper was grateful for the services of John and Johanna Marr, two experienced guides from Boulder who shepherded the conductor up three local mountains: Long's Peak, Lone Eagle Peak, and Halletts Peak.

In 1946, Mitropoulos decided to attempt Grand Teton peak in Wyoming, an unforgiving mountain that is often described as the American Matterhorn. He undertook this strenuous climb under the guidance of Ray Garner, a robust young man who made his living as a professional climber and lecturer. In an interview given in 1950, Garner described the Grand Teton adventure in some detail:

> A mountain is trying to kill you all the time. . . . [People wonder] why does the Maestro risk that priceless neck of his, that peerless brain that can bring deathless music out of a hundred men? [It's] because a mountain is not a pile of rock, but a spiritual challenge. Because the Maestro is seeking God.
>
> I remember the day we got to the mountain. The Maestro felt he could reach out—like this—and touch the infinite. One does not conquer a mountain. One conquers oneself. We see the naked man [on these climbs]. I saw the Maestro in his hour of trial, and I saw greatness.[11]

For the first few thousand feet, Mitropoulos ran ahead "like a mountain goat," bursting with eagerness. But his pre-climb conditioning had been at sea level, and he was, after all, a fifty-one-year-old man who smoked at least two packs of Camels daily and who was, moreover, carrying a heavy pack.

All went well until the ten-thousand-foot level, when the altitude really hit him. He staggered, agonizing cramps knotting his calf and thigh muscles.

He kept struggling, but he was in agony. At one point, as we were crossing a dangerous crevasse, he started to slip. There was a thirty-five-hundred-foot sheer drop below him. My wife, who was behind, managed to help him keep his balance. He turned to her and said, "My dear, I wish you could have seen me just once on the podium!" But we succeeded in getting him across, and it was then I saw the man. I saw sheer courage, but I also saw that he couldn't make it to the top. I practically had to fight him to make him turn back. He was broken-hearted. But the next morning, he was out with rope and axe, practicing on cliffs. For a whole week, he worked out ten hours every day, conditioning himself. At the end of that week, he won the battle of man against mountain, and that's why we have a photograph of the three of us eating beans on the summit of Grand Teton.[12]

The conductor was less successful on his penultimate visit to Tapiola in 1949, when he again set out, without allowing himself sufficient time to become acclimated, to hike to the summit of Long's Peak—a mountain that he could see, every clear day, from his favorite study chair in the lodge. At the beginning of the north-face ascent, altitude 12,500 feet, Mitropoulos completely gave out. While his younger and fitter companions continued to the summit, the conductor found a sunny spot and occupied himself by visualizing, page by page, the entire score of *Elektra*—twice.

As David Cooper remembered:

The "younger and fitter" companions were Jim Dixon and two wranglers from the Long's Peak Inn. Those were really wonderful days. Mitropoulos was in rare form and utterly relaxed. He always took his music stand and his chair either outdoors or to a window where he could gaze at Long's Peak while he worked. He wanted conversation to continue, even when he was studying, and he always joined in when something caught his interest. One summer we had a housekeeper who was Billy Graham's secretary at Northwestern Bible College, early in Billy's ministry, and Dimitri was keenly interested in Graham's evangelism. And while he studied, he could not only converse with her, but with me and my friends about music, and even discuss the fine points of plumbing with me, one time when I was trying to install a new shower.[13]

The subject of mountain climbing also gave critic John Sherman a glimpse of something dark in Mitropoulos's soul: his medieval preoccupation with metaphors of death. Once in the autumn of 1946, when he was being interviewed by Sherman on a live radio broadcast, the conductor was enthusiastically describing his conquest of Grand Teton Mountain, when his remarks suddenly veered off in a morbid direction. The climb had been

exceptionally exhilarating, Mitropoulos said, because Grand Teton was "the most fierceful mountain" in North America—he had been in danger much of the time and one mistake away from death at several points during the climb. "I have often thought," the conductor mused, "that the most perfect way for me to die would be a long fall from the top of a mountain into the cold blue silence of a glacial crevasse." According to Sherman, Mitropoulos continued in this vein "with a kind of somber relish" until the critic, with some difficulty, managed to pull him back and get the interview "lifted to a higher plane."[14]

Prophetically or coincidentally, Mitropoulos could scarcely have chosen a more apt metaphorical description of his own demise.

The conductor maintained a tenuous connection with Tapiola and a stronger one with the Coopers, even after he moved to New York. During his summer visits to Colorado, the conductor had acquired a great fondness for what he described as "mountain trouts." There was a trout farm near Tapiola—a rather well-known one, as it happened, since one of its regular patrons was General Dwight Eisenhower—and the Coopers made arrangements to ship fresh "trouts" to the maestro, by way of the chef of his favorite restaurant, Manhattan's famed La Scala. Shipping was done on a strict schedule. Within minutes of being caught, the trout were iced and delivered in person by the Coopers to the express office in Boulder a quarter-hour or so before the train pulled in; the shipment was re-iced in Chicago, then passed on to New York. When the first half-dozen arrived, Mitropoulos was overjoyed and polished them off rapidly, as recounted in his thank-you letter to the Coopers:

> Your kind and loving trouts arrived in time, and by now, of course, are more than digested! It was a wonderful treat for me, and I must say I was so selfish—or probably it happened that I was alone—that I enjoyed them for two consecutive meals—three at a time. Thank God they were not so big as to give me any stomach disturbance![15]

One of Mitropoulos's strangest attachments was his friendship with a Tennessee mountaineer named Anson Mount. When the Minneapolis Symphony played a tour date in Nashville, the thirteen-year-old Mount heard about it on a portable radio belonging to a neighbor. He didn't know the Minneapolis Symphony from Benny Goodman's band, but the concert sounded interesting, so Mount walked the ninety miles to Nashville.

He arrived just as the trucks carrying the orchestra's instruments pulled up, very late. Observing the flustered condition of the orchestra's manager, Arthur Gaines, Mount pitched in and helped to unload the trucks. He worked so hard that Gaines offered him two tickets to the concert. Perhaps young Mount would care to invite his mother.

Nope, replied Mount. Mother lives in White Bluff and can't get here, but I sure would like one ticket for myself.

At this point, Mitropoulos walked by. Gaines introduced them, and Mitropoulos responded with a perfunctory "How do you do?," then began to excuse himself. Gaines tugged at his sleeve and said: "You know, this boy has never heard a symphony orchestra before, and he traveled ninety miles, walking and hitchhiking, to hear one tonight."[16]

Now Mitropoulos's interest was truly piqued. He sat down with Mount and started asking him all sorts of questions about rural America and local history. Mount was relaxed and talkative; the kid was the bugler in his local Boy Scout troop, he liked to meet new people and he was devoutly religious—was in fact planning to become an Episcopal minister. He also had a hobby that immediately endeared him to the conductor: he collected crucifixes. Mitropoulos by now had become truly fascinated. "Well, sir," Anson Mount said, "if you're really interested in barefooted people and log cabins, you just pack a bag and I'll show you plenty."

Mitropoulos did. He went to White Bluff with Anson Mount, stayed several days, then rejoined the orchestra for its next concert, in New Orleans. Mount's mother made him welcome, shot squirrels for dinner, and gave the exotic visitor a crash course in Appalachian history and genealogy. Mitropoulos took Anson Mount under his wing, brought him to New York, and put him up with a wealthy lady friend who promised to inculcate some of the social graces—at the time Mitropoulos met him, Mount did not even know how to use a fork.

Trombonist John MacKay happened to be in New York on the day Anson Mount was scheduled to arrive by train from Tennessee. MacKay recalled:

> He sent Anson some money to get him to come to New York because the kid wanted to come to New York. The boy was very religious and he was big on crucifixes. Dimitri told me to go down to Grand Central to meet him. I asked how I would know him and Dimitri said: "You can't miss him—he's a real hillbilly." And sure enough, you couldn't miss him—he looked like Ichabod Crane. Maestro set him up on a cot in his hotel suite, until he could find a better place for him. He would give the boy money and the boy would go downtown and shop for crucifixes. . . . About two o'clock in the morning, Anson began eating cherries and plopping the pits into a metal container. Finally, Maestro woke up and said: "Listen, will you cut out that research and go to sleep."[17]

Later, Mitropoulos paid Anson Mount's tuition at the University of the South. Somewhere along the line, Mount's ambition to become an Episcopalian minister faded; he ended up with a high-paying job on the staff of *Playboy*.

A leitmotif through all the recollections of former MSO players and audience members is the memory of Dimitri Mitropoulos's generosity. During the war years, budgetary constraints were severe, and none of the orchestra

members received raises in pay. Several of the more important players, however, received direct cash subsidies from Mitropoulos, just so they would stay in the Minneapolis Symphony and not take their talent elsewhere. In this way, he paid out several thousand dollars per season, over and above his significant contributions to charity. When the seasonal deficit rose to $150,000, the conductor voluntarily took a pay cut instead of the hefty raise to which he was certainly entitled. He never complained about this arrangement in public, but he did unburden himself to Katy in a letter dated May 1, 1946:

> We have days of desperation, even considering abandoning the orchestra, and then at the last minute, as by a miracle, funds are found. Then the generous Dimitri has come in, not only never during these nine years asking for an augmentation of salary, but offering to take a reduction, besides secretly paying the men the difference between their salary and what they asked for. . . . Then the horrible war-time taxes came and are continuing, such as to cut my income to one-third of what it was, so that instead of being a rich man in a way, I am only supposed to be one, and that means that I am expected to contribute to all the philanthropic manifestations, which amounts to a very respectable sum every year, in other words, everything I could have saved. Lately, some of my closest friends, who saw my financial condition, stepped into my life and urged me to save some money by forcing me to take some insurance, which will enable me in my older days to have a way of sleeping and eating.[18]

William Cooper remembered being present at a gathering of orchestra members during which a violinist played what was obviously a carefully prepared showpiece. With characteristic forthrightness, Mitropoulos critiqued the performance like a morning-after reviewer, a response that left the poor musician quite crestfallen. Realizing what he had done, Mitropoulos went out the next day and bought the man the finest violin he could find in Minneapolis, then had the instrument hand-delivered with his own note of apology.

His first gift to the Coopers was memorable: an elaborate, motorized, dinner-table fountain which the Coopers eventually learned would work as well with wine and champagne as with water, and which the Cooper family still maintained in working order forty-five years later.

Composer Morton Gould got a rare glimpse of the conductor's customary, almost daily, generosity—one of many instances that went unobserved by the musical world:

> I had dinner with him often . . . and he seemed to prefer ordinary out-of-the-way places—in some cases, real greasy spoons that seemed to poison everybody else, but he thrived on the fare for some reason or other. After a concert, we would go to one of these schlock places and

sit on stools at the counter. I remember once in Minneapolis, we went to a restaurant where all the waiters and waitresses came over to chat with him. They were either Greek or Italian, I forget which, but they spoke to him as though he were a member of the family, some kind of honorary godfather. Turned out he was actually paying the tuition for one of the kids, a son or a grandson or a daughter, to go to college. Somehow, he had found out that this family had financial problems and couldn't afford college. He found out there was a problem, and very quietly, with no publicity whatever, he just took care of it. He did many things of this nature, and it continued when he went to New York. People came in off the street to see him in Carnegie Hall, and I know he gave most of them money or a letter of recommendation or bought them food or provided some kind of assistance.[19]

When the Minneapolis Symphony was on tour in New Orleans, in the winter of 1941, woodwind player Carl Bergman lost his instrument cases in transit; Mitropoulos bought him a brand new oboe and a new English horn, out of his own pocket. If the conductor learned that one of his musicians was down on his luck, or had an expensive medical emergency in his family, he would quietly see to it that the musician received an infusion of cash to help him through the rough period. There were many months when more of Mitropoulos's paycheck went to help others than to support the man who earned it.

When Clara Roesch Herdt, founder of the Women's Symphony Orchestra, first approached Mitropoulos, she was banking on his reputation as a benign idealist. She went to Minneapolis in a burst of naive enthusiasm, without so much as a letter of introduction, and was startled to learn that the orchestra was away on tour. She waited in the lobby of the Groveland apartments for four days until the orchestra returned, but when the operator buzzed the conductor's rooms, Mitropoulos answered: "Oh, I can't see anybody now. I'm just too exhausted." When the operator explained that the young woman had been hanging around for four days, Mitropoulos agreed to meet her for supper.

At first, the Greek in him balked at the very notion of a female conductor. "I don't teach conducting," he explained to Miss Roesch, "and if I did, I wouldn't teach a woman."

Appealing to his idealism, Miss Roesch began almost immediately to change his attitude. By the end of the meal, Mitropoulos had invited her to come to Minneapolis and learn whatever she could learn. His last words on the subject, as they were rising from the dinner table, were: "Oh, and you don't have to pay me anything." Miss Roesch studied under Mitropoulos for four years, and he never charged her a penny.[20]

Mitropoulos even gave away his car. Just before the United States' entry into the Second World War, the conductor went to Detroit, accompanied by John MacKay, and selected a factory-fresh 1942 Cadillac. He drove it, with more enthusiasm than skill, for about six months, then when wartime ra-

tioning made automobiles troublesome to maintain, Mitropoulos seemed to lose interest. After putting the vehicle on blocks for a while, he simply gave it outright to John MacKay, on the condition that MacKay be available to drive him on those comparatively few occasions when he really needed to be driven—which MacKay, in exchange for an almost-new Cadillac, was happy to do.

Mitropoulos also had a special friendship with the trombonist's son, John (Buddy) MacKay, Jr. When the conductor first heard Buddy MacKay play, at the age of six, he recognized a prodigy. He arranged, and paid for, first-class piano lessons, and later bought the boy a Steinway. When Buddy was ten, he debuted in public at a young people's concert, playing the Mozart Concert Rondo and Variations, K. 382; a year later, at a regular subscription concert, he played the same composer's Piano Concerto No. 21 in C Major, K. 467.

In later years, John MacKay recalled the many times Mitropoulos came to the MacKay household:

One of his favorite things was to mix up the hottest damn spaghetti sauce you have ever eaten. It was good tasting but your stomach wouldn't live on it too long . . . sometimes he was an ascetic and did not eat much, then other times he would stuff himself like a glutton. He was a complex, enigmatic man—talk about a dichotomy of drives and insights and trying to make the real world fit with the world of his mind![21]

MacKay graduated from the University of Minnesota *cum laude*. Many of his educational expenses were paid for by Mitropoulos, who also supported the young man for two years of postgraduate work at Juilliard. At the end of his Juilliard period, MacKay met with his benefactor. Knowing that the conductor would not take monetary repayment, MacKay asked if there was not something he could do to repay Mitropoulos's generosity. Mitropoulos thought for a moment, then replied: "Look, if fate directs somebody to cross your path some time in the future and that person could use help and aid, just render it to him and I would consider that ample repayment for whatever debt you feel toward me."[22]

During the war years, Mitropoulos generally used public transportation. Flutist Anton Winkler and his wife Susan, who did not own a car, had an interesting and typical encounter with him one night when they were returning from the movies on a streetcar. The night was bitterly cold, and at one downtown stop, a tall bald man, bundled in an overcoat and with a small beret perched incongruously on his skull, got in and sat down under a gigantic poster advertising Dimitri Mitropoulos and the Minneapolis Symphony Orchestra. As Anton Winkler remembered:

There was this giant streetcar ad, showing Maestro in full warpaint and with his arms outflung, and sitting underneath it, totally unaware, was the man himself. All around us, other passengers were starting to nudge each other and whisper: "Is that *him?*" So we just went over and sat down and said, "Hello, Maestro!" and started chatting. He probably was not aware until he got up to leave the streetcar that he was sitting under this huge photo of himself.[23]

Although most Minneapolis music lovers were content with the rationale that Mitropoulos was married to his art and therefore had no wife or female companion, other than the motherly Jenny Cullen, and although the circumstantial evidence is strong that the conductor was in fact celibate during the Minneapolis concert seasons (though not always so on tour, if anecdotal evidence is taken into account), the more worldly and sophisticated musicians knew there was more to it than that. But Mitropoulos never made straight males feel uneasy, despite his very European habit of addressing colleagues as "my dear" and of administering affectionate little pinches to people he especially liked. Pianist David Bar-Ilan, a very macho fellow indeed, stated that "He was always able to have fine relationships with other men like me, without the matter of his sexual orientation ever even being in the air."[24]

Composer Leon Kirchner, who first met Mitropoulos when the conductor was guesting in San Francisco, had occasion to make a similar observation. The two met following a chamber music concert that included Kirchner's First String Quartet. Mitropoulos sought him out and praised the work flatteringly, then asked if Kirchner had any orchestral scores. As it happened, he did, a half-finished sinfonia on his desk at home in Los Angeles. That was no problem, Mitropoulos indicated—he would soon be in San Francisco for a two-week guest engagement. Could Kirchner come by his hotel on a certain date, at one o'clock in the morning?

Kirchner showed up at the residential hotel on the appointed evening:

> The clerk told me that the Maestro was expecting me. I went up and rang his doorbell at the appointed time. Again I thought: oh, my, this is a very strange time. I had heard that Mitropoulos was homosexual and was a little apprehensive as to the purpose of this nocturnal visit. He opened the door and the first thing I blurted out, at one A.M., was "I'm sorry my wife couldn't come!" Mitropoulos just burst into laughter, then he gave me the tenderest, friendliest little pinch on the neck—that was a gesture he sometimes made with young people he really liked, or admired, or felt intellectually close to. His laughter put me at ease, dismissed my uncalled-for concern. We came into his study—there was a piano . . . he asked me to play the single movement I had completed. After I finished, the first thing he said was: "I will do this work next season with the Philharmonic."[25]

Usually the conductor's generosity of spirit extended to his colleagues on the podium as well as to those in the orchestra. When Stokowski was forming his All American Youth Orchestra in the summer of 1940, Mitropoulos donated many hours of his own time to audition regional candidates simply because he believed in what Stokowski was trying to do. There was one occasion, however, when MSO board member Leo Pflaum saw Mitropoulos react with uncharacteristic bitterness, and that was when Eugene Ormandy came back through town, on tour with the Philadelphia Orchestra. Mitropoulos tried to wriggle out of going, but Pflaum insisted. At intermission, however, Mitropoulos rose from his seat and said: "I'm going backstage to talk to Ormandy. I'll see you later."

"You're not going backstage," Pflaum chided him. "I know what you're going to do—you're going to sneak out and go to a movie."

Mitropoulos reddened. "How did you know?" he responded.

"You have that look," Pflaum said.

Flustered, Mitropoulos made his way out of the hall. The next day he sheepishly confessed to Pflaum that he "just couldn't take it any more—his orchestra is so much bigger and better than mine."[26]

CHAPTER FIFTEEN

Mitropoulos and Contemporary Composers

During his twelve seasons in Minneapolis, Mitropoulos conducted only one work by American composer David Diamond—his *Rounds for String Orchestra*, a work Mitropoulos had commissioned in 1943 and performed on November 24, 1944—but he nurtured Diamond in many other important ways. Mitropoulos felt a profound empathy for the young American: Diamond was brilliantly gifted, often impoverished, proud and sensitive, and destined to become one of America's greatest composers.

The two men were introduced by Aaron Copland during Mitropoulos's guest-conducting engagement with the New York Philharmonic in 1940. Diamond, dressed in an ocher turtleneck sweater, was walking with Copland toward the Fifty-sixth Street entrance to Carnegie Hall when the door burst open and out strode Mitropoulos. "I can still feel the rush of energy," Diamond recalled five decades later; "I can still feel it physically." The first thing Diamond noticed, beyond the "extraordinary face," were the heavy rubber-soled shoes Mitropoulos wore to and from rehearsals.

Mitropoulos greeted Copland, then Copland introduced Diamond, describing him as an uncommonly gifted young composer and expressing the wish that "David will send you some of his music."

The conductor scrutinized Diamond closely, admired his sweater, then said: "I know you; I know your music. Your publisher sent me your *Psalm* for orchestra." When the two men became friends, Mitropoulos would question Diamond closely about André Gide, to whom Diamond's *Psalm* was dedicated, saying: "You must tell me about him. I wanted so much to meet this man when I was in Paris."

Such exchanges of confidence set the tone for a lifelong friendship between Mitropoulos and Diamond, a friendship that weathered numerous vexations, misunderstandings, and arguments. Diamond explicated Gide, and Mitropoulos read to Diamond the world-weary final sonnets of Michelangelo. Their discussions frequently took a metaphysical turn, when they would discuss "the Magic of the Universe and Man's role in that universe."[1]

They also discussed Greek mythology and the central role played in those myths by conjuring magicians. The Greeks of course had a word for that particular form of conjuring: *Goietie*. Diamond became fascinated with the sonnets and with the connection Mitropoulos had made between them and the magic of Greek mythology. Beginning in 1960, only a few months after Mitropoulos's death, Diamond began to blend these two subjects into a darkly powerful musical statement for baritone and orchestra.

After considerable prodding by Leonard Bernstein, Diamond finished the work in 1985, as his Symphony No. 9 ("To the Memory of Dimitri Mitropoulos.") Bernstein directed the American Composers' Orchestra in the world premiere in New York on November 11, 1985; David Arnold sang the verses. In the program notes for that concert, Diamond wrote:

> Of the poems set to music in this work, all of them were the ones Mitropoulos read to me in Italian and which, as I grew older and as my life and its turbulences grew, became commentaries on my own conflicts. It is natural that this symphony be dedicated to that great man Mitropoulos, and that Leonard Bernstein should give its premiere, for he was as close to Mitropoulos as I was. We loved and admired the man's genius and understood his melancholy nature.[2]

When paying the first installment of his commission for Diamond's most popular work, *Rounds for String Orchestra*, Mitropoulos specified the kind of music he wanted: "David, please write me a happy piece—so much of what I play is depressing!"[3] For both the 1942 and 1943 concerts, Mitropoulos had wanted to schedule either Diamond's First Symphony or his First Violin Concerto, but the intransigence of the MSO's manager, Arthur Gaines, forced the conductor to shorten his wish-list of contemporary works.

In May 1943, Mitropoulos wrote Diamond a longhand letter filled with praise for his new Second Symphony and alerting him, at the same time, that the work might prove impossible to schedule any time in the foreseeable future:

> We will talk things over when I see you next fall in New York. And please, I wanted you to know that no matter what I decide about the performance of this piece, it will make no difference to me if I have the second or (I wish you this) the tenth performance. Don't hesitate to try any place and any conductor you like. It is ok with me. I am not a first performance hunter, you know that. Your work deserves undoubtedly a performance, many performances. Besides, I couldn't decide anything now, and I have to meet first the different trustees and board of directors and manager, see their attitude and their thinking for the next season as far as modern works are concerned. This last season we have been as careful as we could be with our presentation of new works to the public. . . . You know all the difficulties, so don't lose any opportunity of getting a hearing for your work. I suggest to try if you can Bruno Walter. He is one of the most sympathetic artists and I am sure his advice will help you a lot.[4]

One month later, Mitropoulos wrote to Diamond again, offering to pay all the expenses of having the new symphony's orchestral parts copied. In July 1943, Diamond apparently wrote Mitropoulos and chided him for programming the Chausson Symphony in B Minor during his forthcoming New York Philharmonic engagement, rather than something contemporary or American. In his response, Mitropoulos patiently explained that he was not allowed, under the existing ground rules, to program more than one or two "classical" works (in the event, he conducted only one such work, the Beethoven Fourth Piano Concerto with Josef Hoffman), because that repertoire was reserved for Bruno Walter, the *de facto* music director. "I had to choose something not very much played and also something that was more or less new without being modern. . . . It took at least a month of heavy correspondence, of scratching and writing and suggesting, until we finally arrived at some conclusions."[5]

Diamond's original letter not only complained about the Chausson selection, but took Mitropoulos to task rather strongly, accusing all members of the conducting profession of "smug opportunism." The conductor's anguished reply reveals an abiding empathy toward a sensitive young colleague:

> I am afraid that your sentence against conductors unfortunately does not exclude me. In my defense, I can tell you only that my "smug opportunism" is extremely suffering and I feel tortured by my conscience and also question my usefulness to exist as an artist. You, no matter if your work is played or not, at least have pleasure while you are writing it or showing it to some of your close friends. But we [conductors] do not even own the instrument on which we play, and it is granted to us under restricted conditions. It is a hell of a situation, yet we have to make the choice either to be opportunists and have this instrument to play, or not have this instrument and do something else.[6]

In October of the same year, 1943, Diamond wrote to Mitropoulos from Boston, informing him that Koussevitzky had expressed an interest in programming the Second Symphony. On one level, Diamond was of course overjoyed; on another level, he felt uncertain about this opportunity because he had promised the work to the Minneapolis Symphony and Mitropoulos, after all, had paid to have the orchestral parts copied. Mitropoulos unhesitatingly replied:

> accept any performance the Boston Symphony may give you . . . what is important is that the work should be played, and it is not only a question of having this one played, but also the question of having another of your works played by the Boston Symphony, if you get under the protective atmosphere of the Koussevitzky clique. So forget about me. . . . I wish you much luck.[7]

Only two weeks later, the volatile composer unloaded more anger in Mitropoulos's direction, railing, with considerable justification, against backstage politics and their influence over who got played and who did not. Diamond had reason to be bitter: he had just begun to hit his stride as a mature composer, but already he had had to endure criticism that his music was old-fashioned. He also fired some salvos in the direction of Krenek and the other atonalists, who, he contended, were getting preferential treatment in Minneapolis and elsewhere. In reply, Mitropoulos sent a somewhat indignant response:

Although your letter pleased me immensely from one side, with its news that Koussevitzky finally decided to conduct your new symphony himself—from the other side, its allusions about conductors and politics, and me only differing as a man, I would not say that I was quite pleased. And now, let me also be frank with you.

I certainly believe that you have a talent, that you do your best, that you are conscientious and a hard worker. I feel that you deserve any help, and I will always be glad to do it when I think the moment is the right moment. I have already showed, without your interference, how much I can react upon a composition, without the interference of any friendship or politics. I think your second symphony is more advanced in many ways than the first, which means that if I liked and performed the first, I certainly would like to perform the second too. But if in the meantime I happened to have noticed something that interests me more, or that I think is more mature, and for which I think I have to learn something myself—and I mean *Krenek and Company*—I like to play it, no matter what you may think about it . . . and I am sure that when you will think better of it, you will have made a step forward in your life. Besides that, I have to fight for it and I do so with great pleasure, and I consider myself privileged to live in the same town with that great mind and composer . . . Ernst Krenek. Unfortunately, I cannot fight for many things together, but everything will have its time and its place. That's the way I think.

I like you very much and I appreciate you a lot. I am twice your age, although you think you know more. That's your privilege, but because you are my friend, I wish you had a little more respect for those conductors who certainly have long years of career behind them of knowledge and value and struggle, and it is, in a way, very bad taste for a young man to start his career with such an attitude toward his older colleagues. Although I forgave you, I never forgot the impertinent way in which you allowed yourself to rail against my interpretation of the Third Symphony of Brahms, and that time, just as now, you excused yourself under the skin of sincerity. So do I. It depends on how much we think of ourselves when we exhibit sincerity in a harsh way. I know how self-minded you are—that this letter will neither help nor do you any good (in fact it may harm you because I am afraid you will be furious at me), but I think that I deserve also once in a while the right to exhibit my sincere opinion too. I wish you the best of luck always, because I am afraid that with your character, as I many times told you, you may need it a lot.[8]

This correspondence is particularly interesting because Mitropoulos was still sending Diamond money to live on, even while Diamond was snapping at him in letters, out of frustration and disappointment. When Diamond ran out of money, he would write to Mitropoulos, and the conductor would respond with a check sufficient to carry the young man through one more period of crisis. Finally, in the summer of 1945, the cash flow stopped; Mitropoulos had learned that, during the harsh years of the German occupation of Greece, his beloved mother had gone deeply into debt. Every dollar he could spare was sent overseas to restore her fortunes. Even so, Mitropoulos could not quite bring himself to cut Diamond off. In a letter dated June 30, 1945, he said: "In spite of that, my dear David, I would like to help you if you need it badly, but not in the substantial way I did before. Believe me, I cannot do it this time."

By the start of 1946, Diamond was emotionally very troubled. He hit bottom one night in February:

I had been in analysis for several years . . . but as sometimes happens in analysis, I would get very depressed. My depressions were mainly about the run-arounds I would get from conductors. They would have the score of a piece for years, and they'd say they were going to play it, and then they didn't, and this goes on and on. Dimitri was the only one who didn't behave that way, but even Lenny never got around to playing anything of mine during his first year with the City Center Orchestra—even though he performed a number of other American composers. It just depressed me . . . sometimes I would have just ten cents in my pocket. . . . Finally came this evening when I had gone over to Eddie Condon's place because I had gotten to know Eddie rather well, and I found that I could borrow some money from him . . . but he didn't show up. And I thought: well, I can't take another week of being this broke. And I'm not going to bother Dimitri any more about money. . . . I had some sleeping pills, so I just went into the closet and swallowed the Seconals. Then I went to the phone and called Dimitri in Minneapolis, where it was six o'clock in the morning. I told him what I had done, and asked him to take care of all my music. I thought of him as my literary executor.[9]

Fortunately for the future of American music, Mitropoulos was home to answer the phone. He realized the seriousness of the situation, and as soon as Diamond hung up, he telephoned the authorities in New York. Not long after he ended his conversation with Mitropoulos, Diamond heard the downstairs entrance to his cold-water flat being forced open, and a few minutes later he was on his way to a hospital.

Mitropoulos was glad to have helped in saving the young composer's life, but as far as financial support was concerned, the suicide gesture was the final straw. On March 14, 1946, he wrote another long admonitory letter to Diamond:

> To tell you the truth, the absolute truth, my obligations already undertaken, plus a constant solicitation of relatives and dear friends in Greece, have brought me to a financial situation which makes me unable at this time to be of any financial help to you. . . . Have courage [and] try to find a way of existing without the help of anybody, even if that costs you for a while a disappearance from the musical world—I don't think you will lose your contacts. You can stay home with your parents and work and concentrate for yourself. I am sure they might be able to give you some food, so that you don't have to starve while you try to find balance and calm and serenity in yourself.
>
> If you are privileged from chance or from God to live a heroic and martyrized life, you have to go through by yourself. If you don't, you take away the glory and the opportunity that is given to you to do something very outstanding. Otherwise, if you have not the courage to face it, it will mean you have not been chosen.[10]

Mitropoulos's faith in Diamond was not misplaced. Diamond continued to write strong, beautiful works in an accessible yet unmistakably modern American symphonic style. He endured a decade-and-a-half of neglect during the 1950s and early 1960s, when the academic serialists dominated the profession of music. Finally, starting in 1990 (in honor of the composer's seventy-fifth birthday), Delos records began issuing an integral set of his orchestral works, to the highest critical and popular acclaim.

Mitropoulos tried to use his Minneapolis position, and whatever prestige went with it, on behalf of living composers, regardless of nationality. In November 1941, he invited chubby, balding Paul Hindemith to town, to attend rehearsals and performances of his Symphony in E-flat Major—one of Hindemith's most red-blooded works and one whose continued neglect is beyond rational explanation.

As it happened, another composer was in town that week: Sergei Rachmaninoff. During the previous collaboration between Mitropoulos and Rachmaninoff, the two men had engaged in a friendly but heated discussion about the state of symphonic composition in the contemporary world—Rachmaninoff holding the opinion that nothing worth hearing was being produced, and Mitropoulos, of course, hewing to a diametrically opposite point of view. Since Rachmaninoff would be in town for the first performance of the Hindemith symphony, Mitropoulos invited him to sit backstage (where he would not be bothered by autograph seekers) and listen.

This was really a good symphony, the conductor insisted. Rachmaninoff took a chair and stationed himself just out of sight behind the proscenium arch.

At the conclusion of the symphony, which was enthusiastically received by the audience, the perspiring conductor loped offstage, grabbed a cigarette from his secretary, tapped Rachmaninoff on the shoulder, and said: "Well?"

Rachmaninoff looked up at him with a doleful expression and lugubriously intoned: "No gooooood."

Hindemith's visit caused some turmoil behind the scenes. The MSO management quickly discovered that their celebrity guest was arrogant, demanding, and thoroughly unpleasant to work with. When he learned that his travel and lodging expenses did not include funds for his wife—and this was the first time the MSO management had heard about the lady—he pitched a temper tantrum that embarrassed everyone who witnessed it. No contingency funds were available to assuage their guest, and Hindemith was growling about pulling out of the engagement altogether unless he got his way. Quietly, anonymously, Mitropoulos wrote out a check for Mrs. Hindemith's expenses and donated it to the orchestra. The Hindemith concert went on as planned, and the composer left on schedule with wife in tow, without so much as a thank you to Mitropoulos or anyone else.

Of all the composers Mitropoulos championed, only David Diamond was as personally close to the conductor as Ernst Krenek. That Krenek and Mitropoulos should end up in close physical proximity was a coincidence; that together they should work to further the cause of modern music was inevitable. Because of their partnership, the Twin Cities of Minnesota became, for a period of five years, an internationally recognized center of progressive music-making—whether they liked it or not.

Ernst Krenek was born in Vienna in 1900 and studied with Franz Schreker, whose late-romantic idiom characterizes Krenek's earliest works. His most spectacular success was the influential and much-discussed jazz opera *Jonny spielt auf* (Johnny Strikes Up the Band), a seminal musical work of the 1920s. Following its first production in Leipzig in 1920, the opera flared to life in more than one hundred performances during the next two years, including a run at the Metropolitan Opera in New York. Krenek was uncomfortable, even embarrassed, by the easy success of *Jonny spielt auf*. The 1920s saw Krenek, as restless and adventurous a musical spirit as he was a solid and down-to-earth teacher, turning toward the twelve-tone technique and applying it more vigorously and in more varied forms than did any other composer of the day, including his friend and mentor, Arnold Schoenberg.

Krenek first came to America in the autumn of 1937, with a touring company called the Salzburg Opera Guild, who were then performing Krenek's adaptation of Monteverdi's *L'incoronazione di Poppea*. As soon as his contractual obligations were fulfilled, Krenek and his wife headed to California. There he spent time with colleague Roger Sessions, played with a new music ensemble, and supplemented his income by playing in a WPA orchestra in San Francisco.

The Kreneks emigrated to America, this time for good, in the autumn of 1938. One of the artists who helped arrange for the Kreneks' escape was violinist Louis Krasner, himself an American citizen, who would later become concertmaster of the Minneapolis Symphony. Once in the United States, Krenek picked up a variety of jobs, either as a soloist with various orchestras, or as a lecturer. He accepted a teaching job at Vassar College in 1939, and stayed there for three years until he was driven to seek other employment because of an ongoing feud with the reactionary head of the music department.

At this juncture, Krenek learned that a position was coming open at Hamline University in St. Paul, and another—much more prestigious on the face of it—was simultaneously opening at the University of Minnesota in Minneapolis. As it happened, Krenek was in the midst of corresponding with Mitropoulos about the possibility of having one of his works played by the MSO. In a frank, detailed reply, Mitropoulos tried to warn the composer about the reception his more recent, atonal works would likely receive; the letter also included advice that Krenek not seek the University of Minnesota position:

> Your kind letter came right on the day of the first performance of the Hindemith symphony. Certainly I am asking myself what became of the composer of "Jonny spielt auf" and "Orestes," whom I enjoyed so much in Berlin in 1920. You almost complain of being forgotten, but have you asked yourself, too, if you have not forgotten also the public to whom you address yourself. It seems they can't follow you any more, you have deserted them by making yourself more and more abstract, therefore I am afraid they deserted you too. But I am sure all that is easy to remedy, knowing your talent and your genius—and really, believe me, I will be very glad to introduce a score of yours with more human appeal, like those you were writing some years ago.
>
> Excuse me this next: Hindemith with his new symphony was able to touch and to thrill even a Minneapolis *höchst konservativ* public. He didn't need to become cheap; he simply tried to be human, and he succeeded, and so he made the task for us performers easier in helping him. Let us hope it will be the same with you. Please excuse my writing you this advising kind of letter, but I feel deeply moved by the tone of your letter.
>
> As for the position here in Minneapolis, although I spoke to the music director himself who is about to resign, I'm afraid I can't give you much hope for I find out they need an American-born man with an American mind and American fame.[11]

Krenek did not get the University of Minnesota job, and had little choice, if he wished to enjoy continuous employment, but to take the offer from Hamline. Although he had concluded that "I am a little beyond their size, so to speak, and I believe they know that, too,"[12] he would not regret the decision. Still, at the time he made it, there was no sense of answering Destiny's call. As the composer later recalled: "That is how it came about. I had no intentions of reorganizing the middle-west . . . or of carrying the gospel of twelve-tone music to those prairies. I just had to come, and here I was."[13]

Hamline University had barely survived the Great Depression and looked it. Founded in 1854 by the Methodist Episcopal Church, Hamline University in 1942 had a faculty of sixty-six and an enrollment of slightly more than six hundred students. Krenek's duties were to teach theory, composition, and music history, to give piano instruction, and to supervise research projects.

The Austrian composer found his new school "a more remote, and, in many respects, more limited institution" than any other with which he had been associated—Hamline's music department had a budget of five hundred dollars per year with which to purchase books, scores, and instruments. Fortunately, Krenek regarded the situation as a challenge and not a demotion.

Mitropoulos welcomed his famous colleague with a handwritten note:

> I can't tell you enough how happy I am that you are coming to live near us. At least the Music Department of the Hamline University has real artistic intentions, in comparison with the narrowmindedness of the M. Depart., of our University. Thanks for your kind letter and I am looking forward to the day of our meeting.[14]

Among Krenek's first efforts was to get in touch with Mitropoulos about a new orchestral work entitled *Variations on a North Carolina Folk Song "I Wonder as I Wander,"* Op. 94. Treated in twelve-tone fashion, the piece did not sound much like a folk song, but the mere association helped audiences to listen with less prejudice, as did its convenient fifteen-minute length. In accepting the work for performance both in Minneapolis and during his now-annual guest stint in New York, Mitropoulos did add a word of caution: "don't be too harsh or too cruel! Don't think of my ears, better think of those of the poor unsophisticated public."[15]

Minneapolis heard the work on December 11, 1942. Rehearsals were tense and exhausting. Despite the players' considerable reservoir of good will toward Mitropoulos, they manifested a very understandable reluctance to confront a fifteen-minute work that demanded more effort than all the other music on the program combined. Violinist Louis Krasner described the mood thus:

> of course, when we got a new piece to play, whether it was Krenek, or Schoenberg, or Stravinsky, or whatever Mitropoulos put on the stands,

there was always some concern on the part of the players. Other things, they could play easily . . . but now they have to take this home and work on it. But it wasn't just the modern works. I remember once, we did a symphony of Borodin [Symphony No. 2] which was not in the usual repertoire [and] there was almost as much consternation and objection and inability to play as there was with the Krenek.[16]

The audience's response to their first dose of Krenek was predictably befuddled if not actually hostile. They applauded respectfully, if only because the newspapers had told them how famous Hamline's new professor was in Europe. John Sherman's review hit the mark when he wrote: "this work doubtless caused more discussion than any other on the program, for even those who objected to it must have felt it had much to say, and said it with originality and a curiously concentrated and allusive idiom."[17]

Oboist Rhadames Angelucci experienced an embarrassing moment after this concert. He was greeting his wife backstage and immediately blurted out: "What terrible music!" just as Ernst Krenek happened to walk by. Angelucci felt bad about the incident because he rather liked Krenek as a person, finding him "genteel and calm." He sought out Mitropoulos and confessed to inadvertently hurting the composer. "My dear," the conductor said soothingly, "Krenek is a very brilliant man, and it's fine writing. You don't understand it, perhaps, because it's too new to you."[18]

About one year later, when Mitropoulos was enjoying his third and last guest engagement with the Boston Symphony, Angelucci happened to hear the radio broadcast that included another performance of *"I Wonder as I Wander."* This time, his reaction was very different:

I *liked* it. Honestly. I was very surprised. I heard things that I didn't hear sitting in the orchestra playing this composition. I realized that there was actually a lot of thought and insight in what he had written. . . . In those days, we called it very modern music, it was "far out," and people used to tell me they couldn't understand this music; well, I couldn't understand it, actually [when we played it], . . . but when I heard it on that broadcast from Boston, I honestly did like it. . . . I could see there were things in there, that notes were popping out from different parts of the orchestra that I hadn't known existed.[19]

A year went by before Mitropoulos thought it was safe to program another Krenek work, this time the 1922 Symphony No. 2, a brooding, powerful, predominantly somber work, approximately fifty minutes long, drenched in expressionistic *weltschmerz*. The symphony was not a twelve-tone composition, but it was highly dissonant and its melodic content was muted, shadowy, and not easily perceived by ears more used to Brahms and Tchaikovsky.

Now it was the composer who cautioned the conductor: "it's rather aggressive . . . and it's very long. And Mitropoulos put it in his head that he wanted to do this. I even remember I warned him, but no, he said, 'I want to do this thing.' So he did, and of course, it caused a colossal upheaval."[20] The MSO players had to struggle much harder to get the symphony ready than they had for the folk-song variations, but most of them undertook the chore with an attitude of good sportsmanship. After the orchestra had struggled mightily to realize one of the symphony's massive, cacophonous climaxes, a double-bass player hollered out "Happy new year!" with such perfect timing that everyone, including Mitropoulos, broke up with laughter.

A concerted attempt was made to prepare the Minneapolis audience for this stern listening experience. Krenek gave a radio talk, illustrating the symphony's themes on a piano. Much newspaper space was devoted to lecturing the public about Krenek's credentials, his European triumphs, his standing in the music profession. Mitropoulos, in an interview with John Sherman, suggested that the concertgoing public had an obligation to give the Krenek symphony an attentive hearing: "We have made many gifts this season to symphony patrons, of old and cherished favorites from the repertoire. Now we are asking in return a gift of patient and thoughtful hearing. Listeners will not regret such consideration, for the Krenek symphony is music of great power and originality."[21]

Predictably, all of the listen-to-this-because-it's *good-for-you* publicity backfired and the symphony was given a chilly reception. Rarely did anything played by the MSO generate such heated condemnation from both audience and critics. Not many were able to listen past the symphony's harsh dissonance and surface aridity to perceive the expressionistic strength at its core.

A further element of controversy soon erupted behind the scenes. Mitropoulos went to Arthur Gaines, the MSO's hard-nosed business manager, and informed him that, because Krenek's ties to Europe had been severed by the war, the composer was not legally represented by any performing rights agency in America. According to the laws governing such matters, Krenek was to be paid the customary royalty directly from the orchestra's business account. According to Krenek himself, Gaines received this unexpected news with a stony countenance and replied: "We didn't know about that before the concert, so I don't think it is necessary. Besides, the creation of that kind of music ought to be discouraged."[22] Mitropoulos paid the royalty in cash.

Despite the antagonism toward his symphony, Krenek scored big with the skeptical Minneapolis audience only a few months later, with the March 24, 1944, premiere of his *Cantata for Wartime for Women's Chorus and Orchestra,* Op. 95. The unusual scoring was dictated by circumstance: enlistments and the draft had claimed most of Hamline's male voices. In any event, the work was brilliantly scored—some scholars aver that Krenek was a better choral composer than an orchestral one—and the text, derived from five poems by Herman Melville, was stirring.

In the spring of 1945, Krenek surprised everyone by writing an entertaining little piece called *Tricks and Trifles*—twenty-two playful and amusingly scored variations on a little four-note motif Krenek had discovered in a string quartet being composed by one of his students, Virginia Seay. The work was warmly received and interpreted, correctly or not, as a gesture of the composer's good will, a sign that he was willing to meet the Minneapolis public more than halfway.

Krenek's final Minneapolis composition was a major addition to his catalogue, the five-movement Third Piano Concerto. This impressive piece was commissioned by Mitropoulos and dedicated to him. Naturally, he played and conducted its first performance, on November 22, 1946. This extraordinarily compact work of about fourteen minutes fairly bristles with ideas, including one fiercely demanding passage that requires the soloist to reach inside the piano and pluck or strum the naked wires. Fred Gossen, a member of the MSO's chorus, found part of the performance risible: "Mitropoulos was a rather strange-looking man anyway—very skinny with this huge head—and he looked a bit odd from the back. He simply turned around and presented his rear to the audience while he plucked around inside the piano. All you could see was that great bald head and the rear end—the visual image was delightful."[23]

All the reviews cited Mitropoulos for his showmanship and energy. In what must have been a sweet moment indeed for Krenek, John Sherman's morning-after review sounded suspiciously like a fan letter:

> The Krenek work . . . achieved more vital communication with the audience (or at least with me) than any work of Krenek's played at Northrop. Keyless, full of technical mischief and sharp, wry dissonance, sparsely scored, it gained effects [by its] playfulness and lyricism. It had crackling originality, exploited curious textures (including a strumming of piano wires) and voiced its epigrams with pungency and rhythmic bounce.[24]

Soloist-conductor, players, and sharp-eared critics appreciated the brilliance and dash of Krenek's concerto (a work that still awaits its first studio recording, sad to say), but concertmaster Louis Krasner, from his vantage point in the front, was dismayed at the lack of audience response: "I remember being so dumbfounded that when it was over, and I expected the audience response to be so overwhelming, to find that nobody was with us. All this way, we've been driving an empty carriage. The locomotive had been going with all this enthusiasm and there was nobody on the train behind us!"[25]

This concerto was the last Krenek composition to be played by the Minneapolis Symphony for twenty years. Probably the most significant result of the Mitropoulos-Krenek propinquity was the founding, in late 1943, of a Twin Cities chapter of the International Society for Contemporary Music

(ISCM). By the time the chapter was forced to dissolve, after a final concert on March 12, 1947, it had presented thirty-seven works by twenty-four composers, including eight world premieres.

On December 1, 1943, the new ISCM chapter gave its first concert, in Bridgeman Hall on the Hamline campus. On the program were *Four Piano Pieces* by Roger Sessions, nine songs by Charles Ives, the world premiere of Krenek's Third Sonata, and Victor Babin's Sonata Fantasia for Cello and Piano. Subsequent programs showcased, among others, more music by Sessions and Ives, a violin-and-piano arrangement of Alban Berg's Chamber Concerto, a rhapsody for two pianos by Panamanian composer Roque Cordero (whose studies with Krenek were being paid for by Mitropoulos), and the hemispheric premiere of Schoenberg's *Book of the Hanging Gardens*.

Krenek insisted that the ISCM concerts be presented in an informal, open-arms atmosphere, designed to put the audience at ease with the novelties they were about to hear. Krenek usually delivered some introductory remarks, a task he performed with warmth and charm. The formula worked: the ISCM concerts developed a certain in-group cachet which lured new listeners and assured the ongoing loyalty of the already-converted.

Mitropoulos did whatever needed doing. Sometimes he was a featured soloist for piano music, sometimes he accompanied songs, and sometimes he just stood quietly and turned pages for other musicians. Neither Krenek nor Mitropoulos shied away from pure showmanship, as they demonstrated when they delivered a drop-dead performance of a four-hand piano version of Darius Milhaud's *Le Boeuf sur le toit*. Both pianists reveled in the sauciness and rhythmic excitement of the music and turned the performance into a virtuoso romp. According to one audience member "they beat the living tar out of that piano," to such an extent that the piano lid fell down. With an enormous grin, Mitropoulos reared up—still madly banging out his part—and flung the lid back to its upright position.

Even listeners who did not care either for Krenek's teaching methods or his musical style, sensed, thanks to the ISCM concerts and the international attention they received, that something special was going on in their community, something that had to be respected—a conjunction of creative energies that had made the Twin Cities an internationally known center of musical culture. Even a casual glance at the list of repertoire will confirm that Krenek and Mitropoulos, along with some remarkably dedicated colleagues and students, gave their audiences a concert series that any major musical capitol would be proud to claim for itself. That they were able to accomplish so much when and where they did makes their achievement all the more remarkable.

However gratifying his experiences in Minnesota, Ernst Krenek never reconciled himself to one aspect of life in St. Paul—unfortunately, a rather large aspect of life in St. Paul: the long, dark, Scandinavian winters. He coped as well as he could, but visions of California tormented him all the time, and close associates remember that the composer was genuinely miserable during the interminable weeks of January and February. He muted his displeasure when speaking to native Minnesotans, for he was always a man of good manners, but once he did lament to colleague Robert Holliday: "I wonder what desperation drove people to settle in this latitude!"

What finally drove Krenek from Hamline, even more than the winters, were the demands of his own creative muse: he gave so much of his time and energy to his teaching duties that he had too little left for his own creative work. When the opportunity came for him to move to California, to pursue teaching duties that were less demanding of his time, he went, though not without regrets as far as his students and colleagues were concerned. He knew, as they did, that his departure signaled the end of a period that would, in time, become almost legendary. In his later years, Krenek always spoke fondly of his time in St. Paul, saying: "The only time I was able to carry on instruction with full independence, and free of importunity, was when I was given the chance to build up my own music department at Hamline."[26]

Maybe so, but the manner of Krenek's leave-taking generated a great deal of resentment, even hostility, and poor Mitropoulos took the brunt of it. In a rather bitter letter dated January 5, 1948, he reported on the situation to Krenek, who was happily basking in the California sunshine:

> You don't know what I have gone through these last days. I must tell you that everybody in the school had the impression that you would come back for the second semester . . . because there are a lot of people who want to graduate with you . . . everybody at Hamline expected you back and therefore your resignation comes to them like a blow. I have heard comments which are going to the extent of finding that act of yours unethical. Naturally everybody addressed their comments to me as the man responsible for giving them an answer. I would have liked to tell them directly to their faces that this is what they deserved after the way they treated you here. Mrs. Carpenter and some of the other members of the board of directors who never liked your music now think they are fully justified in putting the blame on me. Now I don't know what to say.[27]

Thanks in part to Mitropoulos's unflagging advocacy, Ernst Krenek's reputation began to rise after World War Two. Not only his orchestral and chamber music but also his once-persecuted operas began to have performances during the 1950s. Krenek was in Europe when Mitropoulos died, in November 1960, but he was too busy with an upcoming opera production to take time out to attend the funeral. Evidently, he was also too busy even to issue a statement of gratitude to the memory of the one colleague who stuck by him and who paid a heavy price for doing so, for Krenek's only reaction to the conductor's death was silence and seeming indifference.

As for the orchestra members in Minneapolis, they were glad to have done it and gotten it over with. They had tried their best with a piece most of them regarded as fantastically overcomposed and virtually unintelligible. As the scattered and unenthusiastic applause began to sound, after Mitropoulos had stalked off the stage in a fairly thunderous mood, a man in the violin section was heard to remark: "Gee, is it over? I still had half a page of notes to play."[31]

One American composer Mitropoulos did not perform was Leonard Bernstein—yet another indication of how ambivalent his feelings were toward the "genius boy." When David Diamond sent Mitropoulos the score of Bernstein's Symphony No. 1, *Jeremiah*, for mezzo-soprano and orchestra, hoping to obtain a hearing for that work in Minneapolis during the 1943 season, Mitropoulos rejected the score. In the cover letter that accompanied the returned score, the conductor lamented Bernstein's compulsion to write such "Jewish music." Since Mitropoulos was certainly not anti-Semitic, that turn of phrase should be understood in the context of Mitropoulos's parallel disapproval of any notion that he should be a writer of "Greek music." As he had proven repeatedly in Athens, Mitropoulos saw no particular virtue in musical nationalism, and he found it irritating that Lenny should be so ethnically demonstrative. Of course, the conductor was conveniently forgetting that at the time he was Bernstein's age, he was composing *The Greek Sonata*, a piece that is at least as ethnically motivated as Bernstein's *Jeremiah*.

Mitropoulos never conducted a single Bernstein work, in fact, either in Minneapolis or in New York—a fairly glaring omission considering the Greek conductor's many performances of Sessions, Mennin, Diamond, Gould, Kirchner, and other Americans of Bernstein's generation. Bernstein reciprocated when he composed his cycle of piano portraits entitled *Seven Anniversaries*; the slot that once was to have been dedicated to Mitropoulos was assigned to Serge Koussevitzky.

For all the cloudiness of the two men's relationship, Mitropoulos remained fascinated by Bernstein and generally supportive. When Lenny was studying at the Curtis Institute and struggling desperately to feed and house himself on the paltry forty-dollar-a-month allowance Sam Bernstein sent him, Mitropoulos subsidized Bernstein with monthly checks for seventy-five dollars. Moreover, he was responsible for Bernstein's obtaining two guest-conducting engagements in Minneapolis, in 1943 and 1945. At a reception following the 1945 concert, Bernstein gave such a cruel, tasteless impersonation of Mitropoulos that he was publicly rebuked by the wife of concertmaster Louis Krasner.

In public, both conductors always spoke flatteringly of one another, but Bernstein, with close friends or after a few glasses of wine at a party, often indulged himself by savagely mocking the mannerisms and accents of both Mitropoulos and Koussevitzky. Such behavior was anathema to Mitropoulos.

Nevertheless, his most detailed written reference to Bernstein, in a letter to David Diamond dated July 14, 1943, seems abundantly fair:

I am receiving symphonies every day, and lately one from our friend Bernstein. Decidedly, there is an epidemic of symphomania. Everybody has to write a symphony. Certainly, that is their privilege. By the way, the work of Bernstein shows, as always, that the boy has talent for everything. I wish that God may put into his brain some order and some decision about what he is going to be—pianist, composer, or conductor. I personally think he could be all three, and more, but if he does not decide to do one of those things, he will never do anything good.[32]

Some months later, Arthur Rodzinski announced that God had told him to hire Leonard Bernstein as his assistant conductor at the New York Philharmonic. God's recommendation notwithstanding, Bernstein elbowed his way to the center of attention so often and so obnoxiously that Rodzinski banned him from entering the conductor's lounge. By that time, Bernstein had made his celebrated and seemingly spontaneous (but actually very carefully plotted) last-minute substitution for the supposedly ailing Bruno Walter, and his conducting career was launched, with or without Rodzinski's patronage.

On hearing of Lenny's remarkable success, Mitropoulos wrote to David Diamond, on January 11, 1944: "I am happy that Lenny Bernstein is going places now and that he will also have his happy time like many of us when we began. There is nothing more beautiful than to be a promising, talented, and genius young man."[33]

CHAPTER SIXTEEN

The Postwar Years: Awaiting the Summons

After the Allied liberation of Greece in May 1945, Mitropoulos was able to resume full-scale correspondence with Katy Katsoyanis. Their first rather flurried exchange of letters (only fragments of Katy's have been published, so the dialogue is rather one-sided in print) has a breathless, catching-up quality.

Mitropoulos's wording suggests, between the lines, that he felt he really hadn't missed much, other than the company of a small number of friends, by being away from Greece. Rather than spend time lamenting the chasm created by the war, Mitropoulos was eager to give Katy a very positive impression of his American career, and of the way he was regarded in his new homeland:

> The fact that I have been isolated from you all for so many years was certainly quite hard on me, but lots of interesting things happened to me from an artistic point of view. So I can say that during those years when so many other people were ruined, I feel that I have gained just as much in fame as in personal artistic progress. I can tell you without overestimating myself, that I developed more skill, more concentration, and maybe a more relaxed technique. Many people who knew me in the beginning and now have noticed that difference.[1]

Just below this paragraph, he ventured to explain to Katy the American concept of box office:

> Anyway, from the point of view of circumstances for creating fame, as our friend Rilke says, I can tell you that I have acquired some—quite important may I say. Not only among my colleagues, who seem to like and appreciate me wherever I go, but also from the box office standpoint. In case you don't know that term, it means the income results of every artist who attracts the public and fills the halls. An artist who has a box office must be an artist of value. Certainly, that is not always the case, but in a country where the business side is so important, this fact has lots of consideration.[2]

Not long after the war's end, Arturo Toscanini invited Mitropoulos to accompany him to Italy for a series of benefit concerts, the proceeds from which would go toward rebuilding the bomb-shattered La Scala opera house—a place dear to the hearts of both conductors. The request speared Mitropoulos on the point of a very keen moral dilemma. To most of his Greek friends, Italy was still the enemy—it was, after all, Fascist troops who first invaded Greek soil and who assisted the Germans during their brutal occupation. On the other hand, Toscanini had couched the invitation in such a way as to imply that a rejection would do irreparable harm to Mitropoulos's relationship with his Italian colleague. What finally decided the matter was Mitropoulos's own forgiving nature; he had not been harmed by the Italians, and had many times gone on record with the belief that Italy was basically a great and warm-hearted nation, however cruel and deluded its recent leadership may have been. At the end of a long letter dated May 1, 1946, dictated to his secretary Faith Reed, Mitropoulos tried to sneak the news past Katy in one short rather vague paragraph that included the sentence: "I tremble to know what you think about it."

Katy's reply fairly burst off the page with furious indignation. She could not, she began, find either an excuse or extenuating circumstances to justify his decision. How could Toscanini, dedicated anti-Fascist that he was, fail to understand why Mitropoulos hesitated to conduct in Italy before setting foot in Greece? Katy then reminded her friend of what Greece had endured so recently:

> It's a good thing that you yourself are fully conscious of the implications. It's a good thing that you don't talk about art being above it all. . . . Think: the whole countryside is in ruins; our villagers are living in the wrecks of their houses and in caves from which they come out when it rains to put their animals under shelter; we have no more bridges, nor factories, nor harbors—all of this the result of an infamous invasion and of an honorable defense. . . . If you had fought on the Albanian front, if you had spent here the unbearable years of the occupation, if the Italians had shot your father or your brother, if you had lost your home, and especially if you had been wounded with all the pain of your country—then of course such a gesture would have been in the spirit of the humanist-apostle you want to be.[3]

Mitropoulos was stunned at the vehemence of her attack, but thanked her, in his next letter, for being "a real friend" and rebutting his rather tepid justifications with her "cruel and inexorable" argument. He promptly canceled the Italian engagement, feigning illness as his excuse. Toscanini was probably not fooled, though there is no sign that he took umbrage. Probably he understood the delicacy of Mitropoulos's position better than Mitropoulos himself had at the beginning of the episode.

Throughout the late summer and autumn, the correspondence continued at a more normal temperature. Then, in December 1946, Katy had the painful experience of sending a telegram to Mitropoulos informing him that his mother had died. She went peacefully, quickly, in the middle of eating her breakfast. According to numerous passages in Katy's letters, it seems that Angeliki Mitropoulos had resigned herself to her son's prolonged absence. She knew of his meteoric success in America, and she knew that he loved her, and his regular infusions of money—some of which got through, via the Red Cross, even during the darkest days of the Axis occupation—had enabled her to survive the war years in some degree of comfort and security. Yet there seems to have been a curious distancing on the part of Mitropoulos. He wrote to her comparatively seldom and certainly not nearly as often as he wrote to Katy Katsoyanis or to Maria Negroponte. "Your fame gratified her more than your presence," Katy wrote in a letter sent a day or two after her grim telegram, adding, somewhat curiously: "She never stopped thinking of you, but, believe me, she didn't feel the *need* to see you. If, dear Dimitri, it hurts that you were not able to see her again, as I'm sure it must, you should be comforted with the thought that you were an exceptional son, and that you gratified a mother's ambition as few people have."[4]

Mitropoulos had in fact received Katy's telegram backstage, right after his first rehearsal with the Philadelphia Orchestra for a brief winter engagement during a time when Ormandy was out of action with a sprained shoulder. The wire landed on the desk of the orchestra's manager, who did not have the spine to deliver it. Instead, he deputized a musician named Louis Gesensway (a budding composer whom Mitropoulos had helped, both financially and professionally) to break the news to the conductor. In a moment of true black comedy, Gesensway importuned Mitropoulos with such an elaborate and clumsy preface that Mitropoulos, for a couple of horrified minutes, thought the man was about to ask him for a large sum of money. "I was prepared to be strong and refuse," Mitropoulos wrote of the incident, "if only because I myself was broke. Later on, I thought, ironically, that I would have given the man everything I owned not to have that news."[5]

Mitropoulos was growing increasingly restless as the decade entered its final years. His letters contained many references to the matter—most of them discreetly oblique until midway into 1946, when he began to write and speak much more directly—that he had hoped to have a better and more prestigious orchestra by this stage in his American career. One passage in a letter to Katy dated January 13, 1947, suggests that the conductor still had a somewhat naive idea of how much better circumstances would be in New York, in comparison with the way things were in Minneapolis:

> As far as the New York Philharmonic is concerned, there also Mr. Rodzinski is not very anxious to have me. So you see, my dear, I am afraid I will see my old days always connected with the Minneapolis Symphony Orchestra, which by the way is an excellent orchestra now. I have here lots of friends who love me. That compensates at least for the lack of interesting milieu and the pity of giving so much . . . to a public who loves me but is not quite able to appreciate what I am doing. That

doesn't mean that there is not here a nucleus of very advanced people, but as usual they are not very numerous. Out of the five thousand that the auditorium holds, there might be 200 who really feel and communicate with me.[6]

During the 1946–1947 season, the Minneapolis Symphony gave the largest number of concerts in its history; counting his out-of-town appearances, Mitropoulos conducted 143 concerts—a strenuous schedule indeed, considering the amount of travel and the relatively large number of new or unfamiliar works programmed. The winter tour that season consisted of thirty-five concerts in twenty-seven cities, followed by a tour of the Pacific Northwest that ran from March 22 to April 36, involving thirty-eight concerts in thirty-one cities. Immediately after the conclusion of this tour, he flew to New York and took the Philharmonic on a portion of its spring tour, conducting in a different city every night from May 3 to May 11. Summer brought only a brief vacation at Tapiola, then he was off to Philadelphia, where, in his new capacity as principal conductor of the Dell programs, he led twenty-eight more concerts.

One perhaps predictable result of so much concertizing was a temporary burn-out of enthusiasm for the warhorse repertoire. He confessed as much to Katy:

Now the only thing I look forward to is the new works which I am going to study between mountain climbing. You certainly know this is my only real satisfaction—like an old hard-boiled prostitute looking for new love experiences, because I am sure that you certainly know that it doesn't matter to me any more how beautifully or effectively or incomparably, etc. I might interpret a symphony by Brahms or Tchaikovsky, although the people, sincerely or not, express themselves as if they had never heard them before.[7]

In the very same letter, however, Mitropoulos went on at considerable ecstatic length about how he had just fallen in love with Puccini's *Madama Butterfly* for the first time, blithely unconcerned about the massive self-contradiction.

There were no Philharmonic dates in 1946, but in May, with the sponsorship of the International Society for Contemporary Music, Mitropoulos went to New York to conduct one of the season's most talked-about concerts. In cooperation with the Columbia Theater Associates, the ISCM mounted a full production of Stravinsky's *L'Histoire du soldat* on the stage of Columbia University's Brander Matthews Theater. Also on the program were Walter Piston's Divertimento and Krenek's *Symphonic Piece for Nine Instruments*.

L'Histoire was given a full and creative staging. The production began with the musicians sauntering on stage, smoking and talking, in their shirtsleeves. Narrator, conductor, and ensemble were on stage, fully visible during the piece, and took part in the action—giving advice to the hero, playing solitaire, drinking Cokes. At one point, when the soldier raised his glass to drink some wine, Mitropoulos pulled a bottle out from under the podium and took a drink too.

Reviews of this concert were unanimous in their praise. Both the Krenek and Piston works were taken seriously and measured intelligently for their considerable merits, but the Stravinsky was joyously received: "Those of us who were witnessing Stravinsky's great classic for the first time—and that meant a great many—felt we had been struck by a kind of artistic atomic bomb," wrote one reviewer.[8]

Riding a wave of ebullience from the success of the ISCM program, Mitropoulos headed for Philadelphia and the opening of a seven-week Dell season. For once, the opening night was favored by clement weather, and the Dell's business manager, David Hocker, announced from the stage that the opening night crowd had set a record for these concerts: more than twelve thousand people. As before, Mitropoulos did not serve the standard summery pops fare, but gave his huge *al fresco* audiences meaty and varied programs.

During the nineteen (out of twenty-eight) concerts he conducted, Mitropoulos led an exceptionally varied list of works, including Holst's *St. Paul Suite*, Tchaikovsky's seldom-played *Hamlet*, Milhaud's *Suite Française*, Mahler's First Symphony, Menotti's suite from the ballet *Sebastian*, Verdi's Requiem, Tchaikovsky's Second Symphony, Morton Gould's Concerto for Orchestra, and for the first and apparently only time in his career, Bruckner's Fourth Symphony.

Morton Gould came from New York and guest conducted one of the last concerts in June, the program that included his own compositions along with Oscar Levant's famed interpretation of Gershwin's *Rhapsody in Blue*.

Gould was exceptionally close to Mitropoulos; indeed, Mitropoulos once said that "Morton Gould is the only composer from whom I would accept a brand new work without even looking at the score. I know it will be good before I see the first bar."[9] Their first personal contact came about when Mitropoulos took Gould's *Spirituals* to Boston, where the work was enthusiastically received by audiences and critics alike.

Gould recalled that Mitropoulos spent much of his free time in Philadelphia with members of the artistic and musical community who were gay—including one who had an apparently unrequited crush on the maestro—but that the conductor mostly kept himself free of any attachment.

It was in Philadelphia and we were sitting around having drinks at this party, I think it was after a concert, and there was this young man there who was obviously very much taken with Mitropoulos and was really trying to make a play for him. Now I was sitting on the other side of Mitropoulos and I started to feel a little uncomfortable. I was thinking, maybe I'd better get up and leave. . . . So at one point I said to Dimitri, out of the side of my mouth, "Would you like to be left alone?" and he said, "No, no, don't go. Stay here." Later, when it was time to go, he said, "Let's take a walk around the block," which I was glad to do, because he loved walks and he was always great company on them. As we were walking, he said to me, "You see, I must keep my discipline. You saw that young man—how he wanted to be with me. But no, I must stay with my discipline." Now, I am sure, and I know for a fact, that there were times when he did not stay with it, but very often he was monklike and celibate. He was, I think, constantly torn between his own powerful sensuality, his physical drives, and his self-denial, his very disciplined work schedule.[10]

Another astute professional musician who got a close look at Mitropoulos during this productive summer season was David Amram. Amram's mother was a childhood friend of Henry Gerstley, president of the Dell concerts organization and one of Mitropoulos's closest friends in Philadelphia. On one occasion, when Gerstley happened to be present, the conductor noted that he had a rare break in his schedule, two days in a row without a concert, and expressed to the room at large a desire to go somewhere and relax. Gerstley said he knew of just the place, a commodious beach cottage on the Jersey shore, owned by his friends, the Amrams. They were a musical family and would probably be delighted to welcome the conductor. If Dimitri were interested, he would make a phone call and see if it could be arranged. With the impulsiveness that typified his catch-as-catch-can approach to recreation, Mitropoulos agreed, pending the Amrams' permission.

The Amram family thought this was a fine idea, and plans were made to make their distinguished visitor feel welcome. Young David had never seen Mitropoulos in person before, but he had listened to records and radio concerts from New York, and he looked forward to the meeting keenly. He was not to be disappointed.

"I noticed immediately," Amram wrote twenty years later,

that there was a constant electric energy that seemed to emanate from him . . . when I met him, his eyes seemed to go right through me, through my sister, my family, and the entire little house we lived in. He seemed to be able to see everything at a glance. At the same time there was a hint of a smile that played constantly about the corners of his mouth. He seemed to have life all figured out, with a kind of Olympian chuckle about it all. He seemed totally aware of everything that was happening, and able to cope with any situation.[11]

For the next two days, Amram and his family fell under the spell of Mitropoulos's conversation: "he spoke almost like a priest or a saint. Rabbis I had heard—friends of my father's with their wild Talmudic logic—none of them had this man's burning angelic spirit."

Two days after the end of this beach interlude, David Amram attended a Dell concert as the conductor's guest. He quickly came to understand

> how much the personality of the conductor has to do with the kind of music produced. The program included Debussy's *Iberia* . . . and Brahms's First . . . and when Mitropoulos walked out on stage to conduct, you could tell the musicians were glad to see him there. There was no looking at the floor, no zombie-like stares as if they were being humiliated by someone who was presumably going to lead them. They were *glad he was there*. And from the first downbeat to the last there was a kind of excitement I had never seen before at a concert. He seemed totally involved with the music and with the musicians, completely unaware of the audience. Some of his gestures were unfathomable and bizarre, but the music that came out was really inspired. I had never realized the fire and passion that lay in Debussy's music until I heard this performance. . . . It was possible to visualize great mountains and forests, to hear the wind whistling through the trees, to feel the branches rubbing against one another. Mitropoulos's own roots in God and nature were so deep they seemed to project these true natural feelings into the music and made it sound different from any performance of Debussy I had ever heard.[12]

Much as he adored the Debussy, the Brahms First was, for Amram, the finest experience of the concert. As a French horn player, Amram figured he knew this symphony inside-out, but on this occasion, the work seemed freshly minted, sprung direct from the fires of inspiration.

> The great torrents of energy, the contrasting pastoral and reflective moments sounded completely different. I actually had a vision of Greece (which I had never visited) . . . and it wasn't too much different from what Greece looked like when I did visit it eight years later. . . . I had the uncanny feeling that Brahms would have liked this performance more than any by the so-called Brahms experts, who made him drip with a lugubrious, Germanic, pedantic, heavy-handed sentimentality. Mitropoulos interpreted this as a free piece. I could see that he was trying to show the excitement that Brahms must have felt when he finished his First Symphony in his late forties.[13]

When Amram and his mother went backstage to congratulate the conductor, Amram was flabbergasted when Mitropoulos took him aside, in the midst of a great throng of well-wishers and celebrity-orbiters, and told him that he had read through the score of a horn trio Amram had composed, and that he should learn to modulate better. Amram had seen Mitropoulos browse through the score while visiting the beach cottage and he knew that Mitropoulos could not possibly have spent more than a half-hour glancing at it. Yet he next told the young composer the precise bar where the modulation needed work. Then he patted Amram affectionately and "went back into a trance and stared at the people again."[14]

When Amram next saw Mitropoulos, he was music director of the New York Philharmonic, and his style, in Amram's opinion, had become considerably less flamboyant on the podium, as though there were a new center of calm within him. The main work on the concert was Mahler's First Symphony and the orchestra was the National Symphony of Washington, D.C.—not, at that time, anyone's idea of a first-class ensemble. Amram thought they quite surpassed themselves under Mitropoulos and went backstage to tell him so after the concert.

"Maestro, having studied a little bit now," Amram began, "I'm able to see and appreciate what you're doing."

Mitropoulos replied, somewhat to Amram's surprise:

There is nothing to see, my boy. There is nothing to appreciate. There is really nothing to conducting . . . nothing to learn. It's all in the music. You have to learn the music. Naturally, there are many facets to conducting, to learning about different kinds of beats and different kinds of motions to produce a different kind of sound, many tricks to make players pay attention to you, and infinite ways of achieving different results and making clear what you have in mind. You have to learn how to be able to say it through the baton and your hands and physical gestures, without ever saying anything. But far more important and way beyond that is the music and the understanding and the knowledge of the music. If this is really there, that quality will communicate to the musicians faster than anything.[15]

On July 3, 1946, Mitropoulos and the Philadelphia Orchestra went before the microphones to record his interpretation of Prokofiev's Third Piano Concerto—the only commercial recording of Mitropoulos-the-pianist in the concerto repertoire—and a few days later to record Gian Carlo Menotti's *Sebastian* ballet suite. Both recordings suffer from shrill, coarse, blasty sonics, but at least the Prokofiev captures Mitropoulos's fire-breathing piano technique with some fidelity. Less successful was the Menotti recording—the sound is poor and the performance is uptight and square; Menotti himself hated it.

Mitropoulos was pleased that his Prokofiev interpretation was now preserved for posterity, but—in a long letter to Katy dated October 1, 1947—he expressed doubt that he would perform again as soloist/conductor in the foreseeable future. The added burden of memorizing a complex solo part, along with the orchestral score, had become too onerous; there was never enough time to prepare every element properly and the results were too often "forced" and therefore displeasing to him:

unless the struggle for the achievement is not forced, but natural, the moral purpose is weakened. In better words, it has to be projected not as an achievement but as an easy result of disciplined will, and one should not arrive at the summit of the mountain so exhausted that he cannot enjoy the beauty of the view, but simply say, "Oof! I am glad it is over!" Then it has no meaning. . . . In my mountain climbing it is my privilege to take my time. That doesn't matter, but when it comes to art it matters, and anything that does not totally surpass material difficulties and become spiritualized to the extent of annihilating any material impression is condemnable. . . . so let us summarize our philosophy: the achievement for the achievement, yes—but only for one purpose: to surpass the material, to annihilate it, reduce it to nothing, so that the spiritual achievement becomes an absolute morality, which is the only and unique goal of every man and artist.[16]

Duo-pianists Arthur Whittemore and Jack Lowe came to the Dell in July to perform Poulenc's Two-Piano Concerto, a charming, scintillating score in the composer's best *boulevardier* manner. It was the first Philadelphia performance in twelve years; a year later, the soloists made the first recording of the piece, for RCA Victor. They requested Mitropoulos as their conductor (the orchestra would be the eponymous RCA Symphony, comprising freelance talents and moonlighting musicians from the New York Philharmonic), and RCA told them that was fine, provided Mitropoulos was willing to work for five hundred dollars. He was, and Arthur Whittemore was astounded to learn that this was the first money Mitropoulos had ever earned from a recording:

> We played the Poulenc with him in '46, in Philadelphia. He learned the entire piece in one weekend. Then a year went by and we contacted him about doing the recording for RCA. He said he would do it, and the night before we were to record it, he called and said: "Boys, will you bring your score to the recording session?" And we said yes, we would, and then he said, "I haven't really seen it since last year and there's one spot in the clarinet part I'm a little uncertain about." We were astounded. Here it had been an entire year since he'd seen the score, and the only thing he needed to refresh his memory about was one little E-flat in the clarinet part! The next day, he glanced at that page, put the score down, and went through the entire recording session without even glancing at it again. Everything went so well we couldn't believe it; we finished the session with an hour to spare.[17]

The 1946 season turned out to be the most successful in the seventeen-year history of the Robin Hood Dell concerts. More than two hundred thousand listeners had flocked to the outdoor venue. A lion's share of the credit went to Mitropoulos, whose steady and galvanizing presence was deemed a vast improvement over the earlier arrangement, under which guest maestros flew in for a single rehearsal, conducted their concert, and flew out the next morning, a constant rotation.

At the opening of the 1947 Dell season, Mitropoulos led the Philadelphians through their first-ever performance of Prokofiev's Fifth Symphony. The city's leading music critic, Max de Schauensee, had not cared for the work when he heard Koussevitzky do it with the visiting Boston orchestra two years previous, when the score was brand new. As de Schauensee admitted:

At that time your reviewer didn't have too many kind words to say about Prokofiev's latest large-scale work. Hearing Mr. Mitropoulos's exposition of the symphony last night, he was forced to reverse most of his earlier opinion. . . . The Greek conductor seems like the ideal man for this work. His drive and energy kept the long curving line of the score moving where before it had seemed static, and who but he could so well have realized the long, slow, tortured *adagio* which forms the work's third movement.[18]

Eight thousand listeners turned out to hear soprano Marian Anderson, and close to fourteen thousand attended on the night of July 10, for a concert reading (a performance without sets, costumes, or stage action) of Puccini's *Madama Butterfly*. Eleanor Steber, one of Mitropoulos's favorite singers, played Cio-Cio-San to angelic perfection. The week after the concert, program annotator William E. Smith commented: "This writer has heard numerous productions of *Madama Butterfly* in the past, but never realized the full force and beauty of the work, its thrilling qualities and gorgeous orchestral fabric, until their glorious and thrilling manifestation by Mitropoulos and his splendidly responsive, inspired forces at the Dell."[19]

Although Mitropoulos grouched about conductors who pandered to the common ear, he saw no paradox in his sudden espousal of such an operatic chestnut because *Madama Butterfly* was, to Dimitri Mitropoulos, *new music*, and its charms were not in the least shopworn. He even gushed with pride about the opera in a letter written to Katy about one month after the performance:

strangely enough, my first direct and deep contact with Puccini's *Madama Butterfly*, in spite of its old fashioned almost faded beauty, made me really feel young and aroused in me my long suppressed dramatic and theatrical and emotional qualities. It was a real pleasure to be able, without a stage, almost alone, narrating the whole opera like a huge symphony . . . the effect was undoubtedly contagious and the people and musicians were equally thrilled with the result, without mentioning the fact that all this was achieved in only three and a half hours of rehearsals the same day as the performance. That almost equals any ascent of the Matterhorn or . . . Mt. Everest.[20]

The intense, almost pathological effort needed to achieve such results in so little time brought out the *Gipfelstürmer* in Mitropoulos, caused him to feel a "combination of high emotional necessity of expression" and the "high emotion of the necessity of achievement for itself."[21] Again, as was so often the case when he drove himself to one of these creative "highs," his philosophical justification bordered on outright masochism. He described his motive as "this combination of almost distressing struggle to achieve for the sake of achieving and for the sake of contemplating and absorbing beauty, regardless of the amount of struggle and self-abnegation which are the tributes one pays to be able to contact or touch the untouchable, the infinite."[22]

For the first time in three seasons, Mitropoulos went back to the New York Philharmonic from November 20 to December 14, 1947. His programs were the most stimulating of the year for that orchestra, including Barber's Cello Concerto, the world premiere of Krenek's Fourth Symphony, and the American premiere of Mahler's Sixth Symphony. Krenek had brought the Mahler symphony to Mitropoulos's attention, and its contrasting moods of pastoral yearning and grim, death-haunted struggle instantly appealed to the Greek conductor. Only one orchestral score of this symphony was known to exist in the United States and it was tucked away in the Library of Congress. Mitropoulos had to assemble a complete set of parts from various European contacts, including Katy Katsoyanis.

None of the above-listed works bothered the New York critics as much as Mitropoulos's resurrection of Richard Strauss's *Alpine Symphony*, Op. 64. Mitropoulos originally conceived of flashing each sectional title of the score onto a large screen above the proscenium as the orchestra began playing that portion. Just before rehearsals began, Mitropoulos got a letter from Bruno Walter. Evidently someone high up in the orchestra's management had decided that the slide-show constituted a compromise to bourgeois taste and that if word got out about it, there would be international snickering—another round of ammunition for snooty Europeans to hurl at America's low-brow aesthetics. This was the first, but not the last, time that the Philharmonic's management, through the avuncular Walter, curbed Mitropoulos's plans, the idea being that Mitropoulos was much less likely to get into a public dispute with an esteemed colleague than he was with Arthur Judson, the head of Columbia Artists Management, or Bruno Zirato, the Philharmonic's business manager. Walter's letter is a fascinating document, not only for the bizarre picture it gives of Bruno Walter presuming to lecture Mitropoulos on matters of aesthetics, but also because of the glimpse it affords of the indirect, Machiavellian way the New York Philharmonic's management sought to twist Mitropoulos's arm.

After expressing his "warm sympathy" for the Greek musician's philosophical viewpoint, Walter launched into a pedantic lecture on "the emotional power of music" versus its more circumscribed "descriptive power." In his *Alpensinfonie*, Walter contended, Strauss had debased his art: "seduced by his uncanny descriptive talent, he trespasses the noble limits of Symphonic Music." If the music cannot make its own descriptive points, why reinforce its empty rhetoric with captions? Why explain to the public the score's descriptive intentions and thereby confess the impotence of the music to make itself understood without such a crutch?

Walter's lengthy (and windy) admonition ended with a veiled threat: if Mitropoulos would not voluntarily abandon his slide-show scheme, the concert would be canceled and Walter would place his enormous prestige behind the action. The letter concluded with a ludicrously ironic postscript: "I am very happy that you perform Mahler's Sixth!"[23]

Mitropoulos's reply to this extraordinary supplication has not survived, but he must have been startled that Walter would lecture him so vehemently. He quietly abandoned the slide-show idea in deference to his senior colleague (and, not coincidentally, his superior in the Philharmonic's pecking order).

As things turned out, the slide projection probably would not have mattered one way or the other, for the Manhattan critics were ready to flail the Strauss piece before they had heard a note of the performance. "Empty and tedious" wailed Olin Downes, the most conservative of New York reviewers; only "one-twentieth of it—the aftermath of the thunderstorm—is mellifluous and sentimental in the most bourgeois vein, from which one would have expected Mr. Mitropoulos long since to have graduated." Another critic stated that hearing the Strauss was the closest thing to a "brain concussion" he had ever experienced in a concert hall.

Ernst Krenek had submitted detailed program notes for his Fourth Symphony, scheduled for its premiere on November 27, 1947, but he had written them in language and terminology more suited to one of his graduate courses in theory than to the average member of the New York Philharmonic audience. To avert the inevitable backlash, Mitropoulos felt obliged to write Krenek and ask permission to do a little editing:

> I must tell you about the alarming impression that your program notes . . . made. It went around in gossip and made me alarmed in spite of myself. I asked to read them, and I must confess to you that in spite of my complete acceptance of the whole script, I am afraid that if we print it exactly as you sent it we might alarm the listeners into thinking that they are hearing some kind of laboratory work, and they might thus miss the great message of your drama.
>
> So I ask you to allow me to print in the programs only the analysis of the symphony and nothing more. I really do believe the analysis will be helpful to the comprehension of the work, but the introduction might be, I'm afraid, disastrous. People still, when they hear about the twelve-tone system, always think about something terrible, and they should first listen to music without any prejudice. Then later on we might tell them how it is done.[24]

Despite the less intimidating program notes, Krenek's Fourth was received coldly by the audience, venomously by the reviewers. "A very poor and labored piece of music," wrote Downes, "artificial in method, lacking in invention, ugly and tedious."

In contrast to the Krenek symphony, Mahler's Sixth went over rather well. Some patrons, finding it too long and overheated, did scuttle for the exits before it was over, but most stayed and many of those joined in a standing ovation. Mitropoulos was praised for the seemingly incredible feat of memorizing the entire gigantic score and compelling the Philharmonic to play it accurately and with at least the rudiments of stylistic comprehension. Those who were present in Carnegie Hall on this night witnessed the laying of the foundation of the Mahler boom that erupted fifteen years later, the first rough incarnation of a nascent performing tradition.

Most intriguing of all were the generally ecstatic notices given to Mitropoulos's December 4 performance of Beethoven's Fifth Symphony. Since the conductor's erratic handling of such core repertoire works was among the larger knouts eventually used to flog him out of town, it is interesting to see how terrific the critics thought this early performance to be. "Not a single measure was routine, not a note that did not blaze, not a phrase that did not fail to cut to heart of its meaning," wrote Downes. "Every fermata was the roar, the endless defiance of Beethoven. It was a fresh reading of a masterpiece. . . . This interpretation must be rated as one of Mr. Mitropoulos's greatest achievements in this city."[25]

The only dissenting voice about the Beethoven was, with almost amusing predictability, Virgil Thomson's. Thomson accused Mitropoulos of playing to the gallery, gauging his dynamic effects for the amount of applause they would bring. Soft passages were clean, he admitted, but the loud passages, of which there are so many, were strident and unmusical. "There were no medium-weight passages," said Thomson; "everything was a feather or a ton of bricks."

The Minneapolis Symphony's 1948 winter tour (twenty-seven cities) included, for the first time, stops in New York and Boston. This was followed by an even more strenuous spring tour of thirty-five concerts, lasting from March 27 to April 26. When the orchestra was playing in York, Pennsylvania, a statement by Mitropoulos appeared in the Twin Cities papers and led directly to the opening of an FBI file on the conductor. The occasion was the publication in western newspapers of accounts of the infamous Politburo crackdown and public castigation of seven well-known Soviet composers, including Prokofiev and Shostakovich. They were accused of writing music that "follows the formalist trend—a trend against the people." Spread across fully one-half of the front page of *Pravda* was a resolution sharply critical of "survivals of bourgeois ideology nurtured by the influence of the decadent music of western Europe and America." This despicable trend, it was said, had "engendered in composers an obsession with intricate instrumental symphonic forms to the neglect of opera, choral music, and folk songs."[26]

Mitropoulos's statement, which he issued in reply to the many inquiries he received from the press, was a dizzying blend of rhetorical fuzziness, idealism, wishful thinking, and political naiveté; its tone of wait-and-see tolerance toward the Soviet denunciation was quite enough to cause J. Edgar Hoover to start a dossier on the Greek conductor. Mitropoulos wrote, in part:

to force artists to compose in one way or another is Utopian as well as being an insult to art itself, but certainly opera, choral and folk song forms are more accessible to the masses, therefore I do believe that such forms should be encouraged in order to uplift the people to a degree from which they can be still further raised to the higher form of abstract music.

Undoubtedly the Russian attempt to intrude in a censorial way in the productivity of their contemporary composers is an attack on artistic freedom.

Nevertheless, if Russia has a plan to educate her people, this regimenting way ceases to be an attack on artistic freedom. It simply means a considering of the artist as a worker serving the people, with compositions that will attract their interest and, in the process, educate them.

The composers are merely being ordered, or let us say urged to lay aside—momentarily, I hope—their artistic and no doubt legitimate impulses because the Russian masses are not yet advanced enough to absorb abstract music.

After all, strange as it may look, this attack on the part of the Russian government on artistic freedom is not a procedure at which we can cast the first stone, when here, with principles of democratic freedom of thought as our ideal, we still condemn to starvation those of advanced music thinking because we either do not like or do not understand their thought, not to mention those listeners who stubbornly refuse to be educated.[27]

The conductor was back in New York in May 1948, after the conclusion of the Minneapolis season, for another highly successful ISCM concert. The venue was the Juilliard concert hall; the featured artists were Louis Krasner, violin, and Eduard Steuermann, piano; Stravinsky's *L'Histoire du soldat* was featured, coupled with Alban Berg's Chamber Concerto for piano, violin, and thirteen winds.

The Stravinsky work was fully staged—with costumes, props, and blocking—and Mitropoulos took an even bigger part in the theatrics than he had in the previous performance of *L'Histoire*. He and the Juilliard ensemble were dressed in workers' caps and overalls and often took part in the stage action. "An absolutely first class actor!" wrote Olin Downes of the conductor.

On June 22, 1948, the Robin Hood Dell opened its nineteenth season. As in previous seasons, Mitropoulos offered hearty, challenging musical fare, including Mahler's First and Strauss's *Also Sprach Zarathustra*. Rainy weather limited attendance at some of the early concerts, but twelve thousand patrons showed up on the night of July 12 to hear Lauritz Melchior belt out Wagner selections.

Fourteen concerts had been scheduled for the season. Not only did bad weather cut into the box office receipts, but the 1948 Republican Convention was in town, monopolizing the taxis and absorbing the attention of many Philadelphians who might otherwise have gone to the outdoor concerts. The only attraction that turned a significant profit for the Dell organization was a pops evening conducted by Sigmund Romberg. Mitropoulos knew the Dell concerts were in trouble as early as July 13, when he wrote about the situation to his dear friends, the Coopers:

> Our concerts here so far have been very unsuccessful, partly because of the weather and partly because the people are more interested in conventions and in having a grand time than in coming to listen to our long-beard expressions in music. The Association has so far lost ten thousand dollars, so everything looks very gloomy and I don't know what might happen by the end of the season. Yesterday, however, Romberg . . . did fill the house to capacity, which is about 15,000, and once more the manager realized the futility of trying to inject what we call beautiful serious music into the minds of people who don't want it. There was lots of cheering and happiness yesterday in the audience in which I was present, crying inside of me for the inexorable fate that all people who deal with spiritual values have to go through. The only thought that comforted me, if I can say that, is that the full house gave me some hope that we might get through the rest of the season with the other clownish attractions that are coming, and quieted my fear that I might not get my salary from which I need to live. . . .
>
> The town has been jammed absolutely with Republicans. The hotel in which I live was crowded with bands and choruses singing Stassen's heroism, stature, and deeds in conflict with the bands of Mr. Dewey and some other California fellows. I was in the middle of all this, deploring the day I was born. . . . Believe it or not, seriously, I want to take refuge as soon as I can in the jungles and join Dr. Schweitzer, who is really the wisest of all men.[28]

Three days after Mitropoulos penned those despairing words, the plug was pulled. At intermission during the concert of July 16, the orchestra was informed that the season was being terminated after the next concert. All who were present when the gloomy announcement was made were asked to keep the information private until the Dell's management had released its official press statement the following morning.

Mitropoulos did not wait. Exasperated, even angry, he spontaneously blurted out the story as he was accepting the applause of the audience. After his third bow, he suddenly veered off course to the nearest live microphone and announced: "You might as well enjoy yourselves. Tomorrow night is the last night. The Friends of the Dell have let us down."[29]

Henry Gerstley, president of the Dell concerts, had no choice but to face the press that same evening. Not only reporters but also dozens of upset patrons crowded backstage for confirmation and enlightenment. The numbers told the story, Gerstley said; season ticket sales were off by almost $25,000, recording royalties had not lived up to projections (in large part, one imagines, because of their wretched sonics), the early run of bad weather had cut into attendance badly, and an unknown but presumably large number of potential patrons were sitting comfortably at home, listening to the Republican Convention on their radios. This was also the first political convention to be televised, and even though the number of TV sets in Philadelphia could not have been large, people would squeeze into any room that had one—so compelling was the novelty of this new medium.

Only two thousand listeners showed up at the final concert. After Mitropoulos led his demoralized forces through an intense rendition of Berlioz's *Rakoczy March*, the faithful rose and gave the musicians an ovation that lasted through eight curtain calls.

In his post-mortem analysis of the Dell's premature closing, critic Max de Schauensee called the incident "a disgrace to a city which has always prided itself on being one of the great musical centers of the country."[30]

Mitropoulos would never conduct the Philadelphia Orchestra again. Ormandy saw to it.

"Mitropoulos Takes Whack at 'Tosca'" read one headline after Mitropoulos conducted a "concert performance" of Puccini's opera at Lewisohn Stadium on July 26 and 27, 1948. Although the critics lavished praise on Eleanor Steber's Tosca and were generally kind to the young tenor named Louis Roney who sang Mario, their verdict on the conducting was mixed. Irving Kolodin found the orchestral treatment to be filled with "mathematical, rather angular phrasing—Mr. Mitropoulos seemed to desire the grandiose, the oratorical almost, but though he amply succeeded in obtaining them, he left the bulk of Puccini's *Tosca* in the score, there to await some other opportunity for total release."[31] On the opposite side of the jury were an equal number of reviews that called Mitropoulos's interpretation "stirring" or "notably cogent, pungent, and dramatic . . . he presided over the executants like an inspired madman."[32]

The conductor's decision to program *Tosca* also occasioned another long-distance argument with Katy Katsoyanis. When Mitropoulos casually announced that he intended to mount a concert performance of that opera, first in Philadelphia then in New York, Katy expressed her disapproval in no uncertain terms:

I must admit that with regard to *Tosca* I experience a kind of allergy . . . to me Puccini in that case wallows in the shallow waters of melodrama, lacking Verdi's dramatic elation which might have helped him get unstuck. . . . Do you really think it is consistent with the function of a conductor, as you yourself have conceived it, to adorn a mediocre work with the misleading brilliance of a splendid interpretation and thus present it to the audience with a greatness not in fact its own? I, on the contrary, believe that an artist as genuinely inspired as you has the right to trust his talent to render accessible to the public works which it would otherwise be unable to understand and enjoy.

However, as for this year the die is cast, perhaps I can convince you with regard to next year, because after *Tosca*'s triumphant success the manager will undoubtedly propose . . . *La Bohème!*[33]

As if sensing that she might have castigated him in a manner out of proportion to his sin, Katy softened the ending of this letter with a spirited pat on the back, for what his ongoing crusade on behalf of the difficult and the contemporary:

What pleases me particularly is that against all opposition you carry on presenting avant-garde compositions, in other words, instead of "like Savonarola, threatening the naive with eternal fire," you offer the Hell on this Earth! [Abstract music]—spiritual inferno for the poor listener! Here is a kind of torture that escaped Dante's imagination. But I forget that Dante was a Latin and consequently placed abstraction in Paradise.[34]

Mitropoulos was incapable of carrying on a lengthy epistolary argument in the sustained bantering tone Katy employed. Instead, he had already mounted a serious and closely reasoned defense of his decision:

The matter of the performance of *Tosca* . . . it is unfortunately not exactly my choice, but you must understand it isn't quite a concession from my part either. Such an undertaking is a costly enterprise and, after all, the summer concerts are more on the popular side, although I try symphonically to uplift them with very serious works. But when it comes to such an expensive performance, they have to have some assurance of box office, that is, people's attendance, which will be able to pay the expenses. . . . Unfortunately the Philadelphia [and New York] concerts have not the stuffy and aristocratic and conceited atmosphere of the Berkshires, where Mr. Koussevitzky enjoys a higher type of works with some millionaires. We represent the people. We give music to the people and, like children, we have to give them bonbons so that they will be able to swallow some more bitter medicine, until they arrive at the possibility of enjoying something for which they have to make an effort. . . . Anyway, it can't be done by going around like Savonarola and threatening people with the flames of hell because they smile and laugh and have a good time, and telling them that unless they stop liking Puccini they will be condemned to eternal fire.[35]

Mitropoulos opened the New York Philharmonic's autumn 1948 season on October 7 and stayed through most of November, directing a total of twenty-four concerts. A subtle shift in tone is perceptible in the way Manhattan's critics were now treating Mitropoulos's concerts: seldom encountered is the sense of surprise and discovery—pro and con—that characterized the notices written when he was a little-known and fairly exotic guest, a dark horse in the ever-fascinating conductorial sweepstakes for the Philharmonic.

By the start of the 1948 season, most Manhattan insiders knew it was only a matter of time until the Philharmonic job would be offered to Mitropoulos, if indeed it had not already been. To his critics, he was already damned-if-he-did, damned-if-he-didn't. When he conducted difficult and austere music, he sometimes won accolades, but in the process he had to contend with criticism from the Philharmonic's management about what those programs did to the box office; if he played a program of well-known classical-era favorites, he was open to unfavorable comparison with Toscanini or Bruno Walter or George Szell; if he resurrected pleasant, middling-to-good music that deserved an occasional hearing (Charpentier's *Impressions of Italy* was a prime example during the 1948 season), he was roundly booed by both the liberal and conservative critics. Welcome to New York.

The quality of Mitropoulos's October 7 reading of Brahms's First Symphony quite took Virgil Thomson by surprise, as he confessed in a wildly opinionated notice that was one of the few totally positive reviews he gave to a Mitropoulos concert:

> The program was just chestnuts, and not first quality chestnuts either, unless you consider Brahms' First Symphony a first-class work, which I do not (although the idea that it is not is not original with me). The Philharmonic itself, though unquestionably a first-class orchestra, is not a sensuous or colorful music producing body, and never has been in my memory. And Mr. Mitropoulos, though surely a musician of the first water, has long been a disappointment in performance, because of the cast-iron tone quality he draws from any orchestra and the frequently over-weening nature of his emphasis.
>
> The pleasurable quality of last night's concert came from an ease of execution that has not hitherto been shown in New York by this conductor and that is, heaven knows, not characteristic of our Philharmonic. As if the brilliant mind and powerful director we have all known him to be had come, toward fifty, into serenity. His readings were both straightforward and reserved, alert but impersonal, thoroughly musical and at no point egotistical in expression.[36]

Thomson sustained the critical counterpoint by praising Mitropoulos's decision to perform, on October 21 and 22, Schoenberg's seminal *Five Orchestral Pieces*, Op. 16:

> Arnold Schoenberg's *Five Orchestral Pieces* . . . were written in 1909, nearly forty years ago. Previously they have been played in New York, I believe, one and three-fifths times. They are among the more celebrated works of our time, and yet few musicians or music-lovers have heard them. The present writer, though the owner of a printed orchestral score for twenty-five years, listened to them last night with virgin ears. Having followed the performance score in hand, he is able to certify that Mr. Mitropoulos and the Philharmonic boys read them faithfully and to perfection.[37]

Only a week after the Schoenberg pieces, which a surprising number of Philharmonic patrons found oddly appealing ("music to read science fiction by," was one overheard response), Mitropoulos served up another important twentieth-century work, on October 31: Anton Webern's Passacaglia, Op. 1. This seldom-heard composition—firmly entrenched in the key of D minor and drenched with rich post-Wagner chromaticism—also went over well with critics and commoners alike. The conductor's treatment of this elusive score was judged "beyond praise in all respects."[38]

On October 28, the Philharmonic gave the New York premiere of Morton Gould's Third Symphony, a substantial and serious work first played one year earlier in Dallas and greatly revised during the interim. November opened with the first performance of a work by a forty-one-year-old, one-armed Greek composer named Harilaos Perpessa. Mitropoulos was the first—and ultimately the only—conductor to champion Perpessa's music. Perpessa, though of Greek parentage and claiming Greek nationality for himself, was in fact born in Leipzig and studied under Arnold Schoenberg in Berlin. His music was not at all like Schoenberg's, however, but was strongly romantic in mood, conventional in tonality, and heavy in orchestration. The advocacy of Mitropoulos brought Perpessa briefly out of the cultural shadows and into the limelight, but to no lasting effect. The work played in 1948 was his Prelude and Fugue, and it shared program space with a Wagner overture, the Schumann Cello Concerto, and, after intermission, the Symphony in B-flat Major of Chausson.

Although not especially shapely, the lineup certainly afforded the pleasure of contrast. Olin Downes, in his review of November 5, labeled it "a very queer program," although he declined to elaborate on what, exactly, made it so. The Perpessa work he dismissed as "very difficult to play . . . and of distinctly dubious value." The audience, much to Mr. Downes's patrician dismay, loved the piece, applauded it lustily, and cheered the rather beefy-looking composer when Mitropoulos called him to the stage.

One week after the Perpessa premiere, Mitropoulos boldly programmed Mahler's seldom-played Seventh Symphony, balancing it, on the concert's first half, with a Mendelssohn overture and Poulenc's delightfully fizzy *Concert champêtre* for harpsichord and orchestra. Poulenc himself was at the keyboard, and the work thoroughly charmed its listeners. The critics, rather surprisingly in view of the esteem Poulenc would enjoy only a decade later, responded like a pack of old fogies, clucking their tongues at the work's sprightly, effervescent qualities and implying that, for some strange reason, any work composed for the harpsichord had to be Serious Stuff in order to be worthy of their attention.

Olin Downes, at least, lauded the Poulenc work, mainly because it was so much more digestible than the Mahler symphony that followed. His remarks on the Mahler are quite typical of the entrenched resistance Mitropoulos still met when he programmed works by that Austrian composer: "Under ordinary circumstances, we might say that the Poulenc music was witty and ingenious but rather superficial . . . [but] as the Mahler symphony went on and on, from one dreary platitude and outworn euphemism to another, one regarded Poulenc with ever-increasing esteem."[39]

Italian pianist Arturo Benedetti Michelangeli made his American debut on November 19, playing the Schumann Piano Concerto and scoring an impressive success with audience and reviewers alike. Mitropoulos rounded off his longish engagement by introducing two more new works in his final pair of programs: *Vision dramatique* by Polish composer Karol Rathaus, and Artur Schnabel's *Rhapsody for Orchestra*. This was the first Schnabel work Mitropoulos had conducted since the notorious Minneapolis performance of the First Symphony. Although shorter, by far, than any of Schnabel's symphonies, the *Rhapsody* was equally complex: polytonal, polychordal, frequently and fiercely dissonant. To the delight of both composer and conductor, the piece held the audience's attention, was generously applauded (although some measure of that response was no doubt motivated by respect for Schnabel the great Beethoven interpreter, not Schnabel the composer), and received very respectable reviews.

Before this eventful year was finished, Mitropoulos had to live through two more personal crises; one was painfully wounding but temporary in its effect, the other would alter his very destiny and shorten his life.

One year earlier, a manifesto had appeared in the Athenian press, collectively signed by a group calling itself the Praesidium of Greek Composers, which reproached Mitropoulos in fairly strong language for his lack of interest in the Greek national school. His rejoinder was blunt and went straight to the heart of the matter:

I am ready to take up any composition of value which has been composed in the last ten years—i.e., since the time when I have lived in Athens—however I reserve for myself every right to perform the compositions which I pick out here, and in so doing to take due regard for the taste and level of sophistication of my audience. My [Greek] colleagues should know that everything we bring to performance here is world-class music, with the exception of the new works of young American composers, to whom we are directly committed.[40]

In effect, Mitropoulos was saying to the hometown composers: write something really good, and we'll consider it. He had, after all, performed an entire concert of Greek music in Minneapolis in 1939, and he premiered Greek works in New York in 1948, 1950, and 1954. While audience response was mixed, critical response to everything except the Skalkottas *Four Greek Dances* was not very positive. He felt that the works of Kalomiris, for example, with their heart-on-sleeve nationalistic folksiness, were not likely to wow the tough New York audience. In the poisonous atmosphere of the Manhattan cultural hothouse, only the strongest and healthiest musical blossoms stood a chance of survival. And by presenting works of palpable inferiority, Mitropoulos would have been accused of nationalistic favoritism—another rock for the mob to throw at him.

All of which was true, as far as it went. It seems very odd, though, that the conductor never applied the same argument to the often rather faded specimens of generic romanticism he conducted with such gusto (the Charpentier suites, the early tone poems of Saint-Saëns, the works of Mohaupt, Rabaud, Balakirev, Pfitzner, and d'Indy—the list is a fairly long one), which elicited at least as much condescension from the reviewers, regardless of their inherent worthiness of an occasional hearing, as anything by Kalomiris was likely to do. And such an argument begs the question of Skalkottas's more advanced and challenging scores, not all of which were severely atonal by any means.

One has to venture something of a guess in this matter: that Mitropoulos had become, over the decade of activity that separated him from his Athenian roots, far more embittered about the cultural conditions in Greece than he was willing to admit even to himself. That such an automatic prejudice existed in him, a kind of knee-jerk intellectual aversion to any musical product of that milieu, would not have been an easy thing to admit, even for someone who was ordinarily so ruthlessly honest about himself and his feelings.

This possibility seems confirmed by the renewed flare-up of anti-Mitropoulos articles that appeared in Greece in 1948, following a singularly unpleasant incident after a New York concert. A belligerent correspondent for an Athenian newspaper had tried to corner Mitropoulos backstage after one of his New York concerts, while the conductor was in his usual smiling-but-detached after-concert mode, trying to cope with dozens of fans and hangers-on who had crowded around him. The Greek correspondent kept hurling loud, aggressive questions, in Greek, over the heads of everyone else, needling Mitropoulos until he was provoked to a rare display of public anger. Turning on the reporter, he furiously responded, in English: "You Greeks must understand that I am not your property—that I belong to the people of the world!"[41]

This brief display of all-too-human pique occasioned a renewed barrage of vilification in the Greek papers. Dragged forth into the headlines was a speech Mitropoulos had given in Boston more than a year earlier, lamenting, in his usual Ghandian manner, the way in which the American government was pouring arms and military advisers into Greece to bolster the rightist government in its savage and protracted civil war against a Communist-dominated partisan army of leftists. The conductor was, of course, blissfully unaware of the brutality being inflicted on the Greek peasants by the more ideologically severe partisan commanders, and his remarks had the same idealistic, above-it-all political fuzziness as his ill-considered press release about the Politburo's clampdown on Soviet composers.

Inspired by the lofty tone of Mitropoulos's remarks—so endearingly in keeping with the musical priest image that had grown up around him—his audience had been demonstrably moved. Unfortunately, a representative of the neo-Fascist Greek government was on hand, and he deliberately mistranslated and edited the conductor's statements, making him sound, when this version was splashed across the front pages of the Athens newspapers, callously indifferent to the suffering caused by the conflict, opposed to American aid, and downright unpatriotic.

When the disgruntled Greek reporter filed his vengeful story from New York, the whole issue was fanned into flames again, even more bitterly than it had been the first time around. Even the conductor's most loyal Greek supporters were outraged at some of the things he supposedly said. And to be fair, that "You Greeks must understand that I am not your property" remark, when taken out of context, certainly seemed like a slap in the face to all the pro-Mitropoulos people who had endured first the Nazi occupation, and now the even more barbaric horrors of civil war. An apparently furious letter from Katy Katsoyanis (unfortunately not reproduced in the published version of their correspondence) forced Mitropoulos to defend himself to her:

> So once more, protected in a prosperous country, I again pronounced from my pedestal sentences which offended my compatriots. . . . All this mess started, in my opinion, because the European help that comes from America has one purpose—to bribe people and handicap their making their own decisions. . . . As long as our help consists of guns and more guns, inevitably the result will be catastrophe. . . .
>
> I love Greece as much as you do but I do not love Greece in a purely human way as you do. Your advices have too much of *couleur locale*, and I am not interested any more in such colors; I am only interested in humans in general. Everybody is my compatriot from now on and always has been, and I really do feel that I am the property of everyone. . . . I feel only upset that without wishing to I offended and wounded suffering people. I certainly did not have that in mind when I said what I said. I was emphasizing the necessity for humanity to get together and abandon nationalistic prides, and urged the spiritual values, not of

narrow-minded local content, but of Christian brotherhood. Again you can say that if I were in danger of being decapitated . . . by a Communist fanatic, I would not have the courage to speak of human brotherhood— but who made him a fanatic? How can you expect wisdom when people have been pushed to extremes by the immorality of the powerful groups?[42]

Katy was not letting him off the hook so easily. Her reply to this letter is reproduced in the published collection of letters, and it shook Mitropoulos deeply when he received it:

Your whole letter . . . is permeated with such fanaticism, and your charges against us are so heavy that, if you do want criticism, you'll receive it today.

For me, too, the brotherhood of nations is one of the highest ideals . . . and I think Greece is a beautiful foundation from which to embrace the world. But since you are "not the property of any country, but belong to the people of the world," why is it that when you talk about Americans, you say "we"?

You accuse me of loving Greece in a very human way. I think that love is not an ideal but a feeling, therefore something very human. In any case, I'm not chauvinistic, but I do love this country. . . . I like its nature, I like its people full of substance, exaltation, and unpredictability. They know how to improvise the unerringly right gesture at great moments.[43]

The conductor's response writhed with masochistic humiliation:

I feel spanked, mortified, ashamed, and in American slang, like a heel or a skunk. . . . I accept the horrible punishment with pleasure because it comes from a deep affection like yours. . . . You call me a fanatic; I am not . . . I am only a person who seeks for love, and I also use my art for this purpose. That is why my artistic life has been successful, because it always showed a necessity for communication and love between me and my audiences. The rest is nothing more than a very puerile and amateurish way of making big talks about problems that need greater persons. . . . All I know is to conduct—my thinking is a hobby, and therefore confused—I have to accept with humility my fate of being a prostitute, trying to understand and to feel each time somebody else's mind and interpret it to the best of my ability.

You know me very well by now, you have seen me in my most distressed moments. I always arrive at the edge of a precipice, and I guess before I die I will have to go through the same procedure many times. Therefore, this mistreating myself, as you say, as long as it doesn't go to the extent of committing suicide, is a challenge and a kind of self-imposed penalization and each time I feel it includes in it a germ of progress.[44]

With peace restored between the two correspondents, and the controversy in the Athenian newspapers burning itself out, Katy responded with an ebullient letter that inadvertently contained a line of chilling prophecy:

Let's not lose courage—what man envisioned will sooner or later become reality. For the time being, let's hurry up and exchange a few more letters on this earth, before I am blessed with listening to the concerts you'll give for the angels. I wonder only whether your whole repertoire will have a place in Heaven—or whether you'll be obliged for some of your pieces to take a tour into Hell.[45]

Appropriately, the opening concert of the 1945–1946 Minneapolis season was "A Victory Concert," which Mitropoulos dedicated to the men and women of the U.S. Navy and for which the stage at Northrop had been draped with flags. Attendance set a new record—5100 people, many of them still in uniform. On the program was, naturally, Beethoven's Fifth (in one of its last appearances as "The Victory Symphony") and Ernst Bloch's shaggy but amiable *America: An Epic Rhapsody*, for which the orchestra was joined by three local choruses.

November 1945 was a month of the new and the novel. Both Tchaikovsky's Second Symphony and Schubert's Sixth were played—the former had not been heard in Minneapolis since the days of Verbrugghen, and the Schubert, to the astonishment of the critics who looked it up, had never been played in town before. Also heard in November was the American premiere of Max Reger's Piano Concerto in F. This complex, Teutonic, note-heavy work came blazingly to life as Mitropoulos and Rudolf Serkin played it, and the reviewers, rather to their surprise, enjoyed it hugely. One critic even wrote: "This music has good nerves, good soul, and excellent viscera."[46]

And on the last day of November 1945, Louis Krasner and Mitropoulos presented the Minneapolis premiere of Arnold Schoenberg's Violin Concerto. Many listeners reacted as did critic John Sherman, who tried mightily to keep an open mind but who finally confessed that the whole piece seemed "monotonous, gray and airless." Most of the audience suffered dutifully and applauded politely, but one reviewer, Norman Houk of the *Minneapolis Tribune*, experienced, to his immense surprise, a Road-to-Damascus conversion:

Underneath the complex surface of this difficult piece . . . was not nonsense, but order, and as much emotion as can be discovered in any romantic composition, which this concerto essentially is. That may not have arrived on first hearing, but it was there.

I sincerely hope we are aware of the enormous debt we owe to Dimitri Mitropoulos and Louis Krasner. It is Mr. Mitropoulos's forward looking that makes Minneapolis an important music center. He is probably the only conductor in the country not frightened by the difficulties

of this score, and the only one who could give it a performance equal to that of, say, Beethoven.[47]

Nineteen-forty-six was the year the Minneapolis Symphony Orchestra became stable again, after its wartime stresses and inconsistencies. The orchestra's funding became secure once more, its ranks filled to capacity, and, for the first time, a significant number of women players—five—appeared as regular members of the ensemble. Mitropoulos himself seemed to go from strength to strength; although his programs sometimes offered bizarre juxtapositions, and reviewers sometimes chided him for the stridency and nervousness of his interpretations of the romantics, it seemed that on the whole he was happy in Minneapolis and Minneapolis was still happy with him.

A substantial percentage of the 1946 programs was given over to the new and the unfamiliar, but only a few selections (the Krenek Third Piano Concerto comes most forcefully to mind) presented really formidable challenges to the audience. Once again, Mitropoulos presented scrupulously knowledgeable readings of a cross-section of musical styles: Gould's Concerto for Orchestra, Britten's *Sinfonia da Requiem*, Respighi's *Gregorian Concerto*, and the Third Symphony of Sir Arnold Bax.

Several veteran Minneapolis Symphony players indicated, during their interviews for this book, that Mitropoulos's last three seasons with the orchestra were the smoothest, the most technically secure, and overall the best-programmed. A detailed reading of the week-by-week reviews reinforces this impression. Wartime fluctuations of personnel were a thing of the past, the orchestra's growing prestige—international as well as national—was a source of pride even to people who did not care for the contemporary scores whose performance had engendered that prestige. Mitropoulos himself was more relaxed; his interpretations were now a bit broader, less nervy, less characterized by too much jumpiness in the brass and occasionally indifferent work in the woodwinds. The string sections had bloomed under Louis Krasner's guidance, and while no one would describe this orchestra's string tone as lush (even on the much-admired Mercury recordings under Antal Dorati, made in the early days of stereo, the strings always sound thin), it had become solid, more precise, and had developed a nice sheen. A new recording company, RCA Victor, took the place of Columbia; their first recording, a Rachmaninoff Second Symphony taped in January 1947 that shows off the orchestra to impressive advantage, including string playing that is searingly intense without becoming scrappy.

On the whole, Mitropoulos's final seasons were marked by fairly consistent programming policies. Any new music was of high quality and relatively accessible, works on the order of Barber's heart-rendingly beautiful

Knoxville: Summer of 1915, Webern's fascinating Passacaglia, Op. 1, or Vaughan Williams's spellbinding Sixth Symphony.

Ascending a musical summit once more, Krasner and Mitropoulos gave the Minneapolis premiere of Roger Sessions's Violin Concerto, on November 14, 1947. The stone-faced reactionaries were, on this occasion, vastly outnumbered by an audience that listened with respect and sincere concentration. Again, as he had so often during the Mitropoulos regime, John Sherman of the *Star-Journal* caught the tone of the event in his morning-after critique: "The . . . concerto afforded no easy delights for passive concertgoers, and it was a job of hard listening for those who paid attention. But the effort was its own reward in the experience of meeting a musical mind of high and austere originality in a work of great probity, intensity, and technical finish."[48]

CHAPTER SEVENTEEN

Boston Denied

During the war years, the question for Minneapolis music lovers was not *whether* they would lose Mitropoulos to a bigger, more prestigious orchestra, but *when* and *to which one*. Most heavy betting was on the New York Philharmonic—which was, after all, the out-of-town orchestra that he - conducted with the most regularity and that had the most urgent need for a major full time conductor—but the most knowledgeable insiders fully expected Mitropoulos to end up in Boston, inheriting the crown of Koussevitzky.

For a while, during his most successful seasons at the Robin Hood Dell, there seemed a strong outside chance that he might end up in Philadelphia; the orchestra there plainly loved working with him, and audiences found his style more stimulating than that of the ever-more-complacent Eugene Ormandy. But one reason why Ormandy had become complacent was his rock-solid power base in Philadelphia. His conservative programming pleased most of the well-to-do subscribers as well as the board of directors, which reflected their tastes, and his recordings sold well. The dump-Ormandy-and-hire-Mitropoulos movement, though passionate, was mostly confined to the older orchestra members (many of whom now longed for the days of Stokowski and saw in Mitropoulos a figure of comparable electricity), the hardcore fans of the Robin Hood Dell concerts, and an outnumbered, out-dollared coterie of musical sophisticates. Ormandy had become, perhaps without at first wanting to, a paradigm of bourgeois aesthetic virtues; those who knew how the Philadelphia musical establishment worked, already sensed that he would be the orchestra's music director until he either died or became too incapacitated to continue—which was, in fact, exactly the way things worked out.

There seemed to be no real barrier in the way of Mitropoulos's ascendancy to the Boston job. By 1944, the last year in which Mitropoulos conducted the BSO, Serge Koussevitzky was seventy years old and he clearly could not maintain his demanding schedule forever. The most plausible scenario envisioned him stepping down at the decade's end, perhaps continuing for a while as conductor emeritus, making a few seasonal appearances in Boston, and mainly concentrating his energies on his beloved Tanglewood. Mitropoulos seemed not only the logical successor, but the ideal

one. The BSO players loved working with him, and audiences cheered his Boston appearances.

Two unforeseeable factors intervened, however. The first was Koussevitzky himself, who still had considerable power. The patrician Russian had never quite resigned himself to the success Mitropoulos had scored as a guest conductor, and he was known to have been highly offended by the rumors, true or not, that he had been fiercely jealous of those successes. Indeed, one reason he had permitted Mitropoulos to return in 1944 was precisely to put those rumors to rest. Since those concerts, a tentative date had been set in 1946 for Mitropoulos to guest conduct in Boston yet again, in December, for four weeks. This time, the decision was made by the board of directors, not by Koussevitzky—who considered it expedient to agree but who felt no great joy in doing so.

Unfortunately, and quite by chance, something happened in 1946 to rekindle Koussevitzky's umbrage. In February, *Life* magazine published a profile of Mitropoulos by music critic Winthrop Sargent. Written in the slightly fatuous style typical of the magazine's prose at the time, and slightly skewed in some of its facts (Roque Cordero is identified as a "Cuban" composer), it heavily reinforced the popular image of the conductor as the "El Greco of the concert hall," the musical monk, the "lonely wolf" bachelor whose "work did not leave him time to be a good husband," "a fast eater with an insatiable appetite for cherry pie," and so on. The article is surely no worse than most of its ilk, but three things in it made Koussevitzky furious. One was Sargent's glib (and ethnically insulting) account of Mitropoulos's Boston debut:

> Bostonians, who are inclined to think Greeks are people who run lunch wagons, had never heard of him. But on the advice of their regular conductor, Serge Koussevitzky, they had advanced $500 minus traveling expenses to bring him over from Europe for a guest appearance. As he stepped to the podium, the audience in Symphony Hall assumed the raised eyebrows appropriate to America's proudest and most discriminating musical public . . . the Boston Symphony was playing as even Bostonians had seldom heard it play before. The concert ended in such a burst of applause and cheers that the great Serge Koussevitzky nervously fingered his well-tended laurels.[1]

As if this reminder were not enough to set off Koussevitzky's wrath, he expressed mortal outrage at one typical Dimitri-ism that Sargent had chosen to emphasize: "At the university, Mitropoulos liked to explain his musical philosophy in graphic metaphor. To surprised listeners he averred that the task of a [conductor] is very much like that of a prostitute. It consists in making other people happy no matter how you feel yourself—and then passing the hat."

The tone of *weltschmerz*, and the earthy metaphor framed by it, amounted to blasphemy in Koussevitzky's eyes. *He* certainly did not regard himself as a whore, nor did he see anything relevant or amusing about his colleague's seemingly cavalier remarks.

The final blow was a photograph on the third page of Sargent's article, showing Mitropoulos—utterly absorbed in studying a score on a music stand beside his chair—basking under a sun lamp in his Groveland Street apartment, clad in nothing but a pair of swim trunks, a big cross resting on his fish-white belly, gangling arms and legs sprawled akimbo.

Music lovers who knew Mitropoulos were merely amused by the photo—it just depicted Dimitri being Dimitri. No one, of course, could ever imagine Toscanini, Stokowski, or Koussevitzky allowing themselves to be publicly depicted in such a condition of semi-nude informality, but that was part of the charm of the illustration and doubtless one reason why *Life* chose to publish it.

Koussevitzky was mortified. He reacted as if Mitropoulos had disgraced the entire conducting profession, calling people over to see this "obscene" photo and muttering dire imprecations on Mitropoulos's head in his usual mixture of Russian, French, and tortured English. At Koussevitzky's insistence, Mitropoulos's forthcoming engagement was summarily scrubbed. Even a year later, Koussevitzky's ire still smoldered, as David Cooper found out:

> I met Koussey for the first and only time in June 1947, when the Boston Symphony came to Princeton, at a time which coincided with reunion weekend. Koussey and his wife-to-be, Olga, were staying at the home of the chairman of the Music Department, since there were no available hotel rooms. I was introduced to him there, and was received with the utmost courtliness. Knowing the background of his recent difficulties with Mitropoulos, I asked with fake innocence if I might pass on Koussey's greetings, the next time I saw Mitropoulos in Minneapolis. Said he: "Better say notinks. Dere isss *feelink*!"[2]

It did not take long for the Boston conductor's outrage to be reported to Minneapolis. Although Mitropoulos was reluctant to go into details, he showed up at the Coopers' house one night so glum that his hosts made inquiries. "Koussevitzky is now my enemy," he said, real anguish in his voice. He unburdened himself in more detail to Katy:

> By the way, I wanted to tell you that from Boston things look very dark. The Maestro again showed his teeth by canceling an engagement that the Board of Directors offered me. . . . The reason he gave for his fury was that the man who wrote the article in Life Magazine had made some insinuations about his jealousy when I conducted his orchestra and so on—things for which I am not responsible. I am afraid he caused that himself by letting people see his anxiety and fear. But the result was that he persuaded them to cancel my engagement.[3]

Koussevitzky's sense of moral propriety was fully and rigorously Bostonian. Although he had been a womanizer in his fiery youth, he had long since taken a position of ironclad rectitude. In his conducting classes at Tanglewood, according to Bernstein biographer Joan Peyser, "Koussevitzky emphasized the importance of feeling 'clean' before the conductor mounts the podium. Feeling clean meant, at the very least, feeling heterosexual."[4]

But by 1946, the same year the offending Mitropoulos profile appeared in *Life*, Koussevitzky had begun to feel hemmed in on all sides at Tanglewood by a veritable phalanx of homosexuals. He imported Benjamin Britten in that year to give the U.S. premiere of *Peter Grimes*, the operatic masterpiece that Koussevitzky had commissioned, and was flabbergasted to learn, once Britten was on the grounds, that the respected English composer was gay. Not only that, but several of the most important composers Koussevitzky had sheltered at Tanglewood and championed in Boston were under suspicion, as Koussevitzky somewhat quaintly phrased it, of being "pederasts."

Even while Bernstein was studying with Fritz Reiner at the Curtis Institute, he began maneuvering himself into Koussevitzky's inner circle. On the first occasion he was invited to Koussevitzky's home, he purposely left a scarf behind with his initials on it, so that he would have an opportunity to return. Although there is some anecdotal evidence that Koussevitzky suspected Bernstein's bisexuality, other members of Koussevitzky's entourage, aware of the old man's homophobia as well as his warmly paternal feelings for Bernstein, protected him from exposure to some of the more scurrilous gossip circulating about Lenny. By early 1947 the issue seemed moot, for Bernstein had in January announced his engagement to the lovely and cultured Felicia Montealegre and he had, from all visible signs, gone straight—with a vengeance, for it was not uncommon to hear him indulge in some very vocal and, in the opinion of many of his homosexual acquaintances, needlessly nasty gay-bashing. Having seen at firsthand the anguish Mitropoulos suffered because of his own sexual preference—not to mention the time-bomb threat such orientation could pose for a famous conductor— Bernstein was making a determined effort to suppress his own sexual nature in the interests of furthering his career.

This new and aggressive evidence of heterosexuality comforted Koussevitzky and made it both convenient and emotionally easier for him to dismiss his earlier suspicions about his favorite pupil. And in 1948, when the Boston Symphony's board of directors was trying to finalize a schedule for Koussevitzky's retirement and a choice for his successor, Bernstein's machinations looked to be on the verge of paying off.

Two conductors were in the running, virtually neck and neck: Mitropoulos and the dashing Alsatian conductor Charles Munch, who had— to stretch the horse-racing analogy—come up fast on the outside, propelled by the publicity given to his wartime bravery as a member of the French Resistance.

Crucial to the decision would be the good will of the board of directors, which was dominated by an elderly member of the powerful Cabot family whose reputation for moral rectitude was formidable even by Bostonian standards. (Oliver Daniel, who was producing the BSO radio broadcasts at this time and thus knew what went on behind the scenes in Boston, once described old man Cabot as "the Jerry Falwell of orchestra board chairmen.")

There are two versions of what happened, one of them—astoundingly—recounted to Mitropoulos by Bernstein, out of God-knows-what depth of vengeful rancor and cruelty, and the other recounted by a board member to pianist Jack Lowe.

According to the first version, Bernstein simply went to Koussevitzky at the critical moment in this retirement-replacement process and said: "You do know, don't you, that Mitropoulos is a homosexual?" and armed with that testimony, Koussevitzky went to the board and made sure that Mitropoulos was out of the running.

The other version is, if anything, even more sinister. As Jack Lowe recounted it:

Mitropoulos had been so fascinated by Lenny's talent and potential that, immediately after he urged him to go to Curtis and enroll in Reiner's class, he actually telephoned Reiner and begged him, as one colleague to another, to do whatever he could to guide him in conductorial matters. But Koussevitzky loathed Mitropoulos because of the sensation he had made in Boston, just detested him, and so when the time came, he got hold of Lenny and said, I will do thus and so for you if you will give me some ammunition against Mitropoulos, if you will condemn him publicly—if you will tell me he is a homosexual; that's what I want to hear, and I want to hear it from your lips. And so Bernstein did—told the man what he wanted to hear. Later when we heard about it from Dimitri, all he said was "You have no idea what that did to me. I don't care about my career, or about being maligned, or even the fact that some day I had hoped to get the Boston Symphony—the very fact that that boy would turn on me that way showed how little character he had."[5]

For readers with a taste for poetic justice, there was one final twist to this sad turning of events. What Koussevitzky had promised Bernstein, in return for his willingness to play Judas, was his recommendation that Bernstein be appointed, instead of Charles Munch, to be Koussevitzky's successor. In early 1949, he made good his promise to Bernstein by presenting to the Boston Symphony's board of directors an ultimatum. Certain that the board would never permit the change of power to take place over something as vulgar and untidy as a forced resignation, Koussevitzky went before them and stated that unless they were prepared to accept his very public resignation, they must appoint Leonard Bernstein his successor.

There was a closed-door consultation among the board members during which Bernstein's disqualifying characteristics were once again itemized. He was young; he was American, not European; he was a known Leftist; he was connected with—perish the thought!—Broadway; and, of course, he was a Jew. The last two qualifications were probably almost as bad, in the eyes of the Bostonians, as any sexual deviance.

A spokesman for the board quietly informed Koussevitzky that his resignation had regretfully been accepted.

Stunned, Koussevitzky found himself out of a job at the age of seventy-five. This was a situation he had never envisioned and had not planned for. Despite his physical frailty, he was forced to embark on a degrading and exhausting career as a guest conductor, compelled to accept bush-league engagements with second- and third-rate orchestras just to make his living expenses. He died a year and a half later, a sad and already anachronistic figure.

In December 1948, the New York Philharmonic issued a press release stating that Dimitri Mitropoulos and Leopold Stokowski had been named as co-directors of the orchestra. The news hit Minneapolis like an A-bomb.

CHAPTER EIGHTEEN

Farewell to Minneapolis

On the surface of things, the 1949 changing of the conductorial guard in Minneapolis was accomplished smoothly and with seemly decorum on the part of the principal players.

Backstage and in the board room, however, there was considerable turbulence. Arthur Gaines, the long put-upon business manager of the Minneapolis Symphony, was relieved that Mitropoulos was going—indeed, he had been quietly working toward that end for at least two years, abetted by at least some of the board members.

Although various compromises and formulas had been worked out from season to season, the constant friction between the reactionary requirements of the box office and Mitropoulos's passionate desire to program Sessions, Krenek, Schoenberg, Schnabel, and the like, were never really resolved; and as long as Gaines ran the business end of things, they never would be. Both conductor and manager were weary of this battle of wills; manager, of course, was in a better position to do something about it than conductor.

In the faction headed by Gaines, there was throughout 1946 and 1947 a growing feeling that ten years of Mitropoulos was enough; that both orchestra and community needed someone less stressful, less given to passionate advocacy of the unpopular, less inclined—to be blunt about it—to shoot his mouth off in public with the intemperate zeal of a missionary. Mitropoulos's *ex cathedra* pronouncements about aesthetic ideology in the Soviet Union, about heavy-handed American meddling in the political affairs of postwar Greece, about the musical philistinism of those who refused to give modern composers a fair hearing—each of these incidents caused chagrin and embarrassment to a growing number of board members and financial backers of the Minneapolis orchestra. At least a few of these people may also have learned that the FBI was starting to ask questions about Maestro Mitropoulos's offstage activities, opinions, and associations. The first precognitive shudder of McCarthyism was already going through the body-politic.

Matters came to a head in 1948, when Mitropoulos became a passionate and outspoken apostle of third-party presidential candidate Henry Wallace. Appointed as Roosevelt's secretary of agriculture in 1933 and his vice presidential running mate in 1940, Wallace had evolved a far more liberal political philosophy than that of his boss. Shunned by conservative Democrats in the 1944 election, Wallace remained in a cabinet post as secretary of commerce until his opposition to Truman's get-tough policy toward the Soviet Union compelled his resignation in 1946. He edited the *New Republic* magazine for a year, then formed the ultraliberal Progressive Party and ran in 1948 on a platform of increased cooperation with the USSR, arms reduction, and United Nations supervision of foreign aid programs. He received a million or so popular votes but carried no states.

Wallace's ideals matched Mitropoulos's down the line. The two men had met and enjoyed at least one long conversation that covered both music and politics (in a follow-up letter to Mitropoulos, Wallace referred to "composers . . . who perhaps stand in music like Einstein stands in science" and asked the conductor to send him a list of their names).[1] The conductor was active in the Progressive movement in Minnesota and contributed substantial sums to the third party's coffers.

When Mitropoulos imprudently began using concert stages in Minneapolis and elsewhere as a bully pulpit to plug Wallace's candidacy, the board felt compelled to censure him. It was one thing for him to talk like that in the Minneapolis papers, although every column inch of such coverage made the orchestra board squirm with discomfort, but it was quite beyond endurance that he should say the same sort of things when the orchestra was on tour.

Before leaving for the 1948 winter tour, Mitropoulos assured the board that he would stick to music and say nothing political. By the time the orchestra played the first of two concerts in Atlanta, he was primed to make a political gesture if not a speech. After opening night, there were two parties. One was the official party, hosted by the tour sponsors and the MSO board of directors; the other was a fundraiser hosted by the local Wallace-for-President organization. Mitropoulos spurned the official party and went to the one for Wallace.

Accounts of this indiscretion were phoned in to the Twin Cities' morning papers. That night, at intermission in Atlanta, Mitropoulos received a long-distance scolding by Leonard Carpenter, son of the orchestra's founding patron. Mitropoulos was contrite—he really was naive enough to suppose that his decision to attend the Wallace party was of no real significance—and he behaved himself for the rest of the tour.

In his heart, Mitropoulos did not want to break precipitously with Minneapolis; his block of concerts in New York in the forthcoming season was not large enough to preclude a half-season's work in Minnesota. He advanced this proposal to the board, who rejected it, quite properly from their own point of view—better that the change be total, the break clean. No matter how individual MSO supporters felt about keeping Mitropoulos or letting him go, everyone agreed that the orchestra would suffer under another season of guest conductors. The decision to appoint Antal Dorati, then director of the Dallas Symphony Orchestra, as Mitropoulos's successor was made very quickly—at least a week before anything but rumors appeared in the newspapers—and in conditions of secrecy which some observers found both suspicious and dishonorable. William Cooper was one; he fired off angry letters to the twelve board members with whom he was personally acquainted, protesting the unseemly haste and secrecy and voicing the anguish of thousands of Minneapolis music lovers who felt that Dimitri Mitropoulos was not only a personal friend—regardless of whether they had actually met the man—but also a revered cultural icon whose absence would plunge the city into an intellectual dark age. Eleven board members replied; three of them agreed with Cooper but said they had been outvoted—the other eight stood loyally by the board's actions, but did so in very defensive language.

One of those board members invited the Coopers to dinner so that they could meet the new conductor-designate. Dorati was an hour late. "We still felt that in its haste the Board had made a poor choice," wrote Cooper in his family memoir. "There were two seasons of Dorati before we moved to Colorado; we found his programs inexpressibly dull."[2]

Louis Krasner viewed the change in conductors as marking the end of his own Minneapolis career. He had come there because Mitropoulos had given him the chance to learn and perform important and challenging twentieth-century concertos, and their collaboration had been something special. No one, to judge from his two recordings of the work, has ever set forth the Schoenberg concerto with greater eloquence and insight, and the Krasner-Mitropoulos interpretation of Roger Sessions's Violin Concerto is still talked about in tones of reverence by Sessions's pupils.

Because Krasner was the concertmaster and personally close to Mitropoulos, he was often approached by the musicians as an intermediary:

> They especially came to me on the tours, griping because they had to work too hard. I mean, when the Minneapolis went on tour, we didn't just rotate the same two or three programs from town to town, we recapped the repertoire for the whole season! We all had a pile of parts about two feet high, and he would change the program mix all the time, so nothing would be routine. So the men would come to me, after the fatigue started to get to them, and say, "Louis, why don't you tell him—we're not playing in Carnegie Hall. We got Dubuque, Iowa, and a bunch of fly-blown towns in Texas. Tell him to take it easy, for God's sake!"
>
> Well, two or three years after both Mitropoulos and I had left Minneapolis, the boys came through Syracuse on tour and of course they all piled into my house after the concert and I said to them, "So, is your life on the road any better these days?" And they said, "Well, it may have been exhausting touring with Dimitri, but at least we came alive at night during the concerts. We became human beings again. But, Louis, you know what's worse than that kind of hard work? *Boredom*. Now we have nothing. A tour under Dorati is six weeks of non-existence."[3]

To the press, Mitropoulos was lucid and dignified when speaking of his own departure, and typically generous toward the colleague who had been chosen to replace him:

> I have accepted the position in New York because it is my duty to my artistic career. My sentiments, my heart, are with Minneapolis where I have had such happy years. My friends here mean so much to me.
>
> Now, I must start a new home, practically a new life. Minneapolis will always be close to me. I do not want to say goodbye. Any time Minneapolis needs me for any occasion, a pension fund concert or a special event of any kind, I shall feel it my duty to comply.
>
> Dorati has a fine background as a musician. He is skilled and he is ambitious. He has already accomplished many fine things, and I think his coming here makes the future of the Minneapolis Symphony one of great promise. . . . After much deliberation with the members of the board as to what would be best. . . . I concur in its action wholeheartedly.[4]

But the Coopers happened to be present at the moment Mitropoulos learned for certain that Antal Dorati would be his replacement. At the sound of the name, his complexion changed and he sagged as though hit with a pole-axe. After a moment he shook his head and quietly said: "Oh, my God. . . ."

All the Minneapolis papers were flooded with say-it-isn't-so letters. Typical was the comment in the *Star-Journal*: "We have had a great man among us, and our lives will be richer, our standards of service and workmanship higher because of his example. Dimitri Mitropoulos has lived among us, not as an outsider, but as a man deeply interested in the community."

An anonymous orchestra member was quoted in the same paper as saying: "He is deeply loved by all of his orchestra, man for man. They all mourn not only his leaving but resent his being allowed to leave. He has done more for the Minneapolis orchestra and the public that have heard him than anyone else. He combines the unbelievable—genius with humanity. He actually loves his enemies."[5]

When the orchestra members learned what was happening, a spontaneous movement emerged for the entire ensemble, as a unified body, to approach Mitropoulos and literally beg him to stay; in fact, to threaten to go on strike if he did not at least receive a designation as chief guest conductor. By the time the movement had generated enough steam to get into motion, the board had already acted and presented the city and the orchestra with a *fait accompli*.

The last sad irony is that if such a united front had come into being before the board's decision, Mitropoulos had been prepared to withdraw his name from consideration by the New York Philharmonic.

In a final interview given to his friend John Sherman, Mitropoulos summed up his feelings and the philosophy he had nurtured during his tenure with the Minneapolis Symphony Orchestra: "When I first came here, I was very tense. But the conditions here, and the way I've been able to work with the orchestra, have helped me immeasurably in all the things that develop a conductor and a man."

It was here in Minneapolis that the conductor had deepened his convictions about an artist's responsibility to the people and to himself:

People sometimes chide me and say, "Why do you memorize all those scores, why do you take on the added work of playing chamber music when you don't have to?" My answer is that a man who has something to give the world *must* do more than he has to. He must be more than an opportunist who makes all the correct moves and no more. That is his moral obligation.

I could have conducted without scores, if I wanted to, only in New York, and made an impression where it would have done me the most material good. That would have saved me much work here. But that would have been the easy way and I would have despised myself. To give more than is demanded or expected is not only the higher morality, it is an imperative. . . . Humanity is served by extreme examples, like that of St. Francis embracing poverty and dramatizing the ideals of virtue, love, and service to mankind.

St. Francis did not ask people to do as he did, but his example is nevertheless a beacon that men need to have held aloft even though they cannot be expected to follow exactly in [his] footsteps.

The man of great gifts, then, is "inhuman" in the sense that he does not and cannot pursue the normal rewards and satisfactions of most people. He belongs to the world, not to himself. What's more, he was born to be that way. He is trapped into his role in life, and if he suffers in attaining his goals and appears to be a figure of tragedy, he is really not tragic to himself, and truly his suffering is his deep happiness.

Sherman brought up the subject of World War Two, Hitlerism, and the fall of Germany from its perceived role as a standard-bearer for western culture to its recent condition of barbarism. Mitropoulos replied:

The time has come in history when art must have a moral foundation and when artists themselves must exemplify the highest integrity and morality. Look at Germany. It has given the world some of the greatest music and musicians—Mozart, Beethoven, Schubert and Brahms. If great music could uplift a nation's character, Germany would have been the nation of the greatest ideals, the greatest influence for good. We know now it became the world's most savage destructive force.

We have come to the point where anything without a moral purpose is useless and even dangerous. It might be that football up to now has exerted more moral good than music. Until today, we have allowed artists to be anything they wished to be in their private lives and ideologies, as long as they gave us the products of their exceptional skill and creative imagination.

Now, it seems to me that a change is here, and that these idols whom the public looks to for the inspiration and uplift of music must have greatness of character and spirit. Who else is left to look up to, and who more effectively than the artist could personify human dignity, unselfishness and aspiration?[6]

Mitropoulos conducted his final subscription concert with the Minneapolis Symphony on March 18, 1949. He had been in Minneapolis for twelve years. By the time he arrived, the Twin Cities were already well acquainted with the core repertoire of symphonies, overtures, and concertos. Mitropoulos had not neglected these treasured works; more often than not, his virile, rhythmically dynamic interpretations had illuminated the thrice-familiar from surprising new viewpoints.

Before Mitropoulos came, the regional audience was dimly aware that the basic cultural factors from which this great musical literature had been created had begun to alter. And Minneapolis's music lovers distrusted these changes, which at first seemed to strike, out of mere caprice it seemed, at the very foundation of traditional classical music. But through Mitropoulos's Herculean efforts, according to Donald Ferguson's program notes,

> our incredulous ears and our complacent tastes have become gradually accustomed to the repellent surface and the often bitter substance of this music. We have sometimes resented what seemed to us unwarranted scourgings, but many of us have at last realized that these ordeals were merely awakening us from contented slumber and unproductive dreams.
>
> No one but a consummate musician could have done this. A mere fanatic for the new art would have been repudiated; one merely tolerant of it would have given us no insight into the spiritual upheaval of which even two world wars still remain the unprecedented sign. We had taken the old art, even before Mr. Mitropoulos came, as an evidence and an expression of the human temper—the most potent of historic forces. That the new art has also the same purpose—whatever may be its artistic permanence—was a harder lesson to learn. But we have been kept, more fully than any other musical community of like size, abreast of the times.
>
> Mr. Mitropoulos once spoke of himself as a priest of music, and of us as his congregation. To fulfill that mission, he has often foregone the easier role of entertainer or miracle-worker. It was a daring—indeed, a sacrificial—act. We readily manifest our pleasure in his wonder-working through applause or other conventional vehicles of appreciation. His priesthood we can only acknowledge in silence.[7]

When the conductor came on stage to begin this emotionally charged concert, the mood in the auditorium was hesitant, perhaps puzzled. Many in the audience seemed at a loss; this moment had been coming, they knew, sooner or later, but now that it was upon them, they were bewildered at how quickly the actual process had come to pass. Ferguson, William Cooper, John Sherman, and a few others who were stunned by the enormity of what was ending, rose the moment Mitropoulos strode on stage, but they were alone for an embarrassing half-minute or so, while the rest of the audience came to the realization that this was, in fact, the last time this ritual might be enacted. Then—quickly enough as comprehension sank in—those who were still sitting rose to their feet and a great wave of applause swept across Northrop Auditorium.

As his farewell offering, Mitropoulos conducted Mahler's First Symphony, a work that thousands of Americans learned for the first time thanks to the Minneapolis Symphony's path-breaking, best-selling recording. Many in the hall that night had responded with mixed, even hostile, feelings when Mitropoulos first conducted this symphony; many of those same people now felt a proprietary affection for the piece, a proud sense that the music lovers of Minneapolis were definitely ahead of the national curve with regard to this composer. It was a feeling many cherished and now suddenly realized was going to be taken from them, probably forever.

The performance, by all accounts, was a stupendous one, and at the end of it the audience roared to its feet. After eight curtain calls, Mitropoulos came to the edge of the stage with a live mike in his hands and bid farewell to the city he had served for twelve rather incredible years:

> I feel sad, but I also feel contented. I feel that I have done something for you. I have given you the best years of my life, and I did that with love. What is amazing in the history of humanity is that you recognized it. You honored me with more than I really deserved, and also you loved me, I'm sure.
>
> My going doesn't matter because I know that you have something of my blood in you, and it will go on with you even when I am not here. You helped me grow, and you did grow with me. I'm sure that my message will continue in spite of my going away. Unfortunately, the inexorable laws of destiny for the chosen people (pause on recording) they have to follow their duties and not their heart's desires. So I'm going someplace where I don't know if I'm going to be happy. But I have to go. I have to climb the mountain that is expected from me to climb more, until I go, like everyone else, and find our common father.
>
> And now also, to my friends, colleagues in the orchestra, I want to say that those years for me—they were all like my kids. I was their father, and we loved each other. And please, if I sometimes have been harsh with some of them, please forgive me.
>
> So also to you, if I have ever hurt with some modern compositions, I hope you will not have it—will not keep it in mind because I have to

do it, you see. And besides being a friend of yours and an entertainer, I had some duties also towards art that I could not miss.

So I think that is enough. I keep you all here so late—but I tell you, so long. And God be always with you.[8]

Although the March 18 concert marked the climax of the season, it was not the last time Mitropoulos conducted the MSO. Immediately after the final hometown subscription concert, the orchestra went on tour again, visiting thirty-eight West Coast cities in five weeks.

No sooner had the conductor caught his breath from that marathon, than he entrained once more for San Francisco, where he had been chosen to inaugurate the first-ever Arts Commission Spring Festival. One gets the feeling, when matching Mitropoulos's schedule against the available dates on a calendar, that he was trying to stay as busy as possible to avoid brooding over the great move from Minneapolis to New York.

Two choral works highlighted the San Francisco engagement, both of them conducted by Mitropoulos for the first and last times in his career: Kodaly's *Psalmus Hungaricus* and Honegger's *King David*. In preparing the latter work with the San Francisco Municipal Chorus, Mitropoulos reached back in his memory for some of the staging ideas he had come up with at the time he was writing incidental music for classical Greek dramas, during his last two years in Athens. He assigned stage directions for various sections of the chorus, having them rise and sit in uniform groups, as the time came for them to declaim certain dramatic highlights in the text. To add flair to one potent climax, he instructed the entire chorus to rise, on the crescendo, in a slow, gradual wave, spreading across the stage. The audience found this added effect thrilling, and the critics described it as truly innovative and well within the melodramatic bounds of Honegger's music. So successful was this semi-staged approach, that Mitropoulos would refine it for use in several choral-orchestral programs in New York.

Like so many other visitors, Mitropoulos fell in love with San Francisco—with its radiant natural setting, its fascinating architecture, its free-and-easy cultural ambience. He even hinted, to some who conversed with him during his rare moments of relaxation, that it would not take much to coax him to move to the West Coast as soon as his initial New York contract had expired. Unfortunately for both Mitropoulos and the San Francisco music community, no one took those hints very seriously. Tourists were always saying things like that.

Before Mitropoulos entirely severed his connection with the Minneapolis Symphony Orchestra, one last, very special tour, provided an idyllic, bittersweet experience for both conductor and musicians.

The occasion ("a cultural rodeo," John Sherman called it) was a convocation in Aspen, Colorado, to honor the bicentennial of the birth of Goethe; the purpose was "to examine Goethe's idea of the universality of man in a world tortured and confused by the lack of Goethean spirit."[9] If ever there were a project guaranteed to pique Mitropoulos's interest, this was it. When the festival's organizers, quite shrewdly, invited him and the MSO to Aspen, he accepted with alacrity. When the distinguished guest list was published, Mitropoulos may have thought he was going to Heaven instead of Colorado.

Headline celebrities included Thornton Wilder, Robert M. Hutchins, José Ortega y Gasset, and—from the forests of distant Lambarene, Africa— the legendary Dr. Albert Schweitzer, a man who had been a personal hero of Mitropoulos for years.

Headline lectures and all musical activities took place in a handsome new amphitheater designed by Finnish architect Eero Saarinen. Otherwise, beyond this temple of modernism, visitors found an Aspen that was a far cry from the pricey spa it has become. The town was just starting to acquire a new identity as a ski resort, and in places it still resembled the frontier ghost town it had been not too long before. Housing was at a premium for the Goethe Festival, forcing some orchestra members to lodge in log cabins, and some in a former bordello only recently refurbished and turned into a tourist hotel. When Mitropoulos heard a rumor that his "boys" were going to be put up in a "whorehouse," he protested, until someone actually took him into the building and proved that it was no longer being used for its original purpose.

There was one unpleasant moment during this otherwise perfect inter-lude. Because of the timing of the festival, a substantial number of substitute players had to fill in for MSO regulars who had already made summertime plans. At the first rehearsal, the orchestra sounded palpably inferior to the way it sounded at the end of the regular season. Mitropoulos became un-characteristically abrasive and was even heard to remark that "at least next year I'll have the New York Philharmonic to work with!" Some orchestra veterans still remembered the sting of that verbal slap more than thirty years later.

Mitropoulos was seen everywhere in and around Aspen, rehearsing, at-tending seminars and lectures, roaming the mountain slopes, chatting with leathery local cowboys, himself usually clad in his now-favorite American uniform, a simple shirt and blue jeans. No record survives of the conversa-tions he shared with Ortega y Gasset, Schweitzer, and the other great minds in attendance, but they must have been about as close to Plato's symposia as it was possible for a mid-twentieth-century man to experience, and Mitro-poulos often spoke of this Aspen sojourn as among the most wonderful times of his adult life. As marvelous as it was to converse with Schweitzer, Mitropoulos really brightened up with he learned that one of his favorite movie stars, Gary Cooper, was present and lodged in the same hotel as many orchestra members. For a man addicted to western movies, this was good fortune indeed.

Partial records of the conductor's own speeches do survive, thanks to John Sherman's ability to jot things down in shorthand. Mitropoulos participated in one or two roundtable discussions and at least one formal lecture, probably on July 20, following a talk by Professor Willi Hartner of Frankfurt, entitled "Goethe and the Natural Sciences." After a fairly brief opening speech on the artist's moral obligation to society and humankind and after apologizing for his "amateur philosophizing," the conductor fielded questions from the audience. Given the nature of that audience, the questions were pitched at a gratifyingly high level, and when Mitropoulos got one such as "Is religious faith an important basis for art?," he could hit it out of the ballpark.

"In my case, it was," he responded:

because I was conditioned from early childhood to believe in religion and to need its constant presence within my life. But I know many people who don't have religion, some who are atheists, who have contributed greatly to humanity. The question of whether a man is Christian or not is irrelevant. It is his contribution to his fellow man that counts. To me it is disturbing that so much discussion here has dwelt on whether or not Goethe or even Albert Schweitzer was a true Christian. Their self-sacrificing gifts to humanity should be enough. Socrates was not a Christian, but he died for the truth. An atheist, Sigmund Freud, has contributed as much as any believer in his great book, *Moses and Monotheism*.

Mitropoulos was wound up and so was his audience. The discussion ran overtime, according to Sherman's dispatch from Aspen, and at one point:

the audience gasped. . . . Contending that a conductor must temporarily be in love with the composition he is playing, regardless of his private opinion of it, Mitropoulos asserted that one of the pieces the Minneapolis Symphony had played a few hours ago—Liszt's *Tasso*—was a filthy piece of music. "[It] has an exhibitionism and self-pity that infects the stream of pure music represented by Bach, Haydn, Mozart, and Beethoven, but when I am playing it, I am *loving* it!"

Although to all outward appearances Mitropoulos's appointment as co-director of the New York Philharmonic marked his ascent to one of the three highest peaks in American musical life, he knew there were risks and he knew the grief other famous colleagues had come to in that merciless cultural arena. As recently as 1944, had he not declared to composer Elie Siegmeister that "the Philharmonic is the graveyard of conductors" and that he would never be more than a guest with that orchestra?

Yes he had, but in 1944 the Philharmonic was being slapped fitfully back to life by the mercurial and possibly mad Artur Rodzinski, who showed every sign of settling in for a long reign; Mitropoulos might therefore only have been rationalizing a situation that, at the moment, seemed beyond his influence.

Yet now that the job was actually his, all of his former ambivalence returned, and all of those horror stories about what the orchestra had done to other famous men before him filled his mind with something like a premonition. Outwardly confident and happy about his changed situation, he nevertheless confided some misgivings to Katy, in a letter dictated in late January 1949:

> I don't really know if that change is for my good or not, but anyway destiny brought it and I have to follow it, you understand. Here I was in a secure place for the rest of my life. Now I will go into the middle of intrigues and struggles among so many musicians, who naturally are envious, some of them without a job and without an orchestra, so it is not going to be easy in New York, I know, but I have gone so far, so I have to go ahead and be ready for everything.[10]

Right up until the day the Philharmonic appointment was announced to the newspapers, some of Mitropoulos's closest friends—musicians who were better acquainted with the realities of the New York musical scene than Mitropoulos was, men and women who bore the scars of experience—tried to persuade the conductor to decline the offer. He need not stay in Minneapolis long, they reasoned—once the word got out that he was available and interested, the next vacancy with any major American orchestra could probably be his for the asking; never mind the incredible opportunities that were presented in postwar Europe. Among the musicians who lobbied the hardest was Louis Krasner. As Krasner saw it, Mitropoulos was really wavering right up until the moment came to declare himself, and then, drawn irresistibly by the undertow of his own destiny, he seemed unable to do anything else but allow himself to be swept along.

"It's like a moth to the flame," he explained to Krasner after an intense evening of debate about the New York posting; "I simply can't resist. I am too weak *not* to go, do you understand? Of course, Louis, I know the situation there may not be good, but how can one in his career be *offered* the New York Philharmonic and refuse it? It's not possible! I have to go, even though I know I am probably going to my doom."[11]

INTERMEZZO

New York, New York, It's a Helluva Town!

The conductor's task is really not unlike that of a prostitute; it consists of performing to make other people happy, no matter how you feel yourself . . . and then passing the hat.

—Dimitri Mitropoulos

Don't speak to me about the New York Philharmonic! That orchestra is Murderers' Row! If you don't believe me, just look at what they did to poor Mitropoulos.

—George Szell

The City

New York in 1949 was not Boston or Philadelphia; no indeed. The media's—especially the movies'—fixation on Manhattan made it seem not only the pinnacle of American culture, but the only place that mattered, really. New York was regarded simultaneously as the center of all that was innovative and new, *and* as the cultural bastion *par excellence* of everything enduring, everything that was hallowed by tradition. The twin pillars of the city's musical identity were, and seemingly always had been, the Metropolitan Opera and the New York Philharmonic-Symphony Orchestra. Critic and artist-manager Cecil Smith expressed the matter this way: "As long as they exist . . . many of the fundamental issues of music will be cared for. The Wagner and Verdi operas and the Beethoven and Brahms symphonies will be perpetuated in performances of high, if somewhat routine, excellence."[1]

To those who lived in New York—especially those who chose to live in New York but were originally from somewhere else—the city was unquestionably the center of the musical universe. What happened there *mattered*; all else was mere provincial bustle. And yet, paradoxically, many of these very individuals would flock to hear the visiting bands from Boston and Philadelphia rather than shell out for tickets to the New York Philharmonic.

253

Of course, as the clear-eyed have always known, in matters literary and musical, New York can be among the most provincial and insular cities on earth; yet even writers, composers, and actors who understood that fact sought passionately for the New York stamp of approval; a portfolio of good reviews from the New York critics was to writing, composing, or performing what a made-in-Paris label was to a dress.

By Mitropoulos's second season as sole music director, the Philharmonic was well into a transitional phase, consciously attempting, with Mitropoulos as the standard-bearer and lightning rod, to move off dead-center—to prevent itself from becoming what critics, even then, were beginning to call "a museum." In the realm of orchestral music, the New York Philharmonic had become a cultural icon and an arbiter of taste—other orchestras across the country looked to it for leadership in programming policies, choice of soloists, and the maintenance of satisfactory performer-audience relationships.

If Dimitri Mitropoulos had ended up in Boston or Philadelphia, his fate would surely have been different, because the situation for a conductor in New York was very different from the situation obtaining in the two rival cities. In Boston or Philadelphia, the resident orchestras were seen as *belonging* to those cities; to its patrons, the Philadelphia Orchestra was Philadelphia's very own band, an integral part of what made Philadelphia— Philadelphia. And in Boston, if Charles Munch conducted a mediocre performance of a Beethoven symphony, he would be forgiven, for he was Boston's own choice to lead Boston's orchestra, and the patrons would wait with equanimity until he gave a first-class performance of something else the following week.

And if the particular works played on a given week in Boston or Philadelphia were not precisely what the majority of listeners might have wanted to hear, still, the audiences in those cities accepted with good grace whatever was played, for the unspoken attitude was one of doing anything, putting up with anything, in order to support the orchestra—particularly if the alternative was to endure the embarrassment of a deteriorating ensemble, or no orchestra at all. The New York Philharmonic-Symphony Orchestra could not count on that kind of loyalty and commitment. Neither musicians nor management could escape the sense of inferiority brought about by the ten or so guest appearances made every season by the rival orchestras from Philadelphia, Boston, and Cleveland. These ensembles brought repertoire jewels that were rehearsed and polished to the last semiquaver and interpretations that had been groomed like championship horses before the supportive audiences at home. The Philharmonic could sound a little scruffy, a little coarse, in comparison to those great, gleaming music-machines, capable of unleashing coruscating waves of gorgeous tone with an intimidating consistency that made a mockery of the NYPSO's rough-and-ready timbres. There were also dozens of competing ensembles that visited the city from Great Britain, Scandinavia, Germany, Austria, the Netherlands, and elsewhere, and there was an array of attractions to seduce the orchestra-music audience and compete, with the hard-working but not-as-glamorous Philharmonic, for the ticket-buyers' dollars. The result was that, during the weeks when the heavy competition was in town or had just departed—to glowing reviews and intense cocktail-party praise—the Philharmonic could expect, with depressing regularity, to play before a lot of empty seats.

At the time Mitropoulos was appointed co-director, the New York orchestra played twenty-eight weeks in its regular Carnegie Hall season. Programming, always a mercurial element in Mitropoulos's makeup, was shaped and constrained by three different and sometimes conflicting considerations. First, there was the conservative, even reactionary, taste of the traditional long-term subscribers—a diminishing group in numbers, but a critical one in terms of fundraising and volunteer support. Next came the national radio audience, which was conditioned to regard the Philharmonic as the nation's most prestigious musical showcase. Finally, but perhaps most crucial to the overall health of the orchestra, came the one-shot ticket buyers: a generally sophisticated audience, spoiled to the point of fickleness by the wealth of musical choices available to them in New York, bored by Brahms and blasé about visiting soloists. It was this audience that filled the hall when Mitropoulos led the Philharmonic in *Elektra* and *Wozzeck* yet often chose to spend their time elsewhere on the nights he programmed a balanced assortment of the novel and the comfortable. It was possible to seduce them, even ravish them, on individual nights for individual events, but in the main their response to any given program could never be taken for granted; the same people who gave *Elektra* a standing ovation also stayed away in droves when Mitropoulos offered Milhaud's *Christophe Colomb*. No conductor who ever lived could consistently satisfy an audience so demanding yet so capricious. That was the main reason why, to the uninitiated in such matters, a typical succession of weekly Philharmonic programs might appear anarchistic, unshaped by reason, cobbled together without much thought to the conventional programming formulas that had obtained for decades in other big-orchestra cities. In reality, Mitropoulos and the orchestra board worked desperately hard to find an all-but-impossible, season-long balance that would optimize the support of listeners who mainly wanted musical red meat flung from the stage, as well as those people who wanted to dine on truffles, while still remaining—at least perceptually—the musical showcase of the nation.

Another programming difficulty derived from the insistence, by both the national radio audience and the old-guard subscribers, that the Philharmonic should always, season after season, present the basic concerto repertoire in performances by the big-name soloists of the day. So great a portion of the orchestra's time and resources went into this one narrow aspect of programming that in order to present new or unfamiliar concertos, the ratio of purely orchestral to concerto time had to be skewed even more.

Thus in a typical season, 1951–1952, one reads of an amazing and patently lopsided array of twenty-eight instrumental and seventeen vocal soloists, performing a total of forty-three times, sometimes the same concerto twice in the same season. So ingrained a feature had this become that any sign of retrenchment to a more balanced musical menu brought ominous growls of protest from the various artists-management bureaus—particularly the powerful Columbia Artists Management apparatus—who counted on the Philharmonic, more than any other venue, to showcase their most promising new clients. If these agencies were offended too often, the orchestra might not have such an easy time, down the road, securing the services of Heifetz, Rubinstein, or Francescatti.

Nowhere was the fickleness of the New York audience more evident than in the matter of conductors. To put it plainly, the city's *cognoscenti* of symphonic execution were spoiled rotten by the chance to hear, during any given season, more great and sometimes-great maestros than the inhabitants of any second-tier city got to hear in a decade. Boston's audience, Philadelphia's audience—in keeping with the traditions of those cities—were content to listen to Ormandy and Munch all season long, with a few weeks here and there assigned to prestigious guests—because those orchestras and those conductors were regarded as one entity, one cultural package.

In New York, whatever else he may have been, Mitropoulos was thought of as the Philharmonic's *chief* conductor, never as its personification, its embodiment, its symbol. No matter what he gave them, the New York audience grew restive and truculent after six or seven weeks of *only* Mitropoulos. When Howard Taubman gave the death-blow to Mitropoulos in his notorious "What's Wrong With the Philharmonic?" article, his most ludicrous complaint was that the Philharmonic "suffered" by having the same old roster of guest conductors year after year, citing the names of Bruno Walter, George Szell, and Guido Cantelli. Today, of course, any audience privileged enough to hear four such conductors lead any season's concerts would consider itself blessed beyond measure, so mediocre has the big-name talent become in the conducting profession, and so perverse had the New York audience and critics become by the mid-1950s.

The NYPSO's board hewed to a reasonable philosophy of not simply importing the latest flash-in-the-pan conducting sensation to wow the audience with a single week's worth of carefully prepared specialties; instead, they gave the visiting conductors sizable chunks of time—three to four weeks—in which to make a deeper, more significant impression. The policy foundered on two reefs: the orchestra's intransigent, bully-boy refusal to be impressed by anybody and the persistent fickleness of both the New York audience and the critics who helped to shape its tastes and who tried to give public voice to its inchoate discontents.

When looked at from the vantage point of the late twentieth century, the Philharmonic's roster of conductors seems almost inhumanly good, and the balance afforded by their contrasting styles, close to Solomonic. From the Central European roots of classicism and romanticism came Bruno Walter—the elder statesman who could make Bruckner palatable and who had been a close personal friend of Gustav Mahler—and George Szell, whose bracing, no-nonsense approach to the conservative repertoire gave pleasure to those who had been converted to the interpretive ideology espoused by Toscanini. Embracing that same repertoire, but also capable of giving stupendous readings of Russian, French, and Italian music, was the awesomely talented young Guido Cantelli. Adding spice to the entire mix, and giving the Philharmonic an edge as a living, breathing cultural institution, was Mitropoulos, with his passionate advocacy of the new, the difficult, the challenging, and—one thing he definitely shared with Stokowski—the theatrical. Viewed as a master plan for balancing the conflicting needs of its audience components, the Philharmonic's selection of conductors during the 1950s seems, at least in retrospect, very well-judged.

Writing in 1952, Cecil Smith declared: "The astonishing thing is not that the Philharmonic's programs sometimes look helter-skelter or opportunistic, but rather that the conductors and the management succeed in satisfying so many warring tastes at least part of the time, without losing sight of high musical values."[2]

Mitropoulos was not naive about New York and its difficult orchestra, but when the time came to make his decision, what it all boiled down to was the fact that he had to climb that mountain; and since the long-prayed-for invitation from Boston had never materialized, New York was the only mountain he could ascend. To have turned down the job would have been unthinkable and probably, to Mitropoulos himself, an act of spiritual cowardice. All the same, and even if one factors into the picture the element of masochism so inextricably woven into the conductor's deeply held beliefs about self-sacrifice on the altar of Art, one cannot believe that Mitropoulos would have acted as he did—or would have failed to act—if he had foreseen the depth of the humiliation that awaited him.

The Critics

There were a lot of newspapers in New York in 1949, and each of them had a music critic of one sort or another; there were also weekly columns by Winthrop Sargent in *The New Yorker*, Irving Kolodin in *The Saturday Review*, and the fiercely dogmatic, almost hysterically polemical B. H. Haggin in *The Nation*. In terms of molding public opinion and influencing careers, however, there were only three who really mattered.

Oldest and most influential was Olin Edwin Downes, who was chief music critic for the *New York Times* for thirty-two years, starting on January 1, 1924.

He brought to the job an incorruptible sense of integrity. He did not hesitate to deflate the reputations of public favorites if in his opinion that popularity was undeserved, but when an artist struck him as the genuine article, he could be lavish in his praise. Vladimir Horowitz, Jascha Heifetz, Alexander Brailowsky, and José Iturbi were among the many soloists whose American careers were given tremendous boosts by Downes's enthusiasm.

He was quite open about his prejudices—no phony protestations of critical objectivity for him—so that his readers always had a clear understanding of the context that framed his opinions. He made no apologies for his conviction that the classical and romantic masterpieces constituted the pinnacle of musical culture, and saw no defensible reason why contemporary works should not be weighed in the balance from that perspective. As his successor, Howard Taubman, said in an obituary tribute: "He loved the great masters because he loved what they had to say, because they lifted up his heart and because he knew that they could do the same for all who would listen. But he brought an inquisitive mind to new works and performers, hoping always that they would be revealed as something treasurable."[3] When Adolph Ochs, publisher of the *New York Times*, once marveled that a critic could still find something new to say about performances of Brahms and Beethoven, Downes replied: "Give me thirty competent performances of the *Eroica* in thirty days, and I will find something to say—in fact, that demands saying—about each one."

Downes had blind spots: he admired certain twelve-tone works because of their inventiveness and their capacity to express the grimmer realities of post-World-War-One civilization, but he never quite became comfortable with the likes of Sessions and Krenek. Mahler he detested, finding nearly everything in his output, except for parts of *Das Lied von der Erde*, to be vulgar, excessive, and meretricious. He could on occasion sound pompous and overly patrician, not to say stuffy, but he always wanted to like new and previously unknown music, and when he did not, he at least tried to be constructive and fair in his comments.

His coverage of the Mitropoulos era was fairly even-handed, but he had a dismissive attitude about Mitropoulos's "missionary" stance vis-à-vis some of the thornier contemporary scores. As far back as 1940, he had warned Mitropoulos in print, in words that almost seem chosen to mock the conductor's religious feelings about music, that he "reserved the right to be intolerant of a believer of a different faith." When he thought the conductor did a good job, or presented worthy music that other conductors either shunned or were too lazy to prepare, Downes was generous in his praise. When he found Mitropoulos's interpretations to be too personal or too hard-driven, or the music Mitropoulos presented to be lacking in virtue, he could be as sharp-tongued as any other reviewer. But at least he judged the conductor's work on a case-by-case basis, without any underlying ideological agenda other than his own well-known basic conservatism.

Howard Taubman, the man who succeeded Downes in the *New York Times* job, was not a product of a broad-based musical education but was a genuine newspaper man. Taubman was a New Yorker, born in 1907, a product of that city's schools, and a graduate of Cornell University. He went to work for the *New York Post* after graduation and stayed with that paper until 1930, when he went over to the *Times*, where he would stay until his retirement in 1972. He began as a second-string critic and go-fer in the newspaper's music department and was promoted to music editor in only five years. On paper, the position of music editor may look more elevated in rank than that of chief critic, but the real power and prestige resided in the critic's job, as Taubman learned for himself during the years he edited Olin Downes's copy. Taubman was nothing if not ambitious. He had very keen antennae and was able to detect any significant quiver in the local balance of power. An enthusiastic supporter of Mitropoulos during that conductor's first few seasons with the Philharmonic, he evolved a more skeptical attitude when the honeymoon period was over, and by the time he ascended to the throne of power once held by Olin Downes, he understood that the way to even more power was to ally himself with the factions that were determined to oust Mitropoulos. Members of that loose, informal conspiracy fed Taubman rumors and gossipy news about friction within the orchestra, and about incidents of rebellion and ill-disciplined behavior among the personnel, and finally recruited him to be the Brutus who would deal the killing stroke to the already-wounded Greek conductor.

The sharpest pen in town belonged to composer-critic Virgil Thomson. A native of Kansas City, Thomson had grown up in an all-American atmosphere and had begun playing the piano at age five. While still a youngster, he became organist at his family church, Calvary Baptist, and the many hymns he heard and played remained part of his compositional arsenal, often showing up in sophisticated orchestral or instrumental guise.

After service in World War One he went to Europe in 1921 as a member of the Harvard Glee Club and stayed on in Paris for a year thanks to a John Knowles Paine Fellowship. He landed in the hurricane's eye as far as music was concerned, for while studying counterpoint with the seemingly ubiquitous Nadia Boulanger he met and befriended Erik Satie, Jean Cocteau, and members of Les Six, for whom Cocteau was the catalyst. It was in Paris that he wrote his first music reviews, as an overseas stringer for the *Boston Transcript*. Much of Thomson's later music reflects a chic, ironic, slightly tart aesthetic very much in keeping with the Parisian scene of the 1920s.

In 1926, Thomson met Gertrude Stein, setting the stage for a most fruitful collaboration that resulted in the operas *Four Saints in Three Acts* (1927–1928) and *The Mother of Us All* (1947). In his chamber and orchestral works, Thomson shifted styles like a chameleon, ranging from the austere and elusive piano *Portraits* to the ripe, sweeping folksiness of his award-winning film scores *The River*, *The Plow that Broke the Plains*, and *Louisiana Story*.

In October 1940, Thomson signed on as music critic for the *New York Herald Tribune*—a position he was to hold for the next fourteen years—and rapidly established himself as the liveliest, most stylish, most intentionally provocative reviewer in New York.

History is filled with examples of good or at least passable composers who have written musical criticism, starting with Berlioz and continuing through Havergal Brian. Music criticism written by composers tends to fall into two distinct categories: that written grudgingly, as a means to pay the bills while one waits for one's ship to come in; or that written to advance causes or styles with which the critic-composer feels himself allied.

Thomson broke that mold. He wrote criticism for most of his creative life, and it was criticism that, in its clarity, wit, and capacity to give pleasure, fully complemented his music. As a working composer himself, and one, moreover, intimately acquainted with the political, ideological, and social mechanisms that determine what the public does and does not get to hear, Thomson brought to his reviews a robust and healthy cynicism about superstar performers (conductors were a special *bête noire*) and the gradual encroachment of the dreadful Great Performances syndrome. He was the loudest, clearest, most persuasive voice to speak up against the transformation of Arturo Toscanini from one-great-conductor-among-many into The Only Great Conductor Worth Your Time. Thomson did not suffer fools or poseurs gladly, and penned some of his most acidic, penetrating observations about the smug conservatism of various august performing bodies, including of course the New York Philharmonic.

Thomson's commitment to the music of his time was not a case of soapbox oratory, special pleading, or ideological zeal. He simply cared about it and cared passionately. His columns ground no axes for this school or that; his biases (mostly for French and American works) were cheerfully admitted; readers knew where he stood and trusted him, even if they did not always agree with him. His European background gave him a certain intellectual cachet, while his unmistakably American tone of voice gave him readability—a winning combination of Parisian elegance and Missouri frankness.

Thomson's columns were devoutly scanned by New York's progressive music lovers, who could take cultural cues from his musings; waspish, eminently quotable, on occasion deliciously bitchy, Thomson was always a terrific read. Just as Thomson succeeded in reintegrating music criticism back into New York's intellectual life, so too did he hope that Mitropoulos would do the same thing for the activities of the New York Philharmonic. Why, then, was Thomson so rough on Mitropoulos so much of the time? Why, in the name of musical progressivism, was he not more supportive of what Mitropoulos was trying to do? To be sure, he was quick to praise certain of the conductor's programs, and unlike Downes, he was willing to be swept away by Mahler, but even when he liked some of the music Mitropoulos chose to perform, he often seemed to go out of his way to find fault either with the conductor's interpretation or the orchestra's rendering.

For one thing, he kept his distance from the monumental or the heart-on-sleeve; conductors of the "wow!" school were especially likely to get short shrift. Add to that a certain tough-boy attitude that gradually crept into his tone after five or six years on the New York concert beat, and a certain determination, perhaps, to go the extra rhetorical mile just to prove to his loyal readers that he was not going to be soft on Mitropoulos just because the Greek was a champion of modern music. He said as much in a letter to Moses Smith, the man in charge of making Minneapolis Symphony recordings for Columbia, when Smith expressed puzzlement at Thomson's treatment of so valuable an ally in the cause of modern music:

> I expect that in the Mitropoulos case we are disagreeing about a point of taste rather than a point of fact. I have no prejudice against Mr. Mitropoulos, and I have a pre-disposition in his favor for the large number of new works he has played. I have often said so in print too. His case is an interesting one. I find his workmanship more interesting than the musical result. Many people do not agree with me. It may be, too, that he is more at ease with his own orchestra than with the Philharmonic. Please don't think, though, that I am trying to prove anything more than what I have stated in the reviews of his work that I have published in the last two years. I don't even know what you mean by "hitting below the belt." Is it hitting below the belt to admire a man's musicianship without subscribing to his interpretations? And is it not legitimate to make an effort to describe those interpretations in more general terms than would be involved in merely saying that one admired this detail and not that? I have spent lots of thought on the Mitropoulos question, and I have gone to more of his concerts than I have to those of any other visiting conductor at the Philharmonic. I don't pretend that my diagnosis of his case is final, even for me. But I am beginning to verify what was merely an impression two years ago. I am sorry you question my good will about it.[4]

Many observers who knew Thomson were also puzzled by his on-again, off-again, damning-with-faint-praise treatment of Mitropoulos's concerts. Pianist Oscar Levant, for example, knew Thomson quite well and simply could not understand why his reviews of Mitropoulos's concerts became so "murderous, interminable, [and] unrelieved," particularly when the critic writing them had so often measured other conductors by their willingness to champion modern music. When Levant once brought up the subject of Thomson's seeming enmity toward Mitropoulos, the latter philosophically replied: "It's too bad I am deprived of the company of one of the most civilized men in New York."[5] Mitropoulos then musingly recalled what he described as a "most enjoyable" luncheon he had eaten at Thomson's apartment.

The next time he was with Thomson, Levant mentioned how much Mitropoulos had enjoyed himself at that luncheon; Levant thought that such a neutral subject of conversation might "mollify him toward Mitropoulos," but instead of taking the bait, Thomson merely rolled his eyes, smacked his lips, and replied: "No one in the world can cook a leg of lamb better than I!"

Thomson went on to say that he had recently received a letter from Mitropoulos. "How was it?" Levant asked.

"Typically Greek," said Thomson, refusing to be drawn forth about the subject any more.[6]

The Management

The backstage world of classical music—a realm of managers, booking agents, publicity flacks, boards of directors, power brokers, and hangers-on of every stripe—is where the business part of the music business takes place. Most audience members and music lovers are aware of the business side, but only in a dim and probably unrealistic way. The pure aesthetic experience is sullied by the realization that politics, as much if not more than talent, dictates which musicians get to perform, where they get to play, and what compositions the public gets to hear.

All varieties of politics get dirty from time to time, even musical politics, especially when reality is held up to the mirror of the ideal. In the matter of Dimitri Mitropoulos, backstage politics and managerial policies were of critical importance—the key players were the powerful Columbia Artists Management, Inc., and a remarkable man named Arthur Judson.

Until the late 1920s, no one paid much attention to the idea of managing and merchandising an artist's services in the same general manner as one might manage a corporation. At the start of that decade, a period during which musical activities in the United States expanded tremendously, artists' affairs were handled by fewer than a dozen individuals, independent managers who divided the financial pie into relatively equal slices.

Until the explosion of radio in the 1920s, artists' managers functioned in a civilized and leisurely world, enjoying respectable wealth and often developing long and intimate partnerships with their clients. Radio, however, turned music-making into a big business, for suddenly the audiences were huge and the potential profits correspondingly great. Arthur Judson was one of the first, and surely the most successful, managers to exploit the synergistic possibilities of the new broadcast medium. Described by one close associate as "an ample, florid man with the well-fed poise of a bank president," Judson was a founder of the CBS radio network. Whatever criticisms were later leveled at Judson, it could not be said that he was a philistine: he was a trained violinist with an extensive knowledge of music and had spent seven years on the faculty of Denison University.

Judson crossed from the academic to the business side of music-making gradually, beginning in 1907, when he joined the staff of *Musical America*. For five years, Judson worked in the editorial department, gaining respect for the thoughtfulness and style of his concert reviews. Willingly transferred to the advertising department in 1912, Judson seems to have been strongly attracted to the commercial aspect of the music world, perhaps sensing that he had a greater contribution to make there than he did as just another critic.

He could not have made a smarter move than his first one: moving to Philadelphia in 1915, to take over management of that city's burgeoning orchestra and the affairs of its glamorous new conductor, Leopold Stokowski. As Stokowski began his cometary rise to stardom, Judson's prestige rose correspondingly. In 1918, he opened an office in New York and four years later became manager of the New York Philharmonic Society, a post he would hold for more than thirty years.

Anyone who managed both the Philadelphia Orchestra and the New York Philharmonic was clearly a power to be reckoned with, and Judson very cleverly interwove his activities as a personal manager of soloists with his access to two of the most prestigious orchestras in America. By 1930, he had the most impressive list of clients in the world.

The strategy behind every Judson enterprise was basically the same: the broadcasting corporation and the booking agency would cooperate in every way possible to build the careers and enhance the market value of the artists under contract. With network broadcasts still in their infancy, Judson kept his clients on the road, showcasing them on local radio programs nationwide, then using that exposure to generate demand for personal appearances by those same artists, all while creating an aura of prestige for the network under whose umbrella all this activity was being conducted. Judson's success was so rapid and so remarkable that it was easy to forget the obstacles he had to overcome in the beginning, mostly from skeptics who believed that radio would render all flesh-and-blood performances superfluous.

But Judson saw opportunity where less visionary businessmen saw only problems. As electrical recordings and talking movies began to make an impact on the music audience, Judson moved to enlist those media into his overall strategy, giving Columbia-managed artists an advantage in every form of electronic as well as live performance.

When Columbia Concerts Corporation came into being on December 12, 1930 (as a wholly owned subsidiary of CBS), it merged not only Judson's private agency but also those of five other solidly established independent managers. From its first day of operation, the new Columbia agency could boast a roster of 125 top-notch artists and ensembles—approximately two-thirds of the most successful and respected musical talent in America, making it the General Motors of classical music. Judson himself was chairman of the board, while the titular president was William S. Paley, the head of CBS.

After ten years of successfully applying Judson's marketing strategies, CBS and NBC found themselves under investigation by the Federal Trade Commission for monopolistic practices. To avoid protracted and costly legal entanglements, both networks divested themselves of their artists' management bureaus. Judson and the other managers whose bureaus were originally subsumed under the aegis of CBS pooled their resources and bought the artists' management operation from CBS. There was no name change at the time, but in 1948, Judson's bureau rechristened itself Columbia Artists Management, Incorporated (CAMI, as musicians referred to it). The name was chosen to draw attention to the fact that the bureau's business was that of merchandising *artists*, not of promoting the concerts in which they might appear.

By 1950, Judson and a half-dozen associates, operating from offices near Carnegie Hall, still controlled the careers of the majority of the nation's, perhaps the world's, leading musical artists. CAMI's managers decided who got to perform and where, and how big the fees were. Judson *also* managed an orchestra with whom every solo performer longed to appear. The financial sums involved were large: by 1950, the collective United States audience was purchasing musical talent to the tune of twenty-five million dollars annually, and at least half of that amount went to CAMI, which managed 150 solo artists and conductors and thirty-five groups.

Critic and booking agent Cecil Smith neatly summarized the reality of this situation:

> For decades the American public has been spoon-fed romantic notions of the spotlessness of artistic endeavor and with Hollywood's conception of musical talent as something that inevitably rises to the top like cream in a bottle of milk. Most Americans find it difficult to reconcile the lovely purity of great music with the sordid machinations of musical commerce. But it is the hard fact that commercial concerns preoccupy musical performers in the United States quite as much as artistic ones. Some degree of substantial artistry is, of course, a necessary ingredient of long-term success in the commercial concert field. But dozens of handsomely developed artists never obtain a toehold in the field simply because they have no way of obtaining engagements.[7]

For every successful virtuoso, the conservatories of the world were busily cranking out hundreds of well-trained, highly motivated artists. There was little room at the top of the profession, and dozens of ferociously gifted young men and women were competing for every exposure. Viewed in legal terms, the artist is an independent contractor and the manager is his or her agent. Technically, it is the artist who hires the manager, by agreeing to pay the manager a percentage of the fees garnered by the engagements that manager arranges. In reality, of course, agents like Judson could represent virtually anyone they wanted to, managing as few or as many artists as they liked.

In 1950, Judson stepped down as chairman of the board of CAMI, but the retirement was merely a formality—his power remained undiminished.

Judson retained the title of honorary president and his seat on the board; he also retained control of the New York Philharmonic, although he left the daily chores of running the orchestra to his trusted lieutenant, Bruno Zirato. Since Judson ordered his private files burned at the time of his death, it is impossible to know exactly how much of Mitropoulos's trouble with the Philharmonic originated in Judson's decisions and policies; it is clear, however, that everything Zirato did was cleared by Judson first, and that Zirato often acted as Judson's surrogate in matters pertaining to the running of the Philharmonic.

Judson was vulnerable to conflict-of-interest charges and favoritism in his relationship with the Philharmonic. On one hand, he was the head of an important organization that "bought" artists for its concerts, and on the other hand he was the head of a powerful organization that "sold" them. Chief among the accusations hurled at Judson by Artur Rodzinski, on the occasion of Rodzinski's dramatic resignation from the directorship of the Philharmonic, was that Judson kept packing the seasonal lineup of soloists with CAMI artists, whether Rodzinski happened to want them or not.

Even Judson's enemies, however, admitted his brilliance. And in no other area of musical activity was Judson's pitch-perfect blend of idealism and commercial instinct more astute than in the realm of symphony orchestras and the men who directed them. Any manager who could *start* his career with Stokowski and the Philadelphia could hardly fail to attract the best talent in the field thereafter; at the height of Judson's power, he managed most major conductors in the United States and knew the managers of every first-rate orchestra in the land.

Judson's early promotion of Leopold Stokowski was aided by that conductor's unique flair for self-promotion; his grooming and elevation of Eugene Ormandy—from a theater pit to one of the world's greatest orchestras in less than a decade and a half—was brilliance itself. Instantly attracted by Mitropoulos's headline success in Boston, Judson signed him and deftly steered the Greek conductor into Ormandy's old slot, where Mitropoulos had honed his abilities to the point that Judson deemed him ready for the New York orchestra, and the Philharmonic ready for Mitropoulos.

By the time Mitropoulos started losing control of the Philharmonic, Judson was no longer center stage but had become an *éminence grise* in the wings. The habit of playing God was not easily broken. Where the New York Philharmonic was concerned, no action was taken, no policy promulgated, without Judson's consultation and approval. One writer who knew him well and studied his methods closely summed up Judson thus:

Judson's knack of serving conflicting interests at the same time without betraying either side has made him the most enigmatic figure in the commercial music world. In conversation it is hard to know just whom you are addressing. Is he, at a given moment, the manager of Heifetz or the manager of the Philharmonic? Or is he, as is often the case, neither one, but a detached and dispassionate observer of the endless intrigues and circuitous operations of the music business?[8]

As manager of the New York Philharmonic-Symphony Orchestra, Bruno Zirato was Judson's right-hand man, his ubiquitous go-fer, and the factotum through whom most people, even people such as Rodzinski and Mitropoulos, had to go in order to deal, or even speak, with Judson. Like the White House chief of staff, Zirato exercised far more power than his official job description would indicate.

Outwardly a man of the most courteous manners, capable of great tact and diplomatic grace even when handling the most delicate matters of personnel relations, Zirato was a rather different man inside. Many of the musicians interviewed for this book described him as "a pirate," "a Mafioso type," and "a gangster at heart," and there could have been a bit of literal truth in those descriptions. Zirato had a colorful background as a *giornalista* in Naples, where as a young man, he reputedly counted a number of underworld contacts among his sources.

Then, at a fairly young age, he managed somehow to ingratiate himself with Enrico Caruso and became the great tenor's indispensable private secretary, traveling everywhere with him, handling his correspondence, maintaining his appointment book. In the opinion of Artur Rodzinski's wife, Halina, it was this latter capacity that made Zirato so valuable to Arthur Judson and so powerful over lesser mortals, since it gave Zirato control of access, enabled him and him alone to decide "whom to admit (or not) to [the] exalted presence, and how to make it seem a favor when it might have been a right."[9]

When Caruso died in 1921, Zirato was promptly engaged by Arthur Judson, who spoke no Italian, and soon proved his worth as a go-between with Toscanini, who refused to negotiate in any language other than Italian. Zirato played to the hilt his role as the Don of the Philharmonic. As Halina Rodzinski described that role: "His presence in the Steinway Building offices of the Philharmonic added a touch of humanity to the place, for he was at heart a typical southern Italian, able to sympathize with the widow and orphans of the man he had helped to finish off."[10]

Such were the administrators Mitropoulos would have to deal with on a daily basis; there could hardly have been a greater contrast in personalities. And then, there was the New York Philharmonic.

The Orchestra That Took No Prisoners

The New York Philharmonic (in 1950, the Philharmonic-Symphony Orchestra of New York), was founded in 1842; it is the oldest orchestra in continuous existence in the United States and the third-oldest in the world (the other two are the Leipzig Gewandhaus and the orchestra of the Paris Conservatory). It began humbly enough, as a cooperative venture by a group of musicians seeking ways to improve their livelihood. Its first concert was given on December 7, 1842, under the baton of U. C. Hill; the orchestra numbered sixty-three men and the featured work on the program was Beethoven's Fifth Symphony.

During the Philharmonic's first decade, the orchestra varied in size from fifty to sixty-seven players and was directed by a dozen different men, usually players from the orchestra. Gradually, the conductor's responsibilities devolved to a single individual who showed an affinity for the task. Conductors were elected by the orchestra members and served at their pleasure. The number of players rose steadily, reached one hundred during the 1867 season, and stayed there.

When the twentieth century arrived, the Philharmonic's conductor was Emil Pauer (1898–1902). He was followed by Walter Damrosch (1902–1903), various guests from 1903 to 1909, then for one brief splurge of glory (1909–1911), by Gustav Mahler. The longest-tenured of the Philharmonic's early conductors was Josef Stransky, who directed the ensemble from 1911 to 1923.

The Philharmonic celebrated its one-thousandth concert in 1916, during Stransky's unconscionably long term as music director. Stransky was well-liked by the average concertgoer, but he was a standing joke to New York's musical sophisticates. His repertoire was both narrow and stuffy, and by the end of his reign in 1923, the Philharmonic had dwelt for many seasons in a pit of hopeless mediocrity. An arrogant and fussy little man, operating, largely on bluff, far beyond his abilities, Stransky was a poor technician and a worse interpreter. Oscar Levant, who attended many of his concerts as a lad, once said of him, "his limitations were boundless," and his hold over the orchestra was so shaky that one rebellious player is supposed to have snarled, during a particularly testy rehearsal: "If you don't behave better, we'll follow your beat."

Under the virtuosic leadership of Willem Mengelberg, Stransky's successor (1921–1930), the Philharmonic achieved a level of sheer brilliance beyond anything it had displayed previously, and which it would never display again except under Toscanini, and, sporadically at least, during its later concerts with Bernstein. An implacable drillmaster, Mengelberg turned the Philharmonic into one of the world's best symphonic ensembles.

During the first three decades of the twentieth century, the New York Philharmonic absorbed several ensembles that never really got off the ground; by far the most important merger took place in 1928, when the Philharmonic joined with its only serious rival, Damrosch's Symphony Society, forming the New York Philharmonic-Symphony Orchestra (NYPSO, or nip-so for short), which in turn was known as simply the Philharmonic.

By the 1928–1929 season, Carnegie Hall was the scene of a battle of the titans between Mengelberg and Arturo Toscanini. The Dutch conductor, with his swaggeringly subjective interpretations of the late romantics complete with great dollops of slithering *portamento* in the strings, and his progressive espousal of composers as diverse as Mahler, Debussy, Bloch, Respighi, Honegger, Milhaud, Kodály, Hanson, Goldmark, and early Stravinsky, was increasingly seen as an anachronism from a faded and unfashionable age; Toscanini, despite his incredibly limited repertoire and obsessive focus on a narrow set of musical values (characterized as unassailable moral virtues by those who backed him and stood to profit by his triumph), seemed as modern as Bauhaus chrome, the incorruptible priest of something touted as "objective" interpretation. Tastes were shifting, profoundly and fundamentally, and Toscanini caught the new wave just as it was peaking. He rode it with spectacular aplomb and ended up as music director of the Philharmonic from 1930 to 1936, after sharing the podium with Mengelberg for the 1929–1930 season.

During that period, his name became synonymous with great conducting to the extent that

> in the mind of the average man the name Toscanini was as much a label for all music as that of Einstein was for all mathematics. The New Yorker, watching the traffic cop waving his arms in the middle of the street, could heckle him with "Who do you think you are, Toscanini?" in the assurance that the gag would be understood, though neither he nor the cop might ever have attended an orchestral concert.[11]

Although direct comparison of Mengelberg's and Toscanini's recordings reveals a nearly identical level of skill and discipline, there was a perception, from the first night he stepped on the podium, that Toscanini got the orchestra to play better than anyone else could. There seemed a burning purity to his intensely focused performances: fidelity to the printed score, strict yet electric rhythmic profiles, astonishing transparency combined with tip-of-the-stick precision, the rigorous purging of late-romantic habits—these, combined with the worshipful accolades of critics such as Olin Downes, who heard in Toscanini's performances the sonic equivalent of the Holy Grail—made audiences feel somehow cleansed of their sins when they went to a Toscanini concert. Most of Toscanini's reviews were not sober analyses but worshipful panegyrics larded with references to the Italian conductor's being "the custodian of holy things," the "high priest of beauty"; and his often tense, febrile readings as "miracles of recreative genius." The man himself—a notorious womanizer who could practice backstage intrigue with the suave and murderous dedication of a Borgia prince—was proclaimed one of "the few who are truly consecrated and elect, the priests and guardians of immortal beauty, who are filled with that mystical power of creative faith which can turn an act of service into a miracle of resurrection."[12]

The Italian's temper tantrums were as legendary as his acute musical ear, and the Philharmonic got plenty of experience with both. The edge-of-the-chair discipline that awed the Carnegie Hall crowds and exercised otherwise rational music critics to commune with the ineffable, theorized one hard-bitten violin player, was simply the result of a "continuous psychology of crisis"—that "like people trapped in a sinking ship or a burning building, the members of Toscanini's Philharmonic found themselves capable of prodigious feats, pursuing a necessary course of action out of desperation."[13]

Toscanini gave the Philharmonic greater prestige, greater pride, greater glory, than it had ever known before. He did not, however, bring genuine prosperity. One reason is that he never conducted more than half a season; the sell-out crowds he generated, the attention lavished on him by the worshipful media—and the perception by the public that Toscanini was there a lot more than he actually was—made the concerts given after his departure something of a let-down for both the musicians and the box office.

Nor was the price of glory a bargain. Of all the conductors in the world, only Stokowski commanded as high a salary as Toscanini. For his ten weeks, more or less, of conducting in New York, the maestro was paid about $100,000 dollars; sometimes more, if the per-concert rate took effect. Howard Taubman claimed to have been present on one occasion when the chairman of the Philharmonic's board of directors looked at a projected salary of $102,000 and said to Toscanini, "Let's make it a round figure of $100,000." Without missing a beat Toscanini fired back: "Why don't you make it $110,000—that is also a round figure." One hundred and ten thousand dollars is what the man got, at a time when the average Philharmonic player received take-home pay of approximately ninety dollars a week.

No matter how grubby the backstage machinations, no matter how grasping he was in terms of salary and perks, no matter how many sopranos he slept with, Toscanini's legend never sustained so much as a scratch. To most of the public, and a majority of the critics, he was *the* Maestro; to True Believers such as the seemingly hearing-impaired B. H. Haggin, he was practically God incarnate.

Any criticism in the press was aimed at the Italian conductor's stiflingly narrow repertoire. Beethoven, Brahms, and Wagner comprised forty percent of Toscanini's programming with the NYPSO, and a large slice of the remaining sixty percent was taken by Italian composers, some of whom (Respighi, Rossini, Martucci, and Pizzetti) were worthy of such attention, but others of whom (Sinigaglia, Bossi, and Sonzogno) manifestly were not. During his entire tenure with the New York Philharmonic, Toscanini conducted a grand total of five pieces of music by American composers. Clearly, during Toscanini's reign, the New York Philharmonic achieved its highest peak of renown; just as clearly, the orchestra was forced into a position of near-total irrelevance to contemporary American music. Since the public identified Toscanini with "great music," the natural if subconscious inference was that if Toscanini did not conduct certain kinds of music, that music must not be worth much.

Toscanini enshrined a concept of music-in-a-vacuum; music torn free from its context and cultural roots; a handful of pristine masterpieces floating in the void, unrelated to anything that came after them; isolate, immaculate, infinitely repeatable, all-the-classical-music-you'll-ever-need; the ticket to cultural legitimacy. After the enthronement of Toscanini, no one ever needed to listen to Prokofiev or Schoenberg or Roger Sessions—Toscanini didn't, and there was no higher court in the land to which the curious or bewildered listener, well-intentioned and probably capable of enjoying a much vaster repertoire than what was being served to him, could turn. Thus did a slow but powerful undertow erode the work of other, more progressive conductors and mock their sacrifice of time, energy, and commitment. Toscanini's deification made it not only *okay* to ignore any music written after Puccini, but also gave such intellectual sloth the imprimatur of cultural superiority.

Howard Shanet, historian of the New York Philharmonic, summarized the Toscanini regime and its effect on the orchestra's self esteem:

> Such was the power of Toscanini's musicianship and personality that for the first time since the days of Anton Seidl the Philharmonic was able to capture the full support of the New York public, to rouse up an artistic spirit within its own ranks, and to meet the excitement of the Boston Symphony Orchestra and the Philadelphia Orchestra. Toscanini had made of the Philharmonic—by teaching it, inspiring it, and terrorizing it—a musical instrument that New York could proudly believe to be the best in the world. No longer did sophisticated New Yorkers have to prove the refinement of their tastes by letting it be known that they preferred the Boston Symphony Orchestra to their own. No longer did the Philharmonic musicians, underpaid though they were, have to feel like spiritual charity cases; an orchestra that had been whipped into shape by Toscanini wore the scars of its flagellation in artistic honor.[14]

The members of the Philharmonic had every reason to be proud of what they had accomplished—and endured—playing under Toscanini. But that hard-won pride veiled the orchestra's long-standing inferiority complex; it did not supplant it. The mingling of the two, heated by the surrounding crucible of New York's peculiar cultural circumstances, gave rise to an attitude comprising, in more or less equal parts, paranoia, economic insecurity, pride, touchiness, and tough-guy, chip-on-the-shoulder, arrogance. Oscar Levant, who knew the Philharmonic musicians personally as well as professionally, used to say that they saw their relationship with any conductor, no matter how reputable and before he even stepped on the podium, as that of "one hundred men and a louse."

After Toscanini conducted his final concert as head of the New York Philharmonic, on April 29, 1936, the let-down was tremendous. Granted that Toscanini was unique, there were now two choices before the orchestra's managers: either to seek out a replacement of the highest celebrity and prestige, or to engage a younger man who might grow into the post. Of those already-famous conductors who might be interested, only one seemed available: Wilhelm Furtwängler, who had been a regular guest conductor for the past ten years.

Unfortunately, the great German conductor was already (and unjustly) tainted by his perceived association with the Nazi regime. At the very time his appointment was being vociferously debated, Hitler chose to march into the Rhineland. Furtwängler's name was promptly removed from consideration.

Now that the illustrious German was cut out of the picture, Judson spun the wheel of command a full 180 degrees and gave the job to the thirty-six-year-old John Barbirolli. The reasoning behind that choice seemed murky to say the least, and Judson, as usual, did nothing to explain his motives. At least the Philharmonic was not claiming to have discovered a new Toscanini, but simply a young, promising, and (due to his Englishness) politically sanitary musician.

Promising, Barbirolli certainly was—even those who came to regard his four-year tenure (1937–1941) as a disaster had to admit that he was a gifted, dedicated musician and a decent man—but he was placed in a hopeless, fragile position from the start. He was half Toscanini's age and had only a fraction of Toscanini's experience, but he was required to conduct twice as many weeks out of the season as Toscanini had been asked to handle in his busiest year. The remorseless grind of week-in, week-out rehearsals and subscription concerts, the constant exposure to the merciless basilisk stare of the New York critics, the sheer physical travail of the normal schedule plus two exhausting tours: these would have strained the stamina and judgment of anyone. By the end of Barbirolli's tenure, the general estate of the orchestra had so fallen that its good performances were likened by one observer to "one day's well-being in the life of a neurotic."

By the time Barbirolli was being eased out of the picture, Judson seemed bereft of any coherent management philosophy for the orchestra, much less any long-range plan for its growth and health. For two long, damaging years, the orchestra had no chief conductor, but was led by a round-robin assortment of guest directors. Mitropoulos and Bruno Walter took a month-long chunk of the season in 1940–1941, and for the centennial season of 1941–1942, no fewer than ten conductors were invited to take the reins: Barbirolli, Goosens, Busch, Stokowski, Walter, Koussevitzky, Rodzinski, Damrosch, Mitropoulos, and Toscanini. The surprise hit of the year was Koussevitzky, who charmed the musicians by subtly permitting them to "prove" they could play as well as the Boston Symphony, one of their two most irritating rivals. Mitropoulos, in his segment, took care to present something new on every program, including David Diamond's First Symphony, Hindemith's Symphony in E-flat Major, Copland's *Statements for Orchestra*, and an all-Busoni memorial concert. Stokowski included a new symphony by Roy Harris, and a suite by Henry Cowell. Toscanini's contribution to this anniversary season? A miniature Beethoven festival, what else?

On the whole, however, this arrangement reflected a scandalous lack of leadership on the part of those who controlled the Philharmonic's destiny; the whole thing was monumentally irrelevant. If the public lapped up the spectacle of this conductorial sweepstakes, the more perspicacious critics were appalled at the artistic bankruptcy it symbolized; few music lovers stopped to contemplate how happy they might be if required to perform the same job under ten different bosses during a single year. In an excoriating essay in the *Herald Tribune*, on March 23, 1941, Virgil Thomson called Judson's bluff and summarized, with scathing accuracy, what was wrong with the New York Philharmonic:

> A string of guest conductors, though obviously the first thing the Philharmonic management would think of, is the last thing the Philharmonic musicians need. These have been so thoroughly guest-conducted for twenty years now that they have become temperamental, erratic, and difficult as only first-class musicians can become when subjected to every known form of browbeating and wheedling. The best birthday present the Philharmonic could offer itself and us would be a good permanent full-time conductor, somebody worthy of the job and capable of assuming all its musical responsibilities.
>
> The old Philharmonic is a tricky bird. Give her a good master and she will lay you golden eggs. . . . But, ladies and gentlemen who direct the destinies of the Philharmonic, do you really think another whole year of it is without serious risk? . . . do you really think that the temperamental Philharmonic, if left for a whole year without any conductor of its own at all, won't blow sky-high one day when some equally temperamental guest says "Boo" to it? I do think, birthdays aside, that that venerable institution is tempting Providence to go on playing around with guest conductors when what she really needs is a lord and master who will take some of the jumpiness out of her and put her to work on a five-year plan of some kind, building something in America's musical life that would be worthy of her history and of the city that loves her and supports her and complains about her.[15]

With what seems like a quite astonishing lack of imagination, the Philharmonic management could think of nothing better to offer for its next season (1942–1943) but more of the same: Barbirolli, Toscanini, Rodzinski, Mitropoulos, Walter, Reiner, Howard Barlow, and Efrem Kurtz, with Walter getting the most concerts and poor Barbirolli, in his final lame-duck appearance, getting the smallest slice of the pie.

Shaking itself out of a stupor, the Philharmonic finally made a sound and decisive choice for the 1943–1944 season: Artur Rodzinski. When Judson made him the offer, he told Rodzinski: "There is deadwood and dry rot throughout, and the morale of the orchestra is low, very low. The critics don't call them the 'Dead End Kids' for nothing."[16]

Although not quite a superstar interpreter, Rodzinski was a musician of great integrity and ability, with wide-ranging tastes. He had acquired a solid reputation as an orchestra builder (which can be a quite different thing from an orchestra leader) who had wrought dramatic improvements in both the Los Angeles and Cleveland orchestras and who had, most recently, drilled the fledgling NBC Symphony Orchestra into a state of discipline and ensemble that even Toscanini found admirable when he arrived from Europe to take over.

In appointing Rodzinski, the Philharmonic management gave him a title that had not been given to any previous conductor, even Toscanini: music director. The choice of terminology signaled, as it was intended to, the expansive, long-range aspects of Rodzinski's job, in addition to his routine duties of conducting and rehearsing subscription concerts. As music director, he would supervise all matters of artistic policy, including the hiring and firing of musicians, the selection of guest conductors, the naming of soloists, and the details of the entire seasonal repertoire.

Judson empowered Rodzinski to do a thorough housecleaning. He prepared for the purge by attending other conductors' rehearsals and making a list of recalcitrant and—in a startling number of cases—incompetent players. He finally came up with a list of fourteen musicians whose contracts would not be renewed. The prospect of having personally to confront each man appalled Rodzinski. When he expressed his anguish to Judson, Judson promised that his office would handle the actual notifications.

But before any of the men on the list could be privately contacted, someone in Judson's office leaked the story to the press. All hell broke loose with the Musicians Union. The music-loving public, too, was stunned; everybody knew the Philharmonic had its problems, but was fully fourteen percent of the orchestra truly unfit to play?

If nothing else, the Great Winnowing served to get the orchestra's attention. Once the tumult subsided, Rodzinski was able to establish decent, if somewhat chilly, relations with most of the players. Week by week, season after season, Rodzinski patiently rebuilt the orchestra, working out the ensemble kinks, establishing better discipline, and gradually widening the repertoire until the Philharmonic was at least ankle-deep in the twentieth century.

By the start of the 1946–1947 season, the orchestra looked to be in the best condition it had enjoyed since the glory days of Toscanini. As Virgil Thomson summed up Rodzinski's achievement: "Today the Philharmonic, for the first time in this writer's memory, is the equal of the Boston and Philadelphia orchestras and possibly their superior."[17] Behind the scenes, however, all was not well.

Part of the problem was within the Polish conductor himself. A man of mercurial passions, Rodzinski began exhibiting signs of mental instability. He joined the militantly puritanical Moral Rearmament movement (marital relations with his wife were sometimes preceded by Bible readings and prayers); he began delivering philosophical lectures to his musicians during rehearsals; he began having "transcendental experiences" which he would describe in embarrassing detail to anyone who would listen. One of them took place in an alley behind Carnegie Hall, where Rodzinski thought he had encountered Christ—only to learn that the tall, bearded apparition was the legendary blind street-musician, Moondog.

And he became increasingly paranoid, convinced that Arthur Judson and his minions "had it in" for him. Rodzinski's suspicions grew to such an extent that he actually began carrying a loaded revolver in his overcoat pocket. He constantly complained that the Philharmonic was being forced to showcase too many CAMI-managed artists. He wanted to enlarge the subscription base, in part to respond to the changing cultural dynamics of postwar America, but Judson refused.

By the end of the 1947 spring season, Rodzinski found himself shut off from contact with the board of directors and forced to make his wishes known through Bruno Zirato, who would then pass them on to Judson, who would then—in theory but seldom in fact—pass them along to the board. By now, the orchestral musicians smelled blood: Rodzinski's days were numbered, and the less-principled players figured that they might ingratiate themselves with management by passing along rumors and tales.

One incident, typical but more comic in its outcome than the rest, concerned a complaint brought to the local Musicians Union chapter by one of Zirato's henchmen, stating that Rodzinski had cursed the men in Polish, a language no current member of the orchestra could understand. When called by the union to answer what were labeled as "grave charges," Rodzinski patiently repeated what he had said in Polish, which was dutifully translated to the union representatives as "Where the hell did I put that pencil?"

The situation had exploded in February 1947, when Rodzinski was offered a new contract that in effect stripped him of all the meaningful powers a music director usually has: the authority to select soloists, guest conductors, and overall seasonal programming. Flushed with anger, Rodzinski hurled the pages at Judson and said: "You promised me a contract without strings; instead, you hand me one with chains!"

Rodzinski demanded, and got, permission to speak to the board of directors. Fumbling tensely with a sheaf of notes, he began by lambasting Judson, describing him as "a dictator who made musical progress impossible"[18] and pointing out that "twelve major conductors . . . had marched in a ghostly parade" before the Philharmonic audiences during Judson's reign. All of them, except for Toscanini, had suffered humiliation, while Judson himself remained smugly entrenched in his bastion of power. Rodzinski further blasted Judson for packing the programs with soloists affiliated with CAMI and cynically using the Philharmonic box office as a laboratory in which to measure their commercial potential, all the while lining his pockets with fees, regardless of whether the artists in question went on to enjoy success or faded back into obscurity.

It was unthinkable for a conductor to speak so to these powerful men, even though there was demonstrably more truth than paranoia in Rodzinski's comments. Twenty-four hours later, Rodzinski resigned and called a press conference to explain his action. Hundreds of congratulatory calls and telegrams poured in for the Rodzinskis, many from musicians who wanted to thank the conductor for having the guts to turn over this particular rock in public.

Thanks in part to Judson's influence, Rodzinski lasted only a year in his next job, in Chicago. Other major American podiums were cut off from him—no one wanted to alienate Judson. Rodzinski shifted his activities to Europe, but the damage was done. His personality became impossibly volatile, and his sense of persecution became almost pathological. There were isolated triumphs for him in England and Italy, but his mental and physical health continued to decline. He died, a broken shell of the man he had once been, in 1958.

Like Mitropoulos, Rodzinski deserves a higher rating from posterity than he has yet received.

In no hurry to give to another man the same title or power it had originally given to Rodzinski, the Philharmonic's board came up with the catch-all title of "musical advisor" and gave it to Bruno Walter for the 1947–1948 season. Citing his advancing age as the reason he did not opt for the role of music director, Walter was content to tend his own "small wing of music's museum"[19] while turning over the more adventurous programs to a roster of stimulating guests: Mitropoulos, Stokowski, Munch, Szell.

In his second season as musical adviser, Walter presided over a considerable narrowing of the field, giving Stokowski and Mitropoulos dominating positions in the schedule. Munch, who had scored some sensational triumphs in New York, was now out of the running, having been designated as Koussevitzky's successor in Boston.

When Walter stepped down as musical adviser, in the 1949–1950 season, the management of the New York Philharmonic, in what was clearly intended to be a transitional arrangement, announced that both Stokowski and Mitropoulos would lead the orchestra, as co-conductors.

Mitropoulos at Midpoint

Mitropoulos's move from Minneapolis to New York was headline news, and during the transitional period a great deal was written about him and his style. Predictions were made about his impact on the New York musical scene; his strengths and weaknesses were analyzed in considerable (and often repetitive) detail. The man and his art appear more clearly in focus during this interval between orchestras than they did before or after.

That he was a conductor of genius was obvious to anyone who heard him at his best, in repertoire that was congenial. In contemporary music he

was unsurpassed: intricate rhythms and unconventional balances challenged him and brought out the best in his style. From the densest thickets
of dissonance and experimental harmonic schemes he summoned order,
clarity; his obsessive study of the inner construction of difficult scores allowed him to grasp and project their expressive content with such conviction that he compelled respect from even the most skeptical listeners. His
technique of physical gesture—so charged with energy, so sharp-edged,
even explosive, in its emphatic accents—was ideal for most of the twentieth
century repertoire that fascinated him and engaged his deepest intellectual
commitment. He could physically delineate a score by Richard Strauss or
Alban Berg with such clarity and force that he actually seemed to be a con-
duit through which the music itself flowed like an electrical current.

But the same stylistic qualities, when applied to the vast range of music
between Bach and Brahms, actually got in the way. His performances of
the nineteenth-century repertoire were wildly erratic. He brought to Haydn
a rugged strength and an anachronistic range of dynamics, but in his Mozart and sometimes in his Wagner and Brahms, the interpretations suffered
from the lack of a firm, baton-inflected beat.

In works requiring subtle tone colors—like those of the Impressionists,
say—he imposed a style that fascinated and excited by extracting drama
from music more often considered sensual. His mastery of dynamics enabled him to achieve *pianissimo*s of the utmost transparency, but the overall
tone he drew forth was often harsh in texture, ragged in execution, and
bleak in color. This weakness was not a problem when he conducted the
orchestras of Boston and Philadelphia, both of which had long traditions
of producing rich tone colors; with the New York Philharmonic—and its
"cast-iron tone" as Virgil Thomson described it—the defect was cruelly
magnified.

Virgil Thomson used to proclaim that any experienced concertgoer, if
blindfolded and plunked down in Carnegie Hall, could identify a Mitropoulos-led Philharmonic performance within seconds. "Dimitri Mitropoulos conducting the Philharmonic last night sounded exactly like Dimitri Mitropoulos conducting the Philharmonic," quipped Thomson in a 1949
review. Overall, the sonority Mitropoulos drew from the Philharmonic was
the sonority the orchestra tended to produce anyway: weighty, dark, and
percussive. He played both louder and softer than most conductors. Under
Mitropoulos, passages marked *fff* were massive, thunderous, and tended toward stridency; passages marked *ppp* were remarkably transparent but still
substantial in their timbral presence—dark silk, rather than airy gauze.

Mitropoulos's defects and virtues were eloquently summarized by
Thomson in one of his traditional end-of-season wrap-ups:

> The Mitropoulos concerts were wholly dependable technically. Musi-
> cally they varied a great deal. Some of them were nervous and violent,
> others calm almost to the point of platitude. He played more of the im-

portant new music than any of the other leaders did, played it clearly and efficiently and for the most part convincingly. Of them all, he remains the least decisive. He is a great workman, certainly. He is an interesting musician, certainly. The exact nature of his musical culture and personality remains, however, vague. He seems to be oversensitive, overweening, overbrutal, overintelligent, underconfident, and wholly without ease. He is clearly a musician of class, nevertheless, and a coming man of some sort in the musical world.[20]

Mitropoulos's technical knowledge was unsurpassed—and perhaps unequalled by any other conductor save Toscanini—but there was a lopsidedness to his interpretive results. By 1949, he himself clearly realized the problem. But was he disciplined enough and self-critical enough to achieve, over time, the sobriety, mellowness, and detachment required for him to become as dependable a conductor of Brahms as he was of Berg?

When Mitropoulos once more took on summer engagements in Europe, starting in 1948, Katy Katsoyanis met him in Italy and accompanied him to Rome, Florence, Turin, and Naples. Katy had not seen him conduct since 1939. Making due allowance for her personal closeness to the conductor, there is evidence in her descriptions of a ripening, a maturation, in Mitropoulos's podium style. He was indeed slowly but steadily refining his technique, disciplining his own periodic excesses, consciously striving to become a better conductor:

> It's a great thing for someone to reach self-restraint after passing through and overcoming all the stages of dynamism. . . . There was a time when you were distinguished by an overflow of vitality—today that liveliness is transubstantiated into every note. One could say that every note carries with it, from birth, its own chromatic and dynamic equipment—just as it is sharp or flat, in that same way. This shows especially in the even lines of the plane, where the phrase is not livened by the movement of the chromatization but from its inner intensity. The more I see the frugality of the means you use, the more I say: truly, taste is *mostly subtraction*. Everything seems so natural and unforced—even light and clarity have their mystery! One gets dizzy from the way you build up a phrase, give it expression, breath, meaning. How you weigh precisely the flux of a *rallentando*, the extent of a *piano*, a *forte*, how many gradations in color, weight, quality. How much *content* a pause takes in your hands, what importance an *accent*. Your notes are little springs ready to dart. And all these admirable things happen "by themselves," as though through magic! I ask you again: "How does this miracle come about?" If you answer that's the way it's written, I'll lose my temper![21]

Mitropoulos's focus on self-improvement, however, was soon distracted by the unending demands of his New York job. There, the requirement was for survival and not inner growth; and increasingly, his attention became focused on obtaining basic professional standards of performance and behavior from the unruly musicians of the Philharmonic. The evolution Katy saw in 1948 was suspended by 1950. Mitropoulos did not emerge from this long chrysalis stage until after he had shed the burdens of the Philharmonic post—by which time, it was too late.

PART THREE

Summit and Fall

Where music is, the Demon must be.
—Gustav Mahler

Courage, you may say, but what else do we do in life but draw constantly on our courage and then arrive exhausted at the grave that waits for us.
—Dimitri Mitropoulos to Katy Katsoyanis,
September 10, 1940

CHAPTER NINETEEN

Mitropoulos In, Stokowski Out

By the autumn of 1949, Mitropoulos's first season as co-conductor of the New York Philharmonic, the long-playing record was starting to generate a cultural revolution of enormous impact. Gone were the fragile, heavy 78s, with their limit of four-and-a-half minutes per side. Entire symphonies and concertos were now available on single lightweight vinyl discs. Small labels proliferated, seeking to serve the niche markets that RCA or Columbia found unprofitable.

Although Mitropoulos was seldom at his best in a recording studio, his attitude toward recordings changed as their technology changed. He saw the long-playing record as a valuable medium for spreading the musical gospel. Indeed, his first project in New York was a pioneering record.

Since Stokowski was handling the first eight weeks of Philharmonic concerts, Mitropoulos was free to do the kind of *pro bono* work he most enjoyed: a concert at the Museum of Modern Art, under the auspices of the ISCM, in honor of Arnold Schoenberg's seventy-fifth birthday. On the program was the fascinating Serenade, Op. 24, and the peculiar, somewhat overblown *Ode to Napoleon*, Op. 41.

A full house and good previews greeted this concert. Shortly thereafter, Mitropoulos was approached by cellist Seymour Barab (who played in the septet required by the Schoenberg Serenade) and asked if he would be willing to conduct the first recording of the piece, for a small, independent label aptly named Counterpoint-Esoteric. Mitropoulos told Barab that he would love to record the work, but that he had an exclusive contract with Columbia Records and legally he had to vet the project past them, be turned down, and only then would he be free to record it with another label. If Columbia was agreeable, Mitropoulos told Barab, he would of course conduct for free.

Columbia Records, to the surprise of no one, had absolutely no interest in funding a recording of the Schoenberg piece. Esoteric's recording sessions were therefore organized in mid-December. Barab remembered them vividly even thirty-five years later. "I tell you he was a marvel—an absolute marvel—to work with. Of course, he had the piece memorized—every note, every dynamic mark, every rehearsal number—he never referred to the score at all, it was all up here in my head! My admiration for his talent and abilities had no limit."[1]

Released as Counterpoint-Esoteric 501, this recording of the Serenade stayed in print for more than a quarter-century, achieving the status of an icon. It remains an essential recording for any serious collection of twentieth-century music. There is precision aplenty in the playing, if not quite the brain-surgeon edge Boulez brought to the score, but there is also a unique warmth, pungency, and spirit infusing every bar. For Mitropoulos, this was rock and roll.

Barab remained on friendly terms with the maestro until Mitropoulos's death and was once treated to a rare display of Mitropoulos's oblique, puckish sense of humor. Barab had just picked up some copies of one of his own compositions, a suite of four songs, and was happily wending his way home from the offices of Boosey and Hawkes when

all of a sudden on Fifty-seventh Street I heard myself hailed. I turned around and who was running toward me but Mitropoulos—literally running to catch up. He asked me how I was doing and I said, I'm flying at the moment because I just went up to Boosey and Hawkes and picked up copies of my first published composition. "I didn't even know you composed," he said, "Let me see." He took the score and opened it to the first page and looked at it with an expression of mock-horror, then impishly said: "Hmph! *Key signatures*! Not interested!"[2]

For his first subscription concert of the season, December 11, Mitropoulos offered his public a full, varied, and somewhat ungainly program. Beginning with a Mozart overture and continuing with the Gounod-ish symphonic poem *La Procession nocturne* by Henri Rabaud, the concert's opening half ended with the Krenek Third Piano Concerto, played and conducted by Mitropoulos.

Olin Downes choked on the piano concerto so badly that his entire review had a carping, bilious tone—one that often cropped up in his writing when the music itself had given offense. The Krenek concerto, Downes said, had been "ugly and trivial . . . tedious and disagreeable," even as the program itself had been "long and poorly constructed." It was too bad, he wrote, that the Liszt *Faust Symphony* had come last "for by that time the audience was in a state of weariness too great to respond as excitedly as it should to an uncommonly eloquent reading. It is years since we heard the first movement played with so much fire and Lisztian rhetoric; when the themes were so masterfully projected and inter-related and the whole delivered in such a flamingly romantic spirit."[3]

Mitropoulos did more than conduct on that afternoon broadcast concert—at intermission, just after the Krenek concerto, he puffed his way to the control booth, mopping perspiration from his gleaming head, and sat down for a brief interview with James Fassett, the announcer whose suave narration of program notes made him the "voice of the Philharmonic" to thousands of listeners. The conversation focused on the Krenek concerto and the twelve-tone system; the conductor's answers are noteworthy for their uncompromising intellectual rigor, based on his so-far unshaken belief in the capacity of the average listener to welcome challenge and enlightenment in music, not just entertainment.

Is the Krenek concerto written in a strict twelve-tone system? asked Fassett. Not really, replied Mitropoulos, although it is heavily influenced by that system. He tried to reassure those listening to the broadcast that the twelve-tone system was not a strait-jacket into which composers masochistically thrust themselves, but was instead a natural product of music's evolution. It was a rational system designed to replace the chaos of atonality and polytonality with order and logic, and those who invested some rigorous listening to it would eventually perceive its beauties and expressive content.

Yes, Mitropoulos agreed in reply to one of Fassett's questions, contemporary music was "tough going" for many audience members, but the dilemma it posed for conductors was even tougher: ignore the evolutionary styles and revert to programming nothing but "music for the masses," or continue to present the most distinguished and representative music of today, and let the listener sort things out according to his or her intellectual and spiritual necessities? As for himself, Mitropoulos refused to "deny evolution":

I'm willing to pay the huge effort of making gigantic leaps within the same hour of a performance, from one period to another and fulfill their demands—demands of my audience, I mean—as an honest interpreter, giving my soul and my heart to all periods and serve all people of all intellectual levels; and as far as serving the masses or writing for the masses, I would say this: that the "aristocratic spirit," the high spiritual love, should also be a part of the common man's life. Because I want to believe the "common man" means not something low and mechanical, but that the common man aspires to better himself not only in matters of financial but also in matters of spiritual worth.[4]

This Socratic dialogue with Fassett was a far cry from the usual lightweight intermission banter of a Philharmonic broadcast concert; indeed, no previous Philharmonic conductor had ever spoken this way to the radio audience—reaching out to them, seeming really to embrace them. Starting with the first subscription concert of his first season, Mitropoulos had already elevated both the tone and the substance of the nation's musical dialogue.

Mitropoulos scored one of the great triumphs of his career when he conducted concert performances, on December 22, 23, and 25, of Richard Strauss's *Elektra*. He approached this mammoth score, quite properly, as a vast orchestral tone-poem with voice obbligato, and conducted it so that all the wondrous shades and nuances stood forth clearly while the work as a whole was projected in the grandest, most sweeping lines. This was music he knew well, and the story was in his blood. "I know the tale of Elektra as well as an American knows the story of Huck Finn," he would say, and he proved it in these performances, compelling the Philharmonic to play like souls possessed and turning the orchestra into a kind of Greek chorus. No one could complain about the orchestra's tone on this occasion, for it soared and raged, throbbed and caressed, as the score required, and Mitropoulos found the perfect balance between conductorial control and instrumental freedom of expression. This was one of those occasions when the New York Philharmonic pulled itself together, roused its collective will to a rare level of commitment, and proved to the world—and even to itself—that it could be, if not the suavest orchestra in the land, by God the most formidable.

If some in the audience questioned the appropriateness of performing such a bloodthirsty score on Christmas Day, their complaints were drowned by a tidal wave of accolades, both for the conductor and for his well-chosen soloists: Astrid Varnay as Elektra, Elena Nikolaidi as Klytemnestra, Herbert Janssen as Orestes, and Frederick Jagel as Aegisthus.

The reviewers went scurrying to their thesauruses in search of fresh adjectives as they sounded a chorus of enthusiasm. Irving Kolodin stated that this concert reading of *Elektra* was a musical event "which in beauty of sound and grandeur of expression excelled most others heard here in a score of years, in or out of the opera house."[5] Olin Downes stated simply that Mitropoulos's *Elektra* "must be recorded as one of the legendary musical events in the history of this city."[6] Virgil Thomson proclaimed himself an unabashed Mitropoulos fan when it came to this kind of repertoire:

It was amazing to hear so complex a theater piece as "Elektra" performed as a concert cantata in a foreign language and still to be aware, intensely aware at every moment, from only a modest acquaintance with [the] libretto, of the opera's whole elaborate, dramatic progress. The credit for so astounding a projection belongs equally to the conductor and to the soloists. Such work one does not often hear anywhere.[7]

At some point during the last week of 1949, Mitropoulos wrote to Olin Downes, wishing him the best for Christmas and the new year and expressing his admiration for the intelligence behind Downes's critiques, even on those occasions when they were not altogether favorable. The conductor's letter could not be found, but a copy of Downes's reply tells what was in it, and reveals the sincere respect the two men had developed for one another. The closing paragraph of Downes's letter:

If what I have written of your performances made you feel that there is a greater artistic understanding between us, it helps me very much. If and when, on the other hand, we musically disagree, you know that I can only say what I believe, and say it with all my heart, and that being honest about what one believes and driving that home as hard as possible is the only way in which a man of my profession can be of real cultural service to the community. It is a delightful freedom to me to have this understanding between us . . . and perhaps we can both feel, as I think we do, that in this particularly troubled and confused state of the world, the ministrations of . . . art are a stronghold against evil and stupidity. That I have been able, so far as my abilities extend, to gain your friendship, first as an artist, then as a man, is a great guerdon to me.[8]

The New York Philharmonic management had tried the dual-conductor gambit at two critical junctures in the past, and on both occasions, the situation came down to a man-to-man face-off between one conductor and the other. Two men went into Carnegie Hall; one came out with a job. It had happened first in the 1920s, when Mengelberg displaced the pedestrian Stransky; again several years later, when Toscanini edged out Mengelberg; now, in the 1949–1950 season, Stokowski and Mitropoulos shared one-third of the season each, with Szell, Walter, and Cantelli (all of them, not coincidentally, managed by Arthur Judson), filling out the roster.

There is little information on record as to how Stokowski and Mitropoulos regarded each other; both men were reliably circumspect when speaking about their colleagues in public. Slight anecdotal evidence suggests considerable mutual regard, and the two seemed never to have argued about anything during the two years they shared the Philharmonic job—indeed, they probably never even saw one another. Mitropoulos is on record as being deeply impressed by Stokowski's genius for eliciting gorgeous tone colors (a concern that was definitely not the Greek conductor's highest priority), and Stokowski once expressed in writing his deep "respect and admiration" for Mitropoulos, calling him an "honest, sincere, and very capable musician."[9] Both men were, by temperament, music-director types who wanted hands-on authority with regard to programs, soloists, and orchestra behavior. Both men had wide-ranging tastes in music, and both were keenly interested in spreading the gospel of great music to the largest possible audience. The list of works played during the two seasons of their mutual directorship gives strong evidence that New Yorkers were privileged to experience the most colorful, most stimulating, most far-reaching repertoire played anywhere in the United States.

At first, Stokowski used his customary brand of telepathic charisma to compel the Philharmonic to produce a simulacrum of the luminous, "drenched" string tone he had achieved in Philadelphia during his heyday, and he introduced quite a few major compositions, including the sixth symphonies of Vaughan Williams and Prokofiev. But the magic had little staying power and it was clear to many observers, in 1949, that Stokowski was off his form. His moods vacillated, his treatment of the orchestra seldom contained any warmth, and much of the time he just seemed to be mentally elsewhere.

As always, Stokowski kept his own council, his many-faceted and probably insecure essence wrapped tightly inside layer after layer of self-made myth and protective affectation. Some part of the problem was surely personal. In April 1945, Stokowski had taken his third wife: the willowy, long-legged Gloria Vanderbilt. She was forty-two years younger than he, and she had just fallen heir to four and a half million dollars. By 1950, the marriage was showing signs of strain despite the birth of Stokowski's first son, Stan. Gloria had a strong creative streak in her, but Stokowski suppressed it; any attempt by her to assert her independence only made him colder and more aloof.

It was getting increasingly difficult for Stokowski to pretend that the years did not matter. He read the papers; he knew he was the butt of countless old-enough-to-be-her-grandfather jokes. His response, typically, was to drive himself harder and harder to prove he was not getting old. The result was a certain brittleness of personality which many people found alienating. His work with the Philharmonic, a group that bore him scant good will to begin with, became erratic, although he was still capable of galvanizing the orchestra to tremendous feats, as he did in the Mahler Eighth Symphony (April 1950) that turned out to be his swan song with the Philharmonic.

Oliver Daniel, who produced some of the Philharmonic's radio broadcasts during this and the preceding season, noticed a distinct change in attitude among the players from one season to the next: "That quality of magic that Stokowski was known to possess seemed strangely absent at the beginning of this season. The players who had given him their total cooperation during the previous season now seemed to respond indifferently."[10] Some of the players made no effort to hide that indifference, telling anyone who cared to know that Stokowski was a charlatan and nicknaming him "the old whore."

From his observation post up in the control room, Daniel got a clear view of what happened on stage:

> The orchestra . . . was not prone to give loyalty to anyone, and Stoki, in his sharing role, did not have the force and authority he had had in his Philadelphia days. The players seemed more interested in their backstage card games than in any aspect of music. They resented the introduction of new works which required more work and concentration than the warhorses they could almost play in their sleep. Hence, Bruno Walter with his standard repertoire elicited more cooperation than either Stokowski or Mitropoulos.[11]

If Stokowski was unhappy with the orchestra, the board of directors had become unhappy with Stokowski. It is known, from Stokowski's appointment book, that he lunched with Arthur Judson on December 7 and with Bruno Zirato on the tenth. There was another meeting with Judson, at the Lotus Club on December 28, and a board meeting on December 29. At the conclusion of that meeting, a press release informed the public that Dimitri Mitropoulos had been named sole music director of the Philharmonic for the 1950–1951 season, and that Leopold Stokowski "has made other plans . . . and cannot appear with the orchestra."

Stokowski never publicly alluded to these events, nor did Judson. One can only guess. Oliver Daniel, who studied the incident as closely as possible from the scant surviving documentation, concluded that Stokowski told Judson he was ending their business relationship at about the same time the Philharmonic's management was deciding to go with Mitropoulos alone, despite Judson's oft-quoted belief that the Philharmonic's season was simply too long and too taxing for one man.

There was really no reason other than the personality clash between Stokowski and the orchestra why the duo-conductor arrangement could not have continued indefinitely, much to the benefit of all concerned and to the health of music in general. Had Zirato and Judson really cared, they could have laid down the law to the orchestra members and compelled at least their cooperation if not their affection, where Stokowski was concerned. That they did not, that they let him go completely and threw the whole burden on Mitropoulos, was derided by one of Stokowski's biographers as "a prodigious mistake, a notable example of immeasurable stupidity and treachery."[12]

Conductor Paul Strauss, a protégé of Mitropoulos who went on to lead the orchestra of Liège, Belgium, obtained, quite by chance, a powerful glimpse behind the Wizard-of-Oz curtain Judson kept drawn between his activities and public scrutiny. One morning in 1950 Strauss was sitting in the La Scala restaurant, Mitropoulos's favorite, waiting for the conductor to join him for lunch. That same morning, Mitropoulos and Zirato had had a tense, protracted, ultimately ugly argument about some of the thornier contemporary works Mitropoulos wanted to program during his first season as the Philharmonic's music director.

When the conductor finally appeared, somewhat later than expected, Strauss was startled by his appearance. Mitropoulos's color was normally very rosy—on this occasion, his skin was white with anger and his hands were trembling. Since the conductor rarely used profanity, the impact was powerful when he did. On this occasion, he slammed down into his chair and snarled: "That son of a bitch Zirato!"

"What happened?" Strauss naturally asked.

There had already been complaints from well-heeled subscribers that Mitropoulos had scheduled too much modern music; Zirato had taken it upon himself to deliver their complaints and to forbid the conductor to schedule "excessive" amounts of modern music in the forthcoming season.

"I have to do it," Mitropoulos had told him; "this is my mission!"

"Mission?" Zirato snorted. "Listen: you are not Saint Francis of Assisi and Carnegie Hall is not a church. You're lucky you have the damned job. We took you instead of Stokowski because we thought you'd be more manageable. Now you be a good boy and take care of yourself."[13]

CHAPTER TWENTY

The View from the Great Northern

Nineteen-fifty: new city, new job, new residence—Dimitri Mitropoulos had arrived at the summit that had tantalized him for so long. He was the respected music director of the oldest, and one of the three best, symphony orchestras in the hemisphere. Despite the persistent nagging of some critics, his first half-season as the Philharmonic's man had been well received and had ended, with the sold-out performances of *Elektra*, on a note of genuine triumph. For the moment, the view from this new height was pleasing indeed, and his letter of February 3 to Katy captured a rare mood of ebullience:

> You have heard from people who have been here that I am living in the most inexpensive hotel in New York right next to Carnegie Hall. In the Philharmonic office there is a kind of resentment that the Philharmonic conductor is not living in a palace as the previous ones did. Anyway, I make appeal to the more democratic people as being more royalist than the king himself, so I put them in a spot and they leave me in peace to live the way I want to live and where I want to live.
>
> Everybody seems to like me at the moment. I live in an air of success and understanding. Anyway, I will do my best to keep that situation going, although I can't promise anything because after all, I am also a human being and there is a limit to how much I can be God as they want me to be, or better to say, a man from whom is expected not only the best artistically, but also to take care of all the distressed artistic souls' constant requests for auditions, for engagements, for scores to be examined, for chances to be given to youngsters etc., etc. To be conductor of the Philharmonic I am sure is worse than to be the President of the United States![1]

While it was not quite "the most inexpensive hotel in New York," the Great Northern Hotel was no elite address. A great shabby pile of midtown masonry, it offered few amenities beyond its proximity to Carnegie Hall. Although Mitropoulos could easily have afforded a much classier address, the Great Northern suited him fine, even if it was a source of some embarrassment to the Philharmonic management.

Descriptions of the conductor's Great Northern suite tend to read alike, and no one who visited him in his lair ever forgot it. Clarinetist Sigurd Bockman thought the place "dark and gloomy and messy—but it didn't bother him. Wherever he lived, it was all work, it was just bare walls. Maybe it was a monastic throw-back."[2] Clutter was everywhere: piles of musical scores, overflowing ashtrays, items of clothing, coffee cups, books. There were oriental-style rugs on the floor and a huge high chair by the window with a music stand in front of it. Here the maestro would sit, smoke, and study his scores. In the very early or very late hours, Mitropoulos was usually alone, wrapped in study and meditation; during business hours, however, the place could be filled with people. John MacKay, son of the Minneapolis Symphony's first trombonist, was being put through music school on funds supplied by Mitropoulos, and consequently had to make a monthly visit to the Great Northern to pick up his stipend. MacKay recalled:

> In New York, I thought he might become a little more socially active, but when he wanted to get out of the hotel, it was usually to walk around by himself at odd hours. I once came into the room and there were five or six people there—musicians, composers, Lord knows who—and Dimitri was right in the middle, holding an intense conversation with everybody in at least four different languages![3]

Yehudi Menuhin took his wife, Diana, to the Great Northern to meet Mitropoulos because

> I was very anxious when we first met that she should know the people I loved [in New York]. So she and I went there, and there was this great crucifix hanging in one corner and this shaven man, a symbol of goodness, looking for all the world like a monk. He never went out, you know. He engaged in no social activity whatever. He lived in his rooms, studied his scores, appeared at rehearsals, gave concerts, and in the summer he climbed mountains, at least until his health started to go . . . he was a man made to face mountains, really, not other men. . . .
>
> When one entered that suite at the Great Northern, one entered with Mitropoulos into his world. Secluded, isolated, yet at the same time full and busy and peopled with thoughts and music and with his whole world which he built. So many of us are parasitical in that respect—I mean we live in worlds that other people built and we are dependent on them, whether intellectually or scientifically—we are always living off others who are providing us with our care, our medicine, our thoughts, affiliations, whatever—but here was a man whose complete world was built by himself, and at the same time, it was in no way antagonistic to any other. It was simply there; we admired and revered it.[4]

Mitropoulos walked to Carnegie Hall, usually walked to get his meals, and always went out for his own groceries. Colleague Paul Strauss remembered: "It was not unusual for people to see the conductor of the New York

Philharmonic come walking out of a delicatessen on Sixth Avenue carrying a bag full of groceries. People on the street would see him, wave, and say, 'Hello, Maestro!' and he always nodded and smiled and said 'Hello, hello!' back to them."[5] Of course, there were times when Mitropoulos did not have either the time or the inclination to run a gauntlet of well-wishers or the frequent supplicants who waited for him in the lobby of the Great Northern. On those occasions, he would sneak out of the hotel's back entrance on Fifty-sixth Street and outflank whoever was waiting for him. Again, Paul Strauss:

> If there is one word which would describe the way he lived, the way he thought, the way he worked, I suppose it is "simplicity." There was absolutely no pretension about him, which is amazing for an orchestral conductor, at least in our day. As far as I was able to observe, it amounted almost to an unwillingness to project his own personality. His devotion to music as an art. . . . I don't know whether it was equal to or second to his devotion to religion, but I know he felt the same way about both, about music and religion, even to the point of—how shall I say it?—a kind of self-flagellation.[6]

The announcement of Mitropoulos's appointment as music director of the New York Philharmonic was greeted with enthusiasm. In the pages of *Musical America*, the weekly journal that had been the voice of professional musicians for decades, editor Cecil Smith interpreted the Mitropoulos appointment as a call to arms on behalf of progessivism and tried to launch a preemptive strike on the board of directors:

> Now that the board has made so confident and wise a choice, the development of its prestige depends on its willingness to back him up. Obviously, his sponsorship of contemporary music has by no means damaged him in public esteem. Will the board regard his alignment with today's musical interests as an asset or will it begrudge every hour taken away from the conventional repertoire and instruct him to proceed with care in order not to alienate a minority of subscribers whose musical tastes are wholly traditional? Equally important, will the board, at long last, take a positive stand about the duty and privilege of employing its Sunday afternoon broadcasts as a means of bringing important new and unfamiliar works to the attention of the vast radio audience, which otherwise, in the commerce-ridden present-day scene, has almost no opportunity to hear them?[7]

Mitropoulos lost no time in serving up the unfamiliar, starting with a January 5 concert in which the F minor Piano Concerto of Max Reger received its first New York performance, by Rudolf Serkin—the only pianist of his generation who espoused this piece. Serkin's performance won unanimous praise from all the critics; the concerto itself did not.

On the twelfth of January, Mitropoulos directed the Second Symphony of Roger Sessions. That the honeymoon period was far from over is attested to by the fact that many of the players took their parts home and actually practiced, so conscientious had Mitropoulos made them about their responsibility not only to play this work, but to play it well and with as much comprehension as possible. This occasion was, in fact, the first time any Sessions piece had been performed by one of New York's professional ensembles (the Juilliard orchestra had bravely tackled the First Symphony in the autumn of 1949).[8]

Sessions's symphony received a warm, glowing performance (one preserved on record thanks to a Naumburg Foundation grant), and was greeted with great enthusiasm by the multitude of composers, performers, and academics (John Cage for one) who had come to Carnegie Hall expressly to hear it. There were also some healthy salvos of "Boo!" from pockets of reactionary listeners. The majority of the audience listened to the work with respect and attention, if not enthusiasm; reviewers tried to like it.

For Olin Downes, Sessions was simply beyond the pale; although he acknowledged that the fault might be with his own perceptions rather than any lack of ability on the composer's part. While granting Sessions's "sincerity and lofty purpose," Downes thought the work as a whole to be "artificial and painfully studied."[9]

For once, Mitropoulos took up cudgels with a critic, writing and calling to express his displeasure at what he regarded as willful blindness on Downes's part, and a general conspiracy against contemporary music on the part of the critical brotherhood in general. This exchange of views shaped itself into a heated but gentlemanly debate about broader implications, and the New York Times reprinted much of it in its Sunday edition for January 29, 1950; the exchange is noteworthy because it demonstrates that Mitropoulos's presence in New York had already stimulated some keen intellectual sparring.

Mitropoulos asserted that too many belligerent reviews made it harder for him to perform a reasonable amount of new and unfamiliar music. Downes replied that a conscientious critic must never equivocate—nor does the critic always have time and space to adumbrate all of the reasons, technical and emotional, why he dislikes a work or regards it as bad art. The critic is, in effect, a filtration system between the listener and the performer. Besides, Downes concluded, "No blindness or prejudice of a critic has ever suppressed for long the value of an artistic creation any more than critical trumpeting ever fostered a fake, for any length of time, upon the public."

Mitropoulos: "But you concede that I owe it to my audiences to supply them with new as well as old music?"

Downes: "I do more than that—I consider that you would be unpardonably derelict in your duty if you did otherwise, and that the Philharmonic-Symphony programs have already benefited enormously by your initiative."[10]

Another very controversial program was played on January 26. His first season as head of the Philharmonic was only halfway through and already Mitropoulos was becoming distraught. He had formerly been convinced that he could, in time, find the formula for pleasing most of audience, most of the time, while still being true to what he perceived as his mission and others saw as his mandate to make the orchestra's activities intellectually relevant. He was now realizing that there was no such formula; that whatever he programmed, in whatever proportions, was going to turn off some part of the audience most of the time. He had tried to cover all the bases with a shotgun, helter-skelter approach, and he had been lambasted for it by the critics and by the conservative, monied subscribers.

Now he tried a different approach, a much more conventional bit of programming algebra: one difficult work amply cushioned on both sides by cozier crowd-pleasing selections. Thus the program for January 26, 1950: Cherubini's *Anacreon* Overture, Beethoven's "Emperor" Concerto (with Robert Casadesus), Anton Webern's terse Symphony for Chamber Orchestra, Op. 21, and Rachmaninoff's opulently scored *Symphonic Dances*, Op. 45.

When word got out in the music community that Mitropoulos was going to have the Philharmonic learn the Webern piece, a number of composers and academics showed up for the open rehearsals as well as for the performance. According to Milton Babbitt, nearly half the orchestra section of Carnegie Hall was full at the start of the first rehearsal. Everything went well until the Webern rehearsal. Many of the players made faces and rude noises when Mitropoulos asked them to begin, and some minutes into the score, the Philharmonic's harpist, Theodore Cella, picked up his part, walked forward to the podium, flung the music angrily at Mitropoulos's feet, then stalked off the stage.

In the icy silence that followed, Mitropoulos turned to face the dark auditorium, his shoulders slumped and an expression of bewildered pain on his face. He spread his hands imploringly and said: "What can I do?"

The harpist was persuaded, for the good of the orchestra, to put up with the Webern piece—all ten minutes of it—and the performance went on as scheduled. Babbitt thought the orchestral playing mediocre—clearly, the men's hearts were not in their work on this occasion—but gave Mitropoulos much credit for troubling to learn this recondite score and for mounting its first professional performance in New York. Virgil Thomson gave the performance somewhat higher marks:

> There is every reason to believe the Philharmonic's reading of this tiny but ever so tough work to have been correct. Musicians following the score could question only the size, here and there, of some minute crescendo. The rendering was clear, clean, tonally agreeable and expressive. . . . Once again there was cause to be grateful to Mr. Mitropoulos for his assiduity toward neglected distinction and for his enormous loyalty to the text of a work rare, complex, and in every way difficult.[11]

In a monumental exercise in bad psychology, Cecil Smith's program notes warned the audience that it "probably has never been asked to listen to a more exacting composition, in the whole 108-year history of the Society." Not surprisingly, there was much grumbling and fidgeting in the audience during the performance—one man yelled "No!" so loudly that hundreds of heads turned in his direction. At the end there were hisses and boos aplenty, which only caused the more progressive pockets of listeners to applaud more vigorously.

When this demonstration calmed down, Mitropoulos came out and tried to clear everyone's palate with the lush melodies and billowing climaxes of the Rachmaninoff *Symphonic Dances.*

After the final tam-tam crash that ends the work, Milton Babbitt rushed backstage to congratulate the conductor on the Webern performance. Babbitt was startled to realize that the applause for the Rachmaninoff was scarcely fuller or more enthusiastic than that which greeted the Webern— exactly, and perversely, the opposite of the effect he would have predicted. Backstage, he found Mitropoulos in a state of icy rage, drawing tight-lipped on his cigarette and gesturing furiously in the direction of the audience. "You see?" he cried to Babbitt, "They don't even like *that* shit!"[12]

Mitropoulos had no further engagements with the Philharmonic until April, so he guest-conducted through the spring. In February, he led acclaimed concerts with the Rochester Philharmonic (including Liszt's *Faust Symphony,* not the sort of thing most conductors would choose for a guest engagement), then traveled west for a series of March engagements in Houston and San Antonio. He was pleasantly surprised by the quality of the orchestras in those two cities, describing them as "quick, well-trained, and flexible."

By mid-March he was back in New York, struggling to keep a commitment that turned out to be much more demanding that he had expected. He was roped into "starring" in a twenty-minute movie, the final segment of a four-part anthology film entitled *Of Men and Music* (the first three segments featured Rubinstein, Jan Peerce, and Heifetz). The featured music was the third movement of Liszt's *Faust Symphony,* which Mitropoulos first rehearsed and then performed, the two segments segueing into one another, at which point the musicians in rehearsal mufti suddenly appeared in formal concert garb. The program as a whole was introduced by the inescapable Deems Taylor.

Mitropoulos is shown clad in slacks and a light-colored knit shirt; he looks fit, trim, and full of energy. When the camera closes on just his head, he really does resemble "a Byzantine monk frantically shaking cocktails," but when the camera pulls back, and one sees the hands and arms, the entire Mitropoulos *gestalt* suddenly pops into focus. There's very little of the explosive frenzy noted in his early reviews; but his gestures vividly encompass the overall arc of the music as well as its bar-to-bar incidentals.

The cues are clear (though it is a little jarring to see a conductor mime every single timpani beat), the rhythmic impetus strong, the accents vividly placed, and the general quality of orchestral playing is very high indeed, with a strong inner glow that suits the music well.

The conductor's instructions to the men are patient, clear, and very polite. He smiles sadly when he has to stop them, and always prefaces his remarks with a courteous phrase: "Please, jehnl-men, we have a misunderstanding here." Some of his comments in the film: "No, jehnl-men, not right. Please, the devil is here, Mephistopheles, so make the staccatos more jumpy, alive, nervous!"

Or: "Now we go to the fugue section, where Liszt introduces the theme of Faust in love, but distorted by the devil." The orchestra plays a few bars, then: "No, no, jehnl-men, please. You forget the devil! Take advantage of those accents. Again please. Ah, that's better, that's devilish, all right! Wonderful, you've got it."

The "Margaret theme," he admonishes them to play "like a Verdi aria." They do, and the effect is ravishing.

At all times during this interesting and all-too-brief documentary, Mitropoulos looks and sounds at his best. He hardly breaks a sweat, despite the intense physicality of his actions. One gets the impression of a man totally in control of his own assets and entirely at ease—if such a condition does not sound contradictory—with his own intensity.

In reality, Mitropoulos hated the entire project, as he lamented to Katy in a letter dated March 13, 1950:

> Now I am back here and right now I am under the pressure of the most disagreeable task I had so far in my life, the shooting of a moving picture with me conducting the Philharmonic in an informal rehearsal of the . . . Liszt Faust Symphony, giving the public a taste of what rehearsal is like. I can tell you I thank God that He didn't reserve for me the destiny of having to make my living as a movie actor. I do believe it is the most degrading and insulting profession to human dignity in the world. I do believe that the man who cleans the streets, or the maid who cleans rooms—I will not add those who clean certain smelly places— have more dignity in what they are doing. . . . Anyway, I have to go through it because it might come out good for the Philharmonic.[13]

Mitropoulos's last group of appearances for the 1949–1950 season began on April 13, when the Philharmonic was joined by the Princeton University Chapel Choir for Arnold Schoenberg's searing cantata, A Survivor from Warsaw. Developing some concepts he had first used in Athens and more recently in San Francisco, Mitropoulos asked the chorus to "act" the climax of the piece. As the "Shema Yisroel" chant begins—depicting the Jews lining up for their own extermination—Mitropoulos had the chorus rise, raggedly at first, then in groups until all were standing, and remove their jackets, so that they all stood in the convict-white colors of the condemned. Olin Downes thought the effect "hammy" and the music itself "poor,"[14] though Virgil Thomson and the other regular critics were moved.

So was the audience, which demonstrated so vociferously at the end that Mitropoulos turned and said: "Do you want to hear it again?" They did; score one significant victory for the cause. Schuyler Chapin happened to be sitting in a box next to a gentleman who was on the Philharmonic board of directors, and he observed that when Mitropoulos began to perform the twelve-minute piece for the second time, this board member "turned purple with apoplexy at having not only to listen to the piece again, but at the thought of how much the extra twelve minutes were going to cost!"[15] Cellist Alan Shulman observed another incident: when Mitropoulos went backstage at intermission, Bruno Zirato was waiting for him and ambushed him on the stairs that led to the dressing room. "Zirato came over and chewed him to bits, not only punctured his good mood but virtually left him in tears. Which gives you an idea of what an ugly man, what a son-of-a-bitch Zirato was."[16]

Mitropoulos conducted his last Philharmonic concert for the season on April 23. After snapping at him at least as often as praising him, Virgil Thomson wrote an extremely thoughtful piece that appeared in the *Herald Tribune* on April 30 under the heading "How Mitropoulos's Program Policy Can Either be Supported—or Killed."

After praising Mitropoulos's programming of new and unconventional music, Thomson deplored the common practice of sandwiching the novelty items between over-done warhorses. "Such juxtapositions are rarely becoming to either" the novelty or the warhorses. Box office considerations, Thomson agreed, were probably the reason for such bittersweet programs.

Surely, he reasoned, the need to kow-tow to the box office would be lessened, and the conductor's freedom enhanced, if Carnegie Hall were sold out, or mostly filled, by subscription sales. A heavily subscribed season could be planned with greater freedom than one in which every concert must appeal to single-ticket buyers. Subscribers are more tolerant, Thomson averred, and they seldom ask themselves in advance if they are going to enjoy a concert—they come, out of habit if nothing else, and wait until the program is over to express their likes or dislikes.

Whether such a subscription sale was possible at the Philharmonic, was uncertain. The widening of the subscription base was one of the subjects of argument between Rodzinski and Judson—who wanted to keep on using the Philharmonic box office as a testing ground for his clients. While acknowledging that the issue was thorny, Thomson concluded that it was both the duty and the future of the Philharmonic to continue down the path of "intellectual distinction" with its new conductor, and that a sustained effort over several years toward building as large a subscription base as possible might well mean the difference between the success and the failure of Mitropoulos's enlightened program policy.

If Judson, Zirato, and company were listening, there was no sign of it in their week-to-week handling of the Philharmonic's affairs.

In his three-room aerie at the Great Northern Hotel, Mitropoulos invariably rose at five o'clock in the morning and breakfasted on the customary two raw eggs, black coffee, and perhaps a bit of fruit. He dressed in a white bathrobe with a stitched blue monogram, lit the first of the fifty or so Camels he would smoke during the day, and retired to his favorite study chair beneath a picture of St. Francis. There was a view from the window near him, but not much of one: some decaying brownstones and a big sign reading "The Manhattan Storage and Warehouse Company."

By five-thirty he was deep into scores, laying down the memory tracks in that pressure-cooker of a brain that would enable him to recall, in nanoseconds, any chord, sequence, or individual sharp, flat, or rest from a Mozart score containing 250,000 notes or a Mahler score containing a million. This was the quiet time in his day, when he worshiped his God and his muse; not even he was sure, from day to day, where the line was that separated the two. This was when he was most content, when the world was small and containable; just himself, the music, the sunrise, and the distant mutter and sigh of the city beyond his walls.

He could also continue to study, evidently almost as well, when there was company. Stage designer Andreas Nomikos spent an entire morning sketching him at study, and Mitropoulos appeared for long stretches of time to be absolutely unaware of his presence. His hands moved as he memorized the music, fluttering softly as moth-wings to delineate a *pianissimo*, suddenly jabbing a cue or molding a crescendo; but periodically, he would ask a question or make a comment to the seemingly forgotten visitor. Nomikos found him quite capable of carrying on a conversation and studying at the same time—only a slight time lag between sentences revealed the fact that his attention was in any way divided.

"My subconscious works on the scores while I sleep," he would say, in that intimate, caressing, "furry" voice that reminded so many listeners of actor Charles Boyer. "When I'm at a movie, I turn from a cowboy to a bar in a Strauss tone poem. And when I am going up mountains in the summer, I hear scores all the time as I ascend."[17]

If the visitor remarked on his seemingly photographic memory, the conductor might break concentration long enough to make a deprecating gesture. "It is not photographic, my dear," he would say:

> My secret with a score is just a gift for complete concentration. I take as long as I want. I take a year if I want. Of time and myself, there is no end. Little by little, I arrive at an understanding, without forcing myself. It goes by itself. As soon as I receive a score, I take it to pieces, just as a child takes a clock apart. Then I put it back together, and then, my dear, I know how it is made. Not always everything fits when I put it together

for the first time, or the second. I may have left over bar 155 and bar 223. They represent bits of the clock and I have to find where they go. And when I rehearse, I tighten up every screw, just like a mechanic.[18]

Then, with a hound-dog furrowing of the eyebrows, Mitropoulos might shift focus from music to morality or philosophy, making one of those sudden transitions that so delighted and bewildered his friends: "Life is a big clock. If one part is missing, it doesn't run properly. The man who cleans the streets, the man in the orchestra who only plays the triangle, they should be proud of what they do. They are part of the big clock, part of the glory of life."[19]

Later in the morning, before rehearsals, he might take care of business, or what passed for business in his scheme of things. By 1950, Mitropoulos had earned about three hundred thousand dollars during his eleven years in America. Yet even now, in New York, his own personal living expenses were barely five thousand a year. The rest of his salary, here as in Minneapolis, went to charitable causes, generous impulses, and stipends to young musicians and seminarians—there was, in his mind, little difference between the two callings. In 1950, in addition to young John MacKay, he was supporting at least six full-time music and divinity students. During his next-to-last year in Minneapolis, Faith Reed, his loyal and hard-working private secretary, along with several other close friends, persuaded Mitropoulos to invest in some bonds and annuities—so that he would be at least modestly independent in his old age.

Mitropoulos still felt uncomfortable with that action, even two years later. "Sometimes I feel ashamed to be alive with my fortunate fate, when so many others are suffering," he would say, clearly uncomfortable when the subject of his own good works came up in conversation. "But, then, who knows what stern fate still awaits me in the future?" The interviewer to whom he addressed that last remark thought it was said in a peculiar tone of "hopefulness," as though Mitropoulos enjoyed contemplating future suffering.[20]

When asked a direct question about his multifaceted donations and subsidies, Mitropoulos smiled gently and quoted scripture: "Take heed that ye do not your alms before men, to be seen of them, otherwise ye have no reward of your Father, which is in Heaven. Therefore when thou doest thine alms, do not sound a trumpet before thee, as the hypocrites do in the synagogues and the streets, that they may have glory of men."[21]

Such quotations usually ended that particular train of questioning.

Mixed with his priestly mien was a streak of the vulgarly secular—you could see it in the way he tore into a cheeseburger or in the plebeian way he dealt with a formal dinner (Oscar Levant once saw him pour hollandaise sauce over his chicken and giblet gravy over his asparagus); beneath his air of innocence, his outward manifestations of childlike naivete, was a substratum of something shrewd and sophisticated. Once, when the orchestra

Dimitri Mitropoulos, sketch by Andreas Nomikos, done from life
in the conductor's suite in the Great Northern Hotel, 1956.
Courtesy of the artist.

performance, I thought," but would rather speak in terms of art's moral purpose: "that performance was a significant spiritual victory," or "a fine moral triumph."

"Only life suffered can transform a symphony from a collection of notes into a message for humanity," he would say—putting his own tribulations on a surprisingly utilitarian basis. His persistent compulsion to dwell on the nature of God, the power of moral truth, and the relationship of these concepts to the relatively mundane functions of an orchestra conductor, gave him more than occasional discomfort, even as his openness about these concerns made him vulnerable to the words and deeds of crasser men; but whatever suffering these obsessions caused him to endure, he believed that very suffering to be the cause of whatever transcendental qualities appeared in his music making. In later years, when he was enduring endless travails with the orchestra, he often tended to drift on moods, whims, fancies; when everything jelled, he could still conduct like a house afire; when it didn't, the performances themselves seemed strained and bloated and mired in process rather than achievement—either that, or dry and detached to the point of desiccation. Every private crisis eventually was resolved in and by the music; every private pain he endured sooner or later enriched some musical phrase; every personal sorrow ultimately expanded the range of his communication.

How did he cope with his new fame as the Philharmonic's music director, one of the Beefburger Hall coterie might inquire? And Mitropoulos would answer: "Only by being disinterested can you achieve something worthwhile. If you are big, they will treat you without mercy . . . absolutely without mercy. Take Christ. A holocaust of blood and sacrifice. Or Lincoln. He became a symbol of humanity because Booth shot him."[24]

What about the state of the musical art in America? someone else might ask:

We must have spiritual athletes as well as physical athletes. It is not right that seven-eighths of the American soul should be given to the physical. Why should a good second baseman be paid more than a good second violin? Classical music *is* important. Other people shouldn't hate those who like it or play it, and ordinary music lovers shouldn't hate Schoenberg. What is wrong is to emphasize one thing at the expense of another.[25]

Often, the relationship of music and religion was a topic of conversation. Given the Maestro's upbringing, was it hard for him to separate the two?

Absolutely no separation. My life is absolutely an entity. Everything goes out of one center, and therefore everything is close together. I could not feel art without religion, and vice-versa. I could not feel that I am an artist and not also be worried about certain moral values in the world. I can't believe in artists who are aloof, who only concern themselves with their art. Such art is really useless, in the long run. The artist today has living responsibilities to the rest of the people, because he is a man *in view*, and he should show that his principles, that his artistic integrity if you will, corresponds with human integrity and human feelings.[26]

After the Beefburger interlude, and if there were no additional rehearsals scheduled in the afternoon, Mitropoulos would return to the Great Northern, take a nap for an hour or two, then spend the afternoon dictating correspondence to Faith Reed, and in some cases actually writing the letters himself. He usually ate a hearty meal before returning to Carnegie Hall to conduct a concert, then changed into his white tie and tails in his hotel rooms, and walked the block-and-a-half to the stage entrance.

At the conclusion of the first selection on the program, he darted into the wings, where the loyal Miss Reed waited with a glass of water and a lit cigarette. He downed the water, took a few drags, then bounded back on stage to lead the next selection. The process was repeated between each selection on the program.

After an evening concert, he usually managed to decline all invitations and walked back to his hotel. He bathed, read for an hour or two, and was usually asleep by midnight—at least on the nights when he was ready for sleep. If he was still revved up from the concert, he might take a cab to a movie house and watch a feature or two to unwind.

On May 1, 1950, Mitropoulos flew to Italy for his first postwar tour of that nation. His first engagement was the May Festival in Florence, where he was scheduled to conduct two performances of *Elektra* (May 14 and 16); three concerts were slated for Rome (May 21 and 24 and June 10), one in Bologna (May 27), one in Turin (June 2), and two in Naples before he returned to Florence for a farewell Verdi Requiem on June 6. He would fly back to New York in time to conduct the final week of Lewisohn Stadium concerts, beginning on August 7.

Mitropoulos revisited his old haunts in Rome, a pilgrimage that refreshed his spirit enormously. Unfortunately, he found working conditions at the Florence Festival close to intolerable—an indication of how standards had declined due to the war. The orchestra was horribly overworked, sometimes having to play three operas under three different conductors in a single week. To make matters worse, it wasn't even an especially good orchestra; its playing was frequently out of tune, usually not together, and dreadfully undisciplined when it did not sound simply exhausted. Nor was the situation much better with regard to the vocal soloists; the German singers who had been imported for the production proved to be "arrogant and conceited and very bad musicians, making mistakes constantly."[27]

By the last two days of rehearsal, however, Mitropoulos had somehow whipped this motley assortment into a semblance of professionalism, and the performances of *Elektra* proved to be a great success. "He conducted with the authority of a proud, cruel general, and the outcome was that he achieved a most glorious and merited victory," wrote the critic for *Il Messaggero di Roma*.[28]

After the Rome ordeal, Mitropoulos was grateful to check into "a dream of a hotel" on Capri, where he was tormented night and day by a radio playing loudly outside his window. Fortunately, the rest of the tour went well. Mitropoulos featured a number of new and novel works on this Italian junket, including William Schuman's *Circus Overture*, Morton Gould's Concerto for Orchestra, Malipiero's Seventh Symphony, and Krenek's excoriating *Symphonic Elegy for Strings, on the Death of Webern*, one of that composer's finest works.

Conditions in postwar Italy distressed Mitropoulos. Beggars were everywhere. The middle class was disoriented with its new and chaotic democracy; the working class was openly and vociferously pro-Communist. The only thing propping up the whole tottering nation was American aid money, a situation Mitropoulos felt very uneasy about. In every city where he conducted, dozens of musicians would implore him to help them get jobs in America, any kind of jobs.

He had quite an adventure one night during the Turin leg of the trip. He arrived in town with twenty-four hours to spare, so he hired a cab and asked to be driven to the Matterhorn, about two-and-a-half hours away by car. He planned to check into an inn at the foot of the mountain, in the small Italian village that nestles high up on the Matterhorn's southern flank, at about ten thousand feet. The cab driver swore he knew the way, but he immediately got lost and they did not arrive at the mountain until three o'clock in the morning. Everybody in the village was asleep, and when he reluctantly told the driver to turn back for Turin, he realized the taxi was out of gas. Despite the bone-chilling cold, Mitropoulos spent the night in the cramped back seat of the taxi, his only consolation being the magnificent sight of the Matterhorn rising above him in the moonlight "like a great white tower."[29]

L'Affaire Roxy and the Triumph of *Wozzeck*

The 1950–1951 season, Mitropoulos's first full season as sole music director of the Philharmonic, began not in Carnegie Hall, but with a colorful and controversial experiment that came to be known as L'Affaire Roxy. The Roxy Theater was a Broadway landmark, one of the biggest and swankiest movie palaces in Manhattan, capable of seating six thousand. In addition to showcasing big-budget films, the Roxy offered live stage shows in between movies, featuring comedians, big bands, star vocalists, and sometimes its own army of leggy chorus girls—the Roxyettes—dancing on a full-sized ice-skating rink.

In the spring of 1950, Mitropoulos had been approached by a wealthy countryman named Spyros Skouras, president of Twentieth Century–Fox, member of the board of directors of the Philharmonic, and part owner of a nationwide chain of movie palaces for which the Roxy served as flagship. The plan Skouras laid out for Mitropoulos envisioned the Philharmonic playing a two-week gig at the Roxy before the orchestra's regular season began; four forty-five-minute shows a day, seven days a week. The idea was to broaden the orchestra's audience dramatically, demystify classical music for the hoi polloi, and obtain two lucrative weeks of employment for the orchestra personnel at precisely the time of year they were most in need of it.

Mitropoulos was delighted with the whole concept. It fitted perfectly with his belief in the essentially democratic nature of art, and as soon as he heard the proposal he began to quote Goethe: "Where the muses go, there is their temple."

Some members of the Philharmonic's board, however, were aghast, viewing the Roxy engagement as a debasement of all that the New York Philharmonic stood for. The Philharmonic would be laughed at; it would have to play light music, presumably, in order to keep the untutored masses in their chairs; the newspapers would have a field day taking snide shots at the orchestra, and so on. They were also worried about the expense—thirty thousand dollars per week. If the concerts flopped, it would be a costly flop indeed. Mitropoulos gave the board his word that the dignity of the orchestra would be preserved; the board would have full right of approval for printed advertisements; there would be no compromises in the matter of repertoire; the men would dress formally; all 104 members would be involved; and the music-making would be of the same high caliber displayed at a regular subscription concert.

The Philharmonic was booked to open on September 1, just behind Milton Berle and the Roxyettes. The featured movie would be a Twentieth Century–Fox technicolor costume drama called *The Black Rose*, starring Tyrone Power and Orson Welles. Mitropoulos remained ebullient about the project right up to opening day, and was quoted often in the newspapers. He gave his most detailed response to his friend Louis Biancolli: "We are missionaries," Mitropoulos stated,

> bringing the gospel to people who until now, for one reason or another, have been afraid of us. . . . You see, the people who usually go to the Roxy had thought of us as aloof. They regarded us as the privilege of a certain class. Our aim, the aim of all aristocrats and capitalists of the mind, is to share our spiritual wealth with these people.
>
> We want them to come to listen to our orchestra as we, on our part, would go to a baseball game or to the movies. We want to break down this prejudice against us as a group barricaded in an ivory tower, speaking only to a chosen few. Through our music, we want to say to these people: "This is our capital. With a little patience and effort, it can be your capital too."
>
> This engagement at the Roxy is really about brotherhood—the brotherhood of the mind, the body, and the soul. We are bringing them a beauty that everyone can own, at a very small price. . . . There is a pride in every human being which will not allow him to feel happy knowing that his mind is not developed enough to enjoy spiritual entertainment.
>
> I think we will be among friends at the Roxy.[1]

There were many who wanted the venture to fail and Mitropoulos to get a come-uppance for this "slumming" excursion by the orchestra; only a bare majority of the orchestra board supported the venture, and that guardedly. Letters of complaint poured in from the snootier longtime subscribers —the sort of people who went to Carnegie Hall precisely *because* doing so enabled them to feel superior to the common folk who went to places like the Roxy.

When the curtain rose to reveal the 104 musicians, all spiffily dressed in their penguin suits, every seat in the Roxy was filled, and there was already a long line at the box office for the next show. All four shows were sold out, for a single's day's attendance of just under 24,000. Frank Waldenstein, manager of the Roxy, gave a brief spoken introduction. He outlined the 108-year history of the Philharmonic, reminded the audience that history was being made here today, and when he said the words: "The time or place doesn't matter—it's the music that counts," the audience spontaneously applauded.

Mitropoulos and the Philharmonic share the marquee of the
Roxy Theater with Orson Welles and Tyrone Power, 1950.
Photo by Metropolitan Photo Service, courtesy Dorle Soria.

As *Billboard* described the event, in its usual snappy fashion:

Program-wise and showman-wise, conductor Dimitri Mitropoulos, an
ascetic-looking gent with warm dignity, is making no concessions to
the so-called popular tastes. His program skedded [*Billboard*-ese for
"scheduled"] to change twice weekly, is a solid notch above the usual
pop concert line-up, but nothing appeared too formidable for the enthusiastic audience. Spontaneous applause between the movements of
the Prokofiev Classical Symphony indicated that this was not a trained
audience of habitual concert-goers. They took the music straight, without special staging or lighting.[2]

Indeed they did, and evidently enjoyed what they heard. The big audience was attentive to the music and enthusiastic in its reaction. Fliers de-
tailing the Philharmonic's regular Carnegie Hall season, and emphasizing
the lower tier of ticket prices, were inserted into all the Roxy programs, and
most people took them home.

Far from disparaging the effort, the New York papers treated the Roxy
experiment in a most encouraging and optimistic fashion. The *Times* praised
the venture; bobby-soxers were interviewed as they came out of the theater, resulting in stories like "Jive Bugs Glow at Dimitri's Show"; and the
regular music critics seemed quite disarmed by the whole undertaking,
some of them expressing amazement at how good the (discreetly ampli-
fied) sound was in the cavernous theater.

That first Roxy concert marked the start of long and fruitful association between soprano Eileen Farrell and Mitropoulos. Even thirty-four years later, the memory of that event was fresh and dear:

> When I did "The Last Rose of Summer," he used only a harp. I mean he could be terribly theatrical—like the harp was on Forty-ninth Street and I was on Fiftieth Street, if you know what I mean. I don't think he even conducted. He just stood there, with his head bowed and his hands clasped, and sort of radiated while I sang the song with just a simple harp accompaniment. It was terribly effective.[3]

The conductor had his own rather strange method of measuring the success of the opening program. "I measured the audience with *chewing gum*," he told columnist Jinx Falkenburg.

> Yes, that is correct—chewing gum. I chew gum myself—I *love* to chew gum. But since the chewing effort comes from the brain, when I listen to music, I stop chewing—my brain is occupied with music.
>
> The first thing I noticed at the Roxy, facing this audience of reg'lar guys, was a sea of jaws working up and down, chewing. And then we began to play. In the middle of the concert, I turned around to look again, and I was thrilled to see happening to the audience what happens to me—their brains were so absorbed by the music that they had forgotten even to chew![4]

Opposition to the Roxy experiment faded after the overwhelmingly positive response the programs engendered, but some of the more hidebound patrons and board members nursed a grudge—these were the people who treasured the very elitist attitude Mitropoulos had sought to counteract with the Roxy concerts. One of the viler rumors in circulation was that Mitropoulos had pushed the project through because he was greedy and the Roxy pay scale would give him more money than he could have gotten from two weeks of ordinary concerts. Anyone who actually knew the conductor understood the lameness of that complaint. In any event, the numbers themselves refute it conclusively. Mitropoulos was paid a total of ten thousand dollars for his two weeks' work; half of that sum, he promptly donated to the New York Philharmonic Pension Fund; $1500–$2000 of it he blew on a huge party for the orchestra men and their families; Columbia Artists Management received its usual commission; by the time state and federal taxes took their bite, Mitropoulos actually lost money on the deal.

As for the players of the Philharmonic, there were, for once, no complaints. The gig had been, for a welcome change, *fun*; many of them had been interviewed, too, and had their pictures in the papers; some of them had been asked for autographs by the patrons; all of them had taken home a nice paycheck ($304 for the rank-and-file; slightly more for the first-chair players) at a time during the season when they were used to pinching nickels to get by until the Carnegie Hall concerts began. Seen in relation to the arc of Mitropoulos's tenure with the orchestra, the afterglow of the Roxy concerts probably marked the happiest and most relaxed period of relations with the Philharmonic personnel. The men still could not believe their good luck at having a conductor who not only treated them like human beings, but who actually worked to bring them extra pay and prestige.

A studied attempt had been made by Mitropoulos and the Philharmonic management to plan the 1950–1951 season in a coherent fashion. And perhaps an even more strenuous effort had been made, behind closed doors, to work out a compromise between the amount of unusual music Mitropoulos wanted to conduct and the amount the board was willing to tolerate. In press releases, at least, the resulting arrangement was presented as Solomonic; in private, it was no less acrimonious than the previous year's arguments. The Philharmonic had finished its previous season with a deficit of $81,500, and subscription sales had declined for the second straight year. Olin Downes got the scoop on things: "In light of his experiences, here and abroad, and the returns or lack of returns at the Philharmonic-Symphony box office, [Mitropoulos] has concluded, after a fresh consideration of all the factors involved, that the proportion of two important novelties per month is the approximate measure of the average audience's assimilation."[5]

As to how this arcane formula was derived, Howard Taubman, in a very favorable *New York Times Magazine* profile entitled "The Passionate Calm of Mr. Mitropoulos," gave a more detailed explanation:

> Recently, a group of ladies on the auxiliary board of the Philharmonic-Symphony Society met with Mr. Mitropoulos and suggested that it would be pleasant if he did not assault the ears of his audiences with the horrors of extreme, contemporary music. The conductor listened courteously, and then responded that both he and the orchestra would be derelict in their duty if they did not continue to play such music. Furthermore, he said, he had to conduct it for the good of his own musical soul; it was a challenge which kept him alert and fresh.
>
> However, he went on with the air of a man who could be reasonable, he would be willing to compromise. Since the Philharmonic season is divided into two alternative series, he would include a major modern work only on one of two successive programs in each series. Thus in either series there would be one program devoted to the tried and familiar pieces and one program with a new, perhaps difficult, composition. Every other week the patrons could relax with their established masterpieces, and at least once every fortnight Mr. Mitropoulos would have the satisfaction of performing a sizable new work.
>
> The ladies were relieved by the thoughtfulness of their conductor, and Mr. Mitropoulos was delighted that he could now do an important contemporary work every other week, which was perhaps more than he had hoped for.[6]

In any event, the season's lineup of "novelties" included Milhaud's opera *Les Choéphores*, Malipiero's Fourth Piano Concerto, a two-piano concerto by Robert and Gaby Casadesus, Virgil Thomson's Second Symphony, a symphony by black composer Howard Swanson, Ravel's *L'Heure espagnole*, a tub-thumping epic called the *"Christus" Symphony* by the one-armed Greek composer Harilaos Perpessa, and a concert reading of Alban Berg's *Wozzeck*. Formulaic or not, this was a strong, diverse menu and possibly the most progressive list of works played by any orchestra in the world at that time.

For the opening concert, October 12, Mitropoulos selected Alfredo Casella's orchestration of Bach's Chaconne, Beethoven's Fourth Symphony, and Prokofiev's Fifth. Mitropoulos's way with the Beethoven symphony was a known commodity by now, and there was agreement that he turned the piece into a much more exciting statement than most of his colleagues, despite what Thomson called his "fondling" of the slow movement. Several reviews mentioned patches of roughness in the playing, due in part to the deteriorating skills of the Philharmonic's bassoon player—his inability to cope with his crucial part became notorious, so much so that eventually the orchestra actually had to drop the Beethoven Fourth from its active repertoire for a few years. The "Christus" Symphony of Harilaos Perpessa was one of those now-you-see-'em-now-you-don't pieces that got scheduled and played primarily because their composers caught Mitropoulos in a charitable mood—not such a hard thing to do, given a little persistence. Several times during any given season he said "yes" to importuning musicians, and later was heard to mutter: "Why do I have such a hard time saying 'no'?" Whenever these doubts took hold, and it was too late to back out, Mitropoulos tried to place the questionable work on the less scrutinized Saturday night concerts; a "one-shot special," as these works were known backstage. In the case of Perpessa, what began as a genuine, if temporary, infatuation with the composer's aesthetic gradually changed into detestation.

Composed in Athens, the "Christus" Symphony bears on its title page a quote from Wagner's "Religion and Art": "The ultimate destiny of mankind depends upon the acceptance of the teaching of Christ . . . O, Redeemer, stand by us in Thy immeasurable compassion"—a perfect hook to dangle before Mitropoulos, who promptly committed himself to a performance. By the time the scheduled date rolled around, the conductor was having grave second thoughts. In the interim, Mitropoulos had given his countryman a generous commission for a new orchestral work, and when Perpessa turned in the score, it proved to be nothing more than a new orchestration of Beethoven's Eighth Symphony! Perpessa was not only obstinate and conceited, he was an inexcusably sloppy workman—when the parts to his symphony arrived, they were found to be incomplete, partly illegible, and riddled with obvious mistakes. Rehearsals were stormy as Mitropoulos attempted to piece the score together with little help from the truculent composer. Matters degenerated, at one point, to such an extent that

Mitropoulos began yelling curses at Perpessa in Greek, an absolutely un-precedented spectacle that had many Philharmonic players flashing back to the days of Toscanini. Not coincidentally, this was one of the last times Mi-tropoulos programmed any music by a Greek composer.

Perpessa's symphony is in five movements, three of them prefaced by quotations from the Book of Revelations, the final two by references to "faith, hope, and love." In its spacious orchestration and lofty sentiment, the work suggests Mahler; the juiciness and bombast of its melodic curves sug-gest Miklos Rozsa's epic film scores. With the difficulties of rehearsals be-hind him, Mitropoulos was free to concentrate on the spiritual essence of the symphony; the performance was blazing, luminous, fervent beyond the worth of the material to such an extent that the symphony, as it were, tran-scended itself. At the end of the piece—a seraphic Mahlerian diminuendo—Mitropoulos extended both arms straight out from his body in a gesture of crucifixion; it was pure showmanship. On this occasion, the audience was swept up in the passion of the performance; here was "new music" that spoke to the heart and the solar plexus. Conductor and composer were ap-plauded lustily.

The finest program of the fall season was given its first performance on Thursday, November 9: Darius Milhaud's *Les Choéphores*, coupled with Ravel's delicious satirical opera, *L'Heure espagnole*. For all the whimsicality of many Mitropoulos programs, there were times when his juxtaposition of works was brilliant; this was surely one of them.

Milhaud composed *Les Choéphores* (The Libation-Bearers) in 1920, using a French translation by Paul Claudel of Aeschylus's original, the second of the three parts of the *Oresteia*. In it, the composer deploys some of the bold-est polytonal writing of his oeuvre. Spoken narration and choral chants alternate with more conventionally sung passages, supported by an or-chestral part of great brilliance and vivid timbral color. In the New York performances, Madeleine Milhaud portrayed the main speaker-narrator; her husband, the composer, was present throughout the production, lend-ing it a special authority. Mack Harrell sang Orestes and Eileen Farrell, Elec-tra. The demanding choral part was sung, with enormous gusto and im-pressive French pronunciation, by the Westminster Choir.

Milhaud chose polytonal chords for his main expressive device, ac-cording to his comments in the program notes, because he found them "more subtly sweet, more violently potent," and indeed they are in his han-dling of them. As purely orchestral or choral music, the score could in places sound grating and dense; wedded as it is to a classic tale, its trans-formations and turbulence mated to poetry that sounds magnificent in any language, its power strikes even the least sophisticated listener. No one who was present would ever forget the stark, incantatory power of the "Exhor-tation," when the speaker declaims and the chorus shouts above a roiling, seething instrumental tapestry scored for percussion only.

Audience and critics alike knew they had witnessed something special, just as they had in the previous year's concert performance of *Elektra*, and Olin Downes's notice echoed those of his colleagues:

> "Les Choéphores" . . . is a work of great difficulty for everyone involved. How the soloists and chorus performed with such confidence and virtuosity at a first performance of such a work is hard to explain. . . . But they did it, and the final reason why they did it undoubtedly lies with the conductor. He had to coordinate all the strands and elements of an exceptionally complicated ensemble, and it seemed to us that Mr. Mitropoulos directed with an almost wanton pleasure in the more complicated problems of his task. The more complicated, the more subtle the problems of rhythmics, intonation, balance, and highly dissonant counterpoint, the more interested and satisfied with his lot he seemed to be![7]

Nor did the Ravel opera, so utterly different in subject matter and style, seem anticlimactic. It soothed where the Milhaud disturbed, invoked smiles rather than terror, and in juxtaposition it closed the theatrical circle of the evening and sent the audience home in a satisfied, emotionally replete, mood. Composer John la Montaine thought the Ravel was in every way as exceptional a realization as the Milhaud blockbuster:

> Without question, the finest performance I've ever heard of the Ravel *L'Heure espagnole* was the one that he conducted with the New York Philharmonic, an incredible performance of it, in every last detail. One of the singers told me "It almost threw us at first because he conducted every sixteenth note," and the fact is that the work sounded so fresh, it was as though it were being improvised on the spot. The performance was that opera incarnate, no doubt about it.[8]

At the end of the first week in December, Mitropoulos took a break from his New York activities and traveled out of town for some guest engagements—in Cleveland on December 7, 9, 14, and 16, and then out to San Francisco, a city that charmed him, with an orchestra he enjoyed conducting. His last guest engagement before returning to finish the Philharmonic season was in Buffalo.

On the first two Cleveland dates, Mitropoulos gave the American premiere of Krenek's *Symphonic Elegy* for string orchestra, perhaps the most moving orchestral piece Krenek ever wrote; on the last pair of concerts, he presented the world premiere of a new symphony by Marcel Dick. After attending both rehearsals and concerts, the composer wrote the following letter:

> Still under the great impression your appearance in Cleveland made on all of us, I wish to thank you again for everything you have done for me. Not only for having accepted and played my symphony, the work of an author utterly unknown to the public at large, which in itself is an

almost unbelievable occurrence in today's musical practice; and not only for the deep understanding and loving care with which you projected my music in the two brilliant concert performances. These are qualities we have known you to possess, values for which we have admired you for a long time. Last week I was the fortunate one to benefit by them.

But beyond and above the musical event was the privilege of being with you, and to listen to you. I have not known any human being whose ethical loftiness and intelligence had such an uplifting, stimulating, purifying influence. On me, and everyone around you. When, at parting, I wished God's blessing on you, I realized that you ought to feel blessed enough just for being the kind of man you are.[9]

In between his engagements in Cleveland, Mitropoulos was invited, by the Humanities Department, to be a guest lecturer at the University of Syracuse, where his friend and colleague Louis Krasner was now a professor. More than one thousand people came to Crouse Auditorium, ostensibly to hear a lecture entitled "The Conductor, His Fellow Musicians, and His Community." But Mitropoulos used no prepared text and gave no formal lecture—he sat informally and spoke to the audience as he would have to any friendly group. "I have never tried to become famous," he said.

I have only tried to be useful and to justify my existence as a human being. Ever since I was a kid, I have felt a kind of endless gratitude for being able to breathe, to walk, to mountain-climb, and glory in merely being here. I feel an immense gratitude and a need to do something about this. I feel a great necessity to justify my life, to show that I'm grateful to the one who is responsible for all this.

When I was fifteen, I went to Italy. There I discovered St. Francis and lived in the atmosphere of his work. He was the greatest human being who has lived since Christ. He gave me a life to dream about. . . . I always try to fall back on St. Francis and his godliness.

About his current job, he had this to say:

The Philharmonic is supposed to be the most hard-boiled orchestra in the world. Conductors who finish with them are supposed to be very happy to go away. The players don't like to be ruled, but some conductors have tried to rule and to regiment them. So, although they gave good concerts, they weren't giving their hearts. I treated them as equals; I worked just as hard and harder than they did because a conductor's job requires that he do so. When I first came to the Philharmonic, they were untamed lions. Now they are lambs.

An orchestra is like a community. There is a leader, section leaders, and a triangle player. But each is just as important to the success of the whole. I am there not as leader, but as a man who can do this sort of work, conducting, better than anything else. Since my job is more difficult than that of the triangle player, I must work much harder. I owe as much responsibility to my triangle player as he owes to me.

Turning from music to the world in general, Mitropoulos waxed gloomy: "The church has failed, politics has failed. We don't know what to believe any more. Good doesn't exist any more; it is powerless." Mitropoulos then related how Nathan Milstein, just before a recent concert, had told him that the world situation of the day may well have rendered the professional musician obsolete. "This was a great revelation," the conductor mused. "I soon realized that life without its 'useless occupations' would really not be worth living."

In closing, he summarized the points he wanted to make with his predominantly young audience:

Remember the glory of the unknown. Remember the contentment in having done something to justify passing through this world. Don't always strive to be something for the sake of making money. Remember the contentment which comes from feeling gratitude and giving thanks. And remember to enjoy the good things of life while you're here to enjoy them.[10]

The biggest event of the spring 1951 season, indeed the greatest triumph Mitropoulos scored during his entire tenure with the New York Philharmonic, came on the night of April 12 when he conducted the first of a series of concert performances of Alban Berg's harrowing expressionist opera, *Wozzeck.*

Violent, sardonic, grimly realistic yet full of references to hallucinatory states, *Wozzeck* is a perfect dramatic vehicle for Berg's masterly style—and for the style of Mitropoulos, who gloried in its stark lyricism, its morbid intensity, its alienated treatments of dances, marches, and a lullaby, and its myriad, often gruesome, onomatopoeic effects. Only once before had the opera been performed in New York, back in 1931, when Stokowski brought the Philadelphia Grand Opera Company to the Met. For the Mitropoulos performances, a stellar cast was convened: Mack Harrell sang the title role; Eileen Farrell sang Marie; Ralph Herbert and Frederick Jagel played the doctor and the drum major, respectively, and the choral part was handled by the Schola Cantorum, directed by Hugh Ross.

Mitropoulos astonished everybody by showing up at the first rehearsal with the entire complex score committed to memory. For the opera's first performance, Erich Kleiber required almost fifty hours of rehearsal; Mitropoulos had eighteen. Cellist Anthony Sophos recalled:

Wozzeck was not like your Italian operas, where the music flows along in the same meter for eight bars, sixteen bars; everything is dynamic in the Berg opera, instruments always changing, rhythm always shifting, the voices coming in all over the place. And there Mitropoulos was, just incredibly well prepared and *reveling* in the sheer challenge of it, throwing cues like a computer. It was one of the most incredible conducting feats of our time.[11]

Harry Zaratzian, violinist, remembered how his own feelings and those of his colleagues changed during the first rehearsals:

At the first rehearsal, I hated it. What sort of piece was this? What's so great about it? How can you even tell if you're playing the right notes? I thought the score was crazy, and I thought I was going crazy trying play it. My God, why do we have to learn this stuff? And then it gradually happened. Dimitri began to explain how it was put together, what each detail meant, just patiently untying the knots in the score. By the third rehearsal, I was starting to really understand it—and I could hear the other players going through the same process. By the time we actually performed it, I thought *Wozzeck* was one of the greatest pieces ever composed. Dimitri's ability to explicate and demystify these complex modern scores was just unbelievable.[12]

Milton Babbitt, known to be among the most pitch-acute of composers, agreed that Mitropoulos led a great performance but was conscious, both during rehearsals and performances, of numerous small inaccuracies.

Jacques Monod and I were sitting in the hall, following the score of *Wozzeck* while Dimitri rehearsed. Now, there is a scene in a tavern where Berg uses a cafe band, and in one bar there's a place where the accordionist plays an E minor triad. Well, whoever this guy was, he was brought in as a freelancer and he wasn't very good, because he kept playing an *E major* triad. And Mitropoulos didn't seem to notice it. I turned to Jacques and said, "Should I tell him?" And Jacques said, "Gee, I don't know. Maybe you ought to because other people are certainly going to notice." So I went up to Dimitri at the next break and pointed it out to him in the score, and he was sincerely grateful. He thanked me, and then he went and had a few words with the accordionist. I discovered that this incident was not unique. In fact, that fabulous memory of Dimitri's was accurate mainly with regard to the rhythmic structure of a work—if a sixteenth note were missing, he would notice it. But he was not that scrupulous about pitch, especially in the kind of contemporary scores he loved to conduct. As great as that *Wozzeck* recording is, there are a lot of flubbed notes in it.[13]

There was no scenery, but Mitropoulos made room on the stage, between the podium and the orchestra, for his vocalists to move around, to gesture, to express physically the emotions behind their words. The chorus, too, participated; dressed in simple, working-class attire, its members were drilled to rise and declaim, to gesture, to show expressions of anger, rage, or tenderness as the music required. For the players of the New York

Philharmonic, Berg's score was cruelly demanding, but they went to work on it in precisely the mood of shared creativity, shared challenge, that Mitropoulos strove so tirelessly to inculcate; by opening night, they had the score in their fingers and brains, if not always in their hearts, and they projected both the power and the pity of *Wozzeck* in an unforgettable way.

For once, Mitropoulos's faith in the average listener's intelligence was vindicated. At the end of the opera, there was a moment of breathless silence, as the audience digested the force of the final scene, then a ten-minute ovation began; Mitropoulos and his singers were recalled twelve times. A fiercely demanding, sometimes-atonal opera was suddenly the hottest ticket in Manhattan. Many listeners who came ready to dislike what they heard, left Carnegie Hall stunned by the theatrical power of the opera, ready to admit that Berg's musical idiom was perfect for delineating the elusive, the pathological, the subconscious with all its grisly, guilty secrets and obsessions. Their feelings were summed up neatly by one dumbfounded critic who was so affected by the opening night performance that he returned four days later to hear it again:

> It would be difficult to conceive the opera being written in anything but the contemporary idiom, atonality and all the rest. In *Wozzeck*, it more than makes sense; it is utterly right emotionally. Not that it sounds beautiful. It sounds real. More important, perhaps, the music is the psychological extension of Wozzeck's understandable confusion in a confused world. Berg's transference of this literally into music is a master stroke. It culminates in a third act of indescribable power and remarkable beauty.[14]

Virgil Thomson stated that the production "attracted an audience of music lovers, opera lovers, atonality fans and German literature devotees that should reduce to folly anybody's idea that modern music is not box-office. The occasion also disproved for all time, I imagine, any belief that anybody might have retained that Alban Berg's music is in any way whatsoever recondite."[15] Even Downes quite properly identified the concert "one of the historic achievements in the history of Carnegie Hall."[16]

April was a busy month for Mitropoulos. The excitement of *Wozzeck* had barely worn off, when he was back before the orchestra in his ever-popular dual role as pianist/conductor, this time in the Piano Concerto No. 4 by Malipiero. On April 21, Mitropoulos and the Philharmonic made one of their finest records: the first, and so far only, recording of Krenek's *Symphonic Elegy*.

At the end of the month, the conductor flew to Iowa to help launch the career of his pupil, James Dixon. Born in Guthrie Center, Iowa, Dixon was only sixteen when he met Mitropoulos—he had followed the Minneapolis Symphony from town to town during one of its Midwest tours, until he worked up the courage to go backstage and meet his idol. Mitropoulos, true to his philosophy, did everything he could to discourage Dixon's ambition to become a conductor, but when he realized the young man's determination was unshakable, he agreed to be his mentor. The relationship became strongly paternal (at one point Mitropoulos wanted to adopt Dixon legally), and Mitropoulos subsidized much of Dixon's college education. On April 30, in Davenport, he appeared as soloist in the Prokofiev Third Concerto, while Dixon directed the Tri-City Symphony Orchestra, an ensemble he would lead for the next three decades. While visiting the campus of the University of Iowa, Mitropoulos also delivered two lectures.

Mitropoulos's faith in James Dixon was not misplaced. Dixon made the Tri-City Orchestra into a first-rate ensemble and conducted it until his retirement in 1994. Dixon contributed richly to the cultural life of the Midwest. He followed his mentor's way by presenting numerous world premieres and by championing the difficult and the unfamiliar, and he bore proudly the scars of numerous boardroom battles. Among Dixon's awards were the Elizabeth Sprague Coolidge Medal, the Laurel Leaf Award ("for distinguished achievement in fostering and encouraging American music") of the American Composers Alliance, and the Gustav Mahler Medal, bestowed by the Bruckner Society. Mitropoulos had also received the medal, in 1940.

On May 9, the Philharmonic repeated its visit to the Roxy Theater. The concerts went well, but neither attendance nor publicity reached the same level as they had during the first Roxy gig; nobody tires of novelty quicker than New Yorkers. The Roxy engagements were not repeated in 1952.

In May, detailed appraisals of the season appeared in the papers. Olin Downes called it a "triumph of modernism" and singled out Mitropoulos's three opera performances as highlights not just of the season now ending, but of the past decade.

Louis Biancolli assessed the orchestra's season in terms of its conductor. He noted how much enthusiasm, even passion, Mitropoulos had generated among listeners who were "on his wave length," a panegyric in stark contrast to the sort of critical bludgeoning that became so common, and so brutal, only a few seasons later:

> If I were asked to nominate the conductor of the year, there wouldn't be a moment's hesitation in naming Dimitri Mitropoulos, leader of the symphonic pride of the city—the New York Philharmonic.
>
> This Greek-born batonist has completed what to me was his most brilliant season since his arrival as guest conductor several years ago. Both in program-building and in program presentation, Mr. Mitropoulos rose to new heights this past season. The orchestra played magnificently. . . . If anybody is ever to succeed Arturo Toscanini as the master of masters, it is Dimitri Mitropoulos.[17]

In the summer of 1951, Mitropoulos conducted his customary concerts at Lewisohn Stadium, along with five concerts at the Ravinia Festival in Chicago. At the end of July, he flew to Los Angeles and gave two Hollywood Bowl concerts, all proceeds from which, including his fee, went to the Los Angeles Philharmonic to help bail the orchestra out of its financial troubles. Although he desperately wanted to return to his beloved mountains, Mitropoulos did not have time to exercise and acclimate himself; any serious mountaineering, for a man of fifty-five, was out of the question without a prolonged training period. Sadly, he resigned himself to go without the solace and stimulation of climbing.

The second half of the summer was given over to preparations for the Philharmonic's much anticipated journey to Edinburgh. No American orchestra had ever been invited to the Edinburgh Festival before (and in the opinion of many British orchestral musicians, for whom the festival constituted valuable summertime employment, there was no reason for one to be invited this time, either); much was to be made of the trip in the New York papers.

Much was also being made in the newspapers of London, Edinburgh, Liverpool, and Manchester, as letters of complaint arrived, questioning the need to spend so much money to import a "Yank" orchestra. The Philharmonic would, no doubt about it, have to contend with a long-established English tradition of xenophobia when it comes to conductors, as anyone can verify by reading the record reviews in the pages of that vastly overrated journal *The Gramophone*. Because Otto Klemperer did all of his last work in Great Britain, even his stodgiest, most elephantine, and most rhythmically palsied performances were regularly hoisted to the peaks of Olympus; when Leopold Stokowski lived and recorded in the U.S., *The Gramophone* heaped scorn on his recordings, vilifying him as a buffoon and a charlatan—as soon as Stokowski returned to England to live and record, he suddenly became a Great Conductor once more. There was also the unspoken English preference—scoffed at so royally by Sir Thomas Beecham—for interpretations that are "musical" and correct, rather than performances of high emotional temper. These were the attitudes lying in ambush for the Philharmonic and for its unsuspecting conductor.

Starting on August 22, the Philharmonic would play fourteen concerts in Edinburgh on fourteen consecutive days—a strenuous tour indeed. Bruno Walter would conduct the opening concert, Mitropoulos the second, and so on until the end of the festival. Some of the biggest crowd-pleasers— Beethoven's Ninth Symphony, Mozart's Thirty-Ninth Symphony, and Schubert's Ninth Symphony—would be directed by Walter, a conductor who, after all, was famed for precisely this repertoire; to Mitropoulos went the Mendelssohn "Scottish" Symphony, Prokofiev's Fifth, Vaughan Williams's Fourth, and shorter works by Morton Gould, Howard Swanson, de Falla, and Arnold Bax.

Mitropoulos and the New York Philharmonic playing the national
anthems before a standing audience on opening night of the Edinburgh
Festival, 1951. Scottish Tourist Board photo, courtesy Dorle Soria.

Mitropoulos was showing signs of nervous exhaustion by the time the
tour programs were finalized in midspring; the effort of mastering, rehearsing, and performing *Wozzeck*, near the end of what had already been
a long and demanding season, had drained even his reserves. The fact that
Wozzeck had been both a critical and a box office success seems to have done
nothing to ease Mitropoulos's position relative to offbeat repertoire. He was
still under constant pressure, some of it not in the least subtle, to abandon
his "mission" and become more of an entertainer. He had been counting
on Bruno Walter's support, believing that a man of Walter's education, temperament, and demonstrable decency would uphold his colleague's idealism even if he did not always care for his program selections. But as the
months went by, Walter did nothing to help; if anything, he seemed ever-
so-slightly disdainful of the posture Mitropoulos had been forced to adopt.

Although a dispassionate examination of the Edinburgh programs indicates that each conductor was more or less given the sort of music he felt
happiest with, Mitropoulos saw it differently. The strain appeared during
a pre-tour rehearsal, when Mitropoulos lost his composure totally. He suddenly became distraught, his voice rising in pitch to a querulous screech. He
began complaining about how Bruno Walter had been given all the plums
in the tour repertoire and he had been stuck with the tough-sell pieces. "He
became almost hysterical," recalled Leonard Rose, "complaining bitterly

and peevishly. I hate to use the description, but in this case it's accurate—he sounded like a little old woman ranting about how badly the world treats her. It was not a very pretty sight."[18]

Neither were many of the reviews, following Mitropoulos's debut program on August 23. The *London Times* described Mitropoulos's Beethoven Fourth Symphony, which occupied the first half of that program, as "hateful. He used neither score nor baton and his few manual gestures served to mar the perfection of the ensemble, disrupt the rhythm, and underline the obvious. The finale was taken at such a pace that a public reconciliation between conductor and bassoonist after it was over was certainly called for."[19] Eric Blom, reviewing the August 25 concert for *The Observer*, disliked everything—conductor, Beethoven, and the Prokofiev Fifth Symphony (about which posterity has concluded very differently from Mr. Blom):

> Mr. Mitropoulos as a conductor is original to the verge of freakishness. He not only conducts without a baton, but often without a beat. When he just lets the music plane in the air, the effect can be tense and satisfying, but in Beethoven ("Coriolan" and the fourth symphony), even the New Yorkers could not always save themselves from ragged edges. The finale of the symphony was taken faster then ever one suspected, in order to *épater les Edinburghois*. In Prokofiev's agreeably fanciful but unimportant and overlong symphony, Mr. Mitropoulos's discovery that three or four beats in a bar can be quite useful led to some dazzling orchestra feats.[20]

Time and time again in these Edinburgh Festival notices, one reads comments of astonishment, even wincing discomfort, directed at the Philharmonic's brass section—its weight, its prodigious volumes, the sheer gutsiness of its tone—as though every orchestra in Great Britain had some kind of volume-governor attached to the bells of its brass instruments. Nowhere was this open-mouthed sense of wonder expressed more often, or more fulsomely, than in the notices that followed Mitropoulos's August 27 interpretation of Vaughan Williams's Fourth Symphony.

The review in the *London Times* stated with brevity and magnificent ambiguity, "This heavily scored and essentially linear symphony had a performance from Mr. Mitropoulos such as it has never had here before," and then passed on to another subject. "An aggressive storm of stridency," another critic wrote; "stupendous and immensely exhilarating, for those who could take it!" wrote yet another.

Morton Gould's fizzily exuberant *Philharmonic Waltzes*, played on the August 29 concert, elicited quizzical, sniffy critiques. Gould's *echt*-American sense of musical fun made about as much sense to the English audience as a score composed by a Martian—they missed the gaiety, the spice, the very point of it all, leaving the critics to waffle disdainfully or reach absurdly for comparisons to *La Valse*. Howard Swanson's *Short Symphony* (concert of August 31), which had garnered notices of enormous respect from the New York reviewers, similarly baffled the Brits, some of whom were apparently unable to grasp the idea of a "Negro composer" writing something that did not make references to spirituals or ragtime.

At his final concert of the festival, Mitropoulos relaxed—relatively speaking, anyhow—and served up a warm, luxuriant performance of Rachmaninoff's Second Symphony—apparently another work rarely performed in Great Britain. Even in this highly romantic score, the critics carped about "excessive rubato" and "disturbing intensity."

In the afternoons preceding the various concerts, festival attendees could partake of lectures given by some of the famous and near-famous guests. Mitropoulos's turn came on Tuesday, August 28, when he spoke on the topic "Trends in Modern Music." The tone of his remarks was, for Mitropoulos, rather on the testy side—an indication that the barrage of snooty and uncomprehending reviews had gotten under his skin.

He waved aside the offered microphone and spoke informally, pacing up and down the platform, and speaking, he said, "as a human being interested in all human affairs of which music is one, but not the most important."

In answer to a question about understanding modern music, Mitropoulos replied: "The problem is that most of you are too lazy. You think that you only like Tchaikovsky, and so you get Tchaikovsky. Don't try to understand modern music—try to enjoy it."

On reviewers and their notices: "Most of you go to a concert and then the next day you read the newspapers to see if what you heard was good."

On the musical scene in New York: "It took ten years for the New York Philharmonic to accept me as conductor. I never make any concessions. I try to push as many new things through as possible which are good enough. I often find the orchestra just as reluctant as you are. Take the piece we did by Artur Schnabel. It took me weeks to learn the score, but I had to teach it to the orchestra in one day. It was as if they had taken injections. They played the notes, but they didn't know what they were doing."

Didn't he feel nervous conducting without any railing around the podium? "I don't need one, my dear. Remember, I am a mountain climber—I do not get dizzy at heights."

One final remark to those who criticized his inclusion of modern works: "Don't threaten us that you won't come to the concert."[21]

Near the end of the festival, the regional press devoted several features to Mitropoulos himself, rather than the programs. The most perceptive appeared in *The Observer*:

> He thinks of himself as serving God through music, and frequently says so. He has little to say about the real nature of music, and a great deal to say about its moral purpose. He regards the dedicated artist, including himself, as a member of a race set apart to carry the sins of the world, and frequently says so. To the chosen, life can appear only as a succes-

sion of mountain heights to be scaled with suffering. . . . Here, one would be pardoned for concluding, are all the makings of a mountebank, a kind of pseudo-musical revivalist—or, at best, a crank with transcendentalist leanings. One would be wrong.[22]

After the final concert, the orchestra was entertained at a lavish party thrown by the American consul-general. Toasts were made, speeches rebounded from the walls, and journalists mingled, jotting down remarks, such as Arthur Judson's platitudinous "We brought the best orchestra in America to the best audience in Europe," or Mitropoulos's "jocular" reference to the local critics' reviews, "I hope we will not be in trouble with the Board of Directors when we get home."

The next morning, an honorary bagpipe band was at Waverly Station to give the orchestra a proper Scottish send-off.

When the dust had settled from the event, Neville Cardus, dean of all British music critics, wrote a reflective piece about it for the *Manchester Guardian*:

> It was irony to invite to this year's festival Bruno Walter and Dimitri Mitropoulos—all the more pungent because not designed. Not only are they at extremes as conductors; they represent, almost symbolically, different if not irreconcilable ways of musical thought and feeling; in fact, two different cultures, and one of them seems to be passing away forever.
>
> Walter is of the Old World, Mitropoulos of the New. The culture that nurtured and ripened Walter disciplined self-expression with a sense of proportion. . . . Walter is the last of a tradition; time, that has taken so much away, has given him the nobility of loneliness. To the New York Philharmonic Orchestra he brings a mellow warmth of tone and a civilized poising of phrase which are not there when Mitropoulos takes charge; indeed, we are hearing two orchestras as, in turn, Walter or Mitropoulos conducts.
>
> Mitropoulos gets to work at the top of his voice, so to say; he is demagogic. Without a baton for scepter, he is free to clench his fists or to clutch music and wring the neck of sentiment. He seldom cajoles, though now and then his fingers relax and seem to play individual notes almost as though momentarily in love with them. But mainly he is ruthless, as though beauty were skin deep and therefore must be skinned. He is sincere, obviously, searching for truth at risk of bringing all the heavens of illusion down. . . . Clearly he harbours a daemon of genius, prophetic of some wrath to come. The Zeitgeist has him in thrall.[23]

CHAPTER TWENTY-TWO

The Sinking of *Christophe Colomb*

On October 11, 1951, the New York Philharmonic began its 110th season without a conductor in sight. Patrons beheld not only a leaderless stage, but one that had undergone a strange metamorphosis: a gray curtain had been hung across the back of the stage and the orchestra had been divided into two parts, leaving a triangular area that went from the base of the podium to the center of the gray curtain. As audience members whispered among themselves, a trumpet player rose, unannounced, from the orchestra and unleashed a loud, raucous fanfare. As the last notes sailed into the hall, a figure dressed in a top hat and cape leaped on to the podium and began to orate: "'Tis not for children, not for gods, this play; for understanding people 'tis designed."

Thus began the American premiere of Ferruccio Busoni's "theatrical caprice" *Arlecchino* (Harlequin). Composed just after Busoni visited America in 1915, *Arlecchino* is a sardonic and sometimes wicked satire on the conventions of romantic opera, the World War One era, and humanity in general, all neatly tucked into the stylized framework of *commedia dell'arte*. Harlequin is Faust in a dinner jacket, a philanderer who jealously kills the lover his wife takes in retaliation, while various supporting roles—a Dante-reading tailor, his young wife, a doctor, a priest, and so on—swirl giddily about the main conceit. Busoni's music is terse but frothy, with a bitter scowl beneath the painted smiles.

Mitropoulos staged the work with its full complement of entrances and exits, costumes, and some carry-on props (one of the Philharmonic's librarians appeared in a donkey's head). His cast was superb, including James Pease as the priest, John Brownlee as Harlequin, and Martha Lipton as his wife.

Time had taken some of the satirical edge off of *Arlecchino*, so Mitropoulos played it mainly for laughs; sometimes the musical antics carried the joke—as when the wife's lover delivers a hammy tenor aria and the orchestra stops playing long enough to applaud like a claque—and sometimes the cast resorted to outright slapstick. The opera lasted about one hour and most of the audience spent the hour with smiles on their faces; a few good belly laughs acknowledged the *shtick* Mitropoulos had his singers go through; to be sure, there were a few serious older subscribers who exited the hall midway through the Busoni, evidently disapproving of the japery—but, as Arlecchino himself sings in his epilogue—it is left "to my friends, the newspaper critics, to find the moral of our little play," and all of them had smiles on their faces when they sat down to review this unusual season-opener.

Mitropoulos journeyed to Washington, D.C., with the Philharmonic during the first week in November, to play a benefit concert for the Greek Children's Relief Fund. Again the program was novel: Gabriel Pierne's orchestration of Franck's Chorale, Prelude, and Fugue; d'Indy's *Wallenstein Trilogy*; and Rachmaninoff's Third Piano Concerto, with Gina Bachauer as soloist. One D.C. critic had actually attended a Chicago Symphony performance of the d'Indy score conducted by the composer just before World War One, so he had a valid basis for comparison when he wrote: "I must confess that Mitropoulos discovered beauties in this score that not even the baton of the composer brought to hearing."[1] With the Philharmonic's playing, the D.C. critics found no fault; as for Mitropoulos, whom many in the audience were seeing for the first time, "Certainly . . . he is a master disciplinarian, a technician able to confirm the tonal splendors which this orchestra boasted in the past, but lost for a time"—in other words, just the opposite of what the New York critics would soon be writing.[2]

Back in New York, on November 8, Mitropoulos made a relatively rare excursion into the classical repertoire, conducting Haydn's Symphony No. 104. This kind of music was supposed to bring out the worst in the conductor, and he was already running afoul of the nascent authentic-performance movement, getting slammed by the critics whenever he conducted "big orchestra" Bach or Mozart. There was, however, a body of minority opinion that admitted Mitropoulos's stylistic errors but that also gave him credit for being able, from time to time, to illuminate music of the classical period in surprising and provocative ways. No less an authority than Rudolf Serkin pronounced his accompaniment in Mozart concertos to be "superb."[3] On this occasion, his Haydn interpretation was different enough, yet also persuasive enough, to challenge the basic critical assumptions of Olin Downes, the musical establishment's staunchest defender of traditional values:

> The treatment of the Haydn symphony was individual and challenging, and not from a traditional point of view, or the tradition, as we understand it today, of Haydn's style. It was more theatrical than we have considered Haydn to be in his symphonic works. It was underscored here and italicized there in a new interpretation. The question then arises: Must a symphony composed in the 18th century be presented in the twentieth as if the work had been kept on ice for 200 years, and frozen stiff in the process? . . . Various passages in the symphony were given a new significance that caused one to ask himself whether there was not a hotter blood and a deeper and more personal

emotion in this music than he had believed. And this symphony, the last that Haydn wrote, has certain modern premonitions in it. . . . We don't know whether, after repeated hearings and reconsideration, we would agree with all that Mr. Mitropoulos did with his Haydn. It is more important to have been greatly interested, challenged, excited by his interpretation.[4]

In the second week of November, the conductor began wrestling with one of the most problematic of all Schoenberg's scores: *Erwartung* (Expectation), a "monodrama" for soprano and orchestra. It contains Schoenberg's most extended musical exploration of a pathological, hallucinatory state— some of the eeriest music ever composed; Isolde on a bad drug trip. The libretto is filled with grotesque and sinister imagery—a gibbous moon, the stickiness of blood felt in the darkness, intimations of slithering, crawling beasties in the woods—image crashing into image, as structurally disjointed to the ear as broken glass is to the eye. The musical imagery matches the verbal and requires an unusually big percussion section.

Perhaps it was the cumulative strain of an entire Philharmonic season; perhaps it was the death of Schoenberg only a few months earlier; perhaps it was a sudden crisis of faith brought on by the depressing nature of the score, its unrelieved mood of the neurotic and the deranged, but for whatever reasons, Mitropoulos had a harder time with *Erwartung* than he had ever had with any other work perceived as difficult. For him, the situation was akin to the moment in Minneapolis when he confessed to the orchestra: "Today I hear you as you really sound, not as I think you sound." For a period of several days, he heard this fiercely uncompromising Schoenberg score the way a typical Philharmonic subscriber might hear it, and the experience shook his soul.

David Diamond realized something was wrong when he encountered Mitropoulos backstage after the morning rehearsal:

He was standing alone, in profile, at the top of the stairs, and I had never seen any man in such a state of total despair. I put my hand on his shoulder, and he turned around, and there were tears in his eyes. "Dimitri, what happened? Why are you crying?" I asked. Then he pulled me into his dressing room—I can still feel the tug; he had this way of dragging you in with him; his hands were absolutely like rubber, and you could feel the bones; as far as I was concerned, he could pull down a building—and he looked at me and said: "I don't know what's happening to me. I don't hear anything in this piece! It's total chaos!" "But Dimitri," I said, "you've just gone through the entire performance, and you know the music by heart and you had no problems with the men." "I don't mean that," he said; "that part is easy. I mean I don't hear the *music*. I just don't hear it!"[5]

On November 13, two days before the first performance, he voiced the same emotions to Katy Katsoyanis:

Today I sat down and decided to dictate this letter, but believe me, I am making an effort to think, tired as I am after a long rehearsal struggling with another problematic work, the *Erwartung* of Schoenberg. My ears are aching, my brain is confused, and my nerves are at the point of cracking. . . . Alone in the midst of so many people, with parts badly written and badly annotated, I came to the point of asking myself, what is the use to struggle when you know that the results can't be of any contribution except to a group of sophisticated people who selfishly come to enjoy my tragic struggle. Believe me, I resent them just as much as those who will not understand anything. The price is too big to pay, and I am wondering sometimes if this kind of distorted and screwy beauty is of any transcendental value. I am wondering sometimes if in all that it isn't but the satisfaction of my own ego, that I am trying to realize the impossible, a pure egotistical occupation which has in itself nothing more than the pleasure of self-destruction.

I am doing exactly what a silly cat does who puts her tongue on a saw, licking it with passion, sucking the blood that comes out, and in a frenetic hedonism loses, little by little, her tongue.[6]

Katy replied like the loyal friend she was:

As to whether the value of these modern works is "transcendent" or not—our age is not capable of evaluating them, only time will tell. . . . It's very natural, when you're battling desperately with one of these problematic creations, to question whether they are worth all that great effort; your mission, however, is to play them, solving their problems, explaining them to the audience. The only thing I dare repeat is that you should play them at greater intervals, so that you'll have the time to breathe in between, and the public the time to assimilate them—and that you do not *constantly* provoke the immediate reaction of the Pharisees of criticism. Now I wait anxiously for the notices after the "Erwartung," when the critics will come to judge—from the height of their sterility and according to the mood they woke up in—what you created with your whole being.[7]

In fact, the critics were strong in their praise. More surprisingly, the Carnegie Hall audience seemed to take the piece in stride and there were even some cheers at the conclusion of the performance.

During December and early January of 1952, the Philharmonic hosted guest conductors George Szell and Guido Cantelli; Mitropoulos resumed on the last day of January by presenting the world premiere of Leon Kirchner's first orchestral work, his *Sinfonia in Two Parts.* For Kirchner, the experience of working with Mitropoulos was unforgettable:

I was unable to attend the orchestral rehearsals, but he was such an incredible musician that he could make out almost anything with or without the composer being present, and his critical estimates were pure and visionary. He conducted my music from memory, whereas I had to keep referring to my own score. He knew the mechanics of that music better than I, yet he would ask me to play the score over and over again—not to acquaint him with the notes, for he had those memorized—but to learn the quality of sonority, the phrasing, the psyche of the work. . . . I've played with dozens of conductors since, and I can assure you this is not the usual response. In fact, they often try to show you what *they* know, but rarely would they try to understand what *you* know. Mitropoulos was deeply concerned with the inner nature of a work, so that he would listen over and over again to get the gesture, the intent of the symbols.

I remember he was more than a little bit annoyed with me for not being able to attend the rehearsals, but just before he went on stage I stopped him and said: "The first movement is Savonarola and the second movement is Saint Francis." He broke into a huge grin—he knew exactly what I meant. I know he was identified with St. Francis, but there *was* a duality in him, and when he conducted, he could become Savonarola. Every man has his favorite devil, and when he took command of an orchestra, he *was* a kind of Savonarola. There was something about the way he moved his body, about that powerful command of the spiritual and psychic aspects of the orchestra itself. Yes, there were wrong notes occasionally, and little details that would go wrong, so technically his readings were not always immaculate, but they were so much deeper in terms of understanding than most neater performances are in their presumed exactitudes.[8]

A performance of Monteverdi's *Orfeo*—semi-staged in the same way as *Arlecchino* had been and using Respighi's tasteful orchestration—was the highlight of February's programs, and in March Mitropoulos began rehearsals for the biggest choral-orchestral offering of the season: a semi-staged performance of Mendelssohn's *Elijah* that blew the Victorian cobwebs from the piece and brought it vividly to life. His chorus, the Westminster Choir, was arrayed above and behind the orchestra. Each section rose, sang, gestured, and sat in unison, giving the choruses not their usual air of stuffy rodomontade, but an almost military sense of snap and vigor. Certain arias usually taken at a sedate pace—"O Rest in the Lord" was a startling example—Mitropoulos conducted in a "steamy" manner,[9] sometimes to the point of strain on chorus and soloists. To judge from anecdotes and photographs, the *Elijah* rehearsals must have been lively affairs; unable to obtain the effect he wanted from the chorus when it sings "Help, Lord!" after Elijah's prophecies of disaster, he admonished them to "think of anguish" and then illustrated what he meant by leaping into the air from a chair, arms outstretched, hands formed into claws, jaws gaping, face contorted in a wild rictus of agony. A CBS photographer happened to capture the moment, and the resulting picture, captioned "Airborne Maestro" when it appeared in *Life* magazine in April 1952, is a Mitropoulos classic: the conductor as Dracula (see Figure 47).

Sometimes, the conductor's ideas about blocking conflicted with the literal implications of the score. Tenor David Lloyd, assigned the role of Ahab, remembered Mitropoulos giving him a burst of enthusiastic stage directions, saying: "Now you run over here and sing this and then you run over there and sing this other." Lloyd rechecked his score and said: "You know, Maestro, Ahab was a very, very old man—I don't know if he would be capable of all this running." Mitropoulos responded: "He was? Oh dear . . . then we'll have to figure out something else."[10]

Howard Taubman's review typified the response to this hyped-up interpretation:

> Mendelssohn's "Elijah" was designed as a dramatic oratorio and in the performance that he conducted at Carnegie Hall last night, Dimitri Mitropoulos took that description to heart. This was not a tame reading: it had pace and tension and impact. . . . As for the music . . . it does not belong with the monumental choral works such as Bach's B Minor Mass or Handel's "Messiah." But it is not too far away from these sublime heights. There are places where Mendelssohn's music is sweet and pretty when it should be noble, but there is more dramatic punch to this score than Mendelssohn's belittlers would have you think. . . . Mr. Mitropoulos directed a performance that conveyed the power and sentiment of subject and music. The men of the Philharmonic played with precision and transparency of tone and with a freshness that was surprising in an orchestra nearing the end of a long season.[11]

Concurrent with the spring symphonic programs, Mitropoulos was also involved (for no fee) in the activities of the New York Philharmonic Chamber Ensemble, which gave a series of three highly acclaimed concerts during the spring of 1952. An outgrowth of these activities was one of the most unusual, and now one of the rarest, Mitropoulos recordings. Taped on April 21 and released as Columbia ML-5603, the program consisted of Paul Hindemith's Sonata for Oboe and Piano and Charles Martin Loeffler's Two Rhapsodies for Oboe, Viola, and Piano ("L'Étang" and "La Cornemuse"— The Pool and The Bagpipe).

Milton Katims played the viola in the two Loeffler works; the oboe part in all three pieces was played by Harold Gomberg, the Philharmonic's first-chair oboe. Though universally acknowledged as a supreme master of his temperamental instrument, Gomberg was a strange, moody, individual who was driven by an intemperate desire to stand out, and to be seen as standing out, above the other one-hundred-plus men in the orchestra. He was a devoted and evidently quite talented amateur painter as well as a virtuoso woodwind player.

Gomberg suggested the Loeffler-Hindemith recording during some of the Philharmonic Chamber Ensemble activities, Mitropoulos agreed to do it, and—in a rare and wonderful exception to their usual stinginess where Mitropoulos was concerned—Columbia Records agreed to record the performances for commercial release. Rehearsals took place in the conductor's rooms at the Great Northern, during an early heat wave that left the three participants, in Katims's words, "sweating like pigs." Aside from the stupefying heat, Katims—who had never worked with Mitropoulos before—noticed something very interesting about the conductor's interpretive priorities:

> Harold and I were talking very much about the contour of phrases—as is very understandable with players of instruments that usually just play the melodic line, the horizontal line; talking about the tension up to a certain point and then relaxation and so on . . . breathing in or out, as he had to do, or up-bow and down-bow, as I had to do. What was interesting is that Mitropoulos never said a word during these discussions—I decided he must not have the same approach to making music. I mean, he certainly *understood* what we were talking about, but our concerns just didn't seem to be his.[12]

Both the Hindemith and Loeffler works were new to the domestic record catalogues, and this was in fact the only commercial recording ever made of Mitropoulos in his sometime-role of chamber player. He succeeded in projecting the inwardness, the brooding gothic darkness, of Loeffler's tone poems every bit as well as he did the perhaps-more-sympathetic sparkle of Hindemith's more cosmopolitan score.

The final week of the Philharmonic's spring 1952 season began with another premiere, this time of a two-hundred-year-old work by Handel, his Third Organ Concerto. At the end of this season, only Louis Biancolli was inclined to write a wrap-up review, and he came down firmly in favor of the Philharmonic's programming: "The quota of novelties presented was high and the innovations in the way of opera and oratorio made for good news and better art. . . . It was a season of lofty ideals, reflected both in the repertory and the playing. New York has every reason to be proud of its name-symphony and of the man who conducts it."[13]

The conductor himself looked back on this season as one of the most satisfying in his career. In a letter to Katy dated March 13, he reflected philosophically about this period:

> I, as always, have been very active and, thank God, successful this year with all my musical events and all the new demons that I devolved upon the New York public. Even the critics finally accept that I gave new life to the programs of the Philharmonic concerts that was never there before.

Now I have still four weeks to go and then I rush to Italy to pre-pare *Wozzeck* for La Scala, for which I have been acclaimed these late years as a specialist. It is funny to see how fate or destiny works in peo-ple. . . . If somebody had told me then [in 1929] that one day I will be ac-claimed as a specialist in that particular opera, that I will conduct it all by memory in a concert with the New York Philharmonic, I would not only have laughed at him but I would have considered him a lunatic.[14]

Mitropoulos flew to Europe in early May to begin work, at La Scala in Milan, for what the Italian newspapers would describe as "The Battle of Wozzeck." Before signing the contract, Mitropoulos stipulated, and was given, the same number of rehearsals he had used in New York—six purely orchestral rehearsals and four fully staged ones. At the end of this allotted time, however, not even the first act was in shape to perform. The La Scala orchestra just did not have the experience, the muscle, the sense of quick mastery that the Philharmonic, on its good behavior, could display; even worse, the Italian orchestra's concentration was diluted by the routine per-formances of *Traviata* and *La Bohème* it had to perform on a daily basis. To the astonishment of everyone familiar with the La Scala way of doing things, and to the dismay of many regular patrons who were not ready to admit that *Wozzeck* was a proper opera at all, the management simply shut down the opera house for two weeks, canceling all scheduled perform-ances, so that full attention could be given to *Wozzeck*.

On opening night, June 5, the audience proved so unruly and noisy, expressing their disapproval with such loud, rhythmic whistling, that most of the music was inaudible. Unable to continue, Mitropoulos stopped con-ducting, turned to the crowd and said:

> The decision of whether to applaud or to whistle is a sacrosanct pre-rogative of the audience; however, because this opera requires the utmost mental concentration, I request that spectators refrain from whistling until the end of an act, and that they stop interrupting the performance while it is in progress. As for myself, I ask you please to re-member the signs that hung in the saloons of the American wild west, and which read: "Please don't shoot the piano player—he's doing the best he can."[15]

Chastened and amused at the same time, the crowd quieted, and by the end of the opera, this audience too had been drawn into Berg's dark sound-world to such an extent that the bravos greatly outnumbered the boos and whistles. The Italian press thrived on the controversy, and in the end the reviewers judged the event to have been a triumph for Mitropoulos. "He is a phenomenal director," said Milan's *Il Tempo*, "endowed with prodi-gious ability, interpretive power, and artistic greatness."[16]

In mid-June, Mitropoulos returned to the United States and conducted for three nights at Lewisohn Stadium. From July 8 to July 12, he was in Chicago conducting at the Ravinia Festival; then, after a brief period of rest, he went out to Los Angeles for concerts at the Hollywood Bowl on September 2 and 4. The "Eroica" he conducted at Ravinia was so pulled-about in tempo, so bizarre in accent, that even the most sympathetic critic could only say that it was "interesting." This was, in fact, a summer of bad or at least tepid reviews. On September 2, at the Hollywood Bowl, he directed a very strange performance of Brahms's First Symphony (tapes exist, so the critics' judgment can be verified) which either angered or simply baffled most reviewers. Mildred Norton's review was typical:

> Mitropoulos' desire to gild the lily wrought some excruciating effects in the C Minor Symphony, notably in the flaccid third movement, which was so pushed and pulled into unrecognizable shape that it sometimes came to a dead halt out of sheer agony, and in the stupendous finale, which alternated, like a man with malaria, between chills and fever.[17]

In July, in response to some depressing letters about the musical scene in Athens, the conductor had ordered a complete set of timpani, a trumpet, and several other costly instruments, and donated them to the Athens orchestra; this was no casual act of generosity because, by the time international freight costs had been figured in, the gesture set Mitropoulos back about $2500.

The autumn season of 1952 was a watershed period for Mitropoulos; it marked the beginning of the deterioration of his situation in New York. The spring season had been one of his best: he had given the New York public a series of blockbuster performances of important and intrinsically interesting works that no other conductor would or could take the trouble to learn, and by so doing he had won exceptional respect. He had also programmed more than a few highly accessible modern works which had broadened both the public's taste and the Philharmonic's expertise; Mahler symphonies no longer emptied the hall, and even a work as formidable as *Erwartung* had been appreciated, even if nobody—including the conductor himself, to judge from his letters and comments—had fallen in love with it. *Wozzeck* had been a box-office as well as a critical success. Moreover, he had shown himself capable of giving strong, if sometimes provocative, performances of the more basic repertory—even Olin Downes had said nice things about his Brahms. And the New York Philharmonic, for the first time since the best days of Rodzinski, had become culturally relevant; no other orchestra in the world was presenting so wide a range of music, and doing so on a consistently high level of technical proficiency.

Gradually, in the autumn of 1952, the prevailing critical attitude began to undergo a subtle change. The big opera-based concerts still attracted crowds, but the critics no longer responded with hosannahs; a feeling creeps into the reviews—subtle at first but destined to grow stronger with each passing season—that maybe Mitropoulos was spending too much time and dedication on these one-shot extravaganzas at the expense of more routine conductorial duties. There was no novelty to Mitropoulos any more; the things he had done superbly, the basic repertoire works he had conducted well—no longer were these things *enough*. The cycle of New York's cultural weather had entered a new phase. Fault would be increasingly found where it had not been found before, weaknesses emphasized that had been dismissed hitherto as trivial or incidental or simply inconsequential when stacked against the conductor's virtues. In a sense, Mitropoulos's struggle to win acceptance for himself and his missionary motives had achieved a certain victorious stasis in the spring of 1952, and by the very act of doing so, had triggered a perverse reaction that began with the critics and soon spread to the ranks of the orchestra itself. Taking their leader more and more for granted, *knowing* that he would never treat them sternly or crack the whip of discipline, the men of weaker character began to take advantage; to simply *get by* with their playing instead of making the extra effort required by genuine dedication.

Perhaps these changes were inevitable, an inherent quality in the nature of New York and its cultural significance. Schuyler Chapin, former head of Artists and Repertory for Columbia Records, viewed the phenomenon from a historical perspective:

> You know, there is the cyclical quality to the entire history of the New York newspapers and the key artistic institutions they write about. Back in the Twenties, the critics used to regularly beat up on the Metropolitan Opera. Then, when the regime changed there, the tone of things went up again. Mitropoulos was welcomed, eulogized, then taken for granted, and finally all but assassinated in the press. But the same thing happened to Lenny—he was welcomed and praised and then a prolonged period of carping and nit-picking; same thing with Pierre Boulez—welcomed at first, then attacked—and the same thing happened to Mehta. I think it just goes with the turf. And try to remember, that some of the more adventuresome things Mitropoulos undertook to perform—things like *Christophe Colomb*—were just utterly foreign to many people and once the novelty of those programs wore off, people just started to tune him out.[18]

In early October, Mitropoulos was interviewed about the forthcoming season by a correspondent from the *Herald Tribune*. The conductor took the reporter to lunch at La Scala and began talking as soon as their order was taken.

> You want to know what we are doing this year? I tell you: we are doing what we always do—playing the best contemporary and classical music we can find.
>
> First, we do Mussorgsky's *Boris Godunov*, at least half of it, with George London, the great bass . . . and we will be giving many concertos which are not new but which have not become established as reper-

toire pieces. Violin concertos, for example, by Schoenberg, Walton, Prokofiev and Martin, and cello works by Hindemith and Martinů. . . . And
on November 6, we give the American premiere of Darius Milhaud's
Christophe Colomb. Ah, wait until New York hears "Columbus"! It is one
of the great modern works and we have great singers to do it.[19]

The irony of those remarks about *Christophe Colomb* would haunt him later.

Mitropoulos was off his form during the first week of the season. Despite George London's magnificent singing, the hour-long chunk of *Boris
Godunov* lacked grandeur and the conductor's decision to sandwich it between a Beethoven overture and Strauss's *Also Sprach Zarathustra* made for
a heavy evening indeed. The orchestra's playing, moreover, was thick,
bleak in color, rough, and sloppy.

By the end of October, however, a fervent and well-received performance of Berlioz's *Romeo and Juliet* had the critics again equating the Mitropoulos version with the legendary interpretation of Toscanini. Mitropoulos
seemed to have pulled himself out of a slump—attendance was up and the
reviews were mostly favorable. And then came *Christophe Colomb*.

Not only was *Christophe Colomb* no ordinary opera, in some aspects it
was not an opera at all so much as an extended musical allegory, drenched
in a very sophisticated sort of Catholicism, dealing less with biography than
with matters spiritual and philosophical, and anything but linear in its
structure. The work is in two parts comprising twenty-seven scenes, and
contains about fifty solo roles, in addition to exceptionally complex choral
parts. Although the conventional biographical episodes are depicted, the
main focus of the work is less on Columbus's exploits than it is on certain religious and philosophical concepts that have arisen during the four centuries since the first landings in the New World. Each of the opera-cantata's
twenty-seven scenes is a discrete slice of the whole, unconnected musically
with the scenes before and after; there are flashbacks, flash-forwards, and
largely symbolic episodes that seem to take place outside of historical space
and time—the sort of free-associative narrative scheme that is hard enough
to pull off in prose and immeasurably harder to put across by musical
means. Taken whole, the work is allegorical, historical, mystical, ethical,
and frequently in stylistic or intellectual conflict with itself: a vast stewpot
of concepts, ideas, fancies, and musical devices.

Mitropoulos had to forego scenery and other complex stage trappings,
of course, but he strove at least to suggest the shape of a full-scale production by means of costume, stylized movement, gesture, and blocking. He
had attended the work's first complete performance, in Berlin in 1930, at
the Staatsoper under the baton of Erich Kleiber, and he had been tremendously impressed not only with the spirit of the score, but also by its mon-
umentality. From all indications, it seems clear that he had every bit as
much faith in *Christophe Colomb* as he had in *Wozzeck*, and that he sincerely
expected Milhaud's vast tonal fresco to bowl over the New York audiences.

There was trouble from the start. Although he was using an English translation of Paul Claudel's French original, Mitropoulos had the greatest difficulty getting the choral parts balanced and clear enough to be understood; for much of the time, the members of the chorus might as well have been singing in Estonian. To make matters worse, the orchestral parts were in abominable condition, necessitating much extra labor and time to decipher and make right. The first rehearsal was a shambles, the next only relatively better, and Mitropoulos found himself in the aggravating position of having to approach the Philharmonic's management about paying for extra time. Zirato, who, like so many others, simply could not see what Mitropoulos saw or hear what he, internally at least, heard in this ungainly score, balked. Whereupon Mitropoulos himself paid for several extra hours of rehearsal—a large sum even by 1952 standards, given the number of performers involved.

When the metaphorical curtain went up on opening night, November 6, the audience embarked on a musical journey that went all over the stylistic map, from the bare harmonies of plainchant to some of the most complicated polytonal polyphony Milhaud ever wrote, punctuated—like *Les Choéphores* only to much less effect—with sudden ponderous outbursts of percussion and general clangor. While the musically sophisticated in the audience might have enjoyed figuring out what Milhaud was doing, for most patrons it was simply too much to listen to at one time. The very structure of the piece—a series of more-or-less static tableaux moderated by the narrator, reading from a mystical book—seemed tedious, prolix, and artificial. What the average listener found in this much-touted production was an incomprehensible story only briefly clarified by its occasional references to Isabella's jewels, mutinous sailors, and other traditional aspects of the Columbus story; music that clogged thickly in the ear when it was loud and dramatic, rang hollowly when it was bombastic, and occasionally—very occasionally—caught flame in a brief exhalation of beauty, just enough times to make the rest of the score sound uglier by comparison. At intermission, almost one-half of the audience left; when the chorus of sailors finally cried "Land ho!" a number of patrons cheered and clapped. Those hardy enough to stick it out to the end did not hear the final Te Deum until quarter-past-eleven and did not get out of Carnegie Hall until eleven-thirty.

Next morning, the critics lined up to take their shots: "too much to take," "a blunder, and a monstrous one!" "An endless travelogue moving from Genoa to the Kingdom of Heaven, with far too many local stops along the way," "no focus, no direction, no point!" "the chorus might as well have been reading the Sunday comics," and "a musical hodge-podge—neither fish nor fowl nor good red herring."

Christophe Colomb, and its resounding failure to stir audiences or win critical respect, took a lot out of Mitropoulos. His faith in his own mission, and its gradual but inevitable success, was badly strained by the experience. As Irving Kolodin succinctly put it: "So many things Dimitri conducted because to him they were mentally stimulating. Unfortunately, what was mentally exciting to Dimitri wasn't necessarily so to most of the audience; but because of his own idealism and zeal, he could never quite accept that."[20]

His devotion to Milhaud's elephantine score was as much based on its lofty moral tone and mystico-religious meditations as it was on his technical admiration for Milhaud's accomplishment in setting all this stuff to music; he had run head-on into the realization that the depth and fervor of his personal commitment were, where certain pieces of music were concerned, simply insufficient to sway his listeners. He had driven himself to exhaustion in order to promulgate a three-hundred-pound turkey. His judgment had failed him; his passion for the work's moral subtext had made him deaf to its bombast and turgidity, to the clottedness of its polytonalities (almost as difficult for many listeners to grasp as atonality itself), to the windiness and sheer tedium of its dramatic structure. He had angered the Philharmonic's management, driven half the audience out of Carnegie Hall, wasted several thousand dollars of his own money, and exhausted, with this single enterprise, all the good will he had accumulated in the bank of public opinion. No one seemed to care, any more, about the triumphs of *Wozzeck* or *Elektra*—the only thing people talked about was the colossal flop of *Christophe Colomb*.

Mitropoulos gamely resumed his routine duties, and gave successful performances of Frank Martin's coolly beautiful Violin Concerto, and the Fifth Symphony of Shostakovich (still a relative novelty in 1952) in the weeks immediately following the Milhaud debacle. Louis Krasner joined Mitropoulos on November 30 for the New York premiere of Schoenberg's Violin Concerto.

In December, Mitropoulos's contract was renewed for the 1953–1954 season. Virgil Thomson used this contract renewal as the occasion for writing his most flattering piece about Mitropoulos. He focused on the New York Philharmonic's *sound*, which was precisely where Mitropoulos would take some of his heaviest hits in coming seasons; indeed, one often heard it said that the conductor's obsession with difficult "modern" works had, in some strange alchemical manner, caused the ensemble's tone to become ragged and harsh when applied to more conventional selections. Thomson at least did not hear things that way, at least not in December 1952:

> The Philharmonic's new way, the Mitropoulos way, is to play with more care for musical sound then has previously been the preoccupation of this orchestra. I suspect that this result originates, on the conductor's part, in a care for the intellectual and poetic communication of twentieth-century music rather than any sensuous devotion to orchestral timbres. But the precision which he brings to works which inspire his full mind (and it is a tremendous mind) inspires the orchestra to lend its full attention to what they are doing. And, as a result, the Phil-

harmonic, under his leadership, sounds more and more like the fine musical instrument that it is and less and less like a passing subway express.[21]

Mitropoulos thus had several reasons to feel proud of the season just concluded, despite the humiliating failure of *Christophe Colomb*. But the cumulative stress had taken its toll and whatever pleasure he derived from Thomson's vindicating remarks was fleeting—on December 7, 1952, he suffered a heart attack.

CHAPTER TWENTY-THREE

Recuperation: "Paradise Is Not for Me."

Many of Mitropoulos's close friends regarded his first, comparatively mild, heart attack as a blessing in disguise—the man's staggering workload would have taxed the resources of a young athlete, never mind a middle-aged man with a heavy smoking habit and an indifferent diet; now, perhaps, Dimitri would slow down a bit, take some time off to relax, admit that he was only human and not an instrument of divine purpose.

Under doctor's orders, Mitropoulos quit smoking, at least for a while. Given his nervous temperament, and his life-long dependency on tobacco, this was no easy task. To help ease the transition, his friends donated several sets of *komboli*—rosaries made of hand-carved cherry wood or amber which the conductor could use as worry-beads. He carried a set with him at all times, for the rest of his life. When he was judged once more to be in good health, he eventually returned to his beloved cigarettes, although he did try to limit his consumption somewhat.

When the news broke about Mitropoulos's illness, hundreds of cards, letters, flowers, and gifts poured into the hospital—many from colleagues and Philharmonic people, of course, but most came from ordinary music-lovers who wanted to demonstrate to Mitropoulos that they loved him, in particular, as much as he loved "the people" in the abstract.

He was forced to cancel all conducting engagements for at least three months, including a return engagement to Minneapolis that had been scheduled for February 27. That would surely have been a sweet and triumphant moment for him, but unfortunately he never quite got around to making another date with his former orchestra. Also canceled was a proposed visit to Greece to serve as advisor for the reorganization of the Athens orchestra and opera company. Mitropoulos would not revisit his homeland until 1955.

Among the many visitors who came to his room was Katina Paxinou, who was in Manhattan with the National Theater of Greece, for a production of *Electra*, staged in the original Greek, accompanied by the incidental music Mitropoulos had written in the mid-1930s—probably the last music he completed before abandoning composition altogether. This tour marked, in fact, the only time any of Mitropoulos's music was performed during the American phase of his career. Apparently none of the New York music critics covered the event, but drama critic Brooks Atkinson praised the score in his review.

Paxinou, of course, visited Mitropoulos in the hospital, and the reunion was an emotional one. Several of the conductor's closest friends believed that Mitropoulos still carried a torch for Katina, and that he did so all his life. Eleanor Steber noticed this first when she and Mitropoulos were rehearsing for her Town Hall recital: "We had scheduled this song that was a piece he had played for Katina Paxinou when they were young and when she was training to be an opera singer. I think he was still crazy about her, because every time we did that music, this dreamy sort of light came into his eyes."[1]

Such may well have been the case, for Katina's first hospital visit left the conductor so excited that his doctor restricted her subsequent visits.

By the end of 1952, Mitropoulos had recovered enough to leave the hospital, but he was far from ready to resume his responsibilities. His physician prescribed at least three months of rest in a salubrious climate. For that, California seemed ideal, and several colleagues who had West Coast homes eagerly extended invitations. Mitropoulos considered each one and finally chose to stay with Maxim Gershunoff, head of Artists Management Agency and former trumpet with the NBC Symphony.

Gershunoff actually had not invited him—apparently because he was sure Mitropoulos would prefer to accept the invitations of Spyros Skouras, the head of Twentieth Century–Fox, or Joseph Szigeti, his favorite violinist, who owned a palatial home with swimming pool, that had once belonged to actor Paul Muni. Mitropoulos's doctor approached Gershunoff, however, and said that the conductor seemed to hold him in high regard and felt that he could converse with Gershunoff on a wide range of subjects, including but in no way limited to music. "He keeps saying: 'The thought that makes me smile the most is to stay with Max.'" Loyal friend that he was, Gershunoff agreed on the spot.

When his Constellation touched down at the Los Angeles airport, Mitropoulos was pale, out of breath, and barely able to walk from the passenger ramp to the wheelchair waiting for him. Gershunoff felt that he had been given a strange and wonderful responsibility, and he had a theory as to why:

> He had spent his entire productive life doing his missionary work in music and helping young people with their educations. It was a big problem for him that he had been "rewarded" by fate with a heart attack—he kept speculating on why he had been "punished," what sins he had committed that justified such a plight. And I think that one reason he chose to stay with me rather than with one of his wealthy admirers such as Skouras, was as a kind of atonement for whatever imbalance there had been which had brought this about. Strange reasoning, but then, that was Dimitri.[2]

Gershunoff lived in his parents' former home, above Sunset Strip, overlooking Sunset Boulevard, with a view to the sea. Recuperating on the terrace, Mitropoulos enjoyed a sensation of space, of visual freedom, which helped compensate for the gloomy realization that his mountain-climbing days were over. Gershunoff and his parents, along with the young conductor Paul Strauss, took turns nursing their guest.

One day, Gershunoff, accompanied by Strauss and Eleanor Peters, drove Mitropoulos down to Palm Springs, so that he could see the beauties of the California desert country. "I joined him on the hotel balcony one morning," recalled Strauss,

> and it was one of those special days you get in February in southern California: ideal. No pollution, warm as toast but not too warm; the air so incredibly clear it's almost painful to breathe. Dimitri was standing by the railing, drinking it all in. He said: "This is very beautiful." I agreed with him and suggested, "Dimitri, why don't you live here in the winter, when you're not conducting, or in the summer when you have no orchestral engagements? It would be ideal for you, especially now." But he shook his head wistfully and said, "No, no. This is like Paradise, and Paradise is not for me."[3]

Each day, Mitropoulos walked a little more, regaining his strength. When his condition had improved sufficiently, he began visiting friends and colleagues in the area. One entire day was spent at the Szigetis' palatial home overlooking the Pacific. Szigeti and his wife raised honeybees and possessed a valuable collection of musical instruments. They gave their guest a complete tour.

"It's all so beautiful," Mitropoulos said. "To have such a beautiful view and everything, I would think that one could sleep so peacefully."

"If I didn't have the responsibility of all these things," Szigeti replied, "maybe I *could* get a good night's sleep."

"We went upstairs after seeing the view and the library and all those marvelous instruments," Gershunoff recalled, "and at one point Mrs. Szigeti said: 'Dimitri, this is the room you would have been in if you had chosen to recuperate with us.' Then, for territorial reasons, just like a doggy, he looked around with a little smile and said, 'Well, I will at least go take a pee.'"[4]

John Sherman, critic and historian of the Minneapolis Symphony, visited the recuperating conductor in mid-February. "I was greeted by a healthy-looking convalescent with the bronze-brown complexion of a Hopi Indian—a husky, smiling patient whose cheeks are filled out and whose eyes no longer have under them the black coloring of strain and overwork." Sherman thought the conductor's spirits were excellent, even though he expressed distaste for the idea of slowing down.

"I know ways of economizing my energy, and I'm going to use them," Mitropoulos said. "But as for being relaxed in my work, I can't quite manage that—nothing worthwhile ever came out of a relaxed approach."

"Well, you'll certainly have to tone down the platform-jumps," Sherman said.

"That's unconscious, I don't realize I'm doing it. The doctor said something about slowing down my tempos, but if I have to change my tempos, I'll go into another line of work."[5]

Another day was spent visiting Gertrud Schoenberg, the composer's widow. Mitropoulos had heard rumors that the Schoenberg family had fallen on hard times after the composer's death. When he and Gershunoff found the address however, they discovered a big, pretentious, two-story, Mediterranean-style villa with a circular driveway and a wrought-iron gate. Somewhat taken aback by the contrast between what he had heard about Mrs. Schoenberg's dire needs and the evidence of her true situation, Mitropoulos remarked: "I cannot understand why it is that the wives of great people cannot withdraw to some degree and reduce their standard of living to a realistic level. These are luxuries I wouldn't even offer myself."

Nevertheless, Mitropoulos and Gershunoff enjoyed a cordial visit with Frau Schoenberg; they drank cognac and examined some scores the conductor had not seen before. When they left, Mitropoulos said: "Why don't we have dinner somewhere and then go take in a really bad movie?"

Gershunoff knew at that point that the conductor was truly recovering.

Mitropoulos needed all his rejuvenated spirits to cope with a devastating letter from Bruno Walter, mailed to him at Gershunoff's address. Given that the recipient was only starting to recover from a heart attack, the timing of the missive seems cruel, seems totally at odds with the public's image of Walter as a kind, grandfatherly figure; but this was not the first time the Philharmonic management had used him as cat's paw for their own machinations. In this particular instance, Walter was acting, as well, out of a sincere belief that anyone who sought to propagate atonal music had allied himself with Satan. Gershunoff read the letter many times, with deepening astonishment, and could remember its text confidently even thirty years later: "It is with deep regret that at the suggestion of the Board of Directors I must ask you to confine your future programming to a formula closer to Beethoven, Brahms, and Tchaikovsky. If you find that you should be unable to alter the format of your direction in musical choices, steps would be necessary toward your dismissal."[6]

Mitropoulos agonized over the letter, naturally, and several days later suddenly blurted out: "Well, I've made my decision! From this moment on, I shall no longer be a missionary of music, but a mere entertainer!"

He did not, of course, mean what he said, and by the time he resumed his duties in New York, his missionary zeal was as keen as ever. No additional exchanges between him and Bruno Walter have survived, nor does it appear that Walter allowed himself to be manipulated again in this fashion. Now in his mid-seventies, the Viennese conductor continued his occasional guest appearances with the Philharmonic, but no longer exercised any authority over its daily business after the 1951–1952 season.

The words *heart attack* did not get into the newspapers for several days; the official story handed out by the Philharmonic was "fatigue and overwork," which was at least basically true. Several other conductors, Szell and Walter among them, were hurriedly rounded up to fill in the vacancies now looming in the schedule. Continuity, at least, was now assured. Szell's first concert, interestingly, was roundly panned by several reviewers, who took him to task for not doing what he was supposedly best at: securing disciplined playing from the Philharmonic. "A Mitropoulos concert may be many things," lamented the critic for the *Brooklyn Eagle*, "but it is never dull. Alas, Mr. Szell's was very much so."

With Mitropoulos recovering in California, the New York musical establishment had a chance to replenish its store of good will toward him. After the debacle of *Christophe Colomb*, there had been increasing signs that Mitropoulos was starting to be taken for granted. His sudden absence, however, reminded everyone of how uniquely exciting his programming and many of his performances actually had been. Miles Kastendieck, writing in the *Journal-American*, lamented that "Truth to tell, the [substitutes'] concerts have been a little dull."

When Mitropoulos returned to Carnegie Hall, he was warmly greeted by the orchestra, many of whose players lined up on the second-floor landing outside his dressing room. Man after man stepped forward to greet him, shake his hand, clap him on the shoulder, and say things like: "Maestro, you look like a million bucks!" When the conductor finally closed the door to change into his customary rehearsal uniform—a black turtleneck sweater —one of the violinists scampered down the stairs, beaming, saying: "It's old home week—Papa's back!"

When Mitropoulos strode out on stage, there was renewed applause. He bowed, thanked the men, then said: "You've behaved like angels. For the love and consideration and gifts you gave, I thank you all. I have had two months' rest, and I feel well, so now we can go to the end of the season. Now, jehnl-men, let's begin with the Vaughan Williams. First bar: *Ungh!*" Down came the long, lean arm, and the orchestra exploded.

In addition to the Vaughan Williams Fourth, the concert of April 2 also featured the Fifth Symphony of Prokofiev, in tribute to the recently deceased composer. A capacity audience filled Carnegie Hall with cheers when Mitropoulos came on stage. He conducted with every bit as much energy as he had before his attack and seemingly with a stronger grip on every element of the music. One feature, however, was dramatically different at this concert: he used a small baton. This change, too, was dictated by his doctor, for the sound reason that batonless conducting requires about thirty percent more effort than stick-waving. Although Mitropoulos was sometimes photographed conducting bare-handed in later years, more often than not, he did use a baton from the spring of 1953 until his death.

Only one month remained of the Philharmonic's regular season, but it was a month loaded with interesting repertoire. On April 5, Mitropoulos and his favorite soprano, Eleanor Steber, gave the first complete New York performance of Berlioz's magical song cycle, *Nuits d'été*. Steber enjoyed a special relationship with Mitropoulos (he once wrote that she was "the singer of my soul"), and her voice—though occasionally shrill in the uppermost notes—had a full and voluptuous middle range ideally suited to this music. Mitropoulos, for all his demonstrated indifference to sexy timbre and color for its own sake, could obtain exquisite transparency when he was of a mind. The resulting performance was memorable.

Also performed in April were Scriabin's rarely played *Prometheus: The Poem of Fire*, with Leonid Hambro as the piano soloist (only the second time this work had been given in New York); Gaspar Cassado's cello-concerto arrangement of Schubert's "Arpeggione" Sonata; Arthur Berger's *Ideas of Order* (a Mitropoulos commission that received good notices); an angry, snarling tone poem by Swiss-German composer Gottfried von Einem entitled simply *Orchestra Music*; and the world premiere of George Rochberg's fascinating *Night Music*.

Rochberg had won the George Gershwin Memorial Contest with this composition (actually a leftover segment from a symphony completed in 1949). Working with Mitropoulos made a profound impression on Rochberg:

It was my first orchestral performance, and my first contact with a major orchestra and a great conductor. I came to the first rehearsal and was astonished to learn that he knew every note of it—knew it better than I did in some places—and all the letter placements and measure placements, just *everything*. The reason I found it so utterly incredible is because at that time I was a completely unknown composer, a real nobody, and yet he took my work seriously enough to commit every note to memory, and he conducted it like a god—he really did. I was so overwhelmed by the experience that I never really followed up on that connection—I was so completely in awe of him, that I found it impossible to take advantage of that initial relationship. The result was that he never played anything else by me, but I'm the one to blame for that.[7]

During this, its 111th season, the New York Philharmonic gave 125 concerts. Of that number, three contained world premieres, seven featured American premieres, and six showcased New York premieres. Heart attack or no heart attack, Mitropoulos had certainly not eased back into a full workload—he had dived into his April schedule with full vigor and commitment. Now that the season was over, he felt at the top of his form and in a letter to Katy Katsoyanis, dated May 2, he crowed about it:

I've just finished four weeks of intensive work and, thank God, I feel absolutely well. I'm certain there's no trace of sickness left any more and that with no more smoking and with the help of the *komboli*, my health is better than ever before. Besides this, I had the opportunity to ascertain that the New York public loves me and honors me, except for some who expressed the opinion that I now conduct better and that suddenly I'm more mature than ever before. How much truth there is in this, I don't know. But I know it was to be expected after a prison term of five months. *But the truth always remains the same: privation is the mother of all life and progress!!*[8]

With the season now officially closed, Virgil Thomson did some prophetic gazing into his crystal ball and examined the changing face of American music itself. If the recent season had proved anything, Thomson averred, it was that modern music *as a cause* was as dead as women's suffrage, and for the same reason: the struggle had been won. The last of the modern techniques to achieve admission to the standard concert programs—the twelve-tone system—had finally arrived in the concert halls. It was tolerated more than liked, but its appearance was no longer freakish.

Thomson believed that the still-strong neoclassicists had taken over chromaticism and the dodecaphonic techniques and used them to reinvigorate their own "fading expressive powers." Thomson predicted that *modern music*, as opposed to any other style of music, would no longer have much meaning, simply because there was no other kind of music being written. There would simply be a "twentieth-century style," and everybody would write in it.

Thomson was accurate about that stylistic synthesis, but he was somewhat premature about an "armistice" between the disciples of Schoenberg and the neoclassicists of the Stravinsky-Copland wing. Throughout the 1950s, as competition for the best academic sinecures grew more ruthless, there was more often cut-throat antagonism between those two musical schools. "It may seem silly, and sometimes it seemed pretty absurd to me at the time," recalled Gunther Schuller, "but every professional composer was expected to declare for one ideological camp or the other. And the music Dimitri was presenting in New York was often the kind of music the Copland-Stravinsky axis wanted to suppress."[9]

These ideological rifts had very real and often very serious consequences, in terms of who did or did not prosper in the realm of grants and commissions, and in terms of whose music did or did not get performed. Because of the orchestra's unique status as a cultural icon, a single New York Philharmonic performance might be enough to put a composer on the map; consequently, the Philharmonic's music director wielded great power. The fact was not without consequence that Mitropoulos was identified with the atonalists and that Leonard Bernstein, beginning at the moment he chose to turn away from Mitropoulos and attach himself to Koussevitzky (Aaron Copland's most powerful advocate), would by the mid-1950s be regarded as a champion of the competing musical style. And those who plotted the downfall of one man and the elevation of the other, did so with very little concern for how either man conducted Brahms or Mozart.

Although he felt fully recovered, Mitropoulos did limit his summer engagements for 1953. His continued successes at La Scala led to a signal honor: he was the first non-Italian conductor ever invited to direct a Verdi opera in that house. He conducted five performances of *La forza del destino* in June, along with two orchestral concerts in Milan and two in Florence.

As Mitropoulos was finalizing his plans for the summer, he received an astonishing phone call from Antonio Ghiringhelli, manager of La Scala.

"I'm a little embarrassed about this, Maestro," Ghiringhelli began, "but we are really having to scramble for enough funds to get through the summer season. Would you be willing to take five hundred dollars less for your fee?"

"Well, yes, I suppose so, if it would help, although it will be a little difficult for me at this time."

"Thank you, Maestro. That way I can afford to pay Leonard Bernstein for his La Scala debut. We're trying to get him to do *Medea* with Callas."

"I see," replied Mitropoulos in any icy voice before abruptly terminating the conversation.[10]

After his now-traditional concerts in Italy, Mitropoulos visited, for the first time, the Wagner Festival at Bayreuth. He had long been ambivalent about Wagner's music, and appalled by the political uses to which it had recently been put; because of these feelings and because of his own immense sophistication with regard to twentieth-century music, Mitropoulos did not expect Bayreuth to have much impact. He was wrong; as so many pilgrims had been before him, he was quite bowled over by the place and by the new stylized stage productions then being tried out, with abstract scenery, mood-lighting, and Freudian symbolism.

To Katy, he dashed off the following bedazzled note, dated July 26: "You can't imagine my emotions in this place, in spite of everything that happened in the meantime! Who sent this prodigious spirit into the world? God or Beelzebub?"[11] He was still reeling from the experience when he dictated a remarkably confessional letter to Ernst Krenek in late September—revealing his growing unease with some of the contemporary trends that were already elbowing Schoenberg and Webern from center stage:

> I also had an interesting summer, more as a listener than as a producer or director. The only interesting thing I had to do was to conduct for the first time in my life a Verdi opera, and that was *La forza del destino*. In spite of the outdated material, in spite of the stupidity of the [libretto], this music has an invincible charm, and once more I was assured of the value of that blessed composer, or better to say, blessed human being. But believe it or not, after that kind of bath in sweet waters, in Bayreuth

I found Wagner even more exciting, and I was, to my horror, uncomfortable at hearing what our own era has produced. It really takes a lot
of effort to make that jump from one paradise to the other without
going through the terrible optical illusion which makes you believe that
you went from paradise to hell.

That is the tragedy of us re-creators. In spite of my intellect, which
tries to isolate my ears so that I can hear without [prejudice] the one or
the other side, my ears do hear and therefore in a way enjoy the
3.99/fourths of my daily life, and what a terrible effort it is to adjust
oneself and feel comfortable in the musical atmosphere our times have
created! I don't mean your music, or the music of Hindemith, or Milhaud, or Amadeus Hartmann, or Blacher, or Fortner. You are all very
old fashioned and very outdated before what the new generation is
cooking in a kitchen of noise and desperate complication. God forgive
me for this statement![12]

It was probably during this summer visit to the continent that Mitropoulos engaged Trudy Goth, daughter of Gisella Selden-Goth (a former Busoni pupil and a sometimes-vicious music critic in her own right), as his
European secretary. Goth, known in America primarily as the director of
the Choreographers' Workshop in New York, was a woman of culture and
some wealth; her mother maintained a beautiful Florentine villa that became Mitropoulos's headquarters during his visits to Italy. When weather
permitted, he studied scores in the garden and occasionally frolicked about
with Goth's pet dachshunds.

Trudy Goth not only took care of routine scheduling and travel arrangements, she also performed a perhaps even more valuable service by
protecting Mitropoulos from the constant parade of favor-seekers and in-
fluence-peddlers who besieged the conductor whenever he appeared in
public. Unwilling to be discourteous to anyone, and sometimes hobbled by
his own reputation for generosity, Mitropoulos often said "yes" to too many
people for too many superficial reasons. His privacy and concentration suffered accordingly. Goth had absolutely no trouble saying "no" and she
ruthlessly restricted access to the conductor—too much so, in the opinion of
many acquaintances and colleagues. "She put a wall of armor plate around
him; nobody could penetrate it," recalled Clara Roesch Herdt, a former conducting pupil, "although the wealthier and more socially prominent you
were, the easier it was to gain access. Very much out of character for Dimitri. 'But it makes things easier for me,' he said to me once."[13]

Trudy Goth cared fiercely about Mitropoulos, and often interposed herself between him and the importunities he seemed to attract even when he
tried not to. She made few friends in the process. Oliver Daniel regarded her
as "a terrible hag," David Cooper thought her "dreadful and revolting,"
and numerous interview participants described her as "a real witch," "a
most disagreeable woman," and the like.

But Mitropoulos needed someone to protect him from the consequences of his own generous nature and from his habit of always putting the best possible interpretation on whatever anybody did or said to him. Pianist David Bar-Ilan, who enjoyed fairly cordial relations with her, thought that

> she actually tried to inculcate a sense of paranoia in him, because he seemed so utterly devoid of it. On first meeting, she was not attractive at all, and I have no doubt that she could be a real virago, a ferocious keeper-of-the-gate, when her protective instincts were aroused. But however trying she could be, even for people she liked such as myself, I don't see how anybody could question her devotion to Dimitri.[14]

Exact dates are not known, but it appears that Mitropoulos's professional relationship with Trudy Goth took shape even as his relationship with Faith Reed, his longtime American secretary, was coming to an end. Miss Reed had been with him for more than a decade and had served him devotedly. Her attention to correspondence alone was heroic in its scope, and she also found time to maintain up-to-date files of every review and article that appeared in any newspaper (not for Mitropoulos's vanity, of course, but mainly so that a constant stream of clippings could be fed into Katy Katsoyanis's enormous collection). She was also quite hopelessly in love with him, a situation he remained blithely unaware of for some years and which occasionally gave rise to delicate and painful moments.

On one occasion, in order to surprise and give pleasure, Miss Reed researched the subject of historical Greek costumes, bought the most beautiful material she could find, and laboriously made it into a replica of a Greek gown. Then she walked into the office one morning and the startled conductor, who intended to make a flattering remark about the garment's historical authenticity, instead blurted out: "Oh, you remind me of an old Greek woman!" leaving the chagrined Miss Reed close to tears. On another occasion, fully intending to pay her a compliment, he looked fondly at her and said: "You know, when I'm with you, I think that I'm alone." She knew, of course, what he *meant*, but the words gave pain anyhow.

As the seasons went by, and it became apparent that Mitropoulos, for all his decency and compassion, was simply not ever going to reciprocate Miss Reed's emotional attachment, their working relationship grew strained and eventually it ended.

CHAPTER TWENTY-FOUR

The Honeymoon Ends

Although Mitropoulos had promised several of those closest to him that he would scale back his 1953–1954 workload, he shouldered the burden of a full Philharmonic season as though the heart attack had never occurred. He conducted sixty-eight subscription concerts and all fourteen concerts of the orchestra's spring tour through the South. The percentage of new or unfamiliar music remained the same—about twenty percent—and Mitropoulos won plaudits for some selections.

Paul Hindemith was the featured composer in the concerts of October 22–25, when Mitropoulos gave the New York premiere of his *Die Harmonie der Welt* symphony. Hindemith's polyphonic writing required exceptional clarity to make its case, and his sophisticated deployment of large orchestral forces, often used to deliver heavily accented sonorities, required a conductor who was able to turn the power off and on while maintaining structural clarity—in other words, the symphony played right to Mitropoulos's strengths. The predominantly husky tone and comparatively severe colors so typical of Mitropoulos's New York style were in this case genuine assets, and the performance as a whole was stirring. Here and there throughout Carnegie Hall, disgruntled subscribers ostentatiously sat on their hands at the end of the piece; a few even hissed. These demonstrations of pique were balanced by a smattering of "bravos" from the progressive wing of the audience. A Malipiero pastiche on themes of Vivaldi, entitled simply *Vivaldiana*, soothed everyone with its inconsequential charms, and the concluding work, Borodin's Second Symphony, sounded positively frothy after the Hindemith.

Duo-pianists Arthur Whittemore and Jack Lowe appeared in two very different pieces, both commissioned by the performers and both world premieres, on the program of October 24. First came Ernst Krenek's vigorous and dissonant Concerto for Two Pianos and Orchestra. Due to space limitations, the two pianos were placed perilously close to the edge of the stage, so that both pianists could look down and see the audience practically at their feet. Krenek's concerto begins with a tremendous dissonant blast of a chord, after which the orchestra stops and the soloists begin. Whittemore was already nervous enough when he took his seat in front of the keyboard—he and Lowe had spent a lot of time trying to memorize a very tricky composition, and neither of them was naive enough to expect Krenek to go over like Rachmaninoff. Mitropoulos gave the downbeat, the Philharmonic made a great discordant yowp of a tutti, and a little old lady in the first row leaned toward her companion and said—quite loudly in the sudden silence—"My God, wasn't that awful?"

Morton Gould's *Dance Variations* was the second premiere of the evening—a score as bright and vivacious as the Krenek was grim and dour. Gould cast the composition in four movements: an intense opening chaconne; a playful arabesque that manipulates several traditional dance forms such as the gavotte, polka, and quadrille; a sensuous tango; and a swirling tarantella. Mitropoulos turned in a sultry, swinging, downright sexy accompaniment for the orchestra's half of the repartee and the piano work sparkled.

As to the Krenek concerto, most of the audience, and all of the critics, agreed with the little old lady in the front row. Gould's variations pleased the audience greatly, but the critical condescension toward Gould's style bordered on the priggish. It bespeaks a dreary kind of reverse-provincialism when so many reviewers adopted the same patronizing attitude toward this enormously gifted composer simply because his music was so unfailingly entertaining—especially when the same critics, one paragraph earlier, had thoroughly trashed Krenek for *not* writing communicative music.

October's programs ended with the second-ever New York performance of Arnold Schoenberg's *Pelleas und Melisande*, a lush but painfully strained exercise in late romanticism. It is music that only works when a conductor can project its tumescent arc while simultaneously letting as much light and fresh air as possible into its harmonic density. Every reviewer gave Mitropoulos credit for doing all that could be done to clarify and shape this problematic score.

On November 5 came the long-awaited performance of Beethoven's *Missa Solemnis* which Mitropoulos had originally been scheduled to conduct in the spring of the previous year—a project still-born by his heart attack. Again, the unforgiving nature of the Philharmonic schedule may have undermined his efforts—no conductor could lead four performances of this gargantuan and ungrateful work in four days without losing some of his edge—but the interpretation was muddy, exaggerated, and crude; Mitropoulos labored mightily with the exterior of this elusive masterpiece, but failed utterly to project its spirituality.

Aaron Copland's *Short Symphony* had been scheduled for the concert of November 26, but at the last minute that composition was replaced by Ravel's *Rapsodie espagnole* and Beethoven's Second Symphony. It had been embarrassingly apparent, after the first disastrous rehearsal, that the Philharmonic simply could not do justice to Copland's score—not in the time allotted for rehearsing it, anyway. This had happened before, and it would happen again, in 1956, with Gunther Schuller's Symphony for Brass and

Percussion. To some observers, it seemed little short of scandalous that one of the "Big Three" American orchestras was incapable of performing a work by Aaron Copland; in the ranks of the Philharmonic, however, there was a growing attitude that enough, already, was enough: they had gone the extra mile for Mitropoulos on many occasions, working hard to master music for which they had no enthusiasm or comprehension, and a fair number of them resented having to do that month after month. A mulish intransigence began to permeate the ranks; some of the more antagonistic players intentionally played at a substandard level as subtle acts of rebellion or outright sabotage.

Sometimes the rebellion was not at all subtle. The men knew, by now, that Mitropoulos was never going to yell at them, banish them from the stage, or otherwise behave in the authoritarian manner of his more hard-boiled predecessors. Momentary lapses of intonation, scrappy attacks and releases, rough timbres—all the trademarks of slack discipline—were usually allowed to pass without comment. A natural human tendency slowly manifested itself: to see how much could be gotten-away-with, to avoid hard work and extra practice for compositions, like the Copland symphony, that individual players, in their cynical wisdom, deemed unworthy of the trouble.

A particularly outrageous incident occurred during the morning rehearsal of November 27. The music was Ravel's Piano Concerto in G Major, with Oscar Levant as the soloist. All went well until the orchestra reached a brief but important harp cadenza in the first movement. On the first playing, the harmonics just weren't coming through loudly enough. Mitropoulos clapped for silence and, in his customary courteous way, addressed the Philharmonic's curmudgeonly harpist, Theodore Cella: "My dear Cella, would you give a little more emphasis on the harmonics, please?"

Cella grew red in the face, got up from his chair, walked to the front of the stage, shook the music in Mitropoulos's face, and growled: "I know something about music too, you know!" Then he threw the score down and stormed off the stage.

Incidents of such open insubordination—bordering, in this case, on the childish—were of course not common. But a conductor who permits even *one* such incident to go unchecked, or unpunished, has sent a powerful psychological message to the musicians. The fact that Cella got away with this outburst without suffering anything more than a private tongue-lashing from Bruno Zirato was not lost on the other players.[1]

After witnessing such an incident in a 1954 rehearsal, James Dixon asked Mitropoulos point-blank: "Why do you put up with that crap?"

Mitropoulos replied: "I can afford to forgive him."

Dixon pressed his point: "Yes, that's fine, but your forgiveness does a disservice to all the other players who were behaving themselves!"

Mitropoulos sighed: "You're probably right, but I can't do it any other way."[2]

Mitropoulos may have felt some compensation on the night of the actual Ravel performance, November 29, when he was decorated as a Commander of the Order of the Phoenix by King Paul and Queen Frederica of Greece. Their Majesties arrived at intermission, with great fanfare and a standing ovation from the well-prepared audience, and sat through the concert's second half, comprising the Ravel Piano Concerto and the *Rapsodie espagnole*. When a reporter asked His Majesty how he had enjoyed the concert, the King smiled distantly and replied: "Frankly, I'm not very fond of modern music."

The week-by-week reviews of the autumn 1953 season do not seem dramatically different from those Mitropoulos received during the previous season, but when the midseason summaries were written, between Christmas and New Year's Day, their tone was noticeably cool, even skeptical. The conductor's programming, in particular, was drawing increased fire as his New York tenure lengthened.

Truly, some of Mitropoulos's programs appear capricious or downright perverse. Case in point: the concerts of October 29 and 30, in which Schoenberg's opulent but lengthy *Pelleas und Melisande* was *followed* by two tacked-on excerpts from de Falla's *La vida breve*. The effect was to dilute the impact of the Schoenberg by throwing in what more thoughtful listeners might have regarded as a quick, cheap, sop to the *hoi polloi*. The entire program, which would have been perfectly proportionate if Mitropoulos had just stopped with the Schoenberg composition, was rendered unbalanced and somehow compromised.

And for every program that seemed born of impulse or whimsy, there were two programs that *looked* well balanced on paper but turned out not to be so in practice. This failing was, ironically, linked to one of the conductor's greatest strengths: his ability to focus on each discrete work of music as if it and it alone were the only piece of music that mattered. While this made for striking and memorable results on a piece-by-piece basis, it often destroyed any sense of balance in the overall program. In the more extreme juxtapositions, such as the jump-cut from Schoenberg to de Falla, neither the audience nor the players were able to negotiate those aesthetic hairpin curves as effortlessly, as instinctively, as Mitropoulos.

Up to now, Mitropoulos had more often succeeded than failed, either by accident or design. Through sheer willpower and interpretive persuasion, he had often made curious and ill-balanced programs work. One reason they worked was the cooperation of the orchestra, the majority of whose players had not yet reached the stage of routinely taking advantage of their conductor's temperament and good will; and surely another reason was that the success of certain headline concerts—the blockbuster performances of *Elektra* and *Wozzeck* for instance—was so towering and so unprecedented in the recent history of the New York Philharmonic as to mute much criticism of the way Mitropoulos handled the week-in, week-out subscription concerts.

But by December 1953, there were signs that this was no longer the case; that Mitropoulos's great triumphs no longer weighed as much on the scale of critical opinion as his *perceived* failures in programming, and his *perceived* weakness as an interpreter of the basic concert repertoire—"perceived" is surely the operative term because certain of his performances of Brahms and Beethoven had been extravagantly praised even by Olin Downes, New York's most conservative critic. No doubt about it: in the Beethoven-Brahms-Tchaikovsky repertoire, Mitropoulos was astonishingly erratic and driven, to an extent he simply did not realize, by his own day-to-day mood-swings. On one night, he could project Schumann's "Spring" Symphony with more elan, more virility, more sheer animal exuberance, than any conductor of his generation; a few weeks later, he would perform that same composer's "Rhenish" Symphony with such dry, detached sterility as to astonish even his most charitable supporters. Even making allowances for the known prejudices of the critics, there can be no doubt that the unremitting pressures of the New York job had, by the winter of 1953, begun to reveal themselves in an increasing number of erratic on-again, off-again, performances. Sometimes, especially in the symphonies of Brahms and Beethoven, the level of commitment and interpretive persuasion varied wildly within the same performance. There is only a small semantic and perceptual jump from regarding a conductor as "erratic" to regarding him as "unreliable," and by the end of 1953, some observers of the New York scene were clearly making that transition.

One who already had was critic Miles Kastendieck, who wrote for the *New York Journal-American* and who had been more or less sympathetic to Mitropoulos and his programming philosophy during the first few years of the conductor's residence in New York. But by December of 1953, in a piece for the *Christian Science Monitor*, Kastendieck cast a jaundiced eye over the Philharmonic's fall season and evaluated it in terms that cast an ominous shadow over the future:

> Dimitri Mitropoulos's first eight weeks with the Philharmonic-Symphony appeared a long span, because few of the concerts were wholly satisfying. Each had its bright moments, but usually the program was problematic. While Mitropoulos excelled in the modern field, his individual way with the standard repertory courted reservations on numerous occasions. . . . A performance of Beethoven's *Missa Solemnis* proved disturbing. At times it was difficult to recognize the performance as Beethoven, though Mitropoulos expended a great deal of energy on it. . . . The tendency to contrast old and new music on the same program might have proved more satisfactory, had the works been outstanding. . . . The first New York performance of Hindemith's *Symphony: Die Harmonie der Welt* indicated immediately that several hearings would be necessary to hold public interest. . . . The world premieres of Krenek's Concerto for Two Pianos and Gould's *Dance*

Variations . . . caused no special stir. . . . Neither did Bezanson's Piano Concerto nor Albert's Fantasy for Piano and Orchestra. . . . The American premiere of Blacher's *Ornaments for Orchestra* posed a problem in mathematics, more mathematical than musical. Thus Mitropoulos dutifully presented new works, but unfortunately they offered little that was substantial and less that was stimulating.[3]

Kastendieck's reasoning typifies the damned-if-you-do, damned-if-you-don't syndrome with regard to scores that were new or unfamiliar. He criticized Mitropoulos for programming a new Hindemith symphony that would require "several hearings . . . to hold public interest," but ignored altogether the fact that no composition can have "several hearings" without initially having a *first* performance—which would at least give the more musically sophisticated listeners a sound impression of the work. If it were possible to divine in advance which new works of music would prove to have staying power and which would fade deservedly from sight, the job of music directors would be infinitely easier.

By the last decade of the twentieth century, Morton Gould had long since become one of the most beloved of American composers, yet the critics of Kastendieck's era regularly waved him away as a facile purveyor of "entertaining" music—willfully ignoring the man's awesome craftsmanship—while simultaneously blasting many other composers for writing hermetic, ugly, and inaccessible scores.

For all their eccentricity, Mitropoulos's programs were driven by a coherent purpose: to perform a cross-section of all the different musical styles of his time, from the harsh and "mathematical" score of Boris Blacher, to the middle-class values embodied in Hindemith's monumental symphony (now, of course, recognized as one of his most compelling scores), to the openly and unashamedly crowd-pleasing *Dance Variations* of Morton Gould. Lacking precognition as to which styles and compositions would make the historical cut, and empty of the arrogance that presumes one's personal aesthetic tastes will coincide with the verdicts of history and consensus, Mitropoulos knew that *inevitably* some of the music he conducted would prove to be marginal or ephemeral. But at least *it would have had a hearing.* Too many conductors, by contrast, would adopt the circular, self-fulfilling attitude—advocated, albeit in fairly fuzzy language, between the lines of Kastendieck's piece—that the public wants to hear only the proven masterpieces, or the relatively small number of contemporary works that have, through dint of repeated exposure, gained acceptance. An outgrowth of the Masterpieces Only philosophy of Toscanini, this syndrome holds that if a piece is not already listed in this circumscribed canon, it must not, *ipso facto*, be any good, and therefore why waste time and energy performing it? All the arguments against Mitropoulos's admittedly erratic but enthusiastically open-armed programming policy had triumphed by the mid-1970s (in part, no doubt, because other conductors saw what had happened to

Mitropoulos and drew the logical conclusion). By the end of the century, the
effects of the Masterpieces Only philosophy were clear for all to see: ageing,
dwindling concert audiences, and a possibly terminal decline not only in
the cultural importance of those overplayed masterpieces, but in the level of
inspiration and vitality that characterized their interpretation.

Morton Gould had conversations with Mitropoulos about these
matters:

> This was a very important musical philosophy with Mitropoulos, as it
> was with Stokowski. In discussing . . . the different schools and trends
> that were developing and fighting for a hearing—he admitted that he
> did a lot of pieces by relatively unknown people, including some works
> he thought probably wouldn't last. But he always said: "Look, I know
> that this piece or that piece is probably not good enough to last, but it's
> a significant part of what is happening in music today, for better or
> worse, and it's important that it be heard so that people can make up
> their minds."[4]

As ominous as the Kastendieck article was for Mitropoulos's reputation, an even more depressing aspect of the Greek conductor's situation
was alluded to in a *Saturday Review* article by Irving Kolodin, one of the
more perspicacious and farsighted critics of his time. Kolodin saw beyond
the obvious problems of programming, of trying to please an essentially
unpleasable audience, to the debilitating effects inherent in the nature of
Mitropoulos's job:

> I have no mind for abusing a man obviously swimming upstream, so
> the comments on Mitropoulos will be brief. The prognosis, upon his
> appointment early in 1950, was that he was a man with a valuable in-
> stinct for the sub-standard repertory—the oddities, enormities, and va-
> garies of the symphonic literature—who should be given ample op-
> portunity to show whether there was, in him, a Koussevitzky-like
> growth for other, more exacting things.
>
> Whether three seasons more or less (he was ill a good part of last
> winter) constitutes "ample opportunity" is open to argument; but the
> probability is that we shall never know about his capacity for growth.
> The pressure of the job (especially as Mitropoulos works from mem-
> ory) makes survival, rather than development, the key consideration.
> This is bad for the conductor, and not good for the orchestra he con-
> ducts. Adding economic insecurity to artistic insecurity can only result
> in the kind of tension and lack of repose so contagious in the conductor
> as to infect the stolid group with which he works.[5]

Mitropoulos's first concert of the spring 1954 season was on February 28,
but he had already made the newspapers thrice before that date: on February 25 came the by-now expected announcement that his contract had been

automatically renewed; then came a press release from the Metropolitan Opera stating that an agreement had been reached between that organization and the Philharmonic which would permit Mitropoulos to conduct two operas during the 1954–1955 season; lastly came a spate of enthusiastic reviews about his participation in one of the highly regarded Philharmonic Chamber Ensemble concerts.

He directed and played the piano part of Ernest Chausson's masterful Concerto for Piano, Violin, and String Quartet. The *New York Times* review was unstinting in its praise:

> This reviewer has heard many a presentation of this concerto over the years, but never one that could compare to this in grandeur of conception, fiery intensity, and clarity of architectural design. There was a demonic forcefulness in Mr. Mitropoulos's colorful, virtuosic treatment of the florid piano solo part, that inspired his colleagues to give of their utmost.[6]

According to violinist Leon Temerson, representatives from Columbia Records were on hand for the chamber concert and were so excited by the Chausson concerto—a work which was at that time not well represented in the record catalogues—that they offered to set up a recording session as soon as practicable. Unfortunately for both Chausson and posterity, Columbia's interest peaked at exactly the same time Mitropoulos had to plunge back into the demanding routine of his Philharmonic duties. A tentative date was scheduled for later that spring, but it had to be scrubbed because of the Philharmonic's impending tour of the South. By the time that endurance test was over, the Chausson score was no longer fresh in the players' minds and hands, and the window of time needed to pull the ensemble together again simply never opened.

"That is one of the greatest regrets of my life," Temerson said in his 1985 interview:

> because, although I played that music many times, there was never another performance to equal that one. It was absolutely miraculous. Mitropoulos was playing *fortissimo*, yet I never had the slightest feeling that he was covering me. Normally, what can a violinist do playing against a pianist like that? But with him, there was no balance problem at all—he had such a flair for the instrument that in spite of the power of his playing, he was never too heavy. He also had the colors of the piece at his command in a way that was absolutely incomparable. I never experienced another performance like it, although when I played it later, with other pianists, I tried to make them understand what Mitropoulos had done, especially in the slow movement; but no other performance, for me, ever equaled that one.[7]

By any standard, the Philharmonic concert of February 28 was remarkable. Rudolf Serkin joined the orchestra for three dramatically contrasting works for piano and orchestra, and gave an unforgettable demonstration of the range and depth of his musicianship. First came Mozart's Concerto No. 17 in G Major, K. 453, followed by Richard Strauss's exuberant *Burleske*; Beethoven's Fourth Concerto formed the capstone of the program.

Serkin himself considered this concert a highlight of his career, but reflecting on his long association with Mitropoulos, voiced the opinion that some of the programs they gave in Minneapolis were just as good if not better:

> Yes, when we did the Mozart that night, it was extraordinary, but it was even more so in Minneapolis than in New York. There was less pressure—the orchestra was not so tired. Somehow, we enjoyed it more in Minneapolis. "Relax" is not the right word, because it was always intense. Mitropoulos could never be indifferent. But on the New York concert, for me, the Strauss *Burleske* was the highlight. It was unforgettable, probably the finest performance I've ever known. I don't exactly know how he did it, but the whole thing had a kind of devilish quality—the piece has a demonic element, you know, but he was really the only one who captured that feeling. We understood each other. We had the same ideas, without knowing it, even before we worked together. Playing with him was always a wonderful experience for me.[8]

Peter Mennin's Third Symphony was played on January 30, to generally good reviews. The following week, on February 6 and 7, Debussy's *Iberia* figured on the programs of February 6–7, and the interpretations it received were paradigms of Mitropoulos's way with many "impressionistic" compositions. Sensuality and languor were not in evidence to any great degree, nor, it must be said, were the sort of ravishing timbres Koussevitzky and Stokowski brought to such music. Mitropoulos projected a very different but stimulating style: the music had backbone, sinew, and a slightly hard-edged excitement, always demonstrating a sense of forward momentum, always active and in-the-process-of-becoming. If he was nobody's first choice as a Debussy-Ravel interpreter, he did consistently illuminate their music in ways that could only deepen a thoughtful listener's understanding.

Schoenberg's Piano Concerto received its New York premiere on February 6, without causing much of a stir, and on February 11, 12, and 13, Mitropoulos commemorated the fiftieth anniversary of Richard Strauss's first visit to the United States by directing symphonic pastiches of music from *Arabella*, *Intermezzo*, and *Die Frau ohne Schatten*, together with the *Symphonia domestica*. In marked contrast to the tepid reviews that attended Mitropoulos's first New York performance of the *Domestic Symphony* fourteen years earlier, this one drew lavish praise. "We had not realized before," pontificated Downes, "the exceptional value of this program-symphony, or heard it speak so warmly and poetically."[9]

On February 18, New York got to hear the first American performance of Manuel de Falla's last completed composition, *Homenajes*, a four-part suite of musical portraits (of Ferdinand Arbos, Debussy, Dukas, and an obscure opera composer named Pedrell) written over a twenty-year span and finished in 1939. The first three parts are written in the composer's urbane "late" style and are a somewhat pale mixture of sophisticated technique and thin invention, while the fourth recalls his more popular Andalusian mode of expression.

Although the premiere was respectfully received, *Homenajes* is of interest primarily because it was the subject of a pioneering television broadcast, aired about two weeks after the performance, on Edward R. Murrow's *See It Now* program. Entitled "Anatomy of a Symphony Orchestra," the program made a well-intentioned effort to demystify the work-a-day lives of the Philharmonic men and their leader.

It opens with a closeup shot of Murrow and Mitropoulos chatting on the edge of the stage, both men puffing lustily on cigarettes. They discuss the conductor's function, and Mitropoulos veers off almost immediately into his Franciscan mode, talking about how he tries to reach the "souls of the men," through love and devotion. This was only Dimitri being Dimitri, but the effect is embarrassingly arty and quite at odds with the down-to-earth realism of the rest of the program.

Granted that this kind of show had never been done before, and granted all the good will in the world on the part of Murrow (and of the show's sponsor, the Aluminum Company of America, who graciously volunteered to forego the usual midshow commercial break in the interests of artistic continuity), the show tries to cover too much ground in too little time. And the music chosen is decidedly weak as well as utterly unfamiliar to the presumed audience.

In the context of Mitropoulos's evolving relations with the New York Philharmonic, however, the show is a gold mine of quick, telling glimpses, such as the view of the backstage "bullpen" before the rehearsal begins: Philharmonic men are seen playing chess, occasionally practicing, mostly standing around with cigarettes dangling from their mouths and hands, looking bored and macho. Their deportment is even more revealing during the rehearsal segments. Mitropoulos is shown doing his best to bring the not-terribly-interesting de Falla score to life, making some witty and illuminating remarks ("Please, don't give me so much flesh on those tones"), but the overall impression derived from the facial shots of the musicians is rather appalling. Almost to a man, they look sullen, put-upon, resentful, utterly disinterested, just going through the motions and already figuring out how much extra cash this TV gig might bring in. Perhaps it didn't bring in any; that would at least explain their thuggish scowls and seeming indifference to anything their conductor says to them.[10]

After the close of the Philharmonic season, Mitropoulos went to Milan, as was now routine, to conduct at La Scala. This year, he directed a double bill—Strauss's *Elektra* and Busoni's *Arlecchino*—which proved so popular that four additional performances had to be scheduled. From Milan, he went on to Florence, for five performances of Puccini's *La Fanciulla del West*, in a production directed by Curzio Malaparte. There were also, of course, a scattering of orchestral concerts as adjuncts to these Italian dates.

Noteworthy, too, is the fact that the summer of 1954 marked the first time Mitropoulos conducted orchestral concerts beyond the borders of Italy since his arrival in Minneapolis. On July 9 in Munich, he led the Orchestra of the Bavarian Radio, and one week later the NWDR Symphony Orchestra in Cologne, followed by two concerts in Salzburg with the Vienna Philharmonic (July 21 and 22). For the audiences and critics of mainland Europe, it was the return of a legend, and their response indicated no disillusionment. From that summer of 1954 until the day he died six years later, Mitropoulos was regarded by European audiences, musicians, and critics, as being a conductor on the same exalted plane as Furtwängler or Toscanini.

Such was the intense interest in Mitropoulos's return to mainland Europe that his concerts were covered not only by the reviewers of Cologne, Munich, and Vienna, but by every newspaper in Germany that could get tickets. Typical of the general response was the following, from *Der Mittag* of Düsseldorf: "It would seem inconceivable for a conductor to achieve such great effect with the mass public, to have the effect of a 'star,' and yet remain a faithful servant of music and of the composers' intentions. Yet that is precisely the case with Mitropoulos." Even the jaded Salzburg critics were elated at his two concerts with the Vienna Philharmonic. "He really is first among equals," said the *Salzburger Volkszeitung*, "a musician's musician."[11] For Mitropoulos and the musicians of the Vienna Philharmonic, this marked the beginning of a love affair that lasted until the conductor's death. Many of the VPO players hoped that some way would be found for Mitropoulos to become *their* music director—thus placing him in such select company as Furtwängler, Böhm, and von Karajan. For his part, Mitropoulos experienced intense joy while conducting the Vienna Philharmonic—an orchestra whose sense of tradition, whose tonal qualities, and whose cooperation were so dramatically superior to those of his own orchestra in New York; in conversations with Katy Katsoyanis, he referred to those Salzburg concerts as "some of the happiest moments of my life."

Nor was the Vienna Philharmonic the only European orchestra interested in acquiring his services. As early as 1953, during the period when Mitropoulos was convalescing from his first heart attack, Aristotle Onassis had offered him directorship of the Monte Carlo Opera. Following his European successes in the summer of 1954, other posts were offered, including the RIA Symphony of Rome and the Vienna Philharmonic's plebeian sister orchestra, the Vienna Symphony. In all cases, Mitropoulos's response was that he would consider any offers made to him, but not until "after I leave the Philharmonic." In view of the fact that he was free to terminate his contract at the end of every year, he could have chosen a propitious time, taken the best European offer, and moved his base of operations to Europe, there to enjoy a golden period of music-making in a much less abrasive and hostile ambience. That he did not clearly indicates that in spite of the crushing workload and the vexations of trying to lead an unruly and ill-motivated orchestra, his sense of mission was still firmly focused on New York. He believed that his destiny was to be played out there, for better or worse. The New York Philharmonic was his mountaintop, and he would not leave it until the tempests beat him down from that cold and lonely pinnacle.

CHAPTER TWENTY-FIVE

Operas and Recordings

Throughout his career, Mitropoulos ran hot and cold on Wagner. On the one hand, he was awestruck by the cultural ambience of Bayreuth (much to his own surprise), but on the other hand he doubted whether the music, or the institution, could ever be purged of its associations with Nazism. He harbored a suspicion that the Bayreuth management fawned over foreign visitors mainly because they represented "the victors" and that many of the people who ran the festival were actually nostalgic for the days of the Third Reich.

For these reasons, he limited his Wagner conducting to American venues, where the ideological issue was mostly academic. This attitude enabled him to surrender to the sensuous and dramatic elements in the music, which appealed to him very strongly. In conducting Wagner, of course, Mitropoulos was setting himself up for comparison with the greatest conductors of all time, a consideration that simply did not obtain when he was conducting Roger Sessions or Ernst Krenek. While audiences enjoyed the throaty but powerful sound of his Wagner, critical opinion was decidedly mixed, as the reviews of the October 7 New York Philharmonic concert—first of the 1954–1955 season—amply demonstrated. Mitropoulos directed a complete performance of Act One of *Die Walküre*, with Astrid Varnay, Luben Vichy, and Ramón Vinay as the soloists.

Paul Henry Lang, who had replaced Virgil Thomson when the latter retired from his post at the *Herald Tribune*, was generally impressed by what he heard, but his review included several picky reservations of the kind that were starting to appear more and more frequently:

> Mr. Mitropoulos is a great conductor with an especially well developed sense of the dramatic. His Wagner was fiery and the orchestra responded to his demands. . . . He likes to bite into the music and does so with a firm jaw (albeit with a somewhat less firm beat), but the delicate passages seemed a bit perfunctory, at other times overdone. Yet if it were not for the poetic passages—and they are by no means rare—Wagner would be difficult to take.[1]

With Wagner thus dispatched and the season launched, Mitropoulos scored a triumph on October 14, when he conducted the American premiere of a work that has firmly established itself as a twentieth century classic: the Symphony No. 10 of Dimitri Shostakovich.

A cliche has taken hold to the effect that all great musical masterworks were initially spurned or misunderstood by their audiences. History does not support that notion. Audiences usually know when they are in the presence of the Real Thing. Mitropoulos proved this over and over again, in the presence of an audience more spoiled, more fickle, more potentially vicious than any other in America. By mid-1954, the New York audience was conditioned to listen attentively to novel or difficult works, and despite the fact that many of the works Mitropoulos chose to present were manifestly not masterpieces, a sizable portion of the regular listeners had gradually learned to find aesthetic nourishment and sensual pleasure far beyond the strait-jacket of the Basic Repertoire.

In the case of the Shostakovich Tenth, the Carnegie Hall regulars were prepared to recognize its greatness; their taste had been broadened, their aesthetic wits sharpened to the point where the work made a tremendous impact on its first hearing—so much so that many wrote letters or telephoned the Philharmonic, asking to hear it again. Columbia Records took notice and scheduled a recording session on October 18, just nine days after the premiere. Once again, Mitropoulos had made the New York Philharmonic concerts *matter*; on their best nights together, he and his musicians utterly transcended the vexations of routine and became memorable, provocative, vital. He must have felt, on such a night, that his "mission" had achieved its highest goals, however fleetingly.

Rarely did any Mitropoulos concert generate reviews of such enthusiasm and unanimity. Even *Time Magazine*, not ordinarily an arbiter of matters cultural, was impressed enough to devote an entire column to the symphony and the public's reaction to it. Only two reviews dissented. The *New York Daily News*, which of course didn't have much clout with the city's intellectuals, gave its negative response with a typically telegraphic headline: "Shostakovich Symphony No. 10 a Turkey," and its critic, one Douglas Watt, opined that it was probably unfair to judge the work on a single hearing, "But I guess I'll have to, because I don't ever expect to hear it again. I doubt that many of us will hear it again."

The new guy in the reviewers' bullpen, Paul Henry Lang of the *Herald Tribune*, won the Eduard Hanslick Award for critical boat-missing when he snidely expressed the thought that it was "good to see an orchestra with a tight budget" squander so much on the rights to the American premiere of a modern symphony, and then went on to describe the work in question as "sprawling, noisy, lacking in coherent style, and even culture."

After the Wagner and Shostakovich programs, the remaining concerts of the autumn 1954 season must have seemed rather pedestrian. More and more, the reviewers wrote of deteriorating discipline and shoddy playing by the Philharmonic; more and more, Mitropoulos's interpretations of the basic repertoire were described as being fussier and more mannered than they had been in previous seasons:

> The accompaniment of the Mozart concerto [No. 26 in D major, K. 537] was heavy, coarse, and not too well coordinated . . . [flawed by] slap-dash attacks and lack of balance.[2]

> The conductor's modern, rough-hewn approach to the Eroica had considerable power, and it illuminated certain details in a fresh way. But on the whole it seemed as if the work asserted its greatness by withstanding rock-like Mr. Mitropoulos's aggressive interpretation.[3]

> As is his way with composers of the mid-Romantic epoch, his reading [of Schumann's Second Symphony] was nervous, edgy, and crowded with interpretive oddities. Gruff accents dispelled the symphony's lyricism, swollen dynamics its generous calm. And the genuine Schumann that broke through shone with scant help from the conductor.[4]

The subscription concert of November 14 was the final program in Mitropoulos's 1954 schedule with the Philharmonic. He was now free to plunge into a project that excited him tremendously: his December 20 debut at the Metropolitan Opera, directing *Salome*.

Given the success of Mitropoulos's concert versions of operas, it was only logical that he gravitate to the Metropolitan; many reviews had in fact taken Rudolf Bing's administration to task for not already availing themselves of Mitropoulos's services. One of the criticisms most often leveled at Bing concerned his preference for spending money on big-name vocal stars and then saddling them too often with mediocre conductors, many of whom had no career worth mentioning outside of the Met's orchestra pit.

In his sketchy and blatantly self-serving autobiography (*5000 Nights at the Opera*), Bing takes credit for approaching Mitropoulos and convincing him to divide his energies between Carnegie Hall and the Met. "He was honest and decent and helpful, a wonderful person. A little to his own surprise, he found that he loved working in an opera house."[5]

Mitropoulos had, of course, "worked in an opera house" before, at the beginning of his career, under no less a mentor than Erich Kleiber, and more recently at La Scala. He had also conducted semiprofessional operas in Athens, and his suitability for that medium had been more than adequately tested in his Carnegie Hall performances of *Elektra*, *Boris Godunov*, *Madama Butterfly*, and *Die Walküre*.

Conductor Max Rudolf, who was closely associated with the Met for many years, had a much different account of Mitropoulos's hiring:

> Bing was actually very negative in the beginning, and his account of it in his book is rather unrealistic. The person who suggested it to me was Bruno Zirato, who said: "Max, there's one thing you must do for me.

You must bring Mitropoulos to the Met." I said: "I'll try my best because I believe in it. It's not just a favor to you, because I heard Dimitri conduct *Butterfly* at the Lewisohn Stadium concerts and I think he's an excellent opera conductor."

So then I went to Bing with the proposition, and he was entirely negative about the idea. In fact, it took me two years to convince him. And in his book, he claims it was all his idea, but that's simply not true. He also says that Mitropoulos was his closest advisor about orchestral matters, but in fact Mitropoulos had little contact with him about such things until after I left the Met in 1958.[6]

Rudolf observed Mitropoulos closely when the latter was in the pit. "Everybody liked him, but he didn't go into details the way Reiner did when he rehearsed. Sometimes there were accidents when he was conducting—the orchestra was not always together. But Mitropoulos's great strength, as I saw it, was his complete emotional involvement. He had a very strong personality, and I think he was an excellent opera conductor." As Renata Tebaldi used to remark: "When Mitropoulos is in the pit, one *cannot* be indisposed."

Once, when the Met was touring with a production of *Der Rosenkavalier*, Mitropoulos had a free night and asked Rudolf if he could sit in the orchestra pit for the performance. He sat attentively through the entire opera, and when it was over, he went to Rudolf and said: "You know, Max, tonight something went through my mind. A young conductor watching you might learn something by imitating you. But if they tried to imitate me, it would be a disaster."[7]

Frank Guarrera, a baritone who sang many roles at the Met, remembered that Mitropoulos took to opera

> like a fish thrown into water. When he first came to the Met, there were some raised eyebrows, people wondering why in the world he wanted to cross over into opera at this stage of his career. But he brought with him that wonderful warmth and human understanding, and he won people over immediately. Not that he didn't have some extra work to do, learning some of those things an opera conductor needs to do and a symphonic conductor ordinarily doesn't: little technical things like eye cues and hand cues to the singers on stage.[8]

Edward Downes, well known to radio listeners as the host of the weekly "Metropolitan Opera Quiz," thought Mitropoulos had a special flair for Italian opera. "All those blood-and-thunder Italian things—he was very good at them. Now, a lot of serious musicians were either patronizing or just couldn't fit their temperaments into it. But Dimitri was quite capable of jumping in and doing it wholeheartedly; it was wonderful to experience."[9]

Soprano Licia Albanese found Mitropoulos a joy to work with from the singers' point of view:

His tempo was always such that it enabled an artist to sing beautifully. We never had to go out of our way, because he wasn't too slow or too fast. . . . He used to come into the dressing room and go over a few things and say "Do a beautiful job, but be careful here, and here; we'll just watch each other during the performance and it will be beautiful." Afterwards, he would never forget to say "Thank you, you did beautifully and you are such a fine artist" . . . little compliments like that did not feed your ego so much as they made you feel good about yourself and the opera, and as a consequence, when you went on stage to sing under him, you felt you had an *ally* in the pit.[10]

Rudolf Bing was a notoriously difficult man to get along with, especially for conductors. At the time Mitropoulos came to the Met, Bing had just been embroiled in a well-publicized battle of wills with George Szell. Mitropoulos, of course, had a completely different approach from Szell's, as well as a totally different personality. Robert Herman, Bing's assistant, recalled that the two men established a good working relationship from the start:

Mitropoulos got along with [Bing]; he got along with everyone because he was very quiet and he was not the kind of martinet that George Szell was. He had a warm, friendly acceptance of things, and yet you knew what he wanted—you knew that his taste was good, his judgment was good, and you more or less tended to let him do what he wanted because you had confidence that it would be right.[11]

Some who worked with Mitropoulos at the Met liked to compare him not with Szell, but with another Met stalwart, Erich Leinsdorf. Leinsdorf could deliver perfectly adequate performances night after night; it hardly mattered who the composer was or what opera was playing. With Mitropoulos, the chemistry was always changing, depending on the cast, the work at hand, the conductor's moods. Not all of his Met performances were equally successful: he might be spectacularly good one night, and inexplicably dull one the next. "He could produce performances that came astonishingly alive," remembered Verdi scholar George Martin:

evenings when every note would be vibrant. Then he seemed to inspire in himself and his fellow artists a kind of collective energy. When he was "on," his performances surged with vigor; when he was "off," they would plod, lifeless. I used to sit down close when he was conducting, because I liked to watch the way he shook his arms at the orchestra, as if receiving electric shocks through his fingers. When the music-making was going really well, he would get an almost seraphic, ecstatic look on his face—again, very different from Leinsdorf, who always appeared alert, intent, but also a bit remote and unmoved—the conductor as computer.[12]

A problem with programming Strauss's *Salome* on December 20 was the opera's length—a single act—and the Metropolitan audience wanted a full evening for the price of their tickets. Bing's solution to the problem of what to run with *Salome* took the form of an experiment: an original ballet entitled *Vittorio*, utilizing odds and ends of unfamiliar music by Verdi (arranged by Julius Burger), featuring the Met's *corps de ballet*, and choreographed by Zachary Solov.

The plot was an absurd farrago of grand-opera cliches, and Mitropoulos had to be coaxed into conducting the music. Solov's staging took a very long forty-five minutes to display its inanities and the climactic "duel" had many first-night attendees laughing in derision. It seems clear from the reviews that, after *Vittorio*, anything would have seemed dramatic; *Salome* proved shattering.

The title role was sung by a young, sexy German soprano named Christl Goltz. A trained acrobat as well as a disciplined singer, Goltz delivered a very physical incarnation of Salome; projecting the image of a truly depraved slut, she writhed, crawled, undulated, and teased, reaching a pitch, as one reviewer expressed it, of "feverish, almost unholy intensity." Fortunately, she did not have to rely on bumping and grinding to carry the role, for she possessed a voice capable of surfing on top of Strauss's most effulgent climaxes. At the end, the audience went wild.

Although Olin Downes had a prudish reaction to the staging ("excessively and unnecessarily raw"), he and all his colleagues were stunned by the impact of the opera and awed by Mitropoulos's contribution. Jay S. Harrison, writing for the *Herald Tribune*, spoke for many when he wrote: "Mr. Mitropoulos proved what has long been perfectly clear—that his talent for dramatic expression finds a surging outlet in opera that is not readily available in the symphonic literature . . . he urged sonorities and waves of sound from his crew that were downright blistering in their heat."[13]

Every performance of *Salome* was a sell-out. The audience was thrilled, the cast was excited, the orchestra played like men possessed, and Rudolf Bing was extremely pleased. Clearly, Mitropoulos now had two venues in New York. He conducted at the Met each season, for the rest of his life, and he made a number of successful recordings for the Metropolitan Opera Record Club (a division of the Book-of-the-Month Club). Although he came to opera fairly late in his career, he was acknowledged to be a born opera conductor. Louis Biancolli asserted that this fact should not have surprised

> anyone who had sensed an almost visual drama at work in the "absolute" music he directed in the concert hall. That kind of musician lives and plays leading roles—the other selves of the many composers they interpret—in the music of the masters. They seem to be the medium of great narrative and dramatic conflict and suspense. And so it was that when Mitropoulos began to conduct at the Metropolitan a new electricity pervaded the old house. Whether in Puccini, Verdi, Strauss,

Wagner, it was as if General Manager Rudolf Bing was offering a wholly new repertory. Where there had been acceptable routine, now there was rekindled fire; where listeners had concentrated on the singers, now they were riveted to the orchestra too. I recall vividly, on a double-assignment night as a critic, hurrying down from Carnegie Hall . . . to catch the remainder of Mitropoulos's first *Die Walküre*. I could feel the radiation in the air as I dashed across the lobby and stood by Henry, the dean of ushers. "Stood" is no word for it. Both of us were transfixed, as was the entire house, right up to the compact ranks of standees. . . . That night, Wagner *was* God, and Dimitri Mitropoulos his Prophet.[14]

If Dimitri Mitropoulos was such an inspiring conductor, capable of giving performances that even the most jaded New York critics could described as "incandescent," why haven't his commercial recordings stayed in print as collectors' items in the same way that Furtwängler's and Toscanini's have? Why were there so comparatively few of them to begin with? And why does such a large percentage of his Columbia releases sound, if not exactly inferior to the competition, at least unremarkable, in the sense that few of them capture the "incandescent," "blistering," or otherwise exceptional qualities mentioned in conjunction with his live concert performances?

The matter is complicated but not inexplicable. First, there is the fact that Mitropoulos, even more than other great conductors of his generation, was seldom able to achieve the same level of inspiration under studio conditions as he could with a live audience at his back. He came late to recordings, making his first when he was forty-four years old. The technical constraints of recording sessions, with their fussy requirements of balance, microphonics, time limits, and constant interruptions from the engineers in the control room, had a dampening, inhibiting effect on Mitropoulos. He would just get into his groove, feel his emotions start to soar, and the red light would come on, the orchestra would have to stop, and a disembodied voice from the control room would say something like: "Uh, Maestro, we didn't get the woodwind balances right on that last take, so could you try it again from letter M, please?" He learned to tolerate the demands of the recording studio, to subordinate his natural way of doing things to the uncongenial demands of commerce, but, unlike Stokowski, he never felt entirely at home there.

Second, for reasons of economics, Columbia scheduled most of its New York Philharmonic sessions in the form of one-day marathons, which not only added tension to the process but which must surely have left orchestra and conductor drained of energy long before the end of the day's activity. For example, the recording session of November 11, 1957, included performances of "The Star Spangled Banner" (*why* is unclear; the recording was never issued, in any case), Mussorgsky's *Night on Bald Mountain*, a full LP's worth of music from Prokofiev's *Romeo and Juliet*, Tchaikovsky's

Marche Slav, and Tchaikovsky's Sixth Symphony. No orchestra would attempt a live concert of such length and such demanding material, and no orchestra, no matter how willing, could possibly play so many big-scale pieces in a single stretch without some falling-off of concentration and quality in the latter half of the schedule. In this case, the listener can plainly hear this effect: the Prokofiev ballet excerpts, taped when the performers were relatively fresh, flash and gleam, swagger and strut, all purple and gold; the *Pathétique*, recorded last, is among the worst performances Mitropoulos ever committed to disc—a dry, perfunctory run-through by musicians who have no more to give to the emotional demands of the score.

The most extreme case of this squeeze-'em-dry approach to recordings was the incredible session of November 2, 1952, when no fewer than eight selections were taped: Borodin's Symphony No. 2, de Falla's Interlude and Dance from *La vida breve*, and three dances from *The Three-Cornered Hat*, Mendelssohn's *Ruy Blas* Overture, *Calm Sea and Prosperous Voyage* Overture, *Hebrides* Overture, and the Third and Fifth Symphonies. In this case, at least, the performances don't reflect wear and tear as much as the Prokofiev-Tchaikovsky sessions, probably because the works themselves are shorter and less demanding and because the chemistry between Mitropoulos and the orchestra was vastly better in 1952 than it was in 1957, when he was a lame-duck music director already on his way out of town.

In Columbia's defense, it must be said that Mitropoulos *allowed* these over-long sessions; had he complained or balked, different, more reasonable schedules would have been put into effect. Again, he allowed himself to be taken advantage of. Although he had surprisingly little to say about recordings in either his letters or his published interviews, it seems clear that he regarded the whole process as a chore to be gotten through as expeditiously as possible—if he could do three days' worth of normal recording in one exhausting day, so much the better.

There was also a certain subtle low-priority atmosphere to the Philharmonic's recording sessions with Columbia: here they were, universally acknowledged as the "most important orchestra in America," yet their record company openly treated them as a second-rate attraction, while lavishing much more publicity and easier sessions on the Cadillac of recording teams, Ormandy and the Philadelphia. During the nine years Mitropoulos was under contract with Columbia, he recorded seventy-five works with the Philharmonic, of which only seventy were actually published. Ormandy and the Philadelphia recorded four times that number and enjoyed virtual *carte blanche* to record anything they wanted to. The Mitropoulos Columbia sessions break down by year as follows: 1950, nine; 1951, six; 1952, twelve; 1953, twelve; 1954, seven; 1955, one; 1956, sixteen; 1957, ten; 1958, two.

For all his tolerance and willingness to turn the other cheek, Mitropoulos was quite bitter about the way he and his orchestra were treated by Columbia. Conductor John Canarina, then a student at Juilliard, went backstage to congratulate the conductor after an electrifying 1954 performance of Vaughan Williams's Fourth, and asked him when he would record his by-then-famous interpretation. Mitropoulos cast an angry glance at Bruno Zirato standing nearby and replied: "We won't, apparently. All Columbia is interested in is the Philadelphia Orchestra." Better late than never, Columbia finally did record Mitropoulos's version of the Vaughan Williams Fourth in 1956, and it was hailed, upon its release, as one of the great recordings of the decade.

Mitropoulos received smaller, as well as fewer, royalty payments than Ormandy, especially when Columbia used him as an "accompanist conductor" for a number of rather routine concerto recordings. His special talents were also largely wasted on several recordings of compositions (*Les Préludes*, *Capriccio Italien*, *The Sorcerer's Apprentice*, for example) which were, even in the mid-1950s, egregiously redundant additions to the catalogues—not because he did not conduct this music well, but because he became almost frozen with self-consciousness when asked to compete as a superstar conductor with other superstars who had recorded these warhorses. Several of his most important recordings, such as the Sessions Second Symphony and the Mennin Third, would never have been made without financial underwriting from the Naumburg Foundation—Columbia had little or no interest in doing these works for their own sake.

David Oppenheim, who was in charge of A&R (Artists and Repertory) for Columbia Masterworks, quite naturally viewed things from a different perspective. Ormandy/Philadelphia got the star treatment because their records sold far more copies than those of the Mitropoulos/Philharmonic team, and one reason for that was Mitropoulos's unwillingness to be marketed—not to mention his basic unsuitability as a cultural icon. In his 1985 interview with Oliver Daniel, Oppenheim ventured the opinion that Mitropoulos could have obtained more cooperation from Columbia if he had been willing to fight for it; but, however inappropriately, he responded to second-class treatment with his usual Franciscan passivity and permitted his bitterness to show only rarely and only to close associates.

> Mitropoulos was a very easy person to work with, by and large. In fact, I would say, in some ways, too easy. We made a lot of records with him, but maybe not the records you would consider [vital]. I remember him being very responsive to our problems with the high cost of recording, and that's why we were able to make an incredible number of sides with him at some of those recording sessions. . . . If someone was very fussy and insisted on a lot of re-takes, it got very pricey. But it was very economical if someone just said, "It doesn't matter, let's just play it through." He did that, on a number of occasions. One was when we taped two entire Mendelssohn symphonies in two hours. An absolute record-breaker.[15]

Oppenheim also defended Columbia's relatively stingy allotment of studio time for works that were deemed unprofitable:

He was so very anxious to record the Schoenberg Violin Concerto with Krasner, and that was done in one take without stopping simply because I had no money but I was willing to let the sessions go on that much longer, and so was Krasner, so, boom! the baton came down and off we went and we ran out of studio time within seconds of the end of the concerto. We did some re-takes of the cadenza, of course, but we didn't have to pay for the whole orchestra during that time, so that was acceptable. . . . I know it was hard on Krasner, but it was an opportunity to propagate Schoenberg and that satisfied Mitropoulos; still, it was not a professional way to make a record. That was an example of what I mean by Mitropoulos being more cooperative than he should have been. If he was unhappy with his Columbia catalogue, well, it was partly his own fault because he did not insist on the prerogatives of a great conductor, a star, but rather just another humble musician. A corporation the size of Columbia was not going to be impressed by that attitude.[16]

Louis Krasner remembered that Mitropoulos made an unpalatable deal with Columbia in order to get a shot at recording the Schoenberg concerto. If Mitropoulos agreed to conduct some warhorse selections (*Les Préludes*, the *Polovtzian Dances*, that sort of thing), Columbia would schedule a four-hour recording session, and if there was enough time left over, he and Krasner could squeeze in the Schoenberg.

There was one other small stipulation attached to Columbia's bargain:

both conductor and soloist had to agree in writing to accept no royalties from sales of the recording! The recording session decided upon was held on December 1, 1952. On the night before, Mitropoulos called Krasner and said: "Okay, we're going to do the Schoenberg. I'm obligated to record about two hours' worth of other music, but we have a four-hour session. You be there when we begin at ten A.M., so that whenever the time comes, I can call you in."

Krasner was agreeable and showed up on time. Mitropoulos dispatched the two regularly scheduled works in two hours, then came up to Krasner and said, "Okay, we've got two hours—that's plenty of time for the Schoenberg. Get ready, and I'll call you in a minute."

But the next time Krasner saw Mitropoulos, the conductor was almost crying with frustration. "You know what they did to me?" he cried. "The microphone placement was no good, so the whole thing has to be done over! They've given me an extra hour, though, so we can still do it." Krasner tried to be patient, and went back to practicing the Schoenberg. Finally, he reached the point where he felt he was over-practicing and, wanting to save some spontaneity for the recording, he stopped—and waited.

Mitropoulos came back in at quarter-past-four; the main works had taken more than four hours to tape properly, and now there was not a minute to loose. "Quick, quick," he said, "we must begin the Schoenberg!"

Krasner literally ran to the stage, with barely enough time to tune, and began playing almost immediately. Looking at the score, he saw that he had a two-measure rest coming after the end of the first page, and he started to say something to the conductor. Mitropoulos flashed him a desperate look and indicated that they were going ahead, nonstop.

> I thought perhaps we could stop at the cadenza, but he gave another signal to keep playing, big beats this time. So I played through the whole cadenza and while I was doing so, I had this conversation with myself: on page three, I have to do this section again—over there, the harmonics didn't turn out so good, we have to do this other place pizzicato . . . and all of these things I wanted to say to him at the end of the first movement, before I forgot them. But we plunged into the second movement without stopping, without a word of conversation. I thought, oh well, we do have fifteen minutes extra, since it only takes a half-hour for the whole concerto, and I was desperately trying to prioritize the re-takes, *while I was playing*, so we could get the maximum out of that quarter-hour.

They finished the run-through with exactly fifteen minutes to go. Well, thought Krasner, at least I had the presence of mind to remember the main things we need to do over. But as the last chord of the concerto sounded, to Krasner's astonishment, the entire New York Philharmonic got up and made an angry, resentful rush to the exits, leaving a sweat-drenched Mitropoulos standing there alone with his bewildered soloist.

"Maestro, what's happening?" said Krasner, "we still have fifteen minutes, don't we?"

"No, we don't, Louis. We skipped the fifteen-minute intermission. Union rules—the orchestra agreed to skip it, so we have to let them go now."

By the time Krasner told Oliver Daniel the tale of this bizarre recording session, he had become philosophical about it. But for years after the recording came out, he was deeply offended by the entire experience.

> The irony is that the recording sold out very quickly. Columbia was so reluctant to do it, and then immediately after it was released, it started selling very well. I wrote to Goddard Lieberson (head of the Masterworks division of Columbia) and said, "I can't tell you how embarrassing it is to me and how distasteful the whole thing is—that Mitropoulos and I had to sign this humiliating agreement. It has cost Columbia pennies on the dollar in terms of what you're making off of our labor and commitment." Lieberson never answered me directly, but after a while, I did start to get a trickle of royalties from it, so at least his conscience was in the right place. And do you know, you can't get a copy of that record now, it's in such demand as a collectors' item. About ten years ago, I called a record store and inquired about getting

one for myself, and they said, "Yes, it's one of the real rarities. But we might be able to locate a copy for you if you're willing to spend two hundred dollars."[17]

Mitropoulos's catalogue of Columbia recordings is distinguished primarily by what it does *not* include: none of his concert performances of operas; not the premiere of *Christophe Colomb* and the revival of *Orfeo*; not one of his pioneering Mahler interpretations (other than the prewar Minneapolis recording of the First Symphony), nor the Liszt *Faust Symphony*, nor any of his Busoni—the list goes on and on.

CHAPTER TWENTY-SIX

Return to Athens

Nineteen-fifty-five began for Mitropoulos in the Metropolitan Opera House, where he conducted Verdi's *Un ballo in maschera*. While opera fans anticipated great vocalism from the main singers—Zinka Milanov, Roberta Peters, Leonard Warren, and Richard Tucker—the attention of all America was focused on one of the supporting singers: at the age of fifty-two, contralto Marian Anderson was about to become the first black singer to appear at the Met in its seventy-one-year history.

Although attention was quite properly focused on Miss Anderson's historic debut as the old sorceress Ulrica, on January 7, Mitropoulos's conducting was also praised, with most of the critics seconding Olin Downes:

> for all-around mastery and vividness that suffused not only the orchestra but also every detail of the production, commend us to Mr. Mitropoulos's lyrical, blazing, volcanic interpretation of the score. The theater is evidently in his blood . . . who that heard will ever forget the torrent of orchestral tone that swept the voices and the drama itself forward on its crest, yet ignored no minor issue or detail of the whole?[1]

Back at Carnegie Hall on February 10, Mitropoulos signaled business-as-usual by conducting the first New York performances of Albert Roussel's Third Symphony (February 10 and 11), Peter Mennin's Sixth Symphony (February 17, 18, and 20), and Morton Gould's flashy *Showpiece for Orchestra*. The Gould composition was a theme-and-variations affair commissioned by Columbia Records as a "hi-fi" demonstration piece (not that Columbia bothered to record it for that or any other purpose). Harold C. Schonberg's snippet of a review was a paradigm of the way the New York critics steadfastly refused to relax and enjoy Gould's entertaining music. "The work, about twenty minutes long," wrote Schonberg, "is slick, superficial, and has all the permanence of an ice cube in a glass of hot water. . . . The partiality that Mr. Mitropoulos has shown for Mr. Gould's music through the years is hard to explain."[2]

Mitropoulos went even farther out on his contemporary limb on the night of March 31, when he programmed Rolf Liebermann's Concerto for Jazz Band and Symphony Orchestra. Although the piece sounds amusingly dated now, it was considered a daring Third Stream venture in the mid-

370

1950s, and was taken so seriously that Reiner and the Chicago Symphony recorded it. Liebermann unified the work by means of a twelve-tone row, and so sacrificed the improvisatory qualities at the heart of jazz, but he covered a lot of stylistic ground by incorporating be-bop, blues, boogie-woogie, and a concluding mambo in which the percussion sections of both jazz band and orchestra get a thorough workout. The "concerto" begins with a soft and rather commonplace symphonic introduction, and then the band jumps in. The music passes back and forth, concerto-grosso–like, with much the more interesting ideas going to the jazz ensemble. Leonid Hambro burned up the stage with his foot-stomping traversal of the piano solo in the boogie-woogie movement, and the Sauter-Finegan Orchestra handled the heavy-duty jazz work. Mitropoulos was even more animated than usual, since the piece gave him extra incentive, in the words of *Musical America*'s reviewer, to "lurch, gyrate, whirl and swoon."

Quite a few of the tradition-bound subscribers felt that Mitropoulos had really gone over the line this time; one old fellow was heard to mutter, as he made his way indignantly to the nearest exit, "Pure night club, that's what it is!" On the other hand, the Carnegie Hall audience contained hundreds of younger listeners, and their cheers drowned out the scattered boos.

Olin Downes stayed away that night, knowing full well that anything involving a jazz orchestra would only provoke bile and wrath from himself. Howard Taubman covered the concert for the *Times*; the headline captured the spirit of the evening: "Philharmonic and Sauter-Finegan? Cool!"

Seriousness returned in the following week, when Mitropoulos led a shattering performance of Mahler's Sixth, a work whose American premiere he had conducted, to very mixed notices, seven years earlier. This time, the reviews were lavish in their praise of both music and conductor, but there was unanimous condemnation for the way Mitropoulos had organized the program. For reasons unfathomable, he chose to preface the Mahler symphony with yet another performance of Gould's *Showpiece for Orchestra*. Not only did this frothy diversion get crushed by the Mahler juggernaut, but by juxtaposing it against the Austrian composer's apocalyptic seriousness and high philosophical purpose, Mitropoulos simply made a well-crafted piece of lightweight music seem unbelievably tacky.

Even stranger and more unmusical was Mitropoulos's decision to insert a twenty-minute intermission between the second and third movements of the Mahler Sixth. Carnegie Hall was only half-full when the concert began; a hundred or more patrons took the intermission as a cue for leaving. This strange, off-putting, lopsided program was the clearest instance yet that the pressures of his job and the increasing misbehavior of his orchestra were causing Mitropoulos's judgment to become harmfully, rather than colorfully, erratic. The conductor's ability to focus, to achieve inner balance as well as outward effectiveness, was slowly, week by week, becoming frayed, unreliable to a degree he had never before experienced, and of which he seems to have been only peripherally aware.

After the closing concert of the season, April 17, 1955, the board of directors took stock of the Philharmonic's fortunes and were not pleased. The deficit amounted to $250,000—about the same as for the preceding season. More ominous was the fact that subscription sales had decreased by $21,000. And there was a mounting volume of complaint: from American composers, that they weren't given enough exposure, and from the public about all that "modern stuff." According to one Philharmonic insider, "People would come to the box office, and ask about the length of the modern work on the program. If it was any longer than ten minutes, they wouldn't buy tickets."[3]

Only a day after the final concert of the spring season, the Philharmonic began a grueling cross-country tour starting in Detroit, on April 18. The orchestra gave thirty-one concerts in twenty-nine cities, covering the Midwest, Northwest, and California, with a brief dip south for one concert each in Albuquerque, Tucson, and El Paso. The tour ended in Chicago, on May 21. Mitropoulos led seventeen of the concerts; Guido Cantelli led the remainder.

In several cities, observers who had not seen Mitropoulos since his days with the Minneapolis Symphony remarked on how much more "relaxed" his podium style had become, how comparatively economical his gestures now were. In Minneapolis, where the orchestra played Mendelssohn's Fifth and Shostakovich's Tenth Symphonies, the response was close to hysterical. Naturally, there was much comparison of the visiting orchestra to the home team. One critic observed that "The mellowness, sweetness, body, and richness of the string choir formed the particularly outstanding feature. Aside from that, the sounds of the Philharmonic are not overly superior to those of the Minneapolis orchestra. But the apparent ease with which the sounds roll without tension, the feeling of power only half used, are characteristics in sharp contrast to our local orchestra."[4]

Cantelli was slated to conduct the May 11 concert in Salt Lake City, Utah; since Mitropoulos was fascinated by the Mormon Tabernacle, he asked pianist Grant Johannesen to attend with him:

> There's this great staircase at the back of the tabernacle—what Frank Lloyd Wright had once described as a Victorian quonset hut. We listened to the concert for a while, near the back, and then he said to me, "Let's go take a walk." When he got to the staircase, he began walking backwards, very slowly, head tilted, listening to the sound. It was very strange, very funny actually, to see him slowly backing down the stairs, followed by this trail of music. Back on the temple grounds, he said, "That place has great mystery in it. It is a place for religion."[5]

On the next day, in Provo, Mitropoulos gave a speech to the student body of Brigham Young University. His topic was "My Responsibility." His delivery gave further indication that he was no longer as focused and self-assured as he had been even a year earlier. Woolly in rhetoric, ineffably and somewhat priggishly high-minded in tone, the address rambled on and on like a bad parody of a Khalil Gibran sermon before trailing off to a limp conclusion.

Two days later, May 14, the Philharmonic arrived in Denver. The sponsoring organization for that city had been given its choice of conductors, and it had selected the dashing young Cantelli. William Cooper, who was able to spend a free day before the concert with his old Minneapolis friend, thought that Mitropoulos's feelings were hurt, in view of how warmly received he and the MSO had been by the Denver public on previous occasions. In any event, since Mrs. Cooper was recuperating from illness, Mitropoulos and Professor Cooper went to the concert together. Despite any personal regrets he may have felt about being passed over in favor of his younger colleague, Mitropoulos appeared to be as spellbound by Cantelli's gifts as any other member of the audience, and when the last powerful chord of Brahms's First had died away, he leaned over to Cooper and said, "Wasn't that magnificent?"

Since the Philharmonic had a demanding European tour scheduled in September, Mitropoulos booked no European concerts for the summer. On August 22, 1955, twelve days before the start of the tour, Olin Downes died. He was replaced by the next most senior *Times* critic, Howard Taubman. On the face of it, the shift in power was routine enough, but despite the fact that Taubman had more often than not given favorable notices to Mitropoulos, a slow-building tidal change was gathering force in the currents of New York's musical life, one which became, however decorous and proper it may have seemed on the surface, nothing less than a crusade to drive Dimitri Mitropoulos out of the directorship of the New York Philharmonic. Taubman willingly devolved into its Brutus; many hands proffered him the knife, and when the time came, he drove it home unhesitatingly. As pianist Arthur Whittemore candidly put it: "Taubman had a real hate-on for Dimitri; I don't know where it came from, but it was there."[6]

At four o'clock in the afternoon, September 3, 1955, the first of two chartered buses drove away from Carnegie Hall, bearing the passengers of Plane A—Mitropoulos, Zirato, the administrative staff needed for the tour, and all the first-chair players. A second bus, containing the Plane B passengers (the rank and file musicians), pulled away thirty minutes later. By seven-thirty, both planes were airborne from Idlewild, on their way to Edinburgh's Prestwick Airport. The great European Tour of 1955 was about to begin.

In Edinburgh, the Philharmonic played six concerts, from September 5 to 10. Mitropoulos conducted the first and last; George Szell and Guido Cantelli split the remaining dates. After Edinburgh came two concerts in Vienna (September 12 and 13), followed by dates in Brussels, Berlin, Paris, Basel, Berne, Zurich, Milan, Perugia, Rome, and Naples.

The final concerts of the tour were to be given in London, on October 4 and 5. These London concerts were, in effect, a belated correction of an uncomfortable situation that arose during the first Edinburgh Festival visit in 1951. Under the terms of its agreement with the festival, the orchestra was not permitted to perform anywhere else in Britain. Contract or no, Londoners were indignant that America's leading orchestra had flown all the way across the Atlantic and back without playing a note in the capital.

To represent American composers, on the opening Edinburgh concert on September 5, Mitropoulos chose Morton Gould's *Showpiece for Orchestra*— not perhaps the most felicitous selection, in view of how condescending the New York critics had been toward the work. Edinburgh's reviewers were predictably xenophobic and dispatched the piece in the manner of "Our Music Critic," writing in *The Scotsman*: "Mr. Gould's variations made all the usual noises and a lot more besides, with everything that opens and shuts,and scratches and snorts, having a go, but considering how hard all the band was working, the net result was energetic but surprisingly dreary."[7]

As in 1951, much was made of the power, size, and brilliance of the Philharmonic's sound; many comments were also made about the precision and finesse of its playing—indicating that the orchestra was on its best behavior before its European audiences and implying, rather sadly, that the roughness and out-of-tune playing so carped-about by the New York critics was more a function of attitude than of Mitropoulos's failings as a director.

"The Goliath of symphony orchestras," cried one headline: "Stupendous, colossal, gigantic, terrific." Several observers found the conductor's podium style greatly changed from the wild physicality of his earlier visit. Now, Mitropoulos seemed to control the powerful tonal maelstrom through an intense stillness which some witnesses found almost spooky. At times there was no perceptible beat, and many cues were given with the merest twitch of a finger or lifting of an eyebrow. There were numerous times when Mitropoulos moved his hands to sketch the start of a phrase, then seemed to leave it hanging in air, trusting his instrumentalists to finish from what amounted to a shorthand cue, while the conductor prepared for the next phrase.

Mitropoulos shrewdly programmed the Vaughan Williams Fourth Symphony, a work whose performance had astonished listeners during the 1951 Edinburgh appearance. This time, the power of the Philharmonic's brass section was a known quantity; what caught the critics' attention was the constant stream of string tone—from sixty-four instruments—at Mitropoulos's command, and the use he made of it—expanding or contracting the symphony's oases of lesser tension, achieving remarkable textural clarity despite the rough-hewn quality of much of the scoring.

From Scotland, the orchestra flew to Vienna, for its first visit in almost two decades. There, despite unfeigned hospitality by the men of the Vienna Philharmonic, who threw an *echt*-Viennese party for the visitors after their September 12 concert, the reception was both enthusiastic and guarded—in a word, very Viennese.

Featured symphonies on the two Vienna programs were Brahms's Second, Schumann's Second, and Shostakovich's Tenth Symphonies. The orchestra itself impressed one Viennese critic as occupying a place in the tonal spectrum "between the Vienna and Berlin Philharmonics," and Mitropoulos as resembling "Furtwängler with St. Vitus' dance."[8] Another avowed that the Philharmonic's thrust and brilliance were more suited to Vienna's taste than the "sober perfection" of the Philadelphia Orchestra (which had also visited the city recently). There can be no question but that here, as in Scotland, the orchestra was on its toes, delivering playing that was generally more alert and committed than its patrons heard in New York.

Other Viennese writers went out of their way to demonstrate how hard they were to please. Brahms's Second was described as being "misunderstood, but in an ingenious fashion."[9] The end of that symphony, which is dominated by a hard-to-play top D on the trombone, "had rung out with tone as big as a house," prompting one reviewer to sniff: "It really was a *very* large orchestra," when it was, in fact, exactly the same size as any other major orchestra, including the Vienna Philharmonic. Other critics were less veiled in their terminology, one stating flatly that the orchestra was just "too loud."

According to British writer David Wooldridge, who attended the concerts, Mitropoulos decided, on the night following the "too loud" reviews, to show the audience how delicately and quietly the orchestra could play, by programming as an encore the orchestral version of Rachmaninoff's *Vocalise*. Writing fifteen years after the event, Wooldridge still got goosebumps remembering how the "incredible *ppp* of the final phrase . . . seemed to hang on the final C sharp for an eternity."[10] Unfortunately, few members of the Viennese audience had ever heard of the piece before, so some of the point of the conductor's demonstration was lost.

Wooldridge thought Mitropoulos was also addressing the opening-night reviews when he manifested unusual showmanship during the playing of Verdi's *La forza del destino* Overture. He cued each section with obviously exaggerated motions, just a shade farther ahead of their entries than was his usual wont. Clearly, he was doing this in order to call the audience's attention to each section of his orchestra in turn, for he conducted the rest of the concert in a much more restrained manner. Wooldridge also recalled some inexcusably messy playing by the first clarinet near the start of the Schumann Second Symphony, indicating that not all the players were able to leave their bad habits back in Manhattan.

Whatever the hauteur of the critics, the Viennese public was utterly won over and gave Mitropoulos a thundering ovation, to which he responded, in typical style, by blowing a kiss.

Everywhere the orchestra went in Europe, the response was overwhelming. Many of these European notices, written, presumably, by critics who were used to hearing the greatest orchestras on the continent, are lavish in their praise of the very qualities Mitropoulos was lambasted for by the New York critical establishment.

In Zurich, for example, the critic for the *Neue Zürcher Zeitung* called the performance there:

> a feast of orchestral virtuosity such as one has never heard in Zurich before. What an overwhelming impression—what extraordinary precision of ensemble playing, what purity of intonation! . . . Clearly, Mitropoulos is a man obsessed by music, who transmits to the orchestra, by means of an incomparable sense of concentration, the many intellectual and spiritual tensions of his artistic being.[11]

A similar reception was given in Basel, where critic Werner Oelmann summed up the feelings of many European music-lovers when he wrote: "If, after the death of Furtwängler and the retirement of Toscanini, the question arises as to who is the most important conductor now living, only the name of Mitropoulos and a very few others are even worthy of discussion."[12]

In Berlin, a city whose critics were surely as experienced, as knowledgeable, and on occasion as venomous as their New York counterparts, Mitropoulos and his men were bombarded with praise:

> the precision of their playing is peerless. . . . There can only be words of highest admiration for this orchestra [and for] Dimitri Mitropoulos, their conductor; he radiates deep excitement and aroused our admiration when he conducted modern music in the first concert, and our love when he conducted Schumann and Brahms in the second. Now it becomes understandable why so many call him "the American Furtwängler."[13]

Athens was not on the original itinerary, but the financial support of a wealthy Greek patron (Vasilios Goulandris) made possible a two-day layover on October 1 and 2. Unimpressed by Goulandris's generosity—perhaps even miffed by it—Bruno Zirato let it be known that the Philharmonic's management refused to allocate funds for the orchestra's food and lodging in Athens. Mitropoulos, incredulous at this petty obstructionism, thereupon guaranteed to cover all such expenses out of his own pocket. As Philharmonic trumpet player John Ware recalled the incident:

> We were to be there [Athens] for three nights, and Mitropoulos sent a message to us that said, "I'm going to pay the entire orchestra's hotel bills and food for the three days we're there because this is my home and I want to have you as my guests and therefore that's what I would like to do." So we had an orchestra meeting, because while we really appreciated that offer, we thought we couldn't accept all that, so we sent

him a message back that we would accept his offer of paying our hotel bills—which we did, the whole orchestra for three nights—but that we would respectfully decline to accept money for the food. And after that, we took up a collection. I don't know the amount, but it probably amounted to whatever the hotel bills cost him, and we told him we wanted to donate that to his favorite charity, which he named as an orphanage there in Athens . . . so it was a kind of switching of the funds, but nevertheless, he made the gesture, and it's never been done before or since by any other conductor.[14]

However great the ovations in Europe, the highlight of the tour, for Mitropoulos, was this return to Athens after an absence of seventeen years. When his plane touched down at Helliniko Airport, on Friday, September 30, four hours late because of bad weather encountered in the flight from Naples, he was greeted by a thousand people, crying "*Yassou, yassou!*" (Hello, hello!). Bundles of roses and laurels were thrust at him. He gamely smiled and waved, but his remarks were brief; he apologized for his queasy appearance, telling the crowd that he felt "sick as a dog" from the turbulence.

Several thousand Athenians had camped out overnight in front of the box office. Scalpers circulated with wildly overpriced tickets. Two concerts were scheduled, both at the ancient outdoor theater of Herodus Atticus, where the conductor had led many concerts during his Athenian career. At the acoustical rehearsal on the morning of October 1, Mitropoulos was heard to wish for rain, "so that we don't have to compete with the sight of the Acropolis and the Parthenon." He got his wish: a late-afternoon downpour washed out the concert, which was then rescheduled indoors at the cavernous Orpheus Hall Cinema. There was a mad scramble to get the orchestra repositioned, and when the Philharmonic's long-suffering baggage master, Vincent Jacoby, attempted to carry the covered harp onto an Athenian bus, he was thrown off by the conductor. He finally made it to the theater by hitching a ride on a passing truck.

After conducting the Schumann Second Symphony, Mitropoulos joined the Greek royal family at the theater's bar, where Princess Sophie fetched ice water for him. King Paul and Queen Frederica invited him to lunch the next day; the conductor casually replied: "I'll try to be there, if I'm not too exhausted."

At the end of the concert, the applause was frenzied—a twenty-minute demonstration accompanied by rhythmic foot-stomping and chants of "Mit-tro-POU-los! Mit-tro-POU-los!!"

The conductor soon got his second wind. Every spare moment was spent delivering speeches here and there, sitting before microphones, and dealing with hundreds of well-wishers. He did make time for an emotional reunion with Katy Katsoyanis, and one orchestra member was deeply touched at the sight of the two of them "toddling off together towards the Parthenon."[15]

So great was the demand, so huge were the overflow crowds, that an unscheduled concert was held on the morning of October 2. Mitropoulos was so energized that he decided to accept the royal couple's invitation and was heard to terminate one interview with the words: "I really must go. The King's expecting me, and I hear he serves a good lunch."

In contrast to the tremendous public reception, there was privately an undercurrent of jealousy, a rekindling of old animosities, on the part of the conductor's long-ago Greek colleagues. In 1956 Mitropoulos recalled: "When I went home to Greece, after many years there were a number of old classmates waiting to discuss my luck with thinly veiled bitterness. I cried for them, but they cried for me too when I recalled the terrors and errors that had possessed me in the course of my early trials."[16]

A decidedly ideological and personal tone was set by the various Athenian reviews, as well. As had been the case when Mitropoulos was working in the Greek capital, some critics seemed less interested in being objective chroniclers of the artistic scene than in advancing one cultural faction's agenda against another's. Time, fame, distance, and age had dulled Mitropoulos's vulnerability to such antics, but he was still as disgusted by the situation as he had ever been before the war.

For all its emotional highs and lows, however, Mitropoulos unhesitatingly called this Athenian return "the greatest event of my life." He had left Greece to pursue his career free from the provincialism, sectarian squabbling, and back-biting that had made him so miserable; now, less than two decades later, he had returned in triumph at the head of one of the world's greatest orchestras. Even for a man of humility, there was a mighty satisfaction in such a moment.

After the hullabaloo in Athens, Mitropoulos may have found his visit to London, the last stop on the tour, something of an anticlimax. Certainly the opening concert, on October 4, was a tense, travel-weary affair that generated only lukewarm critical responses. The interpretation of Schumann's Second puzzled the reviewers, who wondered why the conductor gave such prominence to the trumpets even when they did nothing but mark time with tonic-and-dominant punctuation.

Mitropoulos got little praise, either, for including Dvořák's Violin Concerto on his second concert. Nathan Milstein was not the ideal interpreter of this relatively homely piece, nor did Mitropoulos seem terribly involved with the orchestra part. Most of the London critics subscribed to the then-current opinion that Dvořák's "is not a great concerto, not even a very good one" and expressed disappointment that the New Yorkers should bring this to town and not the fabled Vaughan Williams Fourth everyone had read about in connection with their Edinburgh appearances.

Not until the concluding performance of the Shostakovich Tenth—the work's London premiere—did the Londoners hear what conductor and orchestra could do at their best. This performance, at least, was hailed as a revelation in terms of both the music itself and the orchestra's full powers of execution.

No doubt glad to leave London behind, the weary musicians embarked on October 6 for home. Mitropoulos was reeling with exhaustion by this time, yet was still mentally preparing himself for the rigors of the coming Philharmonic season. It was a mercy that he had no foreknowledge of what that season would bring.

CHAPTER TWENTY-SEVEN

A Time of Troubles

Before joining the New York Philharmonic, the distinguished cellist Leonard Rose had played with two other major orchestras: the Chicago Symphony and the Cleveland Orchestra. In Cleveland he was first-chair cello for four years before Artur Rodzinski summoned him to New York during the first year of his reign, to replace a player sacked during the great purge. For the young, idealistic cellist, the transition was startling:

> I was absolutely amazed at what I saw, because during the whole four years I played with the Cleveland Orchestra, it was like being in one big happy family. Yes, of course there were minor differences and disagreements occasionally, but, gee, in the players' room of the Philharmonic, I saw *fistfights*! I learned very quickly that this was one tough bunch of guys. First of all, the orchestra was an ethnic cross-section but there wasn't much of a "melting pot" effect going on. What you mostly had were various factions who barely spoke to each other most of the time.
>
> Secondly, there were many, many Italians, who had come into the orchestra during Toscanini's regime and who had a permanent chip on their shoulders about how things were always rotten compared to the "good old days" under the Maestro. But even the Italians were split into factions—we had Fascists and we had anti-Fascists. We had a few German Nazis and some German anti-Nazis. We had White Russians, and we had a few out-and-out Communists. And there was of course a sizable Jewish contingent who really banded together and kept their guard up toward the other factions, and who put up a real tough-guy facade, sometimes referring to themselves as the "Kosher Nostra." No, the Philharmonic was not one big happy family, I can assure you—all of these factions were constantly bickering and even getting into actual fights with one another.[1]

Thanks to the growing power of the Musicians' Union, the Philharmonic players enjoyed reasonable job security by the mid-1950s—occasional technical lapses and displays of intransigence were no longer grounds for dismissal, not that Mitropoulos would have fired anyone even if he could have. But that is not to say that working conditions were particularly good. The musicians were overworked and underpaid during the main season, and during the summer, except for the Lewisohn Stadium concerts and whatever freelance gigs they could land individually, their income dwindled to the point of real struggle, especially for the men with large families to support.

A rank-and-file New York Philharmonic player, circa 1955, was paid about six thousand dollars per year—roughly on par with the wages of a good plumber. First-chair players, of course, were paid more, but not a lot more; the thinking of management, apparently, was that the prestige of their positions compensated for the niggardly wages.

Because of the high-profile nature of the orchestra's Sunday radio broadcasts, the Sunday programs often were different, featuring, for example, a concerto-and-soloist combination intended to boost the ratings rather than purely orchestral fare. As a result, more often than not, the men had to drag themselves in for a Saturday rehearsal as well as a Sunday concert. Normal weekend activities, as enjoyed by other types of wage-earners and their families, were impossible, resulting in tension and stress at home which often carried over into Carnegie Hall.

Burn-out, emotional and psychological, was widespread among the Philharmonic's musicians. Most professional players begin their careers full of idealistic enthusiasm—they love music and can't wait to put body and soul into its performance. But there were few job openings that paid a living wage, and before a player got a chance to audition for an opening in Boston or Cleveland or New York, he or she would have to put in long seasons with second or third-tier orchestras, making ends meet by teaching, giving lessons, or selling insurance—whatever paid the bills.

Once such a player actually landed a job with a first-rank orchestra, that was usually the top of the ladder. Between the audition and retirement came fifteen, twenty, twenty-five years of routine. Hundreds of concerts under dozens of conductors—good, bad, indifferent—and the orchestral musician sooner or later felt stuck in a rut no longer very different from that endured by a factory worker, and often less well-paid. From a grudging acceptance of the routine, the journey was not far to cynicism and boredom. Given their workload and the stresses on their personal lives, it was logical that the Philharmonic players should manifest an extreme case of this syndrome.

Mitropoulos was keenly empathic to the players' circumstances and did whatever he could to make things better, happier, more full of the spirit of cooperation that was his fixed ideal of the conductor-orchestra relationship. One reason he took the controversial Roxy Theater dates, for example, was to give the men some additional paychecks during a lean time of the year.

He was the first conductor in the orchestra's history to make a policy of rotating the first- and second-chair players on programs that were especially demanding. The first-chair player would perform on the first half, then be able to go home at intermission, while the assistant would take over for the second half of the concert. In this way, the assistant got a chance to perform more solo parts, and the section leaders got a break.

There were displays of solidarity that endeared Mitropoulos to all but the most hard-bitten players. Ranier DeIntinis, a member of the horn section, remembered one such incident:

> He always gave very, very freely from his heart. He threw parties for us, he gave us gifts, and he did something quite remarkable for me. I got married two or three years after I got into the Philharmonic, and just on a lark, I sent him an invitation, never dreaming anything would come of it. But on the Saturday before the wedding, he called me up to his dressing room and said, "Okay, so how do I get there?" "You mean you're coming?" I stammered. "Oh yes, oh yes, of course." And he did. He stayed about a half-hour, long enough to wish everyone well and give his congratulations. He took a taxi all the way over to Brooklyn just to make that gesture.[2]

"He was very easy to talk to," DeIntinis continued:

> And his mode of discipline was simply not recognized as such by many players because it was such an easy, compassionate attempt to impose discipline. If something wasn't going right in the orchestra or with a soloist, he would say, "No, no, we have to be patient—after all, this man has a wife and children to think about, too; many things that he has to think about. So let's be patient and it will all work out fine." And, as far as I'm concerned, it always did—it was always fine in the end, when it counted. If a certain passage wasn't going right in rehearsals, he wouldn't scream and rant about it, he would just say: "No, no, this person has a problem, but if we just work quietly, it will come across." And sure enough, by the Thursday night performance, it was there. As far as I'm concerned, those were the glory days of the New York Philharmonic, and anyone who says the playing deteriorated under Mitropoulos is just plain wrong.[3]

Time and time again, in Oliver Daniel's interviews with retired members of the New York Philharmonic, except for a handful of hard-cases (who, one suspects, would have had nothing good to say about *any* conductor), virtually every man said something like this: "We loved playing under Mitropoulos. He was the kindest, most decent conductor who ever lived, and he would give you the shirt off his back." And yet an overwhelming body of published and anecdotal documentation bears witness to a gradual shift of the orchestra's attitude from grateful cooperation, in the first two or three seasons, to chronic insubordination, slackness, and petty cruelty toward the very man so many professed to love. By 1955, instead of responding in kind to their conductor's decency, kindness, and tolerance, many in the orchestra were openly taking advantage of those very qualities and behaving like spoiled children or petty thugs.

Everyone who worked in or performed with the Philharmonic seemed quite aware of this paradox, and everyone who responded thoughtfully to questions about it had a slightly different perspective.

Composer Gunther Schuller saw the Mitropoulos-Philharmonic relationship as a classic love-hate dichotomy:

> He did not have the ability to discipline the New York Philharmonic. The kind of discipline needed for some of those men was light-years away from his thinking. I, and many others who were close to him, believe that during his last years with the orchestra, both his physical and his emotional health were ruined by the aggravations the orchestra musicians inflicted upon him; they saw him as a softie. They really crucified that man in so many ways, and made fun of him on top of it—even though, in some perverse way, *they also loved him and respected him.* It was a curious kind of love-hate relationship, born, I think, of the circumstances of the Philharmonic's history. They had endured the twin tyrannies of Toscanini and Rodzinski, and then along comes this sweet man who just wanted to make music. And he had no idea at all how to control all those diverse, multinational, conflicting people in the orchestra.
>
> Remember that Rodzinski started off by firing a significant percentage of the whole orchestra, and there was a lot of rough stuff going on behind the scenes the whole time he was there; when Mitropoulos came to them, they saw their chance to win, to take over, and so, gradually, they began to step all over him. I'm not a psychologist, but I think it's fair to say that Mitropoulos was in some ways a masochist. In every case, he did not fight back—no matter what they did to him. He embodied the principle of turning the other cheek. He just took it, whatever anybody meted out to him.
>
> The astonishing thing is how much great music he was *able* to make without being a tyrant like Szell or Reiner. He could take the exact opposite approach and do things like *Wozzeck* and the Webern symphony, against the will of the entire orchestra, the management, and everybody else in New York, and do it in such a way that the music scored a triumph. That took such love and commitment and perseverance, in his soft but dedicated way. It's probably one of the more remarkable phenomena in the annals of music-making.[4]

To violinist Louis Krasner, the situation reflected the danger of emotional burn-out and concomitant cynicism to which all professional musicians can become prey:

> Once you're at that point in your career, what is there that can rekindle the poet in you, ignite that long-ago enthusiasm? It helps if you can play solo, or chamber music, but if you only play in an orchestra, this problem arises for almost every player. The more they see the enthusiasm of

the conductor—the more it expresses his personal feelings—the more they become jealous and resentful that they can no longer relate to music in the same way.

Mitropoulos absolutely understood this, and that is one reason why he devoted so much thought and concern to the welfare of his players. He felt so in debt to them, and so *guilty*. He once said to me, "You know why I work so hard? It's because I'm in a bastard profession, a dishonest profession. The others make all the music and I get the salary and the credit for it." And so he simply didn't *keep* the salary and usually spurned the credit. Every spring, someone would have to lend him money because he didn't have enough to pay his taxes. He had nothing when he died, and I believe he felt he deserved nothing. . . . He provided them with the whips that they used to scourge him.[5]

There were of course some men in the Philharmonic who saw what was happening and who were deeply upset by it. Leonard Rose was one: "I felt very badly about the fact that the Philharmonic, after a certain point, didn't really try to play their best for him. It's not because they didn't *like* him, many of them, it was just that he was simply too nice. And to be too nice to the Philharmonic, that just doesn't work."[6]

It could be argued that at least one "nice" conductor got along with the Philharmonic—Bruno Walter—but even that situation was not what it appeared to be on the surface. Walter would smile and coax and gently admonish at rehearsals, never raising his voice, always the gentleman; but he kept careful mental track of which players did not behave and as soon as rehearsal was over, he was in Zirato's office naming names and recounting offenses. Walter was a useful figurehead for the orchestra, so the offending players would be privately admonished, or threatened, and some semblance of discipline was maintained.

Incompetence or slack performance during rehearsal did not go unnoticed by Mitropoulos—it simply brought no punishment. Rose approached the conductor after one particularly unfortunate rehearsal and asked him: "Maestro, why don't you take these passages a little slower and demand that the men play them properly?" Mitropoulos hung his head a little bit and muttered: "I don't really want to. I would . . ." His voice trailed off, but Rose was certain he had been about to say: "I would incur resentment; I would not be thought of as a nice guy."

Rose contrasted this to Rodzinski's methods:

> If that sort of thing happened in a Rodzinski rehearsal—let's say the strings botched some difficult passage in a Strauss composition—he would stop everything and demand: "First violins alone!" They would play it. "Phooie!" Rodzinski would growl. "That was bad. Spell it out." He would begin to conduct again, slowly. If things still didn't sound good, he would stop and say: "Terrible! Outside players alone." They would play it. "Awful! Inside alone. Dreadful! Last three stands alone.

Terrible, terrible!" Then he would put down his baton and glare at the strings and say: "Gentlemen, if it's not better tomorrow, you'll each play it solo!" By God, the next day it would sound better. Mitropoulos just couldn't lean on them that way. I know it's become a cliche, but it's true: if you're going to get the Philharmonic to play well for you, you have to sit on them and be tough and not give a damn what they think of you personally.[7]

Sometimes it was the best players who took the most advantage of their conductor. According to Louis Krasner:

Part of the trouble is that Mitropoulos was so gentle with all his good players, whom he loved very much. The first-chair players above all. I know of many instances when someone would come to him, before a particularly demanding concert, and say: "You know I can't play so much demanding music and still be at my best for the entire concert. Could you relieve me from playing in this concerto on the last half of the concert, let me go home early?" And usually, he would say: "Sure, take it." I know for a fact that some of the men he treated that way left Carnegie Hall and used that period of free time to play commercial gigs elsewhere, often for radio.[8]

Probably the most egregious example of advantage-taking involved the Philharmonic's first-chair trumpet, William Vacchiano. There were too many inaccuracies in his playing, and too little initiative on his part to correct them. When Mitropoulos talked to him about the problem, Vacchiano claimed that his embouchure—his lip—was suffering because he had to play so many exhausting commercial jobs away from the Philharmonic, just to support his family. Mitropoulos was deeply sympathetic and promised Vacchiano he would speak to the management on his behalf and try to obtain a raise, so that the orchestra's principal trumpet would be able to focus on his Philharmonic activities; and if the raise didn't go through, or was not enough, Mitropoulos personally would make up the difference, on a weekly basis.

For some months afterwards, Mitropoulos supplemented Vacchiano's income out of his own salary. In the meantime, Vacchiano was pocketing the cash and still taking every freelance gig he could find. The scam continued until the day Mitropoulos walked backstage and observed Mrs. Vacchiano showing off a brand new mink coat. The stipends stopped, but Vacchiano was neither punished nor repentant.

Many players took advantage of Mitropoulos's gentleness and generosity, although few were as blatant about it as Vacchiano. Harold Gomberg, the Philharmonic's renowned oboist, talked Mitropoulos into financing a summer trip to Europe, ostensibly to study with some European colleagues, and then spent the entire time pursuing his hobby of oil painting. Gomberg mostly stayed apolitical in the gathering power struggle between pro- and anti-Mitropoulos factions, but he was quick to see which way the wind was blowing and to align himself for maximum advantage. In the final days of Mitropoulos's directorship, Gomberg turned on his benefactor with inexplicable viciousness.

New York Times critic Harold Schonberg witnessed one such incident:

> Gomberg—wow! He could really be brutal. I was at one rehearsal . . . and at one point Mitropoulos stopped the orchestra and politely asked Gomberg if he would re-phrase his part a certain way. Which Gomberg did, but not to the conductor's satisfaction. Mitropoulos stopped again and said, "No, no, Mr. Gomberg, you didn't quite get the idea." And Gomberg looked him straight in the eye and snarled: "If you think you can play it better, come out here and do it yourself." I was astonished. And if I had been the conductor, and a player gave me that kind of sass, I would have sent him packing.[9]

As one fellow-woodwind player put it, on condition of anonymity:

> Harold was a superb instrumentalist, of course, but he always wanted to be treated differently from everybody else. He was personally very boorish, I thought. And I'll never forget how several of us heard him muttering imprecations and "Good riddances" after one of the last concerts with Mitropoulos. I mean, here was this conductor who had been so nice to him, so accommodating, who had actually given him rather a lot of money, and Mitropoulos already had his walking papers, so what was the point in bad-mouthing him like that?

Gomberg's attitude can actually be heard in pirate recordings of the Mahler Third performance of April 15, 1956. His playing, especially at the start of the fourth movement, is so substandard, so patently beneath Gomberg's level of skill, that it can only be deliberate artistic sabotage.

If the Mitropoulos-must-go movement had a ring leader within the orchestra, that individual would have been William Lincer, the first-chair violist. As one colleague expressed it: "Lincer was anti-everybody, but with particular venom towards Mitropoulos."

When Howard Taubman's lethal diatribe was published in April 1956, Leonard Rose was startled to see that many of Taubman's specific accusations repeated, word for word, some of the things Lincer had been saying to other Philharmonic men. Rose realized at once that Lincer had been feeding Taubman a lot of inside information, much of it exaggerated and much of it derived from innuendo rather than fact—knowingly giving Taubman the ammunition he needed to mortally wound Mitropoulos. "I thought it was a rotten, lousy thing to do, a really stinking set-up," Rose told Oliver Daniel in 1984.

Lincer scarcely mellowed with age, as Oliver Daniel's 1985 interview proved. Lincer began by casting aspersions on Mitropoulos's basic competence as a musician, in terms not even Taubman dared to use:

We were never sure he knew what notes he was playing. We never knew whether he knew the notes accurately because he used to do everything from memory. For example, if he wanted to do twenty-three measures before letter P, he would put his hand up to his forehead and mentally turn the score pages back and forth until he found letter P, and then he would tell you what note it was. Nine times out of ten, it was the wrong note. We didn't know whether he could read music, or whether he was really just going by the rhythm.[10]

Composer Seymour Barab once discussed the "discipline" problem with Julius Baker, the Philharmonic's first flute: "I said, 'Julie, what the hell do you guys need discipline for—you're a disciplined musician already, aren't you?' And he replied, 'Well, yeah, I am, but some of the other guys...'"[11]

Leonard Bernstein's description of the so-called decline of the orchestra under Mitropoulos may be taken as a gospel summation of the arguments advanced by the anti-Mitropoulos faction, both within and without the Philharmonic:

> As time went on, Dimitri began to hear more and more in his head what it was he conducted, rather than what was actually coming out. This, combined with his sweet, relaxed relationship with the orchestra, led to something awful, which was the men taking advantage of him, their not ever practicing, their not playing in tune, their not trying to be together. It was a kind of laissez-faire, with empty houses as a result.
>
> There was no audience-orchestra relationship when I arrived. The audience felt remote and left out. People came to a concert, and there would be Dimitri playing a Shostakovich symphony, then a desultory performance of Mozart, although once and a while, brilliant performances—like his Mahler Ninth, *Wozzeck*—things that really engaged him, and nobody could master them that way, and have such fluidity and such instinctive ease. It was really extraordinary. At those moments the orchestra would recover its old fire and love, and it would all work. Then he would go all overboard, program a piece by Ralph Shapey and cancel it because he had bitten off more than he could chew.
>
> As a result of this, with the exception of those very memorable moments, the concerts had become something of a bore. The audience had drifted away, and those that remained felt alienated.[12]

Insofar as the music-loving public of the late twentieth-century thinks of Mitropoulos at all, it is in terms of Bernstein's remarks: a volatile interpreter, capable of magnificent set-piece musical events, like the Mahler symphonies or the concert versions of operas, but not a leader capable of holding either the audience or the orchestra's attention on a week to week basis; and an indifferent disciplinarian under whom the Philharmonic deteriorated grossly.

In fact, if one reads the reviews in chronological order, one sees only a moderate increase in the number of bad-playing incidents mentioned right up until the end of Mitropoulos's tenure, when he was already known to be on his way out. Some of the studio recordings made in the final months of his stewardship—when the orchestra was supposedly falling apart—capture playing that is not only equal to the highest professional standards, but that is palpably richer, more involved, and more characterful than what one hears at the average Philharmonic concert today.

Others who were present during these last, strained years of the Mitropoulos era, 1955–1958, heard little if any actual deterioration. Gunther Schuller:

> The Philharmonic did *not* deteriorate under Mitropoulos. I know because I lived in Carnegie Hall during those years, and I not only played with the orchestra from time to time, but I went to every one of his concerts. Instead of any long-term deterioration, what occasionally manifested itself was obviously attributable to the fact that the players took advantage of Dimitri's generosity and played badly because of that. Frankly, the Philharmonic "deteriorated" much more under Lenny—one of whose problems was that he wanted *everybody* to love him, and he wanted to be "one of the boys" from the very first rehearsal, and that's something you can't do with the Philharmonic.[13]

Schuller cited the Anton Webern symphony as a prime example. Here was a piece the entire orchestra hated on sight. Mitropoulos not only conducted in a clarifying manner, he actually *taught* the score the way a spiritual leader would teach precepts, until the musicians began to see the light.

> The performance is ravishing. Even thirty years later, there is no commercial recording that comes close. My point is that when it came to those performances, somehow his conviction that this was a masterpiece and that he and the orchestra now held it in their sacred trust, compelled them to produce not just a correct performance but a beautiful one. He got a sound out of those violins—even though I was there and saw it happen, I wouldn't be able to tell you in precise detail how he did that. The only way to describe it is as a form of hypnosis. . . . Stokowski did something similar, but it was not with this gentle, pure, quasi-religious manner that Mitropoulos had. I mean, no one was ever afraid of Mitropoulos, as they *were* afraid of Stokie, or Reiner or Szell. Now if fear is absent, then the only explanation for readings such as that Webern piece lies in Mitropoulos's extraordinary ability to convince people that now we must do this, both correctly and beautifully. No, the Philharmonic did not deteriorate during his time and if people are saying that, they should be strenuously opposed and argued-against.[14]

Another long-term witness to the Mitropoulos era was Oliver Daniel, who, as broadcast producer, had to attend both concerts and rehearsals:

So many people say the orchestra went down terribly under [Mitro-poulos], but I was there, riveted to the score so some sudden increase in volume wouldn't knock us off the air. And I never heard any of that so-called "deterioration." Once in a while, you could tell when a player was goofing off or being recalcitrant, but that's not the same thing as a degradation of the whole ensemble. I repeat: I was there; I heard more of that orchestra's playing than any critic in New York, and I heard no deterioration.[15]

There emerges a paradox: more and more reviews mention ragged en-semble, sloppy pizzicatos, rough tone, and eccentric interpretational liber-ties—and yet there is emphatic testimony from some very experienced mu-sicians, as well as the more objective testimony of recordings made during Mitropoulos's last seasons as music director, that the overall playing of the Philharmonic did not deteriorate.

Perhaps the issue boils down to *perception*. What Gunther Schuller and Oliver Daniel—persons who, after all, heard much more of the orchestra's playing than did even the most influential critics—heard as discrete in-stances of misbehavior by individuals or cliques, other listeners interpreted as evidence of institutional decline. Listeners who responded primarily to the breadth and impact of an interpretation did not *mind* the momentary lapses, the lack of uniform bowing, nor were they particularly bothered by Mitropoulos's erratic ventures into the basic repertoire—if the man could give stunning performances of *Elektra* and *Wozzeck*, his peculiarities with Brahms or Mozart were relatively unimportant. The musical world is, and always has been, full of sporadically interesting Brahms conductors, but the virtues of Mitropoulos were much rarer and more precious.

One thing is clear from the surviving reviews: once the anti-Mitropou-los faction began *saying* that the orchestra had gone bad, more and more people started to accept it as being true. What began as a factoid gradually became a symptom: the more the Philharmonic players read about how bad they and their conductor were, the more unsteady their day-to-day per-formances became. As more and more negative comments appeared in re-views of Taubman, Lang, and Sargent, so too did they begin to appear more frequently in the reviews of less powerful critics.

Bernstein's other allegation—that the audiences had started to feel left out and alienated—holds up more strongly and reflects where the true "de-terioration" happened to be: in the conductor's heart.

Mitropoulos's conducting had been grounded on an article of faith that had, until now, seemed rock-solid: that the conductor was not a dictator but a partner in a cooperative creative enterprise, a colleague who should lead through example, persuasion, and love rather than fear. He and the orchestra became, in effect, brother-celebrants at a kind of artistic mass.

And in Minneapolis, that creed had worked—with most of the players, most of the time. In New York, it had worked with some of the players for a while, but as the seasons went by in all their demanding routine, it finally became apparent to Mitropoulos that his philosophy was often in conflict with, if not actually contradicted by, the palpable realities of his situation: a brutal and unrelenting friction that took its toll gradually, week by week, like a spiritual water-torture.

The very foundations of Mitropoulos's art, the beliefs that made him capable of galvanizing a recalcitrant orchestra into radiant performances of works the players actually hated, were gradually undermined. He had *nothing else* to cling to, but maintaining his philosophical stance—in the face of so much evidence that it was bankrupt as far as the New York Philharmonic went—exacted a terrible toll on his nerves and emotions. He had to persuade himself that he was still getting through to the men and the audience, long after it became painfully obvious to outside observers that, most of the time, he was not.

Is it any wonder that, by 1956, his week-by-week performances had become so erratic, so nakedly dependent for their success or failure on his personal swings of mood? When Bernstein asserted that the objective, audible results of a routine subscription concert were markedly different from what Mitropoulos was hearing in his head, he was close to the mark indeed. And on some level (a level which apparently fluctuated almost as much as the conductor's mood swings), Mitropoulos could not help but be aware of the disparity between his fiercely clung-to vision and the actual musical results he was sometimes getting. Yet he could not compromise this aspect of his art any more than he could renounce God or St. Francis; his aesthetic beliefs occupied the same deep psychic terrain as his religious convictions and he could not, while he drew breath, abandon either.

And the consequences of that faith were, by 1956, literally killing him. More to the point in terms of his viability as music director, they were slowly asphyxiating the box office. Subscriptions were in decline; often, the orchestra played to a hall that was half full or less. Although an objective statistical analysis of Mitropoulos's New York repertoire shows that the percentage of new and difficult works on his programs was not, by the standards of a major orchestra and its cultural responsibilities, excessive, still the *reputation* for indigestible programs had grown, by the mid-1950s, to harmful dimensions. Casual music-lovers just assumed there would be something on any Mitropoulos-led concert that they would dislike, and many of them opted to stay home and watch television rather than taking the trouble to go to midtown Manhattan.

To make matters worse, many who did attend, sensed that ideal-versus-reality dichotomy that Bernstein alluded to. Many of Mitropoulos's mid-1950s readings of basic repertoire items sound either strained and bloated (Mozart) or dryly businesslike (Brahms and Tchaikovsky)—the work of a conductor who either has his mind elsewhere or who has grown terminally bored with the composition at hand and is just going through the motions.

Of the conductor's particular strengths and weaknesses, none came under closer scrutiny than his supposed indifference to the highest standards of technique and orchestral discipline—qualities that had become virtual critical fetishes by 1955, thanks to the elevation of Toscanini to the status of demigod.

It is demonstrably true that Mitropoulos did not labor to put the finest possible technical polish on his performances and to those for whom this was a primary matter, it was a dark sin indeed. But to others, the dotting of every *i* and crossing of every *t* in a score was of much less consequence than the aesthetic, philosophical, even moral, heights the conductor sought to reach in performance. Gunther Schuller expressed the matter eloquently:

> There were things like bowing discipline about which he seldom concerned himself at all. He felt that that was the domain of the concertmaster; and in this kind of technical matter he not only displayed little patience but also insufficient knowledge. He could not give the strings bowing instructions that would produce the results he was hearing in his head. He never bothered to acquire that kind of technical knowledge because he felt, "that's *their* job, I don't need to do it." I rarely heard him give any really technical advice to any of the players. His belief was: "I've got my job, up here leading, and your job is to play your instrument properly and since you're a member of a great orchestra, you presumably know how to do that."
>
> Some players criticized him for that, but I personally preferred that kind of leeway and responsibility to the sort of technical meddling some conductors inflict on you. Szell, for instance, gave me *fingerings* for God's sake, as if I didn't know the fingerings of my French horn, of which there are only three anyway! The arrogance of that man! I can't recall a single instance of anything like that with Mitropoulos. Musicians criticized him for it, thinking that this was some kind of great weakness in Dimitri. But the weakness was theirs, for not wanting to bear the responsibilities his conducting style laid upon them.[16]

Jim Fassett, announcer for the Philharmonic radio broadcasts, believed that Mitropoulos was deeply unhappy with his situation even before the murderous Howard Taubman attack in April 1956. "It is no secret," Fassett wrote in his unpublished autobiography,

> that Mitropoulos's last years with the Philharmonic were unhappy ones for him. The atmosphere of dissention and criticism had become increasingly intolerable to a temperament so sensitive and vulnerable. Critics who esteemed him as a musician, and praised him for his perseverance in promoting new music, often found fault with his

performances, particularly with his interpretations of the classics. Rubatos were exaggerated, secondary and tertiary lines profiled too sharply, details lifted out of their context into disproportionate focus. In short, he over-conducted, and more often than not, his concept of a symphony or a tone poem *as a whole*, foundered in the process and never reached the listener at all.[17]

But Fassett and other close observers were certain that these concepts were always clear to Mitropoulos himself. He did not hear music as most people do when their minds start working on sounds perceived through their ears. That kind of aural stimulus was not necessary to him. His perception of a piece began when he saw the patterns of musical symbols on the pages of the score, and his apprehension of the sound-configurations was formed during the process of committing them to memory. Mitropoulos once said something to that effect when conversing with Fassett:

> He told me that he could "hear" a composition while climbing a mountain or walking in the park as completely as he could when he heard it performed in the concert hall or on a phonograph record. Actually, I think he "heard" it much better, because his comprehension of a piece was far more cerebral than emotional. His attempts to reproduce his concept of a composition in orchestral sound was almost bound to fail. The skeleton was there, but putting flesh on it involved the unpredictable and undependable human factor, the cooperation of musicians producing sounds on a large body of purely mechanical instruments. And this striving to reach the ideal, to recreate, for others to hear, the full aural imagery of what had already unfolded, in minutest detail in his own mind, may account for his over-conducting, and by the same token, for his frustration at rehearsals when he felt the players had failed him. "How can you do this to me?" he would plead, wringing his hands, sometimes on the verge of tears.[18]

Composer Morton Gould thought that Mitropoulos's strengths and weaknesses reflected a basic musical instinct too deeply embedded to change:

> It was not that he was an undisciplined musician—he knew every damn note of those scores. But in the actual interpretation, he had this rhapsodic, galvanizing quality when he was in top form. But the downside of that, is that this kind of improvisational performer can sometimes end up with a performance that has a lot of loose ends, that just doesn't come off for one reason or another—the wrong time, the wrong place, the wrong orchestra, whatever it might be. And with the Philharmonic, it could be any or all of those things.[19]

But even after Mitropoulos had stepped down as music director, there were still nights when it all came together; when the conductor was "on," the music was right, and the players were trying. And those nights were unforgettable, according to soprano Frances Greer:

> The first time I actually looked at Mitropoulos during a performance, during a passage in which I was not active, it was as though he had been transformed. He wasn't the same man I knew back at the Great Northern or backstage. His demeanor, his aspect—all of him—was transcendental. It seemed to me that he was exposing his spirit, his very soul, and it was so compelling and so personal, that I could not continue to look at him. It was like looking at the sun.[20]

Gunther Schuller experienced many such moments:

> When he conducted, there simply was nothing else around: there was no auditorium, there was no air, there were no people, there was just the music. When it all worked, it generated a kind of commitment in return from the musicians—you simply had to give, because he mesmerized you. He didn't get you to play because you were being paid or because there was a piece of music in front of you. He simply compelled you to come into his world. Even the most dastardly cynics in the New York Philharmonic—he sometimes conquered them by the sheer force of his personality.
>
> Now I know there are a lot of old Philharmonic musicians who complained that he had a lousy "technique" and was hard to follow. Let me just tell you, those were lazy musicians—or poor musicians—who needed to have everything laid out on a platter for them so they could relax and do their little bits of playing and go home. Yes, you had to meet Mitropoulos half way, and I never had any trouble following him, even in very complex scores.[21]

Schuller never forgot one concert, in which he played third horn for a performance of Rachmaninoff's lush and melodramatic Symphony No. 2. If Berg's music brought out the intellectual in Mitropoulos, Rachmaninoff's brought out the sensualist. "He almost swam in it," Schuller recalled; "it was almost an orgy."

> Anyway, there's this really heroic part in the first movement, where the horns play in unison. Just a bar or so before the horns' entrance, he turned to us and I saw the following: he was in such a state of ecstasy and paroxysm that he looked at us as if he were some Old Testament prophet crying in the desert. He was staring *through* us and into the music—it was like some seer peering into the soul of musical truth. The intensity of his involvement was such that his eyes crossed and the skin on his head started sort of pulling and going up and down as though the brain beneath were responding to the sounds. At that moment, I was completely overwhelmed. I kept playing, of course—I *had* to!—but there were tears running out of my eyes as I did so. That kind of thing

could happen with Mitropoulos, at any time, in any piece of music. He would burn his soul through you at those moments, and I swear to God, it didn't matter *what* his "beat" looked like; it could have been sideways or upside down or not visible at all—when he seized you that way, you simply had to give him your all. Those eyes and that bald head—like some kind of supernatural beacon. Those moments were truly like religious experiences.[22]

At some point, the question must be addressed: what part of Mitropoulos's problems with the New York Philharmonic can be attributed to simple homophobia?

There is no precise answer, of course; yet the impression one gets from reading dozens of interviews with musicians who were on the scene suggests that the conductor's sexual orientation was no secret to the men of the Philharmonic, and that it contributed significantly to the gradual undermining of Mitropoulos's authority.

No problems seem to have arisen in Minneapolis, for the simple reason that the conductor apparently stayed celibate during the months he lived there, and only indulged himself, very occasionally, during tours to other cities; many people knew or at least suspected that Mitropoulos was gay, but since there was no outward manifestation of that lifestyle, no scandals revealed or hushed-up, it required no great effort to pretend that the conductor's bachelorhood was simply a by-product of his priestly dedication to his art. Given the general level of sexual sophistication obtaining in the Midwest in the 1940s, it is doubtful if most of the Minneapolis audience ever gave the matter a second thought. In the tough, worldly wise environment of New York, however, that married-to-his-music dodge probably didn't fool anybody for very long.

Once the notion that Mitropoulos was gay had taken hold of the orchestra's collective imagination, the way was open for the inevitably exaggerated speculations, the nudge-nudge badinage, the telling of jokes, the propagation of rumors, and their inflation to grotesque proportions. Even the music critics joined in, though not, of course, in print. Winthrop Sargent, the powerful critic for *The New Yorker*, used to tell listeners that "Mitropoulos has had every bellboy in the Great Northern Hotel"—a canard as vicious as it was untrue.

There was a terrible irony at work here, in that *most* of the conductor's sexual drive was, and always had been, sublimated ruthlessly into his music-making. It was in those transcendent moments of pure artistic communion with his orchestras that he achieved an almost tantric state of erotic grace, moments of being so saturated with procreative tension and release that they were, in a very real sense, spiritual orgasms.

He had always been very frank about the sexual element in his conducting, often to the acute discomfort of interviewers, especially those who were talking to him in front of an open radio mike. "One must make love to the players," he would say, a metaphysical concept that ran headlong into the deeply macho traditions of the New York Philharmonic. He even did it on television, when he remarked to Edward R. Murrow that when he conducted, he tried to "reach the soul of the musician—in an amorous way—to reach more than his soul, to reach his love." One can only speculate ruefully about the response made by the orchestra's tough-guys when they heard *that* coming from their television sets.

Mitropoulos was never more plainspoken about this phenomenon than he was in a letter to Katy Katsoyanis written in the summer of 1952:

> Believe me, I came to the point of being very, very tolerant when I hear someone else playing music, if he feels it differently from the way I do. I cannot have the courage to accuse anybody for feeling less intensely or liking straightforward things or being afraid to laugh too loud or cry too loud, but I still thank God that I don't tolerate myself to stop being myself, because for me music is another expression of my unlived sexual life, and just as, in such a case, I presume, one is free to express oneself at home in a closed room, I do it on the stage where I feel I am alone in front of a partner with whom I exchange my feelings.[23]

There was, of course, a sizable homosexual subculture in New York—then as now—and if there was any place in the world where Mitropoulos could be himself, it was there. But he was not a great deal more comfortable socializing with groups of gay people than he was attending cocktail parties filled with Manhattan socialites. Only a very few friends, Ned Rorem and David Diamond among them, ever glimpsed the full extent of the conductor's Dionysian torment. He envied Diamond's candor and his fierce, defiant pride. "David, I admire you greatly," he once said: "I think it is a triumph that you came to grips with it so early, that you are always so proud, and that you suffer for it so much."

Overwhelmingly, however, the anecdotal evidence suggests that, in New York as in Minneapolis, Mitropoulos was mostly as chaste and monkish as his public image suggested he was. The indications are very strong that after his first heart attack, he entered a state of celibacy from which he rarely, perhaps never, departed.

Orchestral gossip and innuendo aside, Mitropoulos went to Forty-second Street to see movies, not to cruise. Michael Landis, a Greek-American professional acquaintance and admirer of the conductor, was not naive about Mitropoulos's sexual orientation, but thought that

> he seemed absolutely as straight as could be. In those days Forty-second Street was a very safe place at night—crowded, colorful, and pleasant. I heard it said many times that Mitropoulos went to that part of town to cruise and pick up somebody. I must say that when I was there, I saw him quite often and I never saw anything peculiar going on—I am

very observant, and I assure you, if there was any hanky-panky going on, I would have noticed. No such thing ever crossed my mind, and why should it? I frequented those movie houses at night myself, and I am not a homosexual. Besides, thousands of people went to those theaters, just to relax after work. To say that Mitropoulos went there for anything other than the movies is nonsense. The maestro was there because he, like me, was a night person.[24]

Maxim Gershunoff thought that "Mitropoulos's interest in young people, people such as that kid Anson Mount whom he brought up from White Bluff, Tennessee, was something that may have generated some social condemnation or whispering about his private life *if he had had one*, which as far as I could tell, he simply did not have."[25]

And yet the perception continued to exist, fed by jokes, innuendo, and malice, that Mitropoulos was some kind of rapacious libertine. Leonard Bernstein, in his ongoing campaign to gain control of the Philharmonic, contributed to the stigma by telling everyone he could that the orchestra would be much better off with a married man, a family man—himself, for instance—at its head. Bernstein could smugly, if hypocritically, point to his own marriage and his offspring, and project an image of probity and wholesomeness.

Here was a bitter injustice indeed: the more Mitropoulos behaved like a celibate hermit, the more imaginary sins were attributed to him. He and Gershunoff discussed the problem one time, and Mitropoulos lamented: "What a pity that I am condemned for luxuries I do not have the time to afford!"[26]

Mitropoulos-watchers observed that the conductor was so engulfed by his mission, not to mention the remorseless diurnal demands of his job, that he seldom had a chance to enjoy a carefree day of loafing, visiting, or just going for a walk in Central Park. "One of the saddest things you sensed about him," recalled author and music publisher Hans Heinsheimer, "was that Dimitri just never had any *fun*."[27]

Even those who worked with him on a daily basis, and who enjoyed the most cordial personal relations, felt that their moments of true friendship with Mitropoulos were sporadic and fragile—as though the conductor shied away due to a condition of near-pathological vulnerability. Jim Fassett, the mellow-voiced announcer of the Philharmonic's radio broadcasts, probably socialized with Mitropoulos as much as anyone, yet he too found the moments of genuine closeness to be few and fleeting, and often touched with melancholy.

"He was a soft touch," wrote Fassett in his unpublished memoirs:

Everyone knew it and too many took advantage of it, and yet his true friends were few. Though he longed for genuine friendship, he seldom possessed it. . . . The musicians of the orchestra adored him as a person and admired him as a conductor, but as an artist the divide between them was never really breached. Mitropoulos was the idealist, a mystic dwelling in his ivory tower, and though they regarded him with esteem, they did so from a distance, and from below. Nor did they always demonstrate their respect for him as a conductor by giving their utmost in rehearsals or playing their best in concerts. Such deplorable behavior was a thorn in his side, and he suffered bearing it.[28]

On one occasion, when Fassett had made an appointment to go over a broadcast interview idea with Mitropoulos, he arrived about five minutes late at the La Scala restaurant. Fassett paused a moment to observe the conductor in one of his natural states: bare-headed, wearing slacks, an open-collared plaid shirt, and sandals, pacing slowly up and down the sidewalk and reading intently from a small leatherbound book held close to his formidable nose. Fassett marveled at the utter concentration of the man as he strode to and fro on the busy midtown sidewalk, oblivious to everything except his book, while numerous pedestrians—some annoyed, others amused—were compelled to step around him. Not once did he look up, even when Fassett came close enough to see the title of the book: the *Summa Theologia* of St. Thomas Aquinas.

Mitropoulos's loneliness, his extreme vulnerability to even the most guileless gesture of affection, was brought home to Fassett one day when he called the conductor at his Great Northern suite and asked if he might be free for lunch. He was, and accepted the invitation without a moment's hesitation. They agreed on the hour and place; then, as Fassett was hanging up, Mitropoulos asked a question that made Fassett wince.

"Tell me, my dear, what is the luncheon about? What is it I can do for you?"

Fassett was stunned at this glimpse into the paths along which Mitropoulos's thoughts had to be channeled. After a few seconds of embarrassed hesitation, he replied: "Why, it's not 'about' anything Dimitri. I would just like to have lunch with you, for the pleasure of your company. That's all."

There was no reply. "Did you hear me, Dimitri?" Still silence. "Dimitri? Did you hear me?"

When he replied, the conductor's voice was husky. "Yes, I heard you, Jim. You see, it's so seldom that anyone does this kind of thing for me—I feel, somehow, *released*."[29]

One of the crueler ironies of Mitropoulos's situation was the fact that if he had been sexually attracted to women, he would not have been lonely at all—or at least no more lonely than he chose to be. Throughout his career, he exerted a powerful sexual attraction for precisely the sort of sensitive, intelligent females whose company he most enjoyed. He was not, of course, attractive in the matinee-idol sense—no one would ever have described him as being handsome—but to the sort of woman who perceives deeper beauty, his presence could be devastating. The coarse, earthy sensuality of his features was complemented by an aura of physical strength and grace, and he was one of those men whose virility actually seems enhanced by baldness. Add to this his husky, cello-toned voice, with its light but exotic European accent, his remarkably clear yet penetrating blue eyes, and his charismatic role as a superstar conductor, and he was quite a tempting figure of a man—especially for ladies who harbored fantasies of being attractive enough to change his status as a bachelor.

He was not unaware of his power to attract the opposite sex, and from time to time in letters or conversation, he entertained the possibility of actually marrying. Certainly such a union would have made his life less complicated in many ways and, after all, there was the example of Leonard Bernstein, whose marriage served to deflect rumors of homosexuality and helped to make Bernstein an attractive candidate for music director of the Philharmonic. But Mitropoulos's yearning for domesticity never lasted long; he was too fundamentally honest to enter into such a hypocritical relationship and had he done so, the marriage would likely have been as short-lived and as miserable as Tchaikovsky's.

Mitropoulos did not have much free time, but on some nights, when his restless spirit drove him to leave the confines of his Great Northern lair, he did what many lonely artists have done: he walked the streets of New York. Otto Luening remembered that:

> he used to put on a cap and an old overcoat and go wandering around the Bowery, because he wanted to keep in touch with the wretched of the earth; he did not want to lose his ability to feel compassion for people who were more unfortunate. I guess he came back from those walks with a clearer understanding of his place in the great scheme of things, and probably with empty pockets, too, since he gave money to any indigent that approached him.[30]

The conductor's passion for all-night movies remained in full force, and there were innumerable theaters in New York where he could indulge himself. By the mid-1950s, however, it was difficult to find the old-fashioned westerns that were his favorite fare. Jazz impresario George Avakian, husband of violinist Anahid Ajemian, remembered seeing Mitropoulos squinting painfully at the small print ads in the *Times*, searching for obscure out-of-the-way movie houses that might be showing reruns of a favorite oater, muttering to himself, "They just don't make good westerns any more."

If he couldn't find a western, almost anything else would do. Pianist Earl Wild had a vivid memory of trekking to Forty-second Street one night to catch a late show of *Ben Hur*. Just before the picture started, a seedy-looking drunk wandered into the theater, reeled around a few times, then finally collapsed in the empty seat next to Mitropoulos, who winced not only at this intrusion of his personal space, but at the odor coming from the man. As the credits started rolling, the drunk reached over and slapped Mitropoulos heartily on the back, saying: "How ya doin' tonight, Baldy?"

Wild thought the incident was hilarious; Mitropoulos was not amused. The interloper eventually staggered off to an empty row of seats and the two men were able to concentrate on the biblical epic, wallowing in its sweeping Miklos Rozsa soundtrack. As Wild remembered the evening:

> There's this one scene where Charles Laughton, playing Pontius Pilate, calls Ben Hur (Charleton Heston) before him, and Heston stands there all glistening and muscular in his leather harness and little tunic, and Laughton just ogles him up and down with an unmistakably lascivious leer. Mitropoulos leaned over to me and whispered: "He really likes him, you know." Uh-hunh, I said. "No," Dimitri whispered, "I mean he *really likes him*."[31]

If there was one place in Manhattan where Mitropoulos felt completely at home, it was the La Scala Restaurant, located at 142 West Fifty-fourth Street. Mitropoulos was an investor in the founding of La Scala, whose owners he had come to know when they worked for another restaurant. La Scala's reputation spread fast, once it became known that the Philharmonic's conductor was a regular patron, usually in company with other musical celebrities.

The tone of the place suited him; it was a family business, managed with great pride, specializing in Northern Italian cuisine. Its proximity to Carnegie Hall attracted a great many musicians, and the prices were reasonable enough so that ordinary players could eat there sometimes, along with more illustrious guests. Above all else, La Scala had a tradition of warmth, as though its patrons were all part of some extended family of honorary Italians. Arturo Mirtallo, the manager and co-owner, looked after his regulars. The first thing Mitropoulos did upon entering was to place his worry-beads on his table, marking his territory; then he walked back into the kitchen to greet Orlando Sabatini, the chef, who had served in the Italian army in Greece and who could speak Greek fluently. From the kitchen, Mitropoulos went to the bar, where he was served an ungodly concoction christened (and still served under the name) the Dimitri Cocktail. According to Mirtallo, the drink consisted of two-thirds grappa and one-third vermouth, accented with a twist of lemon. Mitropoulos seemed to thrive on this beverage, but nearly everyone else who tried it reported that it tasted like motor oil. Some of the dishes he enjoyed were beef stew with fava beans, squab, baked Alaska, and a seemingly ghastly specialty made from ricotta cheese, ground coffee, sugar, and rum.

More than the maestro's gustatory peculiarities, Mirtallo remembered Mitropoulos for his warmth and generosity:

> There was a boy who used to deliver our vegetables, and Mitropoulos always had a few words with him whenever they encountered each other in the kitchen. Maestro noticed that the boy's teeth were in bad shape, and one day he came over to me with a check for two hundred

and fifty dollars. He handed it to me and said, "Arturo, would you have the boy go to a good dentist and have his teeth fixed? I want those teeth put in order, no matter what it costs. This is a down payment." Well, the boy went to a first class dentist and had all this work done, and it came to seven-hundred-fifty dollars, and Dimitri paid every cent of it. Later, when the vegetable boy got married, he named his first child Dimitri.[32]

Robert Viola, co-owner of La Scala, remembered the afternoon when Mitropoulos came in and sat by himself, obviously tired from just having conducted a matinee concert. Two out-of-town ladies entered shortly thereafter and took a table across the dining room. It wasn't long before one of the ladies flagged down Viola and asked: "Isn't that Maestro Mitropoulos over there?" Viola replied that it was. "Oh my God, we just came from his concert—it was so wonderful! Do you think he would mind if we go over there and shake his hand to thank him for his beautiful performance?" Viola replied that he did not think Maestro would mind, but that he would go ask.

Mitropoulos listened, a grave little smile on his face, and responded: "'No, it is I who should go over there and thank them.' So the poor man got up, just pushed his own dinner aside, and went over to see the two ladies, rather than have them come to him. That is the kind of heart this man had."[33]

Of all the memories Mirtallo and Viola had of Mitropoulos, none was more poignant than the recollection of their final meeting. Mitropoulos came into La Scala looking haggard and weak and ten years older than his actual age. He had just been released from the hospital after his second heart attack, and he had not yet been able to return to work, for his recuperation was going very slowly. On this afternoon, the restaurant was almost empty, and when Viola approached the conductor's table, he saw there were tears on his cheeks.

"Maestro, what it is? Why are you so *triste*?"

Mitropoulos shook his head in despair. "Roberto, *sono finito*."

"What do you mean?"

"I'm broke. I made over a hundred-thousand dollars last year, but you know me, I gave most of it away. Now I owe the hospital four thousand dollars, and I have nothing to give them. If I don't start working again, I don't know what's going to happen to me!" Mirtallo pulled out his checkbook, made a check out to Mitropoulos, and signed it, leaving the amount blank.

"Here, Maestro, write what you need and don't worry any more about it. You have me and Arturo as your friends forever, along with everyone else at this restaurant. You can eat and drink here for the rest of your life, as long as this establishment exists." Mitropoulos grasped Mirtallo's hand and both men wept.[34]

36   "It seemed to me that he was exposing his spirit, his very soul, and it was so compelling, and so personal, that I could not continue to look at him. It was like looking at the sun." —soprano Frances Greer.

37 Mitropoulos with
ubiquitous cigarette
holder. He smoked
several packs a day,
preferring Camels in
the U.S. and Gauloises
when in Europe. New
York Philharmonic
Archives.

38 Conducting the
New York Philhar-
monic. New York Phil-
harmonic Archives.

39 Mitropoulos studying a score under his favorite goose-neck lamp in his three-room suite in the Great Northern Hotel. Oliver Daniel collection.

40 Mitropoulos switches roles with the conductor of the New York Philharmonic tour train, ca. 1950. Photo by Weiner-Brackman Associates, courtesy Dorle Soria.

41   Mitropoulos, James Miller (Lord Provost of Edinburgh), Bruno Walter, and Floyd G. Blair (president, NYPSO board of directors), Edinburgh Festival, 1951. Courtesy Dorle Soria.

42   Greeting the Greek royal family backstage at Carnegie Hall, probably November 1953, when the maestro was decorated as a Commander of the Order of the Phoenix. From left, Mitropoulos, Zirato, Mrs. Hull, King Paul, Prince Constantine, Princess Sophia, and Queen Frederica. Courtesy Maria Christopoulou.

43   Mitropoulos in Salzburg, 1954, still smoking heavily despite his heart attack. Courtesy Maria Christopoulou.

44   Boarding the plane with Bruno Zirato at the end of the 1955 Athens engagement. Courtesy Dorle Soria.

45   Sun-drenched sculptured features. Photo by Sanford Roth, courtesy Jim Dixon.

46   Mitropoulos rehearsing at the Hollywood Bowl, 1952. Photo by Sanford Roth.

47 The once-famous *Life* magazine "Airborne Maestro" image by CBS photographer Bernard Habermann. During an April 1952 rehearsal of Mendelssohn's *Elijah* with the Westminster Choir, Mitropoulos demonstrates the level of intensity he wants when the music speaks of agony. He leaped off a bench with a shriek. Oliver Daniel collection.

48 Rehearsing the New York Philharmonic. New York Philharmonic Archives.

49　Maria Negroponte, photographed by Jim Dixon, June 17, 1954. Courtesy Jim Dixon.

50　Katy Katsoyanis, photographed by Jim Dixon, June 9, 1945.

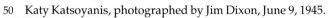

51   Mitropoulos and Katsoyanis aboard a cruise ship, 1955.

52   Mitropoulos, meditative, relaxing in Venice, 1951.

53   Mitropoulos rehearsing with Duke Ellington and Anahid Ajemian, April 1957. Courtesy George Avakian.

54   With Samuel Barber, before the disastrous Vienna performance of *Vanessa* in 1958. Courtesy Jim Dixon.

55 During a recording session for Columbia Records, ca. 1957. Courtesy CBS records.

56, 57, 58   Photographer Elfriede Broneder captured Mitropoulos across the emotional spectrum, from restraint to full cry, as he rehearsed in Vienna in 1958. From the collections of Jim Dixon, Oliver Daniel, and Dimitris Tsitouras, respectively.

59   Carlos Bergonzi, Mitropoulos, Zinka Milanov, in *Simon Boccanegra*, 1960. Photo by Louis Mélançon, courtesy John Browning.

60   Mitropoulos at the Met, ca. 1958. Photo by Louis Mélançon, courtesy Irving Kolodin.

61   Frail and aged, Mitropoulos during his final
summer in Europe. Oliver
Daniel collection.

62, 63   Vienna, October 1960, the final concerts. Those who had not seen Mitropoulos for a year were aghast at how deeply he had aged. Figure 62 by Anton Fischer,
63 by Elfriede Broneder. Courtesy Irving Kolodin and Dorle Soria.

64 Mitropoulos protégé Theodore Vavayannis, conductor of the Athens Symphony Orchestra (successor to the Athens Conservatory Orchestra), receives Mitropoulos's ashes from a representative of the Ministry of Education. Courtesy Mrs. Theodore Vavayannis.

65 Vavayannis leads a funeral procession of the Athens orchestra to the Theater of Herodus Atticus where they played the Funeral March from Beethoven's "Eroica" without a conductor on the podium. Courtesy Mrs. Theodore Vavayannis.

66 Vavayannis bids farewell to his mentor, friend, and colleague, burying the amphora containing Mitropoulos's ashes at the monument in Athens. Courtesy Mrs. Theodore Vavayannis.

CHAPTER TWENTY-EIGHT

The Taubman Attack

In Mitropoulos's last full season as music director of the New York Philharmonic, 1955–1956, the critical attacks became a drum-fire, even as the backstage machinations against him reached the level of a crusade. To be sure, isolated concerts, here and there, won critical praise and generated audience excitement, but the season as a whole displayed a haggard, hit-or-miss quality. In numerous reviews, one reads of concerts that sounded as though two different orchestras were playing: a gang of ill-disciplined semi-professionals on the first half of a concert, and the "real" New York Philharmonic on the second, after the players had settled down to do their jobs. Increasingly, however, no one was sure which of those two orchestras was in fact the real New York Philharmonic.

Mitropoulos's rehearsals were sometimes electrifying ("much better than the concerts," vowed Oliver Daniel), and sometimes a humiliating shambles. The worst offenders—prima donnas like Gomberg and Lincer—set an example of gross misbehavior which infected lesser players. Musicians would wander on and off the stage whenever the whim took them; when not playing, they would carry on *sotto voce* conversations, read magazines, or simply nod off for a quick nap. On embarrassingly frequent occasions, Mitropoulos was reduced to tears, and the sight of their music director—the inheritor of the God-like mantle of such lions as Toscanini and Mengelberg—openly weeping before them generated not pity and contrition, but contempt and revulsion.

British musicologist David Wooldridge, who had attended several of the orchestra's European concerts in September, visited New York during this cruel season and was appalled at what he saw during one rehearsal:

> It was discouraging to visit Carnegie Hall . . . and find that the first clarinet's slip in the Schumann [Second] Symphony a few months earlier (in Vienna) had not been attributable to accident, and that it really was symptomatic of a condition in the orchestra as a whole over which Mitropoulos no longer exercised any control. The rehearsal began with Ravel's *Alborada del gracioso*, where Mitropoulos was at pains to explain that it was perfectly possible—and in fact, clearer—to beat the first and third bars (and analogous bars throughout the work) *in three*, but his

remarks were treated with studied inattention. The point seemed too simple for an orchestra of this caliber to grasp . . . the most that Mitropoulos could do was to suggest that if they did not like it, there was a colleague of his in Cleveland (the frosty disciplinarian George Szell) who would be only too happy to come and conduct them.[1]

When a conductor, in an effort to impose discipline, is reduced to threatening his orchestra with the imposition of *another* conductor, then that conductor is a lost cause.

Mozart was featured on the opening concert of October 20, in homage to the bicentennial of that composer's birth. Rudolf Serkin again proved himself a pianist for all seasons by performing three Mozart concertos. Mitropoulos strove to achieve a semblance of eighteenth-century grace in the orchestral parts, but his solution was a bizarre one: during solo passages, the strings were cut back to Mozartean proportions, but whenever a tutti rolled around, the whole orchestra, including the full complement of sixty-four strings, joined in. As a result, the orchestral accompaniment was characterized by heaviness and by frequently queasy shifts of weight and balance. No one could understand why Mitropoulos didn't just thin out the whole orchestra to begin with.

Astrid Varnay joined the orchestra on October 27 for a concert performance of the final act of Wagner's *Götterdämmerung*. The conductor played Siegfried's Funeral March in honor of the memory of critic Olin Downes. Reviews were bad; the one in *Musical America* was especially brutal:

> The orchestral playing was slovenly throughout; at the very beginning the strings were at sixes and sevens in the rippling figures that accompany the Rhine Maidens; Mr. Mitropoulos's tempos were frequently unorthodox and inconsistent; the Funeral March (played in memory of the late Olin Downes) was muddy; and the final pages did not soar, nor was the masterful combination of themes successfully brought out. Wagner has to be conducted as precisely as Mozart, and no amount of wrist-wobbling and inspirational arm-lifts will substitute for clear cues and meticulously accurate playing.[2]

The barrage continued through November:

New York Times, November 4, 1955: "There is no objection to rough-hewn Beethoven, but he ought not to be coarse and crude. It is a sin to let the Philharmonic play like this."

New York Herald Tribune, November 4, 1955: "What happened to this fine orchestra? [The players] were not together, some of them were out of tune, and the whole business was sloppy and untidy. It simply escapes me why such an incomparable body of musicians is unable to do justice to Mozart. But then, I am a chronicler and cannot fathom the mysteries of the conductorial mind."

New York Times, November 11, 1955: "No one will ever pin a medal on Dimitri Mitropoulos for his program building. No one would have last night. For the ... concert at Carnegie Hall, he assembled trivialities and inoffensive meanderings, seasoned by a helping of grimness. There were a few interesting moments, but not enough for a whole evening. A concert isn't a place for boredom or penitence, and music is not a chore, not a grim, necessary commitment to good works, not a cheerless act of piety."

New York Herald Tribune, November 11, 1955: "How do they make their program selections? By composer's initials, tonalities, or just by flipping a coin?"

After the concert of November 13, Mitropoulos happily escaped for a week to conduct a benefit concert in Syracuse, as a favor to his old friend and former concertmaster, Louis Krasner. There, he received one-hundred percent cooperation from the struggling local orchestra and thunderous approval from a capacity audience.

Buoyed by the midseason break in Syracuse, Mitropoulos returned to the city in late November and threw himself into rehearsals for the Metropolitan Opera's lavish revival of *Tosca*. In contrast to his recent pummeling in the venue of Carnegie Hall, Mitropoulos found himself hailed as a hero. One would think the critics were not writing about the same man.

This was a *Tosca* that is still talked about by opera buffs. The cast was a dream come true: Renata Tebaldi as Tosca, Leonard Warren as Scarpia, and Richard Tucker as Mario—all in the prime of their careers. All the reviewers agreed, however, that the galvanizing force behind the whole stunning production was Mitropoulos. "One of the finest opera conductors in these parts," praised Taubman; other critics agreed.

Here was the same conductor, obtaining brilliant results from a mediocre orchestra, whom these same critics were beating over the head, week after week, for the sloppiness of his work with a much superior ensemble. The obvious conclusion to be drawn was that the Met players were dedicated and cooperative, and the Philharmonic had turned into a band of irresponsible, self-indulgent malcontents; none of the critics, however, saw fit to discuss this dichotomy in print.

The final concert of the year, December 29, was also regarded as a triumph, for it introduced a new masterpiece, Shostakovich's Violin Concerto No. 1, performed by the artist to whom it was dedicated, David Oistrakh (Mitropoulos used a score this time, supposedly because the sight of him conducting without one made Oistrakh nervous). Once again, the Philharmonic audience proved it was capable of absorbing and comprehending a new work when that composition rang true to the highest creative standards. Tumultuous applause greeted the concerto, with the orchestra members joining the ovation; both Oistrakh and Mitropoulos came back for six curtain calls. During the final one, Mitropoulos picked up his copy of the score and held it aloft, symbolically letting the absent composer share the applause.

January 1956 found the conductor venturing into unexplored territory at the Metropolitan Opera: a new production of *Boris Godunov* with Jerome Hines in the title role. The performing edition was a new touch-up of the Rimsky-Korsakov orchestration, done by Karol Rathaus. George Cehanovsky, the Met's longtime Russian coach, thought Mitropoulos captured the essence of Mussorgsky's drama as well as any Russian conductor he had worked with. Unanimously, the critics agreed that it was

> a performance filled with the power and brooding compassion that Mussorgsky poured into it. Once again, the chief architect of a first-rate revival was Dimitri Mitropoulos. It has been many years since the Metropolitan has had a production of "Boris" that was so much all of a piece. Thanks to his dramatic instincts as a conductor, Mr. Mitropoulos has brought urgency, grandeur, and a sense of troubled humanity to this great operatic canvas.[3]

Mitropoulos was constantly moving between Carnegie Hall and the Metropolitan during the late winter and early spring. In March, he conducted for Eleanor Steber's revival of *Manon Lescaut* and won praise for the restrained yet full-bodied tone he secured from the pit orchestra; he also directed *Tosca* and *Un ballo in maschera* as well as additional performances of *Boris Godunov*. During a mid-February performance of *Ballo*, Rudolf Bing made an unannounced appearance in the orchestra pit to lead a rousing version of "Happy Birthday to You" in honor of Mitropoulos's sixtieth birthday.

While all this was going on, he welcomed Katy Katsoyanis to New York, sometime in late January, for a visit of five weeks. She had a suite near his at the Great Northern, and was conspicuous at rehearsals and recording sessions.

On February 18, Mitropoulos's sixtieth birthday was celebrated in Carnegie Hall; David M. Keiser, president of the Philharmonic-Symphony Society, presented the conductor with a copy of the full score for Verdi's *Otello*—a special honor because the House of Ricordi, which owns the rights to Verdi's operas, had an ironclad rule that the material could only be leased, not purchased outright; for Mitropoulos, however, the Italian firm gladly made an exception. A silver plaque was presented on behalf of the orchestra members. The inscription read, in part, "to our beloved director and inspiring leader."

For his part, Mitropoulos gave every member of the Philharmonic a commemorative solid-gold medallion approximately the size of a quarter, with a bas-relief bust of himself on one side, and a personalized inscription on the other.

After the formal ceremonies, Mitropoulos and some close friends, including Katy, adjourned to the La Scala Restaurant, where the conductor ate, among other things, finocchio dipped in a mixture of oil, wine, vinegar, and herbs. Midway through the meal, the entire staff of the restaurant gathered around the table and sang "Happy Birthday" to their favorite guest.

To mark his birthday, Mitropoulos put together a special, symbolic concert, one combining three important elements in his musical personality. First, to mark his early work as a composer, came his orchestration of Bach's Fantasia and Fugue in G Minor (why he chose this out-of-fashion transcription instead of the startlingly advanced Concerto Grosso he actually composed is anybody's guess; the critics ignored or panned the Bach transcription, but the Concerto Grosso might have knocked them on their collective ear); next, symbolizing his commitment to modern music, came Leon Kirchner's Piano Concerto; finally, in homage to the metaphysical elements of mountain climbing, which he could no longer enjoy in a literal sense, came Strauss's *Alpine Symphony*.

Otherwise, the spring 1956 orchestral season was a very mixed bag, perhaps even more so than the autumn season had been. The premiere, on February 2, of Samuel Barber's *Medea's Meditation and Dance of Vengeance* stirred the audience to a wild ovation, but in general the public's response to the spring programs was tepid. It did not escape the critics' notice that Arthur Judson's client-soloists (David Oistrakh, Nathan Milstein, and Michael Rabin) performed the Brahms Violin Concerto three times during this one season.

Originally slated for a February performance was a new piece by American composer Ralph Shapey—a work that Mitropoulos either commissioned outright or at least financially supported at some stages of its development. The Shapey work was listed and promoted right up to the date of the concert, but when patrons opened their programs, they found a hastily mimeographed notice of substitution: instead of Shapey's *Challenge: The Family of Man*, the orchestra would be performing Bizet's *Jeux d'enfants* suite. This may have been the only time in Mitropoulos's career that he actually canceled a modern work on the very eve of its performance, and veteran player John Schaeffer remembered the occasion vividly:

> Now Mitropoulos did conduct some extremely difficult modern music, but this piece was *crazy*. It started out on a low D in the basses and then, the very next note, in a huge glissando, it zoomed up, like a machine being turned on, all the way to the high end of the fingerboard. And *every* measure had an extra 16th-note, or a 32nd-note, or a 3/16ths-note, or something else equally egregious. It was a total mess, and very badly written for the orchestra. Not only could the men not play it, but Mitropoulos, for once, was at a total loss as to how to conduct the thing. He

became intensely exasperated, and finally turned around toward Shapey, who was sitting in the audience, and cried, "Why, why, must you write so difficult?" And Shapey just made this wise-guy gesture and sneered in reply: "This? Oh, this is nothing!" Then he came on stage and sort of pushed Dimitri off the podium and started trying to conduct it himself. It was a total fiasco.[4]

Ralph Shapey was a notoriously prickly character who seemed to delight in writing music guaranteed to make an audience cringe. Oliver Daniel, who had dealings with the composer while he was running BMI, once described Shapey as "the most disagreeable man in the entire music business."[5] He was, however, influential and well-connected, so that the net result of this incident was that yet another modern-music faction withdrew its support from Mitropoulos.

A caustic critical attack greeted the U.S. premiere, on February 25 and 26, of Rolf Liebermann's Music for Orchestra and Speaker, set to poems of Baudelaire. Before that work, Mitropoulos conducted Liszt's orchestrated *Mephisto Waltz*, and after intermission he led Prokofiev's First Violin Concerto (Isaac Stern, soloist) and Kodály's *Háry János Suite*. If one were deliberately setting out to create the lumpiest, most indigestible concert program imaginable, one would be hard-pressed to improve on this pointless juxtaposition of four utterly unrelated pieces. In his *Herald Tribune* review, Lang wrote that this was not a "concert program" but a meaningless "conglomeration." He ended his review with a quotation from one of the Baudelaire poems recited in the Liebermann composition:

> Old Captain, it is time,
> Weigh anchor,
> To sail beyond the doldrums
> Of our days.

Just so no reader could miss the point, Lang dedicated the verse to "our eminent director of the Philharmonic."

Mitropoulos soldiered on through the spring, conducting to houses that were half full on the good nights. There was a brief upsurge of ticket sales in April, when the young Mstislav Rostropovich made a sensational impression with his performances of a recently unearthed cello concerto by Prokofiev, and again for the program of April 12, 13, and 15, when Mitropoulos rolled out his heavy artillery for the first New York performance in thirty-four years of Mahler's Symphony No. 3.

It was a measure of Mitropoulos's long-range achievement that ticket sales for the Mahler concerts were higher than average. Nobody had programmed this work since 1922, when Mengelberg essayed it; no one would do it again until Leonard Bernstein, *building on what Mitropoulos had done*, performed it in 1961 and promptly became identified with it for the rest of his life. To hear the 1956 performance, via one of its numerous commercial incarnations, with all its rough edges, problematical balances, and raw, yawping power, is to be present at the birth of a tradition, a seismic shift in public taste and perception. Mitropoulos, finally, had won his lifelong battle for the honor of Gustav Mahler; most of the credit, and all the medals, would of course go to his successor.

There was, alas, no grand finale to this generally unsatisfying season. Instead, there was a routine concert on April 27, which was given a few tired, dispirited kicks by the increasingly bored, cranky, and disillusioned critical establishment, as typified by Winthrop Sargent's *New Yorker* review:

> On Thursday evening in Carnegie Hall, the Philharmonic opened its final week of concerts with a program that was both remarkably uninteresting and rather typical of the season's routine symphonic doings. Zino Francescatti, an admirable violinist, tackled the trivial rhetoric of the Saint-Saëns Violin Concerto, and Dimitri Mitropoulos, a conductor who shines in rhapsodic and emotional music, gave Rachmaninoff's Second Symphony a loud and only superficially stirring performance. My own reaction to all this was, I fear, one of weariness. I have heard far too many members of impresario Arthur Judson's stable of solo violinists, however admirable, at the Philharmonic concerts this season, and the Rachmaninoff symphony, while a pleasant enough work, is hardly the sort of thing to challenge one's interest.[6]

Mitropoulos was no doubt glad to get the season behind him as well. His energy level had shot up for the Mahler Third, but his internal engine was sputtering unreliably as the season entered its home stretch. His obvious moodiness, and the manner in which his performances seemed to reflect subjective factors whose nature and source his musicians could only guess at, had at times alienated even the players who remained steadfast in their basic loyalty. And even those musicians had grown weary of giving concerts which seemed to incorporate, in their internal dynamics, some dark element of penitence.

Players and conductor alike looked forward to relaxing during the maturing weeks of spring.

And then they all woke up on the morning of Sunday, April 29, and read Howard Taubman's article in the *New York Times*.

It would be inaccurate to speak of a conspiracy formed for the express purpose of ousting Dimitri Mitropoulos and installing Leonard Bernstein in his stead—the very word conjures images of plotters whispering behind locked doors and formulating detailed plans. What happened in the spring of 1956, however, was simply a convergence of interests—vectors of political, social, and artistic force—all of which had as their basic common denominator the elimination of Dimitri Mitropoulos as music director of the New York Philharmonic.

When the orchestra celebrated its 150th birthday in 1993, the numerous documentary features and encomia marking that event usually included (if in fact they included anything about Mitropoulos other than the dates of his tenure) some variation on the idea that Mitropoulos was hounded out of town by the critics. There is of course some truth in that—the conductor had taken some bone-breaking shots ever since Virgil Thomson reviewed his first appearances in the early 1940s—but if one reads all of the reviews, in chronological order, the incidence of really negative notices seems scattered pretty evenly until one comes to the mid-1950s, at which time the carping definitely increases, reaching a climax of sorts during the 1955–1956 season. At no time, however—at least until Taubman's broadside appeared—does there seem to have been a concerted "Dump Dimitri" campaign on the part of the New York critics acting as one body. One important critic—Louis Biancolli—remained steadfast in his belief that Mitropoulos's virtues far outweighed his lapses. And even the nastiest reviewers—Sargent and Lang—did not consistently heap abuse on the conductor's head, week after week.

Once this slain-by-the-cynical-critics theory is put in proper perspective, the main cause of Mitropoulos's troubles seems clearly to have been the rot within his own orchestra, combined with a number of slow-moving political and social forces working in the contextual depths:

• The Ethnic Factor: It was widely believed that either an Italian conductor or a Jewish one would open the purse strings of New Yorkers in a way that the continued presence of a Greek could never do. Guido Cantelli was the favorite candidate until his tragic death in December 1956. With him out of the way, Bernstein loomed as the default candidate;

• The Family Values Factor: Although Bernstein's marriage to Felicia Montealegre was already on the rocks, he projected the public image of a contented, sexually normal husband and father. The musicians were comfortable with that, whatever their private suspicions, and so was everyone else.

• The "Omnibus" Factor: Bernstein had early and cunningly embraced television, and his lecture-concert programs on "Omnibus" were stunning examples of how powerful the new medium could be. The programs earned huge audience numbers, so that Bernstein was known and adored by hundreds of thousands of ordinary Americans—precisely the sort of massive support-base the New York Philharmonic had always wanted but had never quite been able to achieve through its radio broadcasts. Lenny was sexy, warm, witty, and telegenic to a fault; in a word, he was Box Office.

• The Native Son Factor: Bernstein had built a remarkably fervent and loyal base of support during the years he conducted, free of charge, at New York City Center. He had shown himself to be at least as dedicated to modern music as Mitropoulos, but he had also shown a marked interest in American composers, whereas Mitropoulos's championship of the modern had been focused more on European styles and personalities. Mitropoulos had certainly played his share of American works, too, but the perception existed that he favored a handful of difficult composers (Kirchner, Sessions, Schuller) and cared too much for one supposed lightweight: Morton Gould. During his last five years with the Philharmonic, Mitropoulos all but stopped struggling to get modern American composers onto his programs; he conducted nothing by Diamond, Foss, Ives, Persichetti, Bernstein, Carter, Piston, Fine, Riegger, or Ruggles, to name some of the more prominent omissions. Many American composers (William Schuman was perhaps the nastiest and most candid) expressed the belief that their chances of performance by the Philharmonic would increase dramatically if Mitropoulos were out and Bernstein in. Since the perception still existed that, in Gunther Schuller's phrase, "one Philharmonic broadcast could put a composer on the map like nothing else in our society," the anti-Mitropoulos faction had a powerful stake in the matter.

From these circumstances formed a loose, informal, but highly demonstrative pro-Bernstein claque whose members sometimes actually wrangled tickets to Mitropoulos's concerts (easy enough to get, considering how few subscribers actually bothered to show up anymore) for the express purpose of booing and hissing, or ostentatiously walking out in mid-selection.

For men such as David Diamond, who cared deeply for both Bernstein and Mitropoulos and who at times suffered greatly because of it, the outlines of the situation were clear enough: Bernstein was marshalling the clout to make his move on the Philharmonic and was just waiting patiently for the right opening to present itself. Diamond once asked Lenny point-blank why he was plotting with such Machiavellian intent:

> I spoke to him about it one summer in Florence. I said, Lenny, what is going on? Why are you doing this thing? And he replied, "I am not doing a thing. The men in the orchestra feel that Dimitri has been there long enough, that he's bad for discipline, that he lets them get away with playing like pigs. All I want to do is take that orchestra and build them up. I don't think they'll be continuing with Dimitri for very long." Now, mind you, this was in 1953, or 1954, and he was absolutely confident, even then, that the job would be his for the asking, when the right moment came. He had planned very carefully, and of course, he turned out to be right.[7]

Taubman's motives, as seen by Taubman himself, were of course beyond reproach; the fact that he stood to gain, first, by demonstrating both his perspicacity and power, and, second, by allying himself with the nexus of cultural clout forming around Bernstein, was incidental. No doubt that on one level, Taubman was sincerely convinced he was acting for the good of the musical community. Age and reflection mellowed him later, although he gave no sign of it when Oliver Daniel contacted him in 1984; "It's all in the article, Oliver," was his only comment. By 1994, when Taubman's charming book of reminiscences (*The Pleasure of Their Company*) was published, he stated, with honorable frankness, that:

> The conductor on my conscience is Dimitri Mitropoulos. . . . I criticized him for the way in which he as musical director had allowed the orchestra's standards of performance to decline. I was well aware that my observations would do him no good, even cause him pain, but I believed it was my duty to speak out. . . . I did not intend to harm a good man or to open the way for another good man. My aim was to make sure that the Philharmonic would regain its health and prestige.[8]

Be that as it may, Taubman's earlier description of the situation in 1956 sets the scene clearly:

> Olin Downes died in August 1955. I took over the number one spot in September. I began to go to all of the main events of the Philharmonic. . . . I found what was happening deplorable. Mitropoulos was struggling; the orchestra was shot; the entire enterprise was in grave trouble . . . what was needed was shock therapy. . . . In April, 1956, I sat down and wrote that piece. It took me a few days to get it right . . . what I proposed to do, was take over the entire music page . . . the response was enormous. . . . It was a bomb . . . a watershed in the history of the New York Philharmonic. David Keiser, the president, told me it tore them to bits.[9]

The article bore the headline "The Philharmonic—What's Wrong With It and Why," and it took up eight columns of dense print. Under a logical series of subheads, Taubman had systematically marshalled his points, dealing in turn with each of the orchestra's chronic problems.

He began with a summary of the Philharmonic's current estate:

> The Philharmonic-Symphony Society of New York does not have too many reasons for pride in its 114th season, ending today. It does have many reasons for concern.
>
> During the 1955–1956 season the New York Philharmonic-Symphony rarely sounded like an ensemble of the first order. Its programs lacked overall design and were often badly balanced, being either top-heavy or flimsy. Its policy on conductors remained static, and its policy on soloists was planned maladroitly, if it was planned at all. Attendance . . . appeared to fall off; the deficit is bound to be hefty again.
>
> Orchestras, like any other organization, can have poor years. One unsatisfactory season need not cause alarm; it may be written off as unlucky and forgiven. But the Philharmonic's prestige has been waning in recent years and the 1955–1956 season seems to this observer another step in a process of deterioration. Unless an objective, thoroughgoing diagnosis is undertaken and a candid prognosis laid out, the orchestra's affairs may very well worsen.

Taubman listed the audible symptoms of decline:

On a sheer technical level its standards have fallen. Week in and week out, it does not sound as impressive as the Philadelphia and Boston Symphony Orchestras. Compared with those two, or with the London Philharmonic which was here last fall, it is distinctly second class.

The orchestra does not play with precision. Attacks and releases, which are the hallmarks of a smartly drilled ensemble of the first rank, are often careless. The texture of chords is frequently unraveled, with upper, lower and middle voices in inept balance. The weight of the separate instrumental choirs is not always neatly poised, and individual soloists within the ensemble play with varying effectiveness. The orchestral tone has a tendency to coarseness. A pianissimo of shimmering transparency is seldom heard, and fortissimos are apt to be hard-driven.

Zooming in, Taubman put Mitropoulos in his sights and fired:

Because Dimitri Mitropoulos is musical director . . . he bears the heaviest responsibility. He is a serious, dedicated musician, with strong sympathies for the repertory of the late nineteenth century and for certain areas of twentieth-century music. His flair is for dramatic music, and he can communicate an almost feverish intensity. With a Richard Strauss, Mahler, Schoenberg or Berg work at the Philharmonic, or a Puccini opera at the Metropolitan, he can do an outstanding job.

Such virtues, applied to classical and early romantic music, become failings, for these works need proportion, delicacy, occasional repose. In short, Mr. Mitropoulos is not at his best in an important area of the orchestra's repertory. As musical director, he is obliged to conduct a lot of concerts and to cover diverse styles and epochs. He is not the first conductor to be overmatched by the requirements of the Philharmonic post.

Mr. Mitropoulos, moreover, has not established his capacities as an orchestral drillmaster. It may even be asked whether he cares about refinements of execution. It follows that Mr. Mitropoulos may not be the wisest choice for musical director. He would certainly be a valued guest conductor in his specialized repertory.

Why is he re-engaged each year? Obviously, he has his supporters and admirers. It is clear, too, that he is a sweet-natured, agreeable man. He evidently gets along smoothly with management and guests. There are no crises with him like those that occurred when a conductor of Toscanini's iron will and flaming temperament was the music director.

Taubman also listed some specific complaints by the musicians: ethnic favoritism, lousy management relations, personality conflicts that were allowed to deepen until they created chasms across the face of the orchestra's collective good will—in these observations, one sees clearly that Taubman must have had good contacts inside the orchestra, for these family squabbles are of the sort the public seldom gets to see.

He slammed the haphazard nature of the Philharmonic's programming, asserting that three Mozart concertos in one evening, even if they were performed by an artist of Rudolf Serkin's stature, constituted a freakshow, not a legitimate programming concept. Mitropoulos's habit of juxtaposing minor works by famous composers and innocuous contemporary novelties, he excoriated as a source of profound "ennui." And of course, he flogged the conductor for giving time to Morton Gould and the likes of Rolf Liebermann, yet ignoring so many other, worthier, composers.

While Taubman stopped short of accusing Arthur Judson and Bruno Zirato—both managers of the Philharmonic *and* executives of Columbia Artists Management, Inc.—of packing the soloist list each season with CAMI artists, he did observe that more than half of the featured artists in the season just ended were indeed managed by Judson's agency; moreover, the percentage increased when Taubman focused on a lengthy list of soloists who, in his opinion, had "little or no right to solo appearances" in Carnegie Hall. Whatever Judson's intent, the appearance of influence-peddling and impropriety was ineradicable: the Philharmonic was being used to magnify the reputations of CAMI artists, even second-rate ones. How else to explain the insane occurrence of three Brahms concerto interpreters in a single season? Or an uninterrupted spate of violinists that went on for weeks at a time?

However skillfully Taubman deployed his arguments against the Philharmonic's heavy-handed management, the principal target of the article, the man picked out as being responsible for the churlish, unprofessional behavior of the orchestra as well as the skewed, Euro-centric programs, was Dimitri Mitropoulos.

Insulated within his increasingly self-referential shell, sustained only by a threadbare remnant of faith and a seemingly masochistic determination to cling to his mountaintop no matter how badly he got punished for it, Mitropoulos was not expecting anything like this. There are scattered hints and oblique references that suggest he was planning to remain with the Philharmonic until his chosen successor, the brilliant but still-limited Guido Cantelli, was ready to assume the post. Instead, he was publicly identified as the single most detrimental factor in the Philharmonic's declining fortunes by a critic who stopped just short of telling him to pack his bags and leave town; all of the praise he had once received for dragging the orchestra into the twentieth century, all of the towering triumphs of previous years—*Elektra*, *Wozzeck*, the Mahler symphonies—weighed as nothing in the balance when opposed to the fact that his musicians were ill-behaved and that he was not a consistently satisfying Mozart conductor.

He tried to present a stoic face to the world in the days that followed Taubman's bombshell, but a visitor to his rooms in the Great Northern later on the afternoon of April 29 found the conductor pacing back and forth in a state of despondent agitation, his features distorted with pain, clutching the newspaper and repeating over and over again: "Dear God, what does he *want*? WHAT DOES HE WANT??"

CHAPTER TWENTY-NINE

Declining Fortunes

"After the Taubman piece appeared," recalled Morton Gould, "everybody in the New York musical establishment just sort of hung up on Dimitri; it was very, very sad."[1]

Such a furor was unleashed by the article that several New York papers devoted entire pages to letters from concerned readers. Reactions to the article were mixed and fairly even; about half of the printed letters agreed with at least the general thrust of Taubman's piece, and the other half thought he had been too rough on Mitropoulos. Several readers remarked that if Mitropoulos bore most of the responsibility for the Philharmonic's truculent ways, why was it that the Metropolitan Opera Orchestra, a palpably inferior outfit, played so well for him? A large number of readers agreed that the Philharmonic job was too much for one human being, but pleaded that Mitropoulos be retained, at least to conduct the repertoire for which he was so famous.

Of course the other music critics, some of them miffed that Taubman had suddenly acquired such prominence, were compelled to write their own assessments for their own papers. Irving Kolodin reminded his readers that no other musical organization in the world was mandated to serve a public of eight million souls, four nights a week, for eight months out of every year; the quarter-million-dollar deficit was, he agreed, "staggering," and in conclusion he said: "What strikes me as most deplorable is not the cost of keeping the orchestra going . . . but the inferior results at the severe cost . . . it is one thing to have a substantial loss when public attendance is close to capacity (as is the case with the Metropolitan), quite another when the loss is accompanied by definite evidence of public indifference. Then, certainly, it is time for a change."[2]

Paul Henry Lang wrote a two-part follow-up to the Taubman article, in which he, too, concluded that Mitropoulos, and the Philharmonic, might be better off if the Greek conductor moved his base of operations to the Metropolitan Opera:

> Mr. Mitropoulos, the Musical Director of the Philharmonic, is a musician of extraordinary gifts and a gentleman of not only sterling but very engaging character. He has a wonderful sense for the dramatic, the taut,

the fatal—and for the opposite extreme, the sentimental—but is lacking in much that lies between. With music older than the late romantic composers he has no ties, and it is almost as a stranger that he approaches Mozart. This austere and devoted musician is recognized as a master of certain types of contemporary music, but this facet of his talents is frustrated by the policies of the Philharmonic management. Anyway, in order to afford the luxury of presenting contemporary music, a conductor must be equally knowledgeable in other periods in order to provide the balance demanded by our pattern of musical life.

Another severe handicap Mr. Mitropoulos—and his orchestra—must contend with is his lack of manual dexterity, the technique of the baton. His frantic flailing cannot produce order and accuracy, and those who must rely on cues and on unequivocal signs when tempo or meter is changing must be hard put to follow his beat.[3]

While the controversy raged, Mitropoulos sought release through the only anodyne he knew: hard work. During most of May, he was involved in an exhausting tour with the Metropolitan Opera, conducting *Tosca* in Richmond, Atlanta, Memphis, and Dallas, and *Boris Godunov* in Atlanta, Minneapolis, Bloomington, and Chicago.

By the time he returned to New York, he was sufficiently recovered to write about the Taubman affair, with some degree of philosophical detachment as well as residual bitterness, to Katy:

Finally I came back from the tour and found your letters, and thank you for the consolation about the famous article of Mr. Taubman—who became famous overnight with that article. And they speak more about it than about all the productions that I did so far in this town! I received so many condolences from lots of good friends, who would have done better not to write me, to just have ignored it. Anyhow, enough of that . . . it cost me a big grief, but this is a part of life which I always accepted as an inevitable course. Unfortunately, this awful event had lots of repercussions for me, naturally, among the Board of Directors and the management, who got more panicky than I, and they would have replaced me *subito* if there were someone available. They want to find an "all 'round" conductor, as they call it, because they have been told that I am suddenly good only for the opera and so on. There's no use in giving you comments about that stupid remark . . . stupidity is part of the human race and we usually call stupid whatever we don't agree with.[4]

In June, with what must have been a feeling of profound relief, Mitropoulos left for Europe and stayed there until September. With the Vienna Philharmonic, or the forces at La Scala, there were no condescending remarks, no sudden change of attitude based on the now-notorious *New York Times* article. Instead, he was treated with respect and veneration, was even spoken of as the heir-apparent to the mantle of Wilhelm Furtwängler, who had died of pneumonia earlier that spring. The contrast between the scorn being heaped on him in New York and the affection being showed by the members of the Vienna Philharmonic (which also had a reputation for being rough on conductors who did not earn their respect) could not have been greater. Musicians who were acquainted with the New York situation found it baffling and enraging: here was a man whom the Vienna Philharmonic wanted as one of its regular conductors, and the New York Philharmonic wanted to dump him? The matter was inexplicable, unbelievable, and the very existence of such an absurd situation only verified the low opinion many Europeans held of America's musical culture.

Mitropoulos began his summer activities ambitiously, conducting the first Italian performance of Schoenberg's *Pelleas und Melisande*, coupled with Strauss's *Alpine Symphony*. Then, at the end of July, he traveled to Austria for the Salzburg Festival. Furtwängler's absence was keenly felt, and Mitropoulos was hesitant about stepping in to replace the great German conductor in some scheduled performances of Mozart's *Don Giovanni*—a work he had never directed before, and one, moreover, whose composer's style was supposedly alien to him. Musically, however, the Mitropoulos-led *Don Giovanni* was successful, although the production itself was deemed rather dreary.

Before leaving Vienna, Mitropoulos led the Philharmonic in a staggering performance of the Berlioz Requiem, which he dedicated to the memory of Furtwängler in a brief address from the podium. In several Viennese newspaper interviews, Mitropoulos hinted that he might be resigning from the New York Philharmonic in the near future. He never dropped similar hints in his interviews for American papers. Either he was still ambivalent about New York, or he remained stubbornly, even masochistically, determined to remain on his mountaintop as long as he could.

He did not return to work immediately in New York but went instead to Chicago, where he conducted a Lyric Opera revival of Puccini's *La fanciulla del West*, starring Eleanor Steber and Mario del Monaco. In an October 22 letter to Katy, he praised the experience, calling the performance "really . . . perfect . . . much better than in Florence." He was appalled, however, at the behavior of the audience, which gave prolonged applause for the scenery, every aria, the supporting singers, and of course the horses. Finally losing his patience, Mitropoulos shouted to the stagehands to close the curtains and admonished the audience to show some good manners, because "unfortunately, we have some music going on down here in the pit!" After that, he said, "like nice children," the crowd kept silent. "I bless the Almighty," he closed this letter, "that He did not condemn me to live all my life in an opera orchestra pit."

Meanwhile, back in New York, the ponderous machinery of change was moving behind the scenes at the Philharmonic. Despite Mitropoulos's glum assertion that "they would have replaced me *subito* if there were someone available," the Philharmonic's board of directors was not going to give the appearance of haste or unseemliness, or of dancing to the tune of one music critic, no matter how increasingly powerful he might be. Fretful deliberations took place all during the summer.

The first sign of a seismic upheaval came on September 18, when a terse press bulletin announced that Arthur Judson, age seventy-five, had resigned from his position with the New York Philharmonic; on the same day, Bruno Zirato assumed full responsibilities as managing director. To avoid the impression of business-as-usual, Zirato formally severed his ties with Columbia Artists Management, Inc.

One month later, three days after the first concert of the Philharmonic season, a somewhat more dramatic announcement was issued to the press:

> At the request of its musical director, Dimitri Mitropoulos, the New York Philharmonic-Symphony has engaged Leonard Bernstein to share the direction of the orchestra, beginning with the 1957–1958 season. . . .
>
> In a letter to David M. Keiser, president of the Philharmonic-Symphony Society, Mr. Mitropoulos gave as his reasons for requesting the administrative change the large number of invitations he has received to conduct in Europe and a bid to increase his activities with the Metropolitan Opera.
>
> Previously, Mr. Mitropoulos said, he has been obliged to decline these many invitations "because of my heavy Philharmonic duties."
>
> "After thinking the matter over carefully," Mr. Mitropoulos added, "I would like to suggest that my colleague Leonard Bernstein be invited to work with me, and I am sure that together we will be able to prepare a very sound and stimulating season."[5]

When the 1957–1958 programs were announced, Mitropoulos was no longer listed as music director. Instead, he and Bernstein were listed in tandem as principal conductors. Veteran observers of the New York musical scene, like football fans who know the significance of a coach's midseason substitutions, nodded sagely: here came the old double-conductor ploy, used whenever a profound shake-up was looming. Two conductors went into the season; only one would come out. There was, by now, little doubt as to who that would be.

If the Philharmonic's management expected Bernstein to be cautious about programming "modern stuff," they were in for a surprise. Out of the twenty-seven concerts Bernstein conducted during the 1957–1958 season, nineteen of them contained music by eleven contemporary composers (Borishansky, Chavez, Diamond, Foss, Haieff, Macero, Markevitch, Shapero, Shostakovich, Stravinsky, and Webern). During that same season, Mitropoulos directed twenty-three concerts, containing thirty performances of new or neglected works.

On November 24 came news that devastated Mitropoulos. The brilliant young Guido Cantelli had been killed—on his way back to New York to fulfill an upcoming Philharmonic engagement—when his plane went down just after takeoff from Orly Airport outside of Paris.

Mitropoulos wept when he heard the news. Despite Bernstein's apparent inside track, Mitropoulos had continued to hope that Cantelli would be his ultimate successor, even if Bernstein did conduct the orchestra for a few years in the interim. Although the thirty-six-year-old Italian maestro's working repertoire was still limited, he was surely the best-equipped conductor of his generation, blending Toscanini's love of clarity and drama with an ear for orchestral color that had few equals.

Five days after Cantelli's death, Mitropoulos conducted a performance of *Death and Transfiguration* in his memory. People who were in the audience that night still remembered this performance forty years later. Off-the-air recordings of it have circulated widely on both LP and CD, and it can stand as an interpretive paradigm of both the power and the paradox of Mitropoulos's podium style. From the first faltering heartbeat on the timpani, the performance seethes with fever, with delirium barely held in check; Mitropoulos seems to be grappling with a very real Angel of Death, and the orchestra, willing or not, has been dragged into the sulfur and brimstone along with him, for they play like men possessed.

This eschatological mood intensifies and, as the grandiose climax approaches, passes quite beyond the means of musical instruments to express. Mitropoulos has gone into a fugue state; he is somewhere Other: the musical conception in his soul is vaster, greater, than the music can serve as vessel for. A state of barely controlled hysteria permeates the buildup to the great waves of sound that mark the moment of transfiguration, but even though Mitropoulos feels more, transmits more, *wills there to be more*—louder, darker, more and more intense—there is nowhere else for the music to go. The two big climaxes, when they come, do not expand and soar as they should, but implode, their musical molecules collapsing inwardly—hard, tight, muscle-bound, as dense and turbulent with unreleased energy as the core of a neutron star. One finishes listening to this astonishing performance in a state of limp exhaustion mixed with a nagging sense of frustration—a catharsis that has misfired.

Two weeks into the new year, Arturo Toscanini died in his sleep. Mitropoulos joined with many other musicians to pay tribute to the man who had so defined, and so changed, the conducting profession: "The death of my beloved colleague means to the world the loss of a magnificent interpreter, and a man whose spirit has been an inspiring force for all serious artists."

For Mitropoulos, 1957 began auspiciously. He scored one of his greatest triumphs at the Metropolitan Opera by conducting a revival of *Die Walküre* that brought a sold-out house to its feet, shouting. Even Taubman cheered: "There is nothing wrong with Wagner," he quipped, "that a good performance can't cure," and went on to praise the "torrential power" of Mitropoulos's conception.

Mitropoulos was back with the Philharmonic on January 31, to conduct the premiere of yet another work based on biblical themes, *Midrash Esther* by Jan Meyerowitz. The program also juggled a Mozart divertimento, Goldmark's Violin Concerto, and a symphonic fragment from Zandonai's *Giulietta e Romeo*. All the critics except Louis Biancolli heaped scorn on the program, with special venom being spat at the Meyerowitz work. Perhaps the most interesting thing about this concert was the brazen appearance of a pro-Bernstein claque in the audience, which loudly booed the Meyerowitz composition and ostentatiously refused to applaud the more conventional music.

On February 21, Mitropoulos gave—rather astonishingly—his first performance of Berlioz's *Symphonie fantastique*, a work tailored to his style as few others were in the entire repertoire. He lavished on it a dark, somber reading, carefully prepared (no reviewers' jibes about sloppy playing on this occasion) and terrific in its cumulative impact. Fortunately for posterity, Columbia recorded his interpretation three days later, in splendid stereo sound. One can listen to this performance today, on compact disc, and hear no trace of orchestral degeneration; on the contrary, the Philharmonic plays with more vivid color, more character, and—yes—more precision than it played during Bernstein's early years, or during the entire Mehta regime.

As winter yielded to spring, the number of unusual works on the Philharmonic's programs increased: Morton Gould's *Jekyll and Hyde Variations*, Alberto Ginastera's *Overture to a Creole Faust*, a Fantasy for Orchestra by Robert Mann, violinist for the Juilliard Quartet, Gail Kubik's Symphony No. 3, Gunther Schuller's *Dramatic Overture*, Elliott Carter's *Holiday Overture*, and the New York premiere of Walton's Cello Concerto, with Gregor Piatigorsky as the soloist. If this was admittedly a "scatter-gun" approach to contemporary music, it was at least an approach that tried to represent the highest levels of midcentury musical craftsmanship as well as the broadest possible range of styles.

Mitropoulos ventured away from Carnegie Hall during this busy spring, to donate his services to several worthy events: a New York Chamber Ensemble concert in March; a Negro History Week benefit at which he led a freelance orchestra in works by Ulysses Kay and William Grant Still, and the world premiere of Lionel Hampton's *King David* suite; and, at Town Hall, a "Music for Moderns" concert, where he shared the stage with Duke Ellington, whom he professed to admire.

The Philharmonic's season ended on May 12, with a mighty performance of Walton's *Belshazzar's Feast*. Critic Paul Henry Lang, a decent enough fellow, decided to forego any more Mitropoulos-bashing and wrote a rather bland piece about how the Philharmonic ought to give fewer concerts and have more rehearsals.

Howard Taubman, however, thought the sacking of Arthur Judson was not enough; that Mitropoulos, instead of being allowed to gradually and gracefully disengage himself from the Philharmonic, should be packed off immediately and as humiliatingly as possible. No one knows the reason for Taubman's *ad hominem* bile, but as pianist Arthur Whittemore said, the critic did indeed have a "hate-on" for Mitropoulos. Taubman's year-end feature was mean-spirited and sadistic; Mitropoulos was clearly on his way out so it is difficult to see this new onslaught as anything other than kicking a man when he was down:

> It was evident . . . that those of us who yearned for a better day for the orchestra would have to be patient. There were programs and performances during the 115th season when every bit of patience had to be involved. As in the bad old days of recent years, one encountered slovenly playing, dull, turgid and superficial novelties and unworthy soloists. There were evenings when it was difficult to calculate who was more bored—performers or audience.
>
> Who will see to it that standards are raised to their old estate and not permitted to deteriorate again? Certainly not Mr. Mitropoulos. He has had ample opportunity, and has failed. One does not question his sympathies for certain modern schools or his gifts of personality and temperament. But he appears to have neither the interest nor the special talent for the meticulous training or sustained leadership which inspires an orchestra to live up to its highest potentialities, whatever the music.[6]

Glad to be leaving New York, Mitropoulos began his European summer by conducting Verdi's *Ernani* in Florence on June 14, 17, 20, and 23. On June 27–28, he led symphonic concerts with the La Scala Orchestra which were notable because they featured the first-ever Italian performances of Mahler's Sixth. The orchestra "played it very well," he wrote to Katy, "and with good discipline, too, in spite of the natural aversion the Latin musician feels for such music."[7] From Milan, he went to Cologne, then to Salzburg, where he conducted a triumphant *Elektra*. While he was there, he conducted two orchestra concerts at the Mozarteum, on August 14 and 28. A veteran player in the Vienna Philharmonic recalled that "the performance of *Elektra* was one of the orchestra's finest experiences in Salzburg. Mitropoulos was able to shape both the ecstasy and the drama of Strauss's music so that the performance became an all-time highlight, a climax which could hardly be excelled."[8]

He took the Vienna Philharmonic to the Lucerne Festival on September 1, and when the regular Viennese season began on September 21, also under Mitropoulos's direction, there was rife speculation, indeed hope, that in the near future he might become not just a regular guest conductor, but the Vienna Philharmonic's principal conductor. Indications are that he was seriously considering such a career move, once he had finished with his obligations in New York—but he already had Metropolitan Opera dates booked for the next two seasons, as well as a substantial part of the Philharmonic's concerts.

Meanwhile, the Philharmonic's board of directors was preparing to finish what it had started by severing the Arthur Judson connection. The august gentlemen who managed the Philharmonic Society took their own time in these matters; it would not, after all, set a good precedent for the society to act precipitously at the behest of one crusading music critic. Phase one had involved the ousting of Arthur Judson, an act of managerial regicide about which some of the board members had felt queasy. A decent interval—an entire season, in fact—had been allowed to go by before phase two, the sacking of a conductor who was admired, respected, even loved, by a sizable worldwide audience, went into effect.

The actual transfer of power took place six weeks into the season, on November 19, 1957. In the weeks leading up to that date, Mitropoulos had enjoyed another triumph at the Met, conducting for a Peter Brook production of Tchaikovsky's *Eugene Onegin* that Lang described as "sumptuous." And he had opened the Carnegie Hall season by featuring the American premiere of Dimitri Kabalevsky's Fourth Symphony. To all outward appearances, the season was starting off just like any other, except that it was two days behind schedule, due to a wage dispute between the Philharmonic Society and the musicians' union.

Without any preamble, a press conference was announced for November 19, by David M. Keiser, president of the Philharmonic Society. A high-profile location had been chosen: the exclusive, prestigious Century Club in midtown Manhattan. Once the reporters had settled down, Mitropoulos rose and gave a speech that was either: a) a masterpiece of irony; b) a profound exercise in masochism; or, c) a final, and most astonishing, example of the very naiveté that had undone him in the first place. He was, he stated, "abdicating with joy," in order to court "that very tempting mistress, the Metropolitan Opera," and that the decision to appoint Leonard Bernstein "shows that America is now so grown up musically that it can offer such an important post to an American-born and American-trained musician."

One witness, Philharmonic historian Howard Shanet, recalled that "it was touching to hear this kind, generous, and well-intentioned artist make his unconsciously condescending remark from his position of weakness."[9] Given what has subsequently become known about the love-hate relationship between the two men, the remarks might not have been "unconsciously condescending" at all.

Mitropoulos then took the chance to address a few remarks to the members of the musical press. "It is all right to write what you believe. But sometimes you should also think that when you write something disagreeable, it doesn't hurt only the conductor; it also hurts the Philharmonic. The Philharmonic needs more support and less criticism. If too many critical things are said, the public loses faith."

This was a pretty feeble riposte for a man who had been run over by the full power of the *New York Times*. Its very moderation and lack of combativeness reveals the extent to which Mitropoulos was indeed willing to turn the other cheek.

Bernstein also made a few remarks. He paid tribute to the fact that Mitropoulos had been crucial in his own decision to turn to conducting, and spoke with great apparent feeling about his colleague's "heartbreaking situation in New York," without of course alluding to his own part in creating that situation.

From November 20, 1957, Dimitri Mitropoulos was no longer music director of the New York Philharmonic. He would finish his scheduled concerts for that season and would participate in the orchestra's South American tour of 1958, but those were his last official duties. Henceforth, he would be just one of numerous guest conductors.

Leonard Bernstein's ascent to the directorship of the Philharmonic marked a watershed in the history of American music and a crushing, humiliating failure for the man he had once worshiped. In the end, Mitropoulos had been undone by the very qualities that made him such a special musician and such a rare human being. As Shanet summed it up in his history of the Philharmonic: "The breadth of Mitropoulos's musical interests and his acceptance of the conductor's responsibilities as educator had led to hopes that remained partially unfulfilled. The simplicity and naiveté that were so charming in him as a man were . . . unbecoming in a cultural leader of one of the world's most sophisticated cities."[10]

CHAPTER THIRTY

Vanessa Hot and Cold

Mitropoulos labored, his last few years, under the strain of more than one cruel irony. When he was dumped by the Philharmonic, he put the best face he could on the matter by proclaiming that he was abdicating in order to concentrate more on his work at the Metropolitan Opera, but by the autumn of 1957, Rudolf Bing had subtly but pervasively altered the conductor's role with that house, a process which Irving Kolodin, the Met's best historian, described as "the reduction in status of Mitropoulos from a master of special scores to an everyday conductor of almost any."[1] As he led more and more routine bread-and-butter operas, he was taken more and more for granted, and his work in the pit began to show some of the same erratic qualities as his work with the Philharmonic. He was "on" one night and somewhere else the next.

But there was still one triumph to come: the world premiere, on January 15, 1958, of Samuel Barber's *Vanessa*. Gian Carlo Menotti's libretto recounts a Chekovian tale of love and loss among the upper classes of an unidentified "northern country" in or about the year 1905. The original concept was inspired by the *Seven Gothic Tales* of Isak Dinesen. Taken by itself, the libretto is a bit strained—would-be Strindberg without most of the requisite nastiness—but once wedded to Barber's atmospheric, moody, sometimes soaringly lyrical score, it becomes no less plausible, no less a theatrical experience, than many of the Italian operas in the Met's repertoire. The point of the tale, as Barber summed it up, is that "Love only exists as a compromise. . . . Whomever we love, it's not the image of the person we expected."[2] This was certainly a concept that Mitropoulos could identify with.

During his visits to Italy in 1956 and 1957, Mitropoulos spent as much time as he could with Barber, working with him on the orchestration. The conductor was delighted with the score; indeed, he took to Barber's elegantly conservative style with as much enthusiasm as he had once taken to Alban Berg's. In an *Opera News* interview, he proclaimed:

> It is a miracle that a composer had the courage to write music in this style. . . . [Barber] hasn't been contaminated by different kinds of contemporary experimentation. . . . *Vanessa* is highly theatrical, full of orchestra surprises and climaxes, but always at the service of the stage, as any real opera should be. . . . At last, an American grand opera![3]

423

In its final form, *Vanessa* epitomizes everything Samuel Barber was as a composer. Menotti's libretto gave him the chance to write for all the set-piece specialties of grand opera: a ball scene with a waltz, a folk-dance ballet, a coloratura skating aria, a love duet, a shimmeringly beautiful orchestral interlude (the intermezzo to Act Two, which has achieved a life of its own as a concert selection), and the now-famous quintet ("To love, to break, to find, to keep") that is the grand finale and one of the finest climaxes in all twentieth-century opera. Barber met these challenges with a score that begins on a high level of pure craftsmanship and gradually gathers inspiration as it progresses.

Certainly, the premiere and the subsequent recording benefited from one of the finest casts that could have been assembled: Eleanor Steber, Rosalind Elias, Regina Resnik, Nicolai Gedda, Georgio Tozzi, and George Cehanovsky. About Mitropoulos's contribution, opera historian George Martin recalled: "the best music comes late in the opera, but Mitropoulos carried the beginning, emphasizing the drama, so the audience, intrigued, stayed with the opera until Barber's imagination took fire. From then on, it was gorgeous."[4]

George Cehanovsky, who sang under both conductors, compared Mitropoulos to Toscanini:

> When tempi were established in rehearsal with Toscanini, they would be exactly the same in performance. He would not change one iota. But Mitropoulos was a conductor of the moment. When a singer was in good voice, he would suck everything out of that singer, but he would never disturb a singer when he or she was enlarging a phrase. If the singer was in good voice, he would always be with that person. Now in some operas, that is impossible, like in *Tosca*, for example, and it should have been impossible in *Vanessa*. It was very tricky to hold everybody under control, but he could do that because he was so free himself. He seemed to *be* the music itself when he conducted that opera. I can't speak for other singers, but I certainly appreciated it.[5]

On opening night, *Vanessa* was received with a thunderous ovation from a sold-out house sparkling with celebrities. The reviews were ecstatic. In the *New Yorker*, Winthrop Sargent called the opera "one of the most impressive things . . . to appear anywhere since Richard Strauss's more vigorous days."[6] Paul Henry Lang thought it every bit as fine as any opera to be heard on "the Salzburg-Milan axis." The opera's success made national news and was praised as a symbol of American cultural maturity even by publications such as *Time* which were not normally in the business of extolling American culture of the loftier kind; Samuel Barber became a hero. The opera won the Pulitzer Prize, and Barber received several medals and honors, including elevation to the prestigious American Academy of Arts and Letters.

Mitropoulos received his share of glory, too, and the praise must have been a balm to his wounded pride. RCA Victor recorded *Vanessa* in September, using the original cast, and the album became a best-seller. It is, in fact, the only Mitropoulos recording that has never gone out of print, and its beauties can be savored today on compact disc.

Once the high point of *Vanessa* was past, the rest of the spring season of 1958 was, for Mitropoulos, just something to be gotten through as best he could. He had two blocks of time with the Philharmonic in February and early March, and they must have been an ordeal.

On March 1, he gave the world premiere of a symphony by a Greek composer—the last time, as it happened, that he would conduct a work by a fellow countryman—and he might as well have saved himself the trouble. The composer was Yorgos (George) Sicilianos, the work was his First Symphony, and the critics, in fairly harsh terms, expressed their hope that it would be his last. Lang, for instance, fired a massive broadside at both Sicilianos's work and the Benjamin Britten Piano Concerto that was also performed:

> It is well known that Dimitri Mitropoulos is a great believer in contemporary music and a friendly and conscientious servant of its composers. In this he is rare among conductors and deserves full honors. But we cannot always trust the validity of his judgment; the program he selected for Saturday night's Philharmonic concert was atrocious.
>
> The premiere of Yeorgo Sicilianos' First Symphony was a pathetic affair. This composer bows his head to so many masters that his neck must need to be held up by braces . . . Mr. Sicilianos is worse than an eclectic composer—his music is like a mound of shingles upon which the listener must walk, sliding in every direction with every step.
>
> . . . Benjamin Britten's Piano Concerto . . . [is] a truly eclectic trifle without any spiritual content.[7]

Once more, Mitropoulos stunned his audiences and temporarily silenced his critics by conducting searing concert performances of *Elektra* on March 6, 7, and 19. Inge Borkh sang the title role, matching heroic vocalism with a commanding stage presence.

Mitropoulos led his final concert as co-conductor of the New York Philharmonic on March 16. The program was typical: Mahler's Tenth Symphony (the two-movement torso of it, anyway; all that is authentically from Mahler's hand), and accompanied the twenty-five-year-old Glenn Gould in performances of Bach's D Minor Concerto and Schoenberg's singular Piano Concerto.

Mitropoulos was still committed to the Philharmonic's long-planned South American tour, but he was not in good shape: his heart condition was worsening and he was starting to have gall bladder problems. This was one of the most exhausting tours the Philharmonic had ever undertaken—forty-one concerts in twenty-two cities, all in six weeks' time. Moreover, he was humiliatingly assigned to fill in for Bernstein, which often meant that he would have to conduct repertoire that was not especially congenial. Bernstein's treatment of his older colleague was subtly cruel: if Lenny suddenly wanted to scoot off somewhere to sightsee or (as increasingly happened) to flirt with some attractive young man, Mitropoulos was obliged to assume his duties in addition to his own. Bernstein's wife, Felicia, disliked flying and could be heard praying in Spanish whenever the orchestra's plane was crossing a mountain range. When her husband publicly embarrassed her by making passes at young men in Felicia's native country of Chile, she decided she had had enough and angrily flew back to the United States.

Mitropoulos took whatever was dished out to him, and his public complaints, as usual, were mild. Even to his closest friend, Katy, he played down the worst aspects of the trip, summarizing the experience in very temperate language:

> To speak about *success*, that is a very mild word. The South Americans, as you know, are very demonstrative, and they really went haywire. From [Buenos Aires] on, we played every town, because I was alone with the orchestra, Mr. Bernstein having gone to rest in the home town of his wife, Santiago, Chile . . . so I had to conduct every day at all the coast cities of Argentine and Brazil, where the reception was warm, and as exhausting as it could be.[8]

Bernstein may well have been a little miffed at the adoration Mitropoulos received from the Latin American audiences. Pianist Ruth Slenczynska, who was touring the region at the same time as the orchestra, had occasion to observe Mitropoulos's success in several cities where tour dates overlapped:

> Contrary to what everyone expected, Bernstein was not the great popular success with South Americans, but Mitropoulos was. His musicianship apparently just enchanted those people—particularly in Buenos Aires, where they raved over him, absolutely loved his work. In Rio de Janeiro, the same thing took place. Everybody had expected the young Bernstein to captivate those audiences with his looks and whatnot, but it didn't happen. Mitropoulos became the star of that tour.[9]

Mitropoulos in fact proved, on several occasions, that he knew perfectly well how to upstage a colleague if he wanted to. In São Paolo, for example, where music-lovers had camped out all night in front of the box office, Mitropoulos led an open-air concert before a throng of thirty thousand and created a frenzy of enthusiasm when, at the start of the concert, he turned to the public-address microphone and greeted the audience in flawless Portuguese. When he conducted, as an encore, dances from de Falla's *The Three-Cornered Hat*, the crowd went berserk. One Philharmonic veteran was heard to remark to a colleague: "My God, what do they do if they *don't* like you?"

Upon returning to New York, the orchestra received a rather curious reception. Hundreds of family members and fans were on hand; the mayor was supposed to be there, too, but he backed out at the last minute and sent, in his stead, the Department of Sanitation band. A handful of second-tier dignitaries made speeches and presented the two conductors with commemorative medals. In accepting his, Mitropoulos made another of his marvelously indiscreet speeches, calling attention to the mayor's absence and saying that, while medals were fine, they were no substitute for the kind of support these musicians deserved and so seldom got from their city's administration.

After those remarks were greeted with scattered, tentative applause, Mitropoulos moved away from the mike, and Bernstein moved in to hog it, lavishing praise on the musicians, bragging about how they had "played like angels," and so on. Mitropoulos stood in the background while this was going on. Some acquaintances observed that he was all alone; not a single person had stayed by his side; once Bernstein began to speak, all attention was focused on the younger man.

Since his presence was obviously no longer needed nor, apparently, wanted, Mitropoulos began to shuffle off morosely, head down, alone. Shocked at the way Mitropoulos was being treated—virtually as though he had ceased to exist—several friends made their way to his side and offered to take him to lunch. Visibly cheered, he accepted. As they were walking away, the Sanitation Department band began to play once more. Mitropoulos halted, cocked his head to listen, then smiled wearily and said: "Listen to that. The boy must be conducting them—they weren't playing that well before."

And in fact, Bernstein had taken the baton from the band leader and was at that moment launching into a lusty rendition of "The Stars and Stripes Forever."

The early weeks of the summer of 1958 were fairly pleasant ones. Mitropoulos went in June to Israel and conducted concerts in Tel Aviv, Jerusalem, and Haifa. He was overjoyed to be in the Holy Land for the first time, and devoted every spare moment to sightseeing.

From Israel, he flew to Amsterdam for two concerts with the fabled Concertgebouw Orchestra, and in early August, he returned to Vienna for his now-regular appearances at the Salzburg Festival.

This year's festival was to have been very special: the entire Metropolitan production of *Vanessa* had been booked for a performance on August 19. This was the first time since 1910 that a Met production had been seen in Europe, the first time any American opera had been given at Salzburg, and the first time any opera had been sung in English there. This should have been one of the happier engagements of Mitropoulos's career, but instead it proved to be a disaster.

Without having heard a note of *Vanessa*, the Viennese critics began to snipe at the work weeks before opening night, calling it an "unfortunate" choice, and attacking American culture in general. Librettist Gian Carlo Menotti knew there was going to be trouble on the occasion of the first press conference:

> As soon as we arrived in Salzburg, Sam [Barber] and Mitropoulos and Bing were asked to a press conference where they were asked the most embarrassing questions. Things like: "Mr. Barber, do you feel that we Austrians are not good enough to write operas, that you have to bring your operas from New York?" Things like that—really awful. And the whole atmosphere was wrought up to such a state of poison that we just knew we were going to have a hostile, horrible audience. And sure enough, we did. The audience was just frozen; they barely applauded at the end. A whole audience of musicians and critics, and it was one of the worst evenings I have ever been through. The music was still beautiful and the production was possibly even better than in New York. But von Karajan snubbed us afterwards, did not even come backstage to say "Nice job," or "Bravo." Afterwards, we weren't even invited out. Just Mitropoulos, Sam, Bing and I eating all by ourselves in a little restaurant. After all, von Karajan was the director, and he was the one who invited us over, saying what a wonderful opera it was, but he washed his hands of us when he saw which way the wind was blowing. He behaved like an absolute pig.[10]

Some of the worst problems were with the backstage crew. There is a place in Act Three where snow is supposed to blow in from the blizzard raging outside. The Salzburg stagehands made no attempt to use realistic stage-snow, but instead just threw big wads of cotton onto the stage, which of course caused the already-primed audience to break into hoots of derisive laughter.

The press was scathing. Barber's music was derided as "a chromaticized Puccini, plus a few ounces of Strauss, Wagner, and Tchaikovsky, and a shot of Debussy." The libretto was "dated, old-fashioned, Strindbergian. . . a combination of fin de siècle realism and pseudo-psychology." The production as a whole was "disgusting," "wretched," "enough to make one cry." Cecil Beaton's lavishly detailed sets were "insipidly naturalistic," and so on.[11]

Mitropoulos withdrew from public sight for a week or so, terribly bitter about *Vanessa*'s reception from the hitherto-friendly Viennese. In the days that followed, many members of the audience approached him and told him that they, personally, had liked *Vanessa* very much, and some critics wrote follow-up pieces suggesting that the opera was not entirely bereft of musical virtues.

Putting the Salzburg failure behind him, Mitropoulos remained in Europe throughout September. He took the Vienna Philharmonic to Athens for four concerts early in the month, the last concerts he would ever conduct in his homeland. When the Vienna Philharmonic opened its official season, on September 27, Mitropoulos was on the podium, fueling new speculation that he would eventually become that orchestra's principal conductor. As though to make the speculation that much more interesting, he also conducted the Vienna Symphony's first concerts, October 4 and 5.

When he returned to New York, he faced a very busy schedule at the Met. He conducted four *Tosca*s, three *Boris Godunov*s, one *Eugen Onegin*, one more *Vanessa*, and a couple of fairly routine *Cavalleria rusticana—I pagliacci* productions. He was busy, productive, and had started rather to enjoy his freedom from the daily grind at the New York Philharmonic (where his successor was now, in his turn, being accused by the critics of "sloppy discipline").

Mitropoulos spent a quiet Christmas, intensely studying scores for scheduled Met productions of *Macbeth* and *Pelléas et Mélisande* by Debussy, two works for which he felt a strong affinity.

Then, without warning, on January 23, 1959, he suffered a second and far more serious heart attack.

CHAPTER THIRTY-ONE

To Fall from a Mountaintop

Mitropoulos suffered one severe heart attack and several secondary aftershocks. The attacks confirmed what many of his closest friends had thought, ever since his recovery from the first hospitalization: he had done little to take care of himself. He had resumed smoking and had graduated from Camels to Gauloises, a brand of fragrant but potent French cigarettes with one of the highest nicotine contents of any brand on the world market. He continued to wolf down greasy lamb dishes, rare hamburgers, and other cholesterol-rich meals. He existed on five hours of sleep a night. He drove himself relentlessly, moving from the Met to Carnegie Hall, still obsessively memorizing even the most demanding scores. And while doing all of this, he had been subjected to the incalculable stress of being publicly humiliated, driven from his Philharmonic job, and gradually relegated to the status of a work-horse repetiteur at the opera house.

David Bar-Ilan was one concerned friend who was dismayed, but not exactly surprised, when the conductor was felled in January 1959:

> The main thing that worried me at that time, aside from his customary overwork, was that I thought he was eating too much for a man with a heart condition. I really felt he was not taking good care of himself. I suppose he had a certain fatalistic attitude about this. I had the impression that he never really listened to what his doctors told him—that he was determined to live the way he wanted to live. He was not a man who could have lived on his knees, so to speak. He never wanted to be a slave to anything, including his own body's infirmity.[1]

When he recovered from the initial trauma, Mitropoulos began to be terrified, for the first time in his life, of poverty. As usual, he had no savings—he was still supporting a half-dozen students and handing out cash sums to anyone he felt deserved them—and his medical bills were mounting alarmingly. After tip-toeing around the matter for a few days, his doctors finally gave him the official word: no work for six months, total rest, absolutely no conducting. Mitropoulos was distraught. He poured out his feelings in a letter to Katy written only a week after he entered the hospital:

Nobody could ever imagine the greatness of my disaster. Immediate death would have been better than this sudden lightning attack on my moral as well as economic structure! Believe me, there couldn't have been a worse moment literally to destroy me! To remain now, *at this time,* unemployed for six months means to lose $60,000, which after the state has extorted its share, would have paid for my debts of last year and the expenses of the new one till August! . . . I'm condemned to inaction for six whole months, at the end of which I'm not assured of any beneficial future without the sword of Damocles hanging over my head! . . . Believe me, it's a thousand times better to stop abruptly than to be forced to live on credit, both physically and financially. I had a serious talk with my doctor and from our discussion I realize clearly the tragedy of our lives. A chain of circumstances that no one can foresee or prevent, but one has to submit to, like Job. The poor wretch was bewildered that all these disasters were happening to him: what injustice, what harm had he done in his life, when he had tried hard to be perfect, decent, just— and the ironic answer that we all know: exactly because of that![2]

Once the crisis was past, Mitropoulos could at least have some visitors. Louis Biancolli, the one critic who had remained wholly on Mitropoulos's side, spent as much time as he could with the conductor, and found him "distressed at the prospect of enforced inactivity and the specter of mounting bills. What financial reserve he might have accrued had gone over the years to relieve others in a similar plight."

I spent three hours with him . . . at the hospital, going over the direction his life-story would take if he ever got well, and I began taking it down in the Gregg shorthand that has been my own tape recorder since I was a boy. . . . I knew then that Mitropoulos's memoir would be a source of inspiration to young and old alike in its twin theme of whole-souled dedication to music and to the relief of material distress among fellow musicians and their families, and many others. I also knew the book would never be written. Mitropoulos was determined to die *in medias res* of music, as in tragic yet poetic fact, he did, and I was determined to spare him the daily grilling of a relentless ghost. I did not want even the partial guilt of his death on my conscience. So his story has gone untold.[3]

Pianist Byron Janis was also one of the first visitors. He found the conductor "very ill and feeling very alone. In contrast to the first time he had been hospitalized, he had had few cards, almost no visitors. There wasn't even a flower in the hospital room. He was utterly despondent, and kept muttering things like, 'Well, you know, you're only important for a short time in this life . . . people forget so quickly.'"[4]

By early March, Mitropoulos was able to walk around and do light exercise. His doctors were amazed at his recuperation, and one of them even said that he could return to conducting at that moment, provided he only did it once or twice a month. He laughed when he heard that—if he resumed, he would be conducting three or four times a week, just as he always had. He seems never to have seriously entertained the notion of really cutting back just to prolong his physical existence.

His doctors could promise only that he could count on keeping his August–October commitments in Salzburg, Cologne, and Vienna. On March 7, he wrote again to Katy:

> I am walking up and down in my room, which is a big one, and I do my exercise in order to get strong, so that in two weeks I will be able again to go to my movies, to my restaurant La Scala, and naturally, I am going to see the Promised Land of my artistic activities [the Met and Carnegie Hall] from afar, just like a man who is paying a heavy debt for his guilt! You don't know how beautiful is the view from my window, looking down on the river, the boats passing up and down, and in front of me, all the skyscrapers of Manhattan. And in the evenings, sometimes when I am alone, I sit in the window and meditate in front of this gorgeous city.[5]

He began feeling well enough to resume with Katy the on-again, off-again debate/discussion of musical aesthetics the two of them had been engaged in for almost twenty years. Although he doggedly continued to stand on the side of modernist composers, there are signs in his letters that he had finally become disenchanted with the serialists, or perhaps more accurately, with the power so many of them were now starting to wield in academic circles.

For by this time, serialism had achieved a fleeting kind of triumph as its practitioners consolidated their hold over an exhausted postwar Europe, and as a growing number of composers in America strove first to acquire and then justify their academic perks by turning their art into a hermetic quasi-science (something they could do because of the enormous national insecurity engendered by the advent of Sputnik), creating the academic equivalent of the Maginot Line and embroidering on their battle-flags the often-quoted dictum of Milton Babbitt: "Who cares if you listen?"

Above all else, Dimitri Mitropoulos wanted people to *listen*; not only with their emotions, but with their intellects and even their moral sensibilities. It is ironic that the triumph of serialism and its related ideologies came about not for any of the reasons Mitropoulos had predicted, and that its two-decade-long reign resulted not in a broadening of musical tastes and sensitivity, but—at least in the limited arenas where people took such matters seriously—in a mood that verged on the totalitarian and gave birth to a dogmatism of near-Stalinist intolerance.

Mitropoulos would have been alienated by that hollow triumph, by the spectacle of a hundred tenured Babbitts launching salvo after ideological salvo at the empty seats in the auditoriums where concerts of their increasingly ugly and in-bred music was performed. How Mitropoulos's own style, thinking, and programming priorities might have changed is of course a totally conjectural matter; that, had he lived, he would have made a valuable and eloquent contribution to the aesthetic debate, seems a given. His absence from the musical scene simply made the ensuing decades even more dreary and dogmatic, at least for listeners who still, to some extent, gave a damn about music as a form of human communication.

"I was reading Camus' description of the situation in Algiers," he wrote to Katy on March 14:

> and I earned a very pessimistic outlook—I might say hopeless—of humanity ever getting together, that the idea of the brotherhood of man is less and less than Utopia, it is simply pure stupidity . . . with the progress of nihilism and atheism, not only in politics but also in art. I have in mind "electronic" composers and the avant-garde people who refuse the idea of a theme—in other words anything that is human in us [is] to be discarded.[6]

Mitropoulos was released from the hospital at the end of March, but his health was irreparably damaged. He was ordered by his doctors to take tranquilizers, so that he would be forced to lead a more sedate existence for a while. He hated them. He tried to resume studying scores but found that "my brain does not work anymore." He endured bouts of anxiety and depression. He took his telephone off the hook so that well-wishers could not disturb him. "I need my privacy now more than ever," he wrote to Katy on March 31, "in order to fight alone all my problems and doubts about myself."

Friends who had not seen him since before the heart attack were dismayed by his appearance. His monk's-tonsure of hair had turned white; the flesh hung loosely on his face; he looked ten years older than he was.

By April, his condition had worsened. He was plagued by a prostate infection and by bladder stones. The former malady was relieved by an operation on May 5, but because of his generally weakened condition, the second affliction could not be treated surgically. For the remainder of his life, he was plagued with periodic bladder infections and fevers.

Nevertheless, he went back to Europe. He allowed himself a period of rest in Zurich, from August 1 to August 12, then he plunged once more into his work, rehearsing the intense and demanding oratorio of Franz Schmidt, *The Book of the Seven Seals*, which he conducted at Salzburg on August 23, 1959. He conducted twice in Cologne, on August 31 and September 7: the first concert commemorated the centenary of Mahler's birth (with a stunning performance of the Sixth Symphony) and the second was an all-Strauss program in honor of the tenth anniversary of that composer's death. He led two more Strauss programs in Vienna, on September 19 and 20, and followed them with several productions at the State Opera.

Just getting back to work had a revivifying effect on Mitropoulos, but even though he felt much better by September, something had changed profoundly within him, as he expressed to Katy in a letter written from Cologne:

> What can I say to you, my dear Katy, my health is in good shape but I am no longer the same man! I've withdrawn within myself more than ever before and I long for my moments of isolation. I look at the people around me with the same kindness but with more indifference, as though I weren't living among them any more, and was watching them from another world. This frightens me sometimes! I have no certainty that I'm alive or that I will stay alive for very long. It's as though I am expecting the end. I hope this feeling . . . will disappear in time. And I'm terrified that I will re-enter the horrible atmosphere of doctors and nurses.[7]

When he returned to New York, he rested and prepared for the demanding part he would play in the New York Philharmonic's Mahler Festival, scheduled to begin on December 1 and run for eight weeks, in observance of the fiftieth anniversary of Mahler's tenure with the New York Philharmonic.

His first assignment was the Fifth Symphony, to be performed on January 2, 1960. He was welcomed back by the Philharmonic players with demonstrations of real affection by most. During the Mahler Fifth rehearsals, Mitropoulos addressed the horn section with the following startling remarks: "I must apologize to the horns. (Puzzled laughter). No, I am serious. I am always asking them to play more, but some good friends, whose opinion I respect, tell me that the horns are often too loud. So, horns, if I ask for more, please don't do it. (More laughter) I really mean it. I know I will get excited and ask for more but you must resist!"[8]

James Chambers, principal horn at the time, called that "an impossible assignment! We all made a great effort to comply, but it was very difficult to ignore the impassioned pleas of a conductor who in the excitement of performance has forgotten his own admonition!"[9]

Mitropoulos led the Fifth Symphony on December 31 and January 1–3; the First Symphony on January 7–10; the two-movement version of the Tenth on January 14–17; and the valedictory Ninth on January 21–24.

His final performance of the Ninth Symphony was an extraordinary experience. After decades of ignoring or deprecating Mahler's music, the New York audience suddenly seemed to comprehend it on a deeper level; many were moved to their souls by the revelation. After a few seconds of stunned silence at the end, the audience roared to its feet, joined by most of the players. After the performance, concertmaster John Corigliano came to Mitropoulos backstage, tears flowing freely down his face, and embraced him, saying that it was an unforgettable privilege to play this music under his baton.

Henry Levinger, a writer for *Musical America*, joined in the "endless ovation," then went backstage and asked the conductor why he thought "a work which never had been so fully appreciated by [the New York] audience seemed suddenly to have conquered it."

"Well," Mitropoulos answered in perfect sincerity, "maybe Gustav Mahler has led my baton from the beyond."

In parting, Levinger admonished Mitropoulos to take care of himself. Quoting from his beloved western movies, the conductor smiled softly and said: "I cannot and will not live as an invalid. I'd rather die with my boots on."[10]

In these, his final concerts with the New York Philharmonic, Mitropoulos at least had the satisfaction of being praised by his enemies, the critics. Even Taubman was forced to write in his review: "Mr. Mitropoulos's absorption in his task was so thorough, and the orchestra's playing rose so admirably to the challenge, that one felt as if there were no middlemen between the composer and the listener."

Leonard Bernstein dropped in for the Friday afternoon performance of the Tenth, intending only to exchange a few words of business with some people who were using his box seats that day. Having done that, he fell so utterly under the spell of the music that when someone tried to get him to move on, he replied: "It's so incredible, I can't leave," and indeed, he caused such a commotion with his demonstrations of enthusiasm that he distracted a number of nearby listeners from the music itself.

For the rest of that spring of 1960, Mitropoulos put his failing body through an unspeakable regimen of work. Including a sensationally received revival of Verdi's *Simon Boccanegra*, he directed twenty-eight performances at the Met. Many of these, he directed while feverish. He seemed to have turned into a pale, self-consuming flame, his body wasting away as his spirit burned more brightly. At moments, he seemed almost transparent, anchored to this earth only by the determination that showed in his eyes. Katy believed that at this time "he lost not only the possibility, but the *capability* of rest."[11]

On March 20, the Greek poet George Seferis received a letter from Mitropoulos in which the conductor confessed: "Unfortunately, my so-called devotion to my work has taken me practically completely away from life itself. I don't 'live' any more except for those moments when I am on the podium, and except for those moments, I spend the rest of my life preparing myself in excoriating discipline, doubt, and humility."[12]

On the same day, Mitropoulos wrote to the wife of David Cooper, the son of his dear friend William, to acknowledge a recent photo of the Coopers' one-year-old son, for whom the conductor had been named godfather:

Dear Nancy:
     It was indeed a wonderful gesture of a mother to send me the picture of this happy-looking son of hers, who also happens to be—alas

from afar—my godson. I am sure he gives you enormous joy, a joy that always in my life I looked upon in other people, and knew definitely could not be one of my personal joys. I know that it is not fate, but absolutely my personal wish that I remained a bachelor and in spite of that I still can feel the right and the value of such an enjoyment in others.

I wish to you, to David, and to your boy all the happiness that fate can allow you, and I hope I live long enough to meet this boy when he will be grown up, and he will be able to understand me.[13]

In other letters to the Coopers written that spring, he reminisced wistfully about the peaceful days at Tapiola lodge, where he came as close as he could to having a family of his own. Two days before his departure for Europe, he wrote his "dear friends, Dorothy and Bill" an expression of yearning that also seemed a farewell: "Believe me, I will always keep hoping that some day I might be able to come and relax a little in your arms, just like one of the family. It is just a dream, but I hope that we will all live long enough so that I might realize that dream. . . . So I tell you goodbye, and many good wishes for good health for you all."[14]

At about this same time, Mitropoulos attended the opening of Sidney Lumet's production of Albert Camus's *Caligula*, for which David Amram had written some music. At the conclusion, with a twinkle in his eye, Mitropoulos said to the young composer: "I enjoyed your music, David. . . . You have made wonderful strides since that time almost fifteen years ago when we met. You've even learned to modulate."

Then the conductor tried to excuse himself, telling Amram that he ought to go and meet "some of the many important people here."

"Well, Maestro, you're the only important person for me here," replied Amram.

Mitropoulos was touched. "You're a good boy, as you always were. I'm happy that you feel that way about me. It's good to have such loyalty to your old friend. To tell you the truth, I am not feeling very well. I'll go back to the hotel."

Amram insisted on escorting the conductor back to the Great Northern. As they drew near that address, Mitropoulos suddenly turned to Amram and said: "Would you ever want to do anything besides music?"

Remembering Mitropoulos's habit of asking questions in order to voice their answers, Amram answered simply: "No."

"Neither would I," mused Mitropoulos. "I thought about it many times, but the more I work at music, the more I know how fortunate I am to be a musician. Without it, I don't know what I'd do. Without it, I can't imagine my life having meaning. I can't even climb mountains anymore, since my health has been bad. I should not smoke, and even the one big meal I eat every day should be supervised more carefully. Still, music gives me that same joy that it always did."

As Mitropoulos was entering the hotel, he turned once more to Amram, "took another look at me with his wonderful piercing eyes," and quietly said: "Aren't we lucky?"[15]

That was the last time Amram saw him.

In early May, Mitropoulos underwent a painful and slow-healing operation for his bladder condition. He was not allowed to resume activities until the end of July, when he sailed for Europe to keep his engagements at the Salzburg Festival.

He only had one work to conduct at this year's festival, but it was one of the biggest in the repertoire: Mahler's "Symphony of a Thousand," the Eighth. About eighty minutes long, it calls for a huge orchestra, seven soloists, and the biggest chorus that can be assembled.

The normal Salzburg hall was not big enough to contain the performing forces as well as an audience, so the production was mounted in that unique outdoor venue known as the Felsenreitschule (the Outdoor Riding School), an immense quarry-like arena that was once part of the bishop of Salzburg's stables. It was open to the elements, and the back of the "stage" area was a huge cliff that had been fashioned into tiers of stone arcades through which the performers entered and exited. In the early days of the Salzburg Festival, Clemens Holzmeister, a brilliant Viennese stage designer and architect, had made use of these imposing arrangements to construct huge, fabulous, make-believe cities for plays such as *Faust* and operas such as *Don Giovanni*.

Rehearsals were stormy. Mitropoulos had had to endure enormous vexations in arranging the performance with the Viennese bureaucrats. He was in a foul temper when the first rehearsal began late. He raged at the Vienna Philharmonic's concertmaster, at the first trombone, at the soloists, stamping his foot and waving his fists. No one had ever seen him behave like this before.

After the rehearsal, several friends took him to a cafe, where everyone made an effort to calm him down. Present were James Dixon and Felix Eyle, concertmaster of the Metropolitan Opera orchestra, and Eyle's wife. Throughout the luncheon, Mitropoulos complained bitterly: "I can't be alone for a minute! Everybody is always coming to me and asking for this favor and that favor, for letters of introduction to the New York orchestra, for a commitment to conduct this or that piece. And everybody wants money! My God, I can't do it any more! I just can't! I'm so tired, and they never stop coming to me!"[16]

By contrast, the actual performance on August 28 was a stupendous success. The day had been cloudy, but at the exact moment Mitropoulos launched into the titanic final chorus of the "Veni, Creator Spiritus" movement, the sky opened melodramatically and a shaft of golden light shined down on the podium.

Conductor John Canarina, who had followed Mitropoulos's career since his student days at Juilliard, never forgot the demonstration at the end of the symphony:

I had not seen Mitropoulos for a couple of years, and I was shocked at his appearance when he came out on stage. But the performance was tremendous, and the audience went wild, yelling and clapping rhythmically. I remember that Mitropoulos acknowledged the applause only for a few minutes. He came out and shook hands with all the soloists and first-desk people in the orchestra, and he lifted one little chap from the Vienna Boys Choir and kissed him on the forehead, and then he left the stage. He did not come back, although the ovation must have gone on for another fifteen minutes.[17]

He stayed in and around Vienna through the early autumn, and in September he conducted six performances at the Staatsoper of Verdi's *La forza del destino*. These were his farewell performances as an opera conductor, and, as Katy recorded, they seemed to build in magnitude and force from night to night:

The rehearsals were difficult, the last one stormy. His surveillance of the whole and of each scenic detail was immediate and demanding. The first performance was an achievement; it had that exaltation which is the result of overcoming difficulties. The second one was smooth and faultless, but the third! It was one of those miracles you cannot explain, nor even conceive. Never before had I seen him in such eminence. . . . From the very first note it was obvious that something unique was happening—the perfection of it filled us with awe. I asked myself: "Can such things happen on earth?" Yet I felt that this man had to die. Where else could he still go? He had surpassed all human boundaries. Later the musicians in the orchestra and the singers confessed to me: "We don't know why, but we played (or sang) as never before in our lives. He forced us to surpass ourselves."[18]

How had he done it? Katy asked him afterward. Dimitri only replied: "Such performances are gifts of God."

He conducted a pair of orchestra concerts with the Vienna Philharmonic in early October, then went to Cologne for what was to be his final public appearance. His performance there of Mahler's Third, taped on October 31, is much superior to his New York performance of April 1956, and not only because the German oboist was doing his job. This performance, along with the incredible Vienna Mahler Eighth and the *Forza* performance of September 23, bear powerful testimony to the fact that Mitropoulos was still growing as a conductor, maturing in fact, now that he was liberated from the struggle for survival that had been his lot in New York. Had he lived, he would have entered a golden period.

At the intermission of the Cologne concert, Mitropoulos's physical state was so alarming that Trudy Goth and representatives of the Cologne Radio tried to persuade him to cancel the remainder of the performance. Mitropoulos would not even consider it. When the applause began at the end, he gave a quick bow, then ducked out the back door of the hall, suitcase in hand, and took a taxi to the railroad station before anyone could stop him. The next morning, he was in Milan.

In Milan, he was scheduled to perform Mahler's Third again. He began the day by breakfasting in a coffee house near La Scala, where he encountered the orchestra's first-chair oboe, a gentleman named Visai. The conductor greeted his colleague cordially, but Visai immediately noticed that Mitropoulos looked exhausted, that his complexion was unnaturally pale, and that he had trouble getting his breath.

When Mitropoulos arrived to begin the rehearsal, at ten o'clock, he was welcomed with a standing ovation. He could tell from their faces that the players had noticed his condition and were alarmed by it, but he tried to reassure them by saying: "It's true I am fatigued, but I'm like an old automobile whose parts are worn out, but that still works."

As he gave the men his opening instructions, he spoke to them by name: "dear Musetti, dear Caruso, my dear friend Visai." Then he got down to work. He gave the first tempo, then stopped for some technical instructions, then resumed. One musician who was there later said: "I will never forget the great power with which he conducted the celli and contrabasses at bar No. 39 in the score. I can still see him bending to the right with tremendous force and demanding a 'wild effect' from the players."[19]

They reached bar No. 80, where the trombones make a big entrance. A few seconds later, Mitropoulos stopped conducting and sat back down on his high stool. The orchestra fell silent, anticipating further instructions.

Instead, his face froze and he slowly began to pitch forward, "like a statue falling from a pedestal." His head crashed into the music stand in front of the podium, lacerating his scalp and flinging a shower of blood over the stage. The conductor was carried to one side of the stage and a doctor was immediately summoned, along with an ambulance. There may still have been a faint pulse when he was loaded into the ambulance—accounts differ on that detail—but when the vehicle arrived at the nearby Milan Polyclinic, Dimitri Mitropoulos was dead.

An autopsy revealed that the coronary had been so massive it had blown open one of the chambers of his heart.

All during that summer, Mitropoulos had prayed to his stern and personal God, and in the end, God had answered his prayer and granted him precisely the death he would have chosen.

A Brief Recessional

And then he was the best of all things, Greek—
no quality more precious has mankind:
What lies beyond only the gods may find.
> —Cavafy, "The Epitaph of Antiochus,
> King of Kommagene"

Sweet is my sleep—
But more to be mere stone
So long as ruin and dishonor reign
Speak in an undertone.
> —Michelangelo; as set to music in David
> Diamond's Ninth Symphony, dedicated to
> the memory of Dimitri Mitropoulos

On the morning of November 1, 1960, David Diamond and Trudy Goth, in Florence, made plans to travel together to Milan to attend Mitropoulos's Mahler concert. They were making final preparations when the news of his death arrived. It was as though the sun had gone black.

———————

A handwritten letter was found on Mitropoulos's body:

> It is my irrevocable desire that in the event of my death a notice should be published to the effect that flowers should not be sent. If anybody wants to remember me, then he can make a contribution, in my name, and any capital that accrues thereby should be used to support American composers, under the aegis of the New York Philharmonic Society. My mortal remains should not be put on public view; they should be cremated without any ceremony and in a manner which does not give rise to excessive cost. My ashes should be given to Mr. James Dixon, resident of the state of Iowa. They are to be placed in an amphora or

some other suitable container, which shall be purchased for a nominal sum. The aforementioned James Dixon may, if he wishes, donate this amphora in order that burial can take place in Greece.

Since cremation was not legal in Italy, the corpse was taken to Lugano, Switzerland, where the conductor's wish was carried out. The government of Greece sent a C-47 military plane, on the day following the cremation, and the ashes were taken back to Athens by Theodore Vavayannis, friend and protégé of Mitropoulos and conductor of the Athens Symphony Orchestra.

That same afternoon, a ceremony was held in Mitropoulos's honor at the Theater of Herodus Atticus, and the urn was placed on public view for three days at the Athens Conservatory. Mitropoulos's final resting place was within a marble memorial designed by sculptor Giannis Papas. In his address, Mr. Aristotle Kyriakides, president of the Athens Conservatory, said: "We lay these honored ashes in this grave with reverent and loving hands. That was his wish. Let this humble urn be covered by the soil of Greece, and may our great departed friend find in this grave the everlasting peace he sought. Let no lamentations accompany this burial."

Later that same year, a bust of Mitropoulos, on a simple marble pedestal, was erected in a meadow in the province of Arcadia. It remains there today, as solitary in its witness as the man whose visage it bears was in his life. All around rise the wild and ancient hills of the Peloponnesus, and in the distance, Mitropoulos's monument is watched over by his beloved mountains.

The day Mitropoulos died, Arthur Mirtallo, co-owner of the La Scala Restaurant, received a postcard from Milan, in which the conductor specified what he wanted for lunch on the day he would return to New York.

On the night of November 2, composer David Amram went out of his New York apartment to buy a newspaper. On the front page was the news that Mitropoulos had died. Amram walked in a daze for the rest of the night.

> Every time I tried to think of something else, I saw his face. I could see the wing collar he wore when he conducted. I could see him bowing to the orchestra, bowing to the audience, and looking far off, the way he always did when the music was over.
>
> He always heard something no one else did. You could tell it just by being in his presence. Now, no one would ever know his secret. All we could do was remember that face and the eyes that looked as if they were from another time. The half-flickering smile, the great domed head, the compassion and sense of irony that he radiated in his gentle, loving way.

I knew he had simply left his body behind. He didn't need or want it any more. . . . For the rest of my life, I could think of him and try to fathom the secret that he had left his countless friends all over the world. At best, all the thousands of musicians I had met could leave the world their music. Mitropoulos had left the world his soul.[20]

Mitropoulos had been scheduled to lead Mahler's Third Symphony with the New York Philharmonic in April. Of course, Bernstein substituted for him. After ascending the podium, Lenny theatrically bowed his head in apparent reverence for a long minute before launching into the symphony's grandiose opening. The critics chided him for his "shameless exhibitionism" and then went on to praise his masterful conducting. "In his last tribute to Mitropoulos, Bernstein succeeded in ripping the attention away from him as he had done so many times during Mitropoulos's life."[21]

And in September 1960, Howard Taubman was promoted to the most powerful and prestigious reviewing job in the world: chief drama critic for the *New York Times*.

Notes

PREFACE   The Forgotten Giant

1. Isaac Stern, interview by Oliver Daniel, tape recording, August 25, 1985. Unless otherwise specified, all interviews were tape recorded; the Archive of the Performing Arts, University of Minnesota, is the depository for the materials collected in this research.

CHAPTER ONE   Origins

1. Dimitri Mitropoulos, "Missionary of Music," in Hans Reinhardt and Josef Muller-Marein, *Das Musikalische Selbstportrait von Komponisten, Dirigenten, Instrumentalisten, Sängerinnen und Sängern unserer Zeit* (Hamburg: n.p., n.d.), unnumbered pages.
2. Vresthena, also spelled Tristena and Prestena, is the transliteration used in the British Naval Intelligence Geographical Handbook Series, Kathleen Giberd, ed., *Greece* (Cambridge: Cambridge University Press, 1944).
3. Dorle Soria, interview by Oliver Daniel, January 12, 1984.
4. "Philharmonic to Give Party for Mitropoulos," *New York World Telegram*, February 10, 1956.
5. John Collis, "The Greek Come Bearing Gifts," *Symphony Magazine*, May 1951.

CHAPTER TWO   Adolescent Turning Points

1. Maria Christopoulou, interview by Oliver Daniel, August 1, 1985.
2. David Lloyd, interview by Oliver Daniel, April 4, 1984.
3. Paul Strauss, interview by Oliver Daniel, December 15, 1983.
4. Julien Green, *God's Fool: The Life and Times of St. Francis* (New York: Harper and Row, 1985), 70.
5. Dimitri Mitropoulos, "What I Believe," *Hi-Fi Music at Home*, May–June 1956.
6. Green, *God's Fool*, 77.

CHAPTER THREE   The Young Composer

1. From unpublished translation by James Aliferis of portions of Apostolos Kostios, *Dimitri Mitropoulos* (Athens: National Bank of Greece, 1985). This book is based on Kostios's doctoral dissertation but also contains additional anecdotal material (hereafter Kostios, *Mitropoulos*). Kostios's book has been

translated into Italian (Florence: Aletheia, 1994), and the possibility of a French edition has been mentioned in the press.

2. Maria Christopoulou, interview by Oliver Daniel, January 8, 1985.

3. Apostolos Kostios, "Der Dirigent Dimitri Mitropoulos," 10, trans. William Walker, tape recording; originally published as Ph.D. diss., University of Vienna, 1983, (hereafter Kostios dissertation). Kostios quoted Mitropoulos reviews in English.

4. Dimitri Mitropoulos and Katy Katsoyanis, *A Correspondence: 1930–1960* (New York: Martin Dale, 1973), 14. Mitropoulos dictated his letters, in English, to Faith Reed. Presumably Katsoyanis's letters were written in English as well.

CHAPTER FOUR   Berlin and Studies with Busoni

1. Mitropoulos and Katsoyanis, *Correspondence*, 12.

2. Maria Christopoulou, interview by Oliver Daniel, May 19, 1985.

3. Mitropoulos, "Missionary of Music."

4. Geoffrey Douglas Madge's incendiary performance of Mitropoulos's *Greek Sonata* (Paris, Dante Records PSG-9010, 1992) is probably much like the composer's own.

5. Mitropoulos, "Missionary of Music."

6. Gisella Seldon-Goth, "My Friend Mitropoulos," *Opera News*, January 17, 1955.

7. Mitropoulos, "Missionary of Music."

8. Otto Luening, *The Odyssey of an American Composer* (New York: Charles Scribner's Sons, 1980), 169.

9. Otto Luening, interview by Oliver Daniel, December 9, 1984.

10. Roland Gelatt, *Music Makers* (New York: Alfred A. Knopf, 1953), 30.

11. Mitropoulos, "Missionary of Music."

12. Mitropoulos, "Missionary of Music."

13. James Aliferis, interview by Oliver Daniel, May 29, 1984.

14. Mitropoulos, "Missionary of Music."

15. Mitropoulos, "Missionary of Music."

CHAPTER FIVE   Athenian Achievements

1. Konstantine Kydoniatis, interview by Oliver Daniel, May 22, 1985.

2. Mitropoulos, "Missionary of Music."

3. Kostios, *Mitropoulos*.

4. Mitropoulos, "Missionary of Music."

5. Kostios, *Mitropoulos*.

6. Mitropoulos and Katsoyanis, *Correspondence*, 20.

7. Mitropoulos and Katsoyanis, *Correspondence*, 5.

8. Mitropoulos and Katsoyanis, *Correspondence*, 10–11.

9. Carlos Moseley, interview by Oliver Daniel, May 14, 1985. When Oliver Daniel and Don Ott went to Greece in 1984, Katsoyanis tried to discourage them as well, at first refusing to be interviewed, then consenting only after tactful intervention by third parties. Although age had taken its toll and Katy's rambling part of the dialogue failed to provide anything useful, she did allow them to make copies of some 2500 newspaper reviews and articles from her collection of "Dimitriana." Thus the letters and her eloquent in-

troduction to them ended up being the "authorized" version of that re-markable relationship, just as Katy had always intended.

10. Mitropoulos to Katsoyanis, October 29, 1938, in *Correspondence*, 30.
11. Mitropoulos to Katsoyanis, April 23, 1940, in *Correspondence*, 13.
12. Mitropoulos and Katsoyanis, *Correspondence*, 13–14.
13. Kostios dissertation, 13.
14. I am indebted to George Leotsakos for his analysis of the Concerto Grosso. A more detailed version of his analysis appeared as the foreword to the printed score, issued by the Greek Ministry of Culture and Science, 1980.
15. This letter does not appear in the Mitropoulos-Katsoyanis book, but several lines are quoted in the program notes to Madge's performance of the *Greek Sonata*. Dante Records PSG-9010.

CHAPTER SIX Mountains to Climb

1. Mitropoulos, "Missionary of Music."
2. Review excerpts from Kostios dissertation, 20.
3. Mitropoulos, "Missionary of Music."
4. Apostolos Kostios, interview by Oliver Daniel, May 19, 1985.
5. Parisian reviews quoted in Kostios dissertation, 20.
6. Mitropoulos to Katsoyanis, February 19, 1933, in *Correspondence*, 26.
7. Mitropoulos to Katsoyanis, February 19, 1933, in *Correspondence*, 26.
8. Mitropoulos to Katsoyanis, May 30, 1934, in *Correspondence*, 28.
9. Gelatt, *Music Makers*, 37.
10. Gelatt, *Music Makers*, 37.
11. Elie's review is dated December 7, 1944, but his observations are equally applicable to the Mitropoulos of a decade earlier. Quoted in Kostios dissertation, 125.
12. An earlier reviewer quoted in Kostios dissertation, 125.
13. Mitropoulos, letter to Dino (possibly Dino Yannopoulos), date unknown, copy provided and presumably translated by Theodore Vavayannis during interview by Oliver Daniel, May 15, 1984.
14. George Leotsakos to Oliver Daniel, May 26, 1985.
15. George Leotsakos to Oliver Daniel, May 26, 1985.
16. Reprinted in Kostios, *Mitropoulos*, trans. James Aliferis, May 29, 1985.
17. John Papaioannou, interview by Oliver Daniel, May 28, 1985.
18. John Papaioannou, interview by Oliver Daniel, May 28, 1985.
19. Michael Landis, interview by Oliver Daniel, December 13, 1983. Skalkot-tas's *Return of Ulysses* (or *Odysseus*) was recorded for the first time in 1991 (Koch/Schwann CD-31110) in a performance by the Vienna Radio Symphony Orchestra. The disc also includes Kalomaris's stirring First Symphony. Mitropoulos's rousing account of the four *Greek Dances* is long out of print, but the entire set of thirty-six is available in lusty performances by the Urals Philharmonic, conducted by Byron Fedetzis (Lyra CD-52).
20. William S. Cooper, untitled memoir (carbon copy, ca. 1963), 93.
21. All quotations from this 1932 climb are from Tassos Zappas, "Dimitri Mitropoulos on the Peaks of Olympus," mimeographed, ca. 1980.

CHAPTER SEVEN   Triumph in Boston

1. Formosis Pandelis, interview by Oliver Daniel, May 26, 1984.

2. Harold C. Schonberg, *The Great Conductors* (New York: Simon and Schuster, 1967), 302.

3. Mitropoulos's contract specified that the first concert would be on January 21 in Providence, Rhode Island, with concerts to follow in Boston on January 24, 25, and 27, the programs to be identical and of Mitropoulos's choosing. A second program would be given in Boston only on January 31 and February 1.

4. Richard Dyer, "Mitropoulos Says Symphony Here 'Superior to Any in Europe,'" *Boston Herald*, February 10, 1936.

5. This and the following from Cyrus W. Durgin, "Here to Conduct Boston Symphony, Mitropoulos Says Music Should Please, Not Educate," *Boston Globe*, February 10, 1936.

6. John de Lancie, interview by Oliver Daniel, April 20, 1985.

7. Olin Downes in David Ewen, *Dictators of the Baton* (New York: Alliance Book Corp., 1943), 108.

8. Alexander Williams, *Musical Courier*, February 8, 1936.

9. Ewen, *Dictators*, 108.

10. Mitropoulos to Katsoyanis, March 1, 1937, in *Correspondence*, 28.

11. Leonard Bernstein, *Findings* (New York: Simon and Schuster, 1982).

12. Bernstein speech at Mitropoulos benefit, December 2, 1979, quoted in Humphrey Burton, *Leonard Bernstein* (New York: Doubleday & Co., 1994), 36.

13. Joan Peyser, *Bernstein* (New York: William Morrow and Co., 1987), 36.

14. Jean Demos to Joan Peyser, photocopy, n.d.

15. Bernstein, *Findings*, 26–34.

16. Oliver Daniel to John de Lancie, April 20, 1985.

17. Moses Smith, *Musical Courier*, January 1, 1937.

18. John Gruen, *The Private World of Leonard Bernstein* (New York: Viking Press, 1968), 52.

19. Peyser, *Bernstein*, 36.

20. Peyser, *Bernstein*, 349. When Mitropoulos discussed this matter, he was not coy about the sublimated eroticism, but he chose elegant turns of phrase and metaphor. When Bernstein discussed the same phenomenon, he not-so-facetiously told a colleague, "I have one basic criterion for choosing whether or not to conduct a given work: will it give me an orgasm?"

21. Bernstein in *Reflections*, quoted in Peyser, *Bernstein*, 39.

CHAPTER EIGHT   Lightning Strikes in Minneapolis

1. John Sherman, *Music and Maestros: The Story of the Minneapolis Symphony Orchestra* (Minneapolis: University of Minnesota Press, 1952), 16. Sherman's excellent history of the Minneapolis Symphony is detailed, charming, and witty; unfortunately it is out of print and originally was available only regionally. See also: John H. Mueller, *The American Symphony Orchestra: A Social History of Musical Taste* (Bloomington: Indiana University Press, 1951); Molly Foster, "Mrs. Scott Brings Music to the University and Minnesota," privately printed pamphlet, Minneapolis, 1983; and Susan D. Winkler, "Midwest Symphony—the Minneapolis Symphony's 50th Anniversary," *Christian Science Monitor*, October 23, 1953.

2. Sherman, *Music and Maestros*, 85.
3. Sherman, *Music and Maestros*, 228.
4. Sherman, *Music and Maestros*, 230.
5. Sherman, *Music and Maestros*, 277.
6. John Sherman, "Music Notes," *Golfer and Sportsman Magazine*, April 1938.
7. James Davies, "Mitropoulos Acclaimed After Concert," *Minneapolis Tribune*, January 8, 1938.
8. John Sherman, "Mitropoulos Hailed with Ovation," *Minneapolis Journal*, January 8, 1938.
9. John Sherman, "Greek Maestro's Methods Baffle Even the Experts," *Minneapolis Star*, January 10, 1938.
10. John Sherman, "Mitropoulos Offers Seven Overtures," *Minneapolis Star*, January 16, 1938.
11. John Sherman, "Mitropoulos Offers Strauss Works," *Minneapolis Star*, January 14, 1938.
12. James Davies, "Music," *Minneapolis Tribune*, January 29, 1938.
13. James Davies, "Music," *Minneapolis Tribune*, January 15, 1938.
14. Sherman, "Maestro's Methods," January 10, 1938.
15. Johan S. Egilsrud, "Mitropoulos Shows Rare Creative Art in Overtures," *Minneapolis Journal*, January 16, 1938.
16. Sherman, "Seven Overtures," January 16, 1938.
17. James Davies, "Music," *Minneapolis Tribune*, February 18, 1938.
18. Johan S. Egilsrud, review, *Minneapolis Journal*, March 12, 1938.
19. James Davies, "Music," *Minneapolis Tribune*, April 22, 1938.
20. Maxim Gershunoff, interview by Oliver Daniel, October 6, 1983.
21. Alan Shulman, interview by Oliver Daniel, November 19, 1983.
22. Samuel Chotzinoff, "Dimitri Mitropoulos Brings His Forceful Art to New York," *New York Post*, May 31, 1938. One wonders if Chotzinoff chastised his idol, Toscanini, when the latter, in a performance given in March 1941, actually reorchestrated the ending of this same symphony by inserting a bold flourish of trumpets to reinforce the climax.
23. Chotzinoff, "Brings Forceful Art," May 31, 1938.

CHAPTER NINE   Summer and Winter 1938

1. Sigurd Bockman, interview by Oliver Daniel, December 8, 1986.
2. Louis Krasner, interview by Oliver Daniel, July 8, 1983.
3. Sherman, *Music and Maestros*, 235.
4. Sherman, *Music and Maestros*, 237.
5. Christopher Constantakos, interview by Oliver Daniel, December 13, 1983.
6. Sherman, *Music and Maestros*, 239.
7. Brenda Ueland, *Mitropoulos and the North High Band, and Other Pieces on Musical Life* (St. Paul: The Schubert Club, 1983), 13–16.
8. Anton Winkler, interview by Oliver Daniel, November 23, 1984.
9. Burton Paulu, interview by William R. Trotter, July 23, 1993.
10. Anton Winkler, interview by Oliver Daniel, November 23, 1984.
11. John Verrall, interview by Oliver Daniel, July 2, 1983.
12. John Verrall, interview by Oliver Daniel, July 2, 1983.
13. William Cooper, memoir, 35.
14. Leonard Rose, interview by Oliver Daniel, January 7, 1984.
15. Anton Winkler, interview by Oliver Daniel, November 23, 1984.
16. Sherman, *Music and Maestros*, 238.

17. Johan S. Egilsrud, "Mitropoulos Given Ovation at Premiere," *Minneapolis Journal*, November 5, 1938.

18. Mitropoulos to Katsoyanis, December 24, 1938, in *Correspondence*, 31.

19. Mitropoulos to Bernstein, February 5, 1938, quoted in Humphrey Burton, *Leonard Bernstein* (New York: Doubleday, 1994), 45.

20. David Diamond, interview by William R. Trotter, July 11, 1992.

21. David Diamond, interview by William R. Trotter, July 11, 1992.

22. Peyser, *Bernstein*, 38.

CHAPTER TEN   War Clouds Gathering

1. *Time Magazine*, April 24, 1939.

2. Johan S. Egilsrud, "Symphony Plans Fundraising," *Minneapolis Journal*, April 20, 1939.

3. Johan S. Egilsrud, "Symphony Endows Rossini Overture with New Vitality," *Minneapolis Tribune*, January 12, 1939; John Sherman, "Music," *Minneapolis Star*, January 12, 1939.

4. John Sherman, "Music," *Minneapolis Star*, January 12, 1939.

5. James Davies, "The Symphony Orchestra," *Minneapolis Tribune*, March 18, 1939.

6. John Sherman, "14th Symphony Concert," *Minneapolis Star*, April 1, 1939.

7. Moses Smith, "Northwest of Chicago," *Boston Evening Transcript*, April 5, 1939.

8. Herman Devries, "Music in Review," *Chicago American*, February 23, 1939.

9. Edward Barry, "Mitropoulos a Conductor of Fiery School," *Chicago Daily Tribune*, February 22, 1939.

10. Eugene Stinson, "Mitropoulos Debuts," *Chicago Daily News*, February 22, 1939.

11. Dialogue from *Reflections*, quoted in Peyser, *Bernstein*, 45.

12. Burton, *Leonard Bernstein*, 59.

13. Johan S. Egilsrud, "Mitropoulos and Symphony in Fine Fettle," *Minneapolis Tribune*, October 28, 1939.

14. John Sherman, "Music," *Minneapolis Star-Journal*, October 28, 1939.

15. Jack Conklin, "Music," *Minnesota Morning Tribune*, December 16, 1939.

16. Frances Boardmann, "Symphony Gives Season's Most Polished Performance," *St. Paul Pioneer Press*, December 23, 1939.

17. Mitropoulos to Katsoyanis, December 23, 1939, in *Correspondence*, 33.

18. Johan S. Egilsrud, "John Verrall's 'First' Earns Instant Kudos," *Minneapolis Morning Tribune*, January 27, 1940.

19. George Hage, "Rich Musical Treasure Yielded by Weekend," *Columbus Citizen*, February 12, 1940.

20. Quotations from unsigned article, "U.S. is Musical Center Now, Conductor Thinks," *St. Louis Post Dispatch*, February 8, 1940.

21. Edward Barry, "Tone Colorings Mark Concert by Mitropoulos," *Chicago Daily Tribune*, February 8, 1940.

22. Eugene Stimson, "Music Views," *Chicago Daily News*, February 8, 1940.

23. Leonard Bernstein to David Diamond, spring 1940, in Burton, *Leonard Bernstein*, 71.

24. Mitropoulos to Katsoyanis, June 7, 1940, in *Correspondence*, 36.

25. Mitropoulos to Katsoyanis, June 14, 1940, in *Correspondence*, 37.

26. S. R. Wallace, "Mitropoulos Declares Germans World's Best Concert Audiences," *The Michigan Daily*, January 29, 1941.

27. Cecil Smith, "Examines Work of Mitropoulos as Conductor, *Chicago Tribune*, January 28, 1941.
28. Cecil Smith, "Examines Work," February 9, 1941.
29. Sherman, *Music and Maestros*, 277.
30. Anton Winkler, interview by Oliver Daniel, November 23, 1984.
31. Sherman, *Music and Maestros*, 277.
32. Virgil Thomson review in *New York Post* quoted in Sherman, *Music and Maestros*, 279.

CHAPTER ELEVEN   The War Years in Minneapolis

1. Mitropoulos to Katsoyanis, May 1, 1946, in *Correspondence*, 51.
2. Grace Davies, "Orchestra and Audience Unite in Enthusiastic Welcome to Conductor," *Minneapolis Daily Times*, January 17, 1941.
3. Grace Davies, "Symphony Given Ovation on Eve of Departure," *Minneapolis Daily Times*, January 31, 1941.
4. Comments summarized from *Minneapolis Star-Journal*, February 1, 15, and 22, 1941.
5. Mitropoulos quoted in *Minneapolis Morning Tribune*, March 11, 1942.
6. John Sherman, "Szigeti Soloist at 18th Symphony," *Minneapolis Star-Journal*, March 28, 1942.
7. Oscar Levant, *Memoirs of an Amnesiac* (New York: G. P. Putnam's Sons, 1965), 225–226.
8. John Sherman, "Oscar Levant Plays at Pension Concert," *Minneapolis Star-Tribune*, April 16, 1942.
9. John Sherman, "Mitropoulos Conducts Shostakovich 7th," *Minneapolis Star-Tribune*, November 28, 1942.
10. Mitropoulos to David Diamond, July 23, 1943.
11. Mitropoulos quoted in *New York Post*, August 21, 1943.
12. Norman C. Houk, "Sandburg Narrates Lincoln Role," *Minneapolis Morning Tribune*, April 8, 1944.
13. Louis Krasner, interview by Oliver Daniel, August 8, 1983.
14. *Minneapolis Star-Tribune*, March 18, 1945. All the papers carried accounts; the wording differed in some details.
15. Unidentified clipping, *Minneapolis Star-Journal*, March 22, 1945.
16. Unidentified clipping, *Minneapolis Star-Tribune*, March 22, 1945.

CHAPTER TWELVE   The War Years: Guest Engagements

1. Mitropoulos to Katsoyanis, June 25, 1940, in *Correspondence*, 37–38.
2. Mitropoulos to Katsoyanis, September 24, 1940, in *Correspondence*, 41.
3. Mitropoulos to Katsoyanis, September 24, 1940, in *Correspondence*, 41.
4. Mitropoulos to Katsoyanis, September 10, 1940, in *Correspondence*, 40.
5. Mitropoulos to Katsoyanis, October 16, 1940, in *Correspondence*, 43.
6. Unsigned article, "Greek Conductor Shows No Anger toward Italy," *New York Post*, November 20, 1940.
7. Robert A. Simon, "Musical Events," *The New Yorker*, December 15, 1940.
8. Olin Downes, "Mitropoulos Wins Concert Ovation," *New York Times*, December 20, 1940.
9. Virgil Thomson, "Showy Conducting," *New York Herald Tribune*, December 20, 1940.

10. Ross Parmenter, "Guest Conductor by Way of Greece," *New York Times*, December 28, 1940.
11. Olin Downes, "Sinfonia Biblica is Given Premiere," *New York Times*, January 3, 1941.
12. "Gifted Greek," *Time Magazine*, January 25, 1941.
13. C. J. Bulliet, "Ravinia's First War-time Symphonic Opus," *Chicago Daily News*, August 1, 1942.
14. Edward Barry, "Symphony Led by Mitropoulos in Ravinia Bow," *Chicago Daily Tribune*, July 2, 1942.
15. Edward Barry, "Another Look at Mitropoulos," *Chicago Daily Tribune*, July 8, 1942.
16. John Selby, "Mitropoulos Takes Over Symphony," unidentified newspaper.
17. Virgil Thomson, "Music," *New York Herald Tribune*, December 25, 1942.
18. Olin Downes, "Music in Review," *New York Times*, December 25, 1942.
19. Virgil Thomson, "Music," *New York Herald Tribune*, January 7, 1943.
20. Olin Downes, "Mitropoulos Seen in Double Role," *New York Times*, January 7, 1943.
21. Rudolph Elie, Jr., "Mitropoulos: A Mighty Man is He," *Boston Herald*, December 12, 1944.
22. Rudolph Elie, "Music," *Boston Herald*, December 16, 1944.
23. Rudolph Elie, "A Mighty Man is He, Part 2," *Boston Herald*, n.d.
24. Ben de Loache, interview by Oliver Daniel, April 21, 1983.
25. Virgil Thomson, "Music," *New York Herald Tribune*, December 31, 1945.
26. Mitropoulos to Katsoyanis, June 22, 1945, in *Correspondence*, 41.

CHAPTER THIRTEEN There Were Giants . . .

1. This and subsequent quotations in this chapter, unless identified otherwise, are from Mitropoulos, "The Making of a Conductor," *Etude*, January 1954.
2. Schonberg, *The Great Conductors*, 254.
3. Mitropoulos, "The Making of a Conductor."
4. Quoted in Kostios dissertation, 260.
5. Mitropoulos to Katsoyanis, January 26, 1940, in *Correspondence*, 34.
6. Mitropoulos to Leon Kirchner, October 31, 1955.
7. Louis Krasner, interview by Oliver Daniel, July 8, 1983.
8. Sherman, *Music and Maestros*, 239.
9. Mitropoulos quoted in Kostios dissertation, 260.
10. Sherman, *Music and Maestros*, 240–241.
11. Sherman, *Music and Maestros*, 241.
12. David Hall, *The Record Book* (New York: Oliver Durrell, Inc., 1948), 132.

CHAPTER FOURTEEN American Friends, American Ways

1. Mitropoulos to Katsoyanis, December 24, 1938, in *Correspondence*, 32.
2. Burton Paulu, interview by William R. Trotter, July 23, 1993.
3. Sigurd Bockman, interview by Oliver Daniel, December 8, 1986.
4. Sherman, *Music and Maestros*, 283.
5. Sherman, *Music and Maestros*, 284.
6. Leonard Carpenter, interview by Oliver Daniel, November 2, 1985.
7. John Verrall, interview by Oliver Daniel, July 2, 1983.
8. David Cooper, interview by Oliver Daniel, October 31, 1983.
9. David Cooper, interview by William R. Trotter, July 15, 1993.

10. William Cooper, memoir, 95.
11. Ray Garner quoted in Richard O. Boyer, "Maestro on a Mountaintop," *The New Yorker*, April 15, 1950.
12. Boyer, "Maestro on a Mountaintop."
13. David Cooper, interview by William R. Trotter, July 15, 1993.
14. Sherman, *Music and Maestros*, 239.
15. William Cooper, memoir, 100.
16. John MacKay, interview by Oliver Daniel, October 6, 1983.
17. John MacKay, interview by Oliver Daniel, October 6, 1983.
18. Mitropoulos to Katsoyanis, May 1, 1946, in *Correspondence*, 52.
19. Morton Gould, interview by Oliver Daniel, July 16, 1983.
20. Clara Roesch Herdt, interview by Oliver Daniel, April 12, 1984.
21. John MacKay, interview by Oliver Daniel, October 6, 1983.
22. John MacKay, interview by Oliver Daniel, October 6, 1983.
23. Anton Winkler, interview by William R. Trotter, August 25, 1992.
24. David Bar-Ilan, interview by Oliver Daniel, April 6, 1985.
25. Leon Kirchner, interview by Oliver Daniel, July 1, 1984.
26. Leo Pflaum, interview by Oliver Daniel, September 1, 1985.

CHAPTER FIFTEEN Mitropoulos and Contemporary Composers

1. David Diamond, program notes to his Symphony No. 9, New York, November 11, 1985.
2. Diamond, program notes to Symphony No. 9.
3. David Diamond, interview by William R. Trotter, July 11, 1992.
4. Mitropoulos to David Diamond, May 26, 1943.
5. Mitropoulos to David Diamond, July 23, 1943.
6. Mitropoulos to David Diamond, July 23, 1943.
7. Mitropoulos to David Diamond, October 19, 1943.
8. Mitropoulos to David Diamond, November 1, 1943.
9. David Diamond, interview by Oliver Daniel, December 6, 1983.
10. Mitropoulos to David Diamond, March 14, 1946.
11. Mitropoulos to Ernst Krenek, November 25, 1941.
12. Ernst Krenek to Donald Ferguson, May 5, 1942.
13. Ernst Krenek to Olive Jean Bailey, ca. 1979.
14. Mitropoulos to Ernst Krenek, May 25, 1942.
15. Mitropoulos to Ernst Krenek, June 3, 1942.
16. Olive Jean Bailey, "The Influence of Ernst Krenek on the Musical Culture of the Twin Cities" (Ph.D. diss., University of Minnesota, 1980), 11. See also Louis Krasner, interview by Oliver Daniel, October 15, 1983.
17. John Sherman, "Krenek Premiere," *Minneapolis Star-Journal*, December 12, 1944.
18. Bailey dissertation, 143.
19. Rhadames Angelucci, interview by Oliver Daniel, December 28, 1986.
20. Bailey dissertation, 144.
21. John Sherman, "Minneapolis Hails Krenek as One of Big Men in Music," *Minneapolis Star-Journal*, December 22, 1944.
22. Bailey dissertation, 147.
23. Fred Gossen, interview by Oliver Daniel, March 8, 1985.
24. John Sherman, "A Piano-Playing Dimitri," *Minneapolis Star-Journal*, November 23, 1946.
25. Bailey dissertation, 153.

26. Bailey dissertation, 21.
27. Mitropoulos to Ernst Krenek, May 1, 1948.
28. Cesar Saerchinger, ed., *Artur Schnabel* (New York: Dodd, Mead & Co., 1957), 319.
29. Saerchinger, *Schnabel*, 321.
30. Milton Babbitt, interview by Oliver Daniel, March 18, 1985.
31. Anton Winkler, interview by Oliver Daniel, November 23, 1984.
32. Mitropoulos to David Diamond, July 14, 1943.
33. Mitropoulos to David Diamond, January 11, 1944.

CHAPTER SIXTEEN   The Postwar Years: Awaiting the Summons

1. Mitropoulos to Katsoyanis, September 6, 1945, in *Correspondence*, 49.
2. Mitropoulos to Katsoyanis, September 6, 1945, in *Correspondence*, 49.
3. Katsoyanis to Mitropoulos, May 1946, in *Correspondence*, 53–54.
4. Katsoyanis to Mitropoulos, December 19, 1946, in *Correspondence*, 57.
5. Mitropoulos to Katsoyanis, January 13, 1947, in *Correspondence*, 58.
6. Mitropoulos to Katsoyanis, January 13, 1947, in *Correspondence*, 58–59.
7. Mitropoulos to Katsoyanis, August 14, 1947, in *Correspondence*, 60.
8. Alma Lubin, "Stravinsky Work Delights Contemporary Music Audience," *ISCM Bulletin*, May 22, 1946.
9. Oliver Daniel, in Morton Gould, interview by Oliver Daniel, July 16, 1983.
10. Morton Gould, interview by Oliver Daniel, July 16, 1983.
11. David Amram, *Vibrations: The Adventures and Musical Times of David Amram* (New York: Macmillan Publishing Co., 1968; Greenwood Press, 1980), 45.
12. Amram, *Vibrations*, 46–47.
13. Amram, *Vibrations*, 48.
14. Amram, *Vibrations*, 49.
15. Amram, *Vibrations*, 85.
16. Mitropoulos to Katsoyanis, October 1, 1947, in *Correspondence*, 64–65.
17. Arthur Whittemore, interview by Oliver Daniel, October 1, 1983.
18. Max de Schauensee, "Prokofiev Symphony Receives Premiere at Robin Hood Dell," *Philadelphia Evening Bulletin*, June 26, 1947.
19. William E. Smith, "The Conductor's Corner," Robin Hood Dell program brochure, n.d.
20. Mitropoulos to Katsoyanis, August 14, 1947, in *Correspondence*, 60–61.
21. Mitropoulos to Katsoyanis, January 13, 1947, in *Correspondence*, 59.
22. Mitropoulos to Katsoyanis, August 14, 1947, in *Correspondence*, 61.
23. Bruno Walter to Mitropoulos, carbon copy, n.d., New York Philharmonic Archives.
24. Mitropoulos to Ernst Krenek, October 4, 1947.
25. Olin Downes, "Raya Garbusova Concerto Soloist," *New York Times*, December 5, 1947.
26. Quotations from *Pravda* in "Mitropoulos Analyzes Russian Censure of Composers," *St. Paul Pioneer Press*, May 21, 1948.
27. "Mitropoulos Analyzes Censure," May 21, 1948.
28. William Cooper, memoir, 96.
29. Henry Gerstley, interview by Oliver Daniel, September 19, 1983.
30. Max de Schauensee, *Philadelphia Evening Bulletin*, n.d.
31. Irving Kolodin, "Music to My Ears," *Saturday Review*, August 1, 1948.

32. Louis Biancolli, "A Mitropoulos 'Tosca,'" *New York World Telegram*, July 27, 1948.
33. Katsoyanis to Mitropoulos, January 29, 1948, in *Correspondence*, 69–70.
34. Katsoyanis to Mitropoulos, January 29, 1948, in *Correspondence*, 70–71.
35. Mitropoulos to Katsoyanis, January 12, 1948, in *Correspondence*, 68–69.
36. Virgil Thomson, "Music," *New York Herald Tribune*, October 21, 1948.
37. Virgil Thomson, "Music," *New York Herald Tribune*, October 23, 1948.
38. Virgil Thomson, "Music," *New York Herald Tribune*, November 1, 1948.
39. Olin Downes, "Work by Poulenc Concert Feature," *New York Times*, November 16, 1948.
40. Kostios dissertation, 257.
41. Kostios dissertation, 258.
42. Mitropoulos to Katsoyanis, February 27, 1948, in *Correspondence*, 72–73.
43. Katsoyanis to Mitropoulos, March 14, 1948, in *Correspondence*, 75.
44. Mitropoulos to Katsoyanis, April 10, 1948, in *Correspondence*, 77–79.
45. Katsoyanis to Mitropoulos, April 19, 1948, in *Correspondence*, 77.
46. Warren Wirtz, *Minneapolis Daily Times*, November 17, 1945.
47. Norman Hauk, "Schoenberg Innovation Proves Rewarding," *Minneapolis Tribune*, December 1, 1947.
48. John Sherman, "Profitable Session with Sessions," *Minneapolis Star-Journal*, November 15, 1947.

CHAPTER SEVENTEEN   Boston Denied

1. Winthrop Sargent, "Dimitri Mitropoulos," *Life*, February 18, 1946.
2. David Cooper, interview by William R. Trotter, July 2, 1993.
3. Mitropoulos to Katsoyanis, January 13, 1948, in *Correspondence*, 58.
4. Peyser, *Bernstein*, 139.
5. Jack Lowe, interview by Oliver Daniel, November 17, 1984.

CHAPTER EIGHTEEN   Farewell to Minneapolis

1. Henry Wallace to Mitropoulos, carbon copy, March 5, 1948.
2. William Cooper, memoir, 98.
3. Louis Krasner, interview by Oliver Daniel, September 1, 1983.
4. Mitropoulos quoted in *Minneapolis Star-Journal*, March 24, 1949.
5. *Star-Journal*, March 30 and April 1, 1949.
6. Mitropoulos, interview by John Sherman in Schmidtt's Music Store, tape recording, ca. April 1949.
7. Donald Ferguson, MSO program notes for March 18, 1949.
8. Mitropoulos, farewell address to Minneapolis Symphony Orchestra audience, March 18, 1949, transcript of backstage recording by Burton Paulu, engineer for many of the MSO's radio broadcasts.
9. All Aspen quotations from John Sherman, "American Festival at Aspen," *Opera and Concert Magazine*, May 1951.
10. Mitropoulos to Katsoyanis, January 20, 1949, *Correspondence*, 87.
11. Louis Krasner, interview by Oliver Daniel, July 8, 1983.

INTERMEZZO *New York, New York, It's a Helluva Town!*

1. Cecil Smith, *Worlds of Music* (Philadelphia: J. P. Lippincott Co., 1952), 131.
2. Smith, *Worlds of Music*, 226.
3. Howard Taubman, "A Personal Memoir," *New York Times*, August 28, 1955.
4. Tim Page, ed., *Selected Letters of Virgil Thomson* (New York: Summit Books, 1988), 185.
5. Levant, *Memoirs*, 222.
6. Levant, *Memoirs*, 223.
7. Smith, *Worlds of Music*, 14.
8. Smith, *Worlds of Music*, 38.
9. Halina Rodzinski, *Our Two Lives* (New York: Charles Scribner's Sons, 1965), 234.
10. Rodzinski, *Lives*, 275.
11. Howard Shanet, *Philharmonic: A History of New York's Orchestra* (New York: Doubleday, 1975), 258.
12. Lawrence Gilman, review, *New York Sun*, January 15, 1946.
13. Winthrop Sargent quoted in Joseph Horowitz, *Understanding Toscanini* (New York: Alfred A. Knopf, 1987), 111.
14. Shanet, *Philharmonic*, 271–272.
15. Virgil Thomson, "Music," *New York Herald Tribune*, March 23, 1941.
16. Rodzinski, *Lives*, 270.
17. Virgil Thomson, "Music," *New York Herald Tribune*, April 19, 1942.
18. Shanet, *Philharmonic*, 289–290.
19. Shanet, *Philharmonic*, 307.
20. Virgil Thomson, "Conducting Reviewed," *New York Herald Tribune*, April 19, 1942.
21. Katsoyanis to Mitropoulos, September 4, 1948, in *Correspondence*, 85. Emphasis in original.

CHAPTER NINETEEN Mitropoulos In, Stokowski Out

1. Seymour Barab, interview by Oliver Daniel, July 12, 1984.
2. Seymour Barab, interview by Oliver Daniel, July 12, 1984.
3. Olin Downes, "Krenek Concerto Introduced Here," *New York Times*, December 9, 1949.
4. Mitropoulos, interview by James Fassett, transcript of radio broadcast, December 11, 1949, New York Philharmonic Archives.
5. Irving Kolodin, "Music Makers," *New York Sun*, December 23, 1949.
6. Olin Downes, "Strauss' 'Electra' Excels in Concert," *New York Times*, December 23, 1949.
7. Virgil Thomson, "Music," *New York Herald Tribune*, December 23, 1949.
8. Olin Downes to Mitropoulos, December 29, 1949, New York Philharmonic Archives.
9. Paul Strauss, interview by Oliver Daniel, December 15, 1983.
10. Oliver Daniel, *Stokowski: A Counterpoint of View* (New York: Dodd, Mead & Co., 1982), 524.
11. Daniel, *Stokowski*, 525.
12. Abram Chasins, *Leopold Stokowski: A Profile* (New York: Hawthorn Books, 1982), 205.
13. Paul Strauss, interview by Oliver Daniel, December 15, 1983.

CHAPTER TWENTY The View from the Great Northern

1. Mitropoulos to Katsoyanis, February 3, 1950, in *Correspondence*, 94–95.
2. Sigurd Bockman, interview by Oliver Daniel, December 8, 1986.
3. John MacKay, interview by Oliver Daniel, January 10, 1987.
4. Yehudi Menuhin, interview by Oliver Daniel, March 18, 1987.
5. Paul Strauss, interview by Oliver Daniel, December 15, 1983.
6. Paul Strauss, interview by Oliver Daniel, December 15, 1983.
7. Cecil Smith, "The Philharmonic-Symphony Initiates a Hopeful New Era," *Musical America*, January 1, 1950. See also: Miles Kastendieck, "Music," *New York Journal American*, January 8, 1950.
8. David Cooper said that Mitropoulos and Sessions "hit it off personally and professionally," and that Mitropoulos offered to be Sessions's supporter at the Philharmonic. In 1949 in Minneapolis they had discussed a performance of the Second Symphony, but Sessions believed that any efforts to get the parts to Mitropoulos and then to perform the work would be sabotaged by individuals who were not admirers of the composer. He believed these included Hans Heinsheimer and William Schuman at the publisher, G. Schirmer, and even Aaron Copland, of whom Sessions was particularly jealous and suspicious. Thus evolved a complicated and, in retrospect, rather amusing plot in which "a mutual acquaintance named Bill Carlin nabbed the parts from Heinsheimer in a clandestine operation and delivered them into Mitropoulos's hands." David Cooper, interview by William R. Trotter, July 15, 1993.
9. Olin Downes, "Sessions Symphony Given by Philharmonic," *New York Times*, January 13, 1950. Louis Biancolli wrote, "The idiom is a bit hard to take for those not used to Mr. Sessions' language. Yet it is a strong, tangy idiom, steeped in the vernacular, and from one corner of the symphony to the other, it is American." "Mitropoulos Salvages a Classic," *World Telegram and Sun*, January 20, 1950.
10. Olin Downes, "The Case for New Music," *New York Times*, January 29, 1950.
11. Virgil Thomson, "Music," *New York Herald Tribune*, January 29, 1950.
12. Milton Babbitt, interview by Oliver Daniel, March 18, 1985.
13. Mitropoulos to Katsoyanis, March 13, 1950, in *Correspondence*, 96.
14. Olin Downes, "Schoenberg Work is Presented Here," *New York Times*, April 14, 1950.
15. Schuyler Chapin, interview by Oliver Daniel, December 11, 1984.
16. Alan Shulman, interview by Oliver Daniel, November 19, 1983.
17. Details of regimen and rehearsal quotes from Richard O. Boyer, "Maestro on a Mountaintop," *The New Yorker*, April 15, 1950. Beefburger Hall quotes from interview by Martha Dean, broadcast on WOR, August 4, 1950, typescript, New York Philharmonic Archives.
18. Boyer, "Maestro on a Mountaintop," 39.
19. Boyer, "Maestro on a Mountaintop," 39.
20. Boyer, "Maestro on a Mountaintop," 40.
21. Boyer, "Maestro on a Mountaintop," 39.
22. Boyer, "Maestro on a Mountaintop," 46.
23. Boyer, "Maestro on a Mountaintop," 47. *Jehnl-men* substituted for the original *gentlemen*.
24. Dean typescript, August 4, 1950.
25. Dean typescript, August 4, 1950.

26. Dean typescript, August 4, 1950.
27. James Dixon to Faith Reed, May 15, 1950.
28. Kostios dissertation, 45.
29. Kostios dissertation, 46.

CHAPTER TWENTY-ONE   L'Affaire Roxy

1. Louis Biancolli, "Mitropoulos Visiting Roxy to Open Ivory Tower," *World Telegram and Sun*, August 31, 1950.
2. *Billboard*, September 9, 1950.
3. Eileen Farrell, interview by Oliver Daniel, February 8, 1984.
4. Jinx Falkenburg, "New York Close Up," *New York Herald Tribune*, September 20, 1950.
5. Olin Downes, "Mitropoulos in Command as Philharmonic Starts," *New York Times*, September 8, 1950.
6. Howard Taubman, "The Passionate Calm of Mr. Mitropoulos," *New York Times Sunday Magazine*, September 8, 1950.
7. Olin Downes, "2 Operas Offered by Philharmonic," *New York Times*, November 17, 1950.
8. John la Montaine, interview by Oliver Daniel, November 30, 1984.
9. Marcel Dick to Mitropoulos, December 19, 1950.
10. Mitropoulos quoted in student newspaper, n.d., New York Philharmonic Archives.
11. Anthony Sophos, interview by Oliver Daniel, November 27, 1983.
12. Harry Zaratzian, interview by Oliver Daniel, December 18, 1984.   .
13. Milton Babbitt, interview by Oliver Daniel, March 18, 1985.
14. Miles Kastendieck, "Philharmonic at Carnegie," *New York Journal American*, April 16, 1951.
15. Virgil Thomson, "Music," *New York Herald Tribune*, April 13, 1951.
16. Olin Downes, "Berg's 'Wozzeck' Presented Here," *New York Times*, April 13, 1951.
17. Louis Biancolli, "Mitropoulos Rated as First Conductor," *New York World Telegram and Sun*, May 15, 1951.
18. Leonard Rose, interview by Oliver Daniel, January 7, 1984.
19. Unsigned review, *London Times*, September 25, 1951.
20. Eric Blom, "The Arts at Edinburgh," *The Observer*, October 2, 1951.
21. Unidentified clipping, September 28, 1951, New York Philharmonic Archives.
22. "Profile: Dimitri Mitropoulos," *The Observer*, October 2, 1951.
23. Neville Cardus, "Contrasts at Edinburgh," *Manchester Guardian*, December 3, 1951.

CHAPTER TWENTY-TWO   The Sinking of *Christophe Colomb*

1. Glenn Dillard Dunn, "Mitropoulos Shows Mastery in Gala Performance Here," *Washington D.C. Times-Herald*, November 7, 1951.
2. Paul Hume, interview by Oliver Daniel, June 17, 1984.
3. Rudolf Serkin, interview by Oliver Daniel, December 18, 1984.
4. Olin Downes, "Rossini Overture Concert Feature," *New York Times*, November 9, 1951.

5. David Diamond to Oliver Daniel, November 28, 1983.

6. Mitropoulos to Katsoyanis, November 13, 1951, in *Correspondence*, 117.

7. Katsoyanis to Mitropoulos, November 27, 1951, in *Correspondence*, 119.

8. Leon Kirchner, interview by Oliver Daniel, July 1, 1984.

9. Martha Lipton, interview by Oliver Daniel, November 13, 1983.

10. David Lloyd, interview by Oliver Daniel, April 4, 1984.

11. Howard Taubman, "Mendelssohn Opus Presented Here," *New York Times*, April 11, 1952.

12. Milton Katims, interview by Oliver Daniel, November 18, 1984.

13. Louis Biancolli, review, *World Telegram and Sun*, April 21, 1952.

14. Mitropoulos to Katsoyanis, March 13, 1952, in *Correspondence*, 120–121.

15. Mitropoulos, "Missionary of Music."

16. Kostios dissertation, 49.

17. Mildred Norton, "Hollywood Bowl," *Los Angeles News*, September 3, 1952.

18. Schuyler Chapin, interview by Oliver Daniel, December 11, 1984.

19. Mitropoulos in unsigned interview, "Philharmonic to Perform Many New Works," *New York Herald Tribune*, October 5, 1952.

20. Irving Kolodin, interview by Oliver Daniel, December 12, 1985.

21. Virgil Thomson, "Improved Philharmonic," *New York Herald Tribune*, December 5, 1952.

CHAPTER TWENTY-THREE   Recuperation: "Paradise Is Not for Me."

1. Eleanor Steber, interview by Oliver Daniel, February 8, 1984.

2. Maxim Gershunoff, interview by Oliver Daniel, October 6, 1983.

3. Paul Strauss, interview by Oliver Daniel, December 15, 1983.

4. Maxim Gershunoff, interview by Oliver Daniel, October 6, 1983.

5. John Sherman, "Words and Music," *Minneapolis Star*, February 27, 1953.

6. Maxim Gershunoff, interview by Oliver Daniel, October 6, 1983.

7. George Rochberg, interview by Oliver Daniel, June 23, 1985.

8. Mitropoulos to Katsoyanis, May 2, 1953, in *Correspondence*, 129. Emphasis in original.

9. Gunther Schuller, interview by Oliver Daniel, June 14, 1983.

10. Paul Strauss, interview by Oliver Daniel, December 15, 1983.

11. Mitropoulos to Katsoyanis, July 26, 1953, in *Correspondence*, 130.

12. Mitropoulos to Ernst Krenek, October 21, 1953.

13. Clara Roesch Herdt, interview by Oliver Daniel, April 12, 1984.

14. David Bar-Ilan, interview by Oliver Daniel, April 6, 1985.

CHAPTER TWENTY-FOUR   The Honeymoon Ends

1. Paul Strauss, interview by Oliver Daniel, December 15, 1983.

2. James Dixon, interview by William R. Trotter, December 10, 1993.

3. Miles Kastendieck, "Mitropoulos's First Eight Weeks," *Christian Science Monitor*, December 5, 1953.

4. Morton Gould, interview by Oliver Daniel, July 16, 1983.

5. Irving Kolodin, "Music to My Ears," *Saturday Review*, October 31, 1953.

6. Olin Downes, "Chamber Ensemble in Splendid Concert," *New York Times*, February 28, 1954.

7. Leon Temerson, interview by Oliver Daniel, December 11, 1985.

8. Rudolf Serkin, interview by Oliver Daniel, December 18, 1984.
9. Olin Downes, "Strauss Program at Philharmonic," *New York Times*, February 12, 1954.
10. *Anatomy of a Symphony Orchestra*, videocassette, produced by CBS, originally broadcast on *See It Now*, February 18, 1954. Museum of Broadcasting, New York, New York.
11. Düsseldorf and Salzburg reviews quoted in Kostios dissertation, 52, 59.

CHAPTER TWENTY-FIVE   Operas and Recordings

1. Paul Henry Lang, "Wagner in Evening Dress," *New York Herald Tribune*, October 8, 1954.
2. Unidentified review, *Musical America*, October 15, 1954.
3. Unidentified review, *Musical America*, November 15, 1954.
4. Virgil Thomson, "The Philharmonic," *New York Herald Tribune*, November 15, 1954.
5. Rudolf Bing, *5000 Nights at the Opera* (New York: Doubleday & Co. Popular Library Edition, 1972), 177.
6. Max Rudolf, interview by Oliver Daniel, December 30, 1984.
7. Max Rudolf, interview by Oliver Daniel, December 30, 1984.
8. Frank Guarrera, interview by Oliver Daniel, March 5, 1985.
9. Edward Downes, interview by Oliver Daniel, July 4, 1985.
10. Licia Albanese, interview by Oliver Daniel, January 29, 1985.
11. Robert Herman, interview by Oliver Daniel, December 16, 1984.
12. George Martin, interview by Oliver Daniel, March 30, 1985.
13. Jay S. Harrison, "Strauss' 'Salome,'" *New York Herald Tribune*, December 16, 1954.
14. Louis Biancolli in Mitropoulos and Katsoyanis, *Correspondence*, 9–10.
15. David Oppenheim, interview by Oliver Daniel, June 20, 1985.
16. David Oppenheim, interview by Oliver Daniel, June 20, 1985.
17. Louis Krasner, interview by Oliver Daniel, July 1, 1984.

CHAPTER TWENTY-SIX   Return to Athens

1. Olin Downes, "Opera: 'A Masked Ball,'" *New York Times*, January 8, 1955.
2. Harold C. Schonberg, "Philharmonic Plays Gould 'Showpiece,'" *New York Times*, February 21, 1953.
3. *Variety*, April 22, 1955.
4. John M. Harvey, "Mitropoulos Welcomed Back," *St. Paul Pioneer Press*, May 18, 1955.
5. Grant Johannesen, interview by Oliver Daniel, June 30, 1984.
6. Arthur Whittemore, interview by Oliver Daniel, October 1, 1983.
7. "New York Philharmonic-Symphony Opening Concert," *The Scotsman*, September 6, 1955.
8. Review quoted in Kostios dissertation, 56.
9. Review quoted in Kostios dissertation, 56.
10. David Wooldridge, *Conductor's World* (New York: Praeger Publishers, 1970), 321–322.
11. Review in *Neue Zürcher Zeitung*, October 26, 1955, translation, New York Philharmonic Archives.
12. Werner Oelmann, review, *National Zeitung, Basel*, September 22, 1955, in Kostios dissertation, 57.

13. Review in *Berliner Morgenpost*, September 20, 1955, translation, New York Philharmonic Archives.
14. John Ware, interview by Oliver Daniel, January 20, 1984.
15. Anthony Sophos, interview by Oliver Daniel, November 27, 1983.
16. Mitropoulos, "What I Believe," *Hi-Fi Music at Home*, May–June 1956.

CHAPTER TWENTY-SEVEN   A Time of Troubles

1. Leonard Rose, interview by Oliver Daniel, January 7, 1984.
2. Ranier DeIntinis, interview by Oliver Daniel, January 21, 1985.
3. Ranier DeIntinis, interview by Oliver Daniel, January 21, 1985.
4. Gunther Schuller, interview by Oliver Daniel, July 7, 1983.
5. Louis Krasner, interview by Oliver Daniel, July 8, 1983.
6. Leonard Rose, interview by Oliver Daniel, January 7, 1984.
7. Leonard Rose, interview by Oliver Daniel, January 7, 1984.
8. Louis Krasner, interview by Oliver Daniel, July 8, 1983.
9. Harold C. Schonberg, interview by Oliver Daniel, February 27, 1985.
10. William Lincer, interview by Oliver Daniel, September 17, 1985.
11. Seymour Barab, interview by Oliver Daniel, December 7, 1984.
12. John Gruen, *The Private World of Leonard Bernstein* (New York: Viking Press, 1968), 26–27.
13. Gunther Schuller, interview by Oliver Daniel, July 7, 1983.
14. Gunther Schuller, interview by Oliver Daniel, July 7, 1983.
15. Oliver Daniel, interview by Arthur Whittemore, October 1, 1983.
16. Gunther Schuller, interview by Oliver Daniel, July 7, 1983.
17. James Fassett, "Memoirs," typescript, n.d., 58–59.
18. Fassett, "Memoirs," 59.
19. Morton Gould, interview by Oliver Daniel, July 16, 1983.
20. Frances Greer, interview by Oliver Daniel, October 15, 1983.
21. Gunther Schuller, interview by Oliver Daniel, July 7, 1983.
22. Gunther Schuller, interview by Oliver Daniel, July 7, 1983.
23. Mitropoulos to Katsoyanis, July 24, 1952, in *Correspondence*, 122–123.
24. Michael Landis, interview by Oliver Daniel, December 13, 1984.
25. Maxim Gershunoff, interview by Oliver Daniel, October 6, 1983.
26. Maxim Gershunoff, interview by Oliver Daniel, October 6, 1983.
27. Hans Heinsheimer, interview by Oliver Daniel, November 19, 1983.
28. Fassett, "Memoirs," 56–57.
29. Fassett, "Memoirs," 57.
30. Otto Luening, interview by Oliver Daniel, December 9, 1984.
31. Earl Wild, interview by Oliver Daniel, August 25, 1984.
32. Arturo Mirtallo, interview by Oliver Daniel, August 24, 1984.
33. Arturo Mirtallo, interview by Oliver Daniel, August 24, 1984.
34. Arturo Mirtallo, interview by Oliver Daniel, August 24, 1984.

CHAPTER TWENTY-EIGHT   The Taubman Attack

1. David Wooldridge, *Conductor's World* (New York: Praeger Press, 1970), 324.
2. Review, *Musical America*, November 15, 1955.
3. Howard Taubman, "Opera: Boris Godunov," *New York Times*, January 21, 1956.
4. John Schaeffer, interview by Oliver Daniel, March 3, 1985.
5. Oliver Daniel, in Carlos Moseley, interview by Oliver Daniel, May 14, 1985.

6. Winthrop Sargent, review, *The New Yorker*, May 1, 1956.

7. David Diamond, interview by William R. Trotter, July 11, 1992.

8. Howard Taubman, *The Pleasure of Their Company* (Portland, OR: Amadeus Press, 1994), 219–220.

9. Peyser, *Bernstein*, 217–218.

CHAPTER TWENTY-NINE   Declining Fortunes

1. Morton Gould, interview by Oliver Daniel, July 16, 1983.

2. Irving Kolodin, "The Philharmonic Comes Under Fire," *Newark Star-Ledger*, May 18, 1956.

3. Paul Henry Lang, "Seasonal Inventory (II)," *New York Herald Tribune*, June 3, 1956.

4. Mitropoulos to Katsoyanis, May 28 1956, *Correspondence*, 145.

5. "Bernstein Named by Philharmonic," *New York Times*, October 16, 1956.

6. Howard Taubman, "Long Way to Go," *New York Times*, May 12, 1957.

7. Mitropoulos to Katsoyanis, July 7, 1957, in *Correspondence*, 150.

8. Otto Strasser quoted in Kostios dissertation, 66.

9. Howard Shanet, *Philharmonic: A History of New York's Orchestra* (New York: Doubleday, 1975), 327.

10. Shanet, *Philharmonic*, 327.

CHAPTER THIRTY   *Vanessa* Hot and Cold

1. Irving Kolodin, *The Metropolitan Opera: A Candid History* (New York: Alfred A. Knopf, 1966), 587.

2. Barbara Heyman, *Samuel Barber: The Composer and His Music* (New York: Oxford University Press, 1992), 382.

3. Mitropoulos quoted in "Miracle on 39th Street," *Opera News*, January 27, 1958.

4. George Martin, interview by Oliver Daniel, March 30, 1985.

5. George Cehanovsky, interview by Oliver Daniel, February 11, 1984.

6. Winthrop Sargent, "Musical Events," *Saturday Review*, January 25, 1958.

7. Paul Henry Lang, "Music," *New York Herald Tribune*, March 2, 1958.

8. Mitropoulos to Katsoyanis, June 19, 1958, in *Correspondence*, 153.

9. Ruth Slenczynska, interview by Oliver Daniel, June 30, 1984.

10. Gian Carlo Menotti, interview by Oliver Daniel, May 16, 1984.

11. Heyman, *Samuel Barber*, 396.

CHAPTER THIRTY-ONE   To Fall from a Mountaintop

1. David Bar-Ilan, interview by Oliver Daniel, April 6, 1985.

2. Mitropoulos to Katsoyanis, February 4, 1959, *Correspondence*, 154–155.

3. Biancolli in Katsoyanis, *Correspondence*, 6.

4. Byron Janis, interview by Oliver Daniel, December 31, 1984.

5. Mitropoulos to Katsoyanis, March 7, 1959, in *Correspondence*, 158.

6. Mitropoulos to Katsoyanis, March 14, 1959, in *Correspondence*, 160.

7. Mitropoulos to Katsoyanis, September 6, 1959, in *Correspondence*, 166–167.

8. James Chambers, "Mahler and Mitropoulos Remembered," brochure notes for New York Philharmonic Orchestra recordings, 1984–1985 season.

9. Chambers, "Mahler and Mitropoulos Remembered."

10. Henry Levinger, review, *Musical America*, December 1, 1960.
11. Mitropoulos and Katsoyanis, *Correspondence*, 22.
12. Mitropoulos to George Seferis, in *Correspondence*, 1.
13. Mitropoulos to Nancy Cooper, March 20, 1960, in Cooper, memoir, 106–107.
14. Mitropoulos to Dorothy and William Cooper, June 28, 1960, quoted in Cooper, memoir, 108.
15. David Amram, interview by Oliver Daniel, November 19, 1985.
16. Felix Eyle, interview by Oliver Daniel, January 16, 1985.
17. John Canarina, interview by Oliver Daniel, February 28, 1984.
18. Mitropoulos and Katsoyanis, *Correspondence*, 23–24.
19. "The Last Moments of the Life of Maestro Dimitri Mitropoulos as Described by Prof. G. Graghirolli, Violinist of the Orchestra alla Scala di Milano," translated from the Italian (Milan: mimeographed, ca. 1962).

A Brief Recessional

1. Amram, *Vibrations*, 381–382.
2. Peyser, *Bernstein*, 276.

Sketch of Mitropoulos rehearsing *Un ballo in maschera* at the Met in 1956,
at the time of his sixtieth birthday, by Sam Norkin.
Courtesy of the artist.

Selected Bibliography

Books

Amram, David. *Vibrations: The Adventures and Musical Times of David Amram.* New York: Macmillan Publishing Co., 1968; Greenwood Press, 1980.

Anderson, Marian. *My Lord, What a Morning.* New York: Viking Press, 1956.

Bernstein, Leonard. *Findings.* New York: Simon and Schuster, 1982.

Biancolli, Louis, and Herbert F. Peyser. *Masters of the Orchestra.* With an introduction by Dimitri Mitropoulos. New York: G. P. Putnam's Sons, 1954.

Bing, Rudolf. *5000 Nights at the Opera.* Popular Library Edition. New York: Doubleday & Co., 1972.

Bookspan, Martin, and Ross Yockey. *Zubin: The Zubin Mehta Story.* New York: Harper & Row, 1978.

Briggs, John. *Leonard Bernstein: The Man, His Work, and His World.* Cleveland: World Publishing Co., 1961.

Brook, Donald. *Gallery of Conductors.* London: Rockcliff Publishers, 1951.

Burton, Humphrey. *Leonard Bernstein.* New York: Doubleday & Co., 1994.

Carlson, Effie B. *A Bio-bibliographical Dictionary of Twelve-tone and Serial Composers.* Metuchen, NJ: The Scarecrow Press, 1970.

Chasins, Abram. *Leopold Stokowski: A Profile.* New York: Hawthorn Books, 1979.

Christopoulou, Maria. *Dimitri Mitropoulos: His Life and Works.* Athens: n.p., 1971.

Daniel, Oliver. *Stokowski: A Counterpoint of View.* New York: Dodd, Mead & Co., 1982.

Dorati, Antal. *Notes of Seven Decades.* Detroit: Wayne State University, 1981.

Downes, Irene, ed. *Olin Downes on Music.* New York: Greenwood Press, 1968.

Downes, Olin. *Ten Operatic Masterpieces.* With an introduction by Dimitri Mitropoulos. New York: Charles Scribner's Sons, 1952.

Ewen, David. *Dictators of the Baton.* 2nd ed. Chicago: Ziff-Davis Publishing Co., 1948.

Gallup, Steven. *A History of the Salzburg Festival.* Topsfield, MA: Salem House Publishers, 1987.

Gelatt, Roland. *Music Makers.* New York: Alfred A. Knopf, 1953.

———. *The Fabulous Phonograph.* New York: J. B. Lippincott Co., 1955.

Gordon, Eric A. *Mark the Music: The Life and Work of Marc Blitzstein.* New York: St. Martin's Press, 1989.

Gruen, John. *The Private World of Leonard Bernstein.* New York: Viking Press, 1968.

Hall, David. *The Record Book* International edition. New York: Oliver Durrell, Inc., 1948.

Heyman, Barbara. *Samuel Barber: The Composer and His Music*. New York: Oxford University Press, 1992.

Horowitz, Joseph. *Understanding Toscanini*. New York: Alfred A. Knopf, 1987.

Kolodin, Irving. *The New Guide to Recorded Music*. International edition. Garden City, NY: Doubleday & Co., 1950.

———. *The Metropolitan Opera, 1883–1966: A Candid History*. New York: Alfred A. Knopf, 1966.

Kostios, Apostolos. *Dimitri Mitropoulos*. Athens: National Bank of Greece, 1985.

Kupferberg, Herbert. *Tanglewood*. New York: McGraw-Hill Book Co., 1976.

Lebrecht, Norman. *The Maestro Myth*. New York: Birch Lane Press, 1992.

Levant, Oscar. *The Memoirs of An Amnesiac*. New York, G. P. Putnam's Sons, 1965.

Luening, Otto. *The Odyssey of An American Composer*. New York: Charles Scribner's Sons, 1980.

Mitropoulos, Dimitri. "Missionary of Music." In Hans Reinhardt and Josef Muller-Marein. *Das Musikalische Selbstportrait von Komponisten, Dirigenten, Instrumentalisten, Sängerinnen und Sängern unserer Zeit*. Hamburg, n.p., n.d.

——— and Katy Katsoyanis. *A Correspondence: 1930–1960*. New York: Martin Dale, 1973.

Mueller, John H. *The American Symphony Orchestra: A Social History of Musical Taste*. Bloomington: Indiana University Press, 1951.

Olmstead, Andrea, ed. *The Correspondence of Roger Sessions*. Boston: Northeastern University Press, 1992.

Page, Tim, ed. *Selected Letters of Virgil Thomson*. New York: Summit Books, 1988.

Peyser, Joan. *Bernstein*. New York: William Morrow & Co., 1987.

Rodzinski, Halina. *Our Two Lives*. New York: Charles Scribner's Sons, 1976.

Rorem, Ned. *The New York Diary*. New York: George Braziller, 1967.

Sadie, Stanley, ed. *The New Grove Dictionary of Music and Musicians*. London: Macmillan Publishers, Ltd., 1980.

Saerchinger, Cesar, ed. *Artur Schnabel*. New York: Dodd, Mead & Co., 1957.

Schickel, Richard. *The World of Carnegie Hall*. New York: Jullian Messner, Inc., 1960.

Schickel, Richard, and Michael Walsh. *Carnegie Hall: The First One Hundred Years*. New York: Harry N. Abrams, Inc., 1987.

Schneider, Alexander. *Sasha: A Musician's Life*. New York, 1988. Privately printed.

Schonberg, Harold C. *The Great Conductors*. New York: Simon and Schuster, 1967.

Shanet, Howard. *Philharmonic: A History of New York's Orchestra*. New York: Doubleday & Co., 1975.

Sherman, John K. *Music and Maestros: The Story of The Minneapolis Symphony Orchestra*. Minneapolis: University of Minnesota Press, 1952.

Smith, Cecil. *Worlds of Music*. Philadelphia: J. B. Lippincott Co., 1952.

Smith, Moses. *Koussevitzky*. New York: Allen, Towne, & Heath, Inc., 1947.

Starer, Robert. *Continuo: A Life in Music*. New York: Random House, 1987.

Stewart, John L. *Ernst Krenek: The Man and His Music*. Berkeley: University of California Press, 1991.

Stoddard, Hope. *Symphony Conductors of the U.S.A.* New York: Thomas Y. Crowell Co., 1957.

Strasser, Otto. *Und dafür wird man noch bezählt: Mein Leben mit den Wiener Philharmonikern*. Berlin and Vienna: Paul Neff Verlag, 1974.

Taubman, Howard. *Music On My Beat*. New York: Simon and Schuster, 1943.
———. *The Pleasure of Their Company*. Portland, OR: Amadeus Press, 1994.
Thomson, Virgil. *The Musical Scene*. New York: Alfred A. Knopf, 1945.
———. *A Virgil Thomson Reader*. Boston: Houghton-Mifflin Co., 1981.
Ueland, Brenda. *Mitropoulos and the North High Band*. St. Paul: The Schubert Club, 1984.
Wooldridge, David. *Conductor's World*. New York: Praeger Publishers, 1970.

Periodicals

Boyer, Richard O. "Profiles: Maestro on a Mountaintop." *The New Yorker*, April 15, 1950.
Canarina, John. "The Mahler Boom, from Beginning to . . . Endless." *High Fidelity Magazine*, November 1981.
Collis, James. "The Greek Come Bearing Gifts." *Symphony Magazine*, May 1951.
Eyer, Ronald F. "America's Notable Orchestras, Part XIII: The Minneapolis Symphony." *Musical America*, March 10, 1938.
Garrett, Helen F. "Dimitri Mitropoulos: A Portrait." *Music News*, March 1945.
Helm, Everett. "Vanessa in Salzburg." *Saturday Review*, September 13, 1958.
Heymel, Michael. "Ein Heiliger der Musik." *Hellenika: Jahrbuch für die Freunde Griechenlands*, 1991.
Kolodin, Irving. "Farewell to Capricorn." *Saturday Review*, June 1, 1974.
Leadbetter, Ruth Ann. "Variations on a Theme." *The Christian Advocate*, September 28, 1944.
Levinger, Henry. "Dimitri Mitropoulos: 1896–1960." *Musical America*, December 1960.
Marx, Henry. "A Life for Modern Music." *Music News*, January 1949.
Mitropoulos, Dimitri. "The Conductor Looks at the Audience." *WABF Program Magazine*, February 1950.
———. "The Making of a Conductor." *Etude*, January 1954.
———. "The Conductor Speaks." Interview. *Opera News*, January 3, 1955.
———. "What I Believe." *Hi-Fi Music at Home*, May–June 1956.
Pluta, Ekkehard. "Der Dirigent Dimitri Mitropoulos: Augenblicke der Wahrheit." *Fono Forum*, May 1990.
Politis, M. J. "Dimitri Mitropoulos: A Great Musician and a Great Man." *The Ahepan*, January–February 1943.
Sargent, Winthrop. "Dimitri Mitropoulos." *Life*, February 2, 1946.
Serbin, Max. "Great Music is Mightier than Politics." *American Record Guide*, September 1958.
Seldon-Goth, Gisella. "My Friend Mitropoulos." *Opera News*, January 17, 1955.
Sherman, John K. "Music Notes." *Golfer and Sportsman Magazine*, April 1938.
Smith, Cecil. "Personnel Changes." *New Republic*, January 23, 1950.
Stanley, Louis. "The Baton: Appraisals After a Half-century of Batonless Conducting." *Musical America*, February 15, 1955.
Stoddard, Hope. "Dimitri Mitropoulos." *International Musician*, November 1956.
Taubman, Howard. "Before the Maestro Raises His Baton." *New York Times Magazine*, January 4, 1948.
———. "The Passionate Calm of Mr. Mitropoulos." *New York Times Magazine*, October 8, 1950.
———. "Mitropoulos, Unpredictable Maestro." *House & Garden*, October 1952.

————. "What's Wrong with the Philharmonic?" *New York Times*, April 29, 1956.

Williams, Rodney H. "Vanessa . . . as Recorded." *HiFi and Music Review*, September 1958.

Zirato, Bruno. "Recollections of Caruso." *RCA Victor Picture Record Review*, January 1952.

Zottos, Ion. "Remembering Dimitri Mitropoulos." *The Athenian*, December 1985.

Other Sources

Bailey, Olive Jean. "The Influence of Ernst Krenek on the Musical Culture of the Twin Cities." Ph.D. dissertation, University of Minnesota, 1980.

Chambers, James. "Mahler and Mitropoulos Remembered." Brochure notes for New York Philharmonic Orchestra recordings, 1984–85 season.

Cooper, William S. Untitled memoir. Carbon copy, ca. 1963.

Daniel, Oliver. "Mitropoulos Opens Wide the Ivory Tower Doors." Radio script, April 1954.

Fassett, James. "Memoirs." Typescript, n.d.

Foster, Molly. "Mrs. Scott Brings Music to the University and Minnesota." Minneapolis: privately printed pamphlet, 1983.

Graghirolli, G. "The Last Moments of the Life of Maestro Dimitri Mitropoulos as Described by Prof. G. Graghirolli, Violinist of the Orchestra alla Scala di Milano." Translated from the Italian. Milan: mimeographed, ca. 1962.

Leotsakos, George. "Dimitri Mitropoulos's *Concerto Grosso*." *Works by Greek Composers* series. Ministry of Culture and Science, Athens, 1980.

Soria, Dorle. "Mitropoulos Remembered." Brochure notes for recording of *Tosca*, Metropolitan Opera performance, January 7, 1956.

Weber, Ben. Autobiography. Manuscript, n.d.

Weldy, Lloyd. "Music Criticism of Olin Downes and Howard Taubman in the *New York Times* Sunday Edition (1924–1929 and 1955–1960)." Ph.D. dissertation, University of Southern California, 1965.

Zappas, Tassos. "Dimitri Mitropoulos on the Peaks of Olympus." Mimeographed, ca. 1980.

Interviews

NOTE: Most interviews were conducted by Oliver Daniel or William R. Trotter, as indicated in the notes. Those marked with an asterisk were conducted by Dr. Michael Heymel.

Aaron, Arthur (orchestra manager)
Albanese, Licia (soprano, Metropolitan Opera)
Aliferis, James (music professor, University of Minnesota; assistant conductor, Minneapolis Symphony Orchestra)
Aliferis, Viola (first wife of James Aliferis; adminstrative staff, Boston Symphony Orchestra)
Alpert, Victor (violist, MSO and BSO)
Amram, David (composer)
Angelucci, Betty (friend of Mitropoulos)
Angelucci, Rhadames (oboist, MSO)

Antonini, Alfredo (conductor)
Antoniou, Theodore (composer; conductor)
Arrau, Claudio (pianist)
Avakian, George (producer, Columbia Records; husband of Anahid Ajemian)
Babbitt, Milton (composer)
Bailey, Olive Jean (Krenek scholar)
Baker, Julius (flutist, New York Philarmonic Symphony Orchestra)
Bampton, Rose (soprano)
Bar-Illan, David (pianist)
Barab, Seymour (cellist; composer; helped found Esoteric Records)
Barefoot, Spencer (impresario, San Francisco)
Bean, Betty (publicist, NYPSO)
Bernstein, Leonard (conductor; composer)*
Biancolli, Louis (critic; musicologist)
Bockman, Sigurd (clarinetist, MSO, NBC Symphony Orchestra, NYPSO)
Boitano, Gene (administrative staff, NYPSO)
Bonine, Joan (administrative staff, NYPSO)
Bray, Byron (Columbia Artists representative)
Brieff, Frank (conductor)
Brissey, Paul (violinist, MSO)
Brook, Paige (flutist, NYPSO)
Busoni, Hannah (daughter-in-law of Ferruccio Busoni)
Canarina, John (teacher; music critic)
Carpenter, Leonard (board of directors, MSO)
Castagnetta, Grace (pianist)
Cehanovsky, George (singer and Russian coach, Metropolitan Opera)
Chambers, James (first horn, NYPSO)
Chapin, Schuyler (general manager, Metropolitan Opera; head of Columbia
    Records Masterworks Division)
Chardon, Yves (cellist, Athens Symphony Orchestra, BSO, MSO, Metropolitan
    Opera Orchestra)
Chorafa, Maria (pianist; pupil of Mitropoulos)
Christopoulou, Maria (pupil and biographer of Mitropoulos)
Constantakos, Chris (violinist)
Cooper, David (son of Professor William Cooper, University of Minnesota)
Cordero, Roque (composer)
Dayton, Kenneth (board of directors, MSO)
de Lancie, John (oboist, Philadelphia Orchestra; former director, Curtis Insti-
    tute)
de Loache, Ben (singer with Philadelphia Orchestra; music professor, Yale Uni-
    versity)
DeIntinis, Ranier (French horn, NYPSO)
Diamond, David (composer)
Downes, Edward (musicologist; moderator, Metropolitan Opera broadcasts)
Drucker, Stanley (clarinetist, NYPSO)
von Einem, Gottfried (composer; administrator, Salzburg Festival)*
Elias, Rosalind (mezzo-soprano; starred in *Vanessa*)
Erickson, Robert (composer)
Eyle, Felix (concertmaster, Metropolitan Opera Orchestra)
Farrell, Eileen (soprano)
Fassett, James (radio commentator, NYPSO broadcasts)

Finney, Ross Lee (composer)
Firkušný, Rudolf (pianist)
Formosis, Pandelis (biographer of Mitropoulos)
Frahm, Richard (friend of Mitropoulos)
Freund, J. Hellmut (secretary to Fritz Busch, conductor)*
Garbousova, Raya (cellist)
Geanakopolos, Dino (violinist, MSO; Byzantine history professor, Yale University)
Gershunoff, Maxim (head of Artists Management Agency; friend of Mitropoulos; trumpeter, NBCSO)
Gerstley, Henry (president, Robin Hood Dell Concerts)
Gielen, Michael (conductor)*
Goltzer, Harold (bassoonist)
Gossen, Fred (chorus member, MSO)
Gould, Morton (composer; conductor)
Graff, Grace and Kurt (dancers)
Graudon, Joanna (pianist; wife of Jean Graudon, first-chair cello, MSO)
Greer, Frances (soprano)
Gross, Robert (violinist)
Guarrera, Frank (baritone, Metropolitan Opera)
Gullino, Frank (assistant concertmaster, NYPSO)
Gutman, John (assistant manager under Rudolf Bing, Metropolitan Opera)
Hall, David (author and critic)
Hart, Philip (orchestra manager; author)
Harvey, John (stage designer; friend of Mitropoulos, mainly in Philadelphia)
Hedberg, Earl (violist, MSO)
Heinsheimer, Hans (author; music publisher)
Herbert, Ralph (singer in *Wozzeck* and other Mitropoulos productions; music department, University of Michigan)
Herdt, Clara Roesch (conductor; founder, Women's Symphony Orchestra)
Herman, Robert (assistant to Rudolf Bing, Metropolitan Opera)
Hume, Paul (music critic, Washington, D.C.)
Janis, Byron (pianist)
Johannesen, Grant (pianist)
Kallir, Lillian (pianist)
Katims, Milton (violist; conductor)
Katsoyanis, Katy (lifelong friend and correspondent of Mitropoulos)
Keresey, Howard (librarian, NBCSO and NYPSO)
Kilyeni, Edward (pianist)
Kirchner, Leon (composer)
Kirsten, Dorothy (soprano)
Kittleson, Harold (friend of Mitropoulos and Jenny Cullen)
Koch, Karl Otto (chief of classical programming, Westdeutscher Rundfunk, Cologne)*
Kolodin, Irving (author; music critic, *Saturday Review*)
Kostios, Apostolos (biographer of Mitropoulos)
Kramer, Henry (assistant concertmaster, MSO)
Krasner, Louis (violinist)
Krenek, Ernst (composer)
Kydoniatis, Konstantinos (early friend of Mitropoulos and family)
Kyne, Alice (administrative staff, NYPSO)

La Montaine, John (composer)
Landis, Michael (interviewer, Voice of America; friend of Mitropoulos)
Leotsakos, George (musicologist and critic, Athens)
Levin, Sylvan (conductor; impresario)
Lincer, William (violist, NYPSO)
Lind, Gloria (soprano, Metropolitan Opera and Chicago Lyric Opera)
Lipton, Martha (mezzo-soprano)
Lloyd, David (tenor)
Lowe, Jack (duo-pianist with Arthur Whittemore)
Luening, Otto (composer)
MacKay, John S., Sr. (trombonist, MSO)
MacKay, John, Jr. (pianist)
McQuary, Joan (editor, Columbia University Press)
Marcus, Adele (pianist; teacher)
Martin, George (author)
Masselos, William (pianist)
Mauricci, Vincent (violist, MSO and BSO)
Menotti, Gian-Carlo (composer)
Menuhin, Yehudi (violinist)
Meyerowitz, Jan (composer)
Miller, Mitch (oboist)
Mirtallo, Arturo (co-owner, La Scala Restaurant)
Mitropoulos, Dimitri (radio interview by Martha Deane, 1950; radio interview
    by Lee Eitzen, c. 1955)
Modinos, Christakis (conductor; author)
Moseley, Carlos (president emeritus, New York Philharmonic Orchestra)
Nikolaidi, Elena (mezzo-soprano)
Nomikos, Andreas (stage designer; worked with Mitropoulos at Salzburg, Flor-
    ence Festivals)
Norkin, Sam (artist; journalist)
Oppenheim, David (head of Columbia Masterworks Artists and Repertory)
Papaioannou, John (musicologist)
Paris, Matthew (executor, estate of Ben Weber, composer)
Parmentier, Gordon (composer)
Paulu, Burton (trombonist, MSO; Prof. Emeritus of Broadcasting, University of
    Minnesota)
Pennario, Leonard (pianist)
Peters, Roberta (soprano)
Peyser, Joan (biographer of Leonard Bernstein)
Pflaum, Leo (board of directors, MSO)
Ratliff, Neil (music librarian)
Rich, Martin (assistant conductor, Metropolitan Opera Orchestra)
Rieti, Vittorio (composer)
Robbins, Louis (librarian, NYPSO)
Rochberg, George (composer)
Rorem, Ned (composer; author)
Rose, Leonard (cellist)
Rosenberger, Walter (percussionist, NYPSO)
Rudolf, Max (conductor)
Sargent, Winthrop (music critic, *The New Yorker*)
Schaeffer, John (assistant personnel manager, NYPSO)

Schermerhorn, Kenneth (conductor)

Schonberg, Harold (music critic, *New York Times*)

Siegmeister, Elie (composer)

Semsis, Michalis (friend of Mitropoulos, Athens)

Seldon-Goth, Gisella (mother of Trudy Goth; friend of Busoni and Mitropoulos, Berlin)*

Serkin, Rudolf (pianist)

Sessions, Roger (composer)

Shanet, Howard (author; historian of New York Philharmonic Orchestra)

Shaw, Robert (conductor)

Shulman, Alan (cellist; composer)

Slenczynska, Ruth (pianist)

Sophos, Anthony (cellist, NYPSO)

Soria, Dorle Jarmel (press representative, NYPSO)

Starer, Robert (composer)

Starr, Susan (pianist)

Steber, Eleanor (soprano)

Stern, Isaac (violinist)

Stevens, Rise (mezzo-soprano, Metropolitan Opera)

Strasfogel, Ignace (conductor)

Strauss, Paul (conductor)

Stutch, Nathan (cellist, NYPSO)

Temerson, Leon (violinist, NYSPO; founding member, New York Philharmonic Chamber Ensemble)

Tsitouras, Dimitris (Mitroupolos connoisseur and intermediary with Greek sources for Oliver Daniel and Don Ott)

Vavayannis, Theodore (protégé of Mitropoulos; conductor, Athens Symphony Orchestra)

Verrall, John (composer)

Viola, Robert (co-owner, La Scala Restaurant)

Wagner, Friedelind (granddaughter of Richard Wagner)

Walt, Sherman (bassoonist, BSO)

Ware, John (trumpeter, NYPSO)

Whittemore, Arthur (duo-pianist with Jack Lowe)

Wild, Earl (pianist)

Wilford, Ronald (president, Columbia Artists Management)

Winkler, Anton (flutist, MSO)

Wobisch, Hellmut (trumpeter, Vienna Philharmonic)*

Yannopoulos, Dino (stage director, Metropolitan Opera)

Yeend, Francis (soprano)

Zakythinos, Alexis (author, discography of music by Greek composers)

Zaratzian, Harry (violist, NYPSO)

Building a Mitropoulos Record Collection

Mitropoulos's recordings fall into three categories:

- The commercial Minneapolis recordings
- The commercial New York Philharmonic recordings
- Pirate recordings of live performances

The shortcomings and virtues of the first two categories are discussed in the text (see Chapter Thirteen and Chapter Twenty-five). The third category offers treasures galore, but has mostly been available on now-you-see-'em, now-you-don't Italian specialty labels whose distribution in the United States depends largely on the BIG record stores. If you live near a good, large purveyor, you'll certainly find some of this material in stock, some of the time; if you live in a town serviced only by one of the big national chains that has no consistent commitment to classical material, you're probably out of luck unless you want to mail-order from specialty shops who advertise in the back of *Fanfare* or *American Record Guide*. European music lovers should have a much easier time—Mitropoulos CDs are plentiful and varied, once you cross the Atlantic.

I have listed what I consider the greatest Mitropoulos recordings, and have given the label and number of both LP and, where available, CD incarnations. You may never see most of these recordings; on the other hand, you may stumble on one at a yard sale next Saturday. Sony Classical is considering CD releases of some Columbia material; let us hope.

Readers who are seriously interested should obtain a copy of *The Complete Discography of Dimitri Mitropoulos*, by S. A. Arfanis and Nick Nickson. This is a handsome and enormously useful production, a model of how a discography ought to be done: thorough, reliable, and beautifully illustrated. It can be ordered from Nickson Records, P.O. Box 25523, Rochester, New York, 14625-0523.

The Nickson Records

These Minneapolis Symphony recordings really are in a class by themselves. Nickson, a Rochester broadcasting veteran and indefatigable Mitropoulos collector, has gone to great lengths to obtain the quietest, clearest

Mitropoulos during recording session for CBS Records, 1957.
Courtesy CBS Records.

sources of many Minneapolis recordings and has digitized them with great care. Nickson's first issue was an LP, now out of print, but the five CDs he has published since then are the cornerstone of any Mitropoulos collection. Some of the highlights:

NN-1002: Contains Mitropoulos's melodramatic orchestration of Bach's Fantasia and Fugue in G Minor; Milhaud's arrangement of the Couperin Overture and Allegro from *La Sultane*, which Mitropoulos often conducted; and a stirring rendition of Glazunov's *Overture on Greek Themes*, Op. 3, No. 1.

NN-1003: Begins with Busoni's arrangement of Liszt's *Spanish Rhapsody*, in which Mitropoulos leads his old colleague Egon Petri through as stylish and sparkling a performance as one can imagine. Also on this disc is one of the first recordings ever made of Borodin's Second Symphony (better, in some ways, than the later New York recording); a piercingly brilliant account of the "Bridal Procession" from Rimsky-Korsakov's *Le Coq d'or*; and one incredible rarity: Mitropoulos conducting the accompaniment to Jussi Björling's account of "Addio, alla madre" from *Cavalleria rusticana* by Mascagni.

NN-1004: This is my favorite of all Nickson's productions, comprising "Popular Concert Favorites and Encores." There's a wonderfully snooty account of Prokofiev's *Classical Symphony*, Ravel's *Le Tombeau de Couperin*, and the flat-out GREATEST version of Milhaud's *Le Boeuf sur le toit* that has ever been recorded. Among the shorter selections are a rip-snorting *Russian Sailor's Dance*, and a couple of Dvořák's *Slavonic Dances* that demonstrate some marvelously subtle and effective rubato.

NN-1005: This contains the first of the Minneapolis Columbias, a lithe, powerful, husky-toned Franck Symphony in D Minor, along with Elie Siegmeister's somewhat faded-sounding but still charming *Ozark Suite* and Morton Gould's delightful *Minstrel Show*.

NN-1006: Mitropoulos was one of the best interpreters of Rachmaninoff's orchestral music; indeed, these versions of the Second Symphony and the *Isle of the Dead* are paradigmatic of the conductor's lean, muscular, two-fisted approach to romantic music. The *Isle of the Dead* is particularly thrilling; Mitropoulos blows the bogus impressionist cobwebs from this score and gets *serious* with it. The string tone could cut through a brick, the tempos are right on the edge of hysterical, and the climax fairly explodes with released energy. An eccentric reading, to be sure, but utterly gripping from first note to last.

Commercial and Pirated New York Recordings

Fortunately, in view of how few of his studio records have been commercially reissued, a quite extensive alternative discography documents Mitropoulos's art in all its multiplicity and excitement, albeit often in sound that is just barely tolerable. The majority of these recordings are manufactured in Italy, where the copyright laws are, shall we say, less restrictive than they are in the U.S. (I prefer the description "more enlightened," but then I'm not being deprived of any royalties.)

Many of these have been issued on compact disc and are spasmodically available through mail order or through the few retail chains that value their classical customers. Sound quality is insanely variable and seldom first class, but taken as a whole, these off-the-air recordings capture the conductor at his most spontaneous and thus provide a balanced and often moving documentation of his art, revealing that very incandescence that so often eluded him in the confines of Columbia's studios.

Of the commercial and commercially available air-check recordings, the following strike me as the most desirable (all with NYPSO unless noted):

BARBER: *Vanessa* (rec. February 13, April 7, and April 10, 1958; Metropolitan Opera Orchestra)

> RCA LM/LSC-6138 (LP)
> RCA/BMG 7899-2-RG (CD)

Comment: One of the great recordings of twentieth-century opera; a treasure. This is the only Mitropoulos recording that has never gone out of print in the United States.

BERG: Concerto for Violin and Orchestra (rec. December 30, 1945; Joseph Szigeti, violin; NBC S.O.)

> AS Disc-626 (CD)

Comment: Mitropoulos conducting with missionary zeal and working with one of his favorite soloists. Disc also contains the first American performance of Frank Martin's coolly elegant Violin Concerto. Sound quality is OK.

BERG: *Wozzeck* (rec. April 12, 13, and 15, 1951; Eileen Farrell and others)

> Columbia SL-118 (LP)
> Odyssey Y2 33126 (LP)
> CBS 42470 (CD)

Comment: There are newer, more scrupulously accurate recordings, of course, but the special magic of this pioneering version has not faded. In every sense, this was one of Mitropoulos's greatest triumphs; belongs in every serious record collection.

BERLIOZ: *Nuits d'été*, Op. 7 (rec. January 21, 1954, with Eleanor Steber)

> Columbia ML-4940 (LP)
> Columbia ML-5843 (LP)
> Odyssey Y-32360 (LP)

Comment: Lovely. Just lovely.

BERLIOZ: *Symphonie fantastique*, Op. 14 (rec. February 24, 1957)
Columbia MS-6030 (LP)

>Odyssey 32 16 0204 (LP)
>CBS-MPK-45685 (CD)

Comment: No audible "deterioration" here; the Philharmonic plays gloriously and Mitropoulos's somber, rhetorically flexible interpretation builds to a splendid climax. Among the best and best-sounding of all his Philharmonic recordings: vivid, gleaming, rich in color. The CD version, part of a "Masterworks Portrait" series pressed in Europe, is certainly the one to get; although it is out of print officially, copies may still be found in some dealers' stock or in second-hand stores. In any case, this is worth searching for.

KIRCHNER: Concerto for Piano and Orchestra (rec. February 24, 1956; composer as soloist)

>Columbia ML-5185 (LP)
>New World NW-286 (LP)
>New World -286 (CD)

Comment: Although the recording is mono only, this is still a cornerstone for any good collection of either modern or American music. Recorded under stressful conditions, to put it mildly, the performance has a go-for-broke intensity: you can *feel* Mitropoulos and Kirchner pulling it off.

KRENEK: *Symphonic Elegy for String Orchestra on the Death of Webern* (rec. April 21, 1951)

>Columbia ML-4524 (LP)

Comment: A modern masterpiece given a searing interpretation. This is really one of the great recordings of twentieth-century repertoire, and its obscurity today is a crime. CBS/Sony should reissue it, preferably with its original coupling (Schoenberg's *Erwartung*); listening to both sides at one sitting is a harrowing experience.

LOEFFLER: Two Rhapsodies for Oboe, Viola, and Piano ("L'Étang" and "La Cornemuse," The Pool and The Bagpiper) (rec. April 21, 1952; Mitropoulos, piano; Milton Katims, viola; Harold Gomberg, oboe)

>Columbia ML- 5198 (LP)

Comment: The only commercial recording of Mitropoulos as a chamber musician. All three soloists are sensationally good, and the music is hauntingly beautiful. The Hindemith works on the second side, while light-years away from Loeffler in style, are done to perfection.

MAHLER: Symphony No. 1 in D Major (rec. November 4, 1940; MSO)

>Columbia 11609/14D (78s)
>Columbia ML-4251 (LP)
>CSP-P-14157 (LP)

Comment: A historic recording if ever there was one, and a lithe, taut, dramatic interpretation. One hopes that Nick Nickson will get around to this treasure eventually. The sound on the 78s is really not bad, if you can find clean copies and have something to play them on. Columbia Special Products, or CSP, kept old recordings in print for unfathomable reasons; distribution of this product was insanely capricious, the pressings were gritty, and the sound of the originals—not so hot to begin with—was often distorted by fake "stereo." Yet CSP product turns up quite often in used-record bins, and there were some fine things on that label, including a fair number of Rodzinski's recordings. If you find one, do *not* be conned into paying more than five dollars for it.

MAHLER: Symphony No. 3 in D Minor, for Mezzo-Soprano, Orchestra, and Chorus (rec. October 31, 1960; Lucretia West, contralto; Cologne Radio Womens' Chorus; Cologne School Boys' Chorus; Cologne Radio S.O.)

> Cetra Doc 4 (LP)
> Movimento Musica 02.016 (LP)

Comment: Mitropoulos's last public appearance, documented in decent sound. A strong, balanced, well-organized reading of this sprawling score; significantly better than the 1956 New York performances, revealing that Mitropoulos was getting better even as his body was failing.

MAHLER: Symphony No. 8 in E-flat Major, "Symphony of a Thousand" (rec. August 28, 1960, Salzburg Festival; Vienna Philharmonic Orchestra; Vienna State Opera Chorus; Vienna Boys Choir; Mimi Coertse, soprano; Hilde Zadek, soprano; Lucretia West, contralto; Ira Malaniuk, contralto; Giuseppe Zamperi, tenor; Hermann Prey, baritone; Otto Edelmann, bass)

> Everest 3189/2 (LP)
> Ars Nova C 25/125 (LP)
> Hunt 558 (CD)

Comment: A wonderful, transporting musical experience. Sound on the Everest LPs was poor, especially cramped and distorted at the big climaxes; that on the Hunt CD is clean, open, and free from distortion.

MENDELSSOHN: Symphony No. 3, Op. 53, "Scottish" (rec. November 2, 1953)

> Columbia ML 4864
> CSP-14189

Comment: Everything clicked on this recording: the conductor was "on" and the orchestra was up for it. Tremendously exhilarating. My personal favorite of all "Scottish" Symphony recordings.

MENNIN: Symphony No. 3 (rec. January 2, 1954)

> Columbia ML-4902 (LP)
> CRI-S-278 (CD)

Comment: Another landmark recording, which has fortunately been preserved by CRI on a respectable-sounding CD.

PROKOFIEV: Concerto for Piano and Orchestra No. 3, Op. 26 (rec. December 16, 1945; Mitropoulos playing and conducting; NBC S.O.)

AS Disc-512

Comment: There exist three known examples of Mitropoulos blazing through this challengng piece, his great pianist-conductor specialty. The commercial recording of a 1946 Robin Hood Dell performance is so atrocious-sounding that one can scarcely believe Columbia expected people to pay money for it. There is also a 1949 performance with the NYPSO, but that does not appear to be currently available in any format. This one, recorded with Toscanini's orchestra, will suffice to demonstrate how spectacular these dual-role appearances could be.

PROKOFIEV: Symphony No. 5, Op. 100 (rec. July 9, 1954; Bavarian Radio S.O.)

Orfeo C-204891 (CD)

Comment: Heavily interpreted in the first movement, to be sure, but intensely realized at every turn. Mitropoulos's handling of the motoric fourth movement (often a letdown in performance) is a masterpiece of sustained tension and release. The sound is quite good, and the coupling, an authoritative Schoenberg Violin Concerto with Louis Krasner, makes this disc a real value.

SCHULLER: Symphony for Brass and Percussion, Op. 16 (rec. January 14, 1956; freelance orchestra)

Columbia CL-941 (LP)

Comment: A sonic spectacular in its day, the recording still sounds first rate. One of Schuller's best pieces, the symphony makes some demands on the listener but repays the effort amply. Even if you find it tough to get inside this score, the surface brilliance alone will dazzle you.

SCHUMANN: Symphony No. 1, Op. 38, "Spring" (rec. November 11, 1956)

AS Disc-501 (CD)

Comment: The critics hated this one. And, yes, it is over-tense, hard driven, rough toned. It is also the most virile and exciting account of this faded symphony this listener's ever heard. It is an interpretation that is "wrong" but that still works, on its own terms, on at least one screwball level. I am not alone in this; I know other record collectors who treasure this eccentric interpretation. At least you'll stay awake for the whole thing, which is not always the case with this symphony.

SCRIABIN: *The Poem of Ecstasy*, Op. 54 (rec. April 19, 1953)

AS Disc 508 (CD)

Comment: If any reader remains unconvinced that a man literally can sublimate his sex-life into musical performance, just listen to this. Mitropoulos may not conjure the perfumed sensuality from this piece that Stokowski found there, but this white-hot reading builds to a "climax" that is almost embarrassing to hear, so intense and so drenched in eroticism is the moment when it finally arrives. An amazing document.

SESSIONS: Symphony No. 2 (rec. January 16, 1950)

Columbia ML-2120 (LP)
Columbia ML-4784 (LP)
CRI-SD-278
CRI-673 (CD)

Comment: Another landmark recording of a major contemporary American score. While the sound on the original LPs was not bad, the version to get is the CRI compact disc, which gives you three Sessions symphonies in one package.

STRAUSS: *Elektra* (rec. August 7, 1957, Salzburg; Inge Borkh as Elektra; Vienna Philharmonic; Vienna State Opera Chorus)

Cetra LO-83 (LP)
Nuovo Era 2241/42 (CD)

Comment: You can't go wrong with any of the three Mitropoulos recordings of *Elektra*; he was the perfect conductor for this score, and even his detractors knew it. The Salzburg performance is the only one easily obtainable, and that's fine because Borkh's interpretation of the title role is a landmark of operatic art. For a time, the May 1950 Florence performance surfaced in the U.S. on the Vox/Turnabout label (THS 65040/41) and still appears occasionally in bargain bins. The historic 1949 New York performance, alas, was only briefly available on a pirate label and is nowhere in sight as of this writing.

VAUGHAN WILLIAMS: Symphony No. 4 in F Minor (rec. January 9, 1956)

Columbia ML-5158 (LP)
CSP- 5158 (LP)

Comment: Columbia could have recorded this in stereo, easily, but chose not to. A CD edition (coupled with Stokowski's premiere recording of Vaughan Williams's Sixth Symphony) is available in Europe but not in the U.S. It's worth the trouble to purchase from one of the British record shops that advertises in *The Gramophone*. The European catalogue number is Sony SMK-58933.

General Index

Index of Musical Compositions